European Yearbook of International Economic Law

EYIEL Monographs - Studies in European and International Economic Law

Volume 5

EYIEL Monographs is a subseries of the European Yearbook of International Economic Law (EYIEL). It contains scholarly works in the fields of European and international economic law, in particular WTO law, international investment law, international monetary law, law of regional economic integration, external trade law of the EU and EU internal market law. The series does not include edited volumes. EYIEL Monographs are peer-reviewed by the series editors and external reviewers.

More information about this series at http://www.springer.com/series/15744

Tilman Michael Dralle

Ownership Unbundling and Related Measures in the EU Energy Sector

Foundations, the Impact of WTO Law and Investment Protection

Springer

Tilman Michael Dralle
Heidelberg, Germany

ISSN 2364-8392 ISSN 2364-8406 (electronic)
European Yearbook of International Economic Law
EYIEL Monographs - Studies in European and International Economic Law
ISBN 978-3-030-08543-8 ISBN 978-3-319-77797-9 (eBook)
https://doi.org/10.1007/978-3-319-77797-9

Dissertation, Faculty of Law, University of Dresden

Softcover re-print of the Hardcover 1st edition 2018

Printed on acid-free paper

This Springer imprint is published by the registered company Springer International Publishing AG part of Springer Nature.
The registered company address is: Gewerbestrasse 11, 6330 Cham, Switzerland

Meinen Eltern

Contents

List of Abbreviations

AB	Appellate Body
ACER	Agency for the Cooperation of Energy Regulators
BIT	Bilateral investment treaty
CETA	Comprehensive Economic and Trade Agreement between Canada and the European Union
CFR	Charter of Fundamental Rights of the European Union
CPC	Provisional Central Product Classification of the United Nations
CRE	Regulatory Authority for Energy of France
Directives	Directives 2009/72/EC and 2009/73/EC
DSU	Dispute Settlement Understanding
ECHR	European Convention on Human Rights
ECJ	European Court of Justice
ECOSOC	Economic and Social Council of the United Nations
ECT	Energy Charter Treaty
ECtHR	European Court of Human Rights
EEA	European Economic Area
EEZ	Exclusive Economic Zone
Electricity Directive	Directive 2009/72/EC
Electricity Regulation	Regulation 714/2009
EPA	Economic Partnership Agreement
EPCA	Enhanced Partnership and Cooperation Agreement
ERO	Regulatory Authority for Energy of Poland
EU	European Union
FCSC	Foreign Claims Settlement Commission of the United States
FET	Fair and equitable treatment
FTA	Free trade agreement
Gas Directive	Directive 2009/73/EC
Gas Regulation	Regulation 715/2009
GATS	General Agreement on Trade in Services

GATT	General Agreement on Tariffs and Trade
HDSA	Historically disadvantaged South African
ICSID	International Centre for Settlement of Investment Disputes
ICSID Convention	Convention on the Settlement of Investment Disputes between States and Nationals of Other States
IIA	International investment agreement
ILC	International Law Commission
ISDS	Investor-State dispute settlement
ISO	Independent System Operator
ITO	Independent Transmission Operator
LNG	Liquefied natural gas
MA	Market access
MFN	Most-favored-nation
MPRDA	Mineral and Petroleum Resources Development Act of the Republic of South Africa
NAFTA	North American Free Trade Agreement
NRA	National regulatory authority
NT	National treatment
OECD	Organisation for Economic Co-operation and Development
OJ	Official Journal of the European Union
OU	Ownership unbundling
PCA	Permanent Court of Arbitration
PCB	Polychlorinated biphenyl
PTA	Preferential trade agreement
RAE	Regulatory Authority for Energy of Greece
SRI	Internal Revenue Service of Ecuador
STE	State trading enterprise
TEC	Treaty establishing the European Community
TEN-E	Trans-European energy networks
TEP	Third Energy Package
TEU	Treaty on European Union
TFEU	Treaty on the Functioning of the European Union
TPA	Third party access
TSO	Transmission system operator
TTIP	Transatlantic Trade and Investment Partnership between the United States and the European Union
UN	United Nations
UNCTAD	United Nations Conference on Trade and Development
VCLT	Vienna Convention on the Law of Treaties
VIU	Vertically integrated undertaking
WPDR	Working Party on Domestic Regulation
WPPS	Working Party on Professional Services
WTO	World Trade Organization
W/120	Services Sectoral Classification List

Chapter 1
Introduction

Gas and electricity transmission networks are generally considered to be natural monopolies.[1] This means that the transmission of energy through such networks is not typically carried out on a competitive basis, but by a single natural monopolist.[2] Owing to this, energy transmission networks present specific regulatory challenges. In particular, effective regulatory approaches are needed in order to ensure that the lack of competition in the transmission sector does not lead to the creation of monopoly rents, and that other economic actors have access to energy transmission networks on fair and non-discriminatory terms.[3]

The competition-related problems deriving from the natural monopoly character of gas and electricity transmission systems are seriously compounded by the fact that such networks are often controlled by vertically integrated undertakings (VIUs). In the energy sector, vertical integration refers to the situation wherein a company that controls energy transmission networks (an essentially non-competitive activity) also

---

[1]Christopher Decker, *Modern Economic Regulation: An Introduction to Theory and Practice* (Cambridge University Press 2015) 227, 283; Simonetta Zarrilli, 'Multilateral Rules and Trade in Energy Goods and Services: The Case of Electricity' in Janusz Bielecki and Melaku G Desta (eds), *Electricity Trade in Europe – Review of the Economic and Regulatory Changes* (Kluwer Law International 2004) 255; WTO, Council for Trade in Services, Energy Services – Background Note by the Secretariat (09 September 1998) S/C/W/52, [5, 25, 39]; Winfried Rasbach, *Unbundling-Regulierung in der Energiewirtschaft: Gemeinschaftsrechtliche Vorgaben und deren Umsetzung in die deutsche Energierechtsordnung* (C.H. Beck 2009) 34.

[2]This book focuses on the transport of electricity and gas through *transmission* networks, i.e. the long-distance transport of natural gas through high-pressure pipelines and the long-distance transport of electricity on the extra high-voltage and high-voltage interconnected system. In contrast, local or regional *distribution* networks are not specifically addressed.

[3]Thomas W Wälde and Andreas Gunst, 'International Energy Trade and Access to Networks: The Case of Electricity' in Janusz Bielecki and Melaku G Desta (eds), *Electricity Trade in Europe – Review of the Economic and Regulatory Changes* (Kluwer Law International 2004) 185.

T. M. Dralle, *Ownership Unbundling and Related Measures in the EU Energy Sector*, European Yearbook of International Economic Law 5,
https://doi.org/10.1007/978-3-319-77797-9_1

engages in the production/generation or supply of energy (a competitive activity).[4] Evidence has shown that vertically integrated undertakings have an incentive to leverage their market power in the core network activity into the competitive industry segments in order to benefit their affiliated production/generation and supply businesses.[5]

In the European Union (EU), as well as in other countries around the world, policymakers have devised so-called 'unbundling measures' in order to prevent the discrimination, cross-subsidization and distortion of competition which can result from the vertical integration of energy companies. The term 'unbundling' refers to the separation of energy transmission activities on the one hand from energy production/generation and supply activities on the other. Whereas 'light unbundling' merely requires the keeping of separate accounts for transmission activities, the most far-reaching unbundling requirements mandate the complete independence of network operators from producers/generators and suppliers.

This book examines how international economic law,[6] specifically the law of the World Trade Organization (WTO)[7] and international investment law, interacts with the unbundling and unbundling-related measures in the EU energy sector. In carrying out this examination, the book contains a two-pronged approach. On one hand it analyzes whether and how international economic law limits the adoption or maintenance of unbundling and unbundling-related measures. On the other hand, it examines the question whether international economic law positively requires or

[4]EU energy legislation uses the following definition (for the electricity sector): A VIU is defined as 'an electricity undertaking or a group of electricity undertakings where the same person or the same persons are entitled, directly or indirectly, to exercise control, and where the undertaking or group of undertakings perform at least one of the functions of transmission or distribution, and at least one of the functions of generation or supply of electricity'; see Article 2 No. 21 of Directive 2009/72/EC of the European Parliament and of the Council concerning common rules for the internal market in electricity and repealing Directive 2003/54/EC (13 July 2009) OJ 2009/L 211/55. For the gas sector, see Article 2 No. 20 of Directive 2009/73/EC of the European Parliament and of the Council concerning common rules for the internal market in natural gas and repealing Directive 2003/55/EC (13 July 2009) OJ 2009/L 211/94.

[5]See, for example, Decker (n 1) 142, 178–179. In several EU competition law proceedings, the abuse of dominant position was said to derive from the vertically integrated nature of energy companies; see European Commission, Commission Decision relating to a proceeding under Article 82 of the EC Treaty and Article 54 of the EEA Agreement (18 March 2009) Case COMP/39.402 – RWE Gas Foreclosure, [50]; European Commission, Commission Decision relating to a proceeding under Article 82 of the EC Treaty and Article 54 of the EEA Agreement (26 November 2008) Cases COMP/39.388 – German Electricity Wholesale Market, COMP/39.389 – German Electricity Balancing Market, [87]; European Commission, Commission Decision relating to a proceeding under Article 102 TFEU and Article 54 of the EEA Agreement (29 September 2010) Case COMP/39.315 – ENI, [90].

[6]See Ignaz Seidl-Hohenveldern, *International Economic Law* (3rd edn, Kluwer Law International 1999) 1 (who defines international economic law as referring to 'those rules of public international law which directly concern economic exchanges between the subjects of international law', including individuals, multinational enterprises, non-governmental organizations, and international organizations).

[7]See Agreement Establishing the World Trade Organization (15 April 1994) 1867 U.N.T.S. 154.

encourages States to implement some kind of unbundling policies. The main agreements examined include the WTO's General Agreement on Trade in Services (GATS)[8] as well as bilateral investment treaties (BITs) and other international investment agreements (IIAs).

1.1 Private Restraints on Competition and Energy Transmission as a Natural Monopoly

On the worldwide level, the gas and electricity markets were for a long time dominated by vertically integrated State-owned monopolies.[9] This also holds true for the EU, where until the late 1980s the energy markets of most EU Member States continued to be controlled by public monopolies,[10] which were usually VIUs.[11] Since the 1980s, the political climate in many countries has undergone a significant transformation: away from the idea of State-sponsored energy monopolies and towards privatization and liberalization of their energy markets.[12]

At the same time however it has become clear that the formal liberalization of the sector, i.e. the breaking-up of public monopolies, is insufficient to ensure genuine competition. There is the danger that public restraints on competition are being replaced by private restraints. Even after the removal of formal monopoly rights, vertically integrated energy companies are in a position to exploit their *de facto* monopoly power over the energy transmission facilities. The reason for this is the lack of competition in the gas and electricity transmission sectors, which, as stated, constitute a natural monopoly based on the current state of technology.

A natural monopoly exists where a single firm can produce a given amount of output at lower costs than multiple firms engaged in the same activity. This condition is technically referred to as the subadditivity of the cost function, or cost subadditivity.[13] In the context of energy networks, economies of scale and scope are the main drivers of cost subadditivity.[14] In the gas transmission sector, significant

---

[8]WTO, General Agreement on Trade in Services (15 April 1994) 1869 U.N.T.S. 183.

[9]Energy Services – Background Note by the Secretariat (n 1) [3, 7]; WTO, Council for Trade in Services, Energy Services – Background Note by the Secretariat (12 January 2010) S/C/W/311, [5, 79].

[10]Kim Talus, *EU Energy Law and Policy: A Critical Account* (Oxford University Press 2013) 15ff.

[11]Damien Geradin, 'Introduction' in Damien Geradin (ed), *The Liberalization of Electricity and Natural Gas in the European Union* (Kluwer Law International 2001) xvi.

[12]Piet J Slot, 'Energy and Competition' (1994) 31 Common Market Law Review 511, 511; Angus Johnston and Guy Block, *EU Energy Law* (Oxford University Press 2012) [2.09].

[13]Günter Knieps, *Wettbewerbsökonomie: Regulierungstheorie, Industrieökonomie, Wettbewerbspolitik* (3rd edn, Springer 2008) 21ff; Jürgen Kühling, *Sektorspezifische Regulierung in den Netzwirtschaften* (Energie- und Infrastrukturrecht vol 4, C.H. Beck 2004) 37.

[14]Günter Knieps, 'Wettbewerb auf den Ferntransportnetzen der deutschen Gaswirtschaft: Eine netzökonomische Analyse' (2003) 26 Zeitschrift für Energiewirtschaft 171, 172.

economies of scale exist, *inter alia*, because pipeline capacity costs decrease as the diameter of the pipeline increases.[15] Similarly, in the electricity transmission sector, the cost of one km of line per megawatt of transmission capacity (and thus the unit cost of transporting electric power) declines as the voltage level of the line, i.e. its total transmission capacity, increases.[16] What eventually makes the natural monopoly in the energy transmission sector so problematic from a competition perspective, and thus creates the need for sector-specific regulation, is that the natural monopoly is non-contestable. The reason for this is that the construction of gas and electricity networks involve enormous investments.[17] These investment costs are sunk once incurred, which means that they are non-recoverable upon exit from the market. Whereas such costs are no longer relevant for an established incumbent, they are extremely important for potential new market entrants.[18] In short, it is not economically viable for competitors to duplicate energy infrastructure, which leaves the incumbent natural monopolist with a stable market power.[19] In addition, it must also be taken into account that the construction of a competing parallel infrastructure is limited by environmental, safety, and zoning restrictions.[20]

1.2 Anti-competitive Practices by Vertically Integrated Energy Undertakings

Due to the fact that gas and electricity transmission is essentially a non-competitive activity, vertically integrated undertakings have both an incentive and the ability to exploit their position of power in such a way as to favor their affiliated production/generation and supply companies. First of all, and most importantly, vertically integrated transmission system operators (TSOs) can discriminate against competitors as regards network access. In terms of price-related discrimination, integrated operators may, for example, manipulate the tariff regime in such a way that—even though tariff categories are, on their face, based on non-discriminatory criteria—the

[15] Decker (n 1) 283; D. V Gordon, K. Gunsch and C. V Pawluk, 'A Natural Monopoly in Natural Gas Transmission' (2003) 25 Energy Economics 473, 478.

[16] Michel Rivier, Ignacio J Pérez-Arriaga and Luis Olmos, 'Electricity Transmission' in Ignacio J Pérez-Arriaga (ed), *Regulation of the Power Sector* (Springer 2013) 262.

[17] Decker (n 1) 227, 283; Kühling (n 13) 38.

[18] Knieps (n 13) 32.

[19] Energy transmission systems cannot always be characterized as 'perfect' natural monopolies. The German natural gas transmission sector, for example, is characterized by a certain degree of infrastructure competition, see Knieps (n 14). This does not, however, automatically mean that governmental regulation is unnecessary, see Wolfgang Ströbele, Wolfgang Pfaffenberger and Michael Heuterkes, *Energiewirtschaft: Einführung in Theorie und Politik* (Oldenbourg Verlag 2012) 160.

[20] Piet J Slot and Andrew Skudder, 'Common Features of Community Law Regulation in the Network-Bound Sectors' (2001) 38 Common Market Law Review 87, 87.

tariffs applicable to affiliated businesses are overall lower than those applicable to competitors.[21] Furthermore, it is also possible for integrated operators to elevate transmission tariffs to an artificially high level in order to squeeze competitors' margins.[22] Apart from that, third-party network access may also be reduced or obstructed through non-price behavior. The possibilities for non-price discrimination are manifold. In the electricity sector, the use of allocation procedures that fail to bring about maximum use of interconnector capacity and long-term capacity reservations in favor of incumbents has been reported.[23] In the gas sector, there is evidence that integrated TSOs have implemented strategies to make the purchase of capacity more cumbersome, and thus less valuable, for third parties. This has apparently been done by offering capacity on gas pipelines on a fragmented basis, i.e. through a number of incremental sales, even though it would have been possible to offer such capacity on a longer-term basis.[24] Furthermore, VIUs may understate the capacity that is technically available to third party transport customers, implement an ineffective capacity allocation system, or refuse to offer existing available or unused capacity.[25]

Second, there are clear indications that vertical integration has led to discriminatory investment decisions. In many cases, integrated operators have only invested in network reinforcements if it was in the interest of the company as a whole. In contrast, capacity expansions have been avoided in cases where the extra capacity would have mainly benefitted competitors.[26] In one case, a vertically integrated gas company even suspended ongoing construction works for the expansion of a pipeline, which had been initiated by the network branch due to an increased demand for gas capacity on the part of independent shippers, in response to complaints from the company's supply branch.[27]

A third way for VIUs to leverage the market power derived from their network activity to the commercial segments of the energy sector is by misusing commercially sensitive information. In the course of operating the network, vertically

[21]Emmanuel Cabau, 'Unbundling of Transmission System Operators' in Christopher Jones (ed), *The Internal Energy Market – The Third Liberalisation Package* (EU Energy Law Series vol 1, 3rd edn. Claeys & Casteels Publishing 2010) [4.1]. See also Commission Decision relating to a proceeding under Article 82 TEC – RWE Gas Foreclosure (n 5) [33–35].

[22]Ibid [30–32].

[23]European Commission, DG Competition Report on Energy Sector Inquiry (10 January 2007) SEC(2006) 1724, [497].

[24]See, for example, Commission Decision relating to a proceeding under Article 102 TFEU – ENI (n 5) [51–52].

[25]Commission Decision relating to a proceeding under Article 82 TEC – RWE Gas Foreclosure (n 5) [26–27]; Commission Decision relating to a proceeding under Article 102 TFEU – ENI (n 5) [46–48].

[26]DG Competition Report on Energy Sector Inquiry (n 23) [497–498, 502] (for electricity) and [144, 157 159] (for gas). See also Commission Decision relating to a proceeding under Article 102 TFEU – ENI (n 5) [55–60].

[27]DG Competition Report on Energy Sector Inquiry (n 23) [158–159].

integrated TSOs necessarily obtain information that is of high commercial value to energy generators/producers and suppliers. In the electricity sector, for example, this applies to information regarding the maintenance programs of generation plants, load forecasts, and expected congestion levels.[28] If such information were made available only to affiliated companies, or provided to them at an earlier stage, they would have a clear competitive advantage.[29]

Fourth, vertical integration entails the risk of cross-subsidization. By using profits earned from the non-competitive network sector, a vertically integrated undertaking is able to lower sales prices at the wholesale and retail levels.[30] This imposes losses on existing competitors, potentially forcing them to leave the industry, and discourages new competitors from entering the market.

While all of the above-mentioned anti-competitive practices are likely to undermine the level playing field between economic actors in the production/generation and supply of energy, it is discrimination in network access that constitutes the most direct and thus most relevant restriction on competition resulting from the natural monopoly character of gas and electricity transmission systems. It is not surprising, therefore, that governmental regulation in the energy sector has first and foremost attempted to ensure non-discriminatory network access.

1.3 Unbundling Measures in Context: Behavioral and Structural Regulatory Approaches

Regulatory approaches that seek to control the anti-competitive behavior of vertically integrated energy undertakings with respect to network access can be broadly classified into two categories: behavioral policies and structural policies.[31] Behavioral policies are governmental regulations setting forth the terms and conditions under which access to the transmission network by third parties must be negotiated or granted. Structural policies, in contrast, require vertically integrated undertakings to implement some degree of separation between their network activities on the one hand, and the production/generation or supply activities on the other (unbundling). Therefore, whereas behavioral policies primarily reduce the *ability* of the transmission system company to deny or hinder network access (while failing to remove the incentive to do so), structural policies seek to suppress or eliminate the *incentives* of

[28]Cabau (n 21) [4.3].

[29]Cabau (n 21) [4.3]; Rasbach (n 1) 38.

[30]Rasbach (n 1) 38; Cabau (n 21) [4.2].

[31]This classification is used by the OECD, see for example OECD, 'Recommendation of the Council Concerning Structural Separation in Regulated Industries' (C(2011)135 and CORR1 13 December 2011) 2 <http://www.oecd.org/daf/competition/50119298.pdf> accessed 24 June 2015.

the transmission operator to deny or hinder access.[32] More specifically, the latter category of policies aims to restore the 'natural' incentive of network operators, namely to promote competition in the competitive market segment in order to create a growing demand for their non-competitive service. This natural incentive can be and is often supplanted by opposing incentives on the part of other branches of a vertically integrated undertaking, namely to maximize their sales and market shares of production/generation and supply activities. Accordingly, structural policies are meant to solve the 'conflict of interest' between network operations and commercial energy activities.

As regards behavioral policies, the EU has introduced and gradually developed the instrument of third party access (TPA) in its First, Second and Third Energy Packages. TPA implies that eligible third parties have a legal right, subject to certain conditions, to use the grid of an electricity or natural gas transmission/distribution system owner or operator. One can distinguish here between two variants: the weaker variant of *negotiated* TPA, and the stronger alternative of *regulated* TPA.[33]

The electricity and gas market directives of 1996 and 1998 (the First Energy Package) allowed for both options: (1) negotiated TPA on the basis of voluntary commercial agreements; and (2) regulated TPA on the basis of previously published tariffs set by an external authority.[34] The second generation of internal energy market directives (2003) strengthened the provisions on TPA. They no longer provided for the possibility of negotiated TPA, but instead prescribed regulated TPA as the only option. Consequently, this Second Energy Package (SEP) also introduced substantive rules with respect to the applicable transmission and distribution tariffs and the methodologies underlying their calculation. According to these rules, the methodologies used to calculate the tariffs could no longer be determined in a discretionary manner, but were subject to the mandatory prior approval of the national regulatory authorities (NRAs). The NRAs were also empowered to fix or approve the tariffs.[35] The Third Energy Package (TEP; 2009) has provided the basis for the development of EU-wide network codes, which also contribute to enhanced non-discriminatory network access.[36] Therefore, under the current TPA regime in

---

[32]OECD, 'Restructuring Public Utilities for Competition' (2001) 53 <http://www.oecd.org/competition/sectors/19635977.pdf> accessed 20 January 2016.

[33]See Wälde and Gunst (n 3) 187 (who conclude that 'negotiated access usually proves ineffectual' in the energy sector).

[34]A third option, the 'Single Buyer' model, was only available in the electricity sector and has never been used, see Johnston and Block (n 12) [4.03].

[35]Articles 20(1) and 23(2) of Directive 2003/54/EC of the European Parliament and of the Council concerning common rules for the internal market in electricity and repealing Directive 96/92/EC (26 June 2003) OJ 2003/L 176/37; Articles 18(1) and 25(2) of Directive 2003/55/EC of the European Parliament and of the Council concerning common rules for the internal market in natural gas and repealing Directive 98/30/EC (26 June 2003) OJ 2003/L 176/57.

[36]Article 6 of Regulation (EC) No 715/2009 of the European Parliament and of the Council on conditions for access to the natural gas transmission networks and repealing Regulation (EC) No 1775/2005 (13 July 2009) OJ 2009/L 211/36; Article 6 of Regulation (EC) No 714/2009 of the European Parliament and of the Council on conditions for access to the network for cross-border

place, transmission system operators may only refuse access where they lack the necessary capacity, and duly substantiated reasons must be provided for any such refusal.[37]

As regards structural policies, their development at the EU level was somewhat delayed in comparison to the adoption of network access regulation. It was not until 2003 that tangible unbundling requirements were introduced by the second generation of internal energy market directives (both legal and functional unbundling), and it was only the Third Energy Package in 2009 that provided for comprehensive separation requirements. The TEP contains three different unbundling models: Ownership Unbundling (OU); the Independent System Operator (ISO); and the Independent Transmission Operator (ITO). While all of these unbundling solutions impose fairly drastic separation requirements on vertically integrated energy undertakings, ownership unbundling is the most 'radical' option because it requires the *complete* structural independence of transmission activities from production/generation and supply activities, and hence the total breakup of VIUs. However, as mentioned, it is only one of several unbundling models under the TEP.

There are strengths and weaknesses in both the behavioral and structural approaches to dealing with anti-competitive conduct on the part of vertically integrated transmission system operators. While behavioral policies are an essential element in the effort to ensure non-discriminatory network access,[38] their effectiveness is considered to be limited.[39] As the incentive to discriminate against competitors in the competitive market segment persists, the regulator will face an arduous uphill struggle against covert actions on the part of integrated operators, who benefit from an information advantage and will use all possibilities at their disposal (including legal, technical and economic means) in order to somehow delay network access, limit its quality, or raise its price.[40]

Structural measures, in contrast, address the underlying problem by seeking to ensure that the commercial interests of infrastructure operators are in line with those of access-seeking users.[41] A 'clean solution' is provided by the ownership unbundling measures which, as mentioned, bring about a complete structural separation between TSOs and producer/generators and suppliers. Structural measures which fall short of ownership unbundling do not entirely remove the incentive to discriminate, but certainly can go a long way toward suppressing it. They may,

---

exchanges in electricity and repealing Regulation (EC) No 1228/2003 (13 July 2009) OJ 2009/L 211/15.

[37]Article 32(2) of Directive 2009/72/EC (n 4); Article 35(1) of Directive 2009/73/EC (n 4). In the case of gas, access may also be denied where granting access would (i) prevent TSOs from carrying out public service obligations or (ii) lead to 'serious economic and financial difficulties' with take-or-pay contracts.

[38]Kühling (n 13) 359 (who describes third party access rights as the core – 'Herzstück' – of network industry regulation).

[39]Cabau (n 21) [4.4]; Wälde and Gunst (n 3) 185.

[40]OECD, 'Restructuring Public Utilities for Competition' (n 32) 20ff.

[41]See Wälde and Gunst (n 3) 185.

however, involve onerous and detailed prescriptions. Finally, it is important to stress that the relationship between network access regulation (behavioral measures) and unbundling regulation (structural measures) is not 'either/or'. Rather, the two types of regulation are complementary.

This book will focus on the structural measures implemented in the EU energy sector.

1.4 Unbundling as a Cross-Sectoral and Global Policy Approach

The use of unbundling policies is confined neither to the energy sector nor to the European Union. All network-bound industries are prone to similar anti-competitive practices and have therefore elicited similar interventions by policy-makers. Unbundling has thus become a cross-sectoral and global policy approach. Nonetheless, while many countries around the world have adopted unbundling measures as an integral part of their competition policies, this practice is particularly noticeable in the energy sector.

For example, the members of the Energy Community—an international organization which was set up to extend the EU internal energy market to South East Europe—have committed to gradually implement the *acquis communautaire* on energy. By virtue of a decision taken in October 2011 by the Energy Community Ministerial Council, Albania, Bosnia and Herzegovina, Kosovo, Macedonia, Moldova, Montenegro, Serbia and Ukraine agreed to transpose the TEP's unbundling rules by January 2015.[42] The European Economic Area (EEA) countries of Iceland, Liechtenstein and Norway currently apply the unbundling requirements of the EU's Second Energy Package, and the incorporation of the third legislative package is being considered.[43] The Swiss government carried out a major reform of the Swiss electricity transmission sector in 2007 in order to facilitate integration with the liberalized EU energy market. Under its Federal Electricity Supply Act, the newly-established national TSO swissgrid is prohibited from engaging, directly or indirectly, in electricity production, supply and trade.[44]

[42]Ministerial Council of the Energy Community, 'Decision 2011/02/MC-EnC on the Implementation of Directive 2009/72/EC, Directive 2009/73/EC, Regulation (EC) 714/2009 and Regulation (EC) 715/2009 and amending Articles 11 and 59 of the Energy Community Treaty' (6 October 2011) <https://www.energy-community.org/portal/page/portal/ENC_HOME/DOCS/1146182/0633975AB3B67B9CE053C92FA8C06338.PDF> accessed 8 March 2016.

[43]Council of the European Economic Area, Conclusions of the 42nd meeting of the EEA Council (19 November 2014), [16].

[44]See WTO, Trade Policy Review Report by the Secretariat Switzerland and Liechtenstein Revision (16 August 2013) WT/TPR/S/280/Rev.1, [4.37]; Brigitta Kratz and Frederik Kreuzer, 'Ownership Unbundling – A Swiss Perspective' in Dirk Buschle, Simon Hirsbrunner and Christine Kaddous (eds), *European Energy Law: Droit européen de l'énergie* (Dossier de droit européen vol

There are also important developments outside of continental Europe. Despite its critical attitude towards the EU's unbundling policies in the TEP, the Russian Federation has enacted far-reaching separation requirements in its electricity sector,[45] at least on paper. Furthermore, Argentina, some states of Australia (e.g. Victoria and South Australia), Brazil, Chile, New Zealand, and Venezuela have introduced some form of 'ownership unbundling' of their electricity networks.[46] More limited separation requirements in the electricity industry have been or will be introduced by most provinces of Canada,[47] China,[48] Japan,[49] Peru,[50] Turkey,[51] the United States[52] and Zimbabwe.[53]

Yet as indicated, unbundling is also a cross-sectoral policy approach. Apart from the energy sector, unbundling measures have been introduced in other network-bound industries, such as railways and telecommunications. The key regulatory challenges are always similar: Vertically integrated undertakings have an incentive to discriminate against competitors as regards access to a bottleneck infrastructure.[54]

---

22. Helbing Lichtenhahn 2011). However, the 'Swiss solution' allows generation/production or supply undertakings to hold shares in the transmission operator; see Kratz and Kreuzer (n 44) 73.

[45]It seems that the Russian unbundling legislation in the electricity sector largely corresponds to the most intrusive unbundling model in the Third Energy Package (ownership unbundling), see Elena Timofeeva, *Unbundling in der russischen Elektrizitätswirtschaft im Vergleich zum deutschen und europäischen Energierecht* (Veröffentlichungen des Instituts für deutsches und europäisches Wirtschafts-, Wettbewerbs- und Regulierungsrecht der Freien Universität Berlin vol 34, Peter Lang 2012) 157; Anatole Boute, *Russian Electricity and Energy Investment Law* (Law in Eastern Europe, Brill 2015) 216ff. Given that the ownership unbundling model in the EU's Electricity Directive is not mandatory, one commentator concluded that 'Russia goes further in the liberalization of its electricity market than do some member states in the EU', Boute (n 45) 217.

[46]Michael Pollitt, 'The Arguments For and Against Ownership Unbundling of Energy Transmission Networks' (2008) 36 Energy Policy 704, 709, passim; U.S. International Trade Commission, *Electric Power Services – Recent Reforms in Selected Foreign Markets* (USITC Publication 3370, 2000) 20–2ff.

[47]Government of Canada, 'Electricity Infrastructure: About Electricity' (2014) <http://www.nrcan.gc.ca/energy/electricity-infrastructure/about-electricity/7359> accessed 13 September 2016.

[48]WTO, Trade Policy Review – Report by the Secretariat – China – Revision (12 August 2008) WT/TPR/S/199/Rev.1, 122.

[49]WTO, Trade Policy Review – Report by the Secretariat – Japan – Revision (06 May 2015) WT/TPR/S/310/Rev.1, [4.95]; Ministry of Economy, Trade and Industry of Japan, 'Electricity Market Reform in Japan' (2013) 10–11 <http://www.meti.go.jp/english/policy/energy_environment/electricity_system_reform/pdf/201311EMR_in_Japan.pdf> accessed 7 September 2016.

[50]Article 122 of the Republic of Peru, Electric Concessions Law (Ley de Concesiones Eléctricas) (19 November 1992) Decree Law No. 25844, as amended.

[51]WTO, Trade Policy Review – Turkey – Report by the Secretariat (19 November 2003) WT/TPR/S/125, 95, 98.

[52]Neelie Kroes, 'Improving Competition in European Energy Markets Through Effective Unbundling' (2007) 31 Fordham International Law Journal 1387, 1396–1401.

[53]WTO, Trade Policy Review – Report by Zimbabwe (14 September 2011) WT/TPR/G/252, [106].

[54]See Kühling (n 13) 337ff, 359ff (who identifies unbundling measures as an important ingredient for the regulation of network industries).

However, unbundling requirements do not have the same status in all network-bound sectors, mainly due to technological differences.[55]

In order to exemplify the cross-sectoral nature of unbundling policies, it is expedient to look at the example of the EU. As regards the railway sector, the current regulatory framework requires the independence of railway infrastructure managers in legal, organizational and decision-making terms, but only with respect to certain 'essential functions' (decision-making on train path allocation and infrastructure charging).[56] At the beginning of 2013, the Commission put forward a draft legislative package, the Fourth Railway Package.[57] The Commission concluded that the existing separation between railway undertakings, which run the train services, and infrastructure managers, which operate the railway network, is not sufficient to ensure non-discriminatory access to the rail infrastructure.[58] It thus proposed stricter separation requirements in the form of an 'institutional separation' of infrastructure management and transport operation, which is in fact very similar to the strict 'ownership unbundling' model in the Third Energy Package, despite the difference in wording.[59] Although the Fourth Railway Package, as ultimately adopted, does not provide for the concept of an institutional separation, Directive 2016/2370/EU[60] establishes, *inter alia*, a prohibition against holding certain double mandates (such as being a member of the management board of an infrastructure manager and, at the same time, of a railway undertaking), safeguards to ensure that other legal entities within VIUs do not have a decisive influence on appointments and dismissals of persons in charge of taking decisions on the 'essential functions' of the infrastructure manager, a prohibition against performance-based remuneration from other legal entities of the VIU, and several rules on financial transparency according to which,

[55]See Peter Abegg and others, 'Entflechtung in Netzsektoren – ein Vergleich' [2014] Bremen Energy Working Papers No. 19, 30, 35.

[56]Article 7 of Directive 2012/34/EU of the European Parliament and of the Council establishing a single European railway area (21 November 2012) OJ 2012/L 343/32 (in its unamended form).

[57]European Commission, The Fourth Railway Package – Completing the Single European Railway Area to Foster European Competitiveness and Growth (30 January 2013) COM(2013) 25 final.

[58]Ibid 4–5.

[59]According to the Commission proposal, the same legal person or persons would not have been allowed to 'directly or indirectly exercise control . . ., hold any financial interest in or exercise any right over a railway undertaking and over an infrastructure manager at the same time'. See draft Article 7(2)(a) of the European Commission, Proposal for a Directive of the European Parliament and of the Council amending Directive 2012/34/EU of the European Parliament and of the Council of 21 November 2012 establishing a single European railway area, as regards the opening of the market for domestic passenger transport services by rail and the governance of the railway infrastructure (30 January 2013) COM(2013) 29 final, 11. The 'institutional separation' would have acted as a default rule in the Commission's proposal. Member States would have been able to derogate from this general model, if 'Chinese walls' were put in place to guarantee the full independence of the infrastructure manager; see draft Article 7(5) in conjunction with draft Articles 7a, 7b and 7c, ibid 12–15.

[60]Directive 2016/2370/EU of the European Parliament and of the Council amending Directive 2012/34/EU as regards the opening of the market for domestic passenger transport services by rail and the governance of the railway infrastructure (14 December 2016) OJ 2016/L 352/1.

for example, income from infrastructure network management activities may be used only to finance the infrastructure manager's own business and railway undertakings are prohibited from granting loans to infrastructure managers, either directly or indirectly (and *vice versa*). Furthermore, Directive 2016/2370/EU for the first time requires Member States to ensure the impartiality of the infrastructure manager in respect of traffic management and maintenance planning, i.e. beyond the realm of the 'essential functions'.[61] The Directive's additional unbundling requirements must be fully implemented by 25 December 2018.

As regards telecommunications, EU law does not mandate a certain level of regulatory unbundling, but relies primarily on access regulation. One of the reasons for this approach appears to be that the telecommunications sector is much more dynamic and contains relatively significant infrastructure competition.[62] Nevertheless, Directive 2002/19/EC, as amended in 2009, explicitly provides for the availability of functional separation as a possible remedy which can be imposed by the national regulatory authorities in individual cases in order to effectively address persistent competition problems.[63] The imposition of compulsory functional separation for the activities associated with the wholesale provision of access products is subject to approval by the European Commission, and the Directive highlights that this unbundling requirement is an 'exceptional measure'. Despite this rather careful approach at the EU level, a number of incumbent vertically integrated telecommunications providers, such as British Telecommunications (UK), Telecom Italia (Italy) and TeliaSonera (Sweden), have recently agreed to introduce functional unbundling in response to pressure from legislators and regulators.[64] It should also be noted that the International Telecommunications Union stated in 2008 that there has been a 'tremendous amount of interest around the world recently in functional separation as a regulatory remedy in the telecommunication sector.'[65]

---

[61] See Articles 7, 7a, 7b, 7c and 7d of Directive 2012/34/EU (n 56), as amended by Directive 2016/2370/EU (n 60).

[62] Abegg and others (n 55) 23–30.

[63] Article 13a of Directive 2002/19/EC of the European Parliament and of the Council on access to, and interconnection of, electronic communications networks and associated facilities (07 March 2002) OJ 2002/L 108/7, as amended by Directive 2009/140/EC of the European Parliament and of the Council amending Directives 2002/21/EC on a common regulatory framework for electronic communications networks and services, 2002/19/EC on access to, and interconnection of, electronic communications networks and associated facilities, and 2002/20/EC on the authorisation of electronic communications networks and services (25 November 2009) OJ 2009/L 337/37.

[64] OECD, 'Report on Experiences with Structural Separation' (2012) 68ff <http://www.oecd.org/daf/competition/50056685.pdf> accessed 24 June 2015.

[65] Robert W Crandal, Jeffrey A Eisenach and Robert E Litan, 'Vertical Separation of Telecommunications Networks: Evidence from Five Countries' (2010) 62 Federal Communications Law Journal 493, 497 (citing Malcolm Webb, 'The Emergence of Functional Separation' in International Telecommunication Union (ed), *Trends in Telecommunication Reform 2008: Six Degrees of Sharing* (2008) 139).

1.5 The Focus of Previous Research

While it is clear that unbundling measures are designed to fulfil several important public policy objectives (in particular non-discriminatory network access), they have also raised many legal issues. Legal concerns were raised for the first time with respect to the European Commission proposal of 2001, which called for the implementation of legal and functional unbundling as part of the Second Energy Package. The main concern was that the suggested strengthening of unbundling requirements would violate the fundamental right to property in the EU legal order.[66] However, this criticism did not lead to a watering down of the approach advocated by the Commission, and legal and functional unbundling became part of the SEP. However, when the Commission unveiled its plans in 2007 to consider ownership unbundling measures as part of the third legislative package on energy, a vigorous debate erupted about the legality of such policies.

Apart from national constitutional law, a number of controversial issues were raised under EU law. First, the EU's competence to enact ownership unbundling measures was disputed. According to the 'principle of conferral', the European Union can only act within the limits of the powers conferred upon it by the Member States in the Treaty on European Union[67] (TEU) and the Treaty on the Functioning of the European Union[68] (TFEU).[69] Absent such conferral, there is no legal basis for EU action. Some academic commentators felt that an appropriate legal basis could not be established for OU. In particular it was highlighted that specific competences in the area of energy policy were lacking[70] and that reliance on the EU's harmonization competence in the field of the internal market (Article 114 TFEU, ex Article 95 TEC) was misplaced. Article 114 TFEU does not provide a general legislative power to regulate the internal market,[71] but can only be invoked with respect to

[66]Jürgen F Baur and Andreas Lückenbach, *Fortschreitende Regulierung der Energiewirtschaft: Eine kritische Stellungnahme zu den Kommissionsvorschlägen zur Änderung der Binnenmarktrichtlinie Erdgas (98/30/EG)* (Nomos 2002) 79ff; Rupert Scholz, 'Freiheitlicher Binnenmarkt oder diktierte Marktstruktur?: Zur neuen Gasrichtlinie der EG' [2001] Energiewirtschaftliche Tagesfragen 678, 679ff.

[67]European Union, Treaty on European Union (consolidated version) OJ 2012/C 326/13.

[68]European Union, Treaty on the Functioning of the European Union (consolidated version) OJ 2012/C 326/47.

[69]Article 5(1) and (2) TEU (n 67).

[70]Jürgen F Baur and others, *Eigentumsentflechtung der Energiewirtschaft durch Europarecht: Mittel, Schranken und Rechtsfolgen* (Veröffentlichungen des Instituts für Energierecht an der Universität zu Köln vol 138, Nomos 2008) 19; Rupert Scholz, 'Eigentumsschutz und Entflechtung – Zu den Unbundling-Plänen der Europäischen Kommission' (2007) 57 Energiewirtschaftliche Tagesfragen 76, 77; Johann-Christian Pielow, Gert Brunekreeft and Eckart Ehlers, 'Legal and Economic Aspects of Ownership Unbundling in the EU' (2009) 2 Journal of World Energy Law & Business 96, 102; Johann-Christian Pielow and Eckart Ehlers, 'Rechtsfragen zum "Ownership Unbundling"' [2007] InfrastrukturRecht 259, 261.

[71]European Court of Justice, *Germany v. Parliament and Council (Tobacco Advertising)*, Judgment (5 October 2000) C-376/98 [83].

measures that are genuinely designed for 'market-building' harmonization. In other words, disparities between national rules must be of such a nature that they will result in likely obstacles to trade or appreciable distortions of competition.[72] According to one view, the (continuing) existence of obstacles to the functioning of the internal energy market was dubious, in particular because the process of implementation of the Second Energy Package had not yet been completed at the time the TEP was elaborated.[73] According to another view, Article 114 TFEU could not be used for 'system-changing reforms', such as ownership unbundling.[74]

The prevailing view in the literature, however, was that ownership unbundling measures could indeed be based on the EU's harmonization competence, because (1) there was a real threat that, despite the existing regulatory framework, diverging degrees of unbundling among the EU Member States could lead to an unlevel playing field in the energy sector; and (2) ownership unbundling was capable of improving the conditions for the functioning of the internal market for electricity and gas.[75] In the meantime, exploration of the limits of the harmonization powers under Article 114 TFEU has lost much of its relevance. After the entry into force of the Treaty of Lisbon in late 2009, energy falls within the (shared) competence of the EU (Article 194 TFEU). Future unbundling measures could, therefore, be based on

[72]Ibid [86, 106].

[73]Pielow, Brunekreeft and Ehlers (n 70) 103–105; Pielow and Ehlers (n 70) 261–262. This fact was also emphasized in the context of the subsidiarity requirement (Article 5(1) TEU), see Stefan Storr, 'Die Vorschläge der EU-Kommission zur Verschärfung der Unbundling-Vorschriften im Energiesektor' [2007] Europäische Zeitschrift für Wirtschaftsrecht 232, 236–237.

[74]Jürgen F Baur and Matthias Schmidt-Preuß, 'Europarechtliche Grundlagen des Unbundling' in Jürgen F Baur, Kai U Pritzsche and Stefan Simon (eds), *Unbundling in der Energiewirtschaft: Ein Praxishandbuch* (Carl Heymanns Verlag 2006) 78, footnote 70. However, there is nothing in the text of Article 114 TFEU (ex Article 95 TEC) or in the corresponding jurisprudence of the ECJ, which would suggest such a limitation of the harmonization competence. See Ralf Müller-Terpitz and Michaela Weigl, 'Ownership Unbundling – ein gemeinschaftsrechtlicher Irrweg?' [2009] Europarecht 348, 354–355.

[75]See Müller-Terpitz and Weigl (n 74) 353ff; Christian Koenig, Kristina Schreiber and Kristin Spiekermann, 'Defizitäres Entflechtungsregime? Eine kritische Analyse der Entflechtungsvorschriften in dem Entwurf des dritten Liberalisierungspakets der Kommission der Europäischen Gemeinschaften' [2008] Netzwirtschaften & Recht 7, 9; Bernd Holznagel and Pascal Schumacher, 'Großer Eingriff, k(l)eine Wirkung – Die Pläne der Kommission zur eigentumsrechtlichen Entflechtung der Energienetzbetreiber' [2007] Netzwirtschaften & Recht 96, 100; Kim Talus and Michaël Hunt, 'Ownership Unbundling: What End to the Saga?' in Dirk Buschle, Simon Hirsbrunner and Christine Kaddous (eds), *European Energy Law: Droit européen de l'énergie* (Dossier de droit européen vol 22. Helbing Lichtenhahn 2011) 35–37; Kim Talus and Angus Johnston, 'Comment on Pielow, Brunekreeft and Ehlers on "Ownership Onbundling"' (2009) 2 Journal of World Energy Law & Business 149, 151–152. See also Jürgen F Baur, Kai U Pritzsche and Stefan Klauer, *Ownership Unbundling: Wesen und Vereinbarkeit mit Europarecht und Verfassungsrecht* (Veröffentlichungen des Instituts für Energierecht an der Universität zu Köln vol 121, Nomos 2006) 57–58; Baur and others (n 70) 19–20 (who are critical of the ECJ's case-law but appear to come to the same conclusion).

Article 194 TFEU, without the difficulty of having to comply with the requirements for the application of Article 114 TFEU.[76]

A second dimension of the debate over the EU's competence to enact ownership unbundling measures related to the scope of Article 345 TFEU (ex Article 295 TEC). According to this provision, the EU treaties shall in no way prejudice the 'rules in Member States governing the system of property ownership'. As ownership unbundling measures entail an obligation to break-up vertically integrated undertakings, several authors argued that the EU would be prevented from adopting such measures by virtue of Article 345 TFEU.[77] Even though the 2009 Third Energy Package did not in the end make the strict ownership unbundling model mandatory on an EU-wide basis, and thus does not raise any issues under Article 345 TFEU, the limitation on EU competence contained in the Article remains relevant for future policy-making. In particular, should the Union legislator seek to introduce OU throughout the EU as part of a 'Fourth Energy Package', Article 345 TFEU will certainly play an important role once again.

Apart from questions of legal competence, it has also been asserted that the proposed ownership unbundling policies were inconsistent with (1) the right to property under the EU legal order and under the European Convention on Human Rights (ECHR); and (2) the EU's fundamental freedoms, in particular the free movement of capital (Article 63 TFEU, ex Article 56 TEC) and the freedom of establishment (Article 49 TFEU, ex Article 43 TEC). The central argument here is that the adoption of ownership unbundling requirements would not have been proportional at that point in time, in particular because the existing network access and unbundling regulation would need more time to have its intended effect and could in any event be improved.[78] Given that the Third Energy Package, as finally adopted, contains several unbundling models and thus leaves the choice of OU to the decision of individual Member States, it is compatible with primary EU law. However, the fundamental right to property and free movement rules have become relevant in legal proceedings related to mandatory ownership unbundling measures taken *at the national level*. In the Netherlands, for example, domestic energy companies are currently challenging the implementation of OU at the distribution level (the *Essent* case).[79] After the European Court of Justice (ECJ) gave a preliminary ruling in 2013,[80] the Dutch Supreme Court held in 2015 that, contrary to the

[76]For an assessment of the new competence in the area of energy, see Leigh Hancher and Francesco M Salerno, 'Energy Policy after Lisbon' in Andrea Biondi, Piet Eeckhout and Stefanie Ripley (eds), *EU Law After Lisbon* (Oxford University Press 2012).

[77]See references cited in footnote 21, Chap. 3.

[78]See Sect. 3.3.

[79]See Sect. 3.4.

[80]European Court of Justice, *Staat der Nederlanden v Essent NV and Others,* Judgment (22 October 2013) C-105/12 to C-107/12.

lower court's view, the measures do not infringe Article 63 TFEU or Article 49 TFEU.[81] The complainants' contention that the measures also violate the right to property was dismissed by the Amsterdam Court of Appeal in 2016 and 2017.[82]

It should be noted that the previous discourse on unbundling policies in the EU energy sector was largely based on what can be termed as the 'intra-EU perspective'. Little attention was paid to the overall implications of the TEP for foreign companies and energy relations with third countries. The same holds true for the legal issues involved. For example, although the guarantee of the free movement of capital explicitly applies also to foreign direct investments from third countries, the TEP's compatibility with Article 63 TFEU in a third country context has so far played only a marginal role in the academic debate.[83] Likewise, and more importantly, the whole body of international economic law, in particular WTO law and international investment law, has largely been ignored,[84] and where it has been addressed authors have sometimes simply 'assumed' that unbundling requirements are consistent with WTO law[85]; sometimes pointed out that this remains 'unclear'[86]; or even misjudged

[81]Hoge Raad der Nederlanden, *Staat der Nederlanden v. Essent N.V.* Judgment (26 June 2015) 10/03851.

[82]Gerechtshof Amsterdam, *Eneco Holding N.V. v. Staat der Nederlanden,* Judgment (1 November 2016) 200 175 864/01; Gerechtshof Amsterdam, *Delta N.V. v. Staat der Nederlanden,* Judgment (1 November 2016) 200 176 186/01; Gerechtshof Amsterdam, *Delta N.V. v. Staat der Nederlanden,* Judgment (25 July 2017) 200 176 186/01.

[83]For some (in most cases cursory) analysis of this issue, see Matthias Schmidt-Preuß, 'Die Kontrolle des Verkaufs bzw. des Erwerbs von Netzen (Erwerb durch Nicht-EU-Ausländer gem. §4b EnWG; Außenwirtschaftsrecht; Fusionskontrolle)' in Jürgen F Baur, Peter Salje and Matthias Schmidt-Preuß (eds), *Regulierung in der Energiewirtschaft: Ein Praxishandbuch* (2nd edn. Carl Heymanns Verlag 2016) [77ff, 88–90]; Arnoud Willems, Jung-ui Sul and Yohan Benizri, 'Unbundling as a Defence Mechanism Against Russia: Is the EU Missing the Point?' in Kim Talus and Piero L Fratini (eds), *EU – Russia Energy Relations* (Euroconfidentiel 2010) 233–237; Michaël Hunt, 'Ownership Unbundling: The Main Legal Issues in a Controversial Debate' in Bram Delvaux, Michaël Hunt and Kim Talus (eds), *EU Energy Law and Policy Issues* (1st edn. Euroconfidentiel 2008) 73–85; Jörg Gundel and Claas F Germelmann, 'Kein Schlussstein für die Liberalisierung der Energiemärkte' [2009] Europäische Zeitschrift für Wirtschaftsrecht 763, 769–770.

[84]Some academic contributions address selected and limited aspects of the EU's unbundling legislation from the perspective of international economic law, see Thomas Cottier, Sofya Matteotti-Berkutova and Olga Nartova, 'Third Country Relations in EU Unbundling of Natural Gas Markets: The "Gazprom Clause" of Directive 2009/73 EC and WTO Law' in Dirk Buschle, Simon Hirsbrunner and Christine Kaddous (eds), *European Energy Law: Droit européen de l'énergie* (Dossier de droit européen vol 22. Helbing Lichtenhahn 2011); Willems, Sul and Benizri (n 83); Anatole Boute, 'Energy Trade and Investment Law: International Limits to EU Energy Law and Policy' in Martha M Roggenkamp and others (eds), *Energy Law in Europe – National, EU and International Regulation* (3rd edn. Oxford University Press 2016) [3.43–3.47; 3.63–3.65].

[85]Victor van Hoorn, '"Unbundling", "Reciprocity" and the European Internal Energy Market: WTO Consistency and Broader Implications for Europe' (2009) 1 European Energy and Environmental Law Review 51, 70.

[86]Caroline Van den bergh, 'Reciprocity Clause and International Trade Law' (2009) 27 Journal of Energy & Natural Resources Law 228, 256.

the reach of international economic law rules in this connection.[87] As will be shown in this book however, it seems that it would be wrong to disregard or underestimate the 'external perspective' on the EU's unbundling legislation in the energy sector.

1.6 The Subject and Relevance of This Book

The unbundling regime in the Third Energy Package does not affect only domestic energy companies, but also (and sometimes particularly) foreign energy companies active inside the EU, and in this way trade and investment relations with third countries are invariably affected. The potentially problematic issues under WTO law and international investment law are manifold. Most notably they are not only limited to the unbundling requirements as such, but also extend to the unbundling-*related* measures in the EU energy sector, i.e. the certification procedure provided for in the TEP, which was primarily designed to ensure compliance with the unbundling criteria, and the exemption regime, which allows for derogations from the unbundling requirements with respect to certain infrastructure projects. Different aspects of these unbundling and unbundling-related measures could be said to amount to: (1) prohibited market access restrictions; (2) discrimination between domestic and foreign service suppliers or investors; (3) discrimination among foreign service suppliers or investors; (4) unreasonable, non-objective or partial administration of generally applicable measures; (5) the nullification or impairment of specific market access commitments on account of being more burdensome than necessary; (6) unfair or inequitable treatment; or (7) an expropriation without compensation. This book provides a comprehensive treatment of these delicate issues. In doing so, it covers much new ground, given that this topic has not yet received any substantial attention in academic writing or elsewhere. It also incorporates relevant research publications published in the Russian and Italian languages.

The relevance of analyzing the unbundling regime in the EU energy sector from the perspective of WTO law and international investment law is manifest. Energy markets are increasingly outgrowing national and, in the case of the EU, even supranational borders. There are two main drivers of this development. First of all, technological improvements have paved the way for long-distance transmission of natural gas and electricity. Second, the world-wide movement towards liberalization has led to an opening of energy markets. However, whereas energy trade and investment takes place more and more on a regional, and even global, level, the regulation of energy markets is still largely left to individual countries or (exceptionally) regional integration organizations. This gap between 'market integration' and 'regulatory integration' can lead to significant tensions. Viewed in this light, the

[87] See Schmidt-Preuß (n 83) [97] (who discards the relevance of the GATS with respect to the unbundling and unbundling-related measures solely on the basis of an alleged lack of specific commitments and inadequate classification of energy services).

importance of international economic law lies in the fact that it is the only multilateral framework that provides some normative guidance for the regulation of all energy markets across the globe.[88] An additional point is that international economic law remedies are comparatively effective (e.g. compulsory jurisdiction of the WTO dispute settlement bodies, access to international investment arbitration by private investors). Against this background, it is not particularly surprising that a major foreign investor and a third State have sought to test the legality of the unbundling and unbundling-related measures in the EU energy sector by invoking both international investment law and WTO law. In 2012, the Russian gas company Gazprom initiated an investment arbitration against Lithuania on the basis of the 1999 Russia-Lithuania BIT (*OAO Gazprom v. Republic of Lithuania*).[89] The legal challenge related to Lithuania's enactment in 2011 of ownership unbundling legislation in the gas sector in accordance with the relevant provisions of the TEP, although the proceedings were later dropped. However, in April 2014, the Russian Federation initiated the formal complaint procedure of the WTO by requesting consultations with the EU and some of its Member States (the *EU – Energy Package* case).[90] A Panel was established on 20 July 2015 and later composed on 7 March 2016.[91] Amongst other things, Russia's WTO complaint is directed against all three elements of the EU's unbundling legislation, that is the unbundling requirements as such, the certification procedure, and the exemption regime.[92] The final Panel report is expected to be released in 2018.

The initiated investment arbitration against Lithuania and the WTO *EU – Energy Package* case demonstrate that, apart from EU law and national constitutional law, the rules of international economic law may set limits on the EU's freedom to regulate its internal energy market in general and to adopt unbundling and unbundling-related measures in particular. The EU's energy market liberalization efforts in the form of pro-competitive regulation must be in line with global trade

[88]Although international investment law mainly consists of bilateral investment treaties, it effectively forms a multilateral system of law, see Stephan W Schill, *The Multilateralization of International Investment Law* (Cambridge University Press 2009).

[89]Denis Pinchuk and Nerijus Adomaitis, *Gazprom takes on Lithuania in EU policy test case* (Reuters 2012); Gazprom, *Gazprom seeks international arbitration against Lithuanian Government* (2012); Permanent Court of Arbitration, 'OAO Gazprom v. The Republic of Lithuania' (no date) <https://pcacases.com/web/view/47> accessed 14 September 2016. See also the description in European Court of Justice, *'Gazprom' OAO*, Opinion of Advocate General Wathelet (4 December 2014) C-536/13 [35–36].

[90]WTO, *European Union and its Member States – Certain Measures Relating to the Energy Sector*, Request for Consultations by the Russian Federation (8 May 2014) WT/DS476/1, S/L/409, G/L/1067, G/SCM/D102/1, G/TRIMS/D/40.

[91]WTO, 'European Union and its Member States – Certain Measures Relating to the Energy Sector' (3 December 2015) <https://www.wto.org/english/tratop_e/dispu_e/cases_e/ds476_e.htm> accessed 13 April 2016.

[92]See WTO, *European Union and its Member States – Certain Measures Relating to the Energy Sector*, Request for the Establishment of a Panel by the Russian Federation (28 May 2015) WT/DS476/2.

liberalization rules and international investment protection standards.[93] It should be stressed that although this book is specifically concerned with the energy market legislation in the European Union, the problematic legal issues are of a general nature. Therefore, and also taking into consideration that unbundling has become a cross-sectoral and global policy instrument, the analysis presented below applies not only to the specific situation of the EU, but is also relevant to the many other countries worldwide that have implemented, or intend to implement, unbundling legislation, either in the energy industry or in other network-bound industries, such as railways and telecommunications.

Furthermore, apart from the 'limiting' role that international economic law may play in the design of unbundling regimes, WTO law can also have a *positive* normative function in the present context. In addition to prohibiting certain governmental behavior, WTO law likewise contains provisions that require positive action on the part of WTO Members. One of the areas in which such positive norms exist is competition. Competition issues are addressed by WTO law, at least to some degree,[94] because private restraints on competition can significantly undermine the benefits of trade liberalization.

As regards the energy sector, it is clear that the anti-competitive behavior resulting from vertical integration poses considerable barriers to international energy trade.[95] The aim of unbundling measures, such as those introduced through the TEP, is therefore consistent with the rationale and objective of the WTO's competition dimension. Viewed against this background, this book also analyzes whether WTO law, as it currently stands, encourages or positively obliges States to implement some kind of unbundling policies in order to ensure non-discriminatory network access to electricity and gas transmission systems. Moreover, the argument is developed that, *de lege ferenda*, additional pro-competitive regulatory principles for the energy sector could and should be developed within the WTO framework, including in particular shared regimes on unbundling.

1.7 The Course of This Book

This book is structured in the following way:

Chapter 2 traces the gradual development of unbundling policies in the EU energy sector and explains how the current unbundling regime under the Third Energy Package functions, as well as its effect on foreign economic actors.

---

[93]See in this regard also Moritz Wüstenberg, 'An Overview of the Dichotomy between EU Energy Market Liberalisation and the Multilateral Trading System: Case Review of WTO Case DS476 – Certain Measures Relating to the Energy Sector' (2016) 22 International Trade Law & Regulation 8, 17–18.

[94]For a brief overview of the 'competition dimension' of the WTO, see Michael Trebilcock, Robert Howse and Antonia Eliason, *The Regulation of International Trade* (Routledge 2013) 761–762.

[95]See Sect. 6.1.

Chapter 3 briefly outlines and analyzes the legal concerns that have been voiced in the academic literature against ownership unbundling measures, from the perspective of both national constitutional law and EU law. Furthermore, it gives an account of the *Essent* case, which involves a legal challenge against ownership unbundling measures in the Netherlands.

Chapter 4 provides a comprehensive analysis of the ways in which WTO law could limit or prohibit the adoption and/or maintenance of unbundling and unbundling-related measures as provided for in the TEP. In doing so, it focuses on Articles II (MFN Treatment), VI (Domestic Regulation), XVI (Market Access) and XVII (National Treatment) of the GATS.

Chapter 5 analyzes in detail whether, and if so to what extent, international investment law restricts the adoption or maintenance of unbundling and unbundling-related measures in the EU energy sector. The focus of this chapter is on the standards of 'no expropriation without compensation' and 'fair and equitable treatment' (FET).

Chapter 6 examines the question whether international economic law does, or should, oblige WTO Members to take measures in order to prevent VIUs from taking advantage of their *de facto* monopoly position in transmission. To that end, the chapter examines the reach of existing competition-related provisions in WTO law and sets out the case for the development of additional rules on energy services, including common disciplines on unbundling.

Chapter 7 summarizes the key findings.

Chapter 2
The Unbundling and Unbundling-Related Measures in the EU Energy Sector

2.1 The First and Second Energy Packages

The first steps toward the unbundling of generation/production and supply activities from network operations were taken in the mid-1990s. The EU's First Energy Package, consisting of Directives 96/92/EC[1] (electricity) and 98/30/EC[2] (gas), contained pertinent provisions in this regard. Both Directives required integrated electricity undertakings to keep, in their internal accounting, separate accounts for generation, transmission and distribution activities (so-called 'accounting unbundling').[3] They also provided that the Member States shall have access to these accounts.[4] Furthermore, the Directives required Member States to ensure that transmission system operators did not disclose confidential information to other parts of a vertically integrated undertaking or to third parties.[5] In addition, the electricity Directive declared that, unless the transmission system is already independent from generation and distribution activities, 'the system operator shall be independent at least in management terms from other activities not relating to the transmission system.'[6] This requirement was absent in the corresponding gas Directive,[7] although

[1]Directive 96/92/EC of the European Parliament and of the Council concerning common rules for the internal market in electricity (19 December 1996) OJ 1997/L 27/20.

[2]Directive 98/30/EC of the European Parliament and of the Council concerning common rules for the internal market in natural gas (22 June 1998) OJ 1998/L 204/1.

[3]Article 14(3) of Directive 96/92/EC (n 1); Article 13(3) of Directive 98/30/EC (n 2).

[4]Article 13 of Directive 96/92/EC (n 1); Article 12 of Directive 98/30/EC (n 2).

[5]Article 9 of Directive 96/92/EC (n 1); Article 8 of Directive 98/30/EC (n 2).

[6]Article 7(6) of Directive 96/92/EC (n 1).

[7]Peter Cameron, *Competition in Energy Markets – Law and Regulation in the European Union* (1st edn, Oxford University Press 2002) [4.117]. Talus ambiguously writes in this respect that the 'first internal market directives contained mere "management unbundling"', see Kim Talus, *EU Energy Law and Policy: A Critical Account* (Oxford University Press 2013) 78.

T. M. Dralle, *Ownership Unbundling and Related Measures in the EU Energy Sector*, European Yearbook of International Economic Law 5,
https://doi.org/10.1007/978-3-319-77797-9_2

the Commission had originally proposed a similar provision for both sectors.[8] The electricity Directive, however, failed to spell out how the unbundling of management should be achieved in practice.[9]

Directives 96/92/EC and 98/30/EC entered into force in 1997 and 1998 respectively, and had to be implemented into national law within 2 years. Already in early 2001, the European Commission put on the table two proposals for Directives amending the regulatory framework. It concluded that although important progress had been made, the 'ultimate goal of non-discriminatory access to the network' could not be fully accomplished on the basis of the existing unbundling rules.[10] It is interesting to note that during the subsequent legislative process the European Parliament even called for the implementation of ownership unbundling in the electricity sector.[11]

In keeping with the proposals of the European Commission, the Second Energy Package, and in particular Directives 2003/54/EC[12] (electricity) and 2003/55/EC[13] (gas), introduced stricter unbundling requirements.[14] Apart from accounting separation,[15] both Directives provided for 'legal' and 'functional' unbundling. With regard to legal unbundling, the Directives stated that where the transmission system

[8]European Commission, Proposal for a Council Directive concerning common rules for the internal market in electricity and for a Council Directive concerning common rules for the internal market in natural gas (21 February 1992) COM(91) 548 final, 9; European Commission, Proposal for a Council Directive concerning common rules for the internal market in electricity (24 February 1992) OJ 1992/C 65/4, 13; European Commission, Proposal for a Council Directive concerning common rules for the internal market in natural gas (24 February 1992) OJ 1992/C 65/14, 21.

[9]See also Emmanuel Cabau, 'Unbundling of Transmission System Operators' in Christopher Jones (ed), *The Internal Energy Market – The Third Liberalisation Package* (EU Energy Law Series vol 1, 3rd edn. Claeys & Casteels Publishing 2010) [4.5] ('very vague, leaving much room for interpretation').

[10]European Commission, Proposal for a Directive of the European Parliament and of the Council amending Directives 96/92/EC and 98/30/EC concerning common rules for the internal market in electricity and natural gas (13 March 2001) COM(2001) 125 final, 31.

[11]European Parliament, Position of the European Parliament adopted at first reading on 13 March 2002 with a view to the adoption of European Parliament and Council Directive 2002/.../EC amending Directive 96/92/EC concerning common rules for the internal market in electricity (13 March 2002) OJ 2003/C 47 E/351, 359.

[12]Directive 2003/54/EC of the European Parliament and of the Council concerning common rules for the internal market in electricity and repealing Directive 96/92/EC (26 June 2003) OJ 2003/L 176/37.

[13]Directive 2003/55/EC of the European Parliament and of the Council concerning common rules for the internal market in natural gas and repealing Directive 98/30/EC (26 June 2003) OJ 2003/L 176/57.

[14]For an overview, see Eugene Cross and others, 'EU Energy Law' in Martha M Roggenkamp and others (eds), *Energy Law in Europe – National, EU and International Regulation* (2nd edn. Oxford University Press 2007) [5.289ff] (for electricity) and [5.348f] (for gas); Sergey S Seliverstov and Ivan Gudkov, *Энергетическое право Европейского союза* (Аспект Пресс 2014) 117 (for electricity) and 154–155 (for gas).

[15]Article 19 of Directive 2003/54/EC (n 12); Article 17 of Directive 2003/55/EC (n 13).

operator is part of a vertically integrated undertaking, 'it shall be independent at least in terms of its legal form . . . from other activities not relating to transmission.'[16] This did not imply an obligation to separate the ownership of transmission system assets from a vertically integrated undertaking,[17] but meant that the network must be operated through a legally separate entity. The Directives' provisions on functional unbundling further required that the transmission system operator be independent in terms of its 'organisation and decision making',[18] which entailed a number of detailed requirements. Among other things, persons involved in the management of the TSO were prohibited from working simultaneously in a company of the vertically integrated undertaking that was responsible for the day-to-day operation of the generation/production, distribution, and supply of electricity or natural gas.[19] Furthermore, TSOs were required to have effective and independent decision-making rights with respect to the operation, maintenance and development of the network.[20] Certain supervisory rights of the parent company relating to, *inter alia*, the network company's annual financial plan and its level of indebtedness, remained protected.

Directives 2003/54/EC and 2003/55/EC entered into force in August 2003 and had to be fully transposed by July 2004.[21]

2.2 Draft Directives Proposed by the European Commission

In January of 2007 the European Commission released a set of reports relating to the functioning of the internal gas and electricity markets and to corresponding legislative proposals.[22] The qualitative and quantitative data contained therein formed the basis for the subsequent introduction of strengthened unbundling requirements in the Third Energy Package.

[16] Article 10(1) of Directive 2003/54/EC (n 12); Article 9(1) of Directive 2003/55/EC (n 13).

[17] Article 10(1) of Directive 2003/54/EC (n 12); Article 9(1) of Directive 2003/55/EC (n 13). See also 8th recital of the preamble to Directive 2003/54/EC (n 12); 10th recital of the preamble to Directive 2003/55/EC (n 13).

[18] Article 10(1) of Directive 2003/54/EC (n 12); Article 9(1) of Directive 2003/55/EC (n 13).

[19] Article 10(2)(a) of Directive 2003/54/EC (n 12); Article 9(2)(a) of Directive 2003/55/EC (n 13).

[20] Article 10(2)(c) of Directive 2003/54/EC (n 12); Article 9(2)(c) of Directive 2003/55/EC (n 13).

[21] An extended implementation period applied to certain unbundling rules for distribution system operators, see Article 30(2) of Directive 2003/54/EC (n 12); Article 33(2) of Directive 2003/55/EC (n 13).

[22] See European Commission, An Energy Policy for Europe (10 January 2007) COM(2007) 1 final; European Commission, Prospects for the internal gas and electricity market (10 January 2007) COM(2006) 841 final; European Commission, Inquiry pursuant to Article 17 of Regulation (EC) No 1/2003 into the European gas and electricity sectors (Final Report) (10 January 2007) COM(2006) 851 final.

In the Internal Energy Market Communication and the final Report on the Competition Sectoral Enquiry, it was concluded that legal and functional unbundling was insufficient to prevent the distortions of competition that can result from the inherent conflicts of interest created by vertical integration. Three main problems were identified: (1) commercially sensitive information being passed on by the TSOs to the production/generation or supply branch of the vertically integrated undertaking; (2) the persistence of discrimination with respect to network access; (3) distortion of investment incentives.[23] The Commission thus proposed to 'decisively reinforce the current inadequate level of unbundling'.[24]

On 19 September 2007, the Commission presented two draft Directives concerning common rules for the internal market in electricity[25] and natural gas.[26] The draft Directives provided for two unbundling models: Ownership Unbundling (OU) and the Independent System Operator (ISO). The Commission openly favored a strict ownership unbundling model, stating that it is 'clearly the most effective and stable way to solve the inherent conflict of interest and to ensure security of supply'.[27]

In connection with the unbundling provisions, the draft Directives also explicitly addressed certain 'third country aspects'. Article 8a(1) of the draft electricity Directive and Article 7a(1) of the draft gas Directive provided as follows: 'Without prejudice to the international obligations of the Community, transmission systems or transmission system operators shall not be controlled by a person or persons from

[23]Prospects for the internal gas and electricity market (n 22) 10–11.

[24]Inquiry into the European gas and electricity sectors (n 22) 12.

[25]European Commission, Proposal for a Directive of the European Parliament and of the Council amending Directive 2003/54/EC concerning common rules for the internal market in electricity (19 September 2007) COM(2007) 528 final.

[26]European Commission, Proposal for a Directive of the European Parliament and of the Council amending Directive 2003/55/EC concerning common rules for the internal market in natural gas (19 September 2007) COM(2007) 529 final.

[27]Proposal for a Directive amending Directive 2003/54/EC (n 25) 22; Proposal for a Directive amending Directive 2003/55/EC (n 26) 22. See also An Energy Policy for Europe (n 22) 7: 'Economic evidence shows that ownership unbundling is the most effective means to ensure choice for energy users and to encourage investment.'

third countries.'[28] The effect of this so-called 'Gazprom clause'[29] would have prohibited in principle third country entities from acquiring control over EU transmission systems or transmission system operators, or—as the case may be—obliged them to divest any controlling interests they had in such assets.[30] It is important to note that the question of whether the respective third country entity was active in the generation/production or supply business was irrelevant for the purposes of the provision.[31] Therefore, it is true that Articles 8a and 7a were 'less "ownership unbundling" provisions than prohibitions of foreign ownership in ... the gas and electricity transmission systems sector.'[32] The European Commission, however, stated in its explanatory memorandum that the aim of the third country clause was to 'guarantee that companies from third countries respect the same rules that apply to EU based undertakings in both letter and spirit – not to discriminate against them.'[33] This statement can best be understood if one looks at the second paragraph of the third country clause. Article 8a(2) of the draft electricity Directive and Article 7a

[28]According to the text of Articles 8a and 7a, the ban on foreign ownership was '[w]ithout prejudice to the international obligations of the Community'. This qualification, which was clearly designed to prevent breaches of international law, led to discussions regarding the existence of possibly conflicting obligations under international trade and investment law (see for instance August Reinisch, 'Protection of or Protection Against Foreign Investment? The Proposed Unbundling Rules of the EC Draft Energy Directives' in Christoph Herrmann and Jörg P Terhechte (eds), *European Yearbook of International Economic Law 2010* (Springer 2010) 60ff). The Commission itself specifically referred to 'WTO rules' in this regard (European Commission, *Energising Europe: A real market with secure supply* (MEMO/07/361, 2007)). The consistency with WTO rules of Article 8a(1) draft electricity Directive and Article 7a(1) draft gas Directive was apparently also raised by the Council of the EU. In the run-up to the Energy Council of 6 June 2008, the Commission 'gave a number of clarifications to delegations, confirming *i.a.* the compliance of the clause with WTO rules', see Council of the European Union, 'TTE (Energy) Council on 6 June 2008' (9512/1/08 – REV 1, Brussels 27 May 2008), 5. However, within the Commission itself there were diverging views. According to media reports, Commission officials from DG Trade expressed concern about whether the third country clause is in line with WTO rules, see Simon Taylor, 'EU Struggles to Agree on Anti-Gazprom Clause' *Politico* (21 May 2008) <http://www.politico.eu/article/eu-struggles-to-agree-on-anti-gazprom-clause/> accessed 21 June 2016.

[29]See Sanam S Haghighi, 'Establishing an External Policy to Guarantee Energy Security in Europe?: A Legal Analysis' in Ulf Hammer and Martha M Roggenkamp (eds), *European Energy Law Report VI* (Energy & Law vol 8. Intersentia 2009) 178; Caroline Van den bergh, 'Reciprocity Clause and International Trade Law' (2009) 27 Journal of Energy & Natural Resources Law 228, 233; Anatole Boute, 'Wederkerigheid in Europese en Russische energie-investeringen: Een juridische analyse van de "Gazprom-clausule"' [2007] Tijdschrift voor Energierecht 247; Claas F Germelmann, 'Der gemeinschaftsrechtliche Rahmen für Schutzmaßnahmen gegenüber Investitionen aus Drittstaaten im Energiesektor' (2009) 124 Deutsches Verwaltungsblatt 78, 79, 82–83.

[30]Matthias Schmidt-Preuß, 'Energieversorgung als Aufgabe der Außenpolitik?: Rechtliche Aspekte' [2007] Recht der Energiewirtschaft 281, 285.

[31]Ibid.

[32]Reinisch (n 28) 57.

[33]Proposal for a Directive amending Directive 2003/54/EC (n 25) 7; Proposal for a Directive amending Directive 2003/55/EC (n 26) 7.

(2) of the draft gas Directive provided that an agreement concluded with one or several third countries to which the EU is a party may allow for a derogation from the prohibition of foreign ownership contained in Articles 8a(1) and 7a(1). This provision would have enabled the EU to ensure that third country undertakings, which are more difficult to control, also complied with and satisfied the applicable unbundling rules.[34] Apart from this 'equality of competition' rationale, many scholars believed that reciprocity as regards market access conditions likewise constituted a driving force behind the inclusion of the third country clause.[35] After all, this would have provided the EU with a bargaining chip in negotiations with countries which were reluctant to open up their markets to European businesses.[36]

The draft Directives proposed by the European Commission were subjected to several significant modifications. First of all, a number of EU Member States, including France and Germany, pushed for the inclusion of a third unbundling option as an alternative to the OU and ISO models. This led to development of the concept of Independent Transmission Operator (ITO). Furthermore, as regards the third country clause, Member States opposed the outright prohibition of foreign investment in transmission network assets, fearing that the clause might hamper 'benign' investments from abroad.[37] Instead, it was decided to assess third country investors on a case-by-case basis.

2.3 The Third Energy Package

2.3.1 Unbundling Requirements

2.3.1.1 The Three Unbundling Models

Directive 2009/72/EC ('Electricity Directive') and Directive 2009/73/EC ('Gas Directive') provide for three main unbundling models:

---

[34]Germelmann (n 29) 79–80; Schmidt-Preuß (n 30) 286; Van den bergh (n 29) 237. The third country clause could have even been used to impose unbundling on the respective third country undertaking in its country of origin, see Victor van Hoorn, '"Unbundling", "Reciprocity" and the European Internal Energy Market: WTO Consistency and Broader Implications for Europe' (2009) 1 European Energy and Environmental Law Review 51, 58.

[35]Schmidt-Preuß (n 30) 286; Matthias Schmidt-Preuß, 'Die Zukunft der Netze – Szenarien, Modelle, rechtliche Implikationen' in Ulrich Ehricke (ed), *Die neuen Herausforderungen im Lichte des Energierechts* (Nomos 2009) 105; van Hoorn (n 34) 59; Jörg Gundel and Claas F Germelmann, 'Kein Schlussstein für die Liberalisierung der Energiemärkte' [2009] Europäische Zeitschrift für Wirtschaftsrecht 763, 769; Germelmann (n 29) 80.

[36]Helmut Lecheler and Claas F Germelmann, *Zugangsbeschränkungen für Investitionen aus Drittstaaten im deutschen und europäischen Energierecht* (Energierecht vol 1, Mohr Siebeck 2010) 80.

[37]Jan G Westerhof, 'The Third Internal Energy Market Package' in Ulf Hammer and Martha M Roggenkamp (eds), *European Energy Law Report VI* (Energy & Law vol 8. Intersentia 2009) 33.

1. Ownership Unbundling (OU);
2. An Independent System Operator (ISO);
3. An Independent Transmission Operator (ITO).[38]

The main difference between these three unbundling models is that they rely to varying degrees on actual structural separation and/or on structural separation ensured through regulatory solutions.[39] OU is the most intrusive unbundling option. It requires TSOs to be completely independent from producers/generators and suppliers. The ISO model, in contrast, allows undertakings with production/generation or supply interests to continue to own the transmission system, provided that all the functions pertaining to the operation of the network are carried out by an independent entity. Finally, under ITO model, a subsidiary of the vertically integrated undertaking can both own and operate the transmission system. However, the ITO is subject to stringent 'ring-fencing' provisions based on a host of organizational and investment-related measures.

2.3.1.1.1 Ownership Unbundling

The ownership unbundling model is stipulated in Article 9 of Directives 2009/72/EC and 2009/73/EC (also sometimes referred to together as the 'Directives'). The main substantive provisions are found in Article 9(1). First of all, according to Article 9(1)(a) of both Directives each undertaking which owns a transmission system must act as a TSO. In other words, the network cannot be operated by an entity other than the owner of the transmission system. The core requirement of ownership unbundling is then spelled out in Article 9(1)(b) as follows:

> [T]he same person or persons are entitled neither:
>
> (i) directly or indirectly to exercise control over an undertaking performing any of the functions of production or supply, and directly or indirectly to exercise control or exercise any right over a transmission system operator or over a transmission system; nor
>
> (ii) directly or indirectly to exercise control over a transmission system operator or over a transmission system, and directly or indirectly to exercise control or exercise any right over an undertaking performing any of the functions of production or supply;[40]

---

[38] Strictly speaking, there is also a fourth unbundling option under Directives 2009/72/EC and 2009/73/EC. Article 9(9) of the Directives provides that Member States may decide not to apply any of the three main unbundling models provided that the transmission system belonged to a vertically integrated undertaking on 3 September 2009 and that arrangements were in place, at that date, which guarantee more effective independence of the transmission system operator than the specific provisions concerning the ITO model. This unbundling option has only been applied in a very limited number of cases.

[39] European Commission, Commission Decision on the application of Article 9(9) of Directive 2009/72/EC to Transmission System Operation in Scotland (14 May 2012) C(2012) 3284 final, [8].

[40] This is the version contained in the Gas Directive. The Electricity Directive refers to 'generation' instead of 'production'.

Under ownership unbundling, therefore, the same person may not exercise 'control' over a generation/production or supply undertaking and, at the same time, exercise 'control' or any 'right' over a TSO or over a transmission network (lit (b)(i)). Conversely, the same person cannot exercise 'control' over a transmission system or TSO while simultaneously exercising 'control' or any 'right' over a generator/producer or supplier (lit (b)(ii)). Importantly, this prohibition applies across the gas and electricity sectors,[41] thus it also covers situations of joint influence over an electricity generator/supplier and a gas network/TSO, or over a gas producer/supplier and an electricity network/TSO.[42]

The concept of 'control' is legally defined in Article 2 of both Directives.[43] It is taken from and thus equivalent to the definition of control in Article 3(2) of the EU Merger Regulation.[44,45] Accordingly, 'control' refers to 'any rights, contracts or any other means which, either separately or in combination and having regard to the considerations of fact or law involved, confer the possibility of exercising decisive influence on an undertaking'. As can be seen from this definition, control can be exercised on either a *de jure* and/or *de facto* basis.[46] Typically, control is acquired through majority shareholdings which involve the acquisition of a majority of voting rights.[47] Furthermore, situations of so-called 'negative control' are also covered, i.e. where a shareholder has the power to block strategic decisions.[48]

The term 'right', as used in Article 9(1)(b), is legally defined in Article 9(2). The definition includes, but is not limited to, 'the power to exercise voting rights' (lit (a)); 'the power to appoint members of the supervisory board, the administrative board or bodies legally representing the undertaking' (lit (b)); and 'the holding of a majority share' (lit (c)). In accordance with the definition provided, even the possibility to

[41] Article 9(3) of Directive 2009/72/EC of the European Parliament and of the Council concerning common rules for the internal market in electricity and repealing Directive 2003/54/EC (13 July 2009) OJ 2009/L 211/55; Article 9(3) of Directive 2009/73/EC of the European Parliament and of the Council concerning common rules for the internal market in natural gas and repealing Directive 2003/55/EC (13 July 2009) OJ 2009/L 211/94.

[42] European Commission, 'Commission Staff Working Paper – Interpretative Note on Directive 2009/72/EC concerning common Rules for the Internal Market in Electricity and Directive 2009/73/EC concerning common Rules for the Internal Market in Natural Gas – The Unbundling Regime' (22 January 2010) 10 <https://ec.europa.eu/energy/sites/ener/files/documents/2010_01_21_the_unbundling_regime.pdf> accessed 24 September 2016.

[43] Article 2 No. 34 of Directive 2009/72/EC (n 41); Article 2 No. 36 of Directive 2009/73/EC (n 41).

[44] Council Regulation (EC) No 139/2004 on the control of concentrations between undertakings (20 January 2004) OJ 2004/L 24/1.

[45] 13th recital of the preamble to Directive 2009/72/EC (n 41); 10th recital of the preamble to Directive 2009/73/EC (n 41).

[46] See also European Commission, Commission Consolidated Jurisdictional Notice under Council Regulation (EC) No 139/2004 on the control of concentrations between undertakings (no date) OJ 2008/C 95/1, [55, 63].

[47] Ibid [54, 56].

[48] Ibid [54, 58].

exercise a single voting right would be inconsistent with the Directives.[49] This means that an undertaking performing any of the functions of production/generation or supply is allowed only to hold entirely passive financial rights (i.e. the right to receive dividends) related to a minority shareholding in a TSO.[50] The practical significance of the possibility to hold voteless shares can however be doubted, given that, as a general rule, shares carry the right to vote[51] and shareholders will only reluctantly give up their right to participate in the decision-making process of a company in which they hold shares.[52]

Article 9(1)(c) and (d) contain additional prohibitions. According to Article 9(1)(c) the same person or persons are not entitled to appoint members of the supervisory board, the administrative board, or bodies legally representing the undertaking of a TSO or a transmission system, while at the same time directly or indirectly exercising control or any right over a production/generation or supply undertaking. Apart from the partial overlap with Article 9(1)(b), this provision prevents entities that have some influence, but not amounting to control, over a producer/generator or supplier from appointing board members of a TSO.[53] Article 9(1)(d) stipulates that the same person is not entitled to be a member of the supervisory boards, the administrative boards or bodies legally representing a production/generation or supply undertaking and a TSO or a transmission system.

Directives 2009/72/EC and 2009/73/EC specify that the principle of separating network activities from generation/production or supply activities applies throughout the entire EU.[54] The application of the ownership unbundling requirements in

---

[49]European Commission, Commission Opinion pursuant to Article 3(1) of Regulation (EC) No 714/2009 and Article 10(6) of Directive 2009/72/EC – Austria – Certification of Vorarlberger Übertragungsnetze GmbH (29 March 2012) C(2012) 2244 final, 5.

[50]European Commission, Commission Staff Working Document – Ownership Unbundling – The Commission's Practice in Assessing the Presence of a Conflict of Interest including in Case of Financial Investors (08 May 2013) SWD(2013) 177 final, 3, 10; European Commission, 'Commission Staff Working Paper – Interpretative Note on Directive 2009/72/EC concerning common Rules for the Internal Market in Electricity and Directive 2009/73/EC concerning common Rules for the Internal Market in Natural Gas – The Unbundling Regime' (n 42) 9.

[51]See for instance section 12(1) of the German Stock Corporation Act (*Aktiengesetz*): 'Each share confers a voting right.'

[52]The national implementing legislation of EU Member States is not always in conformity with the Directives in this regard. See, for example, section 8(2) of the Federal Republic of Germany, Energy Industry Act (Gesetz über die Elektrizitäts- und Gasversorgung) (07 July 2005) BGBl. I S. 1970, 3621, which only covers the right to exercise voting rights if substantial minority rights are accorded thereby. This allows, in effect, minority shareholdings of up to 25%, see Franz J Säcker and Jochen Mohr, '§ 8 Eigentumsrechtliche Entflechtung' in Franz J Säcker (ed), *Berliner Kommentar zum Energierecht* (vol 1, 3rd edn. Dt. Fachverl. Fachmedien Recht und Wirtschaft 2014) [109ff].

[53]European Commission, 'Commission Staff Working Paper – Interpretative Note on Directive 2009/72/EC concerning common Rules for the Internal Market in Electricity and Directive 2009/73/EC concerning common Rules for the Internal Market in Natural Gas – The Unbundling Regime' (n 42) 10.

[54]See 24th recital of the preamble to Directive 2009/72/EC (n 41); 21st recital of the preamble to Directive 2009/73/EC (n 41).

Article 9(1) of the Directives is not therefore geographically limited to the individual Member States.[55] Accordingly, a person performing the functions of production/generation or supply in Member State A cannot exercise control over a transmission system operator in Member State B, even if it does not exercise control over a production/generation or supply undertaking in Member State B itself.

The legal consequences of ownership unbundling can be described as follows: If the ownership and control structures of an undertaking are already in line with the ownership unbundling regime, Article 9(1) has the effect of preventing the undertaking from making transactions as a result of which it would be able to exercise control or exercise any rights over another entity in a manner inconsistent with the ownership unbundling rules. If, on the other hand, an undertaking is vertically integrated, Article 9(1) translates into an obligation to divest. This can be done either by direct divestiture or by splitting the shares of the vertically integrated undertaking into shares of the network undertaking and shares of the production/generation and supply undertaking.[56] The latter option is only feasible if the resultant distribution of shares is likewise in conformity with the ownership unbundling requirements.

2.3.1.1.2 Independent System Operator

The second unbundling model under Directives 2009/72/EC and 2009/73/EC is the Independent System Operator. Articles 14 and 15 of the Gas Directive and Articles 13 and 14 of the Electricity Directive provide for this model. The main difference between ownership unbundling and the ISO model is that, under the latter, the transmission network assets may remain in the ownership of the vertically integrated undertaking.[57] While the *ownership* rights to the physical network thus remain unaffected,[58] the transmission network must be *managed* by a fully independent company, i.e. the independent system operator.[59]

In order to be approved and designated, the ISO itself must comply with the ownership unbundling rules described above.[60] The transmission system owner, which remains part of the vertically integrated undertaking, must in turn be legally and functionally unbundled.[61]

---

[55] The issue of whether activities in third countries are relevant for the purpose of determining compliance with the OU model is discussed below, see Sect. 2.3.1.4.

[56] 18th recital of the preamble to Directive 2009/72/EC (n 41); 15th recital of the preamble to Directive 2009/73/EC (n 41). Under German law, the splitting of shares would be possible on the basis of section 123(2) of the German Conversion Law (*Umwandlungsgesetz*).

[57] See Angus Johnston and Guy Block, *EU Energy Law* (Oxford University Press 2012) [3.32].

[58] See 16th recital of the preamble to Directive 2009/72/EC (n 41); 13th recital of the preamble to Directive 2009/73/EC (n 41).

[59] Johnston and Block (n 57) [3.32].

[60] Article 13(2)(a) of Directive 2009/72/EC (n 41); Article 14(2)(a) of Directive 2009/73/EC (n 41).

[61] Article 14(1) and (2) of Directive 2009/72/EC (n 41); Article 15(1) and (2) of Directive 2009/73/EC (n 41).

Under the ISO model, the independent system operator acts as a TSO, with all attendant powers and responsibilities. This includes, *inter alia*, granting and managing third-party access; the operation, maintenance and development of the transmission system; and investment planning.[62] It should be stressed that this is the exclusive domain of the ISO; the owner(s) of the transmission system has/have 'no responsibility and no prerogatives' regarding these tasks.[63] In this connection, the Directives require the candidate operator to demonstrate that it has at its disposal all necessary 'financial, technical, physical and human resources to carry out its tasks' as defined in the Directives.[64] Furthermore, it must commit itself to comply with a 10-year network development plan approved and monitored by the regulatory authority.[65] Insofar as ownership and management under the ISO model are in the hands of different persons, some degree of cooperation between the ISO and the owner of the transmission network is indispensable.[66] Therefore the Directives provide that the transmission system owner is under an obligation to cooperate with and support the ISO in the fulfilment of its tasks. This includes, in particular, the provision of all relevant information concerning the network.[67] The transmission system owner is further obliged to either finance the investments decided upon by the ISO and approved by the respective national regulatory authority, or to give its consent to financing by any interested third party.[68] In addition, the owner of the transmission system must cover any liability relating to the network. This does not, however, include liabilities relating to the tasks of the ISO.[69]

2.3.1.1.3 Independent Transmission Operator

The third main unbundling regime is the Independent Transmission Operator, which is provided for in Articles 17 to 23 of the Gas and Electricity Directives. In contrast to the ISO model, the ITO unbundling model permits vertically integrated undertakings not only to own, but also to operate transmission systems.[70] However, a

---

[62] Article 13(4) of Directive 2009/72/EC (n 41); Article 14(4) of Directive 2009/73/EC (n 41).

[63] European Commission, 'Commission Staff Working Paper – Interpretative Note on Directive 2009/72/EC concerning common Rules for the Internal Market in Electricity and Directive 2009/73/EC concerning common Rules for the Internal Market in Natural Gas – The Unbundling Regime' (n 42) 12.

[64] Article 13(2)(b) of Directive 2009/72/EC (n 41); Article 14(2)(b) of Directive 2009/73/EC (n 41).

[65] Article 13(2)(c) of Directive 2009/72/EC (n 41); Article 14(2)(c) of Directive 2009/73/EC (n 41).

[66] Christian de Wyl and Jasper Finke, 'Entflechtung von Energieversorgungsunternehmen' in Jens-Peter Schneider and Christian Theobald (eds), *Recht der Energiewirtschaft* (4th edn. C.H. Beck 2013) [232].

[67] Article 13(5)(a) of Directive 2009/72/EC (n 41); Article 14(5)(a) of Directive 2009/73/EC (n 41).

[68] Article 13(5)(b) of Directive 2009/72/EC (n 41); Article 14(5)(b) of Directive 2009/73/EC (n 41).

[69] Article 13(5)(c) of Directive 2009/72/EC (n 41); Article 14(5)(c) of Directive 2009/73/EC (n 41).

[70] Seliverstov and Gudkov (n 14) 168.

multitude of elaborate rules are put in place by the Directives in order to ensure effective unbundling.

To begin with, the ITO must be 'equipped with all human, technical, physical and financial resources' needed for the fulfilment of its obligations under the TEP.[71] In particular, the ITO must be the owner of the transmission system.[72] The 'leasing of personnel and rendering of services' to the ITO by other parts of the vertically integrated undertaking is prohibited under any circumstances.[73] Furthermore, the ITO is prohibited from sharing 'IT systems or equipment, physical premises and security access systems with any part of the vertically integrated undertaking'. Likewise, the ITO is not allowed to contract 'the same consultants or external contractors for IT systems or equipment, and security access systems'.[74] The Directives also require the ITO to be clearly distinguishable from the vertically integrated undertaking in terms of 'corporate identity, communication, branding and premises'.[75]

In general, the ITO must have effective and independent decision-making rights with respect to the assets necessary for the operation, maintenance, and development of the transmission system.[76] To this end a number of specific and detailed rules apply. The ITO has to have the 'power to raise money on the capital market'.[77] Moreover, all commercial and financial agreements between the ITO and other parts of the vertically integrated undertaking must comply with market conditions and be submitted for approval to the regulatory authority.[78] Furthermore, the ITO is under an obligation to set up and implement a compliance program with a view to ensuring that discriminatory conduct is excluded. The compliance program is subject to approval by the regulatory authority and is monitored by an independent compliance officer.[79] Finally, the ITO cannot have 'any direct or indirect shareholding in any subsidiary of the vertically integrated undertaking performing functions of [generation/production] or supply', nor can it 'receive dividends or any other financial benefit from that subsidiary' (and *vice versa*).[80]

In addition, Directives 2009/72/EC and 2009/73/EC contain detailed rules regarding the independence of the staff and the management of the ITO. Generally, decisions regarding appointment and renewal, working conditions (such as, *inter alia*, remuneration) and termination of the term of office of the management of the

---

[71] Article 17(1) of Directive 2009/72/EC (n 41); Article 17(1) of Directive 2009/73/EC (n 41).

[72] Article 17(1)(a) of Directive 2009/72/EC (n 41); Article 17(1)(a) of Directive 2009/73/EC (n 41).

[73] Article 17(1)(c) of Directive 2009/72/EC (n 41); Article 17(1)(c) of Directive 2009/73/EC (n 41).

[74] Article 17(5) of Directive 2009/72/EC (n 41); Article 17(5) of Directive 2009/73/EC (n 41).

[75] Article 17(4) of Directive 2009/72/EC (n 41); Article 17(4) of Directive 2009/73/EC (n 41).

[76] Article 18(1)(a) of Directive 2009/72/EC (n 41); Article 18(1)(a) of Directive 2009/73/EC (n 41).

[77] Article 18(1)(b) of Directive 2009/72/EC (n 41); Article 18(1)(b) of Directive 2009/73/EC (n 41).

[78] Article 18(6) and (7) of Directive 2009/72/EC (n 41); Article 18(6) and (7) of Directive 2009/73/EC (n 41).

[79] See Article 21 of Directive 2009/72/EC (n 41); Article 21 of Directive 2009/73/EC (n 41).

[80] Article 18(3) of Directive 2009/72/EC (n 41); Article 18(3) of Directive 2009/73/EC (n 41).

ITO cannot be taken directly at the level of the vertically integrated undertaking, but fall within the competence of the ITO Supervisory Board (further elaborated upon in the next paragraph).[81] Furthermore, for a period of 3 years before their appointment, during employment, and for a period of at least 4 years after termination of their term of office, members of the ITO management cannot exercise any 'professional position or responsibility, interest or business relationship, directly or indirectly,' with any part of the vertically integrated undertaking (except for the ITO itself) or its controlling shareholders.[82] The same prohibition also applies to the employees of the ITO, but only for the period of their term of office.[83] Moreover, the ITO management and its employees cannot hold any 'interest in or receive any financial benefit, directly or indirectly, from any part of the vertically integrated undertaking' other than the ITO itself.[84]

Every ITO must have a Supervisory Board. While the Supervisory Board can be composed mainly of representatives of the vertically integrated undertaking, a certain number of its members must comply with the independence requirements outlined above.[85] In addition to its role in the employment of management staff, the Supervisory Board is in charge of taking decisions 'which may have a significant impact on the value of the assets of the shareholders within the transmission system operator', which include, in particular, decisions regarding the 'approval of the annual and longer-term financial plans, the level of indebtedness of the transmission system operator and the amount of dividends distributed to shareholders.'[86]

Finally, the Directives also contain specific provisions relating to investments into the transmission system. Under the ITO model, a 10-year network development plan must be submitted, annually, to the regulatory authority. In its preparation of the plan, the ITO must consult all actual and potential stakeholders, i.e. system users, and make reasonable projections as to how generation/production, supply, consumption patterns, and exchanges with other countries will evolve.[87] The national regulatory authority has the power to demand changes to the 10-year network development plan if, for example, it considers that the plan disregards investment needs identified during the consultation process, or if it is at odds with the

[81] Article 19(1) of Directive 2009/72/EC (n 41); Article 19(1) of Directive 2009/73/EC (n 41).

[82] Article 19(3) and (7) of Directive 2009/72/EC (n 41); Article 19(3) and (7) of Directive 2009/73/EC (n 41). The cooling on period referred to only applies to the majority of the management. For the rest, a less restrictive cooling on period applies. See Article 19(8) of Directive 2009/72/EC (n 41); Article 19(8) of Directive 2009/73/EC (n 41).

[83] Article 19(4) of Directive 2009/72/EC (n 41); Article 19(4) of Directive 2009/73/EC (n 41).

[84] Article 19(5) of Directive 2009/72/EC (n 41); Article 19(5) of Directive 2009/73/EC (n 41).

[85] See Article 20(2) and (3) of Directive 2009/72/EC (n 41); Article 20(2) and (3) of Directive 2009/73/EC (n 41). The independence rules apply to 'at least half of the members of the Supervisory Body minus one'.

[86] Article 20(1) of Directive 2009/72/EC (n 41); Article 20(1) of Directive 2009/73/EC (n 41).

[87] Article 22(3) and (4) of Directive 2009/72/EC (n 41); Article 22(3) and (4) of Directive 2009/73/EC (n 41).

non-binding EU-wide network development plan[88] adopted by the European Network of Transmission System Operators for Electricity and Gas.[89] The national regulatory authority also continuously monitors the implementation of the 10-year network development plan.[90] Moreover, and importantly, if the TSO fails for 3 years to carry out, contrary to the 10-year network development plan, an investment which was to be executed during that time, the regulatory authority is obliged to ensure that the investment at issue is made by taking one of the following measures: First, 'to require the transmission system operator to execute the investments in question'; second, 'to organise a tender procedure open to any investors for the investment in question'; or third, 'to oblige the transmission system operator to accept a capital increase to finance the necessary investments and allow independent investors to participate in the capital.'[91]

With respect to the level of unbundling achieved by the ITO model, in 2014 the European Commission prepared a detailed report in accordance with Article 47(3) of the Electricity Directive and Article 52(3) of the Gas Directive. While cautioning that its findings were of a 'preliminary nature', given that the certification of TSOs under the ITO model only started in 2012, the Commission gave a positive assessment of the ITO unbundling rules, concluding that 'most requirements related to the ITO model seem to work in practice and are usually sufficient and adequate to ensure effective separation of the transmission business from generation and supply activities in the day-today business.'[92]

2.3.1.2 Choice Between Unbundling Models

All TSOs have to comply with one of the three unbundling models outlined above. Despite the fact that the ISO and ITO models are technically framed as derogations from ownership unbundling,[93] in principle there is no hierarchy between the different unbundling models.[94] However, the Directives place some restrictions on the

[88]The non-binding EU-wide network development plan is adopted in accordance with Article 8(3)(b) of Regulation (EC) No 714/2009 of the European Parliament and of the Council on conditions for access to the network for cross-border exchanges in electricity and repealing Regulation (EC) No 1228/2003 (13 July 2009) OJ 2009/L 211/15; Article 8(3)(b) of Regulation (EC) No 715/2009 of the European Parliament and of the Council on conditions for access to the natural gas transmission networks and repealing Regulation (EC) No 1775/2005 (13 July 2009) OJ 2009/L 211/36.

[89]Article 22(5) of Directive 2009/72/EC (n 41); Article 22(5) of Directive 2009/73/EC (n 41).

[90]Article 22(6) of Directive 2009/72/EC (n 41); Article 22(6) of Directive 2009/73/EC (n 41).

[91]Article 22(7) of Directive 2009/72/EC (n 41); Article 22(7) of Directive 2009/73/EC (n 41).

[92]European Commission, Commission Staff Working Document – Report on the ITO Model (13 October 2014) SWD(2014) 312 final, 6.

[93]See Article 9(8) of Directive 2009/72/EC (n 41); Article 9(8) of Directive 2009/73/EC (n 41). See also Cabau (n 9) [4.50].

[94]European Commission, 'Commission Staff Working Paper – Interpretative Note on Directive 2009/72/EC concerning common Rules for the Internal Market in Electricity and Directive 2009/73/

choice of the unbundling model. According to Article 9(8) of the Directives, the ISO and ITO unbundling models may only be chosen '[w]here on 3 September 2009, the transmission system belongs to a vertically integrated undertaking.'[95] If this is not the case, the ownership unbundling rules must be followed. Thus it is clear that the legal framework applicable to 'new' transmission infrastructure, i.e. transmission systems built after 3 September 2009, is the ownership unbundling regime.[96] There has been some uncertainty about whether extensions of existing transmission grids must, or may, be regarded as new transmission systems.[97]

EU Member States can decide: To implement ownership unbundling on an exclusive basis; to offer OU in combination with the ISO or ITO model; or to leave the choice of the unbundling model entirely to the TSOs concerned. By way of example, whereas Lithuania prescribed mandatory ownership unbundling in the gas sector,[98] Germany offers the OU, ISO and ITO models in that sector.[99] Transmission system operators must, however, always be able to choose OU.[100] This model therefore has to be transposed into national law by all Member States. Finally, it should also be noted that the fact that the ISO and/or ITO models are available does not automatically mean that one of these options can in fact be chosen in a given case. As mentioned, the ISO and ITO models can be selected only if the transmission system was part of a VIU on 3 September 2009.

There is no official list of those Member States that only permit the ownership unbundling model. However, according to publicly available information, at least the following Member States have implemented OU as the only available unbundling model in the electricity and/or gas sector: Belgium, the Czech Republic, Estonia, Latvia, Lithuania, the Netherlands, Poland, Portugal, Slovenia, Slovakia,

---

EC concerning common Rules for the Internal Market in Natural Gas – The Unbundling Regime' (n 42) 5.

[95]Article 9(8) of Directive 2009/72/EC (n 41); Article 9(8) of Directive 2009/73/EC (n 41).

[96]European Commission, 'Commission Staff Working Paper – Interpretative Note on Directive 2009/72/EC concerning common Rules for the Internal Market in Electricity and Directive 2009/73/EC concerning common Rules for the Internal Market in Natural Gas – The Unbundling Regime' (n 42) 5.

[97]In principle, the ISO and ITO models can be applied to 'mere extensions' of existing networks; see European Commission, Commission Decision on the exemption of Adria Link s.r.l. (Italy), Holding Slovenske Elektrarne d.o.o. (Slovenia) and E3 d.o.o. (Slovenia) under Article 17 of Regulation (EC) No. 714/2009 for two electricity interconnectors between Italy and Slovenia (17 December 2014) C(2014) 9904 final, [108]. However, the European Commission (correctly) takes the view that extensions of existing transmission grids, for which a new, separate TSO is created, cannot be certified under the ISO or ITO rules; see European Commission, Commission Opinion pursuant to Article 3(1) of Regulation (EC) No 715/2009 and Article 10 of Directive 2009/73/EC – Germany – Certification of the Operators of the Nordeuropäische Erdgas Leitung (NEL) (18 October 2013) C(2013) 7019 final, 4–5.

[98]Republic of Lithuania, Law on Natural Gas (Gamtinių dujų įstatymas) (01 July 2001) Official Gazette, 25.10.2000, No. 89-2743 (as amended), Article 41.

[99]See section 8(1) of the German Energy Industry Act (n 52).

[100]Article 9(11) of Directive 2009/72/EC (n 41); Article 9(11) of Directive 2009/73/EC (n 41).

Spain, and Sweden. In cases where their ownership structures so permitted, transmission system operators in other Member States have also applied for certification in accordance with the OU rules. Based on the certifications issued so far, roughly 70% of all electricity TSOs currently apply the OU model. In the gas sector, 40% of all TSOs have been certified pursuant to this model.[101] Thus in terms of overall usage OU is the most prevalent unbundling model in the energy sector,[102] while second place is occupied by the ITO model,[103] and the least-used unbundling model is the ISO.

2.3.1.3 Unbundling Requirements for State-Owned Entities

In principle, the unbundling requirements of Directives 2009/72/EC and 2009/73/EC apply to both private and public undertakings.[104] However, Article 9(6) of both Directives creates the legal fiction that, in the case of State-owned entities, the ownership unbundling rules will be deemed to be fulfilled if 'two separate public bodies' exercise control over network operations on the one hand, and over generation/production or supply activities on the other. According to the Commission, the two public bodies must be 'truly separate', i.e. not under the 'common influence of another public entity.'[105]

The effect of Article 9(6) of the Gas and Electricity Directives is that the State, which is to be considered as a VIU if it has control over both the competitive and non-competitive parts of the energy sector, does not have to divest the public transmission or production/generation and supply assets to a private person in order to comply with the ownership unbundling rules.[106] This however results in a differential treatment of public and private undertakings. The practical relevance of Article 9(6) becomes clear if one considers that there is substantial degree of public

---

[101]Council of European Energy Regulators, 'Status Review on the Implementation of Transmission System Operators' Unbundling Provisions of the 3rd Energy Package' (C15-LTF-43-04 2016) 13 <http://www.ceer.eu/portal/page/portal/EER_HOME/EER_PUBLICATIONS/CEER_PAPERS/Cross-Sectoral/2016/C15-LTF-43-04_TSO-Unbundling_Status_Review-28-Apr-2016.pdf> accessed 27 September 2016.

[102]Ibid.

[103]The ITO model is much more 'popular' in the gas sector: 44% of gas TSOs have been certified under the ITO model, whereas only 12% of electricity TSOs are currently certified according to this model; see ibid 14–15.

[104]European Commission, 'Commission Staff Working Paper – Interpretative Note on Directive 2009/72/EC concerning common Rules for the Internal Market in Electricity and Directive 2009/73/EC concerning common Rules for the Internal Market in Natural Gas – The Unbundling Regime' (n 42) 10.

[105]Ibid.

[106]Stefan Storr, 'Ownership Unbundling und alternative Entflechtungsmodelle' in Jürgen F Baur, Peter Salje and Matthias Schmidt-Preuß (eds), *Regulierung in der Energiewirtschaft: Ein Praxishandbuch* (Kölner Handbücher zum Energiewirtschaftsrecht. Carl Heymanns Verlag 2011) [6]; Säcker and Mohr (n 52) [33]; Cabau (n 9) [4.156].

ownership in the EU energy sector.[107] In fact, the special OU regime for public undertakings has already been applied for in at least 22 cases.[108]

In the academic literature it is assumed that the incorporation of the tailor-made unbundling model in Article 9(6) of the Directives is based on Article 345 TFEU,[109] which provides that EU law shall in no way prejudice the rules in Member States governing the system of property ownership. Although uncertainties persist regarding the exact scope of Article 345 TFEU, it seems clear that requiring a State to privatize its transmission or production/generation and supply assets would violate this provision.[110]

Inasmuch as Article 9(6) of Directives 2009/72/EC and 2009/73/EC has already been applied in a number of certification decisions, it is now relatively clear under what circumstances the two public bodies can be said to be 'truly separate'. In most cases, two separate ministries will be deemed to have a sufficient degree of separation, provided that each minister has independent decision-making power in his or her area of competence.[111] In this context, a recurrent and problematic issue has been the role of the prime minister. As the prime minister generally has some sort of authority over the individual ministers, one may surmise, or at least speculate, that the transmission, production/generation, and supply activities are thus 'ultimately under the control of one and the same person which does not comply with ownership unbundling.'[112] While in the view of the Commission the power of the prime minister to set political guidelines does not run contrary to the requirements of

[107]See Council of European Energy Regulators, 'Status Review on the Implementation of Transmission System Operators' Unbundling Provisions of the 3rd Energy Package' (n 101) 16–17 (giving an overview of the level of public ownership in the gas and electricity transmission sectors).

[108]The gas and electricity TSOs that have been certified in accordance with Article 9(6) of the Directives are located in Austria, the Czech Republic, Denmark, Estonia, Finland, Germany, Hungary, Italy, Latvia, Lithuania, the Netherlands, Poland, Romania, Slovenia, the Slovak Republic and Sweden.

[109]Dirk Buschle, 'Unbundling of State-owned Transmission System Operators – Effective Remedy or Eyewash?' [2013] European Networks Law and Regulation Quarterly 49, 55, 62; Säcker and Mohr (n 52) [34].

[110]Christian Calliess, 'Ownership Unbundling für alle?: Kritische Überlegungen zu den aktuellen Entflechtungsvorhaben der Europäischen Kommission' (2007) 57 Energiewirtschaftliche Tagesfragen 92, 93–95; Christian Calliess, *Entflechtung im europäischen Energiebinnenmarkt: Zur Vereinbarkeit der europäischen Pläne für ein Ownership Unbundling mit der Kompetenzordnung des EG-Vertrages, insbesondere Art. 295 EGV, und dem allgemeinen Gleichheitssatz* (Bochumer Beiträge zum Berg- und Energierecht vol 50, Boorberg 2008) 19–65.

[111]See for example European Commission, Commission Opinion pursuant to Article 3(1) of Regulation (EC) No 714/2009 and Article 10(6) of Directive 2009/72/EC – Denmark – Certification of Energinet.dk (electricity) (09 January 2012) C(2012) 87 final, 4–6; European Commission, Commission Opinion pursuant to Article 3(1) of Regulation (EC) No 715/2009 and Article 10 (6) of Directive 2009/73/EC – Denmark – Certification of Energinet.dk (gas) (09 January 2012) C (2012) 88 final, 3–5.

[112]Cabau (n 9) [4.162].

Article 9(6),[113] nonetheless the prime minister should not be able to give direct instructions regarding the management of the TSO or the supply branch.[114] In general, based on a review of the certification practice, it appears that the interpretation of the term ‘two separate public bodies’ in Article 9(6) of the Gas and Electricity Directives ‘follows a rather formal approach, relying mainly on general constitutional principles,’[115] while paying less attention to constitutional and political realities.[116]

2.3.1.4 Extraterritorial Application of the Ownership Unbundling Requirements

An important issue relating to the interface between third country companies and ownership unbundling rules is extraterritoriality. The issue of extraterritoriality arises, for example, when a vertically integrated energy undertaking from a third country seeks to acquire control over a transmission system operator or an energy production/generation or supply company in the EU.[117] Is this vertically integrated undertaking required to unbundle itself in its country of origin in order to be able to invest in transmission systems or energy production/generation or supply in the EU? In other words, is the reach of the ownership unbundling requirements in Article 9 of Directives 2009/72/EC and 2009/73/EC geographically limited to the EU, or does it also extend to activities in third countries?[118]

While the Gas and Electricity Directives leave this question open as they do not foresee a specific geographical restriction,[119] the European Commission has taken

[113]European Commission, Commission Opinion pursuant to Article 3(1) of Regulation (EC) No 714/2009 and Article 10 of Directive 2009/72/EC – Latvia – Certification of Augstsprieguma tikls (03 December 2012) C(2012) 9108 final, 2–3.

[114]For a recent example, see European Commission, Commission Opinion pursuant to Article 3 (1) of Regulation (EC) No 715/2009 and Article 10(6) of Directive 2009/73/EC – Lithuania – Amber Grid (23 March 2015) C(2015) 2135 final, 2.

[115]Buschle (n 109) 62.

[116]Ibid 61.

[117]In general terms, the extraterritorial application of ownership unbundling rules is at issue where (i) a foreign person that exercises control over a generation/production or supply company located in a non-EU third country seeks to exercise control or any right over a TSO or a transmission system in the EU; and where (ii) a foreign person that exercises control over a TSO or a transmission system located in a non-EU third country seeks to exercise control or any right over a generation/production or supply company within EU territory.

[118]It will not be discussed here whether the definition of ‘vertically integrated undertaking’, which is contained in Article 2 No. 20 of Directive 2009/73/EC (n 41) and Article 2 No. 21 of Directive 2009/72/EC (n 41) and which is essential for the application of the ITO model, has extraterritorial reach. As the ITO model allows vertical integration, the question of whether the definition of VIU is geographically limited has no significant implications for third country companies.

[119]See Bundesnetzagentur, Beschluss: Zertifizierung eines Fernleitungsnetzbetreibers – GASCADE Gastransport GmbH (05 February 2013) Az.: BK7-12-031, 17; Bundesnetzagentur,

the stance that the ownership unbundling rules in the Directives apply in an extraterritorial fashion. This became obvious for the first time during the certification of National Grid Electricity Transmission, National Grid Gas, and National Grid Interconnectors Limited under the ownership unbundling model.[120] The ultimate holding company of these three TSOs in the United Kingdom also owned subsidiaries in third countries which performed electricity generation activities in the United States. The British national regulatory authority Ofgem considered that the OU requirements were satisfied, given that the national legislation transposing the TEP in Great Britain does not take into account producers/generators and suppliers outside the European Economic Area for certification purposes. The European Commission, however, pointed out 'that Article 9(1)(b)(ii) of the Electricity and Gas Directives is not restricted to generators, producers and suppliers operating in the EEA.'[121] In another case, a third-country investor in a British transmission system operator held shares in electricity generation companies in the US. In its certification decision, the Commission again considered that the definitions of generation or supply in the Electricity Directive are not limited to the EEA.[122] The assumption that the ownership unbundling requirements in Article 9 of the Directives have extraterritorial reach was also reiterated in a recent Staff Working Document of the Commission.[123]

Beschluss: Zertifizierung eines Fernleitungsnetzbetreibers – NEL Gastransport GmbH (20 December 2013) Az.: BK7-12-188, 20; Cécile van Vyve, 'Financial Investors and the Unbundling Provisions for TSOs' (2014) 23 European Energy and Environmental Law Review 63, 70; Tim Heitling and Ann-Christin Wiegemann, 'Fallstrick für Finanzinvestoren? – Die eigentumsrechtliche Entflechtung von Transportnetzbetreibern nach dem neuen EnWG' [2011] Netzwirtschaften & Recht 233, 236.

[120]European Commission, Commission Opinion pursuant to Article 3(1) of Regulation (EC) No 714/2009 and Article 10(6) of Directive 2009/72/EC and to Article 3(1) of Regulation (EC) No 715/2009 and Article 10(6) of Directive 2009/73/EC – United Kingdom – Certification of National Grid Electricity Transmission plc, National Grid Gas plc and National Grid Interconnectors Limited (19 April 2012) C(2012) 2735 final.

[121]Ibid 4.

[122]European Commission, Commission Opinion pursuant to Article 3(1) of Regulation (EC) No 714/2009 and Articles 10(6) and 11(6) of Directive 2009/72/EC – United Kingdom – Certification of TC Westermost Rough OFTO Limited (15 February 2016) C(2016) 975 final, 3–4. For other cases, see European Commission, Commission Opinion pursuant to Article 3(1) of Regulation (EC) No 714/2009 and Article 10(6) of Directive 2009/72/EC and to Article 3(1) of Regulation (EC) No 715/2009 and Article 10(6) of Directive 2009/73/EC – Portugal – Certification of REN Rede Elétrica Nacional S.A. and REN Gasodutos S.A. (12 May 2014) C(2014) 3255 final, 3–4; European Commission, Commission Opinion pursuant to Article 3(1) of Regulation (EC) No 715/2009 and Article 10(6) of Directive 2009/73/EC – France – Certification of TIGF (04 June 2014) C(2014) 3837 final, 2; European Commission, Commission Opinion pursuant to Article 3 (1) of Regulation (EC) No 714/2009 and Article 10(6) of Directive 2009/72/EC – Germany – Certification of 50 Hertz Transmission GmbH (06 September 2012) C(2012) 6260 final, 3–5; European Commission, Commission Opinion pursuant to Article 3(1) of Regulation (EC) No 715/2009 and Article 10(6) of Directive 2009/73/EC – Sweden – Certification of Swedegas AB (30 April 2012) C(2012) 3009 final, 3.

[123](n 50) 5.

At the same time, despite the Commission's position on extraterritoriality it is important to emphasize that in specific instances of extraterritorial application the OU rules are not applied in a mechanical or legalistic manner. Rather, the European Commission has endorsed a flexible approach, arguing that the objective is to remove the *conflict of interest* between generators/producers, suppliers and TSOs. Therefore, in the case of the British National Grid TSOs, the Commission opined that the OU requirements were complied with by virtue of the fact that there was no physical interconnection between the US and the UK electricity systems.[124] In the same way, 'conflicting' assets in Australia, Brazil, China, Pakistan, the Philippines and South Korea were considered not to create a genuine conflict of interest. In other words, if the generation/production or supply activities are geographically removed from, and have no connection with, the transmission activities, there is no obstacle to certification. However, having said that it can be expected that the Commission will take a more restrictive approach if the relevant assets are located in a third country that is geographically close to, or even borders with, one or several EU Member States.[125]

The Commission's approach towards the extraterritorial application of the unbundling requirements is fairly straightforward and has generally been followed by the national regulatory authorities. Nevertheless it remains to be seen whether the corresponding interpretation of the Directives is, in fact, correct. The German regulatory authority *Bundesnetzagentur*, for example, takes the view that the concepts of 'control' and 'right' in section 8(2) of the German Energy Industry Act, which implements Article 9(1)(b) of the Gas and Electricity Directives, are geographically restricted to the EU.[126] This also seems to be the position of the German legislator. The explanatory statement accompanying sections 4a and 4b of the German Energy Industry Act, which implement Articles 10 and 11 of Directives 2009/72/EC and 2009/73/EC, states that the certification procedure applies to transmission system operators that are active within the scope of Union law and that for the purposes of the relevant tests used in the certification process, their scope of application is geographically limited to the territory of the European Union.[127]

---

[124] Commission Opinion – Certification of National Grid TSOs (n 120) 4.

[125] Van Vyve (n 119) 68–69. See also Heitling and Wiegemann (n 119) 236–237.

[126] Bundesnetzagentur, 'Zertifizierungsverfahren – Hinweispapier zur Antragstellung' (BK6-11-157, BK7-11-157 12 December 2011) 17 <http://www.bundesnetzagentur.de/DE/Service-Funktionen/Beschlusskammern/1BK-Geschaeftszeichen-Datenbank/BK7-GZ/2011/2011_0001bis0999/2011_100bis199/BK7-11-157_BKV/BK7-11-157_download.pdf?__blob=publicationFile&v=1> accessed 21 July 2015. However, in the certification of the TSO 50 Hertz the German regulator appears to have accepted that the ownership unbundling provisions under German law (section 8(2) of the German Energy Industry Act (*EnWG*)) have an extraterritorial scope of application, see Bundesnetzagentur, Beschluss: Zertifizierung eines Übertragungsnetzbetreibers – 50 Hertz Transmission GmbH (09 November 2012) Az.: BK6-12-040, 11–24.

[127] See Deutscher Bundesrat, 'Entwurf eines Gesetzes zur Neuregelung energiewirtschaftsrechtlicher Vorschriften' (Drucksache 343/11 6 June 2011) 128 <http://dipbt.bundestag.de/dip21/brd/2011/0343-11.pdf> accessed 26 August 2015. In fact, also a literal reading

Although a detailed examination would go beyond the scope of this book, it is important to note that the extraterritorial application of unbundling requirements also raises issues under public international law. Under international law, a State may only regulate the conduct of natural or juridical persons if an appropriate basis is established for jurisdiction over them. For example, it is generally recognized that a State can claim jurisdiction under the territorial principle, the active or passive personality principle, and the protective principle.[128] These traditional grounds of jurisdiction do not cover the extraterritorial application of unbundling requirements, because the relevant conduct of the third country undertaking occurs in the territory of a third country. However, the so-called 'effects doctrine'[129] could apply in such situations, given that for instance production or supply activities by a company in a third country can produce anti-competitive 'effects' within the territory of an EU Member State if the company or one of its subsidiaries controls a TSO in that Member State. Invoking the effects doctrine in relation to the unbundling requirements in the EU energy sector would be an obvious option, given that the doctrine is gaining traction, particularly in European and international competition law.[130] Despite being controversial, the effects doctrine seems to provide a legitimate basis for jurisdiction under customary international law if the effects are 'substantial, direct and foreseeable.'[131] The fact that the European Commission and the national regulators appear to limit the extraterritorial application of OU requirements to cases in which the relevant EU Member State is geographically connected to the country in which the generation/production or supply activities are carried out reflects this

---

of the German Energy Industry Act suggests that activities in third countries are irrelevant for the purpose of determining compliance with the ownership unbundling requirements as transposed into German law. According to section 8(1) of the German Energy Industry Act (n 52), the ownership unbundling model only applies to 'vertically integrated energy supply undertakings'. The definition of 'vertically integrated energy supply undertaking', in turn, excludes activities that take place outside of the European Union (see ibid, Section 3 No. 38). It is, however, clear that the application of the ownership unbundling requirements only to vertically integrated energy supply undertakings is problematic also for a number of other reasons, see Christian Koenig, Jürgen Kühling and Winfried Rasbach, *Energierecht* (3rd edn, Nomos 2013) [99–101].

[128]James Crawford, *Brownlie's Principles of Public International Law* (8th edn, Oxford University Press 2012) 456ff; Malcolm N Shaw, *International Law* (7th edn, Cambridge University Press 2014) 469ff.

[129]Crawford (n 128) 462ff; Shaw (n 128) 499ff.

[130]Maher M Dabbah, *International and Comparative Competition Law* (Cambridge University Press 2010) 423ff; Thorsten Mäger, 'Einführung und Grundlagen' in Thorsten Mäger (ed), *Europäisches Kartellrecht* (2nd edn. Nomos 2011) 46; Matthias Herdegen, *Principles of International Economic Law* (Oxford University Press 2013) 90; Monica Waloszyk, *Law and Policy of the European Gas Market* (Edward Elgar 2014) 60ff. The German regulator *Bundesnetzagentur* discussed the application of the effects doctrine in relation to the scope of the ITO unbundling model, see Beschluss: Zertifizierung GASCADE (n 119) 16–19; Beschluss: Zertifizierung NEL (n 119) 18–22.

[131]Herdegen (n 130) 91; Thilo Rensmann, 'Völkerrechtliche Grenzen extraterritorialer Wirtschaftssanktionen' in Dirk Ehlers and Hans-Michael Wolffgang (eds), *Recht der Exportkontrolle: Bestandsaufnahme und Perspektiven* (R & W Verlag 2015) 106.

limitation. Thus, the (limited) extraterritorial application of the ownership unbundling requirements in Directives 2009/72/EC and 2009/73/EC appears to be in conformity with public international law.

2.3.1.5 Third Country Companies and Ownership Unbundling Requirements

The unbundling requirements in the Third Energy Package apply equally to EU and non-EU undertakings.[132] Inevitably, therefore, the Gas and Electricity Directives have had an impact on third country companies. In particular, given that the ITO model still allows vertical integration to be maintained and thus largely preserves (foreign) investors' property rights, the main question is to what extent foreign energy companies active within the EU are affected by the far-reaching ownership unbundling requirements.

As a starting point it may be observed that significant third country investments took place predominantly in the EU gas infrastructure sector.[133] Furthermore, OU measures have first and foremost affected the Russian company Gazprom. Being one of Europe's largest suppliers of natural gas, Gazprom is prohibited, under the TEP's ownership unbundling rules, from exercising control or any right over transmission system operators in the EU. Gazprom's business model was, however, for a long time based on the control over pipeline infrastructure.[134] The EU Member States in which ownership unbundling has been, or is being, implemented and in which Gazprom has had or has shareholdings in transmission system assets include Lithuania, Estonia, Latvia and the United Kingdom. Recent Gazprom-sponsored pipeline projects have also been negatively affected by OU legislation.

In Lithuania, which was at the time 100% dependent on Russian gas exports, on 30 June 2011 the legislature passed an amendment to the country's natural gas law with a view to implementing the TEP.[135] The changes entered into force on 1 August 2011.[136] The Natural Gas Act, as amended, requires full ownership unbundling. The deadline for the implementation of OU was 31 October 2014. At the time of adoption

---

[132] 24th recital of the preamble to Directive 2009/72/EC (n 41); 21st recital of the preamble to Directive 2009/73/EC (n 41).

[133] See European Commission, Commission Staff Working Document accompanying the legislative package on the internal market for electricity and gas – Impact Assessment (19 September 2007) SEC(2007) 1179, 40, 107.

[134] Andrey Konoplyanik, 'Russia and the Third EU Energy Package: Regulatory Changes for Internal EU Energy Markets in Gas and Possible Consequences for Suppliers (Including Non-EU Suppliers) and Consumers' [2011] International Energy Law Review 24, 29.

[135] Republic of Lithuania, Law on the Amendment of the Law on Natural Gas (Gamtinių dujų įstatymo pakeitimo įstatymas) (01 August 2011) Official Gazette, 14.07.2011, No. 87-4186.

[136] Lithuanian National Control Commission for Prices and Energy, 'Annual Report on Electricity and Natural Gas Markets of the Republic of Lithuania to the European Commission' (Vilnius 2013), 83 <http://www.regula.lt/en/SiteAssets/ncc-reports/NCC-report-2012.pdf>.

of the implementing legislation, Gazprom held a 37% stake in the Lithuanian vertically integrated gas undertaking AB Lietuvos Dujos. In accordance with the above-mentioned laws, Lietuvos Dujos was required to carry out the unbundling of its gas transmission networks. As a result, the gas transmission network was spun off into a separate company, AB Amber Grid, which began operations on 1 August 2013.[137] In June 2014, Gazprom sold its 37% stake in Lietuvos Dujos and Amber Grid to the State of Lithuania.[138]

In Estonia, which was also characterized by a ‘zero competition environment’, with Gazprom being its sole supplier, the Natural Gas Act was amended in June 2012 in order to implement the provisions of the Gas Directive.[139] The modifications entered into force on 8 July 2012. The Natural Gas Act, as amended,[140] prescribed that full ownership unbundling was to be implemented by 1 January 2015.[141] The decision to implement OU was taken despite the fact that Estonia benefits from an ‘isolated market’ exception under Article 49(1) Directive 2009/73/EC.[142] Gazprom at the time was the largest shareholder (37%) in the vertically integrated energy company AS Eesti Gaas, which operated the Estonian gas transmission system through its subsidiary AS EG Võrguteenus. In July 2013, the de-merger of EG Võrguteenus from Eesti Gaas took place.[143] In June 2015, Gazprom sold its 37% share in the Estonian TSO to the State-owned company Elering.[144] In 2016, Gazprom also sold its shareholding in Eesti Gaas.

In Latvia, which imports all of its gas from Russia, the process of ownership unbundling is still ongoing. Like Estonia, Latvia benefits from an explicit derogation

---

[137]Ibid 85.

[138]Ministry of Energy of the Republic of Lithuania, ‘Comment of the Minister of Energy on Gazprom’s Decision to Sell its Stake in Lithuanian Utilities’ (12 June 2014) <https://enmin.lrv.lt/en/news/comment-of-the-minister-of-energy-on-gazprom-s-decision-to-sell-its-stake-in-lithuanian-utilities> accessed 25 June 2015; Andrius Sytas, *Lithuania Completes Buy of Gas Utility Shares from Gazprom* (Reuters 2014).

[139]See Republic of Estonia, Amendment to the Natural Gas Act (Maagaasiseaduse muutmise seadus) (08 July 2012) Riigi Teataja I, 28.06.2012, 2. See also Ott Ummelas, ‘Estonian Parliament Approves Natural-Gas Unbundling Bill’ *Bloomberg* (6 June 2012) <http://www.bloomberg.com/news/2012-06-06/estonian-parliament-approves-natural-gas-unbundling-bill-1-.html> accessed 23 June 2016.

[140]Republic of Estonia, Natural Gas Act (Maagaasiseadus) (07 May 2014) Riigi Teataja I, 06.05.2014, 11.

[141]European Commission, *Energy Markets in the European Union in 2011* (Publications Office of the European Union 2012) 75; Estonian Competition Authority, ‘Annual Report to the European Commission – Estonian Electricity and Gas Market 2012’ (Tallinn 2013), 53.

[142]Article 49(1) Directive 2009/73/EC (n 41) provides in relevant part: ‘Articles 4, 9, 37 and/or 38 shall not apply to Estonia, Latvia and/or Finland until any of those Member States is directly connected to the interconnected system of any Member State other than Estonia, Latvia, Lithuania and Finland.’

[143]Eesti Gaas, ‘History’ (no date) <http://www.gaas.ee/en/group/history/> accessed 8 May 2015.

[144]Elering, *Elering Acquires Gazprom’s 37 per cent Stake in Estonian Gas Transmission Network* (2015).

under Article 49(1) of the Gas Directive. Nevertheless, the Latvian government decided to opt for ownership unbundling, which was to be fully implemented by the end of 2017. Until recently, the country's gas transmission network was owned and operated by Latvijas Gāze, in which Gazprom is the largest shareholder with a 34% stake.[145] In September 2016, the shareholders of Latvijas Gāze agreed to the creation of a new company, Conexus Baltic Grid, which is now in charge of gas transmission and storage.[146] This decision was made in accordance with the Latvian energy legislation, which required legal unbundling by 3 April 2017.[147] In the second stage, Conexus Baltic Grid had to comply with the ownership unbundling requirements by 31 December 2017.[148] This means that those shareholders of Conexus Baltic Grid which are directly or indirectly engaged in gas production or supply will have to dispose of their shares. This applies in particular to Gazprom. As of early 2018, Gazprom had not yet sold its 34% stake in Conexus Baltic Grid.

In the United Kingdom, Gazprom held a 10% share in Interconnector (UK) Limited (IUK), which owns and operates a sub-sea gas pipeline that links the United Kingdom and Belgium. As IUK was not part of a vertically integrated undertaking on 3 September 2009, it must comply with the requirements of full ownership unbundling. Although some of the non-controlling shareholders of IUK had interests in the production or supply of natural gas (including Gazprom), the divestment route was not initially chosen. Instead, the company decided to implement changes to its corporate governance arrangements, including the Articles of Association and the Shareholders Agreement, in order to ensure that such shareholders are unable to exercise rights in IUK.[149] As a result of these changes Gazprom lost, *inter alia*, its shareholder voting rights and any rights to appoint directors of IUK.[150] In other words, Gazprom relinquished all rights to take part in the decision-making process of the company. Even though the European Commission accepted in 2013 that these arrangements were in compliance with the Gas Directive,[151] Gazprom sold its 10% stake in IUK in late 2015 to the private company Fluxys.[152]

[145]Latvijas Gāze, 'Shares and Trading' (no date) <http://www.lg.lv/index.php?id=189&lang=eng> accessed 23 June 2016.

[146]LETA, 'Latvijas Gaze shareholders back creation of new company in charge of gas transmission, storage' (2 September 2016) <http://www.leta.lv/eng/home/important/133A1865-48EF-844B-16AB-349B536F4803/> accessed 9 September 2016.

[147]Latvijas Gāze, 'Reorganisation Prospectus' (1 July 2016) 15 <http://www.lg.lv/uploads/filedir/File/Jaunumi/2016/Reorganizacija/2016_Latvijas_Gaze_Reorganisation_Prospectus.pdf> accessed 9 September 2016.

[148]Ibid.

[149]European Commission, Commission Opinion pursuant to Article 3(1) of Regulation (EC) No 715/2009 and Article 10(6) of Directive 2009/73/EC – United Kingdom – Interconnector UK Limited (26 March 2013) C(2013) 1872 final, 3ff.

[150]Ibid 6.

[151]Ibid.

[152]Fluxys, 'Fluxys Acquires Gazprom Stake in Interconnector (UK)' (17 December 2015) <http://www.fluxys.com/group/en/NewsAndPress/2015/151217_Interconnector> accessed 23 June 2016.

The ownership unbundling requirements in Directives 2009/72/EC and 2009/73/EC have also affected two major recent Gazprom-sponsored infrastructure projects: South Stream and Nord Stream 2. As mentioned, new interconnectors built after 3 September 2009 must follow the ownership unbundling regime.[153]

The South Stream pipeline was supposed to transport Russian gas directly to the EU, thereby bypassing Ukraine as a transit country. If it had been built as planned, it would have run under the Black Sea, through Bulgaria, Serbia and Hungary to Austria. Starting in the year 2008, i.e. already before the adoption of the TEP, the Russian Federation concluded several international agreements related to the construction and governance of South Stream with both EU and non-EU Member States.[154] Several of these agreements provided for Gazprom's control over the respective pipeline operators.[155] In 2013, the European Commission took the view that the bilateral agreements were incompatible with EU law, in particular on the ground that the ownership unbundling rules of Directive 2009/73/EC were not respected.[156] Although the Russian side sought to invoke the principle of *pacta sunt servanda*,[157] it was made public in December 2014 that Gazprom had stopped the South Stream project.[158]

---

[153] See Sect. 2.3.1.2.

[154] These agreements were published in a compendium, see MENA Chambers, 'South Stream Intergovernmental Agreements: A Compendium' (2014) <http://www.menachambers.com/expertise/energy/South-Stream-IGAs.pdf> accessed 1 May 2015.

[155] See, for example, the Bulgaria-Russia South Stream agreement. Article 2 of this agreement states that '[t]he Company shall own the gas pipeline as well as other assets and facilities constructed and/or acquired in the process of its business activities'. Article 8 of the agreement stipulates that '[t]he functions of the gas pipeline's operator shall be performed by the Company'. Furthermore, Article 3(1) of the Bulgaria-Russia agreement explicitly provides that the 'Bulgarian Founder' (Bulgargas) and the 'Russian Founder' (Gazprom) shall have 50% of the shares in the Company's registered capital each; see ibid 40–41. As Bulgargas and Gazprom are active in the production and/or supply of natural gas in the EU, Article 3(1) of the Bulgaria-Russia South Stream agreement creates a situation where Bulgaria's obligations under the agreement cannot be reconciled with the OU model as foreseen in Directive 2009/73/EC. This finding also applies to the Hungary-Russia (ibid 102ff), Croatia-Russia (ibid 57ff) and Greece-Russia (ibid 79ff) South Stream agreements, which contain essentially identical provisions.

[156] 'South Stream Bilateral Deals Breach EU Law, Commission Says' *EurActiv* (4 December 2013) <http://www.euractiv.com/energy/commission-south-stream-agreemen-news-532120>.

[157] Alexey S Ispolinov and Tatiana Dvenadtcatova, 'Принудительное выделение сетевого бизнеса в рамках Третьего Энергопакета ЕС (unbundling): практика применения' [2014] Закон 111, 119. See also Ministry of Foreign Affairs of the Russian Federation, 'Speech by the Russian Foreign Minister, Sergey Lavrov, and his Answers to Questions from the Mass Media during the Press Conference Summarising the Results of the Negotiations with the Bulgarian Foreign Minister, Kristian Vigenin' (7 July 2014) <http://www.mid.ru/brp_4.nsf/0/E1E909450FC0862F44257D10005BA3C4>; Ministry of Foreign Affairs of the Russian Federation, 'Interview by the Russian Foreign Minister Sergey Lavrov to the Serbian Newspaper "Politics"' (3 February 2014) <http://www.mid.ru/brp_4.nsf/0/5B3D4C4DD2B0BE5744257C75005E82AC>.

[158] 'Russia Says South Stream project is Over' *EurActiv* (2 December 2014) <http://www.euractiv.com/sections/global-europe/russia-says-south-stream-project-over-310491> accessed 26 June

The offshore pipeline Nord Stream 2 is planned to complement the existing Nord Stream pipelines with two additional lines running through the Baltic Sea from Vyborg in Russia to Greifswald in Germany. It is expected that the construction of Nord Stream 2 will be completed by 2019. The corresponding shareholders' agreement was signed in late 2015. Half of the shares in the company that will build and operate Nord Stream 2 are owned by Gazprom.[159] Several EU Member States, which are opposed to the infrastructure project, have argued that the offshore import pipeline is subject to ownership unbundling.[160] Within the Commission there are diverging views on this issue as well.[161] Clearly, if the OU rules were to apply to Nord Stream 2, 'the business case for the project would be destroyed.'[162]

2.3.2 *Certification*

2.3.2.1 General Certification Procedure

In order for an undertaking to be approved and designated as a transmission system operator, it must be certified according to the provisions set out in Article 10 of Directive 2009/72/EC in conjunction with Article 3 of Regulation 714/2009 (for electricity), or Article 10 of Directive 2009/73/EC in conjunction with Article 3 of Regulation 715/2009 (for gas). The objective of the certification procedure is to ensure compliance with the unbundling rules. The procedure is the same irrespective of the applicable unbundling model (OU, ISO or ITO).[163]

The obligation to initiate the certification procedure lies with the respective national regulatory authority. Once the national regulatory authority concerned has decided that the unbundling requirements are complied with, it must notify its

---

2015; 'Russia Confirms Decision to Abandon South Stream' *EurActiv* (10 December 2014) <http://www.euractiv.com/sections/energy/russia-confirms-decision-abandon-south-stream-final-310712> accessed 26 June 2015. See also Jonathan Stern, Simon Pirani and Katja Yafimava, 'Does the Cancellation of South Stream Signal a Fundamental Reorientation of Russian Gas Export Policy?' (2015) 4 <http://www.oxfordenergy.org/wpcms/wp-content/uploads/2015/01/Does-cancellation-of-South-Stream-signal-a-fundamental-reorientation-of-Russian-gas-export-policy-GPC-5.pdf> (writing that the 'TEP (in)compatibility argument ... was the main reason for the South Stream cancellation').

[159]Nord Stream 2, *Gazprom and ENGIE Modify Nord Stream 2 Shareholdings, Equalizing EU-Russian Ownership* (2015).

[160]See Anca Gurzu, 'Nord Stream 2's Opponents Look for Legal Ammunition' (30 December 2015) <http://www.politico.eu/article/nord-stream-2s-opponents-look-for-legal-ammunition/> accessed 23 June 2016.

[161]Karel Beckman, 'Can Nord Stream 2 Be Stopped?' (14 April 2016) <http://www.energypost.eu/can-nord-stream-2-stopped/> accessed 23 June 2016.

[162]Ibid.

[163]Article 13(3) and Article 18(10) of Directive 2009/72/EC (n 41); Article 14(3) and Article 18 (10) of Directive 2009/73/EC (n 41).

(preliminary) decision to the Commission. The Commission will then give its own assessment of compatibility with the unbundling rules.[164] When taking its final decision, the NRA must take 'utmost account' of the Commission's opinion.[165] Subsequently, NRAs have to continually monitor a TSO's respect for the unbundling requirements. To this end, they have the power to open a new certification procedure.[166] Furthermore, TSOs must notify the NRA of any planned transaction which might require a reassessment of compliance with the applicable unbundling model.[167]

2.3.2.2 The Certification Procedure in Relation to Third Countries

Whereas certification requests by TSOs in the EU fall under the general certification procedure outlined above, the situation is different where a transmission system owner or TSO is 'controlled by a person or persons from a third country or third countries'. In such cases, the certification of the TSO concerned follows the procedure provided for in Article 11 of both Directives. As with the unbundling requirements, the concept of 'control' is identical to the one used in the EU Merger Regulation.[168] The term 'third country' is fleshed out in the implementing legislation of the respective EU Member States. Under German and French legislation, for example, the term covers countries which are not part of the European Union or the EEA.[169]

As per Article 11(3) of Directives 2009/72/EC and 2009/73/EC, the certification of third-country-controlled TSOs may be granted only if two conditions have been fulfilled, and the burden of proof in this regard lies with the applicant TSO.[170] First, in accordance with Article 11(3)(a), the foreign-controlled TSO must comply with the corresponding unbundling requirements, i.e. OU, ISO or ITO.[171] Hence third

[164]Article 3(1) of Regulation (EC) No 714/2009 (n 88); Article 3(1) of Regulation (EC) No 715/2009 (n 88).

[165]Article 3(2) of Regulation (EC) No 714/2009 (n 88); Article 3(2) of Regulation (EC) No 715/2009 (n 88).

[166]Article 10(4) of Directive 2009/72/EC (n 41); Article 10(4) of Directive 2009/73/EC (n 41).

[167]Article 10(3) of Directive 2009/72/EC (n 41); Article 10(3) of Directive 2009/73/EC (n 41).

[168]13th recital of the preamble to Directive 2009/72/EC (n 41); 10th recital of the preamble to Directive 2009/73/EC (n 41).

[169]See section 4b of the German Energy Industry Act (n 52); Article L. 111-5 of the French Energy Code (*Code de l'énergie*), reproduced in French Regulatory Authority for Energy CRE, Délibération de la Commission de régulation de l'énergie portant décision de certification de la société TIGF (03 July 2014).

[170]European Commission, 'Commission Staff Working Paper – Interpretative Note on Directive 2009/72/EC concerning common Rules for the Internal Market in Electricity and Directive 2009/73/EC concerning common Rules for the Internal Market in Natural Gas – The Unbundling Regime' (n 42) 23.

[171]But see Lecheler and Germelmann (n 36) 82, and particularly footnote 170, who (erroneously) state that foreign controlled operators cannot choose the ITO unbundling model. Both Directives

country undertakings are subject to the same substantive unbundling rules as EU companies.[172] Second, and in accordance with Article 11(3)(b), it must be demonstrated to the national regulatory authority that 'granting certification will not put at risk the security of energy supply of the Member State and the [EU]'. This is the point in which EU and foreign companies are treated differently. The general certification procedure applicable to EU TSOs lacks a comparable or equivalent requirement to the 'security of energy supply' test contained in Article 11(3)(b).

The Directives further specify which criteria the national regulatory authority shall consider when evaluating whether granting certification to a third-country-controlled TSO will jeopardize the security of energy supply of the respective Member State and the EU. Under Article 11(3)(b) of both Directives, it must take into account: First, the rights and obligations of the EU with respect to the respective third country arising under international law, including any agreement concluded with one or more third countries to which the EU is a party and which addresses the issues of security of energy supply (lit (i)); secondly, the rights and obligations of the respective Member State with respect to that third country arising under agreements concluded with it, insofar as they are in compliance with EU law (lit (ii)); and thirdly, other specific facts and circumstances of the case and the third country concerned (lit (iii)).

The *ratio legis* for the inclusion of the security of energy supply test can be found in recital 22 of the preamble to the Gas Directive and recital 25 of the preamble to the Electricity Directive. It is worth reproducing this common preamble in full:

> The security of energy supply is an essential element of public security and is therefore inherently connected to the efficient functioning of the internal market in gas and the integration of the isolated gas markets of Member States. Gas can reach the citizens of the Union only through the network. Functioning open gas markets and, in particular, the networks and other assets associated with gas supply are essential for public security, for the competitiveness of the economy and for the well-being of the citizens of the Union. Persons from third countries should therefore only be allowed to control a transmission system or a transmission system operator if they comply with the requirements of effective separation that apply inside the Community. Without prejudice to the international obligations of the Community, the Community considers that the gas transmission system sector is of high importance to the Community and therefore additional safeguards are necessary regarding the preservation of the security of supply of energy to the Community to avoid any threats to public order and public security in the Community and the welfare of the citizens of the Union. The security of supply of energy to the Community requires, in particular, an assessment of the independence of network operation, the level of the Community's and individual Member States' dependence on energy supply from third countries, and the treatment of both domestic and foreign trade and investment in energy in a particular third country. Security of supply should therefore be assessed in the light of the factual circumstances of each case as well as the rights and obligations arising under international law, in particular the international agreements between the Community and the third country concerned. Where appropriate the Commission is encouraged to submit recommendations

clearly provide that the ITO model is applicable to certification procedures under Article 11, see Article 18(10) of Directive 2009/72/EC (n 41); Article 18(10) of Directive 2009/73/EC (n 41).

[172]Johnston and Block (n 57) [3.103].

to negotiate relevant agreements with third countries addressing the security of supply of energy to the Community or to include the necessary issues in other negotiations with those third countries.

The procedure for certification in relation to third countries under Article 11 is structured similarly to the general one under Article 10 of both Directives. In the first instance, the competent NRA adopts a draft decision on the certification of the TSO concerned, within a time period of 4 months after certification has been requested.[173] Whereas the responsibility for determining whether the candidate TSO fulfills the relevant unbundling rules lies with the NRA, the security of energy supply test can also be carried out by 'another competent authority designated by the Member State'.[174] A number of Member States have implemented this possibility. In Germany, for example, the security of supply test is implemented by the Federal Ministry for Economic Affairs and Energy,[175] and in France by the Ministry of Energy.[176] This clearly highlights the political nature of the security of supply assessment.[177] The NRA must notify its decision to the Commission. The Commission then has 2 months to issue an opinion as to whether (a) the entity concerned complies with the applicable unbundling requirements; and (b) whether granting certification will put at risk the security of energy supply.[178] If the Commission requests the views of the Agency for the Cooperation of Energy Regulators (ACER),[179] the Member State concerned, or other interested parties, the time period is extended by another 2 months.[180] Subsequently, the NRA must adopt its final decision within a period of another 2 months. In doing so, it is obliged to take 'utmost account' of the Commission's opinion.[181]

[173] Article 11(3) of Directive 2009/72/EC (n 41); Article 11(3) of Directive 2009/73/EC (n 41).

[174] Article 11(3)(b) of Directive 2009/72/EC (n 41); Article 11(3)(b) of Directive 2009/73/EC (n 41).

[175] See section 4b(2) and (3) of the German Energy Industry Act (n 52).

[176] See Article L. 111-5 of the French Energy Code (*Code de l'énergie*), in conjunction with Decree No 2011-1478 of 9 November 2011.

[177] Cabau (n 9) [4.104]. See also Katrin Harjes, '§ 4b Zertifizierung in Bezug auf Drittstaaten' in Franz J Säcker (ed), *Berliner Kommentar zum Energierecht* (vol 1, 3rd edn. Dt. Fachverl. Fachmedien Recht und Wirtschaft 2014) [17] (writing that the assessment of the German Federal Ministry for Economic Affairs and Energy is a 'political judgment').

[178] Article 11(5) and (6) of Directive 2009/72/EC (n 41); Article 11(5) and (6) of Directive 2009/73/EC (n 41).

[179] See Regulation (EC) No 713/2009 of the European Parliament and of the Council establishing an Agency for the Cooperation of Energy Regulators (13 July 2009) OJ 2009/L 211/1.

[180] So far, the Commission has never requested the views of ACER.

[181] Article 11(8) of Directive 2009/72/EC (n 41); Article 11(8) of Directive 2009/73/EC (n 41).

2.3.2.3 Certification Practice in Relation to Third Countries

It may be useful to give an overview of the cases in which the certification procedure in relation to third countries, as set out in Article 11 of Directives 2009/72/EC and 2009/73/EC, has played a role so far.[182]

It seems that Article 11 was applied for the first time in the certification of the German TSO Thyssengas under the ITO model. Thyssengas had been part of the vertically integrated undertaking RWE, but in 2011 it was sold to the Australian investment bank Macquarie Group Limited. The German national regulator *Bundesnetzagentur* determined, in a decision containing just a few sentences devoid of any substantial reasoning, that granting certification would not put at risk the security of energy supply of Germany or the EU.[183] It is also striking that the European Commission, in its opinion on the certification of Thyssengas, appeared to completely ignore the fact that the TSO was controlled by a person from a third country.[184]

In addition, Article 11 of Directive 2009/73/EC was applied in the certification of the French gas transmission system operator Transport et Infrastructures Gaz France (TIGF) under the OU model. When certification was requested, TIGF was owned by Snam (45%), Pacific Mezz Luxembourg (35%) and Société C31 (20%). Pacific Mezz Luxembourg, in turn, was owned by GIC Private Limited, which was controlled by the Ministry of Finance of Singapore. The French regulatory authority CRE and the European Commission declared that GIC, together with Snam (an - EU-based ownership unbundled TSO), exercised joint control of TIGF.[185] This triggered the application of Article 11 of the Gas Directive. It was, however, considered that the joint control by GIC did not jeopardize the security of energy supply of either France or the European Union. The main reasons for this were that Singapore produced no natural gas, that no interconnections to Europe existed, and that trade relations between the EU and Singapore were well-established and reciprocal.[186]

---

[182]Article 11 of the Directives was considered in a number of certification decisions (ENAGAS; REN Rede Eléctrica Nacional and REN Gasodutos; TAP), but as in each case none of the foreign shareholders had, solely or jointly, control over the TSO, the provision was not applied. See European Commission, Commission Opinion pursuant to Article 3(1) of Regulation (EC) No 715/2009 and Article 10(6) of Directive 2009/73/EC – Spain – Certification of ENAGAS, S.A. (gas) (15 June 2012) C(2012) 4171 final, 5; Commission Opinion – Certification of REN and REN Gasodutos (n 122) 3; European Commission, Commission Opinion pursuant to Article 3 (1) of Regulation (EC) No 715/2009 and Article 10(6) of Directive 2009/73/EC – Italy – Greece – Certification of TAP AG (28 January 2016) C(2016) 538 final, 7–8.

[183]Bundesnetzagentur, Beschluss: Zertifizierung eines Fernleitungsnetzbetreibers – Thyssengas GmbH (12 March 2013) Az.: BK7-12-036, 75.

[184]See European Commission, Commission Opinion pursuant to Article 3(1) of Regulation (EC) No 715/2009 and Article 10(6) of Directive 2009/73/EC – Germany – Certification of Thyssengas GmbH (30 January 2013) C(2013) 570 final.

[185]Commission Opinion – Certification of TIGF (n 122) 5.

[186]Ibid 5–6.

Another instance where Article 11 of Directive 2009/73/EC was applied concerns the certification of the Greek gas transmission system operator DESFA under the ITO model. In 2013, the State Oil Company of the Azerbaijan Republic (SOCAR), a company established under the laws of Azerbaijan and controlled by the Republic of Azerbaijan, won a tender to purchase DESFA. According to the terms of the share purchase agreement, SOCAR sought to acquire 66% and thereby exercise sole control of DESFA. These acquisition plans triggered a full-blown analysis under Article 11 of the Gas Directive.

In relation to the issue of security of supply, the European Commission (1) pointed out that the volumes of Azeri gas supplied to Greece and the EU are not insignificant; (2) highlighted the strategic role of the DESFA transmission network as an 'entry gate' for natural gas from different supply sources to the EU and Greece; (3) outlined the potential risk that governmental acts by the Republic of Azerbaijan or acts by SOCAR might hinder compliance by SOCAR or DESFA with EU energy law; and (4) drew attention to the risk that the Republic of Azerbaijan could exercise its ownership rights in a way that could result in SOCAR or DESFA contravening EU law.[187] Furthermore, the European Commission rejected the argument of the Greek regulatory authority RAE that compliance with the unbundling rules in the TEP would in and of itself sufficiently ensure the independence of the network's operation. In this regard, the Commission stressed that 'the EU legislator has clearly established the security of supply assessment in Article 11 as an *additional test* to that of Article 9 Gas Directive (unbundling rules)'.[188]

Against this background, the Commission concluded that additional safeguards were necessary to address the concerns related to the security of energy supply. In particular, it reasoned that certification should not be granted unless it was established 'that RAE has the power to suspend, on its own initiative or upon request of the Commission, all voting rights attached to the shares that SOCAR holds in DESFA should SOCAR and/or the Republic of Azerbaijan take a decision or action that negatively affects the security of supply of Greece and/or the European Union.'[189] In line with the Commission's request, the Greek Parliament ratified a law in September 2014 that gave the Greek regulatory authority RAE the authority to

---

[187]European Commission, Commission Opinion correcting Opinion C(2014) 5483 final of 28 July 2014 pursuant to Article 3(1) of Regulation (EC) No 715/2009 and Article 10(6) and 11(6) of Directive 2009/73/EC – Greece – Certification of DESFA (17 October 2014) C(2014) 7734 final, 4–6.

[188]Ibid 5 (emphasis in the original).

[189]Ibid 7.

impose a suspension of the exercise of voting rights held in DESFA.[190] On September 25, 2014, RAE certified DESFA under the ITO model.[191]

The next example of a certification procedure in relation to third countries involves the Polish section of the Yamal-Europe Pipeline, which runs from Russia to the EU, via Belarus. The gas pipeline section is owned by Europolgaz, which is in turn owned by the Polish State-controlled natural gas company PGNiG (48% of the shares), Gazprom (48%), and Polish Gas-Trading S.A. (4%). It is operated by the fully State-owned company Gaz-System, which applied for certification under the ISO model. While the Polish regulatory authority ERO and the Commission already disagreed over whether Gazprom exercised 'control' over Europolgaz,[192] the application of the security of energy supply test exposed serious discrepancies. ERO took the view that the security of supply analysis 'concerns the entity that is to be granted the certificate of independence – i.e. the transmission system operator'.[193] Accordingly, it held that an examination of the impact of a foreign shareholder in the transmission system *owner* on the security of gas supply to Poland and the European Union 'goes beyond the scope of the analysis to be conducted by the regulatory authority'.[194] Unsurprisingly, ERO thus came to the conclusion that certifying Gaz-System under the ISO model would not put at risk the security of gas supply to either Poland or the European Union.

---

[190]Hellenic Republic, Law 4286/2014 (Νόμος 4286/2014) (2014) Government Gazette, 19.9.2014, No. 194 A. Article 15 of this act introduced Article 65A into the Hellenic Republic, Law 4001/2011 on the Operation of Electricity and Gas Energy Markets, for Exploration, Production and Transmission Networks of Hydrocarbons and other provisions (Νόμος 4001/2011 για τη λειτουργία Ενεργειακών Αγορών Ηλεκτρισμού και Φυσικού Αερίου, για Έρευνα, Παραγωγή και δίκτυα μεταφοράς Υδρογονανθράκων και άλλες ρυθμίσεις) (2011) Government Gazette, 22.8.2011, No. 179 A.

[191]Greek Regulatory Authority for Energy RAE, 'Final Decision on the Certification of the Hellenic Gas Transmission System Operator (DESFA) SA as an Independent Natural Gas Transmission Operator' (Decision No 523/2014 25 September 2014) <http://www.desfa.gr/wp-content/uploads/2015/10/%CF%84%CE%B5%CE%BB%CE%B9%CE%BA%CE%AE-%CE%91%CF%80%CF%8C%CF%86%CE%B1%CF%83%CE%AE-%CF%84%CE%B7%CF%82-%CE%A1%CE%91%CE%95.pdf> accessed 29 June 2015. The acquisition of DESFA by SOCAR was not, however, completed after RAE's decision had been taken. In November 2014, the European Commission announced that it would open an in-depth investigation to determine whether the transaction is consistent with the EU Merger Regulation; see European Commission, *Mergers: Commission Opens in-depth Investigation into Proposed Acquisition of Greek Gas Transmission System Operator DESFA by SOCAR* (IP/14/1442, 2014).

[192]See European Commission, Commission Opinion pursuant to Article 3(1) of Regulation (EC) No 715/2009 and Article 10(6) and 11(6) of Directive 2009/73/EC – Poland – Certification of Gaz-System as the operator of the Polish section of Yamal-Europe Pipeline (09 September 2014) C(2014) 6463 final, 8–9.

[193]Polish Regulatory Authority for Energy ERO, Final Decision on the Certification of the Transmission System Operator Gaz-System (19 May 2015) DRG-4720-2(28)/2014/2015/6154/KF, 71.

[194]Ibid.

The Commission, in contrast, concluded that ERO had failed to carry out a 'true' assessment of the risks to security of supply as required by Article 11(3)(b) of the Gas Directive. It urged ERO to assess Gazprom's joint control over Europolgaz in conjunction with its position as a key supplier, and to evaluate the risk that Europolgaz and/or its shareholders could exercise their ownership rights in a way that could make it more difficult for Gaz-System or Europolgaz to comply with relevant EU law.[195] Similarly to the case of DESFA, the Commission further stressed that, if necessary, 'ERO should be granted additional rights as a necessary safeguard, such as the power to suspend Gazprom's voting rights in Europolgaz.'[196] The transmission system operator was certified on 19 May 2015.[197] Additional safeguards like those contemplated by the Commission were not implemented.

The latest certification procedure in which Article 11 was applied concerns the operator of a transmission link connecting an offshore wind turbine facility in the North Sea with England's onshore transmission system.[198] While the US American investor HELP controlled the transmission operator, it was concluded that the security of supply was not put at risk. The main reasons given were that the offshore transmission line did not form part of the interconnected network, but was linked to the onshore transmission network on a point-to-point basis and that HELP was a financial investor without any control over the operator's day-to-day operations.[199]

Some general conclusions can be drawn from the existing certification practice to date under Article 11 of both Directives. First of all, it is important to highlight that no certification request of a TSO controlled by a person or persons from a third country or third countries has been rejected so far. Where security of supply risks are identified, the European Commission usually calls for the implementation of additional safeguards. The right of the national regulatory authority to suspend the voting rights of the foreign investor in the transmission system owner or TSO has emerged as the standard safeguard in this connection. Furthermore, and on a related point, the security of supply risks assessed under Article 11 are mainly linked to the possibility of non-compliance with EU law, and in particular EU energy law. It is thus the internal dimension of security of supply that takes center stage in the third country certification procedure. Finally, it is interesting to note that the European Commission has taken a stricter approach to the evaluation of security of supply risks than the national regulatory authorities. However, as the case of the Yamal-Europe Pipeline has shown, although the NRAs are required to take 'utmost account' of the Commission's opinion, they have the final say on (third country) certification issues.

[195]European Commission, Commission Opinion pursuant to Article 3(1) of Regulation (EC) No 715/2009 and Article 10(6) and 11(6) of Directive 2009/73/EC – Poland – Certification of Gaz-System as the operator of the Polish section of Yamal-Europe Pipeline (19 March 2015) C (2015) 2008 final, 6.

[196]Ibid.

[197]Final Decision on Certification of TSO Gaz-System (n 193).

[198]Commission Opinion – Certification of TC Westermost Rough OFTO Limited (n 122) 4–5.

[199]Ibid 4.

2.3.3 *Exemptions from Unbundling*

2.3.3.1 General Exemption Procedure

The 714/2009 Electricity Regulation and 2009/73/EC Gas Directive provide for exemptions from certain key obligations under the TEP. According to Article 17 (1) of the Electricity Regulation and Article 36(1) of the Gas Directive, new infrastructure projects may be exempted from, *inter alia*, the unbundling requirements,[200] the third party access regime,[201] and tariff regulation.[202] With respect to the infrastructure eligible for exemption, the Electricity Regulation refers to 'new direct current interconnectors'.[203] The Gas Directive limits possible exemptions to 'major new gas infrastructure, i.e. interconnectors, LNG and storage facilities'.[204]

Similar derogation provisions had already been contained in the 2003/55/EC Gas Directive[205] and the 1228/2003 Electricity Regulation.[206] The main difference between the Second and Third Energy Packages is that under the old law it was not possible to derogate from the unbundling rules. This can be explained by the fact that the functional and legal unbundling rules in the Second Energy Package still preserved incentives for energy producers/generators and suppliers to invest in new transmission infrastructure.[207] Under the new ownership unbundling regime, however, these incentives are largely absent. Their absence leads directly to the economic and regulatory arguments underlying the justification for the derogation rules in general.

[200] Article 9 of Directive 2009/72/EC (n 41); Article 9 of Directive 2009/73/EC (n 41).

[201] Article 32 of Directive 2009/72/EC (n 41); Article 32 Directive 2009/73/EC (n 41).

[202] Article 37(6) and (10) of Directive 2009/72/EC (n 41); Article 41(6), (8) and (10) of Directive 2009/73/EC (n 41).

[203] For a definition of the terms 'interconnector' and 'new interconnector', see Article 2(1) and Article 2(2)(g) of Regulation (EC) No 714/2009 (n 88). In exceptional cases and under certain circumstances, exemptions may also be granted to 'alternating current interconnectors'. Furthermore, exemptions can be granted to 'significant increases of capacity' in existing interconnectors. See ibid, Article 17(2) and (3).

[204] For a definition of the terms 'interconnector' and 'new infrastructure', see Article 2 Nos. 17 and 33 of Directive 2009/73/EC (n 41). Exemptions can also be granted to 'significant increases of capacity' in existing infrastructure and to modifications of such infrastructure 'which enable the development of new sources of gas supply'. See ibid, Article 36(2).

[205] Article 22 of Directive 2003/55/EC (n 13).

[206] Article 7 of Regulation (EC) No 1228/2003 of the European Parliament and of the Council on conditions for access to the network for cross-border exchanges in electricity (26 June 2003) OJ 2003/L 176/1.

[207] Christopher Jones and William Webster, 'Derogations and Exemptions' in Christopher Jones (ed), *The Internal Energy Market – The Third Liberalisation Package* (EU Energy Law Series vol 1, 3rd edn. Claeys & Casteels Publishing 2010) [11.136].

Investments in major new infrastructure are indispensable to complete the internal energy market.[208] At the same time, it is a matter of common knowledge that such investments are highly cost-intensive and risky.[209] Under these circumstances, it is believed that the rigid application of the EU energy regulations could deter third-party investors, i.e. companies other than transmission system operators (so-called 'merchant investors'), from making much needed investments. For example, the *ex post* regulation of access tariffs can significantly lower the expected return for investors, which may lead to the postponement or abandonment of needed investments.[210] Likewise, it is clear that without an exemption from ownership unbundling, undertakings with energy production/generation or supply interests could refrain from building new infrastructure, simply because they could not control it.[211] It is against this background that the European Commission stated that 'ownership unbundling – as much as Third Party Access and tariff regulation – may undermine the commercial viability of a new interconnector if it enhances the risks of the project promoter not to recoup its investment costs and an adequate return on equity.'[212] The 'regulatory holidays' are thus designed to ensure the realization of new infrastructure investments. It is also noteworthy that, viewed against the background of the EU's dependence on imports of natural gas from third countries, Directive 2009/73/EC explicitly states in its preamble that the possibility of derogations 'should apply, *for security of supply reasons, in particular, to new pipelines within the [EU] transporting gas from third countries into the [EU]*'.[213]

Any exemption is temporary[214] and subject to the conditions set out in Article 17 (1) of Regulation 714/2009 and Article 36(1) of Directive 2009/73/EC, as follows: First, the investment must enhance competition in gas/electricity supply. Second, in the case of gas, the investment must also enhance security of supply. Third, the level of risk attached to the investment must be such that the investment would not take

[208]European Commission, Commission Staff Working Document on Article 22 of Directive 2003/55/EC concerning common rules for the internal market in natural gas and Article 7 of Regulation (EC) No 1228/2003 on conditions for access to the network for cross-border exchanges in electricity – New Infrastructure Exemptions (06 May 2009) SEC(2009)642 final, [9].

[209]Johnston and Block (n 57) [4.99].

[210]For a detailed description of this so-called 'truncation problem', see Marek Szydło, 'Regulatory Exemptions for New Gas Infrastructure. A Key Challenge for European Energy Policy' (2009) 18 European Energy and Environmental Law Review 254, 255–256.

[211]Seliverstov and Gudkov (n 14) 177.

[212]European Commission, Commission Decision on the exemption of the "Gazelle" interconnector from ownership unbundling within the meaning of Article 9 of Directive 2009/73/EC (01 December 2011) C(2011) 8777 final, 51; Italian Regulatory Authority for Energy AEEG, Albanian Regulatory Authority for Energy ERE and Greek Regulatory Authority for Energy RAE, 'Final Joint Opinion of the Energy Regulators on TAP AG's Exemption Application' (2013) 41 <http://www.autorita.energia.it/allegati/docs/13/249-13all.pdf> accessed 21 September 2016.

[213]35th recital of the preamble to Directive 2009/73/EC (n 41) (emphasis added).

[214]Article 17(1) of Regulation (EC) No 714/2009 (n 88) – 'for a limited period of time'; Article 36 (1) of Directive 2009/73/EC (n 41) – 'for a defined period of time'.

place unless an exemption was granted. Fourth, the new infrastructure must be owned by an entity legally separate from the system operators in whose systems the infrastructure will be built. Fifth, charges must be levied on users of that infrastructure. Sixth, in the case of electricity no part of the capital or operating costs of the transmission line can come from charges made for the use of transmission or distribution systems linked by it. Seventh, the exemption must not be to the detriment of competition, the effective functioning of the internal market in natural gas/electricity, or the efficient functioning of the regulated system to which the infrastructure is connected.[215]

Although the text of Article 17(1) of Regulation 714/2009 and Article 36(1) of Directive 2009/73/EC refers broadly to the possibility of an exemption from the unbundling rules (which comprises all three main unbundling models in the TEP), new infrastructure for which an exemption can be sought is generally subject to the OU model. The ISO, and in particular the ITO, models are not available because in such cases the investment could arguably take place without the exemption, as it would thus not be strictly necessary for the execution of the project.[216] Furthermore, all new infrastructure projects built after 3 September 2009 have to follow the OU rules in any event.[217] The infrastructure-related exemption regime in the TEP is, therefore, properly called an 'ownership unbundling exemption regime'.

The procedure for the grant of a derogation to ownership unbundling with respect to new infrastructure can be described in the following way. In principle, exemptions are granted only upon application.[218] At the first stage of the procedure, it is the relevant national regulatory authority that takes a decision on the exemption, on a case-by-case basis.[219] If more than one national regulatory authority is involved in granting a derogation, ACER may provide an advisory opinion.[220] So far however it has not made use of this competence. Furthermore, in such cases ACER exercises the decision-making task conferred upon the NRAs where the NRAs are unable to reach an agreement within a specified period of time, or upon a joint request from the NRAs concerned.[221] Once a decision has been reached, the NRA(s) must transmit the decision to the Commission. In the second stage of the procedure, the

[215]Article 17(1)(a)-(f) of Regulation (EC) No 714/2009 (n 88); Article 36(1)(a)-(e) of Directive 2009/73/EC (n 41).

[216]Therefore, the condition in Article 17(1)(b) Regulation (EC) No 714/2009 (n 88) and Article 36 (1)(b) Directive 2009/73/EC (n 41) would not be met.

[217]See Hans Heller, *Neue Erdgasinfrastrukturen und Freistellung von der Regulierung: Ein legitimes Instrument der Investitionsförderung?* (Nomos 2013) 274. See also Szydło (n 210) 267.

[218]Article 17(1) of Regulation (EC) No 714/2009 (n 88); Article 36(1) of Directive 2009/73/EC (n 41).

[219]Article 17(4) of Regulation (EC) No 714/2009 (n 88); Article 36(3) of Directive 2009/73/EC (n 41).

[220]Article 17(4) of Regulation (EC) No 714/2009 (n 88); Article 36(4) of Directive 2009/73/EC (n 41).

[221]Article 17(5) of Regulation (EC) No 714/2009 (n 88); Article 36(4) of Directive 2009/73/EC (n 41).

Commission can require the NRA(s) to amend or withdraw the exemption decision.[222] In contrast to the decision-making procedure regarding the certification of TSOs, it is thus the Commission that has the final say on exemption requests.

A number of projects have already been granted an exemption from ownership unbundling under the TEP, both in the electricity[223] and gas[224] sectors. In lieu of the OU model, the European Commission consistently requires the respective operators to apply the ITO unbundling rules in an 'ad hoc' fashion.[225] Furthermore, in some EU Member States companies are exempted from the unbundling rules in the TEP by virtue of the continued application of exemptions granted pursuant to Article 22 of Directive 2003/55/EC and Article 17 of Regulation 2003/1228.[226] One example is the OPAL pipeline. In 2009, before the entry into force of the TEP, the pipeline had been granted an exemption from third party access and tariff regulation under Directive 2003/55/EC. In such cases, the German legislation implementing the TEP specifically determines that the application of the new unbundling rules, i.e. OU, ISO and ITO, is precluded.[227] In other words, the German legislation extends the benefit of an exemption granted pursuant to the Second Energy Package to the tightened unbundling rules contained in Directives 2009/72/EC and 2009/73/EC, despite the fact that the original exemption decision did not and could not grant unbundling-related exceptions. It should be noted that it is unclear whether this approach is in line with the Directives.[228]

---

[222]Article 17(8) of Regulation (EC) No 714/2009 (n 88); Article 36(9) of Directive 2009/73/EC (n 41).

[223]European Commission, Commission Decision on the exemption of ElecLink Limited under Article 17 of Regulation (EC) No. 714/2009 for an electricity interconnector between France and Great Britain (28 July 2014) C(2014) 5475 final; Commission Decision – Exemption of SI-IT Interconnectors (n 97).

[224]Commission Decision – Exemption of the Gazelle interconnector (n 212); European Commission, Commission Decision on the exemption of the Trans Adriatic Pipeline from the requirements on third party access, tariff regulation and ownership unbundling laid down in Articles 9, 32, 41(6), 41(8) and 41(10) of Directive 2009/73/EC (16 May 2013) C(2013) 2949 final; European Commission, Commission Decision on the exemption of the Slovakian-Hungarian natural gas interconnector from ownership unbundling rules in Article 9 of Directive 2009/73/EC (17 September 2013) C(2013) 6159 final.

[225]See, for instance, Commission Decision – Exemption of the Trans Adriatic Pipeline (n 224) 232.

[226]According to recital 23 of Regulation (EC) No 714/2009 (n 88) and recital 35 of Directive 2009/73/EC (n 41), exemptions granted under Regulation (EC) No 1228/2003 (n 206) and Directive 2003/55/EC (n 13) 'continue to apply until the scheduled expiry date as decided in the granted exemption decision'.

[227]Section 118(7) of the German Energy Industry Act (n 52).

[228]The Directives do not regulate whether, and to what extent, exempted projects under Article 17 of Regulation 2003/1228 and Article 22 of Directive 2003/55/EC are subject to the new unbundling rules, see Heller (n 217) 275–276. In the literature, the extension of the exemptions granted under the Second Energy Package to the unbundling rules in the TEP was rejected, see Jones and Webster (n 207) [11.138]. The Commission takes the view that the unbundling rules can be dispensed with in so far as their application would be incompatible with the exemption pre-dating the Directives, see European Commission, Commission Opinion pursuant to Article 3

2.3.3.2 Exemption Decisions and Third Countries

Based on the experiences so far, the exemption regime under the Third Energy Package (as well as under the old SEP) has a higher practical relevance for foreign economic actors in the gas sector than in the electricity sector. In fact, in the electricity sector there have so far been no exemption decisions with a 'third country dimension'. All of the existing merchant investment projects are intra-EU and without the involvement of any foreign energy investors.[229] At the same time, a number of electricity transmission lines connecting the EU with third countries are presently being built by transmission system operators themselves.[230]

In the gas sector, the possibility to obtain an exemption from ownership unbundling (and/or the third party access rules) has had and continues to be important from the perspective of foreign economic operators. This seems to be due to the fact that while the construction of multi-country pipeline infrastructure is often necessary to transport the natural gas from remote production sites to the customers in the European Union, corresponding demand-driven regulatory procedures for the creation of new pipeline capacity by TSOs are not yet in place.[231] Accordingly, there are several merchant investment projects in the gas sector with a strong third country element.

Under the Second Energy Package, exemptions from TPA were granted to the Nabucco[232] and the OPAL[233] pipelines. The Nabucco pipeline was supposed to run from Turkey to Austria, connecting the EU to significant sources of natural gas in the

(1) of Regulation (EC) No 715/2009 and Article 10(6) of Directive 2009/73/EC – Austria – NABUCCO Gas Pipeline International GmbH (11 December 2012) C(2012) 9575 final, 3–5; European Commission, Commission Opinion pursuant to Article 3(1) of Regulation (EC) No 714/2009 and Article 10(6) of Directive 2009/72/EC – Austria – Certification of Eneco Valcanale S.r.l. (05 March 2015) C(2015) 1547 final, 2–5. This means that decisions on the applicability of unbundling rules (ownership unbundling, ISO, ITO, Second Energy Package) are to be taken on a case-by-case basis.

[229] See also Karolis Gudas, *Intersection of WTO and EU law in International Electricity Trade: Analysis of the Regulatory Environment for Electricity Systems Development* (PhD Dissertation, forthcoming).

[230] See for example the NordLink project between Germany and Norway; the submarine interconnection between Italy and Montenegro; and the interconnector between Croatia and Bosnia and Herzegovina.

[231] Katja Yafimava, *The EU Third Package for Gas and the Gas Target Model: Major Contentious Issues Inside and Outside the EU* (Oxford Institute for Energy Studies 2013) 21–28, 45–46, 49, 51, 55; Simon Pirani and Katja Yafimava, *Russian Gas Transit Across Ukraine Post-2019: Pipeline Scenarios, Gas Flow Consequences, and Regulatory Constraints* (Oxford Institute for Energy Studies 2016) 27–29.

[232] See, for instance, European Commission, Exemption decision on the Austrian section of the Nabucco pipeline (08 February 2008) CAB D(2008)142; European Commission, Exemption decision on the Austrian section of the Nabucco pipeline (22 October 2008) CAB D(2008) 1094, C(2008) 6254.

[233] European Commission, Ausnahmegenehmigung der Bundesnetzagentur für die OPAL-Gasleitung gemäß Art. 22 der Richtlinie 2003/55 (12 June 2009) C(2009) 4694.

Caspian Sea and the Middle East. The project has been abandoned in its current form. The OPAL pipeline is an onshore branch of the Nord Stream pipeline transporting Russian gas from the northeast of Germany to the German-Czech border. It has been in operation since 2011. Under the Third Energy Package, an exemption from ownership unbundling and TPA has been granted to the Trans Adriatic Pipeline.[234] Like its former competitor Nabucco, the TAP is also planned to transport natural gas from the Caspian Sea to European consumers. The pipeline, which is currently being built, will start in Greece, cross Albania and the Adriatic Sea, and then interconnect with the Italian gas transmission network. Apart from that, it was also expected for a long time that Gazprom would apply for an exemption for the (now defunct) South Stream pipeline. In fact, the European Commission even encouraged Gazprom to file such a request,[235] but for various reasons Gazprom chose not to do so.[236]

The development of infrastructure projects with third countries under the OU exemption regime in Directive 2009/73/EC and Regulation 714/2009 is subject to one major limitation. The reason for this can be found in the definition of the eligible type of gas and electricity infrastructure. According to Article 36(1) Directive 2009/73/EC, only 'major new gas infrastructure, i.e. interconnectors, LNG and storage facilities,' qualify, in principle, for the exemption. The central term 'interconnector', in turn, is legally defined as a 'transmission line which crosses or spans a border between Member States for the sole purpose of connecting the national transmission systems of those Member States'.[237] A similar definition applies in the context of electricity.[238] The main consequence of this definition is that gas and electricity transmission lines that connect an EU Member State with third countries cannot benefit from an exemption unless the respective infrastructure *also* crosses or spans a border within the EU.[239] This limitation has already led to the denial of an exemption request.[240] The exclusion of 'EU-third country' gas and electricity transmission projects which have no additional contribution to the interconnection of the EU's *internal* energy infrastructure from the coverage of the exemption regime shows that the exemption provisions in the TEP are drafted in a way that fails to accommodate

[234]Commission Decision – Exemption of the Trans Adriatic Pipeline (n 224).

[235]'EC: Russia Should Apply for South Stream Exemption' *Natural Gas Europe* (7 December 2013) <http://www.naturalgaseurope.com/south-stream-pipeline-exemption-eu-rules> accessed 17 July 2016.

[236]Stern, Pirani and Yafimava, 'Does the Cancellation of South Stream Signal a Fundamental Reorientation of Russian Gas Export Policy?' (n 158) 4.

[237]Article 2 No. 17 of Directive 2009/73/EC (n 41).

[238]Article 2(1) of Regulation (EC) No 714/2009 (n 88).

[239]Seliverstov and Gudkov (n 14) 178.

[240]The NEL pipeline, which is the second onshore extension of the Russian Nord Stream project in Germany (apart from OPAL), did not fulfill the requirement to interconnect at least two national transmission systems of EU Member States, see Bundesnetzagentur, Antrag auf Freistellung von der Regulierung – OPAL NEL Transport GmbH (25 February 2009) Az. BK7-08-009, 20–22.

the specific interests of third countries and third-country energy investors.[241] This is surprising given that, at least in the gas sector, the security of supply rationale underlying the idea of granting 'regulatory holidays' to certain networks applies in particular to new pipelines transporting gas from third countries into the EU.[242]

2.4 Ownership Unbundling and General EU Competition Law

As outlined above, the European Commission was unsuccessful in its attempt to introduce mandatory ownership unbundling as part of the Third Energy Package. There is, however, another avenue through which the Commission has been able to push ownership unbundling in recent years: general EU competition law. While this book focuses on the legal problems connected to (ownership) unbundling as a *regulatory* instrument, it is useful to briefly outline the possibilities of imposing OU in the form of network divestiture as a structural remedy in competition law cases. In addition, this distinction between sector-specific regulation and general competition law will also become important in Chap. 6.

Regulation 1/2003[243] is the main legal framework for enforcement actions based on Articles 101 (dealing with anti-competitive agreements) and 102 (governing abuse of dominance situations) of the TFEU. Under Regulation 1/2003, the Commission has two main avenues for intervention: (1) prohibition decisions pursuant to Article 7; and (2) commitment decisions pursuant to Article 9.

Under Article 7, the Commission can require an undertaking or association of undertakings to cease the infringement. To this end, the Commission can impose behavioral and/or structural remedies. Ownership separation requirements qualify as a structural remedy. Structural remedies may be ordered only if no equally effective behavioral remedies are available, or if the equally effective behavioral remedies are more burdensome for the undertaking. Furthermore, structural remedies must be proportionate to the infringement committed. In the case of enforced changes to the structure of an undertaking, which is the result of ownership unbundling policies, the principle of proportionality is satisfied only if there is a 'substantial risk of a lasting or repeated infringement that derives from the very structure of the undertaking.'[244]

In contrast to Article 7, the application of Article 9 of Regulation 1/2003 does not presuppose the finding of an infringement. Under that provision, companies can

---

[241] See the critical remarks of Ivan Gudkov, 'Газовый диалог России и ЕС: взаимодействие и конфликт международного и европейского права' [2014] Научный журнал Российского газового общества 49, 53 (for the gas sector) and Gudas (n 229) (for the electricity sector).

[242] *Cf.* 35th recital of the preamble to Directive 2009/73/EC (n 41).

[243] Council Regulation (EC) No 1/2003 on the implementation of the rules on competition laid down in Articles 81 and 82 of the Treaty (16 December 2002) OJ 2003/L 1/1.

[244] Ibid, 12th recital of the preamble.

propose certain voluntary commitments in order to settle ongoing antitrust investigations. Once accepted by the Commission, the commitments are binding and enforceable.

As of this time, ownership unbundling has not yet been imposed as a structural remedy under Article 7 of Regulation 1/2003. In fact, the Commission has not adopted structural remedies in any prohibition decision under Article 7 so far.[245] However, the Commission has made it clear that it is generally prepared to make use of such remedies in order to address competition concerns in the energy markets.[246] Furthermore, it indicated that its enforcement powers under Article 7 have 'positively contributed' to the willingness of vertically integrated energy companies to voluntarily offer ownership unbundling commitments under Article 9.[247]

The possibility of commitment decisions under Article 9 of Regulation 1/2003 has proven to be an effective instrument to achieve (partial) ownership unbundling. In the period of 2008 to 2010, three major energy companies (E.ON, RWE, and ENI) committed to divest network electricity/gas transmission assets. All cases related to investigations into the abuse of dominance under Article 102 of the TFEU.

In the case of E.ON,[248] the European Commission expressed concern that the company may have abused its dominant position on the TSO-level by (1) buying more expensive secondary balancing energy from its own production affiliates, while passing on the costs to the final consumer; and (2) preventing the import of balancing energy by unaffiliated power producers from other EU Member States, again with the aim of favoring its own production branch. E.ON committed to divest its extra-high voltage line network (380/220 kV).

In the case of RWE,[249] the Commission produced a preliminary assessment according to which RWE may have abused its dominant position as a transmission system operator by (1) refusing to supply gas transmission services to third customers (understatement of technically available capacity; inefficient congestion

[245] European Commission, Commission Staff Working Document: Ten Years of Antitrust Enforcement under Regulation 1/2003 (09 July 2014) SWD(2014) 230 final, 188.

[246] See, for example, Inquiry into the European gas and electricity sectors (n 22) 44.

[247] European Commission, Commission Staff Working Paper: Report on the functioning of Regulation 1/2003 (29 April 2009) SEC(2009) 574 final, 92.

[248] See European Commission, Commission Decision relating to a proceeding under Article 82 of the EC Treaty and Article 54 of the EEA Agreement (26 November 2008) Cases COMP/39.388 – German Electricity Wholesale Market, COMP/39.389 – German Electricity Balancing Market, [46ff]; European Commission, Summary of Commission Decision (26 November 2008) C(2008) 7367 final; OJ 2009/C 36/8. See also European Commission, *Antitrust: Commission welcomes E. ON proposals for structural remedies to increase competition in German electricity market* (MEMO/08/132, 2008).

[249] See European Commission, Commission Decision relating to a proceeding under Article 82 of the EC Treaty and Article 54 of the EEA Agreement (18 March 2009) Case COMP/39.402 – RWE Gas Foreclosure, [21ff]; European Commission, Summary of Commission Decision (18 March 2009) C(2009) 1885; OJ 2009/C 133/10. See also European Commission, *Antitrust: Commission welcomes RWE proposals for structural remedies to increase competition in German gas market* (MEMO/08/355, 2008).

management system); and (2) implementing a so-called 'margin squeeze' strategy, which entailed increasing transmission tariffs to an artificially high level and manipulating the network tariff structure in such a way as to create disadvantages only for downstream competitors. In order to meet the Commission's competition concerns, RWE offered to sell almost its entire German high-pressure gas transmission network (approx. 4000 km in length).

In the case of ENI,[250] the Commission came to the provisional conclusion that ENI may have infringed Article 102 TFEU by refusing to supply gas transmission services to third parties on certain international gas import pipelines. In particular, the Commission took the view that the company had (1) failed to offer existing available or unused capacity; (2) degraded the quality and value of capacity offered to competitors; and (3) deliberately limited investments in additional capacity that had been requested by third party shippers. With a view to bringing the antitrust proceedings to an end, ENI committed to divest its shareholdings in a number of companies that owned or operated international gas transmission pipelines.

Some scholars have criticized the European Commission by arguing that it misuses the Article 9 procedure under Regulation 1/2003 in order to achieve the political goal of ownership unbundling, i.e. to attain something which it failed to accomplish through legislative action.[251] Against this background, it has been stated that 'while the Commission may have lost the battle on the regulatory front, it is winning the war through the use of general competition law'.[252] The implementation of ownership unbundling 'through the back door'[253] is to some extent facilitated by the recent jurisprudence of the ECJ concerning the limits of commitment decisions under Article 9. Although the Article 9 provision does not, in contrast to Article 7, explicitly provide that the Commission's power to make voluntary commitments binding is subject to the principle of proportionality, it is clear that decisions adopted under Article 9 must comply with that principle.[254] However, in overturning a decision of the General Court the ECJ held in *Alrosa* that Article 9 decisions are not subject to

[250]See European Commission, Commission Decision relating to a proceeding under Article 102 TFEU and Article 54 of the EEA Agreement (29 September 2010) Case COMP/39.315 – ENI, [39ff]; European Commission, Summary of Commission Decision (29 September 2010) C (2010) 6701; OJ 2010/C 352/8. See also European Commission, *Antitrust: Commission welcomes ENI's structural remedies proposal to increase competition in the Italian gas market* (MEMO/10/29, 2010).

[251]Iñigo del Guayo, Gunther Kühne and Martha M Roggenkamp, 'Ownership Unbundling and Property Rights in the EU Energy Sector' in Aileen McHarg and others (eds), *Property and the Law in Energy and Natural Resources* (Oxford University Press 2010) 339.

[252]Talus (n 7) 83.

[253]See Hubertus von Rosenberg, 'Unbundling Through the Back Door...the Case of Network Divestiture as a Remedy in the Energy Sector' (2009) 30 European Competition Law Review 237.

[254]Apart from being a general principle of EU law, the principle of proportionality features in the 34th recital of the preamble to Council Regulation (EC) No 1/2003 (n 243), which states that '[i]n accordance with the principles of subsidiarity and proportionality as set out in Article 5 [TEC], this Regulation does not go beyond what is necessary in order to achieve its objective, which is to allow the Community competition rules to be applied effectively'.

the *same* proportionality requirements as Article 7 decisions. In particular, the ECJ ruled that the Commission is entitled to accept commitments which go further than a decision which it could have adopted under Article 7 of Regulation 1/2003.[255]

In the view of the Court, the application of the principle of proportionality in connection with commitment decisions merely requires the Commission to ascertain (1) whether the commitments offered in the proceedings address the competition concerns at issue, and (2) whether the undertaking concerned has not itself offered less onerous commitments that are also sufficient to adequately address those concerns.[256] In this context, judicial review is limited to verifying that the Commission's assessment was not manifestly incorrect.[257] Importantly, in the absence of an obligation to conduct a fully-fledged proportionality assessment, the Commission is not obliged 'to seek out less onerous or more moderate solutions than the commitments offered to it.'[258]

As a consequence of the *Alrosa* jurisprudence, it is becoming increasingly easy for the European Commission to push ownership unbundling through the use of general competition law. While it is true that the possibility of imposing ownership unbundling under Article 9 of Regulation 1/2003 is based on a voluntary offer by the undertaking concerned, the fact remains however that the Commission is *de facto* in a position to demand such commitments from specific vertically integrated undertakings. Thus the adoption of structural remedies in abuse of dominance cases under Article 102 TFEU will continue to modify market structures. At the same time however, given that the ownership unbundling requirements imposed through EU competition law are not permanent[259] and only operate vis-à-vis specific companies or assets, they cannot be a substitute for lack of action on the regulatory side.[260] The main controversy, therefore, will take place on the regulatory front.

---

[255] European Court of Justice, *European Commission v. Alrosa Company Ltd,* Judgment (29 June 2010) C-441/07 P [35–50] (referring to General Court of the European Union, *Alrosa Company Ltd v. European Commission,* Judgment (11 July 2007) T-170/06 [101, 140]). For an opposing view, see Andreas Klees, 'Das Instrument der Zusagenentscheidung der Kommission und der Fall "E. ON" – Ein (weiterer) Sündenfall' [2009] Wirtschaft und Wettbewerb 374, 378–379.

[256] *European Commission v. Alrosa Company Ltd* (n 255) [41].

[257] Ibid [42].

[258] Ibid [61].

[259] See Commission Decision relating to a proceeding under Article 82 TEC – German Electricity Wholesale Market (n 248) 14. E.ON can reacquire the divested network after a period of 10 years.

[260] Rosenberg (n 253) 254 (who notes that EU competition law 'cannot be used as a vehicle to fulfil regulatory ambitions').

Chapter 3
Ownership Unbundling and National Constitutional Law and EU Law: A Brief Summary of the Relevant Legal Issues

3.1 Introduction

While this book analyzes the unbundling and unbundling-related measures in the EU energy sector from the perspective of international economic law, it is nonetheless important to briefly summarize the main points of the past debate on the legality of ownership unbundling measures under national constitutional law and EU law, a debate which began in 2006 and subsided after the adoption of the Third Energy Package in 2009. This will provide the necessary context and background for the subsequent discussion of WTO law and international investment law.[1]

In this connection, the jurisprudence of the Dutch courts and the ECJ in the *Essent* case should also be examined. Until now, this is the only case in which ownership unbundling requirements have been challenged before domestic courts in the EU. As for the unbundling-*related* measures (certification procedure; exemption regime), their relationship with EU law will not be touched upon here, given that these issues have received only minor attention in the scholarly writings on the TEP.[2]

---

[1]The limits of the EU's harmonization competence under Article 114 TFEU will not be discussed here, as this would not provide any added value for the analysis of WTO law and international investment law.

[2]For a critical analysis of the infrastructure-related exemption regime in the TEP, see Hans Heller, 'Neue Erdgasinfrastrukturen und Freistellung von der Regulierung: Art. 36 der Erdgasrichtlinie 2009/73/EG (§ 28a EnWG) als legitimes Instrument der Investitionsförderung?' (2015) 12 Netzwirtschaften & Recht 66. For a discussion of the certification regime in Directives 2009/72/EC and 2009/73/EC, mainly from a third-country perspective, see Jörg Gundel and Claas F Germelmann, 'Kein Schlussstein für die Liberalisierung der Energiemärkte' [2009] Europäische Zeitschrift für Wirtschaftsrecht 763, 769–770; Arnoud Willems, Jung-ui Sul and Yohan Benizri, 'Unbundling as a Defence Mechanism Against Russia: Is the EU Missing the Point?' in Kim Talus and Piero L Fratini (eds), *EU – Russia Energy Relations* (Euroconfidentiel 2010) 233–237; Matthias Schmidt-Preuß, 'Die Kontrolle des Verkaufs bzw. des Erwerbs von Netzen (Erwerb durch Nicht-EU-Ausländer gem. §4b EnWG; Außenwirtschaftsrecht; Fusionskontrolle)' in Jürgen F Baur, Peter

T. M. Dralle, *Ownership Unbundling and Related Measures in the EU Energy Sector*, European Yearbook of International Economic Law 5,
https://doi.org/10.1007/978-3-319-77797-9_3

3.2 National Constitutional Law

Ownership unbundling measures were first examined in light of national constitutional law, in particular German constitutional law. In that discussion, Article 14 of the German Basic Law (*Grundgesetz*) took center stage. Article 14 enshrines the right to property. In its case-law on Article 14 Basic Law, the German Federal Constitutional Court (*Bundesverfassungsgericht*) distinguishes between regulation of the content and limits of the right to property (*Inhalts- und Schrankenbestimmung*) and an expropriation thereof (*Enteignung*). According to Article 14(3), an expropriation is only lawful if it is made for a public purpose and authorized by a law. Furthermore, the respective law must make provision for, and determine the nature and extent of, just compensation (the so-called *Junktim-Klausel*). In contrast, losses resulting from regulations concerning the content and limits of property rights are generally not compensable.[3] However, if the impact of the measure exceeds a certain threshold, a duty to pay compensation may arise even in such cases.[4] The German Federal Constitutional Court has taken a rather narrow interpretation of the concept of expropriation within the meaning of Article 14(3) of the Basic Law.[5] Interferences with property rights, irrespective of the intensity of the interference, will only be classified as expropriation if individuals are deprived of their property in order to perform certain public tasks.[6]

In the academic literature there was disagreement as to whether ownership unbundling measures constituted regulation of the content and limits of property rights, or an expropriation under German law. Both the former[7] and the

---

Salje and Matthias Schmidt-Preuß (eds), *Regulierung in der Energiewirtschaft: Ein Praxishandbuch* (2nd edn. Carl Heymanns Verlag 2016) [77ff, 88]; Helmut Lecheler and Claas F Germelmann, *Zugangsbeschränkungen für Investitionen aus Drittstaaten im deutschen und europäischen Energierecht* (Energierecht vol 1, Mohr Siebeck 2010) 166.

[3]Hans D Jarass and Bodo Pieroth, *Grundgesetz für die Bundesrepublik Deutschland – Kommentar* (13th edn, C.H. Beck 2014) [53].

[4]German Federal Constitutional Court, *Pflichtexemplar* (14 July 1981) BVerfGE 58, 137; German Federal Constitutional Court, *Denkmalschutz* (2 March 1999) BVerfGE 100, 226 [95ff].

[5]Iñigo del Guayo, Gunther Kühne and Martha M Roggenkamp, 'Ownership Unbundling and Property Rights in the EU Energy Sector' in Aileen McHarg and others (eds), *Property and the Law in Energy and Natural Resources* (Oxford University Press 2010) 346; Markus Perkams, 'The Concept of Indirect Expropriation in Comparative Public Law – Searching for Light in the Dark' in Stephan W Schill (ed), *International Investment Law and Comparative Public Law* (Oxford University Press 2010) 134.

[6]German Federal Constitutional Court, *Baulandumlegung* (22 May 2001) BVerfGE 104, 1 [30]; German Federal Constitutional Court (21 July 2010) BVerfGE 126, 331 [87]. See also Jarass and Pieroth (n 3) [75–77].

[7]Frank Schorkopf, 'Eigentumsrechtliche Entflechtung aus verfassungs- und europarechtlicher Sicht' in Wolfgang Löwer (ed), *Neue rechtliche Herausforderungen für den Strommarkt: Bonner Gespräch zum Energierecht – Band 3* (Bonner Gespräch zum Energierecht vol 3. V & R unipress 2008) 131; Jürgen F Baur, Kai U Pritzsche and Stefan Klauer, *Ownership Unbundling: Wesen und Vereinbarkeit mit Europarecht und Verfassungsrecht* (Veröffentlichungen des Instituts für Energierecht an der Universität zu Köln vol 121, Nomos 2006) 80.

latter[8] views were advocated. It has however also been stressed that the mere classification of ownership unbundling as a regulation of the content and limits of property is not in and of itself a silver bullet to ensure its legality or to avoid the need to pay compensation.[9] First of all, like expropriations,[10] regulations of the content and limits of property must also meet the proportionality test in order to be constitutional.[11] Furthermore, as mentioned, such measures may trigger a duty to pay compensation (or otherwise would be unconstitutional) if the interference with property rights is exceptionally severe.

Against this background, the proportionality of ownership unbundling was discussed at some length in all the relevant literature. Whereas the suitability (*Geeignetheit*) of ownership unbundling to foster competition in the energy sector was not particularly controversial, its necessity (*Erforderlichkeit*) was contested. A number of arguments were put forward. First, it was argued that the rules on third party access already made a contribution to increased competition.[12] Second, authors stressed that the existing unbundling rules, based on Directives 2003/54/EC and 2003/55/EC, were not yet fully operational and that their effectiveness could not be properly evaluated at that point in time.[13] Third, it was recalled that other unbundling models, which were discussed as alternatives (such as the ISO or ITO models), are less restrictive means which could be implemented by the German legislator.[14] As regards the issue of proportionality *stricto sensu* (*Angemessenheit*), some authors took the view that the increased level of competition achieved through ownership unbundling would only be marginal and thus out of proportion to the heavy impact it would have on the right to property.[15]

---

[8]Christian Kahle, 'Die Eigentumsrechtliche Entflechtung (Ownership Unbundling) der Energieversorgungsnetze aus europarechtlicher und verfassungsrechtlicher Sicht' [2007] Recht der Energiewirtschaft 293, 297–299; Thomas Mayen and Ulrich Karpenstein, 'Eigentumsrechtliche Entflechtung der Energieversorgungsnetze: Verfassungs- und gemeinschaftsrechtliche Aspekte des Eigentumsschutzes' [2008] Recht der Energiewirtschaft 33, 37–38.

[9]Mayen and Karpenstein (n 8) 41–42.

[10]Jarass and Pieroth (n 3) [89–91].

[11]Ibid [36–47].

[12]Baur, Pritzsche and Klauer (n 7) 82–83.

[13]Ulrich Büdenbender and Peter Rosin, *Einführung eines Ownership Unbundling bzw. Independent System Operator in der Energiewirtschaft: Rechtliche und rechtspolitische Würdigung der wesentlichen Argumente der Europäischen Kommission* (Verlag Energiewirtschaft und Technik 2007) 115; Winfried Rasbach, *Unbundling-Regulierung in der Energiewirtschaft: Gemeinschaftsrechtliche Vorgaben und deren Umsetzung in die deutsche Energierechtsordnung* (C.H. Beck 2009) 333ff.

[14]Schorkopf (n 7) 131–132; Jürgen Kühling and Guido Hermeier, 'Eigentumsrechtliche Leitplanken eines Ownership Unbundlings in der Energiewirtschaft' (2008) 58 Energiewirtschaftliche Tagesfragen 134, 138–139; Stefan Storr, 'Ownership Unbundling und alternative Entflechtungsmodelle' in Jürgen F Baur, Peter Salje and Matthias Schmidt-Preuß (eds), *Regulierung in der Energiewirtschaft: Ein Praxishandbuch* (Kölner Handbücher zum Energiewirtschaftsrecht. Carl Heymanns Verlag 2011) 1400–1401.

[15]Baur, Pritzsche and Klauer (n 7) 83–85; Mayen and Karpenstein (n 8) 40.

On a final note, it should be emphasized that the scope of application of national constitutional law is generally limited, due to the supremacy of EU law. As recognized in the jurisprudence of the German Federal Constitutional Court, binding legislation at the EU level, as well as corresponding national implementing measures, cannot in principle be scrutinized on the basis of the German Basic Law.[16] However, where Member States are given a certain degree of flexibility in the implementation of Union law, or where the national implementing legislation goes beyond secondary EU legislation, the fundamental rights enshrined in the German Basic Law fully apply.[17] Given that the EU legislator ultimately decided not to prescribe OU as the only available unbundling model in the TEP, but rather to provide a choice to the EU Member States, a decision by the German legislator to adopt mandatory OU would have had to be measured against the standard of the *Grundgesetz*. In line with the critical attitude towards ownership unbundling policies outlined above, several authors stated that the German legislator was simply complying with its obligations under Article 14 of the Basic Law when it transposed not only the OU, but also the ISO and ITO models into national legislation in 2011.[18] In fact, the explanatory memorandum accompanying the implementing legislation in Germany explicitly highlights that all three unbundling models were made available 'for reasons of proportionality'.[19] In other EU Member States, however, such as for example Estonia, national constitutional law has not been recognized as an obstacle to the introduction of OU requirements.[20]

[16]See, for example, German Federal Constitutional Court, *Bananenmarkt* (7 June 2000) BVerfGE 102, 147 [59]; German Federal Constitutional Court, *Treibhausgas-Emissionsberechtigung* (13 March 2007) BVerfGE 118, 79 [68ff].

[17]For a discussion of these principles in relation to unbundling requirements, see Baur, Pritzsche and Klauer (n 7) 99–101; Schorkopf (n 7) 119–120; Johann-Christian Pielow and Eckart Ehlers, 'Rechtsfragen zum "Ownership Unbundling"' [2007] InfrastrukturRecht 259, 262; Matthias Schmidt-Preuß, 'Verfassungsrechtliche Rahmenbedingungen des Unbundling' in Jürgen F Baur, Kai U Pritzsche and Stefan Simon (eds), *Unbundling in der Energiewirtschaft: Ein Praxishandbuch* (Carl Heymanns Verlag 2006) [3–5] (with further references).

[18]Storr (n 14) 1401. See also the references cited in footnote 14 (in this chapter).

[19]Deutscher Bundesrat, 'Entwurf eines Gesetzes zur Neuregelung energiewirtschaftsrechtlicher Vorschriften' (Drucksache 343/11 6 June 2011) 144 <http://dipbt.bundestag.de/dip21/brd/2011/0343-11.pdf> accessed 26 August 2015.

[20]The explanatory memorandum accompanying the law implementing mandatory ownership unbundling in the Estonian gas sector explicitly states that the legislative changes are proportional and thus constitutional, see Republic of Estonia, 'Law on the Amendment of the Natural Gas Act – Explanatory Memorandum – Original Proposal' (2012) <http://www.riigikogu.ee/tegevus/eelnoud/eelnou/5dea306a-39a3-43c7-9d74-e20d79ad6527/Maagaasiseaduse%20muutmise%20seadus/> accessed 18 September 2015.

3.3 EU Law

In addition to their compatibility with (German) constitutional law, ownership unbundling measures have been discussed with respect to their compatibility with EU law. The legal controversies focused mainly on (1) Article 345 TFEU; (2) the general principle of equality; (3) the free movement of capital and the freedom of establishment; and (4) the right to property.

According to Article 345 TFEU (ex Article 295 TEC), '[t]he Treaties shall in no way prejudice the rules in Member States governing the system of property ownership'. Some academic scholars felt that this provision, which functions as a barrier to the exercise of EU competences, would prevent the adoption of ownership unbundling measures at the EU level.[21] However, there was no consensus on this issue.[22] The division of opinion regarding the applicability of Article 345 TFEU to ownership unbundling measures was the result of widely diverging views as to the scope of the Article. Some consider that by referring to Member States' 'rules governing the system of property ownership', Article 345 TFEU encompasses all norms that regulate the granting of property rights and the limitations of these rights. Under this view, Article 345 TFEU could be seen to act as an obstacle to mandatory ownership unbundling. Opponents of this broad interpretation argued that the provision should be understood more narrowly, covering only those situations in which the Union legislator would attempt to define the conditions under which

[21]See Stefan Storr, 'Die Vorschläge der EU-Kommission zur Verschärfung der Unbundling-Vorschriften im Energiesektor' [2007] Europäische Zeitschrift für Wirtschaftsrecht 232, 237, passim; Jürgen F Baur and Matthias Schmidt-Preuß, 'Europarechtliche Grundlagen des Unbundling' in Jürgen F Baur, Kai U Pritzsche and Stefan Simon (eds), *Unbundling in der Energiewirtschaft: Ein Praxishandbuch* (Carl Heymanns Verlag 2006) [78]; Matthias Schmidt-Preuß, 'Der Wandel der Energiewirtschaft vor dem Hintergrund der europäischen Eigentumsordnung' (2006) 41 Europarecht 463, 484; Christian Koenig, Kristina Schreiber and Kristin Spiekermann, 'Defizitäres Entflechtungsregime? Eine kritische Analyse der Entflechtungsvorschriften in dem Entwurf des dritten Liberalisierungspakets der Kommission der Europäischen Gemeinschaften' [2008] Netzwirtschaften & Recht 7, 10; Michael Pießkalla, 'Die Kommissionsvorschläge zum "full ownership unbundling" des Strom- und Gasversorgungssektors im Lichte der Eigentumsneutralität des EG-Vertrags (Art. 295 EG)' [2008] Europäische Zeitschrift für Wirtschaftsrecht 199.

[22]Kim Talus and Angus Johnston, 'Comment on Pielow, Brunekreeft and Ehlers on "Ownership Onbundling"' (2009) 2 Journal of World Energy Law & Business 149, 150–151; Christian Calliess, 'Ownership Unbundling für alle?: Kritische Überlegungen zu den aktuellen Entflechtungsvorhaben der Europäischen Kommission' (2007) 57 Energiewirtschaftliche Tagesfragen 92, 93–95; Christian Calliess, *Entflechtung im europäischen Energiebinnenmarkt: Zur Vereinbarkeit der europäischen Pläne für ein Ownership Unbundling mit der Kompetenzordnung des EG-Vertrages, insbesondere Art. 295 EGV, und dem allgemeinen Gleichheitssatz* (Bochumer Beiträge zum Berg- und Energierecht vol 50, Boorberg 2008) 27ff; Ralf Müller-Terpitz and Michaela Weigl, 'Ownership Unbundling – ein gemeinschaftsrechtlicher Irrweg?' [2009] Europarecht 348, 357–360; Schorkopf (n 7) 121.

private property is converted into public property.[23] In other words, according to the latter view Article 345 TFEU only prohibits privatizations and nationalizations.

The ECJ's existing case-law on Article 345 TFEU does not give a clear indication which of the approaches outlined above is to be preferred. While the ECJ has pointed out on several occasions that the provision cannot be interpreted to the effect that the Member States' rules governing the system of property ownership are exempted from the application of the fundamental rules of EU law, such as for instance the freedom of establishment and the free movement of capital,[24] such pronouncements do not answer the question whether the Union legislator is allowed to prescribe ownership unbundling measures. From a pragmatic perspective, however, this question can be left open for the time being, since Directives 2009/72/EC and 2009/73/EC offer two additional alternative unbundling models and do not mandate the implementation of ownership unbundling.[25] The issue may however become relevant once again in the (near) future, under a prospective 'Fourth Energy Package'.

Furthermore, it is crucial to highlight that Article 345 TFEU has already influenced the formulation of the ownership unbundling provisions contained in the Third Energy Package. As mentioned above, it is undisputed that rules relating to privatization and nationalization fall under Article 345 TFEU. Thus it would be incompatible with Article 345 if an EU Member State were forced to sell either its transmission assets or its production/generation and supply assets to a privately owned company.[26] In this way, Article 345 TFEU served as the justification for the inclusion of Article 9(6) of Directives 2009/72/EC and 2009/73/EC, which creates a special OU regime for publicly-owned companies.[27] However, at the same time Article 9(6) prompted the criticism that the special treatment given to

[23]See Stephan Wernicke, 'AEUV Art. 345 Eigentumsordnung' in Eberhard Grabitz, Meinhard Hilf and Martin Nettesheim (eds), *Das Recht der Europäischen Union: EUV/AEUV* (54th edn. C.H. Beck 2014) [12–14].

[24]European Court of Justice, *Fearon v. Irish Land Commission,* Judgment (6 November 1984) 182/83 [7]; European Court of Justice, *Konle v. Austria,* Judgment (1 June 1999) C-302/97 [38]; European Court of Justice, *Commission v. Germany,* Judgment (18 July 2007) C-503/04 [37]; European Court of Justice, *Commission v. Spain,* Judgment (13 May 2003) C-463/00 [67]; European Court of Justice, *Ospelt and Schlössle Weissenberg,* Judgment (23 September 2003) C-452/01 [24]; European Court of Justice, *Commission v. Portugal,* Judgment (8 July 2010) C-171/08 [64]; European Court of Justice, *Commission v. Poland,* Judgment (21 December 2011) C-271/09 [44]; European Court of Justice, *Commission v. Greece,* Judgment (8 November 2012) C-244/11 [16].

[25]Storr (n 14) 1397.

[26]Calliess (n 22) 94; Calliess (n 22) 65.

[27]See Franz J Säcker and Jochen Mohr, '§ 8 Eigentumsrechtliche Entflechtung' in Franz J Säcker (ed), *Berliner Kommentar zum Energierecht* (vol 1, 3rd edn. Dt. Fachverl. Fachmedien Recht und Wirtschaft 2014) [33–34, 47]; Dirk Buschle, 'Unbundling of State-owned Transmission System Operators – Effective Remedy or Eyewash?' [2013] European Networks Law and Regulation Quarterly 49, 55.

public undertakings was in violation of the general principle of equality under EU law.[28] The general principle of equality, which is recognized in the jurisprudence of the ECJ as a fundamental principle of Union law, 'requires that similar situations shall not be treated differently unless differentiation is objectively justified.'[29] Meanwhile, this principle has also been incorporated into the Charter of Fundamental Rights of the EU (CFR).[30] It is evident that public and private undertakings are treated unequally. Whereas private transmission system operators and commercial energy companies cannot remain part of a vertically integrated undertaking, their public counterparts can continue to be controlled by a VIU, namely the State. According to the predominant view in the literature, there are no objective reasons to justify this difference in treatment.[31]

Furthermore, it must also be mentioned that ownership unbundling measures interfere with the free movement of capital (Article 63 TFEU) and the freedom of establishment (Article 49 TFEU).[32] Persons controlling a production/generation and supply company are prohibited from investing in an undertaking which is active in the transmission of electricity or gas sector (and *vice versa*). Thus the effect of OU is to limit the ability of investors to combine investments in different economic sectors and to sell shares to other private investors.[33] These considerations also apply, *mutatis mutandis*, to the freedom of establishment. In the case of third-country investors, however, the applicability of these two freedoms is unclear, due to their ambiguous interrelationship. In its jurisprudence, the ECJ has occasionally given priority to an *exclusive* application of the freedom of establishment to foreign direct investments, following a 'center of gravity approach'. This effectively implies that foreign market participants are left unprotected in such cases,[34] given that only

---

[28]For a detailed analysis, see Calliess (n 22) 95ff; Calliess (n 22) 67ff. See also Koenig, Schreiber and Spiekermann (n 21) 11; Säcker and Mohr (n 27) [47].

[29]European Court of Justice, *Ruckdeschel and Others v Hauptzollamt Hamburg-St. Annen*, Judgment (19 October 1977) C-117/76 and 16/77 [7].

[30]Article 20 European Union, Charter of Fundamental Rights of the European Union OJ 2012/C 326/391, in conjunction with Article 6(1) European Union, Treaty on European Union (consolidated version) OJ 2012/C 326/13.

[31]Calliess (n 22) 114–129; Säcker and Mohr (n 27) [47].

[32]Kim Talus and Michaël Hunt, 'Ownership Unbundling: What End to the Saga?' in Dirk Buschle, Simon Hirsbrunner and Christine Kaddous (eds), *European Energy Law: Droit européen de l'énergie* (Dossier de droit européen vol 22. Helbing Lichtenhahn 2011) 37; Ivan Gudkov, 'Третий энергетический пакет ЕС: разъединение вертикально интегрированных компаний и ограничение прав инвесторов из третьих стран' [2007] НефтьГазПраво 53, 57.

[33]Angus Johnston, 'Ownership Unbundling: Prolegomenon to a Legal Analysis' in Mielle Bulterman and others (eds), *Views of European Law from the Mountain: Liber Amicorum Piet Jan Slot* (Wolters Kluwer Law & Business 2009) 283–284.

[34]Steffen Hindelang, *The Free Movement of Capital and Foreign Direct Investment: The Scope of Protection in EU Law* (Oxford University Press 2009) 89–108.

Article 63 TFEU applies in a third country context.[35] As regards ownership unbundling, this means that where the freedom of establishment prevails over the free movement of capital, thereby precluding their parallel application, foreign investors in the EU energy sector cannot invoke Article 63 TFEU and thus cannot challenge the OU requirements as set out in Directives 2009/72/EC and 2009/73/EC.[36]

It should, however, be noted that the ECJ's jurisprudence on the applicability of one or both of the freedoms is far from clear. Some authors have taken the view that, based on the court's recent jurisprudence, ownership unbundling requirements would in fact need to be measured against the free movement of capital.[37] Nevertheless, the ambiguity surrounding the relationship between Articles 49 and 63 TFEU leads to legal uncertainty for third country energy investors.[38] Apart from these questions of applicability, the crucial question is whether any restriction on the discussed freedoms, imposed by OU measures, can be justified. In addition to the express derogations found in Articles 52 and 65 TFEU, which cover, *inter alia*, measures taken on grounds of 'public security',[39] OU requirements could also be justified on the basis of 'overriding reasons in the public interest'.[40] In either case, the proportionality of OU thus becomes the decisive factor.

Lastly, commentators have also dealt extensively with the right to property under EU law, which is now expressly enshrined in Article 17 of the Charter of Fundamental Rights. In its (sparse) case-law, the ECJ distinguishes between restrictions on the *use* of property and acts which *deprive* their owners of their property (expropriations).[41] This is consistent with the approach taken by Article 17 CFR. Moreover, it may be inferred from the ECJ's jurisprudence that deprivations of property encompass not only formal expropriations (i.e. where the title to property is transferred to the State or to a third person), but also *de facto* expropriations (i.e. where ownership rights are significantly eroded without a formal transfer of title).[42] Compensation

---

[35] Article 63(1) European Union, Treaty on the Functioning of the European Union (consolidated version) OJ 2012/C 326/47 states that '... all restrictions on the movement of capital between Member States and between Member States and third countries shall be prohibited'.

[36] For a detailed analysis, see Michaël Hunt, 'Ownership Unbundling: The Main Legal Issues in a Controversial Debate' in Bram Delvaux, Michaël Hunt and Kim Talus (eds), *EU Energy Law and Policy Issues* (1st edn. Euroconfidentiel 2008) 73–85. This issue is disregarded by Willems, Sul and Benizri (n 2) 233–234.

[37] Schmidt-Preuß (n 2) [79–82].

[38] Hunt (n 36) 85.

[39] This seems to be the most relevant justification, see also ibid 86.

[40] Schmidt-Preuß (n 2) [89–90].

[41] European Court of Justice, *Hauer,* Judgment (13 December 1979) C-44/79 [19].

[42] *Hauer* (n 41) [19]; European Court of Justice, *Regione autonoma Friuli-Venezia Giulia and ERSA,* Judgment (12 May 2005) C-347/03 [122]; European Court of Justice, *Flughafen Hannover-Langenhagen,* Judgment (16 October 2003) C-363/01 [55–56]. See also Norbert Bernsdorff, 'Artikel 17 – Eigentumsrecht' in Jürgen Meyer (ed), *Charta der Grundrechte der Europäischen Union* (4th edn. Nomos 2014) [20]; Hans D Jarass, *Charta der Grundrechte der Europäischen Union: Kommentar* (2nd edn, C.H. Beck 2013) 201.

must be paid for formal expropriations and arguably also for *de facto* expropriations.[43] In the case of restrictions on the use of property, a duty to pay compensation can, under certain circumstances, be derived from the principle of proportionality.[44] Both deprivations of property[45] and restrictions on its use[46] must be proportional to the aim pursued.

A number of authors considered ownership unbundling measures to constitute a deprivation of property.[47] Following this line of reasoning, some took the view that if the legislative act requiring ownership unbundling does not contain an explicit rule on compensation, the instrument would *ipso facto* violate the right to property guaranteed under EU law.[48] The revenue obtained through the compulsory sale of the transmission assets would not satisfy the compensation requirement.[49] However other authors, while likewise assuming a deprivation of property, nevertheless opined that the sale proceeds could in principle fulfil the compensation requirement, assuming that they do not fall below a certain level.[50]

In contrast to Article 14(3) of the German Basic Law, which requires that the law authorizing an expropriation must explicitly make provision for just compensation (*Junktim-Klausel*), EU fundamental rights law does not contain such a requirement.[51] In accordance with the second group of authors it is therefore submitted that the mere absence of an explicit compensation scheme would not render the EU legislation prescribing OU unlawful, and that the revenue generated through the sale of the network can, as a matter of principle, qualify as compensation.

[43]Ulrich Vosgerau, 'Art. 17 – Eigentumsrecht' in Klaus Stern and Michael Sachs (eds), *Europäische Grundrechte-Charta – Kommentar* (C.H. Beck 2016) [82].

[44]Jarass (n 42) 209–210; Bernsdorff (n 42) [21]; Sebastian M Heselhaus, '§32 Eigentumsgrundrecht' in Sebastian M Heselhaus and Carsten Nowak (eds), *Handbuch der Europäischen Grundrechte* (C.H. Beck 2006) [89].

[45]Heselhaus (n 44) [72]; Jarass (n 42) 205–206.

[46]European Court of Justice, *Alessandrini*, Judgment (30 June 2005) C-295/03 P [86]; *Hauer* (n 41) [23]; European Court of Justice, *Schräder*, Judgment (11 July 1989) C-265/87 [15]; European Court of Justice, *Wachauf*, Judgment (13 July 1989) C-5/88 [17–18].

[47]Kahle (n 8) 294; Jürgen F Baur and others, *Eigentumsentflechtung der Energiewirtschaft durch Europarecht: Mittel, Schranken und Rechtsfolgen* (Veröffentlichungen des Instituts für Energierecht an der Universität zu Köln vol 138, Nomos 2008) 35–37; Mayen and Karpenstein (n 8) 44; Johann-Christian Pielow, Gert Brunekreeft and Eckart Ehlers, 'Legal and Economic Aspects of Ownership Unbundling in the EU' (2009) 2 Journal of World Energy Law & Business 96, 111; Bernd Holznagel and Pascal Schumacher, 'Großer Eingriff, k(l)eine Wirkung – Die Pläne der Kommission zur eigentumsrechtlichen Entflechtung der Energienetzbetreiber' [2007] Netzwirtschaften & Recht 96, 99; Matthias Wohlfahrt, *Ownership Unbundling: Die Vereinbarkeit verschärfter Entflechtungsvorgaben für die leitungsgebundenen Sektoren Elektrizität und Gas mit dem Gemeinschaftsrecht* (Berliner Wissenschafts-Verlag 2009) 162; Rasbach (n 13) 349.

[48]Mayen and Karpenstein (n 8) 44; Baur and others (n 47) 43, 90.

[49]Baur and others (n 47) 92.

[50]Schorkopf (n 7) 128. See also Wohlfahrt (n 47) 131, 199.

[51]Heselhaus (n 44) [74]; Jarass (n 42) 206.

The view was also expressed that ownership unbundling should be classified as a restriction on the use of property.[52] As mentioned above, whereas there is generally no obligation to pay compensation in such cases, an obligation to this effect could arise if such use restriction failed to meet the principle of proportionality. In fact, those who considered ownership unbundling to constitute a restriction on the use of property highlighted that the amount of revenue from the sale of the transmission system assets would play an important role in the proportionality analysis.[53]

The principle of proportionality has thus been at the heart of virtually all discussions. Many of the arguments advanced in this context resemble those made under Article 14 of the German Basic Law. Most importantly, with respect to the necessity of ownership unbundling it was argued that the strengthened unbundling requirements were adopted *prematurely*, in the sense that the effectiveness of legal and functional unbundling and other regulatory instruments (in particular network access regulation) could not have been adequately determined at that point in time.[54] Furthermore, it was argued that the inclusion of the ISO model in the Commission's draft Directives already demonstrated that a less restrictive alternative was in fact available.[55] Other less restrictive alternatives mentioned include a 50%[56] or 10%[57] shareholding cap for production/generation and supply companies (and *vice versa*), as well as general improvements to the effectiveness of the existing unbundling regime provided for in the Second Energy Package.[58] Finally, as regards the issue of proportionality *stricto sensu*, it was stressed that the expected competition-related benefits of ownership unbundling would be small and out of proportion to the massive infringement of property rights.[59]

By way of conclusion, it must be borne in mind that the Union legislator did not ultimately opt for mandatory ownership unbundling. For this reason, the right to property, the free movement of capital and the freedom of establishment are not infringed by Directives 2009/72/EC and 2009/73/EC.[60] This notwithstanding, it is clear that OU measures taken at the *national* level also have to be in conformity with EU law. The *Essent* case, discussed in the next section below, is a good example in this respect.

---

[52] Müller-Terpitz and Weigl (n 22) 363–364.

[53] Ibid 367–368. See also Baur and Schmidt-Preuß (n 21) [80].

[54] Mayen and Karpenstein (n 8) 39–40, 45; Baur and others (n 47) 56ff; Rasbach (n 13) 333ff, 350; Müller-Terpitz and Weigl (n 22) 366; Holznagel and Schumacher (n 47) 102–103; Pielow and Ehlers (n 17) 261–262.

[55] Müller-Terpitz and Weigl (n 22) 366. See also Schorkopf (n 7) 128.

[56] Martin Wachovius, *Ownership Unbundling in der Energiewirtschaft: Vereinbarkeit einer eigentumsrechtlichen Entflechtung in der Energiewirtschaft mit den Grundrechten des Grundgesetzes und des Gemeinschaftsrechts deutscher vertikal integrierter Energieversorgungsunternehmen* (VWEW Energieverlag 2008) 167.

[57] Kahle (n 8) 296.

[58] Baur and others (n 47) 59–60, 62–63.

[59] Baur and others (n 47) 69; Müller-Terpitz and Weigl (n 22) 367.

[60] Storr (n 14) [35] (referring only to the right to property under EU law).

3.4 The Essent Case

The ownership unbundling requirements as set out in the TEP have, to date, not been challenged before the domestic courts of EU Member States. However, in 2008, i.e. before the adoption of the TEP, a legal challenge was brought by three Dutch vertically integrated energy companies after the Netherlands enacted—although not being required to do so under the existing EU law—specific legislation which required mandatory ownership unbundling at the level of *distribution* system operators (the *Essent* case). The lengthy proceedings before the Dutch courts and the ECJ provide valuable insights into how the courts grappled with the issue of whether ownership unbundling requirements are in line with EU and European human rights law.

Although a detailed description of the development of the regulatory framework in the Dutch electricity and gas sectors would go beyond the scope of this book,[61] it should be mentioned that in 2004 the Netherlands transposed Directives 2003/54/EC and 2003/55/EC through the Intervention and Implementation Act,[62] thereby implementing legal and functional unbundling for distribution system operators.[63] However, the Dutch legislator considered it necessary to go one step further, and in 2006 the Independent Network Operation Act entered into force.[64] The Independent Network Operation Act introduced, *inter alia*, the so-called 'group prohibition' into the national electricity and gas acts.[65] Article 10b of the Law on Electricity (and accordingly Article 2c of the Law on Gas) provides, in relevant part, that a distribution system operator (and the companies with which it forms a group) cannot hold any share or interest in a company which generates, supplies or trades in electricity in the Netherlands. Conversely, a commercial energy company is prohibited from holding any share or interest in a distribution system operator (or in a company

[61] For a general overview, see Martha M Roggenkamp, 'Energy Law in the Netherlands' in Martha M Roggenkamp and others (eds), *Energy Law in Europe – National, EU and International Regulation* (2nd edn. Oxford University Press 2007).

[62] The Netherlands, Intervention and Implementation Act (Interventie- en Implementatiewet) (01 July 2004) Stb. 328.

[63] See Article 15 of Directive 2003/54/EC of the European Parliament and of the Council concerning common rules for the internal market in electricity and repealing Directive 96/92/EC (26 June 2003) OJ 2003/L 176/37; Article 13 of Directive 2003/55/EC of the European Parliament and of the Council concerning common rules for the internal market in natural gas and repealing Directive 98/30/EC (26 June 2003) OJ 2003/L 176/57.

[64] The Netherlands, Independent Network Operation Act (Wet onafhankelijk netbeheer) (23 November 2006) Stb. 614.

[65] Another important feature was the prohibition of privatization of electricity and gas distribution system operators, which raised issues under Article 345 TFEU.

belonging to a group of which a distribution system operator is a member).[66] Dutch companies had to comply with this provision by 1 January 2011.[67] The group prohibition in Article 10b of the Law on Electricity and Article 2c of the Law on Gas largely resembles the ownership unbundling model which was subsequently set out in Directives 2009/72/EC and 2009/73/EC. In fact, it is even more far-reaching than the rules on ownership unbundling of transmission system operators under EU law, given that it prohibits a person from holding non-controlling minority shareholdings in both a network operator and a production/generation or supply undertaking.[68]

Shortly after the entry into force of the Independent Network Operation Act of 2006, several affected companies, including Essent NV, Eneco Holding NV and Delta NV, challenged the group prohibition before Dutch courts. They requested the *Rechtbank Den Haag* (The Hague District Court) to declare that the unbundling requirements were incompatible with, *inter alia*, the free movement of capital in Article 63 TFEU, the freedom of establishment in Article 49 TFEU, and the right to property in Article 1 of the First Protocol to the ECHR. In 2009, the *Rechtbank Den Haag* dismissed the claims.[69] As regards the fundamental freedoms, the court, while arguing that the objectives of promoting transparency and free competition could not

---

[66]Article 10b(1) to (3) of the Law on Electricity provides in full:

1. A system operator shall not be a member of a group, within the meaning of Article 24b of Book 2 of the Civil Code, of which a legal person or company which generates, supplies or trades in electricity in the Netherlands is also a member.
2. Legal persons and companies which are members of a group, within the meaning of Article 24b of Book 2 of the Civil Code, of which a legal person or company which generates, supplies or trades in electricity in the Netherlands is also a member shall not own any shares in a system operator or in a legal person which is a member of the same group as that of which a system operator is a member and shall not have any interest in a company which is a member of the same group as a system operator.
3. A system operator and group companies within the meaning of Article 24b of Book 2 of the Civil Code linked to the system operator:

    a. shall not own any shares in a legal person which generates, supplies or trades in electricity in the Netherlands or in a legal person which is a member of the same group as a legal person which generates, supplies or trades in electricity in the Netherlands;
    b. shall not have any interest in a company which generates, supplies or trades in electricity in the Netherlands or in a company which is a member of the same group as a legal person or a company which generates, supplies or trades in electricity in the Netherlands.

Translation taken from European Court of Justice, *Staat der Nederlanden v Essent NV and Others,* Judgment (22 October 2013) C-105/12 to C-107/12 [19].

[67]Article 10b of the Law on Electricity and Article 2c of the Law on Gas did not take effect immediately. Rather, their entry into force was triggered by the adoption of the Act of 21 July 2007, Stb. 273, in conjunction with Article VIII of the 2006 Independent Network Operation Act, see Rechtbank Den Haag, *Essent N.V. v. Staat der Nederlanden,* Judgment (11 March 2009) 306 147/HA ZA 08-756 [2.1–2.6].

[68]For the same view, see European Court of Justice, *Staat der Nederlanden v Essent NV and Others,* Opinion of Advocate General Jääskinen (16 April 2013) C-105/12 to C-107/12 [73].

[69]*Essent N.V. v. Staat der Nederlanden* (n 67).

justify an infringement of the fundamental freedoms because they serve only economic interests,[70] accepted that the considerations concerning the security of energy supply, seen as overriding requirements in the public interest, provided a valid justification.[71] Where the network remained part of a vertically integrated undertaking, its condition would depend on the risks that the generation/production or supply branch faced on the market. Under such circumstances, it could not be guaranteed that profits from the management of the network would be used exclusively to maintain and develop the network.[72]

As regards Article 1 of the First Protocol to the ECHR, it is necessary to bear in mind that, first, the shareholders of Essent NV, Eneco Holding NV and Delta NV were all public entities (provinces and municipalities); and second, that the group prohibition did not prevent the provinces and municipalities from holding shares in both an independent distribution system company and an independent production/generation or supply company.[73] Against this background, the court drew a distinction between the position of the integrated group companies and their shareholders (the provinces/municipalities). It argued that the public shareholders were not deprived of their property rights due to the fact that they were able to have shareholdings in two separate companies instead of in one vertically integrated company. In the court's view, this merely constituted a regulation of the use of property and nothing more.[74] Importantly, and without further explanation, the *Rechtbank Den Haag* then found that this conclusion also influenced the assessment of the impact of the group prohibition at the level of the holding companies, i.e. Essent NV, Eneco Holding NV and Delta NV.[75] Finally, referring back to its finding on the proportionality of the group prohibition with respect to the fundamental freedoms, the court ruled that the unbundling provisions struck a fair balance between the general interests and the private interests of the integrated companies.[76]

The companies subsequently appealed to the *Gerechtshof Den Haag* (Regional Court of Appeal at The Hague), which rendered its judgment in 2010.[77] In its analysis the Court of Appeal focused on the free movement of capital under Article 63 TFEU. After having established that the group prohibition constitutes a restriction on the free movement on capital,[78] the court moved to the issue of justification. First

[70]Ibid [5.10] (citing European Court of Justice, *Commission v. Italy,* Judgment (2 June 2005) C-174/04 [36–37]).

[71]*Essent N.V. v. Staat der Nederlanden* (n 67) [5.11] (citing *Commission v. Italy* (n 70) [40]).

[72]*Essent N.V. v. Staat der Nederlanden* (n 67) [5.11].

[73]Martha M Roggenkamp, 'Ownership Unbundling in the Netherlands: More Haste and Less Speed?' in Jürgen F Baur and others (eds), *Festschrift für Gunther Kühne zum 70. Geburtstag* (Verlag Recht und Wirtschaft 2009) 284.

[74]*Essent N.V. v. Staat der Nederlanden* (n 67) [5.13].

[75]Ibid.

[76]Ibid [5.14].

[77]Gerechtshof Den Haag, *Essent N.V. v. Staat der Nederlanden,* Judgment (22 June 2010) 200 035 392/01.

[78]Ibid [4.6].

of all, it agreed with the lower court that the objectives of preventing distortions of competition through the elimination of cross-subsidization and of protecting the customers of network services through greater transparency were purely economic interests, and therefore not capable of justifying an infringement of a fundamental freedom.[79] It added that, in any event, the Dutch government had not sufficiently established that cross-subsidization occurs in practice or that there is a sufficiently real threat.[80] In contrast to the lower court's ruling, the Court of Appeal rejected the argument that the group prohibition could be justified on grounds of public security under Article 65(1)(b) TFEU or on grounds of ensuring security of supply.[81] It stressed that the existing laws already sufficiently ensured the security of supply. For example, under the Intervention and Implementation Act of 2004,[82] which also implemented Directives 2003/54/EC and 2003/55/EC, the government could require the network operator to invest into a distribution system or could even appoint a trustee to manage the network. The court also referred to additional unbundling-related provisions contained in the Intervention and Implementation Act of 2004 and in the Independent Network Operation Act of 2006,[83] which strengthened the independence of distribution system operators.[84] Thus the court expressed doubt that the group prohibition was able to make an additional contribution to securing energy supply. Having thus found a violation of Article 63 TFEU, the *Gerechtshof Den Haag* held that the claimants had no further interest in a declaration that the same provisions are also inconsistent with Article 49 TFEU or Article 1 of the First Protocol to the ECHR.[85]

The State of the Netherlands lodged an appeal with the *Hoge Raad der Nederlanden* (Supreme Court of the Netherlands), which decided in 2012 to stay the proceedings in order to make a reference to the ECJ.[86] In its judgment of 22 October 2013, the ECJ ruled that the group prohibition constituted a restriction on the free movement of capital within the meaning of Article 63 TFEU.[87] At the same time however the ECJ also found that the objectives of combating cross-subsidization and preventing distortions of competition were not grounds of a purely economic nature, but qualified as 'overriding reasons in the public interest' and could therefore, in principle, justify the restriction.[88] In arriving at this conclusion,

---

[79] Ibid [5.2–5.6] (citing European Court of Justice, *Commission v. Portugal,* Judgment (4 June 2002) C-367/98; *Commission v. Italy* (n 70)).

[80] *Essent N.V. v. Staat der Nederlanden* (n 77) [5.3].

[81] Ibid [5.7–5.14].

[82] Dutch Intervention and Implementation Act (n 62).

[83] Dutch Independent Network Operation Act (n 64).

[84] *Essent N.V. v. Staat der Nederlanden* (n 77) [5.9].

[85] Ibid [6.1].

[86] Hoge Raad der Nederlanden, *Staat der Nederlanden v. Essent N.V.* Judgment (24 February 2012) 10/03851.

[87] *Staat der Nederlanden v Essent NV and Others* (n 66) [47].

[88] Ibid [49–66].

which was not entirely coherent taking into account the relevant case-law,[89] the ECJ stressed that the objectives underlying the group prohibition correspond to the objectives sought by Directives 2003/54/EC, 2003/55/EC, 2009/72/EC, and 2009/73/EC.[90] Finally, the ECJ left it to the *Hoge Raad* to determine whether the group prohibition was *proportional* to the objectives pursued.

On 26 June 2015, the *Hoge Raad* decided that the group prohibition did not go beyond what was necessary to achieve the stated objective, and thus rejected a finding that a violation of Articles 63 and 49 TFEU had occurred.[91] In the court's view the regulatory framework which was in place before the introduction of ownership unbundling was inadequate to effectively prevent cross-subsidization and ensure transparency in the energy market, as well as to ensure security of supply. The State had the right to decide on the degree of protection it wished to afford certain interests and how this should be achieved. In the case at hand, the State aimed to ensure that the possibility of cross-subsidization was *structurally* excluded.[92] In this connection, the Supreme Court emphasized that more regulation and greater supervision did not *structurally* rule out the risk of cross-subsidization.[93] On a related note, and contrary to the judgment of the Court of Appeal, it also held that the State was not obliged to 'prove' that, in the absence of the group prohibition, there would be a practice of cross-subsidization or a sufficiently real threat thereof. The fact that the risk of cross-subsidization is (theoretically) always present in vertically integrated energy companies essentially sufficed.[94] Similar arguments were made with respect to the issue of security of energy supply. Although steps had already been taken to reduce the possibility that investment in commercial activity was made at the expense of network maintenance and development, the group prohibition would guarantee the complete independence of the network management by structurally separating it from commercial energy activities.[95]

The *Hoge Raad* also highlighted that alternative measures had been seriously considered. It noted that the proposal to introduce new disclosure requirements, audits, and intensified supervision had been rejected, because they would lead to significantly higher enforcement and compliance costs, a reduction of transparency, and that conflicts of interest within the integrated energy undertakings would persist.[96] Furthermore, it was also unclear whether anti-competitive activities could be adequately traced through more intensive supervision.[97]

[89]Anne Looijestijn-Clearie, 'Breaking up Is Hard to Do: Dutch Unbundling Legislation and the Free Movement of Capital' (2014) 15 European Business Organization Law Review 337, 348–353.

[90]*Staat der Nederlanden v Essent NV and Others* (n 66) [64–65].

[91]Hoge Raad der Nederlanden, *Staat der Nederlanden v. Essent N.V.* Judgment (26 June 2015) 10/03851 [4.9.1ff].

[92]Ibid [3.17.2].

[93]Ibid.

[94]Ibid.

[95]Ibid [3.22.2].

[96]Ibid [4.9.2].

[97]Ibid.

Inasmuch as Eneco Holding NV and Delta NV had also raised objections on appeal against the rejection of their claims based on Article 1 of the First Protocol to the ECHR, the Supreme Court referred the matter to the Amsterdam Court of Appeal.[98] In a set of judgments handed down in 2016 and 2017, the Amsterdam Court of Appeal ruled that the enforcement of the group prohibition with respect to the complainants was not contrary to the right to property under the ECHR. Under the headings 'lawfulness' and 'general interest', the court pointed out that the interference in the form of the group prohibition was provided for by law and referred to the reasoning of the Supreme Court in the context of Articles 63 and 49 TFEU that the group prohibition was suitable in a general sense and did not go beyond what is necessary to achieve the legitimate objectives pursued.[99] It then moved to the question of proportionality, i.e. whether the legislation had struck a 'fair balance' between the demands of the general interest of the community and the requirements of the protection of the individual's fundamental rights. Given that, according to the jurisprudence of the European Court of Human Rights (ECtHR), compensation is in principle required in the case of a 'deprivation of property', the Court of Appeal began by examining the nature of the group prohibition. It found that the measure did *not* constitute a deprivation of property, but rather a 'control of the use of property'. In a second step, the Court of Appeal assessed complainants' arguments that the group prohibition (1) was not more effective than the legislation that existed prior to its introduction, (2) put them at a disadvantage in comparison with vertically-integrated energy companies (e.g. lower credit rating and therefore increased financing costs), and (3) involved the loss of advantages resulting from vertical integration (e.g. economies of scale and synergies), but ultimately found that this was insufficient to conclude that the requisite 'fair balance' between the competing interests had been upset.[100] Whether Eneco and Delta will appeal the decisions to the Supreme Court is unclear at this point in time.

The relevance of the *Essent* case reaches well beyond the particular Dutch situation. The legal arguments discussed in relation to the group prohibition can also be applied to the ownership unbundling model introduced through the Third Energy Package. When delivering his opinion to the ECJ in *Staat der Nederlanden v*

---

[98]Hoge Raad der Nederlanden, *Staat der Nederlanden v. Eneco Holding N.V.* Judgment (26 June 2015) 10/03852 [4.11]; Hoge Raad der Nederlanden, *Staat der Nederlanden v. Delta N.V.* Judgment (26 June 2015) 10/03853 [4.11].

[99]Gerechtshof Amsterdam, *Eneco Holding N.V. v. Staat der Nederlanden,* Judgment (1 November 2016) 200 175 864/01 [3.6]; Gerechtshof Amsterdam, *Delta N.V. v. Staat der Nederlanden,* Judgment (1 November 2016) 200 176 186/01 [3.5].

[100]*Eneco Holding N.V. v. Staat der Nederlanden* (n 99) [3.7–3.9.5]; *Delta N.V. v. Staat der Nederlanden* (n 99) [3.6–3.8.5]. In the case of Delta, the Court of Appeal examined additional arguments related to Delta's involvement in the operation of a nuclear power plant in Borssele, Netherlands. Ultimately, however, the court concluded that Delta was mainly affected by decisions of a commercial nature as well as strategic choices, and that there was thus no reason to assume that the enforcement of the group prohibition against Delta was in conflict with Article 1 of the First Protocol to the ECHR. See Gerechtshof Amsterdam, *Delta N.V. v. Staat der Nederlanden,* Judgment (25 July 2017) 200 176 186/01.

Essent NV and Others, Advocate General Jääskinen noted that although the TEP was, legally speaking, not applicable given that the enactment of the group prohibition predated the TEP, nonetheless its adoption could not be disregarded.[101] In fact, he went so far as to assert that the group prohibition can 'no longer be challenged, at least as to [its] principle, without directly entailing a review of the compatibility of the 2009 directives with the free movement of capital.'[102] Thus, in his view the real question was whether the OU rules provided for by Directives 2009/72/EC and 2009/73/EC are compatible with the TFEU, and in particular with the freedoms of movement contained therein.[103] Against this background, it is difficult to overestimate the significance of the *Essent* case for the general EU-wide debate on ownership unbundling, as well as the debate concerning the possibility of a 'Fourth Energy Package'. Furthermore, the legal arguments of the Dutch courts can also be usefully applied in the analysis of WTO law and international investment law, which follows below.

[101] *Staat der Nederlanden v Essent NV and Others* (n 68) [71].

[102] Ibid [73].

[103] Ibid [75]. See also Henrik Klement, 'Verstaatlichung statt Regulierung?' [2014] Europäische Zeitschrift für Wirtschaftsrecht 57, 58.

Chapter 4
International Economic Law as a Possible Limit to the Implementation of Unbundling and Unbundling-Related Measures: WTO Law

4.1 Introduction

The law of the World Trade Organization establishes a multilateral framework of principles and rules for the cross-border trade in energy goods and energy services. The WTO framework does not provide any disciplines specifically designed to apply to the energy sector; its rules are general in nature and apply to trade in energy in the same way as they apply to trade in all other goods and services.[1] Thus, all governmental measures which regulate cross-border energy trade must comply with WTO rules on market access, non-discrimination, and domestic regulation.

WTO disciplines could act as a limitation on the adoption and maintenance of unbundling and unbundling-related measures in the EU energy sector. Given that unbundling, certification, and exemption measures have an impact on various service transactions (e.g. transmission, wholesale supply, retail supply) as well as on particular goods (gas/electricity[2]), both the General Agreement on Trade in

---

[1]Thomas Cottier and others, 'Energy in WTO Law and Policy' in Thomas Cottier and Panagiotis Delimatsis (eds), *The Prospects of International Trade Regulation: From Fragmentation to Coherence* (Cambridge University Press 2011) 212.

[2]While it is undisputed that natural gas is a good subject to the GATT (see Andras Lakatos, 'Overview of the Regulatory Environment for Trade in Electricity' in Janusz Bielecki and Melaku G Desta (eds), *Electricity Trade in Europe – Review of the Economic and Regulatory Changes* (Kluwer Law International 2004) 124), there has been a long controversy about the 'goods characteristics' of electricity. In contrast to the NAFTA and the Energy Charter Treaty, which explicitly recognize electricity as a good, the situation under the GATT is more complicated. The drafters of the original GATT 1947, which was later incorporated into the WTO framework, did not treat electric power as a commodity. With respect to the general exceptions provision of (now) Article XX GATT, the New York Drafting Committee Report of March 1947 contains the following statement: 'As it seemed to be generally agreed that electric power should not be classified as a commodity, two delegates did not find it necessary to reserve the right for their countries to prohibit the export of electric power', see World Trade Organization, *GATT Analytical*

T. M. Dralle, *Ownership Unbundling and Related Measures in the EU Energy Sector*, European Yearbook of International Economic Law 5,
https://doi.org/10.1007/978-3-319-77797-9_4

Services (GATS) and the General Agreement on Tariffs and Trade (GATT) are in principle applicable. The scope of application of both agreements may overlap. They are not mutually exclusive.[3] However, although the unbundling regime in the TEP could be scrutinized under both the GATS and the GATT, the respective measures most directly affect the services and service suppliers at issue, and trade in energy goods is only indirectly and partially affected. Therefore, the following analysis will focus on whether the unbundling and unbundling-related measures, maintained by or enacted pursuant to the Third Energy Package, and in particular Directives 2009/72/EC and 2009/73/EC, are consistent with the GATS.

As a starting point, it is necessary to consider the scope of application of the GATS. The GATS applies to all 'measures' of WTO Members 'affecting trade in services' (Article I:1 GATS). The term 'measure' is broadly defined as including any 'law, regulation, rule, procedure, decision [and] administrative action.'[4] Likewise, the notion of 'affecting' has been given a wide interpretation in GATS jurisprudence. In particular, it has been interpreted to be broader in scope than the terms 'regulating' or 'governing'.[5] Finally, the concept of 'trade in services' is legally defined in Article I:2 GATS as the 'supply of a service' through four different modes of supply: (1) cross-border supply; (2) consumption abroad; (3) commercial presence; and (4) the presence of natural persons.

Index: Guide to GATT Law and Practice (Articles I – XXI vol 1, 6th updated edition, 1995) 585. In 1990, a commentator remarked that 'on balance [the evidence] suggests that GATT trade rules do not apply to electricity', see André Plourde, 'Canada's International Obligations in Energy and the Free-Trade Agreement with the United States' (1990) 24 Journal of World Trade 35, 36. It seems that the main reasons for this were that electricity is not tangible and could essentially not be stored using available technology at that time. Nowadays, however, it is widely acknowledged that electrical energy, i.e. the output of the electricity generation process, is a good whose trade is governed by the GATT, see Cottier and others (n 1) 215; Christopher Frey, 'Die Bedeutung des Welthandelsrechts für die Einfuhr von Strom aus Drittländern in den Energiebinnenmarkt' in Thilo Rensmann and Stefan Storr (eds), *Die Energiewende im rechtlichen Mehrebenensystem: Regionale, nationale und internationale Herausforderungen* (Verlag Österreich 2015) 114; Lars Albath, *Handel und Investitionen in Strom und Gas: Die internationalen Regeln* (Schriftenreihe Energie- und Infrastrukturrecht vol 7, Beck 2005) 86–92; WTO, Council for Trade in Services, Energy Services – Background Note by the Secretariat (09 September 1998) S/C/W/52, [9]. More than two thirds of all WTO Members, including Brazil, China, the EU and its Member States, Korea, Mexico, Russia and Saudi Arabia, have undertaken tariff commitments with respect to electricity in their GATT schedules. Electrical energy is classified under the (optional) heading 2716 in the Harmonized System of the World Custom Organization.

[3]WTO, *European Communities – Regime for the Importation, Sale and Distribution of Bananas,* Report of the Appellate Body (9 September 1997) WT/DS27/AB/R [221]; WTO, *Canada – Certain Measures Affecting the Automotive Industry,* Report of the Appellate Body (31 May 2000) WT/DS139/AB/R, WT/DS142/AB/R [159].

[4]Article XXVIII(a) WTO, General Agreement on Trade in Services (15 April 1994) 1869 U.N.T.S. 183. See also ibid, Article I:3(a).

[5]*Canada – Certain Measures Affecting the Automotive Industry* (n 3) [158]; *European Communities – Regime for the Importation, Sale and Distribution of Bananas* (n 3) [220]; WTO, *European Communities – Regime for the Importation, Sale and Distribution of Bananas,* Report of the Panel (22 May 1997) WT/DS27/R/ECU, WT/DS27/R/USA, WT/DS27/R/MEX [7.280].

The first mode of supply covers the supply of a service 'from the territory of one Member into the territory of any other Member.' Mode 2 comprises the supply of services 'in the territory of one Member to the service consumer of any other Member.' Service supply through commercial presence (mode 3) exists where services are supplied 'by a service supplier of one Member, through commercial presence in the territory of any other Member.' Lastly, mode 4 concerns the supply of services 'by a service supplier of one Member, through presence of natural persons of a Member in the territory of any other Member.'[6]

With respect to the unbundling regime in the EU energy sector, the most relevant mode is first and foremost the supply of services through commercial presence. The central question is how foreign service suppliers that have established or seek to establish a commercial presence inside the EU, as well as the services supplied by them, are affected by the unbundling, certification, and exemption measures under the TEP.[7]

Finally, the vital notion of 'service' must be considered. While this concept presents a number of special features in the context of energy trade (which will be explained in the next two sections), there are a number of energy-related 'services', supplied through one of the four modes listed in Article I:2 GATS, which are affected by the rules in the TEP. Therefore, subject to the remarks below, it can be concluded that the unbundling requirements,[8] the certification procedure,[9] and the exemption regime,[10] as well as the laws, regulations or decisions adopted on the

[6]Article I:2(a)–(d) GATS (n 4).

[7]Importantly, the reference in Article I:1 GATS to measures affecting 'trade in services' does not require the existence of actual services trade between the respondent and the complainant or between the respondent and any other WTO Member. It is sufficient that there *may* be trade in services through mode 3; see WTO, *Argentina – Measures Relating to Trade in Goods and Services*, Report of the Panel (30 September 2015) WT/DS453/R [7.85ff]. The GATS disciplines therefore also apply to the entry of service suppliers under mode 3, i.e. service suppliers that seek to establish a commercial presence in the relevant WTO Member; see Martín Molinuevo, *Protecting Investment in Services: Investor-State Arbitration versus WTO Dispute Settlement* (Global Trade Law Series vol 38, Kluwer Law International 2012) 79–80. Article XXVIII(d) GATS (n 4) explicitly defines 'commercial presence' as 'any type of business or professional establishment, including through (i) the *constitution*, acquisition or maintenance of a juridical person, or (ii) the *creation* or maintenance of a branch or a representative office, within the territory of a Member for the purpose of supplying a service' (emphasis added).

[8]See Articles 9 (OU), 13–14 (ISO) and 17–23 (ITO) of Directive 2009/72/EC of the European Parliament and of the Council concerning common rules for the internal market in electricity and repealing Directive 2003/54/EC (13 July 2009) OJ 2009/L 211/55; Articles 9 (OU), 14–15 (ISO) and 17–23 (ITO) of Directive 2009/73/EC of the European Parliament and of the Council concerning common rules for the internal market in natural gas and repealing Directive 2003/55/EC (13 July 2009) OJ 2009/L 211/94.

[9]See Article 11 of Directive 2009/72/EC (n 8); Directive 2009/73/EC (n 8).

[10]See Article 17 of Regulation (EC) No 714/2009 of the European Parliament and of the Council on conditions for access to the network for cross-border exchanges in electricity and repealing Regulation (EC) No 1228/2003 (13 July 2009) OJ 2009/L 211/15; Article 36 of Directive 2009/73/EC (n 8).

basis of such provisions, constitute 'measures ... affecting trade in services' within the context of Article I:1 GATS. Accordingly, they all fall within the scope of application of the GATS.

4.2 Energy Services Within the Meaning of the GATS

It is important to consider *which* energy-related services are subject to the GATS. Determining that an activity constitutes a 'service' within the meaning of the GATS is a precondition for its application. Such a determination is not always straightforward, in particular with respect to certain economic activities in the energy sector. Given that the unbundling regime in the TEP mainly affects the (1) production/ generation, (2) transmission and (3) supply of energy, it must be asked whether these activities qualify as 'services' under the GATS. As will become clear in the discussion below, most of the activities regulated by the unbundling regime are services within the scope of the GATS.

The notion of 'services' is not legally defined in the GATS.[11] This fact is often attributed to the lack of agreement among the Contracting Parties.[12] Article I:3 (b) GATS merely clarifies that except for services supplied in the exercise of governmental authority, the term 'services' includes '*any service* in *any sector*'.[13] This means that no particular service or service sector is *a priori* excluded from the scope of the GATS. The Appellate Body (AB) stated in *EC – Bananas III* that '[t] here is nothing at all in [Article I:3(b)] to suggest a limited scope of application for the GATS.'[14]

Early commentators predicted that the absence of a legal definition would not lead to any practical difficulties,[15] and in fact the question of what a service is under the GATS has not played any major role in WTO dispute settlement proceedings so far.

---

[11]Christian Pitschas, 'Allgemeines Übereinkommen über den Handel mit Dienstleistungen (GATS)' in Prieß, Hans-Joachim and Georg M Berrisch (eds), *WTO-Handbuch* (C.H. Beck 2003) [11]; Martin Michaelis, '§ 20 Dienstleistungshandel (GATS)' in Meinhard Hilf and Stefan Oeter (eds), *WTO-Recht: Rechtsordnung des Welthandels* (2nd edn. Nomos 2010) [23]; Diana Zacharias, 'Article I GATS' in Rüdiger Wolfrum, Peter-Tobias Stoll and Clemens Feinäugle (eds), *WTO – Trade in Services* (Max Planck Commentaries on World Trade Law vol 6. Martinus Nijhoff Publishers 2008) [11]; Matthias Koehler, *Das Allgemeine Übereinkommen über den Handel mit Dienstleistungen (GATS): Rahmenregelung zur Liberalisierung des internationalen Dienstleistungsverkehrs unter besonderer Berücksichtigung des grenzüberschreitenden Personenverkehrs von Dienstleistungsanbietern* (Schriften zum Internationalen Recht vol 106, Duncker & Humblot 1999) 90.

[12]Zacharias (n 11) [11]; Koehler (n 11) 90.

[13]Emphasis added.

[14]*European Communities – Regime for the Importation, Sale and Distribution of Bananas* (n 3) [220].

[15]Dietrich Barth, 'Das Allgemeine Übereinkommen über den internationalen Dienstleistungshandel (GATS)' [1994] Europäische Zeitschrift für Wirtschaftsrecht 455, 455.

However, contrary to what might be suggested by the broad formulation in Article I:3(b) GATS ('any service in any sector') and the lack of definitional disputes, not all economic activities along the energy chain easily qualify as services within the meaning of the GATS. This applies in particular to (1) the production/generation of gas and electricity; and (2) the transmission and distribution of energy.

As regards the production/generation of gas and electricity, the concept of services needs to be distinguished from certain goods-producing activities. Indeed, the view has been widely held that the production of primary and secondary energy does not constitute a service covered by the GATS, but rather results in goods whose trade is governed by GATT rules.[16] Later, drawing upon general discussions within the WTO, some authors identified the ownership of the raw materials necessary for energy production as the main criterion for distinguishing between energy service transactions which are subject to the GATS, and those which are not. According to this approach, the production of energy by an entity owning the necessary inputs does not constitute a service within the scope of the GATS.[17] It is, however, unclear if in fact the ownership of the raw materials is decisive for determining whether energy production activities constitute services. Within the context of the general discussions on the status of manufacturing transactions under the GATS, many WTO Members expressed the view that generally manufacturing activities should not be classified as services, including manufacturing 'on a fee or contract basis', i.e. where the raw materials are not owned by the manufacturer.[18] Similarly, the Panel in *China – Publications and Audiovisual Products* stated in *obiter dictum* that

[16]Energy Services – Background Note by the Secretariat (n 2) [9]; Carlo Gamberale, 'Energy Services', *Guide to the GATS: An Overview of Issues for Further Liberalization of Trade in Services* (Kluwer Law International 2001) 261; United Nations Conference on Trade and Development, Energy Services in International Trade: Development Implications – Note by the UNCTAD Secretariat (18 June 2001) TD/B/COM.1/EM.16/2, [14]; Paolo D Farah and Elena Cima, 'Energy Trade and the WTO: Implications for Renewable Energy and the OPEC Cartel' (2013) 16 Journal of International Economic Law 707, 711; WTO, Council for Trade in Services, Energy Services – Information Note by the Secretariat (22 September 2005) JOB(05)/204, [13].

[17]Mireille Cossy, 'Energy Services under the General Agreement on Trade in Services' in Yulia Selivanova (ed), *Regulation of Energy in International Trade Law: WTO, NAFTA and Energy Charter* (Kluwer Law International 2012) 151; Yulia Selivanova, 'The WTO Agreements and Energy' in Kim Talus (ed), *Research Handbook on International Energy Law* (Research Handbooks in International Law. Edward Elgar 2014) 295; Yulia Selivanova, *The WTO and Energy: WTO Rules and Agreements of Relevance to the Energy Sector* (Issue paper vol 1, International Centre for Trade and Sustainable Development 2007) 21.

[18]See the discussion within the WTO Committee on Specific Commitments, WTO, Committee on Specific Commitments, Report of the Meeting Held on 11 July 2000 – Note by the Secretariat (11 September 2000) S/CSC/M/16, [4–6]; WTO, Committee on Specific Commitments, Report of the Meeting Held on 4 October 2000 – Note by the Secretariat (24 November 2000) S/CSC/M/17, [4–5]; WTO, Committee on Specific Commitments, Report of the Meeting Held on 28 November 2000 – Note by the Secretariat (24 April 2001) S/CSC/M/18/Rev.1, [3–7]; WTO, Committee on Specific Commitments, Report of the Meeting Held on 22 March 2001 – Note by the Secretariat (27 April 2001) S/CSC/M/19, [34–36]. See also Energy Services – Information Note by the Secretariat (n 16) [16].

'[o]bviously, the simple production of a good could not be said to constitute a service.'[19] Therefore, while some uncertainties persist, it seems that to the extent the unbundling and unbundling-related measures in the EU energy sector regulate and affect electricity generation and gas production, they fall outside the scope of the GATS.

As regards the transmission of energy, the WTO Secretariat stated shortly after the conclusion of the GATS that the transportation and distribution of energy constitute services only if they are provided 'independently'.[20] Subsequently it has been suggested by some authors that transportation and distribution are subject to the GATS, and thus carried out 'independently', when these activities are operated by a company that does not own the gas or the electricity to be transported or distributed.[21] Here, the ownership of the goods which are subject to the service performed is once again used as the main criterion to draw a line between transmission activities that fall within the scope of application of the GATS and those that do not. Considering the foregoing, one can get the impression that the GATS effectively 'excludes' vertically integrated service suppliers through the definition of what constitutes a service. This calls for closer examination.

As a first step, it is useful to consider the 'Services Sectoral Classification List' (W/120), which was developed by the GATT Secretariat during the Uruguay Round and was used by most WTO Members to formulate their specific commitments under the GATS. The W/120 provides a categorization of services, drawing upon the 'Provisional Central Product Classification' (CPC) of the United Nations (UN). Where services affect goods, the CPC frequently covers only services which are supplied 'on a fee or contract basis'. For example, services falling into the category '[t]ransportation of fuels' in the W/120 are defined in the CPC as '[t]ransport services via pipeline *on a fee or contract basis* of petroleum and natural gas'.[22] In the same way, '[s]ervices incidental to energy distribution' are specified as 'transmission and distribution services *on a fee or contract basis* of electricity, gaseous

[19]WTO, *China – Measures Affecting Trading Rights and Distribution Services for Certain Publications and Audiovisual Entertainment Products,* Report of the Panel (12 August 2009) WT/DS363/R [7.1189], footnote 659. See also ibid [7.1233].

[20]Energy Services – Background Note by the Secretariat (n 2) [9]. See also Energy Services in International Trade: Development Implications (n 16) [14]; Gamberale (n 16) 261; Simonetta Zarrilli, 'Multilateral Rules and Trade in Energy Goods and Services: The Case of Electricity' in Janusz Bielecki and Melaku G Desta (eds), *Electricity Trade in Europe – Review of the Economic and Regulatory Changes* (Kluwer Law International 2004) 243; Farah and Cima (n 16) 711.

[21]Cossy (n 17) 161, 166–168; Mireille Cossy, 'Energy Transport and Transit in the WTO' in Joost Pauwelyn (ed), *Global Challenges at the Intersection of Trade, Energy and the Environment* (Center for Economic and Policy Research 2010) 117; Mireille Cossy, 'Energy Trade and WTO Rules: Reflexions on Sovereignty over Natural Resources, Export Restrictions and Freedom of Transit' in Christoph Herrmann and Jörg P Terhechte (eds), *European Yearbook of International Economic Law 2012* (European Yearbook of International Economic Law vol 3. Springer 2012) 287.

[22]United Nations, Provisional Central Product Classification (1991) ST/ESA/STAT/SER.M/77, 48, 77 (emphasis added).

fuels and steam and hot water to household, industrial, commercial and other users.'[23] The CPC clarifies that the term 'on a fee or contract basis' means that the services must be supplied by an entity that does not own the raw material concerned.[24] Therefore, the definitions in the GATS classification instruments could provide support for the contention that the transmission of electricity and natural gas is not a service subject to GATS coverage if the transmission system operator owns the respective energy product(s).[25]

The decisive point, however, is that the Services Sectoral Classification List and the CPC have little relevance in determining the scope of application of the GATS. Although it has been stated in academic writing that 'at least those sub-sectors that are explicitly listed in W/120 ... can be considered to fall under the GATS',[26] the *absence* of a service from the W/120 and/or the CPC does not mean that it is *not* subject to the GATS.[27] The view that the GATS classification instruments do not have any legal influence on the scope of application of the GATS is also shared by the WTO Secretariat.[28]

In the end, the problem comes down to the question of what a 'service' is under the GATS. As already indicated, the GATS does not precisely define the concept. In the academic literature, various authors have attempted to define services in a descriptive manner by identifying certain common characteristics (such as intangibility, invisibility),[29] which do not however apply without exception and in addition fail to provide an answer to the issue under consideration. Nevertheless, and at the same time, the ordinary meaning of the notion 'service' offers useful insights, because it clearly presupposes that the relevant activity must be provided by or to a third party.[30] This interpretation is also in line with the writings of economists, according to whom the concept of a service necessarily requires that '*one* economic

---

[23]Ibid 77 (emphasis added).

[24]The category of '[s]ervices incidental to manufacturing' for instance is expressly defined as 'manufacturing *on a fee or contract basis, i.e. manufacturing services rendered to others where the raw materials processed, treated or finished are not owned by the manufacturer*', see ibid 76. See also Cossy (n 17) 151.

[25]It is interesting to note that newer versions of the Central Product Classification contain energy services which are carried out on own account. The latest version of the CPC for instance features the item '[t]ransmission of electricity (on own account)', see code 69111 of the United Nations, Central Product Classification, Ver. 2.1 (2015).

[26]Rudolf Adlung and Weiwei Zhang, 'Trade Disciplines with a Trapdoor: Contract Manufacturing' (2013) 16 Journal of International Economic Law 383, 387.

[27]Pitschas (n 11) [12]; Cossy (n 17) 153.

[28]WTO, Council for Trade in Services, Energy Services – Background Note by the Secretariat (12 January 2010) S/C/W/311, [53]; Report of the Meeting Held on 11 July 2000 (n 18) [4].

[29]See Zacharias (n 11) [16]; Christoph Herrmann, Wolfgang Weiß and Christoph Ohler, *Welthandelsrecht* (C.H. Beck 2007) [812–818].

[30]Tobias Reimold, *Der Handel mit Bildungsdienstleistungen nach dem GATS* (Mohr Siebeck 2010) 45; Cossy (n 21) 117.

unit performs some activity for the benefit of *another*.'[31] Against this background, it becomes clear that it is not so much the ownership of the goods which are the subject of the service, but the requirement of a transaction between different economic actors—typically on the basis of a contract and for remuneration[32]—that is determinative of whether a certain action is a service under the GATS.[33] It can thus be concluded that measures affecting the transport of energy are fully covered by the applicable GATS disciplines if the transport is carried out on behalf of a third party or third parties. In contrast, the transport of energy does not qualify as a service within the meaning of the GATS if it is merely an 'in-house' activity.

The fact that services necessarily occur between different economic actors does not, however, mean that such economic actors cannot be affiliated with each other. The definition (or concept) of a service under the GATS does not envisage a necessity that the economic operators are completely independent from each other, similar to the ownership unbundling model contained in the TEP. In my opinion legal separation is sufficient, and in such circumstances the transportation and distribution of energy is provided 'independently'. Therefore, even if a vertically integrated TSO transports gas or electricity on behalf of another legal entity forming part of the same vertically integrated undertaking, the underlying transaction is subject to the GATS. In contrast, in-house transportation activities within a vertically integrated undertaking that is organized as one legal entity would fall outside the scope of the GATS.

It could be asked: What effect does the definition of 'services' under the GATS have in terms of promoting competition in energy markets? Does it support the adoption of unbundling policies similar to those in the EU energy sector? The primary consequence in a case where the in-house energy transportation activities do not constitute services is that the scope of application of the GATS is reduced. This could imply that certain national treatment or market access barriers cannot be effectively addressed through the WTO dispute settlement system, because these measures are not subject to the GATS disciplines. It seems that this effect is neutral with respect to the decision(s) of WTO Members or individual companies to implement unbundling.[34] As regards this book, it can be briefly highlighted that

---

[31] T. P Hill, 'On Goods and Services' (1977) 23 Review of Income and Wealth 315, 318 (emphasis added). See also Jagdish Bhagwati, 'International Trade in Services and Its Relevance for Economic Development' in Douglas A Irwin (ed), *Political Economy and International Economics* (The MIT Press 1991) 238, 251.

[32] In fact, several authors have taken the view that this is a constitutive element of the concept of 'service' within the meaning of the GATS, see Herrmann, Weiß and Ohler (n 29) [838]; Zacharias (n 11) [22]; Koehler (n 11) 35. But see Reimold (n 30) 48–49.

[33] See also Irene Musselli and Simonetta Zarrilli, 'Oil and Gas Services: Market Liberalization and the Ongoing GATS Negotiations' (2005) 8 Journal of International Economic Law 551, 562–563 (writing that the distinction based on underlying ownership patterns 'is sometimes rather controversial').

[34] Cossy argues that the exclusion of in-house transportation activities has a positive effect on the competitive structure of energy markets. She takes the view that if WTO Members undertake additional commitments on energy services under Article XVIII GATS, such as non-discriminatory

the 'non-service nature' of certain transmission activities does not in any way remove the unbundling and unbundling-related measures in the EU energy sector from the scope of application of the GATS. The unbundling regime of the TEP directly affects the transport, on behalf of a third party, of natural gas and electricity on high-pressure pipelines or high-voltage systems, and thus is fully subject to the GATS.

In conclusion, the scope of application of the GATS covers all energy-related transactions except for (1) the production/generation of gas or electricity; and (2) the transmission of energy 'on one's own account', i.e. not on behalf of third parties. The energy activities which are regulated by the unbundling regime in the TEP are thus largely within the scope of the GATS.

4.3 Are Energy Services 'Services Supplied in the Exercise of Governmental Authority'?

Although it was concluded in the preceding section that the GATS covers services which are regulated by the TEP, this assessment could change as a result of the application of Article I:3(b) GATS. As already alluded to, 'services supplied in the exercise of governmental authority' are carved out from the scope of the GATS according to this Article. Services supplied in the exercise of governmental authority are defined in Article I:3(c) GATS as services which are supplied 'neither on a commercial basis, nor in competition with one or more service suppliers.'

The exception for services supplied in the exercise of governmental authority reflects the controversial question of the extent to which public services should be subject to liberalization under the GATS.[35] There have been claims that the governmental authority exception is valid for the majority of public services.[36] This would mean that, similar to, for example, water, telecommunications and railroads, energy would be exempted from the scope of the GATS.[37] Consequently, the Third Energy

third party access with respect to energy transmission networks, 'companies transporting their own energy goods . . . would not benefit from GATS competition disciplines' (see Cossy (n 17) 168).

Put differently, Cossy's argument seems to be that the TPA commitment could not be invoked by another WTO Member in relation to network access requests by companies seeking to transport their own energy goods. Therefore, there would be an incentive for companies to unbundle in order to benefit from the additional competition-related commitments. In my view, however, the important question is whether the WTO Member undertaking the additional TPA commitment prescribes unbundling domestically or not.

[35]Michaelis (n 11) [27].

[36]See the references in Markus Krajewski, *National Regulation and Trade Liberalization in Services: The Legal Impact of the General Agreement on Trade in Services (GATS) on National Regulatory Autonomy* (Kluwer Law International 2003) 68.

[37]Michaelis (n 11) [27].

Package, as well as national implementing measures, could not be challenged under the agreement.

Article I:3(c) GATS specifies that for a service to be excluded from the scope of the GATS, it is necessary that the service is supplied neither 'on a commercial basis' nor 'in competition with one or more service suppliers,' these requirements being cumulative.[38] This formulation relates to the circumstances surrounding the supply of a service.[39] In contrast, the nature of a service as a service in the public interest or the public ownership of a company are immaterial. Therefore, in order to determine whether energy services, in whole or in part, fall within the purview of this definition, one must look at the way the EU energy market functions.

In this context, it is important to note that substantial structural changes have taken place in the EU energy sector. Traditionally, State-owned vertically integrated monopolies dominated the energy sector, leaving little room for competition. However, in the last 20 years or so there has been a clear trend towards liberalization of the gas and electricity markets.[40] Today, the production/generation and supply sectors are fully competitive. Although the natural monopoly nature of transmission networks could mean that the respective services are, at a given point in time, not supplied in competition with other service suppliers, it is clear that transmission system operators seek to make a profit and thus operate 'on a commercial basis'. In light of these developments, it has been rightfully suggested that 'the GATS article I.3(b)(c) exemption is falling into disuse with respect to large segments of the energy sector.'[41] Whereas the governmental authority exception may have been applicable *before* the structural reforms of the energy markets in the EU, their liberalization and privatization has ultimately led to the dis-application of Article I:3(b) and (c) GATS with respect to most energy services.[42]

Even if nowadays energy services are generally supplied on a commercial basis and/or in competition with one or more service suppliers (Article I:3(c) GATS), the relevance of the phrase 'supplied in the exercise of governmental authority' in Article I:3(b) GATS is still open to question. Can this phrase be interpreted to mean that energy services may be removed from the scope of the GATS? At first glance, it appears that the category of services supplied in the exercise of governmental authority is exhaustively defined in Article I:3(c) GATS.[43] This provision refers only to the notions of commercialism and competition discussed above. However, it seems reasonable to assume that the reference to 'governmental authority' in Article I:3(b) GATS must have some independent function, otherwise the

---

[38]Herrmann, Weiß and Ohler (n 29) [839]; Pitschas (n 11) [13].

[39]Krajewski (n 36) 71–73.

[40]Kim Talus, *EU Energy Law and Policy: A Critical Account* (Oxford University Press 2013) 15ff.

[41]Musselli and Zarrilli (n 33) 576. See also Albath (n 2) 36, 132–133.

[42]On the 'dynamic' scope of application of Article I:3(c) GATS with respect to public services, see Markus Krajewski, 'Public Services and Trade Liberalization: Mapping the Legal Framework' (2003) 6 Journal of International Economic Law 341, 358–359.

[43]Krajewski (n 36) 71.

inclusion of this reference would have been superfluous.[44] But clearly, even if 'some residual importance'[45] is ascribed to the notion of 'governmental authority' in sub-paragraph (b), it cannot override the references to commercialism and competition in sub-paragraph (c). Rather, it supplements Article I:3(c) GATS.[46] Furthermore, the term 'governmental authority' is generally associated with command and control and the power to regulate the conduct of individuals or other entities.[47] Consequently, the mere fact that there is a public interest in the provision of certain energy services is not sufficient.[48]

In conclusion, under Article I:3(b) and (c) GATS, energy services in the EU internal market are not excluded from the scope of application of the GATS.

4.4 Commitments on Energy Services Within the GATS Framework

The preceding sections dealt with the question of whether certain activities which are regulated by the unbundling regime in the Third Energy Package, and in particular by Directives 2009/72/EC and 2009/73/EC, constitute 'services' within the meaning of the GATS. In what follows, the scope of specific commitments with respect to relevant energy services will be elucidated. This is important, since the market access and national treatment obligations (Articles XVI and XVII GATS), as well as most disciplines on domestic regulation (Article VI GATS), only apply if and to the extent that corresponding commitments have been undertaken by respective WTO Members.

Two preliminary points are worth noting. First of all, WTO Members have only rarely agreed to undertake strong commitments in the energy sector.[49] This reluctance certainly stems from the fact that for many WTO Members core energy activities, such as in particular transmission/distribution, are highly sensitive. Second, the service classification under the GATS has failed to provide a coherent and

44 Rudolf Adlung, 'Public Services and the GATS' (2006) 9 Journal of International Economic Law 455, 465–466.

45 Krajewski (n 36) 71.

46 Zacharias (n 11) [64]; Krajewski (n 36) 71–72.

47 Krajewski (n 42) 350; Eric H Leroux, 'What is a "Service Supplied in the Exercise of Governmental Authority" Under Article I:3(b) and (c) of the General Agreement on Trade in Services?' (2006) 40 Journal of World Trade 345, 352.

48 Michaelis (n 11) [28]; Herrmann, Weiß and Ohler (n 29) [839].

49 Frank Schorkopf, '"Energie" als Thema des Welthandelsrechts' in Christian Walter, Stefan Leible and Michael Lippert (eds), *Die Sicherung der Energieversorgung auf globalisierten Märkten* (Mohr Siebeck 2012) 106; Energy Services – Background Note by the Secretariat (n 2) [1, 72]; Energy Services – Background Note by the Secretariat (n 28) [69]; Peter C Evans, *Liberalizing Global Trade in Energy Services* (The AEI Press 2002) 34; Matthias Schmidt-Preuß, 'Energieversorgung als Aufgabe der Außenpolitik?: Rechtliche Aspekte' [2007] Recht der Energiewirtschaft 281, 285.

adequate classification of energy services. As already indicated above, WTO Members were called upon to describe committed sectors and sub-sectors according to the Services Sectoral Classification List (W/120) prepared by the GATT Secretariat during the Uruguay Round.[50] The W/120, in turn, refers to the more detailed Provisional Central Product Classification (CPC) of the UN. As there is no separate category for energy services in the W/120, these services are scattered across a number of different sectors (in particular business, construction, distribution and transport), which results in a 'fragmentation'[51] of energy-related activities and impairs their 'visibility.'[52] While three sub-sectors of the W/120 exclusively refer to energy; namely (1) services incidental to mining; (2) services incidental to energy distribution; and (3) transportation of fuels; other energy services are subsumed under more generic sub-sectors, including construction work for civil engineering, engineering services, scientific and technical consulting services, technical testing and analysis services, storage services, wholesale trade services, and retailing services. A few specific energy services are not covered by the GATS classification instruments. This applies, for example, to wholesale and retail services in electricity.[53]

Several WTO Members, including the United States, Indonesia, Venezuela, the EU and Japan, have put forward proposals aimed at developing a more detailed and comprehensive classification of energy services under the GATS.[54] In the last decade, however, this debate has lost momentum.

The W/120 contains four sub-sectors which are particularly relevant for the issue of unbundling and unbundling-related measures. These are: (1) transportation of fuels; (2) services incidental to energy distribution; (3) wholesale trade services; and (4) retailing services. Each will be addressed in turn.

Services pertaining to the transportation of fuels, which fall into the broader category of transport services, are defined in the CPC as the '[t]ransportation via pipeline of crude or refined petroleum and petroleum products and of natural gas' (CPC 7131).[55] This definition is quite straightforward and squarely covers all activities which are encompassed by the term 'transmission' in the Gas Directive, i.e. the transport of natural gas through a network mainly consisting of high-pressure pipelines with a view to its delivery to customers.[56] In addition, it seems that the

[50]WTO, Scheduling of Initial Commitments in Trade in Services: Explanatory Note, MTN.GNS/W/164 (03 September 1993), [16].

[51]Cottier and others (n 1) 223–225.

[52]Cossy (n 17) 154.

[53]Energy Services – Background Note by the Secretariat (n 28) [47].

[54]For an analysis, see Olga Nartova, *Energy Services and Competition Policies under WTO Law* (Научная Мысль, INFRA-M 2010) 204–213; Pietro Poretti and Roberto Rios Herrán, 'A Reference Paper On Energy Services: The Best Way Forward?' (2006) 3 Manchester Journal of International Economic Law 2, 26–28.

[55]CPC (n 22) 48.

[56]The planning and construction of a pipeline does not, however, fall under the category 'transportation of fuels', see Energy Services – Background Note by the Secretariat (n 28) [45].

transportation of gas through local low-pressure pipelines (distribution) can also be subsumed under CPC 7131. Having said that, the CPC furthermore indicates that the transportation via pipeline has to be carried out 'on a fee or contract basis.'[57] Therefore commitments in this sub-sector only cover situations where the energy products to be transported are not owned by the pipeline transportation service supplier.[58]

'Services incidental to energy distribution', which form part of the broader category of business services, are defined in the CPC as 'transmission and distribution services on a fee or contract basis of electricity, gaseous fuels and steam and hot water to household, industrial, commercial and other users' (CPC 887).[59] This service category has given rise to definitional problems. The word 'incidental' suggests that this sub-sector does not cover energy transmission/distribution *per se*, but instead encompasses services such as the maintenance of networks, consultancy, and metering.[60] The definition in the CPC, however, unambiguously refers to 'transmission and distribution services' (which would perfectly match the corresponding definitions in the Gas and Electricity Directives).[61] There is thus a discrepancy between the literal meaning of the title of the sub-sector and the explanation provided in the CPC. If priority is given to the latter over the former, commitments in this area would also include the actual transmission and distribution of energy.[62] In this case, however, the question arises where to draw the line between, on one hand, the 'transmission and distribution' of natural gas under CPC 887 and, on the other hand, the 'transportation via pipeline' of natural gas under CPC 7131. Such a line would need to be drawn, because the categories in the CPC are mutually exclusive, which means that a given service can be classified in only one category.[63] However, given that the activities covered by CPC 887 and CPC 7131, respectively, are substantially the same (at least with respect to gas), this is a difficult exercise. Finally, it should also be noted that, like the transportation services via pipeline, services 'incidental' to energy distribution under CPC 887 are only covered if they are supplied 'on a fee or contract basis.'

The W/120 also refers to wholesale trade services, a sub-category of distribution services. Wholesale trade services are distributive trade services consisting of 'selling merchandise to retailers, to industrial, commercial, institutional or other professional business users, or to other wholesalers, or acting as agent or broker'.[64]

---

[57]See CPC (n 22) 77.

[58]See discussion in Sect. 4.2.

[59]CPC (n 22) 77.

[60]Energy Services – Background Note by the Secretariat (n 2) [12]. See also Evans (n 49) 39; Zarrilli (n 20) 245; Energy Services – Information Note by the Secretariat (n 16) [18].

[61]Energy Services – Background Note by the Secretariat (n 28) [44].

[62]Gamberale (n 16) 282; Energy Services – Background Note by the Secretariat (n 2) [74].

[63]WTO, *United States – Measures Affecting the Cross-Border Supply of Gambling and Betting Services,* Report of the Appellate Body (7 April 2005) WT/DS285/AB/R [172].

[64]CPC (n 22) 33.

Among other services, this service category includes '[w]holesale trade services of solid, liquid and gaseous fuels and related products' (CPC 62271).[65] In addition, and closely related, the W/120 mentions retailing services, another sub-category of distribution services. Retailing services involve selling goods for personal or household consumption.[66] This group covers, *inter alia*, '[r]etailing services of diverse combustibles, *such as* fuel oils, bottled gas, coal and lignite, wood charcoal and fuel wood, for heating, cooking and other purposes' (CPC 63297).[67] While the reference to 'bottled gas' could suggest a rather narrow scope of the CPC entry, this is only an example of a combustible product (as the words 'such as' indicate). Furthermore, the CPC definition subsequently clarifies that natural gas is a good falling within the scope of retail services under CPC 63297.[68] In sum, the scope of CPC 62271 (wholesale of gas) and 63297 (retail of gas) encompasses virtually all of the activities covered by the notion of 'supply' in the Gas Directive, i.e. the sale and resale of gas to customers, including wholesale or final customers or other natural gas undertakings.

The preceding analysis shows that, on the basis of the W/120 and the CPC, WTO Members can undertake market access and national treatment commitments along the entire spectrum of relevant energy services, at least with respect to the gas sector. The independent 'transmission' of natural gas falls under the transportation of fuels (CPC 7131), and the corresponding 'supply' activities are subject to commitments on wholesale trade services (CPC 62271) and retailing services (CPC 63297) of natural gas.

In contrast however, the classification of electricity services in the W/120 and the CPC is manifestly inadequate. It is unclear whether the transmission of electricity is covered by the sub-sector of services incidental to energy distribution (CPC 887), and wholesale and retail services of electricity are not even represented in the WTO classification instruments. Nevertheless, it is important to emphasize that although these services do not have a (clear-cut) entry in the W/120 or the CPC, they do come within the scope of application of the GATS and thus trigger the application of the MFN treatment obligation.[69]

Having outlined the extent to which TEP-related energy services are included in the GATS classification instruments, the next step is to analyze the pertinent schedules of commitments in order to ascertain whether the EU and its Member States have in fact undertaken specific market access or national treatment

---

[65]Ibid 38.

[66]Ibid 33.

[67]Ibid 43 (emphasis added).

[68]The definition provides that the goods 'classified in CPC 03, 11, 12, 31, 33, 345' are covered by the service commitments under CPC 63297. This includes crude petroleum and natural gas. I do not agree with Teresa M Moschetta, *Il mercato comunitario del gas naturale: Investimenti esteri diretti e diritto internazionale* (Giuffrè 2009) 126, who, in discussing the EU's unbundling measures, suggests that commitments on retailing services are not relevant, because natural gas would not be suitable for retailing due to its particular nature.

[69]Cossy (n 17) 153. See also Sect. 4.2.

commitments in the service sectors outlined above. Before doing so, however, some preliminary remarks are in order.

Due to the division of competences at the time of conclusion of the WTO Agreement, both the European Community (now the EU) and its member states joined the WTO at its founding in 1994.[70] Since then, this dual membership has been retained.[71] This fact, together with the successive enlargement of the EU, has led to a complicated *status quo* regarding the GATS schedules. For the 12 EU Members that became founding members of the WTO in 1994, as well as for the EU, the respective commitments were recorded in a single, combined schedule.[72] The specific commitments in this schedule are composed of the EU12-wide[73] commitments and exceptions, as qualified by the additional limitations attached by the respective Member States. In contrast, all other 16 Member States, which acceded to the EU between 1995 and 2013, have submitted individual schedules to the WTO. While the EU has been working on a consolidated services schedule[74] and also has conducted negotiations with WTO Members on the modification of schedules to this end, this consolidated version has not yet entered into force.[75]

Based on the foregoing, the following observations can be made. First of all, Croatia, Hungary and Lithuania have made commitments with respect to pipeline transport services (CPC 7131).[76] Furthermore, as regards services incidental to

[70]See Article XI of the Agreement Establishing the World Trade Organization (15 April 1994) 1867 U.N.T.S. 154.

[71]Matthias Herdegen, *Principles of International Economic Law* (Oxford University Press 2013) 178–179; Peter van den Bossche and Werner Zdouc, *Law and Policy of the World Trade Organization* (3rd edn, Cambridge University Press 2013) 106–107.

[72]See WTO, European Communities and their Member States – Schedule of Specific Commitments (15 April 1994) GATS/SC/31, including four supplements.

[73]Covering Belgium, Denmark, France, Germany, Greece, Ireland, Italy, Luxembourg, the Netherlands, Portugal, Spain and the United Kingdom.

[74]See WTO, Council for Trade in Services, Communication from the European Communities and its Member States – Certification: Draft consolidated GATS Schedule (09 October 2006) S/C/W/273.

[75]At the end of 2006, the negotiations with WTO Members and the certification of the EC-25 GATS schedule were concluded. However, the consolidated schedule will only enter into force after the internal decision-making procedures of the EU and its Member States, where applicable, have been completed. So far, this has not been done. Therefore, it is the 1994 schedule, which is currently in force. Furthermore, following two further rounds of enlargement (Bulgaria and Romania in 2007 and Croatia in 2013), the GATS schedules of these three Member States have to be consolidated with that of the EU-25. To this end, negotiations under Article XXI GATS (Modification of Schedules) have to be conducted.

[76]WTO, Croatia – Schedule of Specific Commitments (22 December 2000) GATS/SC/130, 33 (full commitment on 'Pipeline Transport Services (CPC 713)' for mode 3 regarding both MA and NT); WTO, Hungary – Schedule of Specific Commitments (15 April 1994) GATS/SC/40, 32 (commitment in the 'Pipeline Transport' sector for mode 3 regarding MA and NT, with the sole reservation (for MA) that '[s]ervices may be provided through a Contract of Concession granted by the state or the local authority'); WTO, Lithuania – Schedule of Specific Commitments (21 December 2001) GATS/SC/133, 23 (full commitment in the 'Pipeline Transport (CPC 713)' sector for mode 3 regarding both MA and NT).

energy distribution (CPC 887), Croatia, Latvia and Slovenia have undertaken specific commitments.[77] All of these countries have self-standing services schedules. Around 13 individual EU Member States, as well as the EU (with respect to another 12 Member States), have undertaken market access and national treatment commitments in the field of wholesale trade services of natural gas (CPC 62271). A similarly high number of commitments (again including the EU) exists in the area of gas retailing services (CPC 63297).[78] In sum, whereas a high level of binding commitments can be found in the non-energy-specific wholesale and retailing sectors, the services schedules of the EU and its Member States feature a comparatively low number of commitments in those sub-sectors that relate exclusively to energy activities. In fact, the EU has not made any commitments on pipeline transportation services or services incidental to energy distribution. Nevertheless, it must be emphasized that while the level of commitments varies, both the EU and almost all of its Member States have undertaken market access and national treatment commitments on services that are relevant to the present analysis of unbundling and unbundling-related measures.[79]

---

[77]Croatia – Schedule of Specific Commitments (n 76) 12 (full commitment on 'Services incidental to energy distribution (CPC 887)' for mode 3 regarding both MA and NT); WTO, Latvia – Schedule of Specific Commitments (22 April 1999) GATS/SC/126, 10 (full commitment on 'Services incidental to energy distribution (CPC 887)' for mode 3 regarding both MA and NT); WTO, Slovenia – Schedule of Specific Commitments (30 August 1995) GATS/SC/99, 18 (commitment on 'Services Incidental to Energy Distribution' (gas only) for mode 3 regarding both MA and NT, with the following reservation: 'Public utility exist; concession rights can be granted to the private operators established in the Republic of Slovenia').

[78]European Communities and their Member States – Schedule of Specific Commitments (n 72) 52–54; WTO, Austria – Schedule of Specific Commitments (15 April 1994) GATS/SC/7, 21; Croatia – Schedule of Specific Commitments (n 76) 18; WTO, Czech Republic – Schedule of Specific Commitments (15 April 1994) GATS/SC/26, 20–21; WTO, Estonia – Schedule of Specific Commitments (05 October 1999) GATS/SC/127, 13; WTO, Finland – Schedule of Specific Commitments (15 April 1994) GATS/SC/33, 22; Hungary – Schedule of Specific Commitments (n 76) 18; Latvia – Schedule of Specific Commitments (n 77) 15; Lithuania – Schedule of Specific Commitments (n 76) 12; WTO, Poland – Schedule of Specific Commitments (15 April 1994) GATS/SC/71, 12–13; WTO, Romania – Schedule of Specific Commitments (15 April 1994) GATS/SC/72, 13; WTO, Slovak Republic – Schedule of Specific Commitments (15 April 1994) GATS/SC/77, 20–21; Slovenia – Schedule of Specific Commitments (n 77) 23; WTO, Sweden – Schedule of Specific Commitments (15 April 1994) GATS/SC/82, 25. In some cases, limitations have been scheduled.

[79]But see Matthias Schmidt-Preuß, 'Die Kontrolle des Verkaufs bzw. des Erwerbs von Netzen (Erwerb durch Nicht-EU-Ausländer gem. §4b EnWG; Außenwirtschaftsrecht; Fusionskontrolle)' in Jürgen F Baur, Peter Salje and Matthias Schmidt-Preuß (eds), *Regulierung in der Energiewirtschaft: Ein Praxishandbuch* (2nd edn. Carl Heymanns Verlag 2016) [97] (who opines that the GATS is not applicable to the unbundling requirements and the certification procedure due to a lack of specific commitments). See also Helmut Lecheler and Claas F Germelmann, *Zugangsbeschränkungen für Investitionen aus Drittstaaten im deutschen und europäischen Energierecht* (Energierecht vol 1, Mohr Siebeck 2010) 100; Caroline Van den bergh, 'Reciprocity Clause and International Trade Law' (2009) 27 Journal of Energy & Natural Resources Law 228, 250–251 (who write state that the EU has not undertaken *any* commitments on energy services; they seem to ignore energy services that are included in non-energy-specific sub-sectors in the W/120, such as wholesale and retail services of electricity and gas).

The scope of commitments by the EU and by Member States may, however, be limited by the inclusion of a horizontal limitation relating to 'public utilities' in the EU's GATS schedule. The market access reservation for mode 3, which the EU consistently takes in all its trade agreements, reads as follows: 'In all EC Member States services considered as public utilities at a national or local level may be subject to public monopolies or to exclusive rights granted to private operators.'[80] An annotated footnote accompanying the reservation contains a non-exhaustive list of sectors which are deemed to fall into this category.[81] Although the exact meaning of the term 'public utilities' remains unclear,[82] it can be said with relative certainty that infrastructure-based services such as electricity and gas transmission, distribution and supply are covered by the reservation.[83] Hence the question arises to what extent the commitments of the EU and of Member States are modified or limited by the inclusion of the public utilities exemption. The effect of this clause is to reserve the right to have monopolies and exclusive rights for public utilities in EU Member States at any level of government, thereby mainly limiting the application of Article XVI GATS.[84]

However, public utilities are not fully exempted from the application of Article XVI GATS. The scheduled limitation only concerns two specific restrictions on market access, i.e. monopolies and exclusive service suppliers. All other prohibited market access restrictions listed in Article XVI, as well as the universe of possible national treatment limitations, are not covered by the 'public utilities' clause.[85] As it is uncontroversial that the unbundling regime provided for in the Third Energy

[80]European Communities and their Member States – Schedule of Specific Commitments (n 72) 2.

[81]The explanatory note states: 'Public utilities exist in sectors such as related scientific and technical consulting services, R&D services on social sciences and humanities, technical testing and analysis services, environmental services, health services, transport services and services auxiliary to all modes of transport. Exclusive rights on such services are often granted to private operators, for instance operators with concessions from public authorities, subject to specific service obligations. Given that public utilities often also exist at the sub-central level, detailed and exhaustive sector-specific scheduling is not practical.'

[82]This view is even shared by the European Commission, see European Commission, Commission Proposal for the Modernisation of the Treatment of Public Services in EU Trade Agreements (26 October 2011) TRADE.B.1/SC/am D(2011), 4.

[83]Markus Krajewski, 'Public Services in Bilateral Free Trade Agreements of the EU' (2011) 25–26 <http://papers.ssrn.com/sol3/papers.cfm?abstract_id=1964288>. See also Modernisation of the Treatment of Public Services in EU Trade Agreements (n 82) 4.

[84]Market access limitations are automatically considered to also provide a condition or qualification to Article XVII, see Article XX:2 of the GATS (n 4).

[85]Krajewski, 'Public Services in Bilateral Free Trade Agreements of the EU' (n 83) 32, 35; Markus Krajewski and Britta Kynast, 'Impact of the Transatlantic Trade and Investment Partnership (TTIP) on the Legal Framework for Public Services in Europe' (2014) 25 <http://papers.ssrn.com/sol3/papers.cfm?abstract_id=2576079> accessed 8 May 2016.

Package does not establish monopolies or exclusive service providers, the EU's public utilities exemption is not applicable in the present context.[86]

Although it can thus be concluded that the EU and its Member States have undertaken pertinent market access and national treatment commitments, the scope of which is not restricted by the EU's public utilities reservation, it is necessary to further specify the applicability of these commitments in relation to the three different measures here in issue (the unbundling requirements as such; the certification procedure; and the exemption regime).

In the case of the unbundling requirements, both the commitments on energy transmission services (CPC 7131 and possibly CPC 887) and the commitments on energy supply services (CPC 62271 and CPC 63297) can be invoked. This is due to the fact that the unbundling requirements are addressed equally to transmission system operators and commercial energy companies.[87] In the case of the certification procedure, on the other hand, only the transmission-related commitments matter, given that the certification provisions apply exclusively to transmission system operations.[88] The same goes for the OU exemption regime. Even though the exemption regime undeniably affects energy producers/generators and suppliers, it regulates the provision of transmission services and not of supply services.

Against this background, and based on the preceding review of the schedules of commitments, the following conclusions can be drawn: First of all, both the EU and

[86]But see Moschetta (n 68) 120–123, 126–127 (who writes that although the ownership unbundling measures proposed by the European Commission in 2007 could be considered as restricting or requiring specific types of legal entity (contrary to Article XVI:2(e) GATS) or as limiting the number of service suppliers in the form of numerical quotas (contrary to Article XVI:2(a) GATS), there would be no violation of specific commitments undertaken by the European Community due to the 'public utilities' exception).

It should also be pointed out that the horizontal limitation only applies to those EU Member States that have a combined GATS schedule, together with the EU. In contrast, it does not have spillover effects on the self-standing services schedules of more recent Member States, such as Lithuania or Croatia, which have undertaken strong commitments in the energy sector. On this point, see also Erich Vranes, 'State Measures Protecting Against "Undesirable" Foreign Investment: Issues in EU and International Law' (2012) 67 Zeitschrift für Öffentliches Recht 639, 669.

[87]In the *EU – Energy Package* case, however, the Russian Federation has not invoked the EU's MA and NT commitments on wholesale and retail services (CPC 62271 and CPC 63297) in this respect; see WTO, *European Union and its Member States – Certain Measures Relating to the Energy Sector,* Request for the Establishment of a Panel by the Russian Federation (28 May 2015) WT/DS476/2. But see WTO, Trade Policy Review – European Union – Minutes of the Meeting (28 November 2013) WT/TPR/M/284/Add.1/Rev.1, 313–314 (where Russia made reference to the EU's commitments on wholesale trade services).

[88]This is also implied in the considerations by Thomas Cottier, Sofya Matteotti-Berkutova and Olga Nartova, 'Third Country Relations in EU Unbundling of Natural Gas Markets: The "Gazprom Clause" of Directive 2009/73 EC and WTO Law' in Dirk Buschle, Simon Hirsbrunner and Christine Kaddous (eds), *European Energy Law: Droit européen de l'énergie* (Dossier de droit européen vol 22. Helbing Lichtenhahn 2011) 279; Anatole Boute, 'Energy Trade and Investment Law: International Limits to EU Energy Law and Policy' in Martha M Roggenkamp and others (eds), *Energy Law in Europe – National, EU and International Regulation* (3rd edn. Oxford University Press 2016) [3.63].

almost all of its Member States have to comply with Articles VI, XVI and XVII GATS with respect to the unbundling requirements as such. Where no commitments on energy transmission services exist, the commitments on energy supply services kick in. The situation is different however for the unbundling-related measures. Here, the EU's lack of commitments in the area of energy transmission becomes relevant, considering that the commitments on wholesale and retail services are not applicable. Therefore, the EU is not required as a WTO Member to adhere to the GATS market access and national treatment obligations, as well as most GATS disciplines on domestic regulation, with respect to the certification procedure and the OU exemption regime.[89] At the same time, it is clear that several EU Member States, including Croatia, Hungary and Lithuania, are bound to apply the said provisions with respect to these measures. Accordingly, it can be stated that while there are specific commitments that allow the Third Energy Package to be examined under Articles VI, XVI and XVII GATS, some challenges against unbundling-related measures would fail simply due to the lack of specific commitments on transmission services at the EU level.

That being said, this book is not primarily concerned with the existence or absence of commitments. It seeks to provide a comprehensive analysis of the substantive legal issues at stake. Therefore, the issue of specific commitments is not further discussed unless a violation of GATS provisions has actually been found in the first place. Finally, it should also be mentioned in this context that the level of commitments on the part of the EU is not cast in stone. In fact, the EU has supported the further liberalization of transmission services in the past.[90]

4.5 Article XVI GATS (Market Access)

Article XVI GATS deals with market access for trade in services. It is one of the key provisions of the GATS. Article XVI is contained in Part III of the Agreement, which means that the market access obligation only applies to the extent specific commitments have been undertaken. As has been shown above, relevant market access commitments exist, both at EU and EU Member State level, relating to the transmission and/or supply of energy.[91]

Under the ownership unbundling model contained in Article 9 of Directives 2009/72/EC and 2009/73/EC, a company engaged in the production/generation or supply of gas or electricity is prohibited from being a service provider supplying energy transmission services. Conversely, a TSO cannot provide wholesale and retail services of gas or electricity. These prohibitions have a clear restrictive impact

[89] See also the references cited in footnote 14 (this chapter).

[90] See WTO, Communication from the European Communities and their Member States – GATS 2000: Energy Services (23 March 2001) S/CSS/W/60.

[91] See Sect. 4.4.

on market access opportunities.[92] Therefore it will be analyzed in this section whether the ownership unbundling model is in conformity with the market access obligations under Article XVI GATS. Given that OU is the most restrictive unbundling solution, the findings below will apply *a maiore ad minus* also to the ISO & ITO models.

At the outset it is convenient to reproduce Article XVI GATS in full. The provision reads as follows[93]:

1. With respect to market access through the modes of supply identified in Article I, each Member shall accord services and service suppliers of any other Member treatment no less favourable than that provided for under the terms, limitations and conditions agreed and specified in its Schedule.
2. In sectors where market-access commitments are undertaken, the measures which a Member shall not maintain or adopt either on the basis of a regional subdivision or on the basis of its entire territory, unless otherwise specified in its Schedule, are defined as:

   (a) limitations on the number of service suppliers whether in the form of numerical quotas, monopolies, exclusive service suppliers or the requirements of an economic needs test;
   (b) limitations on the total value of service transactions or assets in the form of numerical quotas or the requirement of an economic needs test;
   (c) limitations on the total number of service operations or on the total quantity of service output expressed in terms of designated numerical units in the form of quotas or the requirement of an economic needs test;
   (d) limitations on the total number of natural persons that may be employed in a particular service sector or that a service supplier may employ and who are necessary for, and directly related to, the supply of a specific service in the form of numerical quotas or the requirement of an economic needs test;
   (e) measures which restrict or require specific types of legal entity or joint venture through which a service supplier may supply a service; and
   (f) limitations on the participation of foreign capital in terms of maximum percentage limit on foreign shareholding or the total value of individual or aggregate foreign investment.

Furthermore, as a preliminary step it is important to briefly consider the relationship between paragraphs one and two of Article XVI GATS.[94] The question is whether Article XVI:1 creates a self-standing market access obligation which is

[92]In the *EU – Energy Package* case, the Russian Federation takes the view that all unbundling models contained in Directives 2009/72/EC and 2009/73/EC (ITO, ISO and OU) are inconsistent with the market access obligation under Article XVI GATS, see *European Union and its Member States – Certain Measures Relating to the Energy Sector* (n 87) 2. See also Moschetta (n 68) 120; Vranes (n 86) 669.

[93]Footnotes omitted.

[94]Krajewski (n 36) 82–85; Eric H Leroux, 'From Periodicals to Gambling: A Review of Systemic Issues Addressed by WTO Adjudicatory Bodies under the GATS' in Marion Panizzon, Nicole Pohl and Pierre Sauvé (eds), *GATS and the Regulation of International Trade in Services* (Cambridge University Press 2008) 256–258.

separate from Article XVI:2.[95] This would mean that measures which cannot be subsumed under one of the categories mentioned in Article XVI:2 could still run afoul of the first paragraph of Article XVI. Although this issue has not yet been conclusively settled,[96] the correct interpretation would seem to be that the second paragraph of Article XVI exhaustively defines the normative content of the obligation that Article XVI imposes. This view is shared by WTO Panels[97] and the vast majority of legal scholars.[98]

Accordingly, under Article XVI GATS, WTO Members are prohibited from maintaining or adopting those measures explicitly listed in paragraph 2 of the provision. Article XVI:2 covers, broadly speaking, four different categories of quantitative restrictions (lit (a)–(d)), limitations on types of legal entity (lit (e)), and limitations on foreign capital participation (lit (f)). It does not matter whether the measure at issue is discriminatory or non-discriminatory in nature.[99] The following sub-sections analyze whether the OU measures fall within the scope of any of the prohibited market access restrictions of Article XVI:2 GATS, treating each category separately.

---

[95]This interpretation of Article XVI:1 GATS was advocated by Antigua and Barbuda in the *US – Gambling* case, see WTO, *United States – Measures Affecting the Cross-Border Supply of Gambling and Betting Services,* Report of the Panel (10 November 2004) WT/DS285/R [3.124, 3.129–3.130, 3.134, 3.142]; *United States – Measures Affecting the Cross-Border Supply of Gambling and Betting Services* (n 63) [66].

[96]In the *US – Gambling* case, the Appellate Body decided to exercise judicial economy and not pronounce itself on the issue, see *United States – Measures Affecting the Cross-Border Supply of Gambling and Betting Services* (n 63) [256]. Krajewski suggests, referring to ibid [215], that the Appellate Body in fact shared the Panel's view, namely that the restrictions on market access that are covered by Article XVI GATS are only those explicitly listed in paragraph 2 of the provision, see Markus Krajewski, 'Playing by the Rules of the Game?: Specific Commitments after US – Gambling and Betting and the Current GATS Negotiations' (2005) 32 Legal Issues of Economic Integration 417, 431.

[97]*United States – Measures Affecting the Cross-Border Supply of Gambling and Betting Services* (n 95) [6.318]. See also ibid [6.298–9]. Two other Panels simply held that the complainant had failed to meets its burden to present a prima facie case under Article XVI:1 GATS, see WTO, *China – Certain Measures Affecting Electronic Payment Services,* Report of the Panel (16 July 2012) WT/DS413/R [7.628–7.631]; *Argentina – Measures Relating to Trade in Goods and Services* (n 7) [7.434].

[98]Krajewski (n 36) 82–85; Aaditya Mattoo, 'National Treatment in the GATS – Corner-Stone or Pandora's Box?' (1997) 31 Journal of World Trade 107, 109; Pierre Sauvé, 'Assessing the General Agreement on Trade in Services: Half-Full or Half-Empty?' (1995) 29 Journal of World Trade 125, 132; Leroux (n 94) 256–258; Michaelis (n 11) [47]; Koehler (n 11) 124–125. But see Pitschas (n 11) [109].

[99]Krajewski (n 36) 82; Michaelis (n 11) [52]; Scheduling of Initial Commitments in Trade in Services: Explanatory Note (n 50) [4]; WTO, Guidelines for the Scheduling of Specific Commitments under the General Agreement on Trade in Services (GATS), S/L/92 (28 March 2001), [8].

4.5.1 Quantitative Limitations

The ownership unbundling requirements foreseen in Article 9 of Directive 2009/72/EC and 2009/73/EC could constitute a quantitative restriction prohibited by Article XVI:2(a)–(c) GATS, i.e. a limitation on the number of service suppliers (lit (a)), the total value of service transactions or assets (lit (b)), or on the total number of service operations or the total quantity of service output (lit (c)).[100] As the legal issues involved are largely identical, it will be convenient to focus on sub-paragraph (a).

Article XVI:2(a) GATS prohibits limitations on the number of service suppliers in the form of either 'numerical quotas', 'monopolies', 'exclusive service suppliers' or 'the requirements of an economic needs test'. In order to fall under Article XVI:2 (a) GATS, the ownership unbundling requirements would need to take one of these prohibited forms. It is quite clear that ownership unbundling requirements do not provide for or result in the creation of monopolies or exclusive service suppliers.[101] Furthermore, they do not entail the application of an economic needs test.[102] Thus this analysis focuses on whether ownership unbundling requirements could amount to a 'limitation on the number of service suppliers *in the form of numerical quotas*.'

Typical examples of such limitations on market access falling under Article XVI:2(a) GATS include measures which are explicitly framed in quantitative or numerical terms. For example, a measure which establishes an (origin-neutral or origin-specific) annual quota of five new banking licenses would clearly qualify as such a limitation.[103] As ownership unbundling measures do not contain such an express reference to a number of units, one could be led to assume that they fall

[100]Article XVI:2(d) GATS does not seem to be applicable in the present context.

[101]In *US – Gambling*, the Appellate Body suggested that the terms 'monopoly' and 'exclusive service supplier' in Article XVI:2(a) GATS could be defined by reference to Article XXVIII (h) GATS (which provides that 'monopoly supplier of a service' means 'any person, public or private, which in the relevant market of the territory of a Member is authorized or established formally or in effect by that Member as the sole supplier of that service') and Article VIII:5 GATS (which provides that 'exclusive service suppliers' exist where a WTO Member 'formally or in effect, (a) authorizes or establishes a small number of service suppliers and (b) substantially prevents competition among those suppliers in its territory'), see *United States – Measures Affecting the Cross-Border Supply of Gambling and Betting Services* (n 63) [228–230]. For a discussion of the scope of the terms 'monopoly supplier of a service' and 'exclusive service supplier', as defined in these provisions, see Sect. 6.3.1. What is clear is that the existence of monopoly or exclusive service supplier in the EU energy sector, if any, cannot be attributed to the ownership unbundling requirements in Directives 2009/72/EC and 2009/73/EC, but would be the consequence of the natural monopoly character of gas and electricity transmission networks.

[102]The term 'economic needs test' is not legally defined in the GATS. It may however be said that an economic needs test 'refers to a mechanism controlled by a Member or an entity with delegated power ... that allows them to decide whether the entry into the market of new (domestic or foreign) service suppliers is required *on economic grounds*' (emphasis added), see Panagiotis Delimatsis and Martín Molinuevo, 'Article XVI GATS' in Rüdiger Wolfrum, Peter-Tobias Stoll and Clemens Feinäugle (eds), *WTO – Trade in Services* (Max Planck Commentaries on World Trade Law vol 6. Martinus Nijhoff Publishers 2008) [49].

[103]Example taken from Mattoo (n 98) 110.

outside the ambit of Article XVI:2(a) GATS. However, the expression 'in the form of numerical quotas' has been given an extensive interpretation by the WTO dispute settlement bodies in the leading case *US – Gambling*. It is thus necessary to carefully examine the implications of this WTO case in order to be able to reach a conclusion on the legality of ownership unbundling measures under Article XVI:2(a) GATS.

The *US – Gambling* case presented the first opportunity for the WTO dispute settlement bodies to deal with the scope of Article XVI GATS. The main question at issue was whether several US measures banning the cross-border supply by remote means of gambling and betting services constituted a violation of the market access obligation, as alleged by the claimant Antigua and Barbuda. Although the *US – Gambling* case concerned services that were supplied cross-border (mode 1), the interpretation of Article XVI GATS is likewise relevant to services supplied through commercial presence (mode 3).

The background of the case was as follows. Beginning in the mid-1990s, an Internet gaming industry developed in Antigua and Barbuda.[104] The respective gaming and betting services were supplied remotely, that is via Internet, *inter alia* to the United States. In the eyes of Antigua, several federal laws of the US, namely the Wire Act, the Travel Act, and the Illegal Gambling Business Act, constituted a 'total prohibition' on the cross-border supply of gambling and betting services in violation of Article XVI GATS. In particular, Antigua submitted that the United States measures violated Article XVI:2(a) and (c) GATS. According to Antigua, the US measures established, in effect, a 'zero quota' with regard to the number of service suppliers (lit (a)) and the total number of service operations (lit (c)). The United States, for its part, argued that Article XVI does not embody a general rule prohibiting measures that impede market access. Instead, Article XVI:2 would only refer to measures taking a particular form or being expressed in a certain way. Thus the US took the position that the measures at issue did not take the form of 'numerical quotas' (lit (a)) and that they were not expressed 'in terms of designated numerical units in the form of quotas' (lit (c)). Hence the central point of disagreement between Antigua and the US concerned the question of whether limitations on the number of service suppliers and on the total number of service operations only fall within the ambit of Article XVI GATS if they *take the form of* or *are expressed as* numerical or quantitative restrictions, and whether a *de facto* 'zero quota' would amount to such a restriction.

The Panel accepted that the US ban on the cross-border supply of certain gambling services resulted in a 'zero quota' which, although not explicitly couched in numerical terms, could fall within the scope of Article XVI:2(a) and (c).[105] Any other interpretation would, according to the Panel, produce 'absurd results'.[106] The findings of the Panel relating to the interpretation of sub-paragraphs (a) and (c) of

[104] *United States – Measures Affecting the Cross-Border Supply of Gambling and Betting Services* (n 95) [3.2].
[105] Ibid [6.319–6.355].
[106] Ibid [6.332].

Article XVI were subsequently reviewed by the Appellate Body. The Appellate Body also rejected a restrictive interpretation of the words 'in the form of' in Article XVI:2(a) GATS and held that those words 'must not be interpreted as prescribing a rigid mechanical formula'.[107] According to the AB, the emphasis in Article XVI:2 (a) was on the numerical or quantitative *nature* of limitations, and not on their form.[108] Furthermore, 'zero' could be considered to be numerical within the meaning of that provision.[109] In upholding the Panel's finding on this point, the AB concluded that Article XVI:2(a) GATS encompasses measures amounting to a 'zero quota'.[110] Similarly, it also upheld the Panel's finding with regard to Article XVI:2 (c) GATS.[111]

The Panel and Appellate Body reports in the *US – Gambling* case have elicited much criticism. Generally, authors have blamed the Appellate Body for having failed to strike an appropriate balance between market access and domestic regulation. They argued that the broad interpretation of Article XVI GATS adopted in the reports excessively encroaches upon the regulatory autonomy of WTO Members.[112] In particular, they cautioned against 'the slippery slope of confusing form with effect and banning all kinds of domestic regulation not because they *are* quantitative restrictions, but because they have the obvious *effect* of keeping certain services or suppliers off the market.'[113] In the critics' view, this would mean that domestic regulation having a *side effect* of a quantitative restriction on market access for foreign services or service suppliers may be found to violate Article XVI if a market access commitment has been made.[114]

The implications of the *US – Gambling* ruling for the ownership unbundling requirements set out in Article 9 of Directives 2009/72/EC and 2009/73/EC depend, not surprisingly, on how one reads the judgment. Proceeding from the assumption that, after *US – Gambling*, Article XVI GATS covers measures which have the effect of restricting the number of potential service suppliers, the ownership unbundling

---

[107] *United States – Measures Affecting the Cross-Border Supply of Gambling and Betting Services* (n 63) [231].

[108] Ibid [232].

[109] Ibid [227].

[110] Ibid [238–239].

[111] Ibid [252].

[112] See in particular Joost Pauwelyn, 'Rien Ne Va Plus? Distinguishing Domestic Regulation from Market Access in GATT and GATS' (2005) 4 World Trade Review 131; Federico Ortino, 'Treaty Interpretation and the WTO Appellate Body Report in US–Gambling: A Critique' (2006) 9 Journal of International Economic Law 117, 141; Erich Vranes, 'The WTO and Regulatory Freedom: WTO Disciplines on Market Access, Non-Discrimination and Domestic Regulation Relating to Trade in Goods and Services' (2009) 12 Journal of International Economic Law 953, 975ff.

[113] Pauwelyn (n 112) 166 (emphasis in the original).

[114] Vranes (n 112) 976f.

measures in the EU energy sector would amount to a prohibited market access restriction.[115] The number of potential service suppliers supplying gas/electricity transmission services is clearly reduced as a result of the ownership unbundling requirements, as is the number of potential service suppliers supplying gas/electricity supply services. By the same token however, viewed this way a driving test for aspiring taxi drivers would also be inconsistent with Article XVI GATS, because the number of potential taxi drivers is clearly reduced.[116] It is highly doubtful whether the reports of the Panel and the Appellate Body in *US – Gambling* provide a sufficient basis for this type of reasoning.

The facts underlying the case as well as the legal reasoning of the Panel and the Appellate Body show that *US – Gambling* mainly revolved around the 'zero quota' concept. The Panel found that the US legislation 'limits to zero' the number of service suppliers in the gambling and betting sector.[117] In particular, it held that where a WTO Member (1) does not allow market access to the *whole or part of a scheduled sector or sub-sector*[118] or (2) prohibits the use by service suppliers of *one, several or all means of delivery*,[119] this constitutes a 'zero quota' that should be treated as a limitation on the number of service suppliers under Article XVI:2 (a) GATS. If one applies the 'zero quota' concept from *US – Gambling* to the issue under consideration, it becomes evident that the ownership unbundling requirements as set out in Article 9 of Directives 2009/72/EC and 2009/73/EC do not fall under any of the above-mentioned categories. In particular, ownership unbundling requirements do not block market access (through mode 3) to the whole or part of a scheduled sector or sub-sector, given that no activity is *per se* proscribed. Rather, market access is restricted based on *supplier-related characteristics* (i.e. their involvement in production/generation or supply activities or, *vice versa*, in transmission activities). Neither do the ownership unbundling requirements prohibit the use by (mode 3) service suppliers of one, several, or all means of delivery.[120]

[115]It is on this understanding of the *US – Gambling* case that Moschetta argues that the unbundling requirements in the EU energy sector could violate Article XVI:2(a)–(c) GATS, see Moschetta (n 68) 121–123. See also Vranes (n 86) 669 (who writes that 'unbundling requirements relating to legal form, organisation and decision-making . . . may have side effects on market access' and that in view of the *US – Gambling* case, 'there is a risk that other WTO Members could try to challenge the EU regime [i.e. Directive 2009/73/EC] by relying on Art XVI'.

[116]Example taken from Pauwelyn (n 112) 160, 162, 166, 170.

[117]*United States – Measures Affecting the Cross-Border Supply of Gambling and Betting Services* (n 95) [6.330].

[118]Ibid [6.290, 6.335, 6.352].

[119]Ibid [6.287, 6.338, 6.355].

[120]In contrast, the draft Directives originally proposed by the Commission in 2007 would squarely fall within the 'zero quota' concept found in *US – Gambling*. Article 8a of the Commission's draft electricity Directive and Article 7a of the Commission's draft gas Directive provided that, in principle, transmission systems or transmission system operators 'shall not be controlled by a person or persons from third countries', see European Commission, Proposal for a Directive of the European Parliament and of the Council amending Directive 2003/54/EC concerning common rules for the internal market in electricity (19 September 2007) COM(2007) 528 final, 29; European

An example of the former category would be if a WTO Member, having undertaken a full market access commitment under CPC 71310 (transportation via pipeline of petroleum *and* of natural gas), prohibits the transportation via pipeline of petroleum. An example of the latter category would be if a WTO Member, having undertaken a full market access commitment under CPC 887 (transmission and distribution services of electricity),[121] prohibits the transmission of electric power by alternating current.[122] Therefore, it may be concluded on a preliminary basis that it does not automatically follow from *US – Gambling* that ownership unbundling measures are inconsistent with the GATS market access obligation.

Admittedly however, the 'zero quota' concept is far from clear. How is a 'zero quota' defined?[123] Is it possible that the WTO dispute settlement bodies will, in future cases, find that the 'zero quota' rationale equally applies to other situations than the ones described above?[124] It is pertinent to briefly explore this issue. The starting point is the observation that the way in which the Panel construed the 'zero quota' is not grounded in the text of the GATS. In this regard one commentator

---

Commission, Proposal for a Directive of the European Parliament and of the Council amending Directive 2003/55/EC concerning common rules for the internal market in natural gas (19 September 2007) COM(2007) 529 final, 30. This would have effectively blocked 'market access to the whole or part of a scheduled sector or sub-sector' and thus established a 'zero quota' for foreign service suppliers wishing to supply electricity/gas transmission services. See on this, without however referring to *US – Gambling*, Victor van Hoorn, '"Unbundling", "Reciprocity" and the European Internal Energy Market: WTO Consistency and Broader Implications for Europe' (2009) 1 European Energy and Environmental Law Review 51, 66, 72; Van den bergh (n 79) 251–252.

[121]It is assumed here that the transmission and distribution of electricity falls under the sub-sector of 'services incidental to energy distribution', see Sect. 4.4.

[122]It could be questioned whether the 'means of delivery zero quota' reasoning from *US – Gambling* also works in a situation of trade in services through mode 3 (instead of mode 1), but it seems that there are no cogent reasons why it should not. See also the position of the EU and Australia on this issue, WTO, 'Third Party Written Submission by the European Communities: China – Publications and Audiovisual Products: WT/DS363/R' (4 July 2008) [46ff] <http://trade.ec.europa.eu/doclib/docs/2008/august/tradoc_140292.pdf> accessed 28 January 2016; WTO, 'Reply of the European Communities to Third Party Questions: China – Publications and Audiovisual Products: WT/DS363/R' (4 August 2008) 8 <http://trade.ec.europa.eu/doclib/docs/2008/august/tradoc_140294.pdf> accessed 28 January 2016; WTO, 'Australian Responses to Panel Questions to Third Parties: China – Publications and Audiovisual Products: WT/DS363/R' (11 August 2008) <http://dfat.gov.au/international-relations/international-organisations/wto/wto-dispute-settlement/pages/china-measures-affecting-trading-rights-and-distribution-services-for-certain-publications-and-audiovisual-entertainment-pr.aspx> accessed 28 January 2016.

[123]For an excellent discussion, see Douglas A Irwin and Joseph Weiler, 'Measures Affecting the Cross-Border Supply of Gambling and Betting Services (DS 285)' (2008) 7 World Trade Review 71, 85–89.

[124]I.e. a zero quota on the 'whole or part of a scheduled (sub-)sector' or on 'one, several or all means of delivery'.

remarked that 'there is no textual basis for dividing sectors or modes of supply in order to subsequently find limitations to zero in respect of these subdivisions'.[125]

Given that the Panel's 'zero quota' concept is the result of an act of judicial creativity (and thus not based on, or constrained by, the text of the GATS), it is perfectly conceivable that the concept also applies to other similar situations. For example, under ownership unbundling market access to the energy transmission sector is blocked for all service suppliers which are engaged in the supply of energy (and *vice versa*). One could say that there is thus a 'zero quota' in relation to this specific, well identifiable group of service suppliers forming part of the transmission (or wholesale/retail) sector. Generally speaking, it could be argued that if it is possible to divide sectors or modes of supply, as the Panel did, it is also possible to divide the group of service suppliers falling within a given sector, *based on supplier-related characteristics*, in order to later find 'limitations to zero' with respect to one of these subdivisions. Consider the following hypothetical example: WTO Member A undertakes a full market access commitment on gas and petroleum transmission services (CPC 71310). It subsequently enacts legislation which prohibits market access for all new providers of gas and petroleum transmission services which have less than 100 years of experience in the transmission sector. Is Article XVI:2(a) GATS infringed in such a situation, taking into account that the measure imposes a 'zero quota' on all (foreign) service suppliers in the sector at issue which have less than 100 years of relevant experience? Although this limitation is based on supplier-related characteristics, its restrictive impact on market access is similar to a zero quota on the whole or part of the transmission sector.

Taken to its extreme, the 'zero quota' concept of *US – Gambling* could even be interpreted to mean that the prohibition of a *single* service supplier from supplying a specific service breaches the GATS market access obligation.[126] For this individual service supplier, such a prohibition would amount to a zero quota, because it is prevented from entering the market. In commenting on a proposed amendment of the German Foreign Trade and Payments Act (*Außenwirtschaftsgesetz*) and Foreign Trade and Payments Regulation (*Außenwirtschafts-verordnung*), which would have enabled the German government to examine and prohibit acquisitions by

[125]Joel P Trachtman, 'United States – Measures Affecting the Cross-Border Supply of Gambling and Betting Services' (2005) 99 American Journal of International Law 861, 866.

[126]See Bart De Meester, *Liberalization of Trade in Banking Services: An International and European Perspective* (Cambridge University Press 2014) 227–230 (who states: 'Arguably, an individual supervisory decision whereby the access of a service supplier to the market of another WTO member is refused amounts to a violation of Article XVI. Indeed, in the light of the decision by the panel and the Appellate Body in *US – Gambling*, one could conclude that the refusal by a banking supervisor to grant an authorization to supply banking services amounts for this individual applicant to a zero quota. The applicant sees its access to the market refused.'; this interpretation of Article XVI GATS is, however, rejected by De Meester). See also Bart De Meester and Dominic Coppens, 'Mode 3 of the GATS: A Model for Disciplining Measures Affecting Investment Flows?' in Zdenek Drabek and Petros C Mavroidis (eds), *Regulation of Foreign Investment: Challenges to International Harmonization* (World Scientific Studies in International Economics vol 21. World Scientific 2013) 116–118.

non-EU companies in individual cases on grounds of public policy or public security, *Tietje* for instance explicitly referred to the *US – Gambling* case and stated that where specific commitments have been undertaken, WTO Members are in principle prohibited from denying market access to any investor from another WTO Member.[127] Following the view that the prohibited market access limitations under Article XVI:2(a) GATS also include ‘zero quotas’ on specific groups of service suppliers or even individual providers, the ownership unbundling requirements as set out in Article 9 of Directives 2009/72/EC and 2009/73/EC would in fact amount to an impermissible market access restriction.

It is, however, submitted here that such extensions of the ‘zero quota’ concept would unduly broaden the scope of the GATS market access obligation. To demonstrate why this is so, a comparative argument will be presented. Broadening the scope of the *per se* prohibition in Article XVI:2(a) GATS to include ‘zero quotas’ on specific groups of, or individual, service suppliers would result in assimilating the GATS market access regime to an effects-based understanding of market access under EU law. In order to make the fundamental freedoms as effective as possible, the European Court of Justice has adopted a ‘non-hindrance approach’ in its interpretation of the freedom of establishment[128] (Article 49 TFEU) and the free movement of capital[129] (Article 63 TFEU),[130] which are the EU law counterparts to Article XVI GATS and services supplied through mode 3. Clearly, the ‘non-hindrance test’ has been developed with the aim of achieving effective market access. In *Staat der Nederlanden v Essent NV and Others*,[131] for instance, the ECJ applied the

[127] Christian Tietje, ‘Beschränkungen ausländischer Unternehmensbeteiligungen zum Schutz vor “Staatsfonds”: Rechtliche Grenzen eines neuen Investitionsprotektionismus’ [2007] Policy Paper on Transnational Economic Law, 4, 8–9 (who states: ‘Sofern in einem Dienstleitungssektor . . . spezifische Marktzugangsverpflichtungen übernommen wurden . . . ist es gem. Art. XVI:2 (c) GATS unzulässig, einen entsprechenden Marktzugang eines Investors aus einem anderen WTO-Mitgliedstaat teilweise oder vollständig zu beschränken . . .’).

[128] See Ulrich Forsthoff, ‘AEUV Art. 49 Niederlassungsfreiheit’ in Eberhard Grabitz, Meinhard Hilf and Martin Nettesheim (eds), *Das Recht der Europäischen Union: EUV/AEUV* (54th edn. C.H. Beck 2014) [88–118]; Steffen Hindelang, *The Free Movement of Capital and Foreign Direct Investment: The Scope of Protection in EU Law* (Oxford University Press 2009) 118; Paul Craig and Gráinne de Búrca, *EU Law: Text, Cases, and Materials* (5th edn, Oxford University Press 2011) 773–776. For relevant case law, see in particular European Court of Justice, *Kraus v Land Baden-Württemberg,* Judgment (31 March 1993) C-19/92 [32]; European Court of Justice, *Reinhard Gebhard v Consiglio dell'Ordine degli Avvocati e Procuratori di Milano,* Judgment (30 November 1995) C-55/94 [37].

[129] See Georg Ress and Jörg Ukrow, ‘AEUV Art. 63 Freier Kapital- und Zahlungsverkehr’ in Eberhard Grabitz, Meinhard Hilf and Martin Nettesheim (eds), *Das Recht der Europäischen Union: EUV/AEUV* (54th edn. C.H. Beck 2014) [158–186]; Hindelang (n 128) 119–122. For relevant case law, see in particular European Court of Justice, *Commission v. Portugal,* Judgment (4 June 2002) C-367/98 [44–45].

[130] Hindelang (n 128) 115ff.

[131] European Court of Justice, *Staat der Nederlanden v Essent NV and Others,* Judgment (22 October 2013) C-105/12 to C-107/12.

non-hindrance test (using a 'liable to impede/dissuade' standard[132]) to the Netherlands ownership unbundling requirements for electricity and gas distribution system operators, and subsequently found a violation of Article 63 TFEU.[133] Therefore, the concept of 'market access' in EU law focuses primarily on the effects of a measure.[134] This far-reaching approach is, however, counterbalanced by the consideration of a variety of overriding reasons relating to the public interest which may justify restrictions on the fundamental freedoms.[135] In *Staat der Nederlanden v Essent NV and Others*, the ECJ held that the objectives of combating cross-subsidization and preventing distortions of competition may, in principle, justify restrictions on the free movement of capital.[136] In the GATS context, however, Article XIV (General Exceptions) recognizes only a limited number of public interests which may serve as a justification for breaches of the GATS. In particular, the objectives of preventing cross-subsidization and distortions of competition are not included in the 'closed list' of legitimate justifications under Article XIV GATS.[137] It is thus submitted that the inherent balance of the GATS would be completely disturbed if one were to construe the GATS market access obligation in a way similar to the non-hindrance approach adopted by the European Court of Justice. The Appellate Body seems to be aware of this risk and explicitly stated that it would be wrong to assume 'that the words "in the form of" should be ignored or replaced by the words "that have the effect of"'.[138]

In conclusion, even under the expansive interpretation of Article XVI:2 (a) adopted in *US – Gambling*, ownership unbundling requirements as set out in Article 9 of Directives 2009/72/EC and 2009/73/EC are not inconsistent with the GATS market access obligation. They restrict market access based on supplier-related characteristics, and therefore do not involve a 'zero quota' on the whole or part of the energy transmission services sector (or any sub-sector thereof) or on one, several, or all means of delivering such services. A further extension of the GATS market access concept beyond the *US – Gambling* jurisprudence is neither likely nor would it be in keeping with the balance struck by the GATS between national regulatory autonomy and trade liberalization.

---

[132]The ECJ referred *inter alia* to *Commission v. Portugal* (n 129) [45–46].

[133]*Staat der Nederlanden v Essent NV and Others* (n 131) [38–47].

[134]Marcus Klamert, *Services Liberalization in the EU and the WTO: Concepts, Standards and Regulatory Approaches* (Cambridge Studies in European Law and Policy, Cambridge University Press 2015) 265; Jukka Snell, 'The Notion of Market Access: A Concept or a Slogan?' (2010) 47 Common Market Law Review 437, 441–443.

[135]For Article 49 TFEU, see Forsthoff (n 128) [122–124]. For Article 63 TFEU, see Ress and Ukrow (n 129) [225–285].

[136]*Staat der Nederlanden v Essent NV and Others* (n 131) [49–66].

[137]See also Sect. 4.9.1.

[138]*United States – Measures Affecting the Cross-Border Supply of Gambling and Betting Services* (n 63) [232].

4.5.2 Limitations on Forms of Legal Entity

The ownership unbundling requirements as set out in Article 9 of Directives 2009/72/EC and 2009/73/EC could also be challenged as 'measures which restrict or require specific types of legal entity . . . through which a service supplier may supply a service' (Article XVI:2(e) GATS).[139] In contrast to the quantitative limitations discussed above, sub-paragraph (e) concerns measures of a qualitative nature.[140]

In determining whether the OU requirements constitute a limitation within the meaning of Article XVI:2(e), the interpretation of the term 'type of legal entity' plays a crucial role. According to a broad understanding, the term refers to a categorization of legal entities, which could be based on a variety of characteristics or criteria. In particular, whether or not a company exercises, directly or indirectly, control or any right over a generation/production or supply undertaking could be such a criterion.[141] Accordingly, companies that do not exercise control or any right over a generator/producer or supplier could be seen as a distinct 'type of legal entity'. If this were the case, ownership unbundling measures would fall under the *per se* prohibition of Article XVI:2(e) GATS. Therefore, the question arises whether the provision actually has such a broad scope.

WTO jurisprudence has not yet fleshed out the contours of Article XVI:2 (e) GATS.[142] Therefore it does not provide any guidance on how the term 'type of legal entity' ought to be interpreted. The overall scheduling practice of WTO Members supports the view that the scope of Article XVI:2(e) GATS is rather limited. For example, Germany scheduled a limitation according to which the provision of accounting and auditing services is prohibited through the form of a 'GmbH & CoKG'.[143] Similarly, in Belgium a 'Société en Commandite' may not be used to supply auditing services.[144] These are examples of limitations on market access which reflect a narrow understanding of the phrase 'type of legal entity', namely referring to 'distinct types of legal arrangements based on statutory

---

[139]Moschetta for example argues that the ownership unbundling requirements, imposed on legal persons wishing to enter the EU energy market through commercial presence, could be covered by the scope of Article XVI:2(e) GATS, see Moschetta (n 68) 120, footnote 11. See also *European Union and its Member States – Certain Measures Relating to the Energy Sector* (n 87) 2, 9.

[140]Delimatsis and Molinuevo (n 102) 52; Nellie Munin, *Legal Guide to GATS* (Global Trade Law Series vol 31, Kluwer Law International 2010) 199.

[141]As the prohibitions of the ownership unbundling model work both ways, the criterion could also be whether or not a company exercises, directly or indirectly, control or any right over a transmission system operator or over a transmission system.

[142]A brief reference to Article XVI:2(e) GATS was made in *China – Measures Affecting Trading Rights and Distribution Services for Certain Publications and Audiovisual Entertainment Products* (n 19) [7.1356].

[143]European Communities and their Member States – Schedule of Specific Commitments (n 72) 14–16.

[144]Ibid 15–16.

provisions of commercial or company law.'[145] Other frequently scheduled limitations do not relate to specific legal forms in domestic commercial or company law, but nevertheless imply a reference to the range of legal entities available under the host State's laws. For example, Article XVI:2(e) GATS also covers measures which require foreign companies to establish subsidiaries or which prohibit commercial presence through representative offices.[146] The same applies where a WTO Member requires that certain services be supplied exclusively through limited or non-limited liability structures.[147]

However, the question whether the term 'type of legal entity' could have a broader meaning has also been discussed. Some authors referred to Article XVI:2 (e) GATS in the context of State-ownership requirements. They suggested that laws requiring State-ownership might indeed be incompatible with that provision.[148] Such an argument presupposes that the typology of legal entities to which the expression 'type of legal entity' refers may be based on the ownership of a company. The question has also been raised whether Article XVI:2(e) GATS could limit the range of possible government actions in response to the global financial crisis.[149] As one of the policy solutions to tackle the problem of banks which are 'too-big-to-fail', the separation of commercial and investment banking has been proposed. This proposal is designed to isolate basic banking services from speculative banking operations, i.e. line-of-business restrictions. In the United States, such a 'firewall' was for a long time maintained by the Glass–Steagall legislation, which however was repealed in 1999. Critics warned that the introduction or maintenance of line-of-business restrictions in the financial sector could amount to a market access restriction within the meaning of Article XVI:2(e) GATS.[150] Therefore they called for the inclusion of a clarification in the GATS that Article XVI:2(e) 'does not refer to typological distinctions between financial service suppliers based on their specific permitted line of business'.[151]

[145] Krajewski (n 36) 92.

[146] Scheduling of Initial Commitments in Trade in Services: Explanatory Note (n 50) [6]; Guidelines for the Scheduling of Specific Commitments under the GATS (n 99) [12]. See also Friedl Weiss, 'The General Agreement on Trade in Services 1994' (1995) 32 Common Market Law Review 1177, 1210; Sauvé (n 98) 133. Subsidiaries are locally incorporated separate legal entities (i.e. established under the host country's laws), whereas representative offices or branches are usually unincorporated entities, see Krajewski (n 36) 92–93; OECD, *OECD Benchmark Definition of Foreign Direct Investment* (4th edn, OECD 2008) 227ff.

[147] Delimatsis and Molinuevo (n 102) [56].

[148] Tania Voon and Andrew Mitchell, 'Open for Business? China's Telecommunications Service Market and the WTO' (2010) 13 Journal of International Economic Law 321, 359; Van den bergh (n 79) 252; van Hoorn (n 120) 66.

[149] Todd Tucker, 'How to Reform WTO and FTA Rules to Confront Too-Big-To-Fail Banks' (2011) <https://www.citizen.org/documents/memo-gats-conflict-with-bank-size-limits-may-10-2011.pdf> accessed 24 September 2016.

[150] Ibid.

[151] Ibid 27.

There is also some practice at the bilateral and multilateral levels which could be interpreted as supporting the conclusion that Article XVI:2(e) GATS covers line-of-business restrictions. In the US-Chile Free Trade Agreement (FTA), for example, Chile scheduled the following market access reservation in the insurance services sector: 'Insurance services can be provided only by insurance corporations established in Chile *for the exclusive purpose of developing this line of business, either direct life insurance or direct general insurance*.'[152] The Chile-Australia FTA features an almost identical reservation.[153] In the US-Singapore FTA, Singapore scheduled a market access limitation according to which wholesale banks and 'offshore banks' are not permitted to engage in certain activities, such as offering savings accounts.[154] The applicable market access provision in each of these FTAs is, to the extent relevant here, identical to Article XVI GATS.

At the multilateral level, similar reservations can be found in the country-specific schedules of commitments of Armenia,[155] Chile,[156] Laos,[157] Lithuania,[158] Montenegro[159] and Slovenia.[160,161] Armenia, for instance, undertook a full market access commitment (mode 3) on life insurance services, with the sole reservation 'that providers of banking services may not provide insurance services.'

The ownership unbundling requirements in Article 9 of Directives 2009/72/EC and 2009/73/EC clearly establish a line-of-business restriction for companies

[152] Annex III – Non-Conforming Measures of Chile with Respect to Financial Services, US – Chile Free Trade Agreement (06 June 2003) 42 I.L.M. 1026 (2003), 33 (emphasis added). The corresponding market access provision can be found in Article 12.4 (Market Access for Financial Institutions). Example taken from Tucker, 'How to Reform WTO and FTA Rules to Confront Too-Big-To-Fail Banks' (n 149) 14.

[153] See Annex III – Non-Conforming Measures of Chile with respect to Financial Services, Australia – Chile Free Trade Agreement (30 July 2008) <http://dfat.gov.au/trade/agreements/aclfta/pages/australia-chile-fta.aspx> accessed 20 January 2018, 21. The corresponding market access provision can be found in Article 12.5 (Market Access for Financial Institutions).

[154] Annex 10B – Singapore Financial Services Reservations, US – Singapore Free Trade Agreement (06 May 2003) 42 I.L.M. 1026 (2003), 5–6. The corresponding market access provision can be found in Article 10.4 (Market Access for Financial Institutions). Example taken from Tucker, 'How to Reform WTO and FTA Rules to Confront Too-Big-To-Fail Banks' (n 149) 14.

[155] WTO, Armenia – Schedule of Specific Commitments (29 April 2004) GATS/SC/137, 22–24.

[156] WTO, Chile – Schedule of Specific Commitments (15 April 1994) GATS/SC/18, 20.

[157] WTO, Lao PDR – Schedule of Specific Commitments (22 April 2013) GATS/SC/150, 12.

[158] Lithuania – Schedule of Specific Commitments (n 76) 14.

[159] WTO, Montenegro – Schedule of Specific Commitments (05 June 2012) GATS/SC/146, 19.

[160] WTO, Slovenia – Schedule of Specific Commitments – Supplement 1 (26 February 1998) GATS/SC/99/Suppl.1, 8.

[161] None of the mentioned WTO Members has undertaken commitments in accordance with the 'Understanding on Commitments in Financial Services', which provides for additional market access obligations with respect to trade in financial services through commercial presence. For the scope of these additional market access obligations, see Pitschas (n 11) [180]; Armin von Bogdandy and Joseph Windsor, 'Understanding on Commitments in Financial Services' in Rüdiger Wolfrum, Peter-Tobias Stoll and Clemens Feinäugle (eds), *WTO – Trade in Services* (Max Planck Commentaries on World Trade Law vol 6. Martinus Nijhoff Publishers 2008).

engaged in either the transmission of gas or electricity and/or energy production/ generation or supply. Therefore, if Article XVI:2(e) GATS were interpreted as covering such line-of-business restrictions, as the above-mentioned market access reservations suggest, the ownership unbundling requirements would be inconsistent with the GATS market access obligation.

However, there are two main arguments against such an interpretation. First of all, it must be kept in mind that the country-specific schedules represent 'unilateral declarations' of individual WTO Members and cannot, as such, modify the reach of the market access or national treatment obligations laid down in Articles XVI/XVII GATS.[162] Only a large body of concordant practice in such schedules could have an influence on the process of interpretation, in accordance with the well-established rules in the Vienna Convention on the Law of Treaties (VCLT).[163] This is not the case here. Second, and on a related point, the use of 'superfluous language'[164] in country-specific schedules that cannot be reasonably linked to one of the categories mentioned in Article XVI:2 is relatively frequent. A review of GATS schedules has shown that almost 30% of all scheduled market access limitations could not be subsumed under one of the provisions contained in Article XVI:2 (a)–(f) GATS.[165] This can be explained by the fact that WTO Members have been overly cautious in their approach to scheduling limitations. Why risk unintentionally broad commitments which may have the result of foreclosing options for the future?[166] Given that many unnecessary reservations were thus scheduled in order to preserve regulatory autonomy, it would seem manifestly absurd to treat such reservations as evidence that the corresponding WTO Members have a broad understanding of the market access obligation.

In any event, interpreting the *per se* prohibition in Article XVI:2(e) GATS as covering every restriction of a specific activity is not supported by the plain meaning

---

[162]Krajewski (n 36) 79.

[163]According to Article XX:3 GATS, the schedules of specific commitments form an 'integral part' of the GATS. In interpreting the GATS, they can thus be taken into account as 'context' within the meaning of Article 31(1) of the Vienna Convention on the Law of Treaties (23 May 1969) 1155 U.N.T.S. 331. In *US – Gambling*, the Appellate Body held that 'Members' Schedules constitute relevant context for the interpretation of subsector 10.D of the United States' Schedule', which was, in its view, the 'logical consequence of Article XX:3' (see *United States – Measures Affecting the Cross-Border Supply of Gambling and Betting Services* (n 63) [182]). However, in quoting the Panel, it cautioned that the 'use of other Members' Schedules as context must be tempered by the recognition that "[e]ach Schedule has its own intrinsic logic, which is different from the US Schedule."', see ibid.

[164]Rudolf Adlung and others, 'Fog in GATS Commitments – Boon or Bane?' (Staff Working Paper ERSD-2011-04 2011) 12 <https://www.wto.org/english/res_e/reser_e/ersd201104_e.pdf> accessed 29 January 2016.

[165]Rudolf Adlung and Martin Roy, 'Turning Hills into Mountains? Current Commitments Under the General Agreement on Trade in Services and Prospects for Change' (2005) 39 Journal of World Trade 1161, 1177–1178. See also Adlung and others, 'Fog in GATS Commitments – Boon or Bane?' (n 164) 12.

[166]For similar considerations, see ibid 5.

of that provision, and would excessively overstretch its scope.[167] Indeed, following such an interpretation many qualitative regulations in the services sector would translate into a prohibited market access restriction. For example, a law requiring taxi companies to have a license to provide taxi services clearly does not amount to a measure which restricts or requires 'specific types of legal entity ... through which a service supplier may supply a service.' The typological distinctions contemplated by Article XVI:2(e) relate exclusively to the forms of legal establishment permitted to supply the services at issue. This interpretation is also confirmed by the Scheduling Guidelines.[168] Thus it may be concluded that line-of-business restrictions, as well as other qualitative restrictions on specific activities, including ownership unbundling measures, fall outside the scope of Article XVI:2(e) GATS.

4.5.3 Limitations on Foreign Capital Participation

The next relevant provision is Article XVI:2(f) GATS.[169] According to this provision, 'limitations on the participation of foreign capital in terms of maximum percentage limit on foreign shareholding or the total value of individual or aggregate foreign investment' are prohibited in sectors where market access commitments have been undertaken.[170] Like sub-paragraphs (a)–(c), sub-paragraph (f) of Article XVI:2 relates to measures of a quantitative nature.

A classic example of a measure that falls within the scope of Article XVI:2 (f) GATS is a foreign equity ceiling of x percent for a particular form of commercial presence.[171] In *China – Publications and Audiovisual Products*, for instance, the Panel was faced with various Chinese measures which required that in contractual joint ventures for the distribution of audiovisual products, the Chinese party must hold a minimum of 51% of the investment.[172] The Panel ruled that these measures constituted violations of Article XVI:2(f) GATS.[173]

In contrast to the measures in *China – Publications and Audiovisual Products*, the ownership unbundling regime of Directives 2009/72/EC and 2009/73/EC does not contain a plain ceiling on foreign equity. Although OU measures can clearly have a limiting effect on the inflow of foreign capital, there is no doubt that the OU

---

[167]See Krajewski (n 36) 92.

[168]Guidelines for the Scheduling of Specific Commitments under the GATS (n 99) [5].

[169]The Russian Federation invokes this provision as part of its Article XVI GATS claim, see *European Union and its Member States – Certain Measures Relating to the Energy Sector* (n 87) 2, 9.

[170]For a general commentary on this provision, see Munin (n 140) 199–200; Krajewski (n 36) 93–94; Delimatsis and Molinuevo (n 102) [62–66].

[171]Guidelines for the Scheduling of Specific Commitments under the GATS (n 99) [5].

[172]*China – Measures Affecting Trading Rights and Distribution Services for Certain Publications and Audiovisual Entertainment Products* (n 19) [7.1350–7.1397].

[173]Ibid [7.1395–7.1397].

requirements *per se* do not set a 'maximum percentage limit on foreign shareholding' nor establish a 'total value of ... aggregate foreign investment'.

One could, however, ask whether a specific decision whereby a foreign energy company is not allowed to hold shares in a domestic TSO[174] as a result of OU requirements would amount to a limitation on the participation of foreign capital in terms of 'the total value of *individual* ... foreign investment'. The argument could be made that this situation is in fact covered by Article XVI:2(f) GATS, because the total value of foreign capital participation allowed in that individual case would be 'zero', which is reminiscent of the 'zero quota' language used by the WTO dispute settlement bodies in *US – Gambling*. In the scholarly literature there appears to be some limited support for this view. Two authors, for example, when discussing the legal constraints on States' power to control the entry of sovereign wealth funds, seem to argue that Article XVI:2(f) GATS is violated if a specific investment is completely prohibited.[175]

However, this interpretation of Article XVI:2(f) GATS is not persuasive. Where a specific decision is based on a generally applicable law or regulation, the analysis under Article XVI:2(f) should not focus on the individual decision at issue but rather on whether the generally applicable law or regulation involves a 'maximum percentage limit on foreign shareholding' or a 'total value of individual or aggregate foreign investment'.[176] If individual decisions are viewed in isolation from the general criteria underlying them, the scope of the *per se* prohibition in Article XVI:2(f) GATS would be excessively broad. Furthermore, it is already clear from the ordinary meaning of the terms 'maximum percentage limit on foreign shareholding' and 'total value of individual or aggregate foreign investment' that the provisions presuppose a generally applicable limitation on foreign capital, which by definition cannot be found (but can only manifest itself) in a specific decision addressed to a single service supplier. In the absence of such a limitation, restrictions on foreign investment 'in individual cases' fall outside the scope of Article XVI:2 (f) GATS.[177] The reference to limitations on the 'total value of *individual* ... foreign

[174]Or, *vice versa*, in a domestic energy production/generation or supply undertaking.

[175]See Michael Schäfer and Thomas Voland, 'Staatsfonds: Die Kontrolle ausländischer Investitionen auf dem Prüfstand des Verfassungs-, Europa- und Welthandelsrechts' [2008] Europäisches Wirtschafts- und Steuerrecht 166, 171 (who conclude that: 'Eine Beeinträchtigung des Marktzugangs ist gem. Art. XVI:2(f) GATS u.a. dann gegeben, wenn ... eine Investition im Einzelfall komplett verboten wird.').

[176]See De Meester (n 126) 218ff, and in particular 229 (with respect to Article XVI:2(f) GATS).

[177]It is recalled that the Commission's proposal for a Third Energy Package would have completely prohibited foreign investment in electricity and gas transmission systems. The draft Directives stated that transmission systems or transmission system operators 'shall not be controlled by a person or persons from third countries', see Proposal for a Directive amending Directive 2003/54/EC (n 120) 29; Proposal for a Directive amending Directive 2003/55/EC (n 120) 30. It is important to note that the prohibition on foreign investment in the draft Directives did not refer to an explicit numerical threshold. The lack of such a reference does not, however, dis-apply Article XVI:2 (f) GATS. In *China – Publications and Audiovisual Products*, the Panel also examined a Chinese measure that did not set a clear numerical limitation. In that context, the Panel observed that

investment' simply serves to include measures which, while not prescribing a maximum ceiling on foreign equity participation *per se*, set for example a certain percentage limit on each individual investor.[178]

Finally, it should also be noted that Article XVI:2(f) GATS applies to limitations on the participation of *foreign* capital. Based on this wording some authors have convincingly argued that the provision only covers 'inherently', i.e. *de jure*, discriminatory measures affecting the supply of services through commercial presence.[179] In accordance with this view, the ownership unbundling regime in the TEP, as well as corresponding decisions, fall *a priori* outside the scope of Article XVI:2 (f) GATS, given that the OU requirements apply equally to both EU and non-EU companies.[180]

In conclusion, the ownership unbundling regime as set out in Article 9 of Directives 2009/72/EC and 2009/73/EC does not entail a violation of Article XVI:2(f) GATS.

4.5.4 PTAs Addressing the Relationship Between Ownership Unbundling and Market Access Obligations

It is interesting to note that the relationship between ownership unbundling requirements and GATS-type market access obligations has recently been addressed outside the WTO in the context of preferential trade agreements (PTAs). The Comprehensive Economic and Trade Agreement (CETA) between the EU and Canada, which is currently in the process of ratification, is the first PTA that contains a provision to that effect.

'"holding a majority of shares" means simply that one must hold over 50% of the shares' (see *China – Measures Affecting Trading Rights and Distribution Services for Certain Publications and Audiovisual Entertainment Products* (n 19) [7.1392]; see also De Meester and Coppens (n 126) 115–116). Accordingly, the draft Directives would have constituted a violation of Article XVI:2(f), because 'shall not be controlled' effectively implies that foreign service suppliers cannot obtain more than 49% of the shares with voting rights of a transmission system operator (European Commission, Commission Consolidated Jurisdictional Notice under Council Regulation (EC) No 139/2004 on the control of concentrations between undertakings (no date) OJ 2008/C 95/1, [54, 56]). This results from the definition of the term 'control' provided in the draft Directives, which corresponded to the concept of control in the EU Merger Regulation. In this way, the draft Directives would have amounted to a limitation on foreign equity in the form of a maximum percentage of capital that can be held by foreign investors, in violation of Article XVI:2(f) GATS (for the same result, see van Hoorn (n 120) 66; Moschetta (n 68) 121; see also Schmidt-Preuß (n 49) 285).

[178] Delimatsis and Molinuevo (n 102) [64].

[179] Vranes (n 86) 666; Delimatsis and Molinuevo (n 102) [62].

[180] 24th recital of the preamble to Directive 2009/72/EC (n 8); 21st recital of the preamble to Directive 2009/73/EC (n 8).

Apart from the 'textual innovations' which will be described shortly, the market access clause in paragraph one of Article 8.4 of CETA's investment chapter is, for all practical purposes, identical to Article XVI GATS. The scope of prohibited market access restrictions is therefore the same under both provisions. CETA's market access clause is, however, supplemented by an additional paragraph 2, which mentions a number of measures which are deemed *not* to constitute one of the prohibited market access limitations under paragraph one. The relevant passage for our purposes is Article 8.4(2)(b), which is reproduced in its context below[181]:

> Article 8.4
> Market access
>
> 1. A Party shall not adopt or maintain with respect to market access through establishment by an investor of the other Party ... a measure that: ...
> 2. For greater certainty, the following are consistent with paragraph 1:
>
>   (a) ...
>   (b) a measure requiring the separation of the ownership of infrastructure from the ownership of the goods or services provided through that infrastructure to ensure fair competition, for example in the fields of energy, transportation and telecommunications;
>   (c) ...

The term 'For greater certainty' indicates that the insertion of paragraph two does not in any way limit the scope of paragraph one. Indeed, the European Commission takes the view that 'even in the absence of these clarifications, the measures related to ownership unbundling would normally be considered as compatible with the market access obligation'.[182] Therefore, paragraph two is meant as a clarification, not an exception.

This so-called 'Ownership Unbundling Clarification' in Article 8.4(2)(b) CETA is noteworthy in many respects. First of all, the European Union felt it necessary to amend the rules on services. This seems to reflect a concern that the scope of GATS-type market access provisions could be broader than originally assumed. Generally, the rules on market access in services trade or investment in preferential trade agreements only rarely deviate from the provisions in Article XVI GATS.[183] Second, the 'Ownership Unbundling Clarification' highlights that OU requirements play an important role not only in the energy sector, but also in the transportation and telecommunications sector. Third, Article 8.4(2)(b) CETA shows that OU measures

---

[181]Comprehensive Economic and Trade Agreement between the European Union and Canada – Consolidated text (2016) <http://trade.ec.europa.eu/doclib/docs/2014/september/tradoc_152806.pdf> accessed 20 January 2018, 43.

[182]E-mail from me to DG Trade (6 February 2015).

[183]Among the rare exceptions are a number of bilateral preferential trade agreements concluded by Korea (with, *inter alia*, the US, EU, Colombia, Canada and Australia). An understanding appended to each of these PTAs lists several measures which are declared consistent with the applicable market access provision. Interestingly, the list includes, *inter alia*, 'regulations that prohibit an enterprise from concurrently holding two or more business licenses to supply different services'. This description covers line-of-business restrictions and thus also ownership unbundling measures.

have two 'faces'. On one hand, OU policies are designed to safeguard market access opportunities. In a background note on energy services by the WTO Secretariat, for instance, the unbundling of vertically integrated energy companies is hailed as '*the first market access issue* on the road of multilateral liberalization' in the energy sector.[184] On the other hand, CETA's 'Ownership Unbundling Clarification' is a clear reminder that vertical separation measures also constitute restrictions on the entry of foreign service suppliers and thus limit market access.

In purely legal terms, Article 8.4(2)(b) CETA will have no impact on the assessment of ownership unbundling measures under the GATS. According to the principle *pacta tertiis nec nocent nec prosunt*, bilateral preferential trade agreements cannot add to or diminish the rights and obligations of WTO Members provided in the WTO agreements.[185] Moreover, the analysis in this section has demonstrated that CETA's 'Ownership Unbundling Clarification' is, in fact, a 'clarification', and thus superfluous language that was not strictly necessary to introduce. Nevertheless it serves the purpose of legal certainty, at least in the limited context of the CETA.

4.6 Article XVII GATS (National Treatment)

The unbundling regime under the Third Energy Package could also be deemed to be inconsistent with Article XVII (National Treatment, also referred to herein as NT) of the GATS. The national treatment obligation is an expression of the central principle of non-discrimination in WTO law, which is also reflected in Article II GATS (Most-Favored-Nation Treatment) and in several other WTO agreements.

With a view toward eliminating discrimination between foreign and domestic services and service suppliers, Article XVII:1 GATS requires WTO Members to

> accord to services and service suppliers of any other Member, in respect of all measures affecting the supply of services, treatment no less favourable than that it accords to its own like services and service suppliers.

As with the market access obligation in Article XVI GATS, Article XVII GATS applies only in sectors where specific commitments have been undertaken by the respective Member.

In the academic literature a number of authors have discussed the third-country certification procedure in Article 11 of the Gas and Electricity Directives in relation to Article XVII GATS.[186] This is not surprising given that the certification procedure

[184]Energy Services – Background Note by the Secretariat (n 2) [6] (emphasis added).

[185]Isabelle Van Damme, 'What Role is there for Regional International Law in the Interpretation of the WTO Agreements?' in Lorand Bartels and Federico Ortino (eds), *Regional Trade Agreements and the WTO Legal System* (Oxford University Press 2006) 559.

[186]See Cottier, Matteotti-Berkutova and Nartova (n 88) 279; Alexey S Ispolinov and Tatiana Dvenadtcatova, 'Принудительное выделение сетевого бизнеса в рамках Третьего Энергопакета ЕС (unbundling): практика применения' [2014] Закон 111, 120; Monica

under the Directives is different for companies from third countries than for EU companies. There are, however, several other situations in which Article XVII could be relevant. Issues could arise if, for example, one or more domestic energy companies are exempted from the application of ownership unbundling requirements as a result of case-by-case decisions, whereas a foreign energy undertaking is not. More generally it could also be asked whether the TEP's OU exemption regime as a whole is in conformity with the GATS national treatment obligation. Finally, Article XVII GATS may play a role when domestic *State-owned* vertically integrated undertakings are unbundled pursuant to the relaxed ownership unbundling requirements in Article 9(6) of Directives 2009/72/EC and 2009/73/EC, whereas foreign *privately-owned* vertically integrated energy companies have to comply with the more stringent OU requirements in Article 9(1) of the Directives.[187] In sum, therefore, the NT obligation is of importance for all three aspects of the unbundling regime in the TEP, i.e. certification, exemption, and the unbundling requirements as such.

In order to establish a breach of Article XVII GATS, the following four-pronged test applies, which can be distilled from the GATS case law[188]: First, the European Union or one of its Member States needs to have made a commitment on national treatment in the relevant sector and mode of supply. NT commitments have been undertaken by the EU and by Member States in the energy transmission and/or supply sector. Their applicability to the various measures at issue has been discussed above.[189] Second, the impugned measure must be a 'measure affecting the supply of services' in the relevant sector and mode of supply. This phrase is not legally defined in the GATS. However, considering the almost identical expression in Article I:1 GATS ('measures affecting *trade* in services'), which describes the agreement's general scope of application, it is logical to conclude that measures that affect 'trade' in services *ipso facto* also affect the 'supply' of such services.[190] Third, it needs to be established whether foreign services or service suppliers are 'like' domestic services or service suppliers. Fourth, the unbundling or unbundling-related measures must be shown to accord treatment less favorable to the foreign services or service suppliers than to the 'like' domestic services or service suppliers. These latter two elements are discussed in detail below.

Waloszyk, *Law and Policy of the European Gas Market* (Edward Elgar 2014) 70–71; Guillaume Van Der Loo, 'EU-Russia Trade Relations: It Takes WTO to Tango?' (2013) 40 Legal Issues of Economic Integration 7, 21; Boute (n 88) [3.63]. The third country certification procedure is also challenged by the Russian Federation in the *EU – Energy Package* case, see *European Union and its Member States – Certain Measures Relating to the Energy Sector* (n 87) 3.

[187] This point is raised by the Russian Federation in the *EU – Energy Package* case, see ibid 2.

[188] *Cf. China – Certain Measures Affecting Electronic Payment Services* (n 97) [7.641]; *China – Measures Affecting Trading Rights and Distribution Services for Certain Publications and Audio-visual Entertainment Products* (n 19) [7.942, 7.956, 7.1272]; *European Communities – Regime for the Importation, Sale and Distribution of Bananas* (n 5) [7.314].

[189] See Sect. 4.4.

[190] *Argentina – Measures Relating to Trade in Goods and Services* (n 7) [7.474].

4.6.1 Likeness Analysis

According to the third element of the test under Article XVII GATS, foreign services or service suppliers need to be 'like' domestic services or service suppliers. Only a finding of such 'likeness' gives rise to the obligation to treat the former no less favorable than the latter. The notion of 'likeness' is also a key concept in the GATT and has given rise to a number of interpretive challenges for Panels and the Appellate Body. It seems, however, that the application of the concept of 'likeness' under the GATS is generally more intricate than under the GATT.[191] This may be ascribed to: the intangibility of services, which precludes the comparability of services transactions on the basis of physical characteristics; the lack of a sufficiently detailed nomenclature comparable to the Harmonized System (HS) for goods and tariffs; the conceptual distinction between four different modes of supply; and the customized nature of many service transactions.[192] Furthermore, in contrast to the GATT, which (merely) refers to 'like products', the GATS contains a combined reference to 'like services and service suppliers'. This inclusion of services *and* service suppliers makes the likeness analysis under the GATS even more complex.

4.6.1.1 Relationship Between Likeness of Services and Likeness of Service Suppliers

First of all, the reference to 'like services and service suppliers' raises the question of how the conjunction 'and' should be interpreted. The answer to this question has a critically important impact on the scope of the national treatment obligation. Four main different approaches to interpretation can be distinguished. Under the first approach (the 'cumulative test'[193]), the conjunction 'and' is interpreted as requiring that, in a given case, *both* domestic and foreign *services* as well as domestic and foreign *service suppliers* must be like.[194] This restrictive reading of Article XVII GATS would reduce the scope and practical value of the national treatment obligation, because it will typically be more difficult to show the likeness of both services and service suppliers. In contrast to the cumulative test, Article XVII GATS can also be interpreted as establishing two *separate* obligations, namely (1) to accord no less

[191] Mireille Cossy, 'Some Thoughts on the Concept of "Likeness" in the GATS' in Marion Panizzon, Nicole Pohl and Pierre Sauvé (eds), *GATS and the Regulation of International Trade in Services* (Cambridge University Press 2008) 327.

[192] Nicolas F Diebold, *Non-Discrimination in International Trade in Services: 'Likeness' in WTO/GATS* (Cambridge International Trade and Economic Law, Cambridge University Press 2010) 4; Cossy (n 191) 327.

[193] The terminology is adopted from Diebold (n 192) 204ff.

[194] See, for example, Markus Krajewski and Maika Engelke, 'Article XVII GATS' in Rüdiger Wolfrum, Peter-Tobias Stoll and Clemens Feinäugle (eds), *WTO – Trade in Services* (Max Planck Commentaries on World Trade Law vol 6. Martinus Nijhoff Publishers 2008) [36] (referring to a 'narrow cumulative test').

favorable treatment to 'like' foreign services; and (2) to accord no less favorable treatment to 'like' foreign service suppliers. The second and third interpretative approaches are based on this idea of having two distinct obligations. Under the second approach (the 'combined test'), Article XVII would be violated if either foreign 'like services' *or* foreign 'like service suppliers' are treated less favorably. This implies a strong NT obligation. Even if a certain measure, which primarily addresses service suppliers, lawfully treats foreign service suppliers differently because they are not 'like', it could be argued that the *services* supplied are in fact 'like' and that the measure discriminates between these like services, giving rise to a violation of the NT obligation.[195] It is for this reason that the combined test has been criticized by many academics as being insufficiently deferential to national regulatory autonomy.[196] The third approach to interpreting Article XVII GATS (the 'disjunctive test') accommodates these concerns. Under the disjunctive test, the WTO dispute settlement bodies would be required to determine whether a given measure is mainly aimed at regulating the service or rather the service supplier. If the measure at issue is aimed at regulating the service, it is only the likeness of services that is analyzed. In contrast, if the measure is aimed at regulating the service supplier, the likeness of service suppliers has to be demonstrated.[197] The decisive difference between the disjunctive approach and the combined test is that the complainant is not in a position to freely decide whether the likeness and less favorable treatment analysis should focus on the services or the service suppliers at issue. Finally, recently a fourth interpretative approach has been put forward, which stresses the inseparability between the service supplier and the service (the 'merged test'). According to the merged test, the likeness of services and the likeness of service suppliers should not be regarded as separate elements. Rather, it is proposed that the reference to 'like services and service suppliers' be 'read *en bloc*', forming one merged element.[198]

For a long time, WTO case-law was unclear as to the proper relationship between the likeness of services and the likeness of service suppliers. In 2016, the Appellate Body held, in *Argentina – Financial Services*, that Article XVII (and Article II:1) GATS should be interpreted according to the merged test. In particular, it stated that the likeness analysis embodied in the phrase 'like services and service suppliers'

---

[195] See, for instance, Diebold (n 192) 209–210.

[196] See, sometimes using different terminology, Krajewski (n 36) 106–107; Krajewski and Engelke (n 194) [35]; Kalypso Nicolaïdis and Joel P Trachtman, 'From Policed Regulation to Managed Recognition in GATS' in Pierre Sauvé and Robert M Stern (eds), *GATS 2000: New Directions in Services Trade Liberalization* (Brookings Institution Press 2000) 253–254; Joel P Trachtman, 'Negotiations on Domestic Regulation and Trade in Services (GATS Article VI): A Legal Analysis of Selected Current Issues' in Ernst-Ulrich Petersmann and James Harrison (eds), *Reforming The World Trading System: Legitimacy, Efficiency, and Democratic Governance* (Oxford University Press 2005) 209–210; Diebold (n 192) 209–210.

[197] Nicolaïdis and Trachtman (n 196) 254.

[198] Diebold (n 192) 217–219.

constitutes an 'integrated element', requiring a 'holistic analysis of "likeness"'.[199] Regarding the issue of the relative importance which should be given to considerations relating to the service and those relating to the service supplier, the Appellate Body explained that this will be determined on the basis of the 'particular features' of the competitive relationship of the services and service suppliers at issue, 'in the circumstances of any specific case'.[200]

4.6.1.2 Interpretation of Likeness: GATS Jurisprudence

Having described the correct interpretation of the 'like services and service suppliers' requirement, it is useful to now give an overview of the existing case-law on determining the likeness of services and service suppliers, respectively, in a specific situation.

In the *EC – Bananas III* case, the Panel did not delve into a deep analysis of the likeness criterion under Article XVII GATS. It accepted that the wholesale services at issue were 'like services', based on a somewhat vague reference to their 'nature' and 'characteristics'.[201] In a second step, it made the controversial assertion that 'to the extent that entities provide these like services, they are like service suppliers',[202] thereby equating the 'likeness of services' with the 'likeness of service suppliers'. In the *Canada – Autos* dispute, the Panel endorsed this finding in the context of claims under Article II:1 GATS, albeit only 'for the purpose of [the] case'.[203] In *China – Publications and Audiovisual Products*, the factual circumstances of the case led the Panel to apply a simplified likeness test. In the measures in issue, service suppliers were treated differently based exclusively on their origin. Relying on jurisprudence in the context of trade in goods,[204] the Panel held that in such circumstances 'the "like" service suppliers requirement in Article XVII is met, as long as there will, or can, be domestic and foreign suppliers that under the measure are the same in all material respects except for origin.'[205]

---

[199]WTO, *Argentina – Measures Relating to Trade in Goods and Services,* Report of the Appellate Body (14 April 2016) WT/DS453/AB/R [6.29].

[200]Ibid.

[201]*European Communities – Regime for the Importation, Sale and Distribution of Bananas* (n 5) [7.322].

[202]Ibid.

[203]WTO, *Canada – Certain Measures Affecting the Automotive Industry,* Report of the Panel (11 February 2000) WT/DS139/R, WT/DS142/R [10.248].

[204]WTO, *Argentina – Measures Affecting the Export of Bovine Hides and the Import of Finished Leather,* Report of the Panel (19 December 2000) WT/DS155/R [11.168–11.169]; WTO, *Canada – Measures Relating to Exports of Wheat and Treatment of Imported Grain,* Report of the Panel (6 April 2004) WT/DS276/R [6.164–6.167].

[205]*China – Measures Affecting Trading Rights and Distribution Services for Certain Publications and Audiovisual Entertainment Products* (n 19) [7.975–7.976].

The Panel conducted a more thorough analysis in *China – Electronic Payment Services*. First, with respect to the likeness of services, it cautioned against transferring the analytical framework used to determine 'likeness' in the context of trade in goods to trade in services, without first examining the appropriateness of such a transposition.[206] The main criteria for establishing likeness under the GATT were first outlined in the Report of the Working Party on Border Tax Adjustments, and subsequently developed by the WTO dispute settlement organs. They consist of (1) the physical characteristics of a product; (2) the end-uses of a product; (3) the tastes and habits of consumers; and (4) the tariff classification of a product.[207] Furthermore, the Panel in *China – Electronic Payment Services* explained that only services which are in a competitive relationship with each other could be considered to be 'like services'.[208] Second, with respect to the 'likeness of service suppliers' it referred to *EC – Bananas III* and agreed that 'in some cases' the fact that service suppliers provide like services 'may' create a presumption that they are also like service suppliers.[209] In addition, it noted that the domestic and foreign service suppliers at issue would 'describe their business scope in very similar terms' and perceive each other as competitors in the world market.[210] The Panel concluded by ruling that for the purposes of the case, the suppliers are 'like' within the meaning of Article XVII, 'at least to the extent that they provide "like" services'.[211]

In *Argentina – Financial Services*, the most recent case dealing with likeness under Article XVII GATS, the Appellate Body clarified a number of important points. First, the Appellate Body strongly emphasized the notion that the concept of likeness is concerned with the competitive relationship with respect to both services and service suppliers.[212] Furthermore, it accepted that the analytical tools used to determine likeness in the context of trade in goods could also be usefully employed in assessing likeness under the GATS, but only to the extent that they help to evaluate the competitive relationship of services and service suppliers.[213] Finally, it agreed with the Panel in *China – Publications and Audiovisual Products* that likeness can be presumed where the measure at issue provides for a distinction which is exclusively based on origin.[214]

[206] *China – Certain Measures Affecting Electronic Payment Services* (n 97) [7.698].

[207] WTO, *European Communities – Measures Affecting Asbestos and Asbestos-Containing Products,* Report of the Appellate Body (12 March 2001) WT/DS135/AB/R [101].

[208] *China – Certain Measures Affecting Electronic Payment Services* (n 97) [7.700].

[209] Ibid [7.705].

[210] Ibid [7.706].

[211] Ibid [7.708].

[212] *Argentina – Measures Relating to Trade in Goods and Services* (n 199) [6.22–6.25; 6.34].

[213] Ibid [6.30–32].

[214] Ibid [6.35ff]. The Appellate Body, however, cautioned that for different reasons, the scope for such a presumption of likeness under the GATS would be more limited than under the GATT.

4.6.1.3 Likeness of Service Suppliers in the Context of the TEP

The existing WTO case-law, supplemented with some additional considerations, will now be applied to the present context of unbundling and unbundling-related measures. First, the likeness of service suppliers will be discussed. It is important to recapitulate that already three Panels (*EC – Bananas III*, *Canada – Autos*, and *China – Electronic Payment Services*) have embraced the idea that the likeness of service suppliers depends to a large extent, or even exclusively, on the likeness of the services provided by them. Although it is true that likeness was not the deciding factor in any of these cases,[215] the Panel reports clearly reflect a reluctance on the part of the WTO dispute settlement bodies to factor in supplier-related characteristics. The Appellate Body in *Argentina – Financial Services* seemed to implicitly suggest that some independent considerations relating to the service suppliers should be undertaken,[216] but at the same time held that the likeness of services will have an impact on the likeness of service suppliers.[217] Consequently, the likeness of energy service suppliers is, to an appreciable extent, influenced by or contingent upon the likeness of the energy services that they supply.

It should be noted that the approach of linking the likeness of service suppliers to the likeness of the underlying services has been heavily criticized in the literature.[218] The main line of criticism is that establishing the likeness of service suppliers by reference to the likeness of the services they supply would constrain the regulatory autonomy of WTO Members.[219] Obviously, if one were to take into account the characteristics of the service suppliers, the obligation to provide 'treatment no less favorable' would apply in a smaller number of cases. In particular, it would be easier for domestic regulators to make regulatory distinctions not only on the basis of the different characteristics of services, but also on the basis of different characteristics of the service suppliers.[220] In contrast, disregarding the characteristics of service suppliers would 'undoubtedly enhance the liberalizing effect of GATS and put many regulatory regimes under increased pressure.'[221]

---

[215]Diebold (n 192) 195–197.

[216]*Argentina – Measures Relating to Trade in Goods and Services* (n 199) [6.28–6.29].

[217]Ibid [6.29].

[218]Michaelis (n 11) [68]; Krajewski (n 36) 104–105; Gaëtan Verhoosel, *National Treatment and WTO Dispute Settlement: Adjudicating the Boundaries of Regulatory Autonomy* (Hart Publishing 2002) 60–63; Diebold (n 192) 195ff; Werner Zdouc, 'WTO Dispute Settlement Practice Relating to the GATS' (1999) 2 Journal of International Economic Law 295, 332ff; Krajewski and Engelke (n 194) [34].

[219]Werner Zdouc, 'Streitigkeiten über den Dienstleistungsverkehr vor dem DSB' in Dirk Ehlers, Hans-Michael Wolffgang and Marc Lechleitner (eds), *Rechtsfragen des internationalen Dienstleistungsverkehrs: Tagungsband zum 10. Münsteraner Außenwirtschaftsrechtstag 2005* (Verlag Recht und Wirtschaft 2006) 134.

[220]Verhoosel (n 218) 60.

[221]Krajewski (n 42) 104.

While the predominant view is that service supplier-related factors should be taken into account, there is no consensus as to which criteria should be used for this purpose.[222] Possible criteria include the size of a company, the number and qualifications of its employees, assets and equipment, its traditional line of business, its legal form, and other distinctions made by the respective regulatory regime.[223] Furthermore, the public or private ownership of a company could have a bearing on the likeness analysis.[224]

At the same time, while the inclusion of supplier-related characteristics may be desirable from the perspective of regulatory autonomy, it also has a major downside. Given that, even on a global level, no two companies are ever entirely identical,[225] a rigid application of the above-mentioned criteria would lead to a situation whereby it would be almost impossible to prove the likeness of service suppliers. This would excessively curtail the reach of the GATS non-discrimination disciplines.[226] Furthermore, *Argentina – Financial Services* dictates that supplier-related characteristics can be taken into account only in order to assess the competitive relationship of service suppliers. Therefore, for this reason and for other reasons relating to the overall structure of the GATS,[227] the public or private ownership of a company will

[222]Herrmann, Weiß and Ohler (n 29) [866].

[223]Krajewski (n 36) 105; Werner Zdouc, 'WTO Dispute Settlement Practice Relating to the General Agreement on Trade in Services' in Federico Ortino and Ernst-Ulrich Petersmann (eds), *The WTO Dispute Settlement System 1995–2003* (Kluwer Law International 2004) 400.

[224]The issue of likeness of public and private companies has surfaced in WTO dispute settlement practice. In *US – Gambling*, the United States argued that its State-owned lotteries were unlike the private, non-State suppliers of gambling services of Antigua, see *United States – Measures Affecting the Cross-Border Supply of Gambling and Betting Services* (n 95) [3.154]. In contrast, Antigua and the European Union argued that the ownership structure of a company has no bearing on the likeness of service suppliers, see ibid [3.170, 4.39].

[225]Cossy (n 191) 337.

[226]Werner Zdouc, *Legal Problems Arising under the General Agreement on Trade in Services – Comparative Analysis of GATS and GATT* (Dissertation Nr. 2608, Difo-Druck 2002) 166–167.

[227]Although some authors have stressed that distinguishing between public and private companies could be vital in order to protect public services (see Krajewski (n 42) 360–361; Diebold (n 192) 200; Katherine Connolly, 'Finding Space for Regulatory Autonomy in GATS Article XVII after EC – Seals: Public Services and the 'Likeness' of Public and Private Service Providers' (2015) 42 Legal Issues of Economic Integration 57, 69ff), the structure of the GATS likewise suggests that the public or private nature of a company should play no role in determining likeness. It is recalled that the GATS already contains a clause that indirectly deals with services provided by public entities, namely Article I:3(b) GATS. According to this provision, services supplied in the 'exercise of governmental authority' are removed from the scope of application of the GATS. However, and importantly, the GATS governmental service exclusion was *not* drafted so as to cover *a priori* all services supplied by State-owned undertakings. Public services are only caught by Article I:3 (b) GATS if they are 'supplied neither on a commercial basis, nor in competition with one or more service suppliers' (Article I:3(c) GATS). Conversely, services are subject to the GATS disciplines if they are supplied on a commercial basis or in competition with other suppliers, irrespective of whether ownership is in public or private hands; see WTO, Environmental Services – Background Note by the Secretariat (06 July 1998) S/C/W/46, [53] (where the Commission stated with respect to Article I:3 GATS that 'if services were deemed to be supplied on a commercial basis, then,

generally not be a valid criterion, in and of itself, for determining likeness. Accordingly, (foreign) privately-owned TSOs and energy suppliers subject to the 'classic' ownership unbundling model in Article 9(1) of Directives 2009/72/EC and 2009/73/EC are not automatically unlike (domestic) public TSOs and energy suppliers, respectively, which are subject to the special OU requirements in Article 9(6) of the Directives.

Even if certain supplier-related characteristics are incorporated into the analysis, this does not necessarily make the relevant energy service suppliers unlike. For example, companies that supply or seek to supply energy transmission services in the EU will generally not be small-sized enterprises. Moreover, the regulatory regime itself indicates likeness. Energy transmission service suppliers are all subject to the same regulatory regime, i.e. they fall within the scope of the TEP, and particularly Directives 2009/72/EC or 2009/73/EC, and have to comply with the rules on unbundling and third party access. In terms of staff, assets, and equipment the companies will also be roughly the same, given that the supply of transmission services requires a certain infrastructure. The same considerations likewise apply, *mutatis mutandis*, to energy supply companies.

Thus, while the Third Energy Package draws regulatory distinctions between service suppliers (such as between public and private[228] or between foreign and domestic[229] companies), these regulatory distinctions do not in and of themselves justify a finding of 'unlikeness'. As mentioned, the public or private ownership of a company is not a valid supplier-related criterion for the purpose of determining likeness under the GATS. If it were otherwise, the practical effectiveness of the GATS specific commitments would be largely undermined, since WTO Members would be free to treat public enterprises more favorably than private suppliers, regardless of their competitive relationship.[230] As regards the distinction between foreign and domestic companies, *China – Publications and Audiovisual Products* and *Argentina – Financial Services* have confirmed that where a measure provides for differential treatment based exclusively on origin, a presumption of likeness applies.[231]

---

regardless of whether ownership was in public or private hands, the sector would be subject to the main GATS disciplines and to the negotiation of commitments under Articles XVI and XVII'). Against this background, it appears contradictory to assume that the likeness test operates to the effect that services supplied by public companies are, to a large extent, exempted from GATS disciplines.

[228]This applies to the special ownership unbundling regime for public companies in Article 9(6) the Directives.

[229]This applies to the third-country certification procedure in Article 11 of the Directives.

[230]Cossy (n 191) 337 and footnote 30 (who also writes that Article XXVIII(h) and (l) GATS 'suggest that the GATS is neutral with respect to ownership').

[231]*Argentina – Measures Relating to Trade in Goods and Services* (n 199) [6.35ff]. See also *China – Measures Affecting Trading Rights and Distribution Services for Certain Publications and Audiovisual Entertainment Products* (n 19) [7.975].

4.6.1.4 Likeness of Services in the Context of the TEP

Having discussed the likeness of service suppliers, the analysis will now shift to the likeness of services in the context of unbundling and unbundling-related measures. Following the approach of the Panel in *EC – Bananas III*, there is nothing to suggest that the various energy transmission or supply service transactions, respectively, are not 'like'. In principle, they have the same 'nature' and share the same 'characteristics'. This initial assessment is not altered by the application, *mutatis mutandis*, of further criteria forming part of the GATT framework for likeness. In particular, likeness is indicated by the fact that in each case the respective service transactions fall into the same services classification category of the CPC.[232] For instance, there is no reason not to assume that activities that meet the definition of CPC item 71310 (transportation via pipeline of natural gas) also fulfill the likeness requirement.

Where the TEP draws regulatory distinctions between certain services (such as in the context of the infrastructure-related exemption regime[233]), these distinctions do not make the respective services unlike. For example, whether a particular transmission service enhances competition in gas or electricity supply, based on the European Commission's interpretation of this requirement, will arguably not affect the likeness analysis, given that the competition in energy supply is an externality and public policy issue that is completely unrelated to the competitive relationship of transmission services as such.

On a concluding note, the likeness of transmission services calls for some additional considerations.[234] As emphasized by *China – Electronic Payment Services* and *Argentina – Financial Services*, services are 'like' when they are in a competitive relationship with each other. This also means that '[i]f there is – or could be – *no* competitive relationship' between services, the likeness requirement is not met.[235] It is obvious that wholesale and retail services of gas/electricity supply can be in a competitive relationship with each other. However, the case is less clear for energy transmission services. The natural monopoly nature of electricity and gas transmission networks implies that, in principle, there is and can be no genuine competition between different transmission services in a given geographic market.[236] It is, however, submitted here that this should not lead to a conclusion of

[232]That the CPC can play a role in determining likeness has been accepted by the WTO dispute settlement organs, see *Argentina – Measures Relating to Trade in Goods and Services* (n 199) [6.32] (referring to the Panel report in *European Communities – Regime for the Importation, Sale and Distribution of Bananas* (n 5) [7.322, 7.346]). See also Michaelis (n 11) [67].

[233]The requirements for an exemption from the OU requirements, laid down in Article 17 of Regulation (EC) No 714/2009 (n 10) and Article 36 Directive 2009/73/EC (n 8), seem to relate mainly to the conditions for the supply of services (and not to the service providers).

[234]These considerations also apply to the likeness of transmission service *suppliers*.

[235]*Argentina – Measures Relating to Trade in Goods and Services* (n 199) [6.25] (referring to *European Communities – Measures Affecting Asbestos and Asbestos-Containing Products* (n 207) [117]; emphasis in the original).

[236]Thomas W Wälde and Andreas Gunst, 'International Energy Trade and Access to Networks: The Case of Electricity' in Janusz Bielecki and Melaku G Desta (eds), *Electricity Trade in Europe –*

'unlikeness' between the natural monopoly services in question for the purposes of Article XVII (or Article II:1) GATS. Otherwise, WTO Members would be entirely free to discriminate, at least *de facto*, against foreign suppliers in favor of their incumbent natural monopolist. This would significantly inhibit the objectives and purpose of the GATS non-discrimination disciplines.

4.6.2 No Less Favorable Treatment

According to the fourth element of the test under Article XVII GATS, foreign service suppliers must be accorded 'treatment no less favorable' than that accorded to like domestic service suppliers. Article XVII:2 GATS clarifies that this can be achieved either through formally identical or formally different treatment. Article XVII:3 GATS further states that formally identical or formally different treatment shall be considered to be less favorable 'if it modifies the conditions of competition in favour of services or service suppliers of the Member compared to like services or service suppliers of any other Member.' Paragraphs 2 and 3 of Article XVII GATS therefore clarify that the national treatment obligation not only covers cases of *de jure* discrimination, i.e. where a measure distinguishes between service suppliers on the basis of their origin, but also extends to cases of *de facto* discrimination, i.e. where an origin-neutral measure *de facto* results in less favorable treatment.[237] This has been confirmed in WTO jurisprudence.[238]

In the following sub-sections, various aspects of the unbundling regime in the EU energy sector will be tested for compliance with the 'no less favorable treatment' standard. In doing so, different dimensions of this standard will also be highlighted.

4.6.2.1 Certification Procedure in Relation to Third Countries

To begin with, Article 11 of Directives 2009/72/EC and 2009/73/EC is examined. Article 11 lays down the certification procedure for transmission system owners and transmission system operators which are controlled by a person or persons from a third country. In this way the third-country certification procedure accords formally different treatment to foreign service suppliers. However, contrary to the finding of an early Panel stating that '[a]ny regulatory distinction that is based exclusively on

---

Review of the Economic and Regulatory Changes (Kluwer Law International 2004) 184–185; Christopher Decker, *Modern Economic Regulation: An Introduction to Theory and Practice* (Cambridge University Press 2015) 227, 283.

[237] Weiss (n 146) 1211; Herrmann, Weiß and Ohler (n 29) [867]; van den Bossche and Zdouc (n 71) 405, 413.

[238] *European Communities – Regime for the Importation, Sale and Distribution of Bananas* (n 3) [233]; *Argentina – Measures Relating to Trade in Goods and Services* (n 199) [6.105].

criteria relating to the nationality or the origin of the products is incompatible with Article III [GATT]'[239] (a finding later reversed on appeal[240]), a formal difference in treatment between foreign and domestic service suppliers does not, in and of itself, amount to less favorable treatment.[241] Under the GATS this is explicitly confirmed by paragraph 2 of Article XVII. In order to show less favorable treatment, it is necessary to determine whether the difference in treatment also modifies the conditions of competition to the detriment of the foreign services or service suppliers.[242]

Under Article 11 of Directives 2009/72/EC and 2009/73EC, foreign service suppliers are subject to the additional 'security of supply' test. In *Thailand – Cigarettes (Philippines)*, the Appellate Body held that 'the mere fact that the additional administrative requirements are imposed on imported cigarettes, and not on like domestic cigarettes, provides, in itself, a significant indication that the conditions of competition are adversely modified to the detriment of imported cigarettes'.[243] Relying on this statement, the Panel in *Argentina – Financial Services* ruled that a rebuttable legal presumption applicable to the entry of funds from certain jurisdictions constituted an 'additional requirement', which, in its view, amounted to less favorable treatment in the area of trade in services.[244]

The security of supply test clearly creates an additional administrative burden for foreign service suppliers: They have the burden of proof to show that granting certification will not put at risk the security of energy supply of the Member State and the European Union.[245] Therefore, the third-country certification procedure contained in Article 11 of Directives 2009/72/EC and 2009/73/EC modifies the conditions of competition to the detriment of foreign service suppliers,[246] and thus constitutes *de jure* discrimination in violation of Article XVII GATS. Indeed, the

---

239 WTO, *Korea – Measures Affecting Imports of Fresh, Chilled and Frozen Beef*, Report of the Panel (31 July 2000) WT/DS161/R, WT/DS169/R [627].

240 WTO, *Korea – Measures Affecting Imports of Fresh, Chilled and Frozen Beef*, Report of the Appellate Body (11 December 2000) WT/DS161/AB/R, WT/DS169/AB/R [137–138].

241 Krajewski and Engelke (n 194) [42].

242 *China – Certain Measures Affecting Electronic Payment Services* (n 97) [7.687]; *China – Measures Affecting Trading Rights and Distribution Services for Certain Publications and Audiovisual Entertainment Products* (n 19) [7.1130].

243 WTO, *Thailand – Customs and Fiscal Measures on Cigarettes from the Philippines*, Report of the Appellate Body (17 June 2011) WT/DS371/AB/R [138].

244 *Argentina – Measures Relating to Trade in Goods and Services* (n 7) [7.298–7.299] (the finding was made in the context of Article II:1 GATS).

245 European Commission, 'Commission Staff Working Paper – Interpretative Note on Directive 2009/72/EC concerning common Rules for the Internal Market in Electricity and Directive 2009/73/EC concerning common Rules for the Internal Market in Natural Gas – The Unbundling Regime' (22 January 2010) 23 <https://ec.europa.eu/energy/sites/ener/files/documents/2010_01_21_the_unbundling_regime.pdf> accessed 24 September 2016.

246 Cottier, Matteotti-Berkutova and Nartova (n 88) 279; Waloszyk (n 186) 70–71; Boute (n 88) [3.63].

third-country certification procedure was scheduled as a NT limitation in several preferential trade agreements concluded by the EU.[247]

It should be recalled at this point that the European Union, as a WTO Member in its own right, has not undertaken any specific commitments on energy transmission services.[248] The additional security of supply requirement does not, therefore, violate the EU's own obligations under WTO law.[249] In contrast, several EU Member States have included services related to energy transmission in their self-standing schedules of specific commitments. These Member States thus may be acting inconsistently with their WTO obligations, which would also have indirect spillover effects on the EU itself, given that the respective Member States would be torn between conflicting obligations under EU law on the one hand, and WTO law on the other. However, it will be shown below that the violation of Article XVII GATS can be justified under the GATS exception provisions, thus obviating this dilemma.[250]

4.6.2.2 Individual Ownership Unbundling Exemption Decisions

The next potential inconsistency with the GATS national treatment obligation relates to the possibility to apply for an exemption from the ownership unbundling rules under Article 36 of Directive 2009/73/EC or Article 17 of Regulation 714/2009. The OU exemption regime under the TEP allows third-country energy production/generation or supply companies to build and operate new gas or electricity transmission lines in accordance with their commercial needs. Conversely, the denial of an individual exemption application can lead to significant economic losses if existing interconnection capacity is lacking or inadequate and if the failure to execute the planned transmission project leads to the consequence that energy cannot be supplied and sold.

Against this background, the question arises whether the individual ownership unbundling exemption decisions can be challenged on the grounds that they violate the national treatment provision in Article XVII GATS. Although the exemption rules do not formally discriminate between foreign and domestic service suppliers, there could be a situation of *de facto* discrimination. Consider the following scenario: A foreign-owned energy company applies for an exemption from ownership unbundling with respect to a planned transmission project. The relevant national regulatory authority rejects the application. If other applications for exemption filed

[247]See, for example, Association Agreement between the European Union and the European Atomic Energy Community and their Member States, of the one part, and the Republic of Moldova, of the other part (27 June 2014) OJ 2014/L 260/4, 349; Association Agreement between the European Union and the European Atomic Energy Community and their Member States, of the one part, and Georgia, of the other part (27 June 2014) OJ 2014/L 261/4, 215.

[248]See Sect. 4.4.

[249]This is highlighted by Cottier, Matteotti-Berkutova and Nartova (n 88) 279; Boute (n 88) [3.63].

[250]See on this Sect. 4.9.

by domestic energy companies have been fully granted in the past, does this amount to a violation of the national treatment principle in Article XVII GATS?

In principle, individual administrative decisions—qualifying as 'measures' affecting trade in services[251]—fall within the scope of the GATS and are thus subject to its provisions that prohibit discrimination. In *Canada – Administration of the Foreign Investment Review Act*, the GATT Panel stated that in determining whether a given measure is contrary to the NT obligation with respect to trade in goods, 'it is not relevant whether it applies across-the-board or only in isolated cases.'[252] Furthermore, it noted that '[a]ny interpretation which would exclude case-by-case action would ... defeat the purposes of Article III:4 [GATT]'.[253] Arguably, the same holds true for the national treatment principle in the GATS. However, in order to be able to apply the GATS non-discrimination disciplines to individual administrative decisions, there must necessarily be a domestic basis for comparison. It would thus seem to be required that an exemption decision which is directed against a third country applicant company also affects one or more other domestic companies. This is not directly obvious here, as there is no limit on the number of exemption decisions under Article 36 of Directive 2009/73/EC and Article 17 of Regulation 714/2009. It could, however, be argued that a decision whereby an exemption is denied to an applicant indirectly affects those commercial energy companies that have been granted 'regulatory holidays', due to the fact that the latter are protected from increased competition on the supply side.[254] Viewed in this light, it is thus possible to identify a domestic basis for comparison. The main question then is how the 'less favorable treatment' standard under Article XVII GATS operates in such circumstances.

In the GATT context, there have been a number of Panel reports which seem to have proceeded from the assumption that if *one* imported product receives less favorable treatment than *any* like domestic product, *de facto* discrimination exists.[255] One case in point is *EC – Asbestos*.[256] The *EC – Asbestos* Panel was faced with a French measure that banned asbestos and products containing asbestos. Canada alleged that the measure favored substitutes for asbestos, such as PVA, cellulose and glass fibres, and thereby violated Article III:4 GATT. As a first step, the Panel concluded that asbestos, on the one hand, and PVA, cellulose and glass fibres, on the

---

[251] Article XXVIII(a) GATS (n 4) provides that the term 'measure' includes decisions and administrative action.

[252] GATT, *Canada – Administration of the Foreign Investment Review Act*, Panel Report (7 February 1984) [5.5].

[253] Ibid.

[254] See De Meester (n 126) 233–234.

[255] Lothar Ehring, 'De Facto Discrimination in World Trade Law: National and Most-Favoured-Nation Treatment – or Equal Treatment?' (2002) 36 Journal of World Trade 921, 940–943, 948; Ole K Fauchald, *Environmental Taxes and Trade Discrimination* (International Environmental Law & Policy Series vol 50, Kluwer Law International 1998) 220–224.

[256] WTO, *European Communities – Measures Affecting Asbestos and Asbestos-Containing Products*, Report of the Panel (18 September 2000) WT/DS135/R.

other hand, were 'like products' within the meaning of Article III:4 GATT.[257] Then, in a second step, the Panel held that the French asbestos ban resulted in 'less favorable treatment' and thus violated the national treatment obligation. Crucially, its finding of less favorable treatment was based on the simple fact that the French decree treated imported asbestos products less favorably than the like domestic substitute products. In other words, it was sufficient for the Panel that *some* asbestos products imported from Canada were subject to the ban and that *some* asbestos substitute products of French origin were not.[258] The Panel did not inquire whether there was a heavier overall burden on the entire group of imports as compared to the entire group of like domestic products.

Another case in point is *Canada – Periodicals*.[259] In that case, the Panel was faced with an alleged breach of Article III:2 GATT. Canada had levied an 80% tax on the advertising revenues from so-called 'split-run' periodicals, i.e. periodicals that are issued in other countries with the same, or substantially the same, editorial material. According to the Panel, such (imported) 'split-run' periodicals and (domestic) non-'split-run' periodicals would be 'like'. As regards the decisive issue of less favorable treatment, Canada argued that the taxation of imported products in excess of like domestic products should be determined 'in terms of classes of products' and that 'isolated instances of differential taxation' would be irrelevant for the purposes of Article III:2 GATT.[260] The Panel, however, stated baldly that imported split-run periodicals were subject to an internal tax in excess of that applied to domestic non split-run periodicals, and that this amounted to a violation of Article III:2 GATT.[261] Therefore, like in *EC – Asbestos* the Panel did not assess whether the imported products 'as a class' were taxed in excess of the like domestic products 'as a class'.[262]

The way in which the Panels in *EC – Asbestos* and *Canada – Periodicals* applied the national treatment obligations in Articles III:2 and III:4 GATT has been dubbed by Ehring as the 'diagonal test'.[263] Under this test, once likeness has been established, the national treatment obligation is violated if some imported products fall into the disfavored regulatory category and some like domestic products receive the more favorable treatment. Clearly the diagonal test comprises a very broad construction of the national treatment standard. Indeed, applying the NT principle

---

[257]Ibid [8.144, 8.150].

[258]*European Communities – Measures Affecting Asbestos and Asbestos-Containing Products* (n 256) [8.154–8.157]; Ehring (n 255) 942–943.

[259]WTO, *Canada – Certain Measures concerning Periodicals*, Report of the Panel (14 March 1997) WT/DS31/R.

[260]Ibid [3.101–3.103].

[261]*Canada – Certain Measures concerning Periodicals* (n 259) [5.28, 5.30]; Ehring (n 255) 941.

[262]The Panel report in *United States – Malt Beverages* contains similar reasoning, see GATT, *United States – Measures Affecting Alcoholic and Malt Beverages*, Report of the Panel (19 June 1992) DS23/R – 39S/206 [5.19].

[263]Ehring (n 255) 924.

'to the relationship between each individual imported product and any like domestic product'[264] would greatly enhance the liberalizing effect of the national treatment obligation. Transferring this approach to the GATS context, it would mean that less favorable treatment of just one foreign service supplier vis-à-vis one like domestic service supplier amounts to *de facto* discrimination in violation of Article XVII GATS, which would need to be justified under the exception provisions.

On the basis of such an understanding of Article XVII GATS, individual exemption decisions under Article 36 of Directive 2009/73/EC and Article 17 of Regulation 714/2009 could easily be challenged. In a situation where, in the past, energy companies from the EU have been granted an exemption from the obligation of ownership unbundling (see for instance the case of the 'Gazelle' interconnector[265]), the refusal of an exemption request lodged by an energy company of non-EU origin would be a breach Article XVII GATS.

Under the 'diagonal test' described above, the national treatment principle in Article XVII GATS would come very close to the 'non-hindrance' test developed by the ECJ in the context of the fundamental freedoms.[266] As already noted in the discussion of the GATS market access obligation, the non-hindrance approach in EU law has fully 'emancipated' itself from the principle of non-discrimination. With respect to the freedom of establishment (which is the counterpart to services provided through mode 3 of the GATS), the ECJ held that a measure violates Article 49 TFEU 'where that measure, *even though it is applicable without discrimination on grounds of nationality, is liable to hamper or to render less attractive* the exercise by Community nationals . . . of fundamental freedoms guaranteed by the Treaty.'[267] It must be recalled that it was on this basis that the ECJ in *Staat der Nederlanden v Essent NV and Others* found that the Dutch ownership unbundling measures in the energy distribution sector constitute restrictions on the free movement of capital.[268]

However, equating the national treatment principle in Article XVII GATS with the diagonal test produces a number of major difficulties. The first difficulty concerns the balance between the scope of Article XVII GATS and the scope of the general exceptions contained in Article XIV GATS. It is undisputed that a broad reading of Article XVII GATS is only possible if it is complemented by a flexible catalogue of policy grounds on the basis of which otherwise violative measures can be justified.[269] Mandatory or imperative requirements, which have a prominent place in EU law, are however alien to WTO law. What could have become a functional

[264]Fauchald (n 255) 221.

[265]European Commission, Commission Decision on the exemption of the "Gazelle" interconnector from ownership unbundling within the meaning of Article 9 of Directive 2009/73/EC (01 December 2011) C(2011) 8777 final.

[266]Diebold (n 192) 41.

[267]*Kraus v Land Baden-Württemberg* (n 128) [32] (emphasis added).

[268]*Staat der Nederlanden v Essent NV and Others* (n 131) [39–47].

[269]Verhoosel (n 218) 93 states that 'once a measure is considered discriminatory because it causes adverse effects unnecessary to achieve the regulatory objective, exhaustive lists do not work any longer'. See also Piet Eeckhout, 'Constitutional Concepts for Free Trade in Services' in Gráinne de

equivalent in WTO law of mandatory or imperative requirements is the so-called 'aims and effects' test.[270] The 'aims and effects' test, which is based on an interpretation of the words 'so as to afford protection' in Article III:1 GATT, would make it possible to take into account the regulatory purpose of a given measure, i.e. whether the measure has the aim of affording protection to domestic markets.[271] References to a measure's regulatory purpose first appeared in the GATT Panel reports in *United States – Measures Affecting Alcoholic and Malt Beverages* and *United States – Taxes on Automobiles*.[272] The Appellate Body, however, firmly rejected the 'aims and effects' test in *Japan – Alcoholic Beverages II* (with respect to trade in goods)[273] and in *EC – Bananas III* (with respect to trade in services).[274] In 2016 the Appellate Body confirmed, in *Argentina – Financial Services*, that the concept of 'treatment no less favorable' under both the NT and MFN provisions of the GATS 'does not contemplate a separate and additional inquiry into the regulatory objective of, or the regulatory concerns underlying, the contested measure.'[275]

Consequently, under the GATS measures can only be justified on the basis of Article XIV GATS, which features a *closed* list of legitimate public policy objectives and which is rather limited in nature.[276] Against this background, adopting an extensive interpretation of the national treatment principle would threaten a broad range of regulatory instruments. In the case of the ownership unbundling exemption regime this would produce absurd results. Under the diagonal approach to national treatment, once a single domestic service supplier is granted an exemption from ownership unbundling, *all* foreign service suppliers would have a *right*, from that point in time onwards, to be exempted from the application of the OU requirements. In such a case the whole exemption regime under Article 36 of Directive 2009/73/EC and Article 17 of Regulation 714/2009 would thus be rendered patently unworkable.

Búrca and Joanne Scott (eds), *The EU and the WTO: Legal and Constitutional Issues* (Hart Publishing 2001) 232–233; Krajewski (n 36) 110.

[270]For an overview, see Robert E Hudec, 'GATT/WTO Constraints on National Regulation: Requiem for an "Aim and Effects" Test' (1998) 32 The International Lawyer 619; Diebold (n 192) 75–80; Munin (n 140) 177–178; van den Bossche and Zdouc (n 71) 366–367, 392–393.

[271]Note that the 'aims and effects' test has its origin in the likeness analysis under Article III:2 GATT. The 'aims and effects' of a measure can, however, also be considered as part of the analysis of 'treatment no less favourable', see Cossy (n 191) 347–348.

[272]*United States – Measures Affecting Alcoholic and Malt Beverages* (n 262) [5.23–5.26, 5.70–5.77]; GATT, *United States – Taxes on Automobiles*, Report of the Panel (11 October 1994) DS31/R (unadopted) [5.10].

[273]WTO, *Japan – Taxes on Alcoholic Beverages*, Report of the Appellate Body (4 October 1996) WT/DS8/AB/R, WT/DS10/AB/R, WT/DS11/AB/R, Sections G and H.

[274]*European Communities – Regime for the Importation, Sale and Distribution of Bananas* (n 3) [215–216, 240–248].

[275]*Argentina – Measures Relating to Trade in Goods and Services* (n 199) [6.106].

[276]Krajewski (n 36) 160–161.

The second difficulty associated with the broad approach to *de facto* discrimination relates to the relationship between Article XVII and Article VI:4 GATS.[277] Article VI:4 GATS stipulates that negotiations shall be conducted with a view to developing disciplines for domestic regulation. These disciplines shall ensure, *inter alia*, that measures relating to qualification requirements and procedures, technical standards, and licensing requirements are not more burdensome than necessary to ensure the quality of the service. If *de facto* discrimination under Article XVII GATS would cover all situations where one foreign service supplier is treated less favorably than any like domestic service supplier, the development of future disciplines on domestic regulation would become largely futile.[278]

Apart from the fact that the diagonal test is at odds with the overall structure of the GATS, there is also considerable authority militating in favor of a different understanding of the national treatment principle under GATT and GATS. In particular, the Appellate Body in *EC – Asbestos* indicated that the Panel had wrongly interpreted the 'less favorable treatment' requirement by applying the diagonal approach. It pointed out, in *obiter dictum*, that 'less favorable treatment' within the meaning of Article III:4 GATT would require that the measure at stake 'accords to the *group* of "like" *imported* products "less favourable treatment" than it accords to the *group* of "like" *domestic* products.'[279] The Appellate Body's pronouncement shows that it would be insufficient to merely state that one imported product is adversely affected by the national measure at issue and that one domestic product is favored by it.[280] Rather, by making reference to the *group* of imported products and the *group* of like domestic products, the Appellate Body called for an examination of the *overall* impact on imported and like domestic products, with both examined *as a whole*.

In the academic writing this approach has been referred to as the 'asymmetric impact test'.[281] Commentators take the view that the reasoning of the Appellate Body in *EC – Asbestos*, made with respect to the national treatment principle in Article III:4 GATT, can be transposed to the sphere of trade in services, in particular to Article XVII GATS.[282] Accordingly, a situation wherein an individual foreign service supplier is accorded less advantageous treatment compared to any like

[277]Ibid 111–112.

[278]Ibid 112.

[279]*European Communities – Measures Affecting Asbestos and Asbestos-Containing Products* (n 207) [100] (emphasis in the original retained; emphasis added).

[280]Jochem Wiers and James Mathis, 'The Report of the Appellate Body in the Asbestos Dispute: WTO Appellate Body Report 12 March 2001, WT/DS135/AB/R, European Communities – Measures Affecting Asbestos and Asbestos-containing Products' (2001) 28 Legal Issues of Economic Integration 211, 222–223; Federico Ortino, 'The Principle of Non-Discrimination and its Exceptions in GATS: Selected Legal Issues' in Kern Alexander and Mads Andenas (eds), *The World Trade Organization and Trade in Services* (Martinus Nijhoff Publishers 2008) 181–182.

[281]Ehring (n 255) 924–925.

[282]Munin (n 140) 159; Krajewski and Engelke (n 194) [44]; De Meester and Coppens (n 126) 121–122.

domestic service supplier does not automatically constitute a violation of Article XVII GATS.[283]

This interpretation is also in line with the fact that the 'no less favorable treatment' standard is intimately linked to the concept of 'conditions of competition' between like services and like service suppliers. Article XVII:3 GATS provides, and the WTO dispute settlement jurisprudence has confirmed,[284] that there is less favorable treatment only if a measure modifies the conditions of competition to the detriment of foreign services or service suppliers. This notion of 'conditions of competition', which reflects the overall character of WTO law as an exchange of trade opportunities between States,[285] is not concerned with protecting individual service transactions or individual service suppliers. As DiMascio and Pauwelyn have stated in the context of Article III:4 GATT, '[b]ecause trade law's goal is to increase liberalization and market access for imports in the interest of overall welfare, *not to guarantee rights or trade flows to individual exporters ...*, national treatment in GATT is focused upon equalizing the *competitive opportunities* of imports as compared to domestic products.'[286]

Inasmuch as the 'no less favorable treatment' standard under Article XVII GATS must be applied in accordance with the 'asymmetric impact test', the GATS national treatment obligation cannot be usefully applied to individual administrative decisions. In such cases the favored or the disfavored group will invariably consist of only one service supplier, which prevents a meaningful comparison between groups.[287] This is also the case for individual ownership unbundling exemption decisions. Here, the disfavored group is composed of only one entity, namely the third country service supplier whose application under Article 36 of Directive 2009/73/EC or Article 17 of Regulation 714/2009 was denied. In principle, therefore, it is impossible to challenge individual OU exemption decisions on the basis of Article XVII GATS.

The only way whereby Article XVII GATS can conceivably be applied to a specific decision on an exemption request is if the complainant in a WTO dispute can demonstrate the existence of a protectionist intent.[288] In other words, it must show

[283]Krajewski and Engelke (n 194) [44]; Karl Sidhu, *Die Regelung von Direktinvestitionen in der WTO: Das TRIMs-Abkommen und das GATS* (Schriften zum europäischen und internationalen Recht vol 12, V & R unipress 2004) 256.

[284]*Argentina – Measures Relating to Trade in Goods and Services* (n 199) [6.106].

[285]Nicholas DiMascio and Joost Pauwelyn, 'Nondiscrimination in Trade and Investment Treaties: Worlds Apart or Two Sides of the Same Coin?' (2008) 102 American Journal of International Law 48, 54, 61–62.

[286]Ibid 61–62 (emphasis added).

[287]De Meester (n 126) 233–234.

[288]Claus-Dieter Ehlermann and Lothar Ehring, 'WTO Dispute Settlement and Competition Law: Views from the Perspective of the Appellate Body's Experience' (2002) 26 Fordham International Law Journal 1505, 1529; De Meester (n 126) 234–235; Bart De Meester, 'The Global Financial Crisis and Government Support for Banks: What Role for the GATS?' (2010) 13 Journal of International Economic Law 27, 51.

that the less advantageous treatment was based on the foreign origin of the particular service supplier. In practice this will be difficult to accomplish. Protectionist motives could be said to exist if the European Commission, in a specific exemption decision concerning a third-country energy company, significantly deviates from its prior decision-making practice without giving any explanation therefore. The same could be assumed if the Commission applies certain provisions in a manifestly unreasonable manner.

However, it must be kept in mind that a determination that the treatment accorded by a particular exemption decision is based on origin necessarily implies a measure of subjectivity on the part of the respective Panel.[289] Therefore it can be expected that in the absence of tangible evidence, the WTO dispute settlement bodies will be extremely reluctant to find that an individual exemption decision violated the national treatment principle in Article XVII GATS. This reluctance will be even higher if the factual issues involved are highly complex and if the relevant provisions are open to several interpretations, all of which are reasonable and rational, and thus equally 'correct'. This applies generally to the ownership unbundling exemption procedure. The requirements of 'enhancing competition in gas/electricity supply' and 'enhancing security of supply', for example, are broad and flexible notions, which translate into a considerable margin of discretion on the part of the national regulatory authorities and the European Commission.[290] This means that, first of all, the exemption criteria are to some extent susceptible to a politically motivated application, and second that it is particularly difficult for the WTO dispute settlement bodies to determine whether a particular exemption decision had an underlying protectionist objective. To conclude, there has been no exemption decision rendered to date under the Third Energy Package[291] in which a discriminatory intent could be inferred so as to result in a violation of Article XVII GATS.[292]

---

[289]De Meester (n 126) 235.

[290]Katja Yafimava, *The Transit Dimension of EU Energy Security: Russian Gas Transit Across Ukraine, Belarus, and Moldova* (Oxford University Press 2011) 127. See also Jürgen F Baur, 'Ausschließliche Nutzungsrechte an bestimmten Großinvestitionen im Gas- und im Elektrizitätsbereich' in Jürgen F Baur and others (eds), *Festschrift für Gunther Kühne zum 70. Geburtstag* (Verlag Recht und Wirtschaft 2009) 70–71; Katja Yafimava, 'Transit: The EU Energy Acquis and the Energy Charter Treaty' in Kim Talus (ed), *Research Handbook on International Energy Law* (Research Handbooks in International Law. Edward Elgar 2014) 606. The discretion on the part of NRAs and the European Commission is also criticized by the Russian Federation, see *European Union and its Member States – Certain Measures Relating to the Energy Sector* (n 87) 4; Trade Policy Review – European Union (n 87) 313.

[291]Or, for that matter, under the TPA-related exemption regime in the Second Energy Package.

[292]See also in this connection the decision-making practice concerning the notion of 'interconnector' in the Gas Directive in Sect. 4.8.1.1.

4.6.2.3 The Ownership Unbundling Exemption Regime

Although it was shown in the preceding sub-section that individual ownership unbundling exemption decisions that accord less advantageous treatment to a particular service or service supplier cannot, without more, lead to a finding of 'less favorable treatment' within the meaning of the GATS national treatment obligation, the question still remains whether the OU exemption regime as a whole is consistent with Article XVII GATS.[293]

The general conditions under which an infrastructure project can be exempted from the ownership unbundling requirements (and TPA provisions) are clearly set out in Article 36(1) of Directive 2009/73/EC and Article 17(1) of Regulation 714/2009: status as an 'interconnector'; enhancement of competition in supply; enhancement of security of supply [gas only]; level of risk; basic unbundling; levy of charges; no recovery of capital or operating costs [electricity only]; and the exemption's effect on competition.[294] Judging from the design, structure and expected operation, none of these criteria suggest that the conditions of competition are modified to the detriment of foreign service suppliers. Accordingly, taken at face value there is no indication of less favorable treatment.

Having said that, any evidence regarding the actual effects of the contested measure also has to be taken into account.[295] If, in practice, foreign services or service suppliers are disproportionately disadvantaged, i.e. subject to an 'asymmetric impact', that would be evidence of less favorable treatment.[296] A good example in this regard is *EC – Bananas III*. In that case, Ecuador, Guatemala, Honduras, Mexico and the United States alleged, *inter alia*, that the EU's licensing system for the importation of bananas from certain ACP (African, Caribbean and Pacific) States, which were not traditional suppliers of the EU, and from other third countries violated Article XVII GATS. The EU licensing system differentiated between operators, i.e. wholesale traders of bananas, on the basis of the quantities of bananas marketed during the most recent 3-year period for which data was available. Operators would be classified as 'category A' if they had marketed bananas from third countries and/or from ACP countries which were not traditional suppliers of the EU. 'Category B' was comprised of operators which had marketed bananas from the EU or from ACP countries, which were traditional suppliers of the EU. Category A operators were allocated 66.5% of the import licenses for the importation of third-country and non-traditional ACP bananas at in-quota rates, whereas category B operators were allocated 30% of such import licenses. It is important to note that

---

[293]Some authors have suggested that the infrastructure-related exemption regime is discriminatory; see, for example, Ivan Gudkov, 'Газовый диалог России и ЕС: взаимодействие и конфликт международного и европейского права' [2014] Научный журнал Российского газового общества 49, 53.

[294]Article 36(1)(a)–(e) of Directive 2009/73/EC (n 8); Article 17(1)(a)–(f) of Regulation (EC) No 714/2009 (n 10).

[295]*Thailand – Customs and Fiscal Measures on Cigarettes from the Philippines* (n 243) [134].

[296]Ortino (n 280) 185–186.

the differential treatment under the EU's licensing system was based on the origin of the bananas and not of the service suppliers. Therefore, there clearly was no formal discrimination against the complainants' wholesale traders of bananas.[297] However, with respect to *de facto* discrimination the Panel held (and the Appellate Body confirmed[298]) that:

> Under the EC rules, ... Category B operators are eligible for 30 per cent of the licences required for the importation of third-country (i.e., Latin American) and non-traditional ACP bananas at lower in-quota duty rates, regardless of whether they have previously traded in the latter market segment. Therefore, *most beneficiaries of this allocation to Category B operators are service suppliers of EC origin*. At the same time, *most Category A operators, who historically traded third-country and non-traditional ACP bananas but who are eligible to receive only 66.5 per cent of the licences allowing in-quota imports of bananas from these sources, are service suppliers of third-country origin*. Furthermore, we also note that there is no allocation of an EC/ACP market share for Category A operators equivalent to the allocation of 30 per cent of the third-country and non-traditional ACP import licences to Category B operators. Thus, at first sight it appears that the operator category rules would seem to modify conditions of competition in the EC wholesale services market for bananas in favour of service suppliers of EC origin.[299]

The Panel thus ruled that the EU's licensing system for the importation of bananas *de facto* discriminated against the service suppliers of the complaining WTO Members, in violation of Article XVII GATS. It did so on the basis of its observation that (1) the licensing system favored category B and disfavored category A operators; and that (2) most of the beneficiaries were EU service suppliers and most of the disfavored operators were third-country service suppliers. In a nutshell, the Panel found a violation because the EU banana regulations predominantly disadvantaged foreign service suppliers.[300]

It follows from *EC – Bananas III* dispute that the ownership unbundling regime under the TEP would be inconsistent with Article XVII GATS if the exemption practice demonstrated that there is an asymmetric impact on foreign energy service suppliers. As discussed,[301] the asymmetric impact test requires a comparison of the group of foreign service suppliers vis-à-vis the group of like domestic service suppliers, both taken as a whole, against the background of the relevant regulatory distinction. *In casu*, the category of favored service suppliers would consist of energy companies that have received an exemption, and the group of disfavored service suppliers would be composed of companies whose application request has been rejected.

---

[297] *European Communities – Regime for the Importation, Sale and Distribution of Bananas* (n 5) [7.324].

[298] *European Communities – Regime for the Importation, Sale and Distribution of Bananas* (n 3) [244].

[299] *European Communities – Regime for the Importation, Sale and Distribution of Bananas* (n 5) [7.335] (emphasis added).

[300] Ortino (n 280) 179.

[301] See footnotes 279–281 (this chapter) and accompanying text.

	Domestic service suppliers	Like foreign service suppliers
Advantageous treatment	○○○	-
Less advantageous treatment	-	-

Fig. 4.1 *De facto* discrimination in a situation with '*de facto* exclusivity'

In the first instance the exemption regime under Article 17(1) Electricity Regulation is considered here. It has already been mentioned that in the electricity sector there has been no exemption decision or request with a 'third country dimension'.[302] In other words, third country service suppliers have not yet applied for an exemption and no exemption request has been either denied or granted which would have affected foreign services or service suppliers. In contrast, exemptions have been given to EU energy companies (ElecLink[303] and the Italian-Slovenian interconnectors[304]). How then does the 'less favorable treatment' standard operate in such circumstances? Is there an 'asymmetric impact'? Figure 4.1 presents the situation in the abstract.

Although all of the favored operators are domestic service suppliers, this cannot support a finding that foreign services or service suppliers are treated less favorably. The fact that the existing exemptions exclusively favor economic operators of EU origin cannot be attributed to the eligibility criteria of the exemption regime, but results from the initiative, or rather the lack thereof, of private market actors. The national treatment obligation under Article XVII GATS does not, however, deal with competitive advantages or disadvantages of services or service suppliers which are not the result of any governmental measure.

In the context of the NT principle in the GATT, the Appellate Body therefore requires a 'genuine relationship' between the adverse impact on competitive opportunities and the measure in issue.[305] The requirement of a 'genuine relationship' is supposed to ensure that the detrimental impact on the conditions of competition in

[302]See Sect. 2.3.3.2.

[303]European Commission, Commission Decision on the exemption of ElecLink Limited under Article 17 of Regulation (EC) No. 714/2009 for an electricity interconnector between France and Great Britain (28 July 2014) C(2014) 5475 final.

[304]European Commission, Commission Decision on the exemption of Adria Link s.r.l. (Italy), Holding Slovenske Elektrarne d.o.o. (Slovenia) and E3 d.o.o. (Slovenia) under Article 17 of Regulation (EC) No. 714/2009 for two electricity interconnectors between Italy and Slovenia (17 December 2014) C(2014) 9904 final.

[305]WTO, *European Communities – Measures Prohibiting the Importation and Marketing of Seal Products,* Reports of the Appellate Body (22 May 2014) WT/DS400/AB/R, WT/DS401/AB/R [5.101] (with further references).

fact results from the governmental measure in issue. In *EC – Seal Products*, the Appellate Body inquired whether there was a 'genuine relationship' between the *de facto* exclusivity of an exemption for indigenous communities, which only indigenous communities from Greenland had used, and the EU Seal Regime, which otherwise prohibited the importation and placing on the market of seal products. The Appellate Body stated that 'if the current *de facto* exclusivity of the [indigenous communities] exception could be attributed *entirely* to private choice, there would be no "genuine relationship" between this exclusivity and the EU Seal Regime,' and that the non-discrimination obligations in the WTO agreements 'are only concerned with ... *governmental* intervention'.[306] Similarly, in quoting a passage from the *Korea – Various Measures on Beef* case, the Appellate Body in *US – COOL* stated that 'changes in the competitive conditions in a marketplace that are "*not* imposed directly or indirectly by law or governmental regulation, but [are] rather solely the result of private entrepreneurs acting on their own calculations of comparative costs and benefits", cannot be the basis for a finding that a measure treats imported products less favourably than domestic like products'.[307] The rationale of these judgments can also be applied to the sphere of trade in services.[308] Accordingly, the ownership unbundling exemption regime of Regulation 714/2009 cannot be found *de facto* discriminatory merely because foreign service suppliers have not yet taken advantage of it.

Now the exemption regime under Article 36(1) Gas Directive must be assessed.[309] In 2013 the European Commission approved an OU exemption for the Trans Adriatic Pipeline project, which is supposed to transport Azeri gas to Europe.[310] The relevant project company was a foreign service supplier within the meaning of the GATS. As regards domestic service suppliers, two OU exemptions have so far been granted, to the Gazelle pipeline[311] and the SK-HU Interconnector.[312] No exemption request by either a domestic or foreign service supplier has been denied. Consequently, the existing exemptions under Directive 2009/73/EC benefit both domestic and third country services and service suppliers.

---

[306]See ibid [5.336] (emphasis in the original). The Appellate Body made these statements in applying the chapeau of Article XX GATT.

[307]WTO, *United States – Certain Country of Origin Labelling (COOL) Requirements*, Reports of the Appellate Body (29 June 2012) WT/DS384/AB/R, WT/DS386/AB/R [270] (citing *Korea – Measures Affecting Imports of Fresh, Chilled and Frozen Beef* (n 240) [149]).

[308]See also Ortino (n 280) 186.

[309]Exemptions for LNG terminals and gas storage facilities are excluded from the analysis.

[310]See European Commission, Commission Decision on the exemption of the Trans Adriatic Pipeline from the requirements on third party access, tariff regulation and ownership unbundling laid down in Articles 9, 32, 41(6), 41(8) and 41(10) of Directive 2009/73/EC (16 May 2013) C (2013) 2949 final.

[311]Commission Decision – Exemption of the Gazelle interconnector (n 265).

[312]European Commission, Commission Decision on the exemption of the Slovakian-Hungarian natural gas interconnector from ownership unbundling rules in Article 9 of Directive 2009/73/EC (17 September 2013) C(2013) 6159 final.

	Domestic service suppliers	Like foreign service suppliers
Advantageous treatment	○○	○
Less advantageous treatment	-	○

Fig. 4.2 *De facto* discrimination in a situation with only a few economic operators

There is thus no asymmetric impact to the detriment of foreign services or service suppliers. However, the question arises whether this assessment would change if, *ceteris paribus*, a third country energy company applied for an exemption and the request was not approved by the relevant national regulatory authority. Following the logic of *EC – Bananas III*, it could be argued that, technically speaking, there is an 'asymmetric impact' considering that 'most' of the beneficiaries of exemptions are EU service suppliers (two domestic projects v. one foreign) while 'most' of the disfavored operators are of third country origin (one foreign project v. zero domestic) and that, consequently, the exemption regime violates Article XVII GATS. Figure 4.2 provides a general illustration of this hypothetical, but nevertheless possible, scenario.

Although a finding of an asymmetric impact, once found to exist, cannot be 'explained away' by reference to certain legitimate factors,[313] the fundamental problem in applying Article XVII GATS in such a situation is that the number of affected service suppliers is too small to establish 'less favorable treatment' within the meaning of that provision. In my opinion, the GATS national treatment obligation cannot be usefully applied in such a factual setting. A certain threshold number of affected service suppliers is needed in order for the 'asymmetric impact test' to work properly, because otherwise there are insufficient grounds to conclude that the *conditions of competition* have been modified to the detriment of foreign service suppliers and that, therefore, there is discrimination *based on origin*.[314]

Thus, based on the existing exemption practice under the Third Energy Package there has been no asymmetric impact to the detriment of foreign services or service suppliers and thus no *de facto* discrimination under Article XVII GATS. Furthermore, even if an exemption request of a third country company is rejected in the future, this would not automatically translate into an 'asymmetric impact' and

[313] *Argentina – Measures Relating to Trade in Goods and Services* (n 199) [6.106]; *European Communities – Measures Prohibiting the Importation and Marketing of Seal Products* (n 305) [5.117].

[314] The non-discrimination disciplines in GATT and GATS are, ultimately, about discrimination *based on origin*; see Joost Pauwelyn, 'Comment: The Unbearable Lightness of Likeness' in Marion Panizzon, Nicole Pohl and Pierre Sauvé (eds), *GATS and the Regulation of International Trade in Services* (Cambridge University Press 2008).

therefore not lead to a finding of 'less favorable treatment', irrespective of whether there has also been a denial of a request by a domestic service supplier. Only if the number of service suppliers of both domestic and foreign origin which are affected by approval and rejection decisions reaches a certain threshold will it be possible to apply the 'asymmetric impact' test in a way that allows the WTO dispute settlement bodies to draw conclusions about the underlying conditions of competition. In conclusion, it would be very difficult for a complainant to show that the OU exemption regime contained in Article 36(1) of Directive 2009/73/EC and Article 17(1) of Regulation 714/2009 violates the GATS national treatment obligation.

4.6.2.4 Special Ownership Unbundling Requirements for Public Companies

The ownership unbundling regime in the TEP could be found to be discriminatory in terms of Article XVII GATS because the OU rules applicable to (domestic) State-owned TSOs and commercial energy companies are different from the OU rules applicable to (foreign) privately-owned TSOs and energy producers/generators or suppliers.[315] It will be recalled that according to Article 9(6) of Directives 2009/72/EC and 2009/73/EC, the State can remain in control of both a TSO or a transmission system and, at the same time, an undertaking performing any of the functions of generation/production or supply, provided that the two activities are actually controlled by 'two separate public bodies'. Therefore, in contrast to privately-owned VIUs subject to Article 9(1) of the Directives, the State is not under an obligation to divest either the generation/production or supply branch, or the transmission network. It is this formal difference in treatment between public and private companies that has been widely considered to violate the general principle of equality under EU law.[316]

The main issue that needs to be discussed in this regard in the context of the GATS is whether Article 9(6) of the Directives gives rise to less favorable treatment within the meaning of Article XVII GATS, i.e. whether the conditions of competition are modified to the detriment of foreign services or service suppliers. In general, all unbundling models, including the special unbundling option for public undertakings, are designed to ensure the separation of network activities from generation/production or supply activities.[317] In this way unbundling seeks to avoid discrimination, cross-subsidization and distortions of competition. Therefore the unbundling

[315] This argument is made by the Russian Federation, see *European Union and its Member States – Certain Measures Relating to the Energy Sector* (n 87) 2.

[316] See Sect. 3.3.

[317] With respect to Article 9(6) of the Directives, the Commission stated that 'the reason for the obligation to strictly separate the public bodies is to ensure independence with regard to transmission on the one hand and generation and supply on the other'; see European Commission, Commission Opinion pursuant to Article 3(1) of Regulation (EC) No 714/2009 and Article 10 (6) of Directive 2009/72/EC – the Netherlands – Certification of TenneT TSO B.V. (01 July 2013) C(2013) 4206 final, 4; European Commission, Commission Opinion pursuant to Article 3(1) of

rules aim to create a 'level playing field' and thus equality of conditions of competition among commercial energy companies and transmission system operators, respectively.

Against this background it would *prima facie* be implausible to argue that the different unbundling models, including Article 9(6) of the Directives, generate a competitive imbalance between the respective economic operators. At the same time, however, it is a matter of fact that the unbundling models provide different ways to ensure the independence of network operations. Whereas 'classic' ownership unbundling under Article 9(1) leads to an absolute structural separation of transmission activities and generation/production or supply interests, 'public' ownership unbundling under Article 9(6), despite being framed as a variant within the OU model, allows the State to control both transmission and generation/production or supply. The discrepancy between Article 9(1) and Article 9(6) is most visible in cases where the relevant EU Member State has prescribed mandatory ownership unbundling, i.e. to the exclusion of the ISO and ITO models.

It is nevertheless doubtful whether the possibility of 'vertical integration within the State' under Article 9(6) of the Directives modifies the conditions of competition in favor of the undertakings to which that provision applies. To begin with, it is important to point out that only the State is allowed to own and control both a TSO and a generation/production or supply undertaking. The public generation/production or supply undertaking itself cannot remain in control of a TSO (and *vice versa*). The State as an abstract entity, however, is not a 'service supplier' under the GATS.[318] It would thus be wrong to compare the Member State government, as a 'vertically integrated undertaking', with foreign private vertically integrated companies.[319] Rather, it is necessary to focus on the legal entities that actually supply the relevant energy services. Therefore, less favorable treatment could only be shown to exist if (1) foreign private providers of energy supply services are at a competitive disadvantage vis-à-vis domestic public ones; or, inversely, if (2) foreign private providers of transmission services are placed at a disadvantage, in competitive terms, vis-à-vis domestic public transmission service suppliers.

Regulation (EC) No 715/2009 and Article 10(6) of Directive 2009/73/EC – the Netherlands – Certification of Gas Transport Services B.V. (01 July 2013) C(2013) 4205 final, 4.

[318]According to Article XXVIII(g) GATS (n 4), a 'service supplier' is defined as 'any person that supplies a service', which includes natural and juridical persons (see lit (j)). A 'juridical person', in turn, means 'any legal entity duly constituted or otherwise organized under applicable law, whether for profit or otherwise, and whether privately-owned or governmentally-owned, including any corporation, trust, partnership, joint venture, sole proprietorship or association' (see lit (l)).

[319]But see *European Union and its Member States – Certain Measures Relating to the Energy Sector* (n 87) 2 (where the Russian Federation appears to frame the argument in precisely this way, stating that Article 9(6) of the Directives 'permits a Member State government to own and control both the TSO and the production or supply portions of the VIU, whereas third-country service suppliers, including those of Russia, may not' and that this measure is inconsistent with the obligations 'under GATS Article XVII to accord services and service suppliers of any other Member treatment no less favorable than they accord to their own like services and service suppliers').

Given that TSOs operate in a non-competitive, regulated environment, a modification of the conditions of competition would in practice manifest itself only in the production/generation or supply sector. In particular, the adverse treatment could consist of the fact that, in contrast to the public entities concerned, private commercial energy companies cannot benefit from collecting network access tariffs, because they are required to sell the transmission network.[320] While the TPA rules in the TEP provide that network access charges must generally be cost-reflective,[321] which means that TSOs are not able to generate monopoly rents, the collection of network access tariffs is still considered to be a profitable source of revenue. Notably, it appears that the return on revenues generated from the sale of the transmission system assets is generally lower than the network access tariffs.[322] However, even though the State acts as a 'vertically integrated undertaking' due to its control over both the public body owning the commercial energy company and the public body owning the TSO, the generation/production or supply undertaking itself will not be able to benefit from the collection of network access charges. The main reason for this is that direct financial flows between producers/generators or suppliers on the one hand, and transmission operators on the other, would clearly violate both the letter and spirit of the unbundling requirements, which require a true separation of the two public bodies concerned.[323]

In addition, every EU Member State must respect the State aid rules contained in Articles 107 and 108 of the TFEU. Article 107(1) TFEU declares that, except as otherwise provided, 'any aid granted by a Member State or through State resources in any form whatsoever which distorts or threatens to distort competition by favouring certain undertakings or the production of certain goods shall, in so far as it affects trade between Member States, be incompatible with the internal market.' The ECJ has repeatedly emphasized that actions by public undertakings established or appointed by a State are equally subject to the EU State aid rules. Therefore, in the determination of whether a given measure amounts to State aid, 'no distinction is to

---

[320]Christian Calliess, *Entflechtung im europäischen Energiebinnenmarkt: Zur Vereinbarkeit der europäischen Pläne für ein Ownership Unbundling mit der Kompetenzordnung des EG-Vertrages, insbesondere Art. 295 EGV, und dem allgemeinen Gleichheitssatz* (Bochumer Beiträge zum Berg- und Energierecht vol 50, Boorberg 2008) 113–114.

[321]Article 37(6)(a) in conjunction with 36th recital of the preamble to Directive 2009/72/EC (n 8); Article 41(6)(a) in conjunction with 32nd recital of the preamble to Directive 2009/73/EC (n 8). See also Article 14(1) of Regulation (EC) No 714/2009 (n 10); Article 13(1) of Regulation (EC) No 715/2009 of the European Parliament and of the Council on conditions for access to the natural gas transmission networks and repealing Regulation (EC) No 1775/2005 (13 July 2009) OJ 2009/L 211/36. For more details, see Floris Gräper and Christof Schoser, 'Third Party Access' in Christopher Jones (ed), *The Internal Energy Market – The Third Liberalisation Package* (EU Energy Law Series vol 1, 3rd edn. Claeys & Casteels Publishing 2010) [3.45ff].

[322]Calliess (n 320) 114.

[323]European Commission, 'Commission Staff Working Paper – Interpretative Note on Directive 2009/72/EC concerning common Rules for the Internal Market in Electricity and Directive 2009/73/EC concerning common Rules for the Internal Market in Natural Gas – The Unbundling Regime' (n 245) 10.

be drawn between cases where the aid is granted directly by the State and those where it is granted by public or private bodies which the State establishes or designates.'[324] Direct financial contributions on a regular basis from a public TSO to a public commercial energy undertaking would thus clearly constitute State aid within the meaning of Article 107(1) TFEU.[325] Thus it can be said by way of summary that public generation/production or supply undertakings cannot in any way benefit from the network access tariffs collected by public TSOs and that, in this respect, the possibility of 'vertical integration within the State' under Article 9(6) of the Directives does not modify the conditions of competition in favor of any domestic undertakings.

In addition to the above considerations which have been examined, the existence of less favorable treatment could also be based on the assertion that the OU model contained in Article 9(6) is overly lenient, lacks effectiveness, and in practice allows the public TSO to discriminate in favor of a public commercial energy company. After all, the mere fact that a TSO is publicly owned is no guarantee that no discrimination or distortions of competition will occur.[326] A tentative assessment of the effectiveness of unbundling under Article 9(6) of the Directives can be carried out by contrasting the 'Article 9(6) option' to the ITO model. Given that Article 9 (6) allows both transmission activities and generation/production or supply activities to be controlled by the same 'vertically integrated undertaking' (i.e. the State), the permissible ownership and control structures under that provision are very similar to the ITO model. For this reason, it would seem that the ITO model constitutes the appropriate yardstick for determining the effectiveness of the unbundling provision in Article 9(6).[327]

Due to the fact that vertical integration is allowed under both Article 9(6) and the ITO model, the risk that the independence of the TSO is compromised is equally high in both cases. It is precisely this risk that led the EU legislator to prescribe, in the case of the ITO model, an array of detailed rules designed to ensure the TSO's

---

[324]European Court of Justice, *French Republic v. Commission,* Judgment (16 May 2002) C-482/99 [23]. See also European Court of Justice, *Italy v. Commission,* Judgment (21 March 1991) C-305/ 89 [13].

[325]See also Eugene Cross and others, 'EU Energy Law' in Martha M Roggenkamp and others (eds), *Energy Law in Europe – National, EU and International Regulation* (2nd edn. Oxford University Press 2007) [5.129].

[326]Jürgen F Baur and others, *Eigentumsentflechtung der Energiewirtschaft durch Europarecht: Mittel, Schranken und Rechtsfolgen* (Veröffentlichungen des Instituts für Energierecht an der Universität zu Köln vol 138, Nomos 2008) 67–68; Jürgen F Baur, Kai U Pritzsche and Sebastian Pooschke, 'Ownership Unbundling von Energienetzen und der europäische Schutz des Eigentums' [2008] Deutsches Verwaltungsblatt 483, 492 (both referring to Monopolkommission, 'Strom und Gas 2007: Wettbewerbsdefizite und zögerliche Regulierung' (2007), Sondergutachten 49, [611], footnote 598); Franz J Säcker and Jochen Mohr, '§ 8 Eigentumsrechtliche Entflechtung' in Franz J Säcker (ed), *Berliner Kommentar zum Energierecht* (vol 1, 3rd edn. Dt. Fachverl. Fachmedien Recht und Wirtschaft 2014) [47].

[327]Dirk Buschle, 'Unbundling of State-owned Transmission System Operators – Effective Remedy or Eyewash?' [2013] European Networks Law and Regulation Quarterly 49, 63.

independence in terms of, *inter alia*, assets, equipment, staff, management, identity and network investment, as well as close supervision by the national regulatory authorities. Viewed in this light, it is striking that Directives 2009/72/EC and 2009/73/EC do not contain any detailed rules on how to ensure unbundling within the State. The text of both Directives confines itself to requiring that the two public bodies be 'separate'. There is much to suggest that this was not an unintentional regulatory gap, but rather 'the will of the legislature'.[328]

In its opinions on the certification decisions of national regulatory authorities, the European Commission has generally refrained from trying to modify the substance of the 'two separate public bodies' test by reading into the provision new substantive requirements.[329] It is prepared to accept that two different ministries constitute bodies with a sufficient degree of separation, as required by Article 9(6), provided that the ministers have independent decision-making powers for their respective areas of responsibility and that the prime minister is precluded from giving direct orders or instructions to the ministers. With respect to these two requirements, the Commission mainly relies on the constitutional law of the respective Member State, without engaging in a thorough discussion of the 'reality on the ground.'[330]

At the same time, the fact that additional safeguards would be feasible and desirable can be clearly inferred in a number of Commission opinions. One case in point is the certification of Energinet.dk, which is the TSO for gas and electricity in Denmark. After having essentially confirmed that the requirements of Article 9 (6) were complied with, the European Commission elaborated on several other elements which, in its view, reinforced the separation of transmission activities from generation/production and supply interests. It stressed that the board and management of Energinet.dk is 'prohibited from having commercial interests or cross-directorships in generation, production, or supply activities.'[331] Furthermore, the Commission commended the existence of a monitoring program, which had been developed to prevent discriminatory conduct. In addition, it observed that the TSO's financial resources are kept separate from the State's budget and that the State does

[328]Ibid 64.

[329]In one specific case the Commission took the view that 'the separation of the interests concerned must be ensured not only at the level of the members of government, but also at the level of supporting staff and administration', see European Commission, Commission Opinion pursuant to Article 3(1) of Regulation (EC) No 714/2009 and Article 10(6) of Directive 2009/72/EC – Austria – Certification of Vorarlberger Übertragungsnetze GmbH (29 March 2012) C(2012) 2244 final, 6.

[330]See Sect. 2.3.1.3.

[331]European Commission, Commission Opinion pursuant to Article 3(1) of Regulation (EC) No 714/2009 and Article 10(6) of Directive 2009/72/EC – Denmark – Certification of Energinet.dk (electricity) (09 January 2012) C(2012) 87 final, 5; European Commission, Commission Opinion pursuant to Article 3(1) of Regulation (EC) No 715/2009 and Article 10(6) of Directive 2009/73/EC – Denmark – Certification of Energinet.dk (gas) (09 January 2012) C(2012) 88 final, 5.

not receive any dividends from Energinet.dk.[332] All of these precautions noted by the Commission, many of which have their counterpart in the ITO model, clearly enhanced the independence of the TSO in the Article 9(6) setting. However, they are not systematically required by the Commission. As alluded to above, this restraint on the part of the Commission seems to be the logical consequence of the fact that the EU legislator decided against the introduction of ITO-like ‘ring-fencing provisions’ for State-owned companies under Article 9(6).[333]

Thus, based on this brief analysis one may have the impression that the unbundling regime provided for in Article 9(6) of the Directives does not entirely eliminate the incentive for anti-competitive practices on the part of the State-owned TSO, which could theoretically benefit the public commercial energy company. However, this remains at this point a mere possibility. In the absence of empirical evidence, it seems difficult to accept that the conditions of competition are modified to the detriment of (foreign) private generation/production or supply undertakings simply because the separation arrangements within the State may not completely remove the incentive to discriminate in favor of other public entities as regards network access and investment. Moreover, it must also be taken into account that any anti-competitive behavior by the TSO is, in any event, prohibited under general EU competition law, in particular Article 102 TFEU. Viewed against this background, the proposition of inherent ‘less favorable treatment’ is unconvincing.

In conclusion, the special OU model in Article 9(6) of the Directives should be deemed to be in line with the national treatment obligation in Article XVII GATS.

4.7 Article II GATS (Most-Favored-Nation Treatment)

The most-favored-nation principle, embodied in Article II GATS, is a manifestation of the overarching non-discrimination principle, which is also reflected in Article XVII GATS and in several other WTO agreements. Whenever a WTO Member confers any benefit to services or service suppliers of either a WTO Member or non-WTO Member, it must, as per Article II GATS, extend that benefit to the like services or service suppliers of every other WTO Member. Article II:1 GATS reads as follows:

[332]Commission Opinion – Certification of Energinet.dk (electricity) (n 331) 5–6; Commission Opinion – Certification of Energinet.dk (gas) (n 331) 5. See also European Commission, Commission Opinion pursuant to Article 3(1) of Regulation (EC) No 714/2009 and Article 10(6) of Directive 2009/72/EC – Czech Republic – Certification of ČEPS (electricity) (04 October 2012) C(2012) 7059 final, 4; European Commission, Commission Opinion pursuant to Article 3(1) of Regulation (EC) No 714/2009 and Article 10(6) of Directive 2009/72/EC – Slovak Republic – Certification of Slovenská elektrizačná prenosová sústava a.s (09 August 2013) C(2013) 5376 final, 4.

[333]See also Buschle (n 327) 64.

> With respect to any measure covered by this Agreement, each Member shall accord immediately and unconditionally to services and service suppliers of any other Member treatment no less favourable than that it accords to like services and service suppliers of any other country.

Unlike Articles XVI and XVII GATS, which only apply if and to the extent that specific commitments have been undertaken, the MFN principle in Article II:1 GATS applies generally to all measures covered by the GATS, regardless of whether specific commitments have been inscribed in a Member's schedule.[334] While it should be noted that at the time of joining the WTO Members were allowed to specify certain exemptions from the MFN obligation,[335] there are however hardly any MFN exemptions that specifically relate to energy services.[336]

Article II GATS plays a central role with respect to all three dimensions of the unbundling regime in the TEP, i.e. certification, exemption, and the unbundling requirements as such. First of all, as regards the third-country certification procedure set forth in Article 11 of Directives 2009/72/EC and 2009/73/EC, it has been suggested that the security of supply test is not entirely static, but depends to some extent on the country of origin of the applicant transmission system operator.[337] Furthermore, with respect to the exemption regime under the TEP, the argument has been advanced that the granting of individual exemptions from the ownership unbundling requirements could violate Article II:1 GATS.[338] Finally, the EU-wide implementation of the unbundling requirements in the TEP could be inconsistent with the EU's MFN obligation due to the fact that the three unbundling models (OU, ISO and ITO) have different degrees of restrictiveness and that, consequently, foreign services and service suppliers are impacted differently depending on which unbundling model was chosen by the respective EU Member State in which they are located.[339]

The determination of whether the MFN treatment obligation of Article II:1 GATS has been violated involves a three-step test, as follows[340]:

---

[334]In particular, it also applies to the pre-entry phase, see Sidhu (n 283) 229–230; Aly K Abu-Akeel, 'The MFN as it Applies to Service Trade: New Problems for an Old Concept' (1999) 33 Journal of World Trade 103, 124–126; Vranes (n 86) 667. For a different view, see Lecheler and Germelmann (n 79) 100–101; Wulf-Henning Roth, *Investitionsbeschränkungen im deutschen Außenwirtschaftsrecht – Europa- und völkerrechtliche Probleme* (Rechtspolitisches Forum – Legal Policy Forum vol 47, Institut für Rechtspolitik an der Universität Trier 2009) 55.

[335]See Article II:2 GATS (n 4).

[336]Cossy (n 17) 161–162.

[337]This was argued by the Russian Federation, see Trade Policy Review – European Union (n 87) 313.

[338]Ibid 313.

[339]*European Union and its Member States – Certain Measures Relating to the Energy Sector* (n 87) 2–3; Trade Policy Review – European Union (n 87) 313.

[340]*Canada – Certain Measures Affecting the Automotive Industry* (n 3) [170–171]. See also van den Bossche and Zdouc (n 71) 336–337.

First, the measure at issue needs to fall within the scope of application of Article II:1 GATS. As the provision applies with respect to 'any measure covered by this Agreement', its scope of application is identical with the scope of application of the GATS as such, as defined in Article I:1.[341] Consequently, unbundling and unbundling-related measures fall within the scope of application of Article II:1 GATS.[342] Second, it has to be assessed whether the services or service suppliers of WTO Member B are 'like' the services or service suppliers of WTO Member (or country) C. Third, it needs to be examined whether the EU or its Member States accord to services or service suppliers of WTO Member B treatment no less favorable.[343] The last two points will be addressed in turn below.

4.7.1 Likeness of Services or Service Suppliers

As under the national treatment obligation contained in Article XVII GATS, the likeness test plays an important role. The obligation to provide MFN treatment is only triggered if the services or service suppliers of WTO Member B are 'like' the services or service suppliers of WTO Member (or country) C. In terms of the basis of comparison, the likeness analysis under Article II:1 GATS is different from that carried out under Article XVII. Whereas Article XVII GATS refers to the likeness of both domestic and foreign services and service providers, Article II:1 GATS is concerned with the likeness of foreign services and service suppliers.

While the substance of the likeness analysis can vary from provision to provision,[344] it seems that in the field of trade in services the WTO dispute settlement organs do not differentiate between the notion of likeness in Article II:1 and Article XVII GATS.[345] In *EC – Bananas III*, the Panel simply referred to its findings under Article XVII in order to establish a definition of likeness for the purposes of Article II:1.[346] In this light, the considerations developed above[347] are applicable, *mutatis*

[341] *Cf. Canada – Certain Measures Affecting the Automotive Industry* (n 3) [170].

[342] See Sect. 4.1.

[343] In terms of the following analysis, it is the MFN obligation of the EU as a whole that is particularly relevant.

[344] In *Japan – Alcoholic Beverages II*, the Appellate Body stated that the concept of likeness evokes the image of an accordion which 'stretches and squeezes in different places as different provisions of the *WTO Agreement* are applied'. It further noted that the 'width of the accordion in any one of those places must be determined by the particular provision in which the term "like" is encountered as well as by the context and the circumstances that prevail in any given case to which that provision may apply'; see *Japan – Taxes on Alcoholic Beverages* (n 273) 21. See also *European Communities – Measures Affecting Asbestos and Asbestos-Containing Products* (n 207) [88].

[345] See Krajewski (n 36) 121–122.

[346] *European Communities – Regime for the Importation, Sale and Distribution of Bananas* (n 5) [7.346, 7.322].

[347] See Sect. 4.6.1.

mutandis, to the present context. Here it suffices to note that to the extent that the Third Energy Package (allegedly) draws or results in regulatory distinctions between service suppliers (such as between energy companies based on criteria related to their country of origin[348] or based on their location within the EU[349]) or between services (such as between transmission services based on whether they enhance competition in gas or electricity supply[350]), these regulatory distinctions do not make the respective services or service suppliers unlike.

4.7.2 *No Less Favorable Treatment*

The crucial part of the MFN treatment analysis under Article II:1 GATS is the question of whether less favorable treatment can be shown to exist. In contrast to Article XVII GATS, and in particular paragraphs 2 and 3 thereof, there is no explicit indication in Article II:1 GATS that the provision also applies to *de facto* discriminatory treatment.[351] However, in *EC – Bananas III* the Appellate Body held that origin-neutral measures may also violate the MFN obligation.[352] All possible inconsistencies of the unbundling regime with Article II:1 GATS discussed below relate to *de facto* discrimination.

4.7.2.1 Individual Ownership Unbundling Exemption Decisions

The first issue under the 'less favorable treatment' standard is whether the MFN standard in Article II:1 GATS extends to individual instances of privileged or less favorable treatment. If this were the case, individual ownership unbundling exemption decisions could easily be challenged, for example where two companies from third countries apply for an exemption, but only one of the applications is approved. It is clear that in principle Article II:1 GATS fully applies to individual exemption decisions as 'measures affecting trade in services.'

Looking at the text of the GATS itself, one may be tempted to interpret the words 'treatment no less favorable' in Article II:1 GATS in a similar fashion to Article

---

[348]It has been argued that the security of supply test in Article 11 of the Directives involves such a distinction.

[349]This relates to the fact that energy companies can be subject to different unbundling models (OU, ISO, ITO), depending on the EU Member State in which they are located.

[350]See the requirements for an exemption from OU in the Electricity Regulation and the Gas Directive.

[351]Michaelis (n 11) [76].

[352]*European Communities – Regime for the Importation, Sale and Distribution of Bananas* (n 3) [233–234]; *Argentina – Measures Relating to Trade in Goods and Services* (n 199) [6.105]. See also Pitschas (n 11) [53]; Herrmann, Weiß and Ohler (n 29) [853].

XVII GATS, which likewise speaks of 'treatment no less favorable.'[353] As a reminder, it was concluded above that the national treatment obligation in Article XVII GATS does not apply to situations where one domestic service supplier is *de facto* privileged vis-à-vis *any* foreign service supplier.[354] In fact, the 2016 Appellate Body report in *Argentina – Financial Services* has confirmed that, as under the NT obligation, the concept of 'treatment no less favorable' under Article II:1 GATS is focused on a measure's modification of the conditions of competition.[355] Accordingly, the GATS MFN obligation does not apply to situations where an individual service supplier of one WTO Member is treated less favorably than a service supplier of another WTO Member.[356] Just because a particular foreign service supplier from WTO Member B receives less advantageous treatment in a specific instance does not mean that, in general, service suppliers from that WTO Member do not have opportunities to obtain an ownership unbundling exemption on terms equal to those enjoyed by service suppliers from WTO Member C.

In accordance with the notion of 'conditions of competition', and following the reasoning of the Appellate Body in the *EC – Asbestos* case,[357] the MFN obligation prohibits discrimination between the *group* of services or service suppliers of WTO Member B vis-à-vis the *group* of services or service suppliers of WTO Member C. Article II:1 GATS is thus violated if there is an 'asymmetric impact' on the group of services or service suppliers of a particular WTO Member. However, given that a meaningful application of the asymmetric impact test is impossible in the case of individual administrative decisions,[358] Article II:1 GATS cannot be usefully applied to specific exemption decisions. Consequently, the mere fact that the ownership unbundling exemption request of one third-country undertaking is granted, while the exemption request of another is rejected, does not in and of itself amount to a violation of MFN.

At the same time, as under the national treatment principle it is also clear that individual administrative decisions will be inconsistent with the MFN obligation if

[353]In fact, the Panel in *EC – Bananas III* construed the GATS MFN obligation in the light of Panel reports interpreting Article XVII GATS, see *European Communities – Regime for the Importation, Sale and Distribution of Bananas* (n 5) [7.301–7.304].

[354]See Sect. 4.6.2.2.

[355]*Argentina – Measures Relating to Trade in Goods and Services* (n 199) [6.106]. See also WTO, *European Communities – Regime for the Importation, Sale and Distribution of Bananas – Recourse to Article 21.5 by Ecuador,* Report of the Panel (12 April 1999) WT/DS27/RW/ECU [6.133]; van den Bossche and Zdouc (n 71) 335; Ortino (n 280) 195.

[356]This view is shared by De Meester and Coppens (n 126) 120–122. See also Sidhu (n 283) 236–238 (who, however, mainly refers to the interpretation of the MFN principle in the context of international investment law).

[357]*European Communities – Measures Affecting Asbestos and Asbestos-Containing Products* (n 207) [100].

[358]See Sect. 4.6.2.2.

the complainant in a WTO dispute is able to show the existence of a protectionist intent.[359] For example, protectionist motives could be said to exist if the European Commission rejects a certain exemption request although the facts of the case are identical to those underlying a previous positive decision. It must, however, be stressed that the WTO dispute settlement bodies will only rarely find that an individual exemption decision had an underlying protectionist objective, because this will in many cases require a subjective assessment, which in turn entails the risk of 'second-guessing' the decisions of domestic authorities.[360] So far there has been no exemption decision under the Third Energy Package[361] from which the existence of protectionist intent could be deduced so as to result in a violation of Article II:1 GATS.[362]

4.7.2.2 Variety of Unbundling Models (OU, ISO & ITO)

The next issue relating to the MFN obligation concerns the unbundling requirements as such. The possibility of *de facto* discrimination contrary to Article II:1 GATS stems from the fact that there is no uniform unbundling standard, i.e. the TEP provides for three main different unbundling models—ITO, ISO, and ownership unbundling. Thus, depending on the EU Member State, some foreign service

[359] De Meester (n 126) 234–235.

[360] Ibid 235–236.

[361] Or under the TPA-related exemption regime provided for in the SEP. The Russian Federation, however, argues that through the OPAL and NEL exemption decisions, both rendered under the SEP, 'the EU accorded Russian services and service suppliers less favorable treatment than it accorded to like services and service suppliers of other third-countries pursuant to relevant decisions granting exemptions to those suppliers', contrary to its obligations under Article II:1 GATS; see *European Union and its Member States – Certain Measures Relating to the Energy Sector* (n 87) 4. While the merits of this claim will be analyzed in detail by the WTO dispute settlement bodies in the *EU – Energy Package* case, I take the view that the claim is unfounded. As regards the NEL pipeline, it is reasonably clear that the pipeline does not constitute an 'interconnector' within the meaning of Directive 2009/73/EC and that no exemption was granted to other pipelines that also do not meet the definition (for more, see Sect. 4.8.1.1). As regards OPAL, the 'gas release requirement' that was identified by Russia to be discriminatory has also been imposed in other infrastructure-related exemption decisions, such as in the case of the Trans Adriatic Pipeline, see Italian Regulatory Authority for Energy AEEG, Albanian Regulatory Authority for Energy ERE and Greek Regulatory Authority for Energy RAE, 'Final Joint Opinion of the Energy Regulators on TAP AG's Exemption Application' (2013) 63–67 <http://www.autorita.energia.it/allegati/docs/13/249-13all.pdf> accessed 21 September 2016.

[362] But see Ispolinov and Dvenadtcatova (n 186) 119–120, who write that in comparison to the exemption decision relating to the OPAl pipeline, the exemption granted to the Trans Adriatic Pipeline is a good example of a 'highly selective, if not discriminatory' approach of the EU, in violation of the WTO's MFN principle. In my view, however, the same restrictions on dominant undertakings imposed in the case of OPAL were also applied in the case of the TAP; see furthermore the remarks in footnote 361 (this chapter).

See also, in this connection, the decision-making practice with respect to the notion of 'interconnector' in Sect. 4.8.1.1.

suppliers may be in a position to choose the less restrictive ITO model, whereas other foreign service suppliers may be required to apply the more intrusive OU requirements. How does the EU's MFN obligation operate in such a situation?[363]

In the first instance the question arises whether the application of different unbundling models among EU Member States actually entails less favorable treatment in the sense that it modifies the conditions of competition to the benefit of some and detriment of other economic actors. This question is similar to that discussed in the context of the NT obligation, namely whether private energy companies subject to 'classic' OU under Article 9(1) of the Directives receive less favorable treatment than public energy companies that can avail themselves of the special OU model in Article 9(6). As mentioned, all unbundling models contained in the TEP are designed to ensure equal conditions of competition for all electricity and natural gas undertakings. However, whereas the ownership unbundling model forces vertically integrated undertakings to divest the transmission system, the ITO model permits vertical integration, but with strict 'ring-fencing provisions'. Therefore it could be argued that the OU model provides less favorable treatment compared with the ITO model. In particular, the adverse treatment may be said to result from the fact that, in contrast to the OU model, the generation/production or supply companies under the ITO model can continue to benefit from the network access charges collected by the respective TSO.[364] In general, the network access tariffs exceed the return on revenues generated from the sales from the transmission system.[365] Against this background, it may be concluded that the absence of a uniform approach to unbundling could, in fact, give rise to less favorable treatment within the meaning of Article II:1 GATS.

Secondly, the application of the 'no less favorable treatment' standard must be analyzed with respect to measures taken at the EU Member State level, i.e. by 'sub-supranational' entities. It is clear that the EU, in its capacity as a WTO Member in its own right, bears responsibility for EU Member States' actions, even if the respective Member State has discretion in implementing the EU regulation and its actions merely fall within the scope of Union law.[366] The adoption of the ITO model *by an*

---

[363]The Russian Federation argues that the application of different unbundling models among EU Member States violates Article II:1 GATS, see Trade Policy Review – European Union (n 87) 313; *European Union and its Member States – Certain Measures Relating to the Energy Sector* (n 87) 2–3.

[364]Calliess (n 320) 113–114.

[365]Ibid 114.

[366]Frank Hoffmeister, 'Litigating against the European Union and Its Member States – Who Responds under the ILC's Draft Articles on International Responsibility of International Organizations?' (2010) 21 European Journal of International Law 723, 737–738. In *EC – Asbestos*, for example, the Panel accepted that the EU was responsible for a 1996 French decree banning asbestos and products containing asbestos, see *European Communities – Measures Affecting Asbestos and Asbestos-Containing Products* (n 256) [2.3, 3.4]. Likewise, in *EC – Approval and Marketing of Biotech Products*, the Panel held that the independent safeguard measures of several Member States prohibiting the import and marketing of specific biotech products within their respective territories were attributable to the EU under international law, see WTO, *European Communities – Measures*

individual EU Member State therefore, in principle, constitutes 'treatment' that is 'accorded' *by the European Union.*[367] However, even accepting that EU Member State legislation under the TEP may be attributed to the EU does not predetermine the way in which Article II:1 GATS is applied in relation to sub-supranational entities. The main question here is whether the EU's MFN obligation under the GATS should be interpreted to the effect that any favorable treatment granted autonomously by Member State A (an EU Member State) within its territory to the services and service suppliers of a third country must be accorded immediately and unconditionally to like services and service suppliers of all WTO Members in the territory of Member State B (another EU Member State).

The text of the GATS does not clarify the application of the MFN obligation with respect to sub-supranational entities, and the WTO dispute settlement bodies have not yet had the possibility to address the issue.[368] However, some countries have clarified the scope of the MFN obligation in their international investment agreements,[369] and the non-discrimination obligations of preferential trade agreements have also been modified in this regard. The EU-Canada CETA is an example in point. Article 9.5(1) of the chapter on cross-border trade in services provides that each party shall accord MFN treatment to the services and service suppliers of the other party. This is the standard MFN formula. Article 9.5(2) CETA then provides that, '[f]or greater certainty, the treatment accorded by a Party pursuant to paragraph 1 means, with respect to a government in Canada other than at the federal level, or, with respect to a government of or in a Member State of the European Union, the treatment accorded, in like situations, by that government in its territory to services or service suppliers of a third country.'[370] The effect of this clarifying provision is that the 'treatment' independently accorded to the services and service supplier of any third country by the government of EU Member State A in its territory is irrelevant for determining the applicable 'MFN treatment' to be accorded to Canadian services and service suppliers in the territory of EU Member State B.

In order to protect the regulatory autonomy of the EU and of EU Member States, the GATS MFN obligation should be interpreted in the same way. Therefore, given

Affecting the Approval and Marketing of Biotech Products, Reports of the Panel (29 September 2006) WT/DS291/R, WT/DS292/R, WT/DS293/R [7.101].

[367]It is thus irrelevant that the regulatory framework adopted at EU level, i.e. Directives 2009/72/EC and 2009/73/EC, is the same for all (foreign) service suppliers.

[368]Also, it has received only little attention in academic writing. Abu-Akeel (n 334) 121–122 identified the problem, stating that the 'broad language' of the GATS MFN clause 'seemingly requir [es] uniformity at the national, regional or local level, of measures affecting the activities of foreign service suppliers'.

[369]See Government of Canada, '2004 Canada Model Foreign Investment Promotion and Protection Agreement' (2004) <http://www.italaw.com/documents/Canadian2004-FIPA-model-en.pdf> accessed 13 April 2015. Article 4 on MFN treatment is supplemented by the following footnote. '[F]or greater certainty, the treatment accorded by a Party under this Article means, with respect to a sub-national government, treatment accorded, in like circumstances, by that sub-national government to investors, and to investments of investors, of a non-Party.'

[370]CETA – Consolidated text (n 181) 76–77.

that it is the Member States that choose between the different unbundling models and enact relevant legislation, the term 'treatment no less favorable' in Article II:1 GATS must be taken to refer to the treatment accorded by *the EU Member State concerned* to like services or service suppliers of any third country, regardless of the fact that it is the EU's MFN obligation which is at issue. Otherwise, Article II:1 GATS could be used as a lever to enforce a requirement of substantive uniformity throughout the EU of all measures affecting trade in services.[371] Apart from the specific situation of the EU and its Member States, this would also have a detrimental effect on the federalist structure of other WTO Members (e.g. Canadian provinces, US states, Swiss cantons).

Finally, it must also be kept in mind that in order to establish a breach of Article II:1 GATS it is insufficient to merely show that one third-country service supplier is disadvantaged vis-à-vis another third-country service supplier. Therefore, the fact that the Greek gas transmission system operator DESFA (a service supplier of Azerbaijan) was allowed to choose the unbundling rules of the ITO-model,[372] while other third-country service suppliers may be forced to comply with the ownership unbundling requirements, is not as such problematic under the GATS MFN principle. One would need to show that the way in which the TEP has been implemented by the EU Member States resulted in an 'asymmetric impact', i.e. where most of the service suppliers of one WTO Member were obliged to implement ownership unbundling whereas most of the service suppliers of another WTO Member benefited from the less restrictive ITO unbundling rules.

4.7.2.3 The Certification Procedure in Relation to Third Countries

The final issue relating to the application of the GATS MFN obligation is the certification procedure in relation to third-country undertakings, contained in Article 11 of the Gas and Electricity Directives. Although the third-country certification procedure applies equally to all foreign service suppliers seeking to acquire control over a transmission system or a TSO, the security of supply test that applies by virtue of Article 11(3)(b) of the Directives could be understood to involve *de facto* discrimination.[373] There are two main potentially problematic aspects, each of which is addressed in turn below.

First, in order to determine whether granting certification will threaten the security of energy supply of the respective EU Member State or the EU as a whole, the national regulatory authority and the European Commission must take

[371] Abu-Akeel (n 334) 121–122.

[372] European Commission, Commission Opinion correcting Opinion C(2014) 5483 final of 28 July 2014 pursuant to Article 3(1) of Regulation (EC) No 715/2009 and Article 10(6) and 11(6) of Directive 2009/73/EC – Greece – Certification of DESFA (17 October 2014) C(2014) 7734 final, 2–3.

[373] This seems to have been argued by the Russian Federation, see Trade Policy Review – European Union (n 87) 313.

into account the rights and obligations of the EU and of the Member State with respect to the third country under international law, in particular under agreements with a bearing on the security of energy supply.[374] This requirement is not supposed to address the possibility of a conflict of norms (such as, for example, between the NT obligation under the GATS and the third-country certification procedure) or, for that matter, to avoid violations of international law.[375] Rather, it requires that international law agreements be taken into account with a view toward evaluating whether granting certification will put at risk the security of energy supply. This suggests that the existence, or negotiation, of a bilateral or multilateral agreement with the home State of the third-country investor could have an important impact on the outcome of the security of supply test. Indeed, commentators have concluded that 'in practice the security of supply test . . . should *to the extent possible* be dealt with in international agreements between the EU and third countries',[376] and that 'the absence of such an agreement will make an approval *much less likely*.'[377]

In addition to providing a clear, straightforward foundation for the conclusion that granting certification will not put at risk the security of energy supply, the significance of international agreements may also result from certain considerations of reciprocity in terms of market access.[378] In this connection, it has been suggested by some authors that an agreement between the EU and the third country concerned could 'in particular relate to an *identical treatment being granted to EU companies in*

[374]Article 11(3)(b)(i) and (ii) as well as Article 11(7)(b) of Directive 2009/72/EC (n 8); Article 11 (3)(b)(i) and (ii) as well as Article 11(7)(b) of Directive 2009/73/EC (n 8).

[375]Therefore, the phrasing differs from the formulation used in Articles 7a(1) and 7b(2) of the Commission's draft gas Directive and Articles 8a(1) and 8b(2) of the Commission's draft electricity Directive, which provided that the foreign ownership prohibition was '[w]ithout prejudice to the international obligations of the Community'; see Proposal for a Directive amending Directive 2003/54/EC (n 120) 29; Proposal for a Directive amending Directive 2003/55/EC (n 120) 30. For a different view, see Schmidt-Preuß (n 79) [25]; Polish Regulatory Authority for Energy ERO, Final Decision on the Certification of the Transmission System Operator Gaz-System (19 May 2015) DRG-4720-2(28)/2014/2015/6154/KF, 52.

[376]Emmanuel Cabau, 'Unbundling of Transmission System Operators' in Christopher Jones (ed), *The Internal Energy Market – The Third Liberalisation Package* (EU Energy Law Series vol 1, 3rd edn. Claeys & Casteels Publishing 2010) [4.105] (emphasis added).

[377]Silke Goldberg and Henrik Bjørnebye, 'Introduction and Comment' in Bram Delvaux, Michaël Hunt and Kim Talus (eds), *EU Energy Law and Policy Issues* (vol 3. Intersentia 2012) 20 (emphasis added).

Even the European Commission stated in 2010 that '. . . an agreement between the EU and the third country concerned *would clearly be the best basis* allowing to come to the conclusion that granting certification will not put at risk the security of energy supply of the EU', see European Commission, 'Reply to Questions from Mr Shmatko on the Third Package' (29 June 2010) 9 <http://www.asktheeu.org/de/request/168/response/558/attach/3/Annex%20reply%20GHP%20Shmatko%203rd%20package%202.pdf> accessed 24 September 2016 (emphasis added).

[378]See, for example, Jörg Gundel and Claas F Germelmann, 'Kein Schlussstein für die Liberalisierung der Energiemärkte' [2009] Europäische Zeitschrift für Wirtschaftsrecht 763, 770 (referring to 25th recital of the preamble to Directive 2009/72/EC (n 8); 22nd recital of the preamble to Directive 2009/73/EC (n 8)).

the third country (i.e. EU companies being authorised to acquire the third party network) and to requirements relating to *energy market opening* allowing access for EU producers and suppliers in the third country concerned.'[379]

Making the granting of certification contingent on the existence or negotiation, between the EU and the respective third country, of a treaty which regulates security of supply issues in a general fashion would however violate the MFN obligation in Article II:1 GATS. The MFN principle prohibits WTO Members from modifying the conditions of competition in the marketplace to the detriment of like services or service suppliers of any other WTO Member. Conditioning the provision of more favorable treatment to a group of services or service suppliers of a particular WTO Member on any criterion which is inextricably linked to their country of origin necessarily modifies the conditions of competition. Therefore, it is impossible for WTO Member A to open its domestic energy market to WTO Member B (based on the fact that that Member has entered into a bilateral treaty with WTO Member A), but not to WTO Member C (with which no such treaty exists).[380] In the same vein, WTO Member A cannot selectively open its energy market to services and service suppliers of WTO Member B (on the grounds that that country is party to the Energy Charter Treaty (ECT)), but not to services and service suppliers of WTO Member C (because that country has not yet acceded to the ECT).[381] Viewed against this background, it is clear that the 2007 draft gas and electricity Directives of the European Commission, according to which third-country companies would have been prohibited from acquiring control over TSOs and transmission system assets unless an international agreement between the EU and the third country allowed for a country-specific derogation from that rule, would have resulted in a clear violation of Article II:1 GATS.[382]

The question which thus arises at this point is whether the application of the security of supply test contained in Article 11 of Directives 2009/72/EC and 2009/73/EC in fact indicates that certification will only be granted if the country of origin of the TSO applying for certification has concluded a treaty with the EU or one of its Member States relating to general security of supply issues. Contrary to what has been suggested in the academic writing, the existence or non-existence of such agreements has played an almost negligible role in those certification proceedings in which the security of supply test has been applied so far. Often the issue was not

[379]Cabau (n 376) [4.105] (emphasis added).

[380]For an example related to the EU's emission trading system, see Lorand Bartels, 'The WTO Legality of the Application of the EU's Emission Trading System to Aviation' (2012) 23 European Journal of International Law 429, 447, 464; Joshua Meltzer, 'Climate Change and Trade – The EU Aviation Directive and the WTO' (2012) 15 Journal of International Economic Law 111, 138, 149–150.

[381]The Polish Ministry of Foreign Affairs has pointed out that, within the framework of the third-country certification procedure, the Energy Charter Treaty could be considered as an agreement which addresses the issues of security of energy supply, see Final Decision on Certification of TSO Gaz-System (n 375) 52.

[382]Van den bergh (n 79) 250; van Hoorn (n 120) 64–65.

even mentioned.[383] The only relevant case is the certification of the gas transmission system operator DESFA by the Greek national regulatory authority RAE. As a reminder, the State Oil Company of the Azerbaijan Republic (SOCAR), which was controlled by the Republic of Azerbaijan, sought to acquire a 66% stake in DESFA. During the certification process, stakeholders reported that the conclusion of an intergovernmental agreement between Greece and the EU on the one hand, and the Republic of Azerbaijan on the other, was one of the '*prerequisites* set by the EC for the conclusion of the certification' of DESFA.[384] However, although the Commission in fact recommended the opening of negotiations with Azerbaijan, it quickly became clear that such an agreement was not a necessary precondition for certification. Furthermore, the Commission merely sought to negotiate a context-specific agreement governing only the control of DESFA by SOCAR.[385] Given that such a treaty would have affected only a particular service supplier from Azerbaijan, it seems that the conditions of competition would not have been modified in favor of Azerbaijani services or service suppliers.

In its opinion on certification, the European Commission stressed that the Greek regulator RAE had failed to take into account in its assessment the issue of intergovernmental agreements, and further stated that 'the unbundling rules and other regulatory provisions do not, by themselves, provide sufficient guarantees *in the absence of additional safeguards such as an intergovernmental agreement addressing security of supply*.'[386] On that basis, but also on the basis of various other aspects, the Commission took the view that RAE should have the power to suspend all voting rights attached to the shares that SOCAR holds in DESFA. To summarize, the absence of an international agreement did not preclude certification and was only one of several factors that led to the imposition of additional safeguards. This link to the origin of the service supplier is thus very weak. Furthermore, DESFA is the only case where the issue of intergovernmental agreements has been addressed at all. Finally, it seems that the EU would seek, if at all, to negotiate context-specific agreements regulating the particular case at issue. Such treaties do not necessarily lead to a modification of the conditions of competition, hence the possibility of an MFN violation seems therefore out of question.

The second problematic aspect under Article 11 of Directives 2009/72/EC and 2009/73/EC relates to the fact that the NRAs, as well as the Commission, are also required to take into account 'other specific facts and circumstances of the case and

---

[383] See, for example, the cases of TIGF and WMR.

[384] George Lagaris and Alexia Trokoudi, 'Application of Article 11 of the Gas Directive – TSOs Controlled by Companies from Non-Member States' (2014) 19–20 <https://www.energy-community.org/portal/page/portal/ENC_HOME/DOCS/2950031/0633975AD7C27B9CE053C92FA8C06338.PDF> accessed 18 April 2016 (emphasis added).

[385] See European Commission, Recommendation for a Council Decision authorising the opening of negotiations on an Agreement between the European Union and the Republic of Azerbaijan on a legal framework governing the control of DESFA by SOCAR (12 February 2014) COM(2014) 68 final.

[386] Commission Opinion – Certification of DESFA (n 372) 6 (emphasis added).

the third country concerned.'[387] Such specific facts and circumstances relating to 'the third country concerned' carried a significant weight in the certification of the French gas transmission operator TIGF. In that case, one of the shareholders of TIGF, GIC, was controlled by the Ministry of Finance of Singapore. In what could be interpreted as a statement of general application, the Commission declared that 'if the non-EU country concerned produces no energy, or does so but it can be excluded with reasonable certainty that energy will be supplied to the European Union', then security of supply concerns are less likely to arise.[388] In applying this reasoning to the facts at hand, the Commission noted that Singapore produced no natural gas and that it had no interconnections to Europe, and accordingly concluded that it was 'unlikely' that the control of GIC put at risk the security of supply of France or the European Union.[389] This reasoning could suggest that the security of supply test will be, in practice, met if the country of origin of the third-country investor does not export energy to the EU. This would mean that the test *de facto* only applies to a pre-determined group of WTO Members, on the basis of geographical factors, thereby modifying the conditions of competition to the detriment of service suppliers from those countries which have (close) energy trade relations with the EU.[390] However, so far the certification of TIGF is the only decision in which such origin-related considerations have played a role. In addition, the Commission's final determination that the security of supply of France and the EU is not put at risk was also based on other criteria, such as the limited importance of the TIGF network for the French gas transmission system as a whole and considerations relating to the TSO's shareholder structure.[391] Therefore, it seems very difficult to develop an MFN argument here.

In conclusion, it would seem that the security of supply test does not modify the conditions of competition to the detriment of services or service suppliers from any particular WTO Member. The third-country certification procedure contained in Article 11 of Directives 2009/72/EC and 2009/73/EC is thus consistent with the MFN obligation contained in Article II:1 GATS. As a final point, it should also be noted that both the existence of security of supply-related rights and obligations under international law, as well as energy trade relations with the EU or the Member State concerned, are criteria that have a rational nexus to the objective of ensuring

---

[387] Article 11(3)(b)(iii) Directive 2009/72/EC (n 8); Article 11(3)(b)(iii) Directive 2009/73/EC (n 8) (emphasis added).

[388] European Commission, Commission Opinion pursuant to Article 3(1) of Regulation (EC) No 715/2009 and Article 10(6) of Directive 2009/73/EC – France – Certification of TIGF (04 June 2014) C(2014) 3837 final, 5.

[389] Ibid.

[390] See, with similar reasoning in a different context, Bartels (n 380) 445, 464.

[391] These additional elements are not, however, mentioned in the final decision of the French regulator CRE, see French Regulatory Authority for Energy CRE, Délibération de la Commission de régulation de l'énergie portant décision de certification de la société TIGF (03 July 2014).

'security of supply'. This would make it easier to justify any potential MFN violation under the GATS exception provisions.[392]

4.8 Article VI GATS (Domestic Regulation)

Article VI GATS is concerned with establishing general disciplines on domestic regulation. It is of particular relevance for energy services inasmuch as this sector, like other network-based industries, is highly regulated.[393] The underlying rationale of Article VI GATS is that even measures that are non-discriminatory according to Article XVII GATS and do not impede market access within the meaning of Article XVI GATS can significantly inhibit trade in (energy) services if such measures are inconsistent with certain standards of 'good regulation'.

4.8.1 Article VI:1 GATS: Reasonable, Objective and Impartial Administration

Article VI:1 GATS sets out the general rule that in sectors where specific commitments have been made, WTO Members 'shall ensure that all measures of general application affecting trade in services are administered in a reasonable, objective and impartial manner.' The formulation of Article VI:1 GATS resembles Article X:3 (a) of the GATT, which provides that trade regulations of general application shall be administered in a uniform, impartial and reasonable manner.[394] Given the paucity of the case-law on Article VI:1 GATS, appropriate references will be made to the jurisprudence relating to Article X:3(a) GATT.

A number of aspects of the unbundling regime in the Third Energy Package could raise issues with respect to the requirements of Article VI:1 GATS. This relates in particular to the decision-making practice regarding the approval of ownership unbundling exemption requests, and to the application of the unbundling requirements to the offshore sections of international gas pipelines. Although an unreasonable, subjective or partial administration of these measures could also be framed as a violation of the non-discrimination disciplines in Articles II:1 and XVII GATS,[395]

---

[392]See Sect. 4.9.

[393]Gabrielle Marceau, 'The WTO in the Emerging Energy Governance Debate' in Joost Pauwelyn (ed), *Global Challenges at the Intersection of Trade, Energy and the Environment* (Center for Economic and Policy Research 2010) 29.

[394]Note, however, that Article X:3(a) GATT and Article V:1 GATS are not congruent: The former refers to the criteria '*uniform*, impartial and reasonable', whereas the latter uses the words 'reasonable, *objective* and impartial'.

[395]See Sects. 4.6.2.2, 4.6.2.3 and 4.7.2.1.

the domestic regulation disciplines have the advantage that they do not require a showing that the conditions of competition have been modified to the detriment of services or service suppliers of the complainant's origin and that, in consequence, there has been discrimination based on origin.

Before examining the application of Article VI:1 GATS to the unbundling and unbundling-related measures in the EU energy sector, some general comments should be made. First, as mentioned, the provision only applies in sectors where specific commitments exist. The EU and its Member States have undertaken relevant commitments on energy services, whose applicability to the measures at issue here has been discussed above.[396] Second, it must be stressed that Article VI:1 GATS disciplines the *administration* of domestic regulation, not its substantive content.[397] This was confirmed by the Panel in the *US – Gambling* case.[398] Therefore, the regulation itself does not have to be reasonable, objective and impartial.[399]

Third, considering that Article VI:1 GATS applies to 'measures of general application', the question arises whether individualized instances of unreasonable, non-objective or partial administration can result in a violation of that provision. Several authors have taken the view that, given its wording, Article VI:1 GATS covers only measures of general application and does not apply to measures 'addressing specific situations'.[400] The scope of application of the provision would

[396]See Sect. 4.4.

[397]Panagiotis Delimatsis, 'Due Process and "Good" Regulation Embedded in the GATS – Disciplining Regulatory Behaviour in Services Through Article VI of the GATS' (2007) 10 Journal of International Economic Law 13, 18; Michaelis (n 11) [96, 99]; Herrmann, Weiß and Ohler (n 29) [880]; Pitschas (n 11) [129]; Munin (n 140) 273; *European Communities – Regime for the Importation, Sale and Distribution of Bananas* (n 3) [200] (regarding Article X:3(a) GATT); WTO, *European Communities – Measures Affecting the Importation of Certain Poultry Products,* Report of the Appellate Body (13 July 1998) WT/DS69/AB/R [115] (regarding Article X GATT).

[398]*United States – Measures Affecting the Cross-Border Supply of Gambling and Betting Services* (n 95) [6.432].

[399]The substance of a measure could, however, be challenged if it is administrative in nature. For the (to some extent inconsistent) case-law on this issue, see *Argentina – Measures Affecting the Export of Bovine Hides and the Import of Finished Leather* (n 204) [11.69–11.72]; WTO, *European Communities – Selected Customs Matters,* Report of the Panel (16 June 2006) WT/DS315/R [7.102–7.119]; WTO, *European Communities – Selected Customs Matters,* Report of the Appellate Body (13 November 2006) WT/DS315/AB/R [190–201].

[400]Delimatsis (n 397) 20; Markus Krajewski, 'Article VI GATS' in Rüdiger Wolfrum, Peter-Tobias Stoll and Clemens Feinäugle (eds), *WTO – Trade in Services* (Max Planck Commentaries on World Trade Law vol 6. Martinus Nijhoff Publishers 2008) [8]; Andrew Mitchell and Tania Voon, 'Reasonableness, Impartiality and Objectivity' in Aik H Lim and Bart De Meester (eds), *WTO Domestic Regulation and Services Trade: Putting Principles into Practice* (Cambridge University Press 2014) 69–71. For a different view, see De Meester (n 126) 239–240, who concludes that 'if a complainant is able to show that the administration of a measure of general application in an individual case is "unreasonable, not objective or not impartial", *this administrative act "as such" already violates Article VI:1*' (emphasis added). See also Torje Sunde, *Möglichkeiten und Grenzen innerstaatlicher Regulierung nach Art. VI GATS* (Beiträge zum Transnationalen Wirtschaftsrecht vol 59, 2006) 13–14.

thus exclude measures that apply to a single service transaction or to a specific company.[401] Nevertheless, it may very well be that the application of a general measure in an individual case demonstrates that the measure of general application is not administered in compliance with Article VI:1 GATS.[402] In fact, in *US – Hot-Rolled Steel*, the Panel held, in the context of Article X:3(a) GATT, that 'it is not inconceivable that a Member's actions in a single instance might be evidence of lack of uniform, impartial, and reasonable administration of its laws, regulations, decisions and rulings.'[403] However, the Panel went on to state that 'the actions in question would have to have a significant impact on the overall administration of the law, and not simply on the outcome in the single case in question',[404] thereby limiting the reach of its previous pronouncement. A similar approach can be applied to Article VI:1 GATS. In conclusion, whereas an individual measure as such cannot be inconsistent with the obligation contained in Article VI:1 GATS, it may nonetheless constitute sufficient evidence to show that the WTO Member concerned does not honor its obligations under that provision.

Fourth, each of the requirements mentioned in Article VI:1 GATS (reasonable, objective, impartial) embodies a self-standing obligation.[405] In other words, it would be sufficient for a complainant in a WTO dispute to show that another WTO Member's administration of laws and regulations does not comply with any one of the three standards.

Fifth, and finally, the notions of reasonableness, objectivity and impartiality will be briefly elucidated. Panels have understood the term 'reasonable' to mean 'in accordance with reason', 'not irrational or absurd', 'proportionate', 'sensible', and 'within the limits of reason, not greatly less or more than might be thought likely or appropriate.'[406] Furthermore, the case *Dominican Republic – Import and Sale of Cigarettes* suggests that the administration of a measure is unreasonable if, firstly, the authorities of a WTO Member deviate from a standard methodology or practice

[401] *Cf.* WTO, *European Communities and its Member States – Tariff Treatment of Certain Information Technology Products,* Reports of the Panel (16 August 2010) WT/DS375/R, WT/DS376/R, WT/DS377/R [7.1034]; WTO, *European Communities – Measures Affecting the Importation of Certain Poultry Products,* Report of the Panel (12 March 1998) WT/DS69/R [269]; *European Communities – Measures Affecting the Importation of Certain Poultry Products* (n 397) [113].

[402] Krajewski (n 400) [10].

[403] WTO, *United States – Anti-Dumping Measures on Certain Hot-Rolled Steel Products from Japan,* Report of the Panel (28 February 2001) WT/DS184/R [7.268].

[404] Ibid.

[405] Munin (n 140) 277; Molinuevo (n 7) 162–163; Panagiotis Delimatsis, *International Trade in Services and Domestic Regulations: Necessity, Transparency, and Regulatory Diversity* (International Economic Law Series, Oxford University Press 2007) 101–102.

[406] See for example WTO, *United States – Certain Country of Origin Labelling (COOL) Requirements,* Reports of the Panel (18 November 2011) WT/DS384/R, WT/DS386/R [7.850].

or from a provision in a law, and secondly if the authorities do not have the discretion, under the laws in place, to so deviate from the legal rules.[407]

The requirement of objectivity basically entails the absence of arbitrariness.[408] The application of a measure may not be influenced by irrational, emotional or personal elements.[409] In other words, the authorities are prohibited from taking factors into consideration that are unconnected with the subject matter of the decision. Furthermore, one commentator argued that 'a deviation from the standard practice – that is, lack of uniformity in the administration of the measure – may create a presumption that the measure is not being applied objectively.'[410]

The notion of impartiality has been interpreted as 'not partial', 'not favouring one party or side more than another', 'unprejudiced', 'unbiased' and 'fair'.[411]

4.8.1.1 Exemptions from Ownership Unbundling: Interpretation of the Notion of 'Interconnector'

Issues regarding the 'reasonable, objective and impartial' administration of Directive 2009/73/EC could arise with respect to exemptions granted from the obligation of ownership unbundling.[412] According to Article 36 of the Gas Directive, exemptions may be granted to major new gas infrastructure, including, *inter alia*, so-called 'interconnectors'. The term 'interconnector' is legally defined as 'a transmission line which crosses or spans a border between Member States for the sole purpose of connecting the national transmission systems of those Member States.'[413] This definition is central to the exemption regime. Only gas transmission lines that satisfy the definition can be exempted from the provisions of ownership unbundling (and third party access). If the European Commission decides that a specific gas pipeline is not an interconnector, the sponsor of the pipeline will not be granted an exemption, regardless of whether the project would theoretically fulfil all other criteria mentioned in Article 36(1)(a)–(e) of Directive 2009/73/EC.

It has been suggested that the concept of interconnector has in some cases been interpreted and applied in a manner that deviates from the underlying provisions in the law, and that is inconsistent with previous practice.[414] If so, the administration of

---

[407]WTO, *Dominican Republic – Measures Affecting the Importation and Internal Sale of Cigarettes,* Report of the Panel (26 November 2004) WT/DS302/R [7.378–7.388].

[408]Krajewski (n 400) [12].

[409]Ibid.

[410]Molinuevo (n 7) 165.

[411]WTO, *China – Measures Related to the Exportation of Various Raw Materials,* Reports of the Panel (5 July 2011) WT/DS394/R, WT/DS395/R, WT/DS398/R [7.694].

[412]Given that so far there are no exemption decisions with a 'third country dimension' under the Electricity Regulation (see Sect. 2.3.3.2), the focus here will be on the Gas Directive.

[413]Article 2 No. 17 of Directive 2009/73/EC (n 8).

[414]See below footnotes 423, 428–429 (this chapter), and accompanying text.

the generally applicable exemption regime under the TEP could thus violate Article VI:1 GATS. In order to determine whether the administration of the exemption regime does in fact raise issues under Article VI:1 GATS, it is necessary to give a brief overview of the European Commission's decision-making practice under the Second and Third Energy Packages.[415]

The first main question that arose in the interpretation of the term 'interconnector' was whether a pipeline, the main function of which is to transport natural gas from third countries into the EU, can be said to cross or span a border between Member States *for the sole purpose of connecting the national transmission systems of those Member States*.[416] In other words, does a pipeline which connects the national transmission systems of at least two Member States in a merely physical sense, but not primarily with a view to facilitating gas trade between the Member States, constitute an interconnector? In the case of the OPAL pipeline, which was constructed to transport Russian gas through Germany to the Czech Republic (and not German gas to the Czech Republic or *vice versa*), the German national regulatory authority (*Bundesnetzagentur*) decided that preference should be given to a broad reading.[417] In particular, as regards the ordinary meaning of the text, it held that the term 'for the sole purpose' cannot be interpreted to refer to the national transmission systems of the Member States concerned. Rather, it interpreted the term to refer to the word 'connecting', which would thus exclude gas infrastructure also serving other purposes (e.g. distribution).[418] Hence, it accepted that OPAL fulfilled the definition of an 'interconnector' and could thus in principle benefit from an exemption. In coming to this conclusion, the German national regulator also noted that the Nabucco pipeline, which was supposed to bring natural gas from sources in the Caspian Sea and the Middle East to the EU, was exempted by the Austrian regulator *Energie-Control*,[419] and that the European Commission had not taken issue with this decision.[420] The European Commission subsequently endorsed the reasoning of the *Bundesnetzagentur* and upheld its conclusion that the OPAL pipeline qualified as an interconnector.[421]

[415]For a detailed overview, see Hans Heller, *Neue Erdgasinfrastrukturen und Freistellung von der Regulierung: Ein legitimes Instrument der Investitionsförderung?* (Nomos 2013) 223ff.

[416]Bundesnetzagentur, Antrag auf Freistellung von der Regulierung – OPAL NEL Transport GmbH (25 February 2009) Az. BK7-08-009, 22–34.

[417]Ibid.

[418]Ibid 26.

[419]Ibid 30–32. For the exemption decisions of the Austrian national regulatory authority, see Energie-Control Kommission, Bescheid – Nabucco Gas Pipeline International GmbH (09 April 2008) GZ K NIS G 01/07; Energie-Control Kommission, Bescheid – Nabucco Gas Pipeline International GmbH (26 November 2008) GZ K NIS G 01/08.

[420]European Commission, Exemption decision on the Austrian section of the Nabucco pipeline (08 February 2008) CAB D(2008)142; European Commission, Exemption decision on the Austrian section of the Nabucco pipeline (22 October 2008) CAB D(2008) 1094, C(2008) 6254.

[421]European Commission, Ausnahmegenehmigung der Bundesnetzagentur für die OPAL-Gasleitung gemäß Art. 22 der Richtlinie 2003/55 (12 June 2009) C(2009) 4694, 23–24.

In my opinion, the approach taken by both the national regulators and the Commission is in full conformity with the provisions of Directive 2009/73/EC, in particular considering the preamble to the Gas Directive, which states that '[t]he possibility of temporary derogations should apply, for security of supply reasons, in particular, to new pipelines within the Community *transporting gas from third countries into the Community*.'[422] Accordingly, one can conclude that the assertion in the academic literature that the Nabucco pipeline 'is not an interconnector' because it 'originates outside the EU borders'[423] is mistaken. The corresponding exemption decision was therefore not a 'political decision'.

A second and related issue that arose in connection with the notion of 'interconnector' concerns the geographical element of the definition ('transmission line which crosses or spans a border between Member States'). In accordance with this element of the definition, only projects that cross or span a border *between EU Member States* can be exempted.[424] The German national regulatory authority was, therefore, correct in holding that the NEL pipeline, which runs from Lubmin near Greifswald (in the northeast of Germany) to Rehden (in the northwest of Germany), did not qualify as an 'interconnector', even assuming that the pipeline forms part of the larger Nord Stream project and thus interconnects Russia and Germany.[425] Furthermore, in the exemption decision relating to the Trans Adriatic Pipeline, which will start in Greece, cross Albania (a non-EU Member State) and eventually connect to the Italian natural gas network, the European Commission stated that 'the concept of "interconnectors" must be understood as comprising, inter alia, gas pipelines which span the borders of (at least) two EU Member States, *regardless as to whether the territory of an non-EU Member State is crossed in between*.'[426] The Commission added that an overly narrow reading of the definition provided in Directive 2009/73/EC 'would exclude the pipelines which connect the EU Member States, but happen to start, end, or cross a third country.'[427] Contrary to what has been suggested in the academic literature,[428] the Commission's interpretation is not contrary to the plain meaning of the exemption provision, as there is no requirement of a *direct* connection.

Considering what was said in the preceding paragraphs, and taking into account the other exemption decisions rendered under the Gas Directive, it is furthermore clear that there is no basis for the (unspecific) assertion of a WTO Member that

---

[422] 35th recital of the preamble to Directive 2009/73/EC (n 8) (emphasis added).

[423] See Yafimava (n 290) 127–128; Katja Yafimava, *The EU Third Package for Gas and the Gas Target Model: Major Contentious Issues Inside and Outside the EU* (Oxford Institute for Energy Studies 2013) 50; Yafimava (n 290) 606–607.

[424] Heller (n 415) 225.

[425] Antrag auf Freistellung von der Regulierung – OPAL NEL (n 416) 20–21.

[426] Commission Decision – Exemption of the Trans Adriatic Pipeline (n 310) 55 (emphasis added).

[427] Ibid.

[428] Ivan Gudkov, 'Проблемы международноправового регулирования энергетических отношений на примере взаимодействия России и Европейского союза' [2015] Закон 84, 92.

'exemption requests were granted to the third-country service suppliers or owners of ... pipelines, which ... do not meet the definition of an interconnector in the Directive (and in the SEP).'[429]

In conclusion, the existing decision-making practice of the NRAs and the European Commission is coherent and in line with the underlying provisions in the Gas Directive. None of the exemption decisions interpreting the term 'interconnector' display unreasonable, non-objective or partial elements. It is obvious, therefore, that there has been no violation of Article VI:1 GATS. But even assuming that an exemption decision will be taken in the future which clearly exhibits such features, it is doubtful whether Article VI:1 GATS would be violated. It must be borne in mind that Article VI:1 GATS only obliges WTO Members to administer 'measures of general application' in a reasonable, objective and impartial manner. Accordingly, the Panel report in *US – Hot-Rolled Steel* found that a decision on a specific exemption request can only result in a violation of Article VI:1 GATS if the measure has a '*significant* impact on the overall administration of the law, and not simply on the outcome in the single case in question.'[430] Individual exemption decisions are unlikely to have such an impact.

Moreover, it should also be noted that the WTO dispute settlement bodies will only rarely find that the administration of an exemption regime in a particular case was unreasonable or non-objective due to an alleged departure from domestic laws or settled practice. In *US – Stainless Steel*, where Korea claimed that the US authorities had departed from its established policy in two anti-dumping investigations and thereby administered its anti-dumping laws and regulations in an unreasonable manner, the Panel stated, in *obiter dictum*, that the GATT counterpart of Article VI:1 GATS was 'not ... intended to function as a mechanism to test the consistency of a Member's particular decisions or rulings with the Member's own domestic law and practice.'[431] It added that that would be 'a function reserved for each Member's domestic judicial system, and a function WTO panels would be particularly ill-suited to perform.'[432] Similar statements were also made in other dispute settlement cases.[433]

In consequence, and drawing upon the jurisprudence in *US – Hot-Rolled Steel* and *US – Stainless Steel*, it would be very difficult to (indirectly) challenge a specific ownership unbundling exemption decision by arguing that the interpretation and application of the notion of 'interconnector' in that particular measure

[429]This is the argument of the Russian Federation in the *EU – Energy Package* case, see *European Union and its Member States – Certain Measures Relating to the Energy Sector* (n 87) 4.

[430]*United States – Anti-Dumping Measures on Certain Hot-Rolled Steel Products from Japan* (n 403) [7.268] (emphasis added).

[431]WTO, *United States – Anti-Dumping measures on Stainless Steel Plate in Coils and Stainless Steel Sheet and Strip from Korea*, Report of the Panel (22 December 2000) WT/DS179/R [6.50].

[432]Ibid (footnotes omitted).

[433]See WTO, *Peru – Additional Duty on Imports of Certain Agricultural Products*, Report of the Panel (27 November 2014) WT/DS457/R [7.494]. For a similar statement, see also *United States – Anti-Dumping Measures on Certain Hot-Rolled Steel Products from Japan* (n 403) [7.267].

constitutes a departure from the applicable law or practice and that, consequently, the generally applicable measure on which the decision is based was administered in a manner inconsistent with Article VI:1 GATS. This observation also applies to the other exemption requirements contained in Article 36(1)(a)–(e) Gas Directive.

4.8.1.2 Application of Unbundling Rules to Offshore Sections of Gas Import Pipelines

Another issue that needs to be discussed within the context of Article VI:1 GATS relates to the application of the unbundling requirements foreseen in Directive 2009/73/EC to the offshore sections of gas import pipelines that originate in third countries and transport natural gas to the EU.[434] A WTO Member wishing to challenge the unbundling requirements in the Third Energy Package may argue that the EU takes an inconsistent approach in this regard.

I should state at the outset that, in my opinion, both of the following two interpretations of the Third Energy Package are equally valid. On the one hand, it could be argued that the unbundling requirements in the TEP also apply to the offshore sections of international gas pipelines in the territorial waters of EU Member States.[435] It seems that this approach would be most in line with the effort to introduce competition in the EU energy sector and to fight anti-competitive practices resulting from vertical integration. On the other hand, given that the TEP is concerned with establishing rules for the *internal* market in natural gas and electricity, the opposite view is also possible.[436] However, regardless of which interpretation is adopted, the application of the unbundling rules must be consistent. Otherwise, it could be argued that they are administered in an 'unreasonable' or 'non-objective' manner and thus contrary to the requirements of Article VI:1 GATS.

In the case of the (now defunct) South Stream project, the European Commission seems to have taken the position that the respective offshore section must comply

---

[434] As of now, there is no relevant practice in the electricity sector.

[435] See Simon Pirani and Katja Yafimava, *Russian Gas Transit Across Ukraine Post-2019: Pipeline Scenarios, Gas Flow Consequences, and Regulatory Constraints* (Oxford Institute for Energy Studies 2016) 31; Alan Riley, 'Nordstream 2: Too Many Obstacles, Legal, Economic, and Political to be Delivered?' (2015) 7 <http://www.atlanticcouncil.org/images/publications/Nordstream_2_web_1125.pdf> accessed 31 July 2016.

[436] Pirani and Yafimava (n 435) 31; Deutscher Bundestag, 'Ausarbeitung: Nord Stream 2 – Vorgaben des europäischen Energierechts' (2016) 5–6 <https://www.bundestag.de/blob/420194/7f62ba1e54f37cacaab01d4db4d1f65a/pe-6-027-16-pdf-data.pdf> accessed 1 August 2016. It seems that there are diverging views even within the European Commission. Whereas the Commission's Legal Service opined that the Gas Directive does not apply to the part of a pipeline running through the exclusive economic zone and territorial waters of an EU Member State, DG Energy adopted a contrary position; see Karel Beckman, 'Can Nord Stream 2 Be Stopped?' (14 April 2016) <http://www.energypost.eu/can-nord-stream-2-stopped/> accessed 23 June 2016.

with the unbundling requirements in the Gas Directive to the extent that it is located within EU territory. It may be recalled that the South Stream was planned to originate in the Russian Federation, cross the Black Sea, and reach land near Varna, Bulgaria. On its way to Bulgaria, the pipeline was to run through the Turkish Exclusive Economic Zone (EEZ) and through the Bulgarian EEZ and territorial sea. In 2014, the Bulgarian energy minister publicly expressed the view that the Third Energy Package does not (fully) apply to the offshore section of South Stream in Bulgarian territorial waters,[437] which was to be constructed and operated by the Gazprom-controlled company 'South Stream Transport'. At the same time, the National Assembly of Bulgaria approved the first reading of a law which was supposed to modify and supplement the national energy act.[438] The draft law introduced the new category of 'sea water gas pipelines' (*Морски газопровод*). This category included pipelines that are located within the internal waters and/or the territorial sea of Bulgaria, including the (small) land section of such pipelines up until the point of attachment to an onshore gas infrastructure.[439] According to the draft law, the 'sea water gas pipelines' would be exempted from most of the rules set out in the TEP, including third party access, price regulation, unbundling requirements, and certification.[440] The corresponding explanatory memorandum stated that unidirectional sea water gas pipelines, whose purpose is to transport natural gas to Bulgaria from non-EU countries and which are primarily located outside the EU, would not be subject to the full weight of Directive 2009/73/EC, which would regulate only the *internal* gas market of the EU.[441]

The European Commission, however, questioned the compatibility of the proposed amendments with the Gas Directive. EU officials, speaking on behalf of former EU Energy Commissioner Günther Oettinger, 'insisted that EU law applied to infrastructure under EU jurisdiction, including Bulgarian territorial waters and Bulgarian exclusive economic zones',[442] and further stated that 'should the amendments enter into force as adopted by Parliament, we would have strong concerns as

[437]'Bulgaria, Commission, Lost in Translation over South Stream' *EurActiv* (25 April 2014) <http://www.euractiv.com/sections/energy/bulgaria-commission-lost-translation-over-south-stream-301751>.

[438]Republic of Bulgaria, Draft Law on the Amendment and Supplement of the Energy Act (Законопроект за изменение и допълнение на Закона за енергетиката) (2014) 454-01-23.

[439]Ibid 3.

[440]Ibid 2. Specifically, the draft law specified that the following provisions of the Energy Act shall not apply to 'sea water gas pipelines': Section IV of Chapter Three (price regulation), Chapter Four (licenses), Chapter Eight 'a' (certification of TSOs; rules for investment execution; independence of TSOs), Article 170 (obligation of TSOs), Articles 172–172e (third party access; exemption) and Article 197 (interconnection).

[441]Ibid 4–8.

[442]'Bulgaria, Commission, Lost in Translation over South Stream' (n 437).

regards [their] compliance with EU law.'[443] In that case, the Commission would 'need to take the necessary legal steps'.[444]

The firm stance of the European Commission regarding South Stream is in fact somewhat surprising. Consider, for example, the Nord Stream project. The Nord Stream gas pipeline has not been exempted from the application of the unbundling rules (nor, for that matter, from the requirement of third party access) contained in Directive 2009/73/EC and the transmission system operator, Nord Stream AG, has not been certified as being in compliance with the unbundling rules.[445] Therefore, the Nord Stream pipeline is treated by the relevant national regulatory authorities and by the European Commission as if it were not subject to the core provisions of the TEP. Nord Stream, however, very much resembles the offshore section of South Stream. The starting point of the gas pipeline is Vyborg, Russia. It comes ashore at Lubmin near Greifswald, Germany. On its way to the German coast, the pipeline runs through the territorial sea of two EU Member States, namely Denmark and Germany.[446] According to the public statements of the European Commission in the case of South Stream, one would assume that Nord Stream is also subject to the provisions of the Third Energy Package.[447]

The inertia of the German national regulator (*Bundesnetzagentur*) and the European Commission might in fact be connected with political, rather than legal factors. Although Poland and the Baltic States were in opposition to the project, the

---

[443]Martin Banks, 'Battle Rages between Bulgaria and Brussels over Future of Energy Supplies' *EU Reporter* (7 May 2014) <http://www.eureporter.co/world/2014/05/07/battle-rages-between-bulgaria-and-brussels-over-future-of-energy-supplies/>.

[444]Ibid.

[445]See European Commission, DG Energy, 'Exemption Decisions and Pending Notifications of National Exemption Decisions for Gas and Electricity' (no date) <https://ec.europa.eu/energy/sites/ener/files/documents/exemption_decisions_15.pdf> accessed 24 September 2016; European Commission, DG Energy, 'Opinions and Decisions on Operator Certifications' (no date) <https://ec.europa.eu/energy/sites/ener/files/documents/certifications_decisions.pdf> accessed 24 September 2016. See also Philipp Offenberg, 'The European Neighbourhood and the EU's Security of Supply with Natural Gas' (2016) 19 <http://www.institutdelors.eu/media/euneighbourhoodandgas-offenberg-jdib-jan16.pdf?pdf=ok> accessed 31 January 2016; Riley, 'Nordstream 2: Too Many Obstacles, Legal, Economic, and Political to be Delivered?' (n 435) 7; Yafimava (n 290) 128, 328; European Union, Question for Written Answer E-001009/14 to the Commission – Radvilė Morkūnaitė-Mikulėnienė (PPE) – European Law Exemptions for Energy Infrastructure Projects with Russia (31 March 2014) OJ 2014/C 300/290.

[446]Nord Stream, 'The Pipeline' (no date) <https://www.nord-stream.com/the-project/pipeline/> accessed 21 April 2015.

[447]It seems that the Nord Stream AG as the gas transmission system operator would have to comply with the ownership unbundling requirements foreseen in Directive 2009/73/EC. The construction of the Nord Stream pipeline commenced on April 9, 2010, see Nord Stream, *Nord Stream: "The First Three Kilometres Are Laid"* (2010). Therefore, as the transmission system did not exist on 3 September 2009, the ISO and ITO models are not available, see Article 9(8) of Directive 2009/73/EC (n 8) and European Commission, 'Commission Staff Working Paper – Interpretative Note on Directive 2009/72/EC concerning common Rules for the Internal Market in Electricity and Directive 2009/73/EC concerning common Rules for the Internal Market in Natural Gas – The Unbundling Regime' (n 245) 5.

German government has always actively supported the construction of Nord Stream.[448] Nord Stream also enjoyed the political support of the European Union, being designated as a 'project of European interest' in the context of the Trans-European Energy Networks (TEN-E).[449] In contrast to the powerful advocates for Nord Stream, the European Commission was clearly critical of the South Stream project from the very beginning.

One hypothetical explanation for the non-application of unbundling and third party access rules to Nord Stream could be that the pipeline qualifies as an 'upstream pipeline network'. Under Directive 2009/73/EC, an 'upstream pipeline network' is defined as 'any pipeline or network of pipelines operated and/or constructed as part of an oil or gas production project, or used to convey natural gas from one or more such projects to a processing plant or terminal or final coastal landing terminal.'[450] The unbundling and third party access provisions of the Gas Directive do not apply to such upstream pipeline networks.[451] However, taking into account that Nord Stream receives natural gas from Russia's mainland gas transmission system (Unified Gas Supply System), there is little to suggest that it falls within the scope of the 'upstream pipeline' category.[452]

Apart from Nord Stream, it seems that the rules of third party access and unbundling are also not applied to the offshore sections of other natural gas import pipelines coming from African countries, such as Transmed or Greenstream.[453] The

---

[448] 'Nord Stream: A View from Poland' *Natural Gas Europe* (9 November 2011) <http://www.naturalgaseurope.com/nord-stream-a-view-from-poland-3421>; Hanna Smith, 'Russian Foreign Policy and Energy: The Case of the Nord Stream Gas Pipeline' in Pami Aalto (ed), *Russia's Energy Policies – National, Interregional and Global Levels* (Edward Elgar 2012) 124, 134.

[449] See European Union, Decision No 1364/2006/EC of the European Parliament and of the Council laying down guidelines for trans-European energy networks and repealing Decision 96/391/EC and Decision No 1229/2003/EC (06 September 2006) OJ 2006/L 262/1.

[450] Article 2 No. 2 of Directive 2009/73/EC (n 8).

[451] The reason for this is that the definition of the term 'transmission', which triggers the application of the unbundling and third party access obligations, explicitly excludes upstream pipeline networks; see ibid, Article 2 No. 3. Some disciplines regarding access to upstream pipeline networks nevertheless apply, see ibid, Article 34.

[452] See also Offenberg, 'The European Neighbourhood and the EU's Security of Supply with Natural Gas' (n 445) 19 (who writes that the Commission 'could well identify Nord Stream 1 as transmission network and apply the Third Energy Package on the pipeline'). In contrast, Cho and Geelhoed assume that the Nord Stream pipeline qualified as an upstream pipeline within the meaning of Directive 2003/55/EC, see Nichola Cho and Fausta Geelhoed, 'The Nord Stream Pipeline Project – A Brief Overview of its Legal and European Relevance for Supply Security' in Ulf Hammer and Martha M Roggenkamp (eds), *European Energy Law Report VI* (Energy & Law vol 8. Intersentia 2009) 244.

[453] The Russian foreign minister Sergey Lavrov made the following statement in a press conference on 21 January 2015: 'The South Stream situation is utterly clear: the project, regrettably, has been cancelled – primarily because of the European Commission's discriminatory stance. The exemptions from the Third Energy Package (TEP) that were made for other projects confirm that, given the political will and elementary willingness, all the barriers could have been removed. ... *[The European Commission] made an exception ... for maritime sections of a number of other pipelines*

Italian energy company Eni, which is active in the production and supply of natural gas, currently holds 50% of the shares in the transmission system operators of both offshore pipeline sections.[454] Despite this vertical integration situation, the TSOs concerned have not been certified under any of the unbundling models.[455] It is unclear whether Transmed and Greenstream could qualify as 'upstream pipeline networks'.

As a final point, it should be mentioned that there is currently a debate about whether the TEP's unbundling rules apply to Nord Stream 2, the latest Gazprom-sponsored project that is planned to run parallel to the first Nord Stream pipeline.[456] Several EU Member States,[457] as well as academic commentators,[458] have argued that Nord Stream 2 must comply with the OU model in Article 9 of the Gas Directive.

In the context of this sub-section, the question arises what implications the preceding observations have in terms of Article VI:1 GATS. To recapitulate: On the one hand, the European Commission does not apply the unbundling requirements foreseen in Directive 2009/73/EC to the transmission system operators of Nord Stream, Transmed and Greenstream,[459] either because it proceeds on the assumption that the core provisions of the TEP do not apply to the offshore sections of international gas import pipelines, or because it considers these pipelines to be 'upstream pipelines', although at least the Nord Stream project clearly does not constitute an upstream pipeline. On the other hand, the Commission announced that the exemption of the South Stream offshore section located within EU territory from certain key obligations of the EU energy *acquis* would be incompatible with EU law and threatened to initiate an infringement procedure against Bulgaria. Although it seems doubtful whether the public pronouncements of the European Commission

---

in the Mediterranean, such as Transmed, Greenstream, and others. There were many cases, in which the European Commission made exceptions from the Third Energy Package, but not for Bulgaria. I won't go into detail – South Stream has been cancelled.', see Ministry of Foreign Affairs of the Russian Federation, 'Foreign Minister Sergey Lavrov's Address and Annual News Conference on Russia's Diplomatic Performance in 2014' (2015) <http://www.mid.ru/brp_4.nsf/0/D1AFD0A22ABD9AB443257DD4004F33B5> (emphasis added). See also Christian Oliver and Jack Farchy, 'Gazprom Criticises EU over South Stream Gas Pipeline' *Financial Times* (30 May 2014) <http://www.ft.com/intl/cms/s/0/949eb796-e7f2-11e3-9af8-00144feabdc0.html>.

[454]Eni, 'Interim Consolidated Report' (30 June 2016) 146 <https://www.eni.com/docs/en_IT/enicom/publications-archive/publications/reports/reports-2016/interim-consolidated-report-as-of-june-30-2016.pdf> accessed 31 July 2016.

[455]See European Commission, DG Energy, 'Opinions and Decisions on Operator Certifications' (n 445).

[456]See Beckman, 'Can Nord Stream 2 Be Stopped?' (n 436).

[457]Anca Gurzu, 'Nord Stream 2's Opponents Look for Legal Ammunition' (30 December 2015) <http://www.politico.eu/article/nord-stream-2s-opponents-look-for-legal-ammunition/> accessed 23 June 2016.

[458]Riley, 'Nordstream 2: Too Many Obstacles, Legal, Economic, and Political to be Delivered?' (n 435) 7–8. But see Pirani and Yafimava (n 435) 31.

[459]To the extent that the offshore sections of these pipelines are located within EU jurisdiction.

with respect to the South Stream pipeline would be sufficient to be able to conclude that the unbundling requirements in Directive 2009/73/EC are not administered in a reasonable or objective manner within the meaning of Article VI:1 GATS (mainly because it is not entirely clear on what *exact* grounds the 'proposed amendments' of the Bulgarian parliament were allegedly incompatible with EU law), the complete absence of a legal regime governing and clarifying the applicability of the core provisions of the TEP to offshore gas import pipelines has clearly led to a situation of legal uncertainty. Apart from that, Article VI:1 GATS would almost certainly be violated if the designated transmission system operator of Nord Stream 2 were compelled to implement ownership unbundling. In that case, there would be a clear lack of uniformity in the administration of the TEP's unbundling requirements, contrary to the requirements of reasonableness and objectivity in Article VI:1 GATS.

4.8.2 Article VI:4/5 GATS: Substantive Disciplines on Domestic Regulation

Article VI:4 GATS stipulates that the Council for Trade in Services of the WTO shall develop disciplines on domestic regulation. These disciplines shall ensure that qualification requirements and procedures, technical standards, and licensing requirements are (1) 'based on objective and transparent criteria, such as competence and the ability to supply the service' (lit (a)); (2) 'not more burdensome than necessary to ensure the quality of the service' (lit (b)); and (3) 'in the case of licensing procedures, not in themselves a restriction on the supply of the service' (lit (c)).

In accordance with its mandate, the Council for Trade in Services established a Working Party on Professional Services (WPPS) in 1995.[460] The WPPS elaborated disciplines on domestic regulation in the accountancy sector, which were adopted by the Council for Trade in Services in 1998.[461] It is expected that they will be integrated into the GATS at the end of the Doha Round.[462] In 1999 it was decided to replace the WPPS by the Working Party on Domestic Regulation (WPDR), which

[460] WTO, Decision on Professional Services – Adopted by the Council for Trade in Services on 1 March 1995 (04 April 1995) S/L/3.

[461] WTO, Decision on Disciplines Relating to the Accountancy Sector – Adopted by the Council for Trade in Services on 14 December 1998 (15 December 1998) S/L/63. For the text of the disciplines, see WTO, Disciplines on Domestic Regulation in the Accountancy Sector – Adopted by the Council for Trade in Services on 14 December 1998 (17 December 1998) S/L/64.

[462] The GATS Council for Trade in Services does not have any law-making authority. Any disciplines adopted by the Council are not *ipso facto* binding on the WTO Members, but have to be formally integrated into the GATS. See on this Pitschas (n 11) [140]; Michaelis (n 11) [102]; Herrmann, Weiß and Ohler (n 29) [882].

was tasked with developing generally applicable disciplines.[463] The negotiations within the WPDR have, however, proven to be difficult. The latest progress report on the negotiations on trade in services notes that 'disagreement persists on important and basic issues.'[464] Thus the elaboration of horizontal disciplines on domestic regulation remains a still pending task, and therefore they do not place any restrictions on the introduction or maintenance of unbundling and unbundling-related measures in the EU energy sector.

Viewed against this background, the following analysis concentrates on Article VI:5 GATS. Article VI:5 GATS was designed to ensure the provisional application of the disciplines contained in Article VI:4 GATS in order to provide an interim solution. In that sense, the provision can be seen as 'an effort to operationalize the objectives' in Article VI:4.[465] Article VI:5(a) GATS provides as follows:

> In sectors in which a Member has undertaken specific commitments, pending the entry into force of disciplines developed in these sectors pursuant to paragraph 4, the Member shall not apply licensing and qualification requirements and technical standards that nullify or impair such specific commitments in a manner which
>
> i. does not comply with the criteria outlined in subparagraphs 4(a), (b) or (c); and
> ii. could not reasonably have been expected of that Member at the time the specific commitments in those sectors were made.

On the basis of Article VI:5 GATS, it could be argued that the objectives underlying the ownership unbundling measures set out in Directives 2009/72/EC and 2009/73/EC could be achieved in a less burdensome manner and that, consequently, the OU model constitutes a governmental measure that is 'more burdensome than necessary to ensure the quality of the service', thus resulting in a violation of Article VI:5 in conjunction with Article VI:4(b).[466] In fact, Article VI:4(b)/5 GATS is the only obligation in the GATS which allows for an assessment of the intrusive effects of the OU model in the light of some kind of proportionality considerations. Given that OU is the most restrictive unbundling solution, the outcome of such an assessment will apply *a maiore ad minus* also to the ISO and ITO models. Therefore, with a view to evaluating the legality of OU under Article VI:4(b)/5 GATS, the following remarks are in order.

First of all, Article VI:5 GATS only applies in sectors in which a WTO Member has undertaken specific commitments. As has been established, MA and NT com-

[463]WTO, Decision on Domestic Regulation – Adopted by the Council for Trade in Services on 26 April 1999 (28 April 1999) S/L/70.

[464]WTO, Council for Trade in Services, Negotiations on Trade in Services – Report by the Chairman, Ambassador Fernando de Mateo, to the Trade Negotiations Committee (21 April 2011) TN/S/36, [2].

[465]WTO, Working Party on Domestic Regulation, Report on the Meeting Held on 11 May 2001 – Note by the Secretariat (07 June 2001) S/WPDR/M/11, [29].

[466]This argument was raised by the Russian Federation, see Trade Policy Review – European Union (n 87) 313–314.

mitments have been undertaken by both the EU and its Member States in the energy transmission and/or energy supply sector.[467] Furthermore, the scope of application of Article VI:5 GATS covers licensing and qualification requirements and technical standards.[468] In the present context, licensing requirements constitute the relevant category. The GATS does not provide a legal definition of this term, but the following description is used in the negotiations in the WPDR: 'substantive requirements, other than qualification requirements, with which a natural or a juridical person is required to comply in order to obtain, amend or renew authorization to supply a service.'[469] The OU requirements in Directives 2009/72/EC and 2009/73/EC clearly fall within the category of licensing requirements. They are therefore subject to Article VI:5 GATS.

In order for a measure of a WTO Member to be found to be inconsistent with its obligations under Article VI:5 GATS, it must in the first instance be shown that the application of the measure in dispute has 'nullified or impaired' specific commitments. As there is considerable uncertainty regarding the interpretation of this element, a closer analysis is necessary. The concepts of 'nullification' and 'impairment' have their origins in the dispute settlement system of the WTO.[470] Article XXIII GATT provides that a case may be brought to dispute settlement only if the Contracting State 'consider[s] that any benefit accruing to it directly or indirectly under this Agreement is being nullified or impaired or that the attainment of any objective of the Agreement is being impeded.' With a view to lowering the obstacles to *violation complaints* (i.e. claims that an obligation of a WTO Member under a WTO agreement has been violated), Article 3(8) of the Dispute Settlement Understanding (DSU) later clarified that where an obligation assumed under a WTO agreement has been infringed, 'the action is considered *prima facie* to constitute a case of nullification or impairment.' In other words, if the complainant can demonstrate that another WTO Member acted inconsistently with its obligations under the

---

[467]See Sect. 4.4.

[468]In addition, although not explicitly mentioned, Article VI:5 GATS arguably also covers licensing and qualification *procedures*; see Delimatsis (n 405) 118. For an opposing view, see Michaelis (n 11) [106].

[469]WTO, Working Party on Domestic Regulation, Disciplines on Domestic Regulation Pursuant to GATS Article VI:4 – Chairman's Progress Report (14 April 2011) S/WPDR/W/45, 10. Qualification requirements are described as 'substantive requirements relating to the competence of a natural person in relation to the supply of a service, and which are required to be demonstrated for the purpose of obtaining authorization to supply a service' (ibid 12).

[470]For a comprehensive study of this concept, see Frieder Roessler, 'The Concept of Nullification and Impairment in the Legal System of the World Trade Organization' in Ernst-Ulrich Petersmann (ed), *International Trade Law and the GATT/WTO Dispute Settlement System* (Kluwer Law International 1997); Ernst-Ulrich Petersmann, *The GATT/WTO Dispute Settlement System: International Law, International Organizations and Dispute Settlement* (Kluwer Law International 1997) 135–176.

WTO, this creates a presumption regarding the nullification or impairment of benefits.[471] Theoretically this presumption is rebuttable, but practice has shown that it is virtually immune to rebuttal.[472] In keeping with the approach taken in Article 3(8) DSU, the requirement to show nullification or impairment of a benefit in violation complaints has been completely omitted from the text of Article XXIII GATS (Dispute Settlement and Enforcement).[473] In consequence, under both GATT and GATS, the role of the concept of nullification or impairment is nowadays largely confined to the area of so-called *non-violation complaints*, a special feature of the WTO dispute settlement system. The notion of a non-violation complaint refers to the possibility that a measure of a WTO Member can be challenged even if it is not in conflict with one or more provisions of the GATT/GATS. As regards the GATS, such a complaint can be brought under Article XXIII:3, which presupposes, as indicated, that benefits are either nullified or impaired.

Coming back to Article VI:5 GATS, some authors believe that by virtue of Article 3(8) DSU, the nullification or impairment of specific commitments under Article VI:5 is to be presumed.[474] Such a presumption would clearly strengthen Article VI:5 GATS. In the present situation under discussion, a complainant in a WTO dispute would not have the burden of proving that nullification or impairment has occurred as a consequence of OU measures. This interpretation of Article VI:5 GATS is, however, contentious.[475] A number of authors take the opposing view—that Article VI:5 embodies a non-violation concept of nullification or impairment[476] and that, consequently, Article 3(8) of the DSU is not applicable.[477] It is submitted here that neither of these competing views are entirely convincing and that a middle

---

[471]On Article 3(8) DSU, see Peter-Tobias Stoll, 'Article 3 DSU' in Rüdiger Wolfrum, Peter-Tobias Stoll and Karen Kaiser (eds), *WTO – Institutions and Dispute Settlement* (Max Planck Commentaries on World Trade Law vol 2. Martinus Nijhoff Publishers 2006) [71–77].

[472]GATT, *United States – Taxes on Petroleum and Certain Imported Substances (Superfund),* Report of the Panel (17 June 1987) L/6175 – 34S/136 [5.1.7]; *European Communities – Regime for the Importation, Sale and Distribution of Bananas* (n 3) [249–254]; Delimatsis (n 405) 120.

[473]Rainer Grote, 'Article XXIII GATS' in Rüdiger Wolfrum, Peter-Tobias Stoll and Clemens Feinäugle (eds), *WTO – Trade in Services* (Max Planck Commentaries on World Trade Law vol 6. Martinus Nijhoff Publishers 2008) [1, 9]. See also WTO, *Mexico – Measures Affecting Telecommunications Services,* Report of the Panel (2 April 2004) WT/DS204/R [8.4].

[474]Pitschas (n 11) [138]; Michaelis (n 11) [106]; Sunde (n 400) 60–63.

[475]Herrmann, Weiß and Ohler (n 29) [882a].

[476]Jan Wouters and Dominic Coppens, 'GATS and Domestic Regulation: Balancing the Right to Regulate and Trade Liberalization' in Kern Alexander and Mads Andenas (eds), *The World Trade Organization and Trade in Services* (Martinus Nijhoff Publishers 2008) 258; Markus Krajewski, 'Disziplinen für innerstaatliche Regulierung nach Artikel VI GATS' in Dirk Ehlers, Hans-Michael Wolffgang and Marc Lechleitner (eds), *Rechtsfragen des internationalen Dienstleistungsverkehrs: Tagungsband zum 10. Münsteraner Außenwirtschaftsrechtstag 2005* (Verlag Recht und Wirtschaft 2006) 197.

[477]Joel P Trachtman, 'Lessons for the GATS from Existing WTO Rules on Domestic Regulation' in Aaditya Mattoo and Pierre Sauvé (eds), *Domestic Regulation and Service Trade Liberalization* (Oxford University Press 2003) 67; Trachtman (n 196) 212–213; Krajewski (n 400) [68].

way can be found between the two. First, the argument that the application of Article 3(8) DSU to Article VI:5 GATS should be rejected because the latter contains a 'non-violation nullification or impairment' concept stands on weak grounds. The GATS already contains a provision on the basis of which 'non-violation nullification or impairment' cases may be brought, namely Article XXIII:3 GATS. It seems illogical that there should be two separate provisions in the GATS covering such non-violation complaints.[478] In this light, and taking other factors into consideration,[479] the better view would be that Article VI:5 GATS covers only violation complaints.[480] However, this does not necessarily mean that Article 3(8) DSU applies to the 'nullify or impair' language in Article VI:5 GATS. By its own terms, Article 3(8) DSU only applies '*[i]n cases where there is an infringement* of the obligations assumed under a covered agreement.'[481] However, in the case of Article VI:5 GATS, nullification or impairment of specific commitments is a substantive element of that provision.[482] In other words, Article VI:5 GATS is not violated, *unless* nullification or impairment of specific commitments has been shown. Therefore, the presumption contained in Article 3(8) DSU cannot apply at the stage of determining whether the various criteria of Article VI:5 GATS have been fulfilled.[483] Any other interpretation would also contradict the intention of the parties to the GATS, who clearly sought to operationalize only a watered-down version of the disciplines in Article VI:4 GATS.[484]

In conclusion, under Article VI:5 GATS, the complaining WTO Member bears the burden of proving that the application of the disputed measure has 'nullified or impaired' the specific commitments at issue. There can be no doubt that the contours of these concepts are quite blurry, to say the least.[485] It might be possible to draw some guidance from the jurisprudence relating to non-violation nullification or impairment complaints under Article XXIII:1 GATT. The leading case in this regard is *Japan – Film*.[486] Summarizing the approach taken in several previous GATT

---

[478]Delimatsis (n 405) 122.

[479]Ibid 122–123.

[480]This view is also shared by De Meester (n 126) 196 (footnote 554); Petersmann (n 470) 148–149. Furthermore, Roessler notes that Article VI:5 GATS 'establishes the *legal obligation* not to apply measures that nullify or impair specific commitments, thereby reducing the need to resort to the non-violation nullification and impairment provisions of the GATS', see Roessler (n 470) 135 (emphasis in the original).

[481]Emphasis added.

[482]Delimatsis (n 405) 123–124.

[483]On a side note, even if the WTO dispute settlement bodies established that Article VI:5 GATS is breached, Article 3(8) DSU would not apply, because the GATS does not condition access to WTO dispute settlement in such cases on showing that a benefit has been nullified or impaired, see Article XXIII:3 GATS (n 4) and *Mexico – Measures Affecting Telecommunications Services* (n 473) [8.4].

[484]Trachtman (n 196) 213; Krajewski (n 400) [68].

[485]Trachtman (n 196) 213 ('an extremely vague standard').

[486]WTO, *Japan – Measures Affecting Consumer Photographic Film and Paper*, Report of the Panel (31 March 1998) WT/DS44/R.

Panel reports, the Panel in *Japan – Film* held that nullification or impairment could be equated with '"upsetting the competitive relationship" established between domestic and imported products as a result of tariff concessions.'[487] One author has taken the view that it is 'unclear whether the same reasoning would apply to trade in services', but that there are 'no obvious reasons why it should not.'[488] This would mean that Article VI:5 GATS requires that the relative conditions of competition which existed between domestic and foreign services and service suppliers as a consequence of the relevant specific commitment must have been upset. It seems, however, that this test is too narrow for the purposes of Article VI:5 GATS, because it focuses exclusively on a relative comparison between domestic and foreign services and service suppliers. Measures that do not modify the competitive relationship between domestic and foreign services and service suppliers to the detriment of the latter, but nevertheless frustrate specific market access commitments in *absolute* terms, would be excluded from the scope of Article VI:5. Therefore it seems more appropriate to focus more generally on the value of specific commitments.[489]

In the present context, market access commitments are particularly pertinent with respect to the nullification or impairment test. Lithuania, for example, has undertaken a full market access commitment on pipeline transport services.[490] The main value of such a market access commitment is that it provides an assurance of the absence of certain measures of a quantitative or qualitative nature that would impede market entry. This effect of a market access commitment should not be offset in any way. A complainant could thus argue that Lithuania's specific market access commitment on pipeline transport services was nullified or impaired as a result of the introduction of ownership unbundling measures, which ban all gas supply and production companies from providing gas transmission services in Lithuania and which, therefore, to some extent prevent the full implementation of the commitment on market access opportunities of foreign services and service suppliers.[491] However, given that unbundling measures are meant to induce competition and prevent discrimination, it could also be said that OU measures *preserve* the value of market access commitments in the energy sector. In fact, it is clear that the market access opportunities of foreign services and service suppliers can be significantly

---

[487]Ibid [10.82]. The Panel *inter alia* referred to GATT, *Follow-Up on the Panel Report "European Economic Community – Payments and Subsidies Paid to Processors and Producers of Oilseeds and Related Animal-Feed Proteins"*, Report of the Members of the Original Oilseeds Panel (31 March 1992) DS28/R – 39S/91 [77].

[488]David Luff, 'Regulation of Health Services and International Trade Law' in Aaditya Mattoo and Pierre Sauvé (eds), *Domestic Regulation and Service Trade Liberalization* (Oxford University Press 2003) 202.

[489]See Krajewski (n 400) [67].

[490]See Sect. 4.4.

[491]*Cf.* GATT, *European Economic Community – Payments and Subsidies Paid to Processors and Producers of Oilseeds and Related Animal-Feed Proteins*, Report of the Panel (25 January 1990) L/6627 – 37S/86 [148].

undermined through private anti-competitive practices, such as those resulting from vertical integration, unless there is effective competition regulation.[492]

It is precisely for this reason that, in the telecommunications sector, WTO Members have developed additional pro-competitive regulatory disciplines within the WTO framework.[493] As regards the energy sector, the WTO Secretariat clearly stated in its first background paper on energy services that the unbundling of vertically integrated companies is 'the *first market access issue* on the road of multilateral liberalization.'[494] In sum, therefore, it is highly questionable that OU policies 'nullify or impair' market access commitments within the meaning of Article VI:5 GATS.[495]

For a claim to be successful under Article VI:5 GATS, the complainant also needs to show that the way in which the licensing requirements were applied by the respondent WTO Member 'could not reasonably have been expected of [the respondent] at the time the specific commitments in those sectors were made.' This limitation essentially excludes all measures that were in force at the time the specific commitments were scheduled from the scope of Article VI:5.[496] Conversely, this means that measures that were adopted after the specific commitments were made are in principle subject to Article VI:5 GATS, as it can be assumed that such measures 'could not reasonably have been expected.'[497] This would encompass the Third Energy Package (and, by implication, any national implementing legislation), which was adopted after the EU Member States and the EU had drawn up their respective GATS schedules of specific commitments. Thus a presumption arises that other WTO Members could not reasonably have expected the application of the OU requirements.[498]

Finally, Article VI:5 GATS requires that it must be shown that the ownership unbundling requirements were applied in a manner which does not comply with the criterion in Article VI:4(b) GATS, namely that domestic regulation shall not be more burdensome than necessary to ensure the quality of the service. This standard could have far-reaching implications for many regulatory instruments, because it not only establishes a necessity test for domestic regulation ('not more burdensome than *necessary* ...'), but also limits the range of permissible regulatory goals ('... to ensure the *quality of the service*').[499] In the context of this book it is crucial to note

[492] See Sect. 6.1.

[493] See Sect. 6.4.1.

[494] Energy Services – Background Note by the Secretariat (n 2) [6] (emphasis added).

[495] It should also be noted in this connection that although a number of non-violation complaints have been brought under the GATT, alleging nullification or impairment of benefits, none of them has been successful; see van den Bossche and Zdouc (n 71) 175.

[496] Wouters and Coppens (n 476) 258; Michaelis (n 11) [106]; Herrmann, Weiß and Ohler (n 29) [882a]; Delimatsis (n 405) 119; WTO, Article VI:4 of the GATS: Disciplines on Domestic Regulation Applicable to All Services – Note by the Secretariat (01 March 1999) S/C/W/96, [11].

[497] De Meester (n 126) 196–197; Luff (n 488) 203.

[498] See *Japan – Measures Affecting Consumer Photographic Film and Paper* (n 486) [10.79].

[499] Trachtman (n 477) 68.

that Article VI:4(b) GATS only refers to one legitimate policy objective, that is, the quality of the service. Whereas it is plausible that OU measures contribute to the objectives of non-discriminatory network access, combating cross-subsidization and preventing distortions of competition, their nexus to the 'quality of the service' is less evident.[500] The absence of an open-ended or at least extended list of legitimate objectives becomes all the more evident when considering that the existing accountancy disciplines broadly refer to 'legitimate objectives', which include the protection of consumers, the quality of the service, and professional competence and the integrity of the profession.[501]

An attempt could of course be made to give a broad construction to the term 'quality of the service'. It could for example be interpreted to include 'reliability, efficiency, comprehensiveness, or objectives associated with externalities and public policy.'[502] While it is clear that the meaning of the word 'quality' cannot be broadened *ad libitum*, a good argument can be made that the notion refers not only to the quality of the service in a purely technical sense. Therefore, measures that seek to ensure that access-seeking users have non-discriminatory access to transmission networks should be considered to relate to the 'quality' of transmission services.

While OU requirements may thus be considered to relate to the quality of transmission services (*sensu lato*), they would also need to be 'not more burdensome than necessary' to ensure that objective. In this connection it is unclear whether the 'burdensomeness' of a measure is a concept equivalent to, or different from, its 'trade-restrictiveness'.[503] Given that it is the object and purpose of the GATS to expand and liberalize trade in services and that the *chapeau* of Article VI:4 GATS explicitly highlights the aim of removing unnecessary barriers to such cross-border trade,[504] a measure should only be found to be 'more burdensome than necessary' if it creates an unnecessary barrier to trade in services through one of the four modes of supply. The applicable necessity test is not further defined in the provision, but WTO

---

[500]For another example in the context of hospital services, see Adlung (n 44) 480.

[501]Disciplines on Domestic Regulation in the Accountancy Sector – Adopted by the Council for Trade in Services on 14 December 1998 (n 461) [2].

[502]Panagiotis Delimatsis, 'Towards a Horizontal Necessity Test for Services: Completing the GATS Article VI:4 Mandate' in Marion Panizzon, Nicole Pohl and Pierre Sauvé (eds), *GATS and the Regulation of International Trade in Services* (Cambridge University Press 2008) 376 (referring to WTO, Working Party on Domestic Regulation, Communication from Australia (19 July 1999) S/WPDR/W/1, [7]).

[503]The WTO Secretariat opines that there is a difference in meaning, see WTO, Working Party on Domestic Regulation, Report on the Meeting Held on 29 November 2000 – Note by the Secretariat (12 March 2001) S/WPDR/M/9, 8. Similarly, Krajewski takes the view that the concept of 'burdensomeness' is broader than the concept of 'trade-restrictiveness' and that, accordingly, a measure could be found to be more burdensome than necessary, while not being overly trade-restrictive. In his view, such an application of the necessity test in Article VI:4(b) GATS could have a detrimental effect on national regulatory autonomy, see Krajewski (n 36) 141–142. WTO Members, however, appear to treat the two terms as synonymous, see Delimatsis (n 502) 387.

[504]Krajewski (n 36) 142.

jurisprudence on Article XX GATT and Article XIV GATS is applicable *mutatis mutandis*.

Inasmuch as it was shown above that OU measures most likely do not 'nullify or impair' market access commitments in the energy sector, as required by Article VI:5 GATS, only some fundamental proportionality considerations will be given here.[505] Due to their inherent limitations, behavioral measures (network access regulation) cannot completely rule out the possibility that integrated operators will discriminate against competitors. It is thus necessary to suppress, or ideally remove, the incentive of the TSO to give preferential treatment to certain network users. This can only be achieved through unbundling measures.

The decisive issue is thus whether OU is *necessary* to safeguard non-discriminatory network access, or whether there are other, less trade-restrictive unbundling solutions that could achieve the same objective. While it is evident that the ownership unbundling model in the TEP is more effective than, for example, functional separation, the preambles to Directives 2009/72/EC and 2009/73/EC,[506] as well as European Commission documents and decisions,[507] are based on the assumption that all three main unbundling models in the TEP (ITO, ISO and OU) are equally effective in terms of separating the network activities from other activities not related to transmission. This assumption of equal effectiveness means that, in comparison to ownership unbundling, the ITO model could be perceived as a less trade-restrictive and reasonably available alternative, even under a deferential standard of review. However, the EU Member States that have adopted OU through national implementing legislation are not bound by the EU legislator's assumption of equal effectiveness and may provide their own assessment.[508] Moreover, at least from a theoretical perspective, the ownership unbundling model in the TEP will

[505]For a full proportionality analysis, see Sect. 5.7.3.2.

[506]9th, 11th-12th, 16th and 19th recital of the preamble to Directive 2009/72/EC (n 8); 6th, 8th-9th, 13th and 16th recital of the preamble to Directive 2009/73/EC (n 8). See also Cabau (n 376) [4.24]; Buschle (n 327) 54, 62.

[507]European Commission, 'Commission Staff Working Paper – Interpretative Note on Directive 2009/72/EC concerning common Rules for the Internal Market in Electricity and Directive 2009/73/EC concerning common Rules for the Internal Market in Natural Gas – The Unbundling Regime' (n 245) 4; European Commission, Commission Decision pursuant to Article 3(1) of Regulation (EC) No 714/2009 and Article 10(6) of Directive 2009/72/EC – Ireland – Eirgrid/ESB (12 April 2013) C(2013) 2169 final, [17]; European Commission, Commission Decision on the application of Article 9(9) of Directive 2009/72/EC to Transmission System Operation in Scotland (14 May 2012) C(2012) 3284 final, [8]; European Commission, Commission Decision pursuant to Article 3(1) of Regulation (EC) No 714/2009 and Article 10(6) of Directive 2009/72/EC – United Kingdom (Northern Ireland) – SONI/NIE (12 April 2013) C(2013) 2170 final, [11].

[508]In doing so, the Member States could point to statements of the European Commission and the European Parliament, which were made during the legislative procedure leading to the adoption of the TEP and which suggest that ownership unbundling is, in fact, superior to other unbundling options, see European Commission, Inquiry pursuant to Article 17 of Regulation (EC) No 1/2003 into the European gas and electricity sectors (Final Report) (10 January 2007) COM(2006) 851 final, [55]; European Parliament, Resolution on Prospects for the Internal Gas and Electricity Market (10 July 2007) P6_TA(2007)0326, [2].

always be more effective than other regulatory solutions, because it creates TSOs that are completely structurally independent from production/generation or supply interests.[509] Therefore, it will be difficult to show that there is an alternative, less trade-restrictive, measure.

In conclusion, the OU measures as set out in the TEP should be deemed not inconsistent with the domestic regulation disciplines of Article VI:5 in conjunction with Article VI:4(b) GATS.

4.9 Article XIV (General Exceptions)

GATS-inconsistent unbundling and unbundling-related measures could be justified under the general exception provision of Article XIV GATS. According to the analysis conducted in this chapter, the additional security of supply test in the third-country certification procedure provided by Article 11 of Directives 2009/72/EC and 2009/73/EC is the only provision of the TEP that is GATS-inconsistent and thus requires justification under the agreement.[510] A comprehensive analysis of the relationship between the unbundling regime in the TEP and the general exception provision under the GATS is nevertheless instructive and important in order to provide a full assessment of the scope of WTO Members' national regulatory autonomy under the WTO agreements.

The general exception provision in Article XIV GATS reads as follows:

> Subject to the requirement that such measures are not applied in a manner which would constitute a means of arbitrary or unjustifiable discrimination between countries where like conditions prevail, or a disguised restriction on trade in services, nothing in this Agreement shall be construed to prevent the adoption or enforcement by any Member of measures:
>
> 4.10. necessary to protect public morals or to maintain public order;
> 4.11. necessary to protect human, animal or plant life or health;
> 4.12. necessary to secure compliance with laws or regulations which are not inconsistent with the provisions of this Agreement including those relating to:
>
> (i) the prevention of deceptive and fraudulent practices or to deal with the effects of a default on services contracts;
> (ii) the protection of the privacy of individuals in relation to the processing and dissemination of personal data and the protection of confidentiality of individual records and accounts;
> (iii) safety;
>
> 4.13. inconsistent with Article XVII, provided that the difference in treatment is aimed at ensuring the equitable or effective imposition or collection of direct taxes in respect of services or service suppliers of other Members;

---

[509]See the reasoning of the Dutch *Hoge Raad* in Hoge Raad der Nederlanden, *Staat der Nederlanden v. Essent N.V.* Judgment (26 June 2015) 10/03851 [3.20].

[510]See Sect. 4.6.2.1.

> 4.14. inconsistent with Article II, provided that the difference in treatment is the result of an agreement on the avoidance of double taxation or provisions on the avoidance of double taxation in any other international agreement or arrangement by which the Member is bound.[511]

Like its counterpart in the GATT, Article XIV GATS reflects the rationale that WTO Members should be allowed to pursue certain legitimate non-economic policy goals. Apart from lit (d) and (e), which relate to measures that are inconsistent the NT and MFN principles respectively, Article XIV entitles WTO Members to derogate from all provisions and specific commitments.[512] Its structure follows that of Article XX GATT: It contains an introductory paragraph (*chapeau*) and a closed list of public policy objectives.[513] In correspondence with its two-part structure, Article XIV GATS calls for a two-tier analysis.[514] Under the first part of this test, it needs to be assessed whether the measure at issue can be provisionally justified under one of the specific exceptions listed in lit (a) to (e). In the second step, it must be examined whether the general requirements of the *chapeau* are met.

4.9.1 Public Interest Grounds and the Unbundling Regime Under the TEP

In the context of this book, the exhaustive nature of the list of public policy objectives in Article XIV GATS is thrown into stark relief. Under EU law there is an evolutionary list of overriding reasons in the public interest which could justify the various elements of the unbundling regime contained in Directives 2009/72/EC and 2009/73/EC (the *Cassis de Dijon* doctrine).[515] For instance, the restrictions on the free movement of capital and the freedom of establishment resulting from ownership unbundling requirements can, in principle, be justified with reference to the objectives of combating cross-subsidization and preventing distortions of competition. This was confirmed by the ECJ in the *Staat der Nederlanden v Essent NV and Others* case.[516]

Under WTO law, in contrast, there is no *Cassis de Dijon* equivalent.[517] Although it might be desirable to complement the treaty-based exceptions in the WTO

[511] Footnotes in the original omitted.

[512] Michaelis (n 11) [109].

[513] Pitschas (n 11) [154].

[514] Herrmann, Weiß and Ohler (n 29) [884]; Pitschas (n 11) [154].

[515] See European Court of Justice, *Rewe v Bundesmonopolverwaltung für Branntwein*, Judgment (20 February 1979) C-120/78.

[516] See *Staat der Nederlanden v Essent NV and Others* (n 131) [66].

[517] Gaines and Olsen see this as '[o]ne of the most striking differences between the two legal systems', see Sanford E Gaines and Birgitte E Olsen, 'Trade and Social Objectives' in Sanford E Gaines, Birgitte E Olsen and Karsten E Sørensen (eds), *Liberalising Trade in the EU and the WTO: A Legal Comparison* (Cambridge University Press 2012) 208, 230.

agreements with court-made justifications,[518] to date the WTO dispute settlement organs have been unwilling to do so. As alluded to, in *EC – Bananas III* the Appellate Body held that the 'aims and effects' of a measure are irrelevant for the determination of whether that measure is consistent with Articles II or XVII of the GATS.[519] In 2016, the Appellate Body stressed in *Argentina – Financial Services* that the concept of 'treatment no less favorable' under both the MFN and NT provisions of the GATS 'does not contemplate a separate and additional inquiry into the regulatory objective of, or the regulatory concerns underlying, the contested measure.'[520] As a consequence, the objectives of combating cross-subsidization, preventing distortions of competition and providing non-discriminatory network access cannot (and do not) constitute self-standing legitimate public interest grounds under the GATS.

Despite the foregoing, unbundling and unbundling-related measures inconsistent with the GATS can be justified under Article XIV GATS as long as they can be subsumed under lit (a)–(e). In the case of OU requirements, one possibility would be that such measures could fall under Article XIV(c) GATS, which serves as a justification for measures which are 'necessary to secure compliance with laws or regulations which are not inconsistent with the provisions of [the GATS]'. OU measures could be deemed necessary to secure compliance with general EU competition law and in particular with Article 102 TFEU, which prohibits the abuse of dominant market positions. In general, *ex ante* sector-specific regulation can be necessary to enforce *ex post* competition rules, such as Article 102 TFEU. Accounting unbundling, for example, is an essential instrument for competition authorities in order to detect and prevent illegal cross-subsidization.

In the case of OU, however, the situation is different. Ownership unbundling policies go far beyond general competition law. Here, all undertakings are affected. There is no requirement to show that a particular market player abused its dominant position. In this sense, OU effectively 'replaces' proceedings pursuant to Article 102 TFEU and constitutes a stand-alone policy approach. Such a stand-alone policy is not designed to 'secure compliance' with Article 102 TFEU and thus cannot be justified under Article XIV(c) GATS.[521] The fact that OU is aimed at ensuring the attainment of the *objectives* of Article 102 TFEU, namely the prevention of distortions of competition in the internal market, is not sufficient. WTO jurisprudence has clarified that a measure cannot be said to 'secure compliance' with laws or

---

[518]Thomas Cottier, Panagiotis Delimatsis and Nicolas F Diebold, 'Article XIV GATS' in Rüdiger Wolfrum, Peter-Tobias Stoll and Clemens Feinäugle (eds), *WTO – Trade in Services* (Max Planck Commentaries on World Trade Law vol 6. Martinus Nijhoff Publishers 2008) [18].

[519]*European Communities – Regime for the Importation, Sale and Distribution of Bananas* (n 3) [240–248].

[520]*Argentina – Measures Relating to Trade in Goods and Services* (n 199) [6.106].

[521]For a similar argument in a different context, see Martin Nettesheim, 'Unternehmensübernahmen durch Staatsfonds: Europarechtliche Vorgaben und Schranken' (2008) 172 Zeitschrift für das gesamte Handels- und Wirtschaftsrecht 729, 739, footnote 17.

regulations when it only promotes the general policy objectives underlying such laws or regulations.[522] Rather, the measure at issue must secure compliance with specific rules or obligations.[523]

Apart from Article XIV(c) GATS, the exception for measures which are 'necessary . . . to maintain public order' (lit (a)) is especially relevant in the present context. In particular it could be argued that measures which are aimed to enhance the security of energy supply could fall into this category.[524] Given that the ownership unbundling requirements,[525] the third-country certification procedure,[526] and the infrastructure-related exemption regime[527] all allegedly contribute to security of supply, Article XIV(a) GATS could serve to justify potential breaches of the GATS. Thus the question becomes whether security of supply considerations fall within the scope of the 'public order' concept as it appears in that provision, and whether the unbundling and unbundling-related measures are 'necessary' to achieve that aim. This is explored in the following sub-section.

4.9.2 *Unbundling and Unbundling-Related Measures and the Security of Energy Supply*

The first issue is whether measures that aim to ensure security of energy supply can be considered to fall under Article XIV(a) GATS. This requires a closer look at the notion of 'public order' as used in that provision.

The public order exception in Article XIV(a) GATS is supplemented by a clarification (footnote 5), which provides that the exception 'may be invoked only where a genuine and sufficiently serious threat is posed to one of the fundamental interests of society.'[528] In *US – Gambling*, the Panel held that the footnote's

---

[522]Cottier, Delimatsis and Diebold (n 518) [40] (referring to *United States – Measures Affecting the Cross-Border Supply of Gambling and Betting Services* (n 95) [6.538]). See also GATT, *EEC – Regulation on Imports of Parts and Components,* Report of the Panel (16 May 1990) L/6657 – 37S/132 [5.14–5.18].

[523]*Argentina – Measures Relating to Trade in Goods and Services* (n 199) [6.203].

[524]Security of supply considerations could also play a role under Article XIV(b) GATS. See, for instance, Albath (n 2) 122 (who briefly discusses whether the security of energy supply could fall within the scope of Article XX(b) GATT).

[525]See 11th recital of the preamble to Directive 2009/72/EC (n 8); 8th recital of the preamble to Directive 2009/73/EC (n 8).

[526]See 25th recital of the preamble to Directive 2009/72/EC (n 8); 22nd recital of the preamble to Directive 2009/73/EC (n 8).

[527]Here, the security of supply dimension is particularly strong in the gas sector. According to ibid, Article 36(1)(a) an infrastructure-related exemption can only be granted if the new infrastructure enhances security of supply. See also ibid, 35th recital of the preamble.

[528]The official German translation of this footnote reads: 'Die Ausnahmeregelung in bezug auf die öffentliche Ordnung kann nur in Anspruch genommen werden, wenn eine wirkliche, ausreichend schwerwiegende Bedrohung der Grundwerte der Gesellschaft vorliegt.', see Federal Republic of

reference to 'fundamental interests' should be understood to relate, *inter alia*, to 'standards of law, security and morality.'[529] On the basis of this (admittedly rather broad) formulation, a good argument can be made that the security of energy supply can be considered as a fundamental interest relating to 'standards of security.'[530] It merits adding in this context that the Panel in *US – Gambling* also stated that WTO Members 'should be given some scope to define and apply for themselves the concepts of "public morals" and "public order" in their respective territories, according to their own systems and scales of values.'[531] Therefore, WTO Members have some 'wiggle room' in their interpretation of the notion of public order. Accordingly, it is not without relevance that the preambles to Directives 2009/72/EC and 2009/73/EC each highlight that security of energy supply is a crucial element of public order.[532] Considering furthermore that interruptions in energy supplies may have serious consequences for the stability and normal functioning of public institutions, the provision of basic public services, and even the avoidance of violent damage and disorder in the public domain,[533] it is reasonable to assume that the objective of 'security of energy supply' falls under the notion of 'public order'

Germany, Act concerning the Agreement of 15 April 1994 Establishing the World Trade Organization and concerning the Amendment of other Laws (Gesetz zu dem Übereinkommen vom 15. April 1994 zur Errichtung der Welthandelsorganisation und zur Änderung anderer Gesetze) (09 September 1994) BGBl. II S. 1438, 1650. The translation is partially inaccurate, as 'Grundwerte' would usually be translated as 'fundamental *values*' and not as 'fundamental *interests*'. This has led some authors to (erroneously) state that Article XIV(a) GATS refers to *ethical categories* of fundamental conceptions of social order, see Mario Martini, 'Zu Gast bei Freunden?: Staatsfonds als Herausforderung an das europäische und internationale Recht' (2008) 61 Die Öffentliche Verwaltung 314, 321.

In accordance with the English text, the equally authentic Spanish and French language versions refer to 'intereses fundamentales' and 'intérêts fondamentaux', respectively.

[529] *United States – Measures Affecting the Cross-Border Supply of Gambling and Betting Services* (n 95) [6.467].

[530] Some commentators have opined that the Panel's statement regarding standards of security should not be taken to mean that national security interests also fall within the scope of Article XIV GATS. In their view, such interests would only be covered by the security exception in Article XIV *bis* GATS, see Cottier, Delimatsis and Diebold (n 518) [22]; Krajewski (n 36) 158. This clarification relating to the scopes of application of Articles XIV and XIVbis GATS should not, however, be understood so as to imply that State security interests cannot overlap with societal interests. While 'pure' national security interests are covered exclusively by Article XIVbis GATS, it is submitted here that the security of energy supply can be seen as a fundamental interest of both the State *and* the society.

[531] *United States – Measures Affecting the Cross-Border Supply of Gambling and Betting Services* (n 95) [6.461].

[532] 25th recital of the preamble to Directive 2009/72/EC (n 8); 22nd recital of the preamble to Directive 2009/73/EC (n 8).

[533] See European Court of Justice, *Campus Oil,* Judgment (10 July 1984) C-72/83 [34–35]; European Court of Justice, *Commission v. Belgium,* Judgment (4 June 2002) C-503/99 [46]; European Court of Justice, *Commission v. Italy,* Judgment (2 June 2005) C-174/04 [40]; *Staat der Nederlanden v Essent NV and Others* (n 131) [59] (holding, moreover, that Treaty-based justifications in relation to 'public security' in principle also cover measures taken to enhance

within the meaning of Article XIV(a) GATS.[534] The argument that the objective of security of energy supply is essentially economic in nature and therefore falls outside the scope of Article XIV GATS seems unconvincing. Although security of supply policies aim to ensure that economic activity in the energy sector is not impeded, this is only a means to achieve a non-economic end, namely to guarantee public order.[535]

It is important to note that the security of supply objective, when viewed in the light of Article XIV(a) GATS, not only covers external threats (such as, for example, the insecurity of energy sources in third countries or the insecurity of energy transit routes) but also has a strong internal dimension (such as, for example, the lack of investment into the energy transmission infrastructure).[536] Therefore, even measures that have absolutely no effect on the security of foreign energy sources or the security of energy transit routes can contribute to the 'security of energy supply' objective, as protected (indirectly) by Article XIV(a) GATS. This is crucial here because OU requirements, the third-country certification procedure, and the infrastructure-related exemption regime all deal mainly with the internal aspects of security of supply.

The pivotal issue is thus the 'necessity' of the measures at issue. Under Article XIV(a) GATS, the determination of necessity involves 'a process of weighing and balancing a series of factors',[537] which includes the relative importance of the interests or values furthered by the challenged measure; the contribution of the measure to the realization of the ends pursued by it; and the restrictive impact of the measure on international commerce.[538] Accordingly, the more vital or important the objective, the greater the contribution of the measure to the achievement of that objective, and the smaller the level of trade-restrictiveness, the more likely it is that the measure is 'necessary' within the meaning of Article XIV(a) GATS.[539] After this

---

security of energy supply and that the security of energy supply is recognized as being an overriding reason in the public interest).

[534]The question whether the objective of ensuring the security of energy supply comes within the ambit of Article XIV(a) GATS has received some treatment in the literature. Some authors have answered the question in the affirmative (see Felix Geiger, *Beschränkungen von Direktinvestitionen aus Drittstaaten* (Schriften zum Öffentlichen Wirtschaftsrecht vol 4, Nomos 2013) 280; Nettesheim (n 521) 739), others have left the issue open (see van Hoorn (n 120) 71; Cottier, Matteotti-Berkutova and Nartova (n 88) 280–282).

[535]*Cf. Campus Oil* (n 533) [35] (where the ECJ held that 'the aim of ensuring a minimum supply of petroleum products at all times is to be regarded as transcending purely economic considerations').

[536]For the internal and external dimensions of the security of energy supply, see Kim Talus, *Vertical Natural Gas Transportation Capacity, Upstream Commodity Contracts and EU Competition Law* (Kluwer Law International 2011) 60ff, 65ff; Sanam S Haghighi, *Energy Security: The External Legal Relations of the European Union with Major Oil and Gas Supplying Countries* (Modern Studies in European Law vol 16, Hart 2007) 18ff.

[537]*United States – Measures Affecting the Cross-Border Supply of Gambling and Betting Services* (n 63) [305].

[538]Ibid [306].

[539]*Korea – Measures Affecting Imports of Fresh, Chilled and Frozen Beef* (n 240) [162–163].

preliminary assessment, the measure must be compared with possible alternatives.[540] A measure less inconsistent with GATS is not considered ‘reasonably available’ if it does not achieve the desired level of protection with respect to the objective pursued.[541] WTO Members have the right to determine for themselves the level of protection they deem appropriate in relation to the public policy objective at issue.[542]

The ownership unbundling requirements remove the incentives for discrimination in the transmission sector, which means that existing network capacity should be used in an efficient manner (allocative efficiency). This is beneficial to security of supply.[543] Furthermore, and more importantly, a strong point is that OU improves investment incentives.[544] Vertical integration can lead to under-investment, in particular when an integrated TSO deems that additional transmission capacities would be used predominantly by non-affiliated competitors.[545] A similar view was taken by the Dutch Supreme Court (*Hoge Raad*) in the *Essent* case, which concerned OU measures in the Dutch energy distribution sector. The *Hoge Raad* accepted that in a situation of vertical integration there would be the possibility that investment in commercial activity is undertaken at the expense of network maintenance and development, taking into account that the ‘investment capacity’ of a vertically integrated energy undertaking will be distributed among commercial activities on the one hand and network operation on the other. Generally speaking, there would be no guarantee that the funds obtained through network operation are re-invested in the network.[546] The court also embraced the government’s argument that an ownership unbundled TSO would be in a better position to ‘concentrate’ on the management and maintenance of the network, which would, in turn, be positive for security of supply.[547]

At the same time however, there are also serious reasons to doubt the positive relationship between OU and investment spending (and thus security of supply). First of all, it has been suggested that in contrast to an integrated TSO, which will

---

[540]WTO, *Brazil – Measures Affecting Imports of Retreaded Tyres*, Report of the Appellate Body (3 December 2007) WT/DS332/AB/R [156, 178].

[541]*United States – Measures Affecting the Cross-Border Supply of Gambling and Betting Services* (n 63) [308].

[542]*Brazil – Measures Affecting Imports of Retreaded Tyres* (n 540) [140]; *European Communities – Measures Affecting Asbestos and Asbestos-Containing Products* (n 207) [168].

[543]See, for instance, the statement of the Polish national regulator ERO, which argued that granting a certificate of independence under the ISO model to a particular TSO will ‘contribute to an increased level of security of gaseous fuel supply both to Poland and to the European Union as a whole’, see Final Decision on Certification of TSO Gaz-System (n 375) 75 (translation provided by the European Commission).

[544]See, for example, Monopolkommission (n 326) [606].

[545]OECD, ‘Report on Experiences with Structural Separation’ (2012) 111 <http://www.oecd.org/daf/competition/50056685.pdf> accessed 24 June 2015.

[546]*Staat der Nederlanden v. Essent N.V.* (n 509) [3.22.2].

[547]Ibid. See also ibid [4.4, 4.8.1–4.8.2].

seek to reduce network failures as much as possible in the interest of the affiliated supply branch,[548] a fully independent TSO does not have the same incentive to preserve the infrastructure and may be tempted to increase the profitability of the network at the expense of security of supply.[549] Furthermore, although economic research has not yet produced definite results[550] recent econometric evidence suggests that ownership unbundling reduces aggregate investment in the electricity sector due to the diseconomies of vertical integration and non-internalization of network spillovers.[551] While the specific effect of OU on investment in the energy network sector has not yet been researched,[552] a negative causal relationship between infrastructure investment and ownership unbundling has apparently been observed, in some instances, in the rail sector.[553] Therefore, the contribution of ownership unbundling to security of supply appears to be limited, which negatively contrasts with its obvious trade-restrictiveness.

As regards the lack of availability of alternative measures which are less GATS-inconsistent, it would need to be demonstrated that the less GATS-inconsistent ITO unbundling model, which also seeks to prevent discriminatory investment behavior, fails to achieve the desired level of protection. At first glance this appears to be difficult, because a recent survey has shown that the level of investment by TSOs subject to the ITO model seems to be equivalent to that of ownership unbundled TSOs.[554] Furthermore, although the rules of the ITO model are quite burdensome for both the national regulatory authorities and the TSOs involved, the ITO model cannot be considered to impose an 'undue burden' and is thus, in principle, 'reasonably available'.[555] However, based on the assumption that the respondent WTO Member seeks to enhance security of supply 'as much as possible', it is certainly possible to maintain the view that unbundling options other than ownership unbundling do not guarantee that network operations are completely structurally independent from commercial activities, leaving open the possibility that funds

---

[548]Baur and others (n 326) 51. See also Monopolkommission (n 326) [609].

[549]Christian Koenig, Kristina Schreiber and Kristin Spiekermann, 'Defizitäres Entflechtungsregime? Eine kritische Analyse der Entflechtungsvorschriften in dem Entwurf des dritten Liberalisierungspakets der Kommission der Europäischen Gemeinschaften' [2008] Netzwirtschaften & Recht 7, 12.

[550]For an overview of economic literature on the impact of unbundling on investment, see European Commission, *The Economic Impact of Enforcement of Competition Policies on the Functioning of EU Energy Markets* (Publications Office of the European Union 2016) 14–15, 17.

[551]Klaus Gugler, Margarethe Rammerstorfer and Stephan Schmitt, 'Ownership Unbundling and Investment in Electricity Markets – A Cross Country Study' (2013) 40 Energy Economics 702, 711–712.

[552]Ibid 711.

[553]OECD, 'Report on Experiences with Structural Separation' (n 545) 110.

[554]European Commission, Commission Staff Working Document – Report on the ITO Model (13 October 2014) SWD(2014) 312 final, 6.

[555]*Cf. United States – Measures Affecting the Cross-Border Supply of Gambling and Betting Services* (n 63) [308].

generated through the operation of the network are spent on commercial energy activities.[556]

The additional security of supply test contained in Article 11 of the Directives provides a legal tool with which to identify and address security of supply risks arising from the acquisition of control by foreign investors over domestic transmission systems or TSOs. In practice, the provision is used to deal with internal security of supply issues linked to the possibility of non-compliance with EU energy law, other relevant EU law, and obligations under primary EU law (such as, for instance, EU competition rules).[557] It has been used to provide additional rights to national regulatory authorities, such as the right to suspend the voting rights of the foreign investor in the respective TSO under certain pre-defined circumstances. The restrictive impact on international (services) trade is rather minor.[558] Also, there is arguably no alternative measure available. The ordinary instruments of enforcement lack effectiveness vis-à-vis TSOs which are controlled by persons from a third country. According to the territoriality principle, a State may only exercise sovereign authority within the limits of its own territory. The problems of extraterritorial enforcement are well-known in the field of competition law. Domestic competition authorities cannot conduct official investigations beyond the State's jurisdiction, nor can they enforce decisions, sanctions or remedies by legally-sanctioned means.[559] National regulatory authorities seeking to enforce EU energy law against third-country companies would encounter similar obstacles. The third-country company could not, for example, be obliged to finance certain investments into transmission infrastructure.[560] Thus the ordinary enforcement mechanisms do not constitute an alternative that is reasonably available, because they do not achieve the desired level of protection.

The infrastructure-related exemption regime enables the EU and its Member States to accord preferential regulatory treatment to certain infrastructures and their owners/operators, which is supposed to stimulate major new investments in gas and electricity transmission infrastructure (1) between Member States; and (2) between Member States and third countries (i.e. diversification of sources and

---

[556]See the reasoning of the Dutch *Hoge Raad* in *Staat der Nederlanden v. Essent N.V.* (n 509) [3.21, 3.22.2, 4.9.1].

[557]Commission Opinion – Certification of DESFA (n 372) 4–7; European Commission, Commission Opinion pursuant to Article 3(1) of Regulation (EC) No 715/2009 and Article 10(6) and 11 (6) of Directive 2009/73/EC – Poland – Certification of Gaz-System as the operator of the Polish section of Yamal-Europe Pipeline (19 March 2015) C(2015) 2008 final, 5–6.

[558]The third-country certification procedure provides for a case-specific examination of security of supply concerns. Certification is denied only if security of supply risks actually exist in the specific case at hand and if such risks cannot be counterbalanced by additional safeguards. To date, there has not yet been a case in which certification was denied under Article 11 of the Directives.

[559]Oliver Budzinski, *The Governance of Global Competition: Competence Allocation in International Competition Policy* (Edward Elgar 2008) 37–38; Florian Wagner-von Papp, '§ 11 Internationales Wettbewerbsrecht' in Christian Tietje (ed), *Internationales Wirtschaftsrecht* (De Gruyter 2015) [82ff].

[560]See Schmidt-Preuß (n 79) [98].

supply routes). Even though it is difficult to see why new transmission links between an EU Member State and a third country that do not also interconnect the transmission systems of at least two Member States cannot benefit from an exemption,[561] given that they clearly contribute to the stated objective,[562] still the exemption regime overall contributes to security of supply.[563] It must, however, be pointed out that granting 'regulatory holidays' to certain infrastructure projects may also decrease market liquidity and thus have negative effects on security of supply. The primary focus of the infrastructure exemption regime lies on the creation of new transmission capacity. The fact that there may be negative competition and security of supply-related effects in allowing certain parts of the infrastructure to be used on an exclusive and vertically-integrated basis is deliberately accepted.[564] While the infrastructure-related exemption regime may have a (limited) distortive effect on international commerce, in that it gives more favorable regulatory treatment to some service suppliers while excluding others, there is no clearly less-restrictive alternative.

In sum, it may be concluded that security of supply measures can, in principle, be justified under the 'public order' exception contained in Article XIV(a) GATS. However, the application of the embedded 'necessity test' to the unbundling and unbundling-related measures provided for in the TEP reveals a mixed picture. On one hand, a good case can be made that the third-country certification procedure and the infrastructure-related exemption regime are 'necessary' within the meaning of Article XIV(a) GATS. On the other hand, it would be more difficult to justify the ownership unbundling requirements on security of supply grounds, in particular given that the evidence concerning positive effects in terms of network investment is mixed and the impact on international trade is not insignificant. This finding once again highlights the limiting nature of the 'closed list' of public policy objectives in Article XIV GATS. It would seem that there is a stronger nexus between OU policies and other public policy grounds, such as non-discriminatory network access, which however cannot be subsumed under one of the Article XIV justifications.

The *chapeau* of Article XIV GATS, which prohibits arbitrary and unjustifiable discrimination as well as disguised restriction on trade in the application of a particular measure,[565] does not raise any particular issues in the present context.

---

[561] This is due to the definition of the term 'interconnector', see Article 2(1) of Regulation (EC) No 714/2009 (n 10); Article 2 No. 17 of Directive 2009/73/EC (n 8).

[562] See Sergey S Seliverstov and Ivan Gudkov, *Энергетическое право Европейского союза* (Аспект Пресс 2014) 178; Gudkov (n 293) 53.

[563] Marek Szydło, 'Regulatory Exemptions for New Gas Infrastructure. A Key Challenge for European Energy Policy' (2009) 18 European Energy and Environmental Law Review 254, 254.

[564] Hans Heller, 'Neue Erdgasinfrastrukturen und Freistellung von der Regulierung: Art. 36 der Erdgasrichtlinie 2009/73/EG (§ 28a EnWG) als legitimes Instrument der Investitionsförderung?' (2015) 12 Netzwirtschaften & Recht 66, 71.

[565] *United States – Measures Affecting the Cross-Border Supply of Gambling and Betting Services* (n 95) [6.581].

4.10 Article XIVbis (Security Exceptions)

Apart from Article XIV, violations of the GATS arising from the application of unbundling and unbundling-related measures could also be justified under Article XIVbis:1 GATS. This provision, which is largely identical with its counterpart in the GATT (Article XXI),[566] allows WTO Members to derogate from their obligations under the GATS for security reasons. So far, Article XIVbis:1 GATS has never been invoked in a WTO dispute.[567]

Before analyzing the provision, it is useful to reproduce it in full:

> Nothing in this Agreement shall be construed:
>
> (a) to require any Member to furnish any information, the disclosure of which it considers contrary to its essential security interests; or
> (b) to prevent any Member from taking any action which it considers necessary for the protection of its essential security interests:
>
> (i) relating to the supply of services as carried out directly or indirectly for the purpose of provisioning a military establishment;
> (ii) relating to fissionable and fusionable materials or the materials from which they are derived;
> (iii) taken in time of war or other emergency in international relations; or
>
> (c) to prevent any Member from taking any action in pursuance of its obligations under the United Nations Charter for the maintenance of international peace and security.

The elaborate structure of Article XIVbis:1 GATS reveals that it would be wrong to characterize it as a *general* national security clause.[568] Rather, like Article XXI GATT, 'it provides for *specific* exceptions to cover *specific* instances.'[569] Article XIVbis:1(a) and (c) GATS relate to the disclosure of information contrary to essential security interests and measures under Chapter VII of the UN Charter. It is evident that these clauses are not applicable in the present context. The focus is thus on Article XIVbis:1(b) GATS. Whereas lit (b)(i) and (ii) relate to security interests involving military establishments and nuclear fission and fusion, lit (b)(iii) could possibly provide a justification for measures which are aimed at enhancing the security of energy supply of the EU or of EU Member States. It will thus be necessary to analyze in more detail the exact scope of Article XIVbis:1(b)(iii) GATS, which has been described as a 'rather ambiguous and potentially all-encompassing provision.'[570]

---

[566] Pitschas (n 11) [159]; Michaelis (n 11) [112].

[567] Van den Bossche and Zdouc (n 71) 599.

[568] See, with respect to the negotiating history of Article XXI GATT, World Trade Organization (n 2) 600.

[569] Dapo Akande and Sope Williams, 'International Adjudication on National Security Issues: What Role for the WTO?' (2003) 43 Virginia Journal of International Law 365, 384 (emphasis added).

[570] Thomas Cottier and Panagiotis Delimatsis, 'Article XIVbis GATS' in Rüdiger Wolfrum, Peter-Tobias Stoll and Clemens Feinäugle (eds), *WTO – Trade in Services* (Max Planck Commentaries on World Trade Law vol 6. Martinus Nijhoff Publishers 2008) [14].

As a starting point, it is essential to briefly comment on the possibility of judicial review in relation to the security exception. There are proponents of the view that the use of the words 'action which it *considers* necessary' in Article XXI GATT effectively means that its invocation is not subject to judicial review by the WTO dispute settlement organs.[571] Under this view, Article XXI GATT is either a completely self-judging clause (which translates into granting WTO Members unfettered discretion in terms of its interpretation and application), or even bars the WTO dispute settlement organs from exercising jurisdiction over cases involving the invocation of that Article.[572] Given that Article XIVbis:1(b) GATS contains identical language ('action which it *considers* necessary'), the same reasoning would also apply in the context of trade in services.

The WTO dispute settlement bodies have not yet had the opportunity to pronounce themselves on the scope of judicial review in relation to the security exceptions in the GATT/GATS. However, it has been convincingly argued in academic writing that the wording of Article XXI GATT, viewed in its context and in the light of the treaty's object and purpose, does not support an interpretation that would allow a WTO Member to unilaterally determine the scope of its obligations under WTO law in a manner that is patently at odds with a rule-based system.[573] The same applies to Article XIVbis:1 GATS. Accordingly, it has been rightly stated that the 'perception of unfettered discretion cannot be sustained in connection with the security provisions of WTO law, including Art. XIVbis'.[574]

Having said that, it is beyond doubt that certain parts of Article XIVbis:1(b) GATS are in fact, to a large extent, self-judging. After all, some effect must be given to the words '*which it considers* necessary for the protection of its essential security interests'. Views diverge as to whether the term 'considers' relates only to the necessity of the measure adopted or also extends to the determination of the existence of essential security interests.[575] However, regardless of which view is

[571]See, for example, the position of the United States in GATT, *United States – Trade Measures Affecting Nicaragua,* Report by the Panel (13 October 1986) L/6053 [1.2, 4.6, 5.2].

[572]For the relevant discussion, see van den Bossche and Zdouc (n 71) 596–598; Holger Hestermeyer, 'Article XXI GATT' in Rüdiger Wolfrum, Peter-Tobias Stoll and Holger Hestermeyer (eds), *WTO – Trade in Goods* (Max Planck Commentaries on World Trade Law vol 5. Martinus Nijhoff Publishers 2011) [17ff]; Hannes L Schloemann and Stefan Ohlhoff, '"Constitutionalization" and Dispute Settlement in the WTO: National Security as an Issue of Competence' (1999) 93 American Journal of International Law 424, 431ff.

[573]Akande and Williams (n 569) 379ff; Schloemann and Ohlhoff (n 572) 438ff; Andrew Emmerson, 'Conceptualizing Security Exceptions: Legal Doctrine or Political Excuse?' (2008) 11 Journal of International Economic Law 135, 145; Hestermeyer (n 572) [20].

[574]Cottier and Delimatsis (n 570) [8].

[575]In line with the former view, some authors have taken the position that the concept of essential security interests 'amounts to an objective criterion' and that judicial review is possible in this regard (see ibid [17–18]). Others, following the latter view, have opined that, except for an examination of whether the WTO Member was acting in good faith, panels should not second-guess its definition of what constitutes an essential security interest (see Akande and Williams (n 569) 396–399). Although the latter approach is preferable in my opinion, it seems that under both

adopted, the requirement that such measures be taken 'in time of war or other emergency in international relations' (lit (b)(iii)) is clearly not self-judging.[576] In other words, the notion of 'other emergency in international relations', which is relevant here, constitutes an objective prerequisite and must be defined using the interpretative tools provided by Article 31 VCLT. Its meaning cannot be unilaterally determined by the WTO Member invoking the provision.[577] Thus the questions arise: (1) What exactly is meant by 'other emergency in international relations'?; and (2) Does a security of supply risk fall within the scope of that concept?

At the outset the definitional exercise starts with the observation that the inclusion of the word 'other' between 'war' and 'emergency' suggests that the principle of *ejusdem generis* applies.[578] A situation of war is thus a specific instance of the broader category of emergency situations.[579] This implies that an 'emergency' within the meaning of Article XIV*bis*:1(b)(iii) GATS must be of the same kind as a war, i.e. of 'comparable gravity and impact.'[580] While the notion of 'emergency in international relations' therefore covers instances of the use of force between States which amount to an international armed conflict but are short of war, the crucial question is whether situations *not* involving the use of force can constitute an emergency within the meaning of Article XIV*bis*:1(b)(iii) GATS. In principle, there is no apparent reason why this should not be the case.[581] Provided that the gravity and impact reach a certain level, there is nothing in the provision to suggest that military force must be present or imminent.

At the same time however, the concept of 'emergency' also requires a certain proximity between the detrimental event and the moment at which the State decides to take an action. Specifically, the detrimental event must have already occurred or be imminent or proximate.[582] This conclusion has important ramifications for the justification of security of supply related measures under the TEP. The security of energy supply test in Article 11 of Directives 2009/72/EC and 2009/73/EC, for example, is essentially preventive in nature. The national regulatory authorities, as

---

views the security of energy supply could be relied upon as an 'essential security interest' within the meaning of Article XIV*bis*:1 GATS.

[576] Lorand Bartels, 'The Separation of Powers in the WTO: How to Avoid Judicial Activism' (2004) 53 International and Comparative Law Quarterly 861, 871.

[577] Michael J Hahn, 'Vital Interests and the Law of GATT: An Analysis of GATT's Security Exception' (1991) 12 Michigan Journal of International Law 558, 588–589; Akande and Williams (n 569) 398ff; Schloemann and Ohlhoff (n 572) 445–446.

[578] See Schloemann and Ohlhoff (n 572) 446, who opine that the adjective 'other' creates a 'connection to the term "war"'. See also Cottier and Delimatsis (n 570) [28].

[579] Hestermeyer (n 572) [34].

[580] Cottier and Delimatsis (n 570) [28].

[581] See Michael J Hahn, *Die einseitige Aussetzung von GATT-Verpflichtungen als Repressalie* (Beiträge zum ausländischen öffentlichen Recht und Völkerrecht vol 122, Springer 1996) 357. The issue is left open by Schloemann and Ohlhoff (n 572) 446; Hahn (n 577) 589.

[582] Cottier and Delimatsis (n 570) [28]. See also Hahn (n 581) 357.

well as the European Commission, identify potential risks that could materialize.[583] In the case of the OU requirements and the infrastructure-related exemption regime there is no clear temporal nexus between the regulatory action and the underlying security of supply risks that the regulation addresses. It would therefore appear that the unbundling and unbundling-related measures cannot be said to have been undertaken in a time of 'emergency'.

Furthermore, it should be noted that the words 'in international relations' also have a limiting effect. The term 'international relations' can be defined as '[g]lobal political interaction, *primarily among sovereign nations*.'[584] This would thus seem to require an inter-State emergency, to the exclusion of domestic emergencies. Indeed one author, taking the words 'in international relations' at face value, opined that a non-international armed conflict would not be covered.[585] It should be noted that, in contrast to the language in the GATS, some preferential trade agreements contain broader formulations. The security exception in Article 76 of the Agreement between New Zealand and Singapore on a Closer Economic Partnership, for instance, refers to any action 'taken in time of war or other emergency in *domestic or* international relations'.[586] If the drafters of the GATS had wished to include such broad language in Article XIVbis:1 GATS (or Article XXI GATT) they could have or would have done so.

External threats to security of supply, such as disruptions of energy imports from abroad, undoubtedly have a certain cross-border dimension in the sense that the threat emanates from a third country. However, it is difficult to see why such a situation should amount to an emergency 'in international relations'. This assessment is not altered by the fact that the foreign electricity or gas supply company triggering the security of supply crisis may be a State-owned entity.[587] The same

[583]See for instance Commission Opinion – Certification of DESFA (n 372) 6. In that case, the Commission explicitly stated that '[i]n the case at hand, [it] is of the view that at least the following *potential risks* should have been assessed . . .' (emphasis added).

[584]Bryan A Garner (ed), *Black's Law Dictionary* (9th edn) 893 (emphasis added).

[585]See Christoph Schreuer, 'The Protection of Investments in Armed Conflicts' in Freya Baetens (ed), *Investment Law within International Law: Integrationist Perspectives* (Cambridge University Press 2013) 18 (referring to Article 24(3)(a)(ii) Energy Charter Treaty (17 December 1994) 2080 U.N.T.S. 95).

[586]Emphasis added.

[587]According to the ILC's Commentary to the Articles on State Responsibility, government ownership, in and of itself, is not sufficient to attribute acts of corporate entities to the State (see paragraph 6 of the commentary to Article 8 of the International Law Commission, Draft Articles on Responsibility of States for Internationally Wrongful Acts, with Commentaries (2001) YBILC 2001/II(2), 48, where the ILC states that '[s]ince corporate entities, although owned by and in that sense subject to the control of the State, are considered to be separate, *prima facie* their conduct in carrying out their activities is not attributable to the State unless they are exercising elements of governmental authority within the meaning of article 5'). This is also the position of the Appellate Body (see WTO, *United States – Countervailing Duty Investigation on Dynamic Random Access Memory Semiconductors (DRAMS) from Korea,* Report of the Appellate Body (27 June 2005) WT/DS296/AB/R [112], footnote 179; In that case, the Appellate Body dealt with the attribution of conduct to the State under Article 1.1 of the SCM Agreement). By way of example, even though

considerations apply, *a fortiori*, to internal threats. An internal security of supply crisis resulting from discriminatory investment decisions, non-compliance with domestic energy law, or a lack of infrastructure investment does not amount to an 'emergency in international relations', as required by Article XIV*bis*:1(b)(iii) GATS.

All in all, the following conclusions can be drawn from the preceding observations. Due to the missing inter-State element, the security of supply risks addressed by the OU requirements, the third country certification procedure, and the infrastructure-related exemption regime would not usually translate into an emergency 'in international relations' within the meaning of Article XIV*bis*:1(b)(iii) GATS. Moreover, if there is no actual or imminent threat, but only a *potential* security of supply crisis, the security exception cannot be invoked either, as there is no 'emergency'. In conclusion, GATS-inconsistent unbundling or unbundling-related measures provided for by the TEP cannot be justified under Article XIV*bis*:1 (b)(iii) GATS.[588]

4.11 Conclusions

This chapter has analyzed whether, and if so to what extent, WTO law limits the adoption or maintenance of unbundling and unbundling-related measures in the EU energy sector. The findings of this analysis are summarized below.

The unbundling regime set out in the Third Energy Package falls within the scope of the GATS as it affects trade in a number of energy services, including wholesale and retail services of gas and electricity and transmission services (if carried out 'independently', i.e. on behalf of a third party). The governmental authority exception in Article I:3(b) GATS does not remove the TEP from the scope of application of the GATS, given that energy services within the EU are generally supplied on a commercial basis. Furthermore, to the extent that the EU and its Member States have undertaken specific commitments on energy transmission and/or energy supply services, the market access and national treatment obligations as well as the domestic regulation disciplines are applicable, in addition to the horizontal MFN obligation.

The unbundling requirements provided for in Directives 2009/72/EC and 2009/73/EC do not constitute an impermissible market access restriction within the

---

Gazprom is majority-owned by the Russian Federation, its conduct cannot automatically be attributed to the Russian State. The involvement of a State-owned entity cannot substitute for the lack of an inter-State dimension.

[588]This conclusion is supported by Nikolay Mizulin, 'EC Experience in Creating an Internal Energy Market: Lessons for the WTO' in Joost Pauwelyn (ed), *Global Challenges at the Intersection of Trade, Energy and the Environment* (Center for Economic and Policy Research 2010) 73 (who states that 'nothing in [Article XXI GATT] appears to provide for the security-of-supply justification'). For a different view, see Waloszyk (n 186) 71 (who, without having discussed the scope of Article XIV*bis* GATS, writes that 'the introduction of a supplementary condition in article 11 of Directive 2009/73/EC regarding security of supply is justified by article XIV bis GATS').

meaning of Article XVI GATS. OU policies do not prohibit the supply of transmission or wholesale/retail services in a general manner, but only for specific service providers, depending on supplier-related characteristics. Even following the far-reaching *US – Gambling* jurisprudence, this is not a limitation on the number of service suppliers in the form of numerical quotas (Article XVI:2(a); similarly lit (b) and (c)). Neither do OU measures restrict or require a specific type of legal entity through which a service supplier may supply a service (Article XVI:2(e)), because that provision does not cover every restriction on particular activities, but only restrictions on the forms of legal establishment. Finally, OU requirements do not constitute limitations on the participation of foreign capital within the meaning of Article XVI:2(f) GATS, given that OU measures do not set a generally applicable limitation on foreign shareholding and that restrictions on foreign investment 'in individual cases' fall outside the scope of Article XVI:2(f). Furthermore, the TEP's ownership unbundling measures are not inconsistent with the substantive domestic regulation disciplines applicable to licensing requirements (Article VI:4/5 GATS). Even assuming—which is highly questionable—that OU 'nullifies or impairs' market access commitments on energy services (in fact, the opposite could be argued), it cannot be considered to be more 'burdensome', i.e. trade-restrictive, than necessary to ensure non-discriminatory network access. As regards the special OU requirements for public undertakings, it has been shown that the corresponding provision does not amount to a national treatment violation (Article XVII GATS). Although EU Member States can act as 'vertically integrated undertakings', the State as an abstract entity is not a 'service supplier' under the GATS and cannot be compared to foreign private vertically integrated companies. If one focuses on the economic operators that actually supply the relevant services, it becomes apparent that neither the public TSOs nor the public production/generation or supply companies, respectively, have a competitive advantage vis-à-vis foreign privately-owned service suppliers.

Moreover, the variety of unbundling models among EU Member States is in linc with the most-favored-nation treatment obligation of Article II:1 GATS. The main reason for this is that the MFN principle should not be interpreted to the effect that the EU must ensure that any favorable treatment autonomously accorded by *any* EU Member State within its territory to the services and service suppliers of a third country is granted immediately and unconditionally to the like services and service suppliers of *all* WTO Members in the territory of *all* EU Member States. The EU's obligation under Article II:1 GATS cannot be used as a mechanism to enforce a requirement of substantive uniformity throughout the entire EU of all measures affecting trade in services.

Finally, the EU's application of the unbundling requirements to offshore sections of international gas import pipelines is not inconsistent with the domestic regulation disciplines in Article VI:1 GATS. Although the public statements of the European Commission with respect to the South Stream offshore pipeline might provide some support for an assertion of inconsistency, they are not manifestly inconsistent with the (EU-approved) non-application of the unbundling requirements in other cases (such as the Nord Stream pipeline), and thus are insufficient to show that the unbundling regime is administered in an unreasonable or non-objective manner. Nevertheless, in view of the precedent set by the first Nord Stream pipeline, there would be a violation of Article VI:1 GATS if the EU applied the unbundling requirements in the TEP to, for example, the current and highly controversial Nord Stream 2 project.

The second dimension of the unbundling regime in the TEP relates to the exemption of gas or electricity infrastructure from the OU requirements. However, these take the form of individual exemption decisions, which can hardly be challenged under the MFN and NT provisions of the GATS. The non-discrimination provisions in Articles II:1 and XVII GATS only protect the equality of competitive opportunities and do not apply to individual instances of less advantageous treatment of foreign service suppliers. Although exemption decisions with protectionist intent are capable of violating the non-discrimination provisions, the WTO dispute settlement bodies will only rarely determine that a particular decision was based on the origin of the respective service supplier. Existing exemption decisions under the TEP (and, for that matter, under the SEP) do not reflect a protectionism which could result in a violation of Article II:1 or Article XVII GATS. Moreover, as regards specifically the gas sector, all the existing exemption decisions are compliant with the domestic regulation disciplines of Article VI:1 GATS. In particular, the notion of 'interconnector', which defines the types of gas infrastructure that are eligible for an exemption, has been interpreted and applied in a coherent manner and in conformity with the underlying provisions in the Gas Directive. What's more, the unreasonable, non-objective or partial administration of an individual exemption measure does not *ipso facto* amount to a breach of Article VI:1 GATS, given that the provision only applies to measures of general application. Finally, the exemption regime as a whole is not discriminatory within the meaning of the national treatment obligation of Article XVII GATS. It does not contain any criteria which are indirectly related to origin and the existing exemption practice does not allow for the conclusion that there is an asymmetric impact to the detriment of foreign services or service suppliers.

The third and last dimension of the unbundling regime in the TEP concerns the certification procedure. The third-country certification procedure infringes the NT principle of the GATS due to its additional 'security of supply test', which applies only to foreign service suppliers. This is a straightforward case of *de jure* discrimination. Apart from that, however, there are no further inconsistencies. In particular, the application of the security of supply test, as set out in the Directives and as interpreted by the national regulatory authorities and the European Commission, does not depend on (criteria related to) the country of origin of the respective foreign service supplier, such as security of supply related agreements between the third country concerned and the EU, or its geographic location. Therefore, there is no violation of the MFN principle in Article II:1 GATS.

In conclusion, in accordance with the analysis conducted in this chapter, the unbundling regime in the TEP is fully in conformity with the GATS, except for the certification procedure in relation to third countries, which breaches the NT standard. And while GATS-inconsistent unbundling and unbundling-related measures could theoretically be justified under the general exception provision of Article XIV GATS, in the case of the unbundling requirements in particular it becomes apparent that this is very unlikely. Article XIV GATS contains only a closed list of public policy objectives that can justify government intervention with respect to trade in services. The objective of providing non-discriminatory network access would seem not to constitute a legitimate public interest under the provision. Nevertheless, the various measures under the TEP could be justified as being 'necessary to maintain public order' (Article XIV(a) GATS), given that the notion of public order can be interpreted to encompass security of supply objectives. In particular, it can be argued that the additional security of supply test for third-country-controlled TSOs is justifiable under Article XIV(a). In contrast, the GATS security exception provision cannot be invoked with respect to the issues under consideration, because the unbundling and unbundling-related measures were not taken during the time of an 'emergency in international relations' within the meaning of Article XIVbis:1(b)(iii) GATS.

Chapter 5
International Economic Law as a Possible Limit to the Implementation of Unbundling and Unbundling-Related Measures: International Investment Law

5.1 Introduction

International investment law aims to provide a stable framework for cross-border investment, including in the energy sector. It has gained relevance in recent years, as more and more investment treaty arbitrations have been initiated by foreign investors. In fact the year 2015 witnessed a record number of new treaty-based investor-State dispute settlement (ISDS) cases. As of 2016 there are now almost 700 publicly-known ISDS claims.[1] This proliferation is mainly thanks to increasingly common and increasingly popular dispute settlement provisions in international investment agreements (IIAs) which explicitly allow foreign investors to resort to arbitration against their host State in cases of alleged non-compliance with any of the substantive treatment standards. Currently, the 'universe' of IIAs consists of more than 3300 agreements. Around 2900 of these agreements are bilateral investment treaties (BITs).[2] Apart from that, there a number of bilateral and regional preferential trade agreements (PTAs) which contain investment chapters, with a prominent example being the North American Free Trade Agreement (NAFTA).[3] Finally, there are sector-specific treaties with investment provisions, such as the Energy Charter Treaty.[4] A general multilateral agreement on investment has not yet come to fruition.

In essence, IIAs seek to shield foreign (energy) investors from undue governmental interference. The core investment protection standard generally found in IIAs is the protection against expropriation without compensation. IIAs also protect foreign investors and their investments against treatment that is unfair or inequitable

[1]United Nations Conference on Trade and Development, *World Investment Report 2016: Investor Nationality: Policy Challenges* (United Nations 2016) 104.

[2]Ibid 101.

[3]See North American Free Trade Agreement (17 December 1992) 32 I.L.M. 289 (1993).

[4]See Energy Charter Treaty (17 December 1994) 2080 U.N.T.S. 95.

T. M. Dralle, *Ownership Unbundling and Related Measures in the EU Energy Sector*, European Yearbook of International Economic Law 5,
https://doi.org/10.1007/978-3-319-77797-9_5

and against discrimination by the host State in favor of its own investors or investors of another State. Given that investments in the energy sector are often capital-intensive, long-term and risky, investment protection guarantees and the possibility to bring an ISDS case serve an important function here.[5] In fact, more than 40% of all cases decided under the Convention on the Settlement of Investment Disputes between States and Nationals of Other States (ICSID Convention) are energy-related.[6] In the year 2015 alone more than 20 energy-related ISDS cases have been filed.[7]

The State conduct that has given rise to energy-related proceedings under IIAs is diverse. Examples include (1) a policy decision to phase out nuclear energy[8]; (2) the revocation or modification of support schemes for renewable energy investors[9]; (3) termination of long-term power purchase agreements in the electricity generation sector[10]; (4) the reintroduction of administrative pricing in electricity generation after administrative prices had been abolished[11]; and (5) price regulation in the gas transportation and distribution sector in the face of a severe economic and financial crisis.[12]

The unbundling and unbundling-related measures in the EU energy sector could lead to investment arbitration claims under applicable IIAs. On several occasions the Russian Federation has made clear that it regards the unbundling measures in the TEP as a violation of the obligations of the EU and its Member States contained in agreements on investment protection.[13] In an article for the Journal of Common

---

[5]For a general overview of the relevant case-law, see Achim-R. Börner, 'Investment Law and Energy' in Marc Bungenberg and others (eds), *International Investment Law* (C.H. Beck; Hart; Nomos 2015); Markus Krajewski, 'The Impact of International Investment Agreements on Energy Regulation' in Christoph Herrmann and Jörg P Terhechte (eds), *European Yearbook of International Economic Law 2012* (European Yearbook of International Economic Law vol 3. Springer 2012).

[6]International Centre for Settlement of Investment Disputes, 'The ICSID Caseload – Statistics (Issue 2016-1)' (2016) 12 <https://icsid.worldbank.org/apps/ICSIDWEB/resources/Documents/ICSID%20Web%20Stats%202016-1%20(English)%20final.pdf> accessed 25 April 2016. 26% of the cases fall within the category of 'Oil, Gas & Mining' and another 17% of the cases relate to 'Electric Power & Other Energy'.

[7]United Nations Conference on Trade and Development (n 1) 106.

[8]*Vattenfall AB and others v. Federal Republic of Germany* ICSID Case No. ARB/12/12.

[9]*Nykomb Synergetics Technology Holding AB v. The Republic of Latvia,* Arbitral Award (16 December 2003); *Charanne and Construction Investments v. Spain,* Final Award (translation) (21 January 2016) SCC Case No. 062/2012.

[10]*Electrabel S.A. v. Republic of Hungary,* Decision on Jurisdiction, Applicable Law and Liability (30 November 2012) ICSID Case No. ARB/07/19.

[11]*AES Summit Generation Limited and AES-Tisza Erömü Kft v. The Republic of Hungary,* Final Award (23 September 2010) ICSID Case No. ARB/07/22.

[12]*CMS Gas Transmission Company v. The Republic of Argentina,* Award (12 May 2005) ICSID Case No. ARB/01/8; the other Argentine cases.

[13]Ministry of Foreign Affairs of the Russian Federation, 'Speech by the Minister of Foreign Affairs of Russia Sergey Lavrov During a Meeting with Representatives of the Association of European Businesses in the Russian Federation' (8 October 2012) <http://archive.mid.ru//bdomp/brp_4.nsf/0/52A9A0EC716E909344257A94002EBF18> accessed 5 August 2016.

Market Studies, the Russian Minister of Foreign Affairs Sergey Lavrov pointed to the retroactive effect of the unbundling requirements in Directives 2009/72/EC and 2009/73/EC and stated that '[i]n some cases, we see *de facto* expropriation of Russian companies' assets.'[14] In addition, some Russian[15] as well as some other academics[16] have criticized the Third Energy Package, and in particular the certification procedure for third-country-controlled TSOs and the OU requirements, as being in violation of the national treatment standard, the protection against expropriation without compensation, and the fair and equitable treatment standard.

Unbundling measures have already played a role in three different sets of arbitral proceedings, although in none of these cases did the respective tribunal reach the merits of the measures. The first case is *OAO Gazprom v. Republic of Lithuania*. This case related directly to the implementation of Directive 2009/73/EC. In 2011, Lithuania enacted ownership unbundling in its gas sector in accordance with the relevant provisions in the TEP. In March 2012, Gazprom initiated arbitral proceedings against the government of Lithuania on the basis of the bilateral investment agreement between the Russian Federation and the Republic of Lithuania of 1999.[17,18] Gazprom availed itself of the ISDS mechanism contained in Article 10 of the Russia-Lithuania BIT with a view to challenging the Lithuanian legislation which required Gazprom to sell its 37% stake in the country's national gas transmission system.

---

[14]Sergey Lavrov, 'State of the Union Russia–EU: Prospects for Partnership in the Changing World' (2013) 51 Journal of Common Market Studies 6, 8.

[15]Ivan Gudkov, 'Третий энергетический пакет Европейского союза' [2010] НефтьГазПраво 58, 65; Alexandra Anufrieva, *Регулирование иностранных инвестиций в ЕС: Общие вопросы и инвестирование в энергетический сектор* (Зерцало-М 2014) 84–88; Alexey S Ispolinov and Tatiana Dvenadtcatova, 'Принудительное выделение сетевого бизнеса в рамках Третьего Энергопакета ЕС (unbundling): практика применения' [2014] Закон 111, 117.

[16]Arnoud Willems, Jung-ui Sul and Yohan Benizri, 'Unbundling as a Defence Mechanism Against Russia: Is the EU Missing the Point?' in Kim Talus and Piero L Fratini (eds), *EU – Russia Energy Relations* (Euroconfidentiel 2010). See also August Reinisch, 'Protection of or Protection Against Foreign Investment? The Proposed Unbundling Rules of the EC Draft Energy Directives' in Christoph Herrmann and Jörg P Terhechte (eds), *European Yearbook of International Economic Law 2010* (Springer 2010) 63; Richard Happ, 'The Legal Status of the Investor vis-a-vis the European Communities: Some Salient Thoughts' (2007) 10 International Arbitration Law Review 74, 74; Teresa M Moschetta, *Il mercato comunitario del gas naturale: Investimenti esteri diretti e diritto internazionale* (Giuffrè 2009) 82–83; Anatole Boute, 'Energy Trade and Investment Law: International Limits to EU Energy Law and Policy' in Martha M Roggenkamp and others (eds), *Energy Law in Europe – National, EU and International Regulation* (3rd edn. Oxford University Press 2016) [3.43–3.47].

[17]Agreement between the Government of the Russian Federation and the Government of the Republic of Lithuania on the Promotion and Reciprocal Protection of Investments (29 June 1999) <investmentpolicyhub.unctad.org/download/treatyfile/1921> accessed 20 January 2018.

[18]See Denis Pinchuk and Nerijus Adomaitis, *Gazprom takes on Lithuania in EU policy test case* (Reuters 2012); Gazprom, *Gazprom seeks international arbitration against Lithuanian Government* (2012); Permanent Court of Arbitration, 'OAO Gazprom v. The Republic of Lithuania' (no date) <https://pcacases.com/web/view/47> accessed 14 September 2016. See also the description in European Court of Justice, *'Gazprom' OAO*, Opinion of Advocate General Wathelet (4 December 2014) C-536/13 35–36.

In April 2015 it became known that Gazprom had discontinued the arbitration.[19] The reason given for the withdrawal was that the arbitration case 'was no longer relevant' because Gazprom had sold the assets that formed the subject of the proceedings.[20]

The second arbitration case is *Slovak Gas Holding et al. v. Slovak Republic*. In 2012, shareholders of Slovakia's vertically integrated gas undertaking Slovenský Plynárenský Priemysel (SPP) brought an arbitration case against the Slovak Republic, alleging that certain measures violated Article 10(1) ECT on fair and equitable treatment and Article 13 ECT on expropriation. While many of the claims related to the price regulation in the gas sector, the proposed transposition into Slovak law of Directive 2009/73/EC also formed part of the request for arbitration.[21] However, it remains unknown which particular measures were challenged. At the end of 2012, the shareholders of SPP and the Slovak Republic agreed on a 'Settlement Deed'. Interestingly, the Settlement Deed contains a significant carve-out in that it does not include 'any claim that the Current Foreign Shareholders may subsequently make in respect of decisions, determinations or orders made or issued by the Slovak Republic under [the Energy Act] or [the Regulation Act] (including but not limited to decisions or orders in respect of the implementation of Ownership Unbundling or the Independent System Operator model for SPP).'[22] While no such claims were made,[23] the carve-out in the Settlement Deed clearly highlights the possibility of investment arbitration in relation to the EU's ownership unbundling policies.

The third case in point is *Cementownia v. Turkey*, which concerns the introduction of unbundling requirements in Turkey. In that case a Polish investor alleged it had acquired shares in two Turkish vertically integrated electricity companies, 'CEAS' and 'Kepez'. In 1998, these companies had entered into concession agreements with the Turkish Ministry of Energy and Natural Resources, which granted them concession rights for the generation, transmission, distribution and marketing of electricity. The agreements provided that the facilities necessary to carry out the activities under the concessions would remain in State ownership and revert to the State at the end of the concession period.[24]

[19]Юрий Барсуков and Андрей Райский, '"Газпром" отказался судиться с Литвой' *Kommersant* (3 April 2015) <http://www.kommersant.ru/doc/2699980>; 'Gazprom Drops One Arbitration Case Against Lithuania' *Natural Gas Europe* (5 April 2015) <http://www.naturalgaseurope.com/gazprom-lithuania-arbitration-case-23046>.

[20]'Gazprom Drops One Arbitration Case Against Lithuania' (n 19).

[21]*Slovak Gas Holding BV, GDF International SAS and E.ON Ruhrgas International GmbH v. Slovak Republic*, Settlement Deed (14 December 2012) ICSID Case No. ARB/12/7, recital F, point 4.

[22]Ibid.

[23]In January 2013, E.ON Ruhrgas and GDF International sold their 49% joint stake in SPP.

[24]*Cementownia "Nowa Huta" S.A. v. Republic of Turkey*, Award (17 September 2009) ICSID Case No. ARB(AF)/06/2 [5–9].

In 2001, Turkey enacted a new electricity market law. Following the example of the then-existing Directive 96/92/EC, the law introduced certain unbundling requirements in the electricity sector. In particular, it provided that the entire transmission network would be operated by the State-owned Turkish Electricity Transmission Joint Stock Company (TEIAS). As a consequence, vertically integrated undertakings were no longer allowed to engage in transmission. CEAS and Kepez, however, took the position that (1) the concession agreements could not be revoked unilaterally; (2) they had made large investments into the transmission sector, with the legitimate expectation that the concessions would remain in force until the year 2058; and (3) the request for transfer of transmission infrastructure would be illegal, because no compensation would be provided for the compulsory transfer of their transmission rights.[25] After repeated requests by the government to transfer the transmission facilities and rights to TEIAS, the Turkish State terminated the concession agreements and seized the transmission facilities in June 2003. In 2006, the claimant instituted proceedings before the International Centre for Settlement of Investment Disputes (ICSID), alleging expropriation in violation of Article 13 ECT.[26]

Due to its finding that the Polish investor failed to prove its shareholding in CEAS and Kepez, the ICSID tribunal did not pronounce itself on the merits of the case.[27] Nonetheless the *Cementownia v. Turkey* case is highly instructive. Notably, it shows that even unbundling measures that fall short of full ownership separation can lead to international investment arbitration, particularly if they entail an early termination of corresponding concessions.

In light of the foregoing it is clear that the unbundling regime in the TEP may well come into conflict with the rights of third country energy investors. Accordingly, this chapter will analyze whether the unbundling and unbundling-related measures in the EU energy sector are consistent with the investment protection standards in applicable IIAs, and whether they may trigger a duty to pay compensation to aggrieved investors.

5.2 The Framework for Investor-State Claims

This section will provide some brief comments on the general framework for investor-State dispute settlement claims against unbundling and unbundling-related measures. Investors could bring an ISDS claim either directly against the EU (under an investment agreement between the EU and one or more third countries), or

---

[25] Ibid [10–12].

[26] Ibid [13–14, 16, 24–25, 105].

[27] In fact, the tribunal found that the claimant's claim was fraudulent and brought in bad faith.

against one of the EU Member States (under an agreement between the respective Member State and one or more third countries).[28]

As it was not until the entry into force of the Treaty of Lisbon in 2009 that foreign direct investment came under the exclusive competence of the EU,[29] there are only few IIAs to which the EU itself is a contracting party. The most notable example in this regard is the Energy Charter Treaty (ECT), which was concluded as a mixed agreement, i.e. by the EU and all of the Member States.[30] The ECT is a plurilateral energy-related trade and investment agreement, which contains a full-fledged investment chapter, including the possibility of investor-State dispute settlement. As of now 48 States and the European Union have ratified, and another four have signed, the ECT.[31] The ISDS mechanism of the ECT is being actively used, with 97 cases currently registered.[32] In fact, in terms of arbitration the ECT is the most frequently invoked IIA worldwide.[33]

While the conclusion of IIAs between the EU and third countries has now become the exclusive domain of the EU, the EU Member States have been very active in negotiating bilateral investment treaties in the past; in total around 1200 agreements are in place.[34] These 'extra-EU' Member State BITs still represent the vast majority

---

[28]Theoretically, it is also possible that an investor-State arbitration is brought against an EU Member State under a so-called 'intra-EU' BIT. This would however give rise to a host of problems under EU law, see Hanno Wehland, 'Intra-EU Investment Agreements and Arbitration: Is European Community Law an Obstacle?' (2009) 58 International and Comparative Law Quarterly 297; Christian Tietje, *Bilaterale Investitionsschutzverträge zwischen EU-Mitgliedstaaten (Intra-EU-BITs) als Herausforderung im Mehrebenensystem des Rechts* (Beiträge zum Transnationalen Wirtschaftsrecht vol 104, 2011). As this book takes the perspective of extra-EU investors, this possibility is not examined further here.

[29]For an overview, see Marc Bungenberg, 'Going Global? The EU Common Commercial Policy After Lisbon' in Christoph Herrmann and Jörg P Terhechte (eds), *European Yearbook of International Economic Law 2010* (Springer 2010); Wenhua Shan and Sheng Zhang, 'The Treaty of Lisbon: Half Way toward a Common Investment Policy' (2010) 21 European Journal of International Law 1049. There is some controversy about the exact scope of the new exclusive competence over foreign direct investment. Some legal writers argue that the usage of the term 'foreign direct investment' in Article 207(1) TFEU implies that portfolio investment is not covered, see for instance Christian Tietje, *Die Außenwirtschaftsverfassung der EU nach dem Vertrag von Lissabon* (Beiträge zum Transnationalen Wirtschaftsrecht vol 83, 2009) 15–16; Jan A Bischoff, 'Just a Little BIT of "Mixity"? The EU's Role in the Field of International Investment Protection Law' (2011) 48 Common Market Law Review 1527.

[30]See European Union, Council and Commission Decision on the conclusion, by the European Communities, of the Energy Charter Treaty and the Energy Charter Protocol on energy efficiency and related environmental aspects (23 September 1997) OJ 1998/L 69/1.

[31]Energy Charter Secretariat, 'The Energy Charter Treaty' (no date) <http://www.energycharter.org/process/energy-charter-treaty-1994/energy-charter-treaty/> accessed 6 August 2016.

[32]Energy Charter Secretariat, 'List of all Investment Dispute Settlement Cases' (no date) <http://www.energycharter.org/what-we-do/dispute-settlement/all-investment-dispute-settlement-cases/> accessed 6 August 2016.

[33]United Nations Conference on Trade and Development (n 1) 105.

[34]European Commission, Towards a Comprehensive European International Investment Policy (07 July 2010) COM(2010)343 final, 4. This number excludes intra-EU BITs.

of IIAs that can give rise to ISDS claims concerning the adoption of unbundling or unbundling-related measures under the Third Energy Package. They remain in force even though the EU's Common Commercial Policy was subsequently broadened to also cover foreign direct investment. In this connection Regulation 1219/2012 explicitly authorized Member States to retain their existing BITs with third countries.[35] Like the ECT, the extra-EU Member State BITs typically contain a broad ISDS clause.[36] Finally, in addition to this extensive network of bilateral investment treaties, all EU Member States except Italy are also contracting parties to the Energy Charter Treaty.

5.3 Admission Rights

International investment law distinguishes between the pre- and post-entry phases of an investment. The 'pre-entry' phase relates to the making of new investments by foreign investors. This includes the takeover of, or participation in, existing enterprises. In contrast, the 'post-entry' phase relates to the treatment to be given to foreign investors once the investment has been made.[37]

Some of the measures of the unbundling regime in the Third Energy Package can take effect in the pre-entry phase. For example, in a situation where a foreign investor seeks to make a financial transaction or transactions that would result in non-compliance with applicable ownership unbundling requirements, the certification procedure would 'intervene *ex ante*'.[38] The flipside of this is that, depending on the existence and nature of admission rights, unbundling and unbundling-related measures could be problematic from the viewpoint of international investment law.[39]

---

[35]Article 3 of the Regulation (EU) No 1219/2012 of the European Parliament and of the Council establishing transitional arrangements for bilateral investment agreements between Member States and third countries (12 December 2012) OJ 2012/L 351/40.

[36]Some EU Member State BITs do not however provide unqualified access to ISDS. This applies in particular to a number of BITs with the Russian Federation, which were concluded during the Soviet-era. Under these agreements, the right to initiate arbitration proceedings is restricted to disputes relating to the amount or mode of payment of compensation for expropriation. For a full analysis, see August Reinisch, 'How Narrow are Narrow Dispute Settlement Clauses in Investment Treaties?' (2011) 2 Journal of International Dispute Settlement 115.

[37]Sometimes the notions 'pre-establishment' and 'post-establishment' are used. However, referring to the 'admission' and 'entry' of foreign investments is preferable, because these terms are wider than the expression 'establishment', see Armand de Mestral, 'Pre-Entry Obligations under International Law' in Marc Bungenberg and others (eds), *International Investment Law* (C.H. Beck; Hart; Nomos 2015) [6].

[38]Emmanuel Cabau, 'Unbundling of Transmission System Operators' in Christopher Jones (ed), *The Internal Energy Market – The Third Liberalisation Package* (EU Energy Law Series vol 1, 3rd edn. Claeys & Casteels Publishing 2010) [4.73].

[39]See for example Reinisch (n 16) 63 (who writes that '[w]here market access obligations exist, ownership unbundling . . . may become unlawful from an investment law perspective').

Therefore, the question arises whether, and if so to what extent, international law puts limits on the State's ability to regulate the entry of foreign investment.

It is clear that from the perspective of customary international law States are under no obligation to admit foreign investment into their territory.[40] As a corollary, they are free to make the entry of foreign investment contingent on the fulfilment of certain conditions. The situation under IIAs, however, is more nuanced. While admission rights are not contained in all investment instruments, some BITs—in particular those concluded by Canada[41] and the United States[42]—do contain such provisions. European States, in contrast, have generally preferred to retain the right to fully control the admission and establishment of foreign investors.[43] To give an example, Article 2(1) of the German Model BIT reads:

> Each Contracting State shall in its territory promote as far as possible investments by investors of the other Contracting State and *admit such investments in accordance with its legislation.*[44]

As the obligation to 'admit' investments is qualified by the words 'in accordance with its legislation', the State enjoys total discretion to enact laws that do not give foreign investors any enforceable admission rights.[45] Under the Energy Charter Treaty, the whole issue of pre-entry obligations was deferred to a yet-to-be-negotiated 'supplementary treaty'.[46]

It should be noted, however, that a very limited number of BITs concluded by EU Member States contain admission-related provisions. One example is the Italy-

[40]Ibrahim F I Shihata, 'Recent Trends Relating to Entry of Foreign Direct Investment' (1994) 9 ICSID Review – Foreign Investment Law Journal 47, 47; Giorgio Sacerdoti, 'The Admission and Treatment of Foreign Investment under Recent Bilateral and Regional Treaties' (2000) 1 Journal of World Investment 105, 105.

[41]See Articles 3 and 4 of the '2004 Canadian Model Foreign Investment Protection Agreement' <http://www.italaw.com/documents/Canadian2004-FIPA-model-en.pdf> accessed 9 June 2015.

[42]See Articles 3 and 4 of the '2012 U.S. Model Bilateral Investment Treaty' (no date) <http://www.state.gov/documents/organization/188371.pdf> accessed 24 September 2016.

[43]Martín Molinuevo, *Protecting Investment in Services: Investor-State Arbitration versus WTO Dispute Settlement* (Global Trade Law Series vol 38, Kluwer Law International 2012) 85; Mestral (n 37) [4]; (n 34) 5.

[44]'2009 German Model Bilateral Investment Treaty' (no date) <http://www.iilcc.uni-koeln.de/fileadmin/institute/iilcc/Dokumente/matrechtinvest/VIS_Mustervertrag.pdf> accessed 9 June 2015 (emphasis added).

[45]Ignacio Gómez-Palacio and Peter Muchlinski, 'Admission and Establishment' in Peter Muchlinski, Federico Ortino and Christoph Schreuer (eds), *The Oxford Handbook of International Investment Law* (Oxford University Press 2008) 240–241; Otto Sandrock, 'The Right of Foreign Investors to Access German Markets: The Meaning of Article 2(1) of the German Model Treaty for the Promotion and Protection of Foreign Investments' (2010) 25 ICSID Review – Foreign Investment Law Journal 268.

[46]Thomas W Wälde, 'International Investment under the 1994 Energy Charter Treaty' in Thomas W Wälde (ed), *The Energy Charter Treaty: An East-West Gateway for Investment and Trade* (International Energy and Resources Law and Policy Series. Kluwer Law International 1996) 277–284.

Nicaragua BIT, which extends the NT and MFN principles to the right of access to investment activities.[47] This resembles the approach taken in the US and Canadian BITs.[48] The extension of the NT and MFN obligations to the establishment, acquisition, and expansion of investments gives rise to *relative* pre-entry rights, in the sense that admission must be granted on terms no less favorable than those accorded to domestic investors or other third-party investors. Therefore, the required analysis is identical to the one pertaining to the NT and MFN principles. Reference is thus made to those sections which deal with these treatment standards.

5.4 National Treatment Obligation

The overwhelming majority of IIAs contain a provision on national treatment. Although the wording and scope of NT clauses can vary significantly,[49] EU Member States' BITs typically require the State to accord foreign investors and their investments treatment no less favorable than that which it accords to its own investors and their investments.[50] National treatment implies a relative or contingent standard of treatment. It prohibits nationality-based discrimination, both *de jure* and *de facto*.[51]

In terms of the Third Energy Package, the same issues that were discussed in relation to Article XVII GATS also need to be addressed in the context of the national treatment obligation in international investment law. These include: (1) individual ownership unbundling exemption decisions; (2) the special OU requirements for public undertakings; and (3) the certification procedure in relation to third countries. Given that the NT standard in international investment law operates somewhat differently than under Article XVII GATS, this is not merely a repeat academic exercise.

Like under the GATS national treatment analysis, the application of the NT standard in international investment law involves two important steps: In the first place it is necessary to identify an appropriate comparative basis. Secondly the question arises whether less favorable treatment has occurred. As regards the

---

[47]See Articles I(9), II(2) and III(1) of the Agreement between the Government of the Republic of Nicaragua and the Government of the Italian Republic on the Promotion and Protection of Investments (20 April 2004) <investmentpolicyhub.unctad.org/download/treatyfile/3591> accessed 20 January 2018.

[48]See footnotes 41 and 42 (this chapter).

[49]Andrew Newcombe and Lluís Paradell, *Law and Practice of Investment Treaties: Standards of Treatment* (Wolters Kluwer Law & Business 2009) 156.

[50]Rudolf Dolzer and Christoph Schreuer, *Principles of International Investment Law* (2nd edn, Oxford University Press 2012) 198. See also Article 10(7) Energy Charter Treaty (n 4).

[51]Andrea K Bjorklund, 'National Treatment' in August Reinisch (ed), *Standards of Investment Protection* (Oxford University Press 2008) 30; August Reinisch, 'National Treatment' in Marc Bungenberg and others (eds), *International Investment Law* (C.H. Beck; Hart; Nomos 2015) [57–59].

determination of a comparative basis, some BITs explicitly provide that the domestic and foreign investor/investment must be in 'like situations' or 'like circumstances'.[52] Where such an express comparative clause is missing, the requirement to show that the allegedly discriminated foreign market actor and a domestic market actor are actually in like circumstances is implicit in the national treatment obligation.[53] As regards the determination of whether less favorable treatment has occurred, the prevailing view in arbitral practice[54] is that the obligation to accord national treatment is not limited to an aggregate group analysis, but in fact implies that the foreign investor/investment must not be treated less favorably than *any* domestic investor/investment (the so-called 'most favored domestic investor' standard).[55] This stands in stark contrast to 'asymmetric impact test' under the GATS.[56] As the investment tribunal in *Archer Daniels Midland Company v. Mexico* explained, the 'most favored domestic investor' standard effectively means that foreign investors and their investments 'are entitled to the best level of treatment available to any other domestic investor or investment operating in like circumstances.'[57]

The preceding observations do not, however, conclusively settle the issues of 'like circumstances' and 'less favorable treatment'. In contrast to WTO jurisprudence, which categorically rejects the 'aims and effects' test, investment tribunals are prepared to consider the regulatory purpose of a governmental measure as part of

[52]See for example Article 3 of the '2012 U.S. Model Bilateral Investment Treaty' (n 42).

[53]*Nykomb Synergetics Technology Holding AB v. The Republic of Latvia* (n 9) [34]; *Consortium RFCC v. Royaume du Maroc,* Arbitration Award (22 December 2003) ICSID Case No. ARB/00/6 [53]; *Parkerings-Compagniet AS v. Republic of Lithuania,* Award (11 September 2007) ICSID Case No. ARB/05/8 [369]; *Total S.A. v. The Argentine Republic,* Decision on Liability (27 December 2010) ICSID Case No. ARB/04/01 [213]. See also Bjorklund (n 51) 38; Newcombe and Paradell (n 49) 160–161; Nicolas F Diebold, 'Standards of Non-Discrimination in International Economic Law' (2011) 60 International and Comparative Law Quarterly 831, 841.

[54]Jürgen Kurtz, 'The Merits and Limits of Comparativism: National Treatment in International Investment Law and the WTO' in Stephan W Schill (ed), *International Investment Law and Comparative Public Law* (Oxford University Press 2010) 266.

[55]*Pope & Talbot Inc. v. The Government of Canada,* Award on the Merits of Phase 2 (10 April 2001) [42–72]; *Methanex Corporation v. United States of America,* Final Award of the Tribunal on Jurisdiction and Merits (3 August 2005), part IV(B), [20–21]; *Loewen Group, Inc. v. United States,* Award (26 June 2003) ICSID Case No. ARB(AF)/98/3 [140].

[56]The significant differences between the 'most favored domestic investor' standard in international investment law and the group-based approach under the WTO/GATS arguably result from the fact that investment agreements on the one hand and the WTO agreements on the other have different purposes. Whereas the WTO agreements aim to guarantee equal conditions of competition in general, investment agreements seek to protect the individual foreign investor from nationality-based discrimination, see Nicholas DiMascio and Joost Pauwelyn, 'Nondiscrimination in Trade and Investment Treaties: Worlds Apart or Two Sides of the Same Coin?' (2008) 102 American Journal of International Law 48, 78, 82, 88–89, passim; Newcombe and Paradell (n 49) 187–188.

[57]*Archer Daniels Midland Company v. Mexico,* Award (21 November 2007) ICSID Case No. ARB (AF)/04/05 [205].

their national treatment analysis.[58] Systemically speaking, this consideration of a measure's regulatory purpose can be seen either as part of the 'like circumstances' or the 'less favorable treatment' prong of the NT standard.[59] Accordingly, if there is a legitimate public policy goal that can justify the differential treatment complained of, the national treatment claim fails.

In the *Pope & Talbot v. Canada* case, the investment tribunal stated that even if a measure provides differential treatment to a domestic and foreign investor, the measure does not violate the NT provision in Article 1102 NAFTA provided that it has a 'reasonable nexus to rational government policies that . . . do not distinguish, on their face or *de facto*, between foreign-owned and domestic companies.'[60] Similarly, in *GAMI Investments v. Mexico* a NAFTA tribunal accepted that the national treatment standard is not violated if the impugned measure is 'plausibly connected with a legitimate goal of policy . . . and . . . applied neither in a discriminatory manner nor as a disguised barrier to equal opportunity.'[61] In *Parkerings-Compagniet v. Lithuania*, a case under the Lithuania-Norway BIT, the arbitrators held that to constitute a violation of international law, 'discrimination must be unreasonable or lacking proportionality, for instance, it must be inapposite or excessive to achieve an otherwise legitimate objective of the State.'[62] In its view, less favorable treatment of a foreign investor could thus be justified on the basis of an 'objective justification'.[63] Importantly, and contrary to the situation under the GATS, the range of policy goals that States may rely on in order to justify differential treatment is not limited in any way. In principle, an investment tribunal can consider *any* policy objective it considers relevant.

There is still some ambiguity regarding the appropriate standard of review.[64] In *GAMI Investments v. Mexico* a 'plausible connection' was required to the objective sought to be achieved; in *Pope & Talbot v. Canada* a 'reasonable nexus'; and in *Parkerings-Compagniet v. Lithuania* the tribunal stated that the measure 'must [not] be inapposite or excessive'. Overall, this seems to suggest a weaker nexus

[58]Bjorklund (n 51) 30, 37; Dolzer and Schreuer (n 50) 202–203; Newcombe and Paradell (n 49) 162, 176–180; Reinisch (n 51) [62–67].

[59]Diebold (n 53) 839–841, 846–849.

[60]*Pope & Talbot Inc. v. The Government of Canada* (n 55) [78]. This approach was also adopted by *William Ralph Clayton, William Richard Clayton, Douglas Clayton, Daniel Clayton and Bilcon of Delaware Inc. v. Government of Canada,* Award on Jurisdiction and Liability (17 March 2015) PCA Case No. 2009-04 [720ff].

[61]*Gami Investments, Inc. v. The Government of the United Mexican States,* Final Award (15 November 2004) [114].

[62]*Parkerings-Compagniet AS v. Republic of Lithuania* (n 53) [368].

[63]Ibid. In the same vein, several other investment tribunals found that only 'unreasonable' distinctions between foreign and domestic investors in like circumstances would amount to a violation of the national treatment obligation, see *Marvin Feldman v. Mexico,* Award (16 December 2002) ICSID Case No. ARB(AF)/99/1 [170, 182]; *Archer Daniels Midland Company v. Mexico* (n 57) [205]; *Total S.A. v. The Argentine Republic* (n 53) [214].

[64]Newcombe and Paradell (n 49) 178.

requirement in comparison with the 'necessity' standard used in Article XIV GATS and Article XX GATT.[65]

Against this background, the question arises how the national treatment standard applies to the measures at issue here. As regards individual OU exemption decisions, it is clear that there must be a rational basis for exempting one commercial energy company, but not another. The 'rational basis' is found in Article 17 of Regulation 714/2009 and Article 36 of Directive 2009/73/EC, which outline objective and non-discriminatory criteria for granting an exemption. Therefore, there is no NT violation unless the decision to deny an exemption request of a foreign investor cannot be plausibly or reasonably connected to the exemption criteria. Presumably this will only very rarely be the case. Nevertheless, international investment tribunals will conduct a comprehensive and in-depth review of the factual record in order to determine whether there is an appropriate justification, bearing in mind that the investment regime focuses on *individual* investors and thus pays attention to the 'micro-issues of attracting and protecting investments made by individual investors.'[66]

With respect to the special ownership unbundling requirements for public undertakings in Article 9(6) of Directives 2009/72/EC and 2009/73/EC, in the first place it is questionable whether there is 'less favorable treatment'. As discussed, domestic public generation/production or supply undertakings do not have any advantage over (foreign) private ones as a result of Article 9(6). The same applies to domestic public TSOs and their (foreign) private counterparts.[67] Moreover, it is possible that the existence of a discriminatory intent may be required. Although investment tribunals generally agree that discriminatory intent is not a prerequisite for a finding of a national treatment violation,[68] some tribunals have used the absence of a discriminatory intent in order to deny a breach of NT. In *Genin v. Estonia*, the tribunal stressed that the foreign investor was not 'specifically targeted' and that there had been no intention, on the part of the State organ, to treat the investor in a discriminatory way.[69] Similar remarks were made by the tribunal in *LG&E v. Argentina*. In that case, the arbitrators concluded that the claimants failed to prove that the

[65]DiMascio and Pauwelyn (n 56) 76, 88.

[66]Ibid 56.

[67]See Sect. 4.6.2.4.

[68]See, for instance, *William Ralph Clayton, William Richard Clayton, Douglas Clayton, Daniel Clayton and Bilcon of Delaware Inc. v. Government of Canada* (n 60) [719]; *Marvin Feldman v. Mexico* (n 63) [181]; *Parkerings-Compagniet AS v. Republic of Lithuania* (n 53) [368]; *Siemens A.G. v. The Argentine Republic,* Award (17 January 2007) ICSID Case No. ARB/02/8 [321]; *Bayindir Insaat Turizm Ticaret Ve Sanayi A.S. v. Islamic Republic of Pakistan,* Award (27 August 2009) ICSID Case No. ARB/03/29 [390]; *International Thunderbird Gaming Corporation v. The United Mexican States,* Arbitral Award (26 January 2006) [177]; *Occidental Exploration and Production Company v. The Republic of Ecuador,* Final Award (1 July 2004) LCIA Case No. UN 3467 [177].

[69]*Alex Genin, Eastern Credit Limited, Inc. and A.S. Baltoil v. The Republic of Estonia,* Award (25 June 2001) ICSID Case No. ARB/99/2 [369].

governmental measures 'targeted Claimants' investments specifically as foreign investments.'[70] Relying on this stream of jurisprudence, it could be argued that the special OU regime contained in Article 9(6) of the Directives is in line with the national treatment obligation, as it does not specifically target foreign investors.[71]

Finally, the third country certification procedure in Article 11 of the Gas and Electricity Directives must be examined. Several Russian scholars have taken the view that the third country certification procedure breaches the national treatment standard in IIAs by reason of its additional 'security of energy supply' test.[72] Since there clearly is less favorable treatment, the decisive issue is whether an appropriate justification can be provided. In the discussion under Article XIV GATS, it was concluded that the measure was 'necessary' to ensure the security of supply of the EU and its Member States, and thus to maintain public order, and that the measure was therefore justifiable under Article XIV(a) GATS.[73] Given that international investment law applies a more deferential standard of review, i.e. only a 'plausible connection' or 'reasonable nexus' between the measure and the objective pursued, a NT claim would surely fail.[74]

5.5 MFN Treatment Obligation

The most-favored-nation treatment obligation is the second non-discrimination provision commonly found in IIAs. It requires host States to treat investors and investments from the other Contracting Party no less favorable than investors from any third State.[75] Like the NT standard, the concept of MFN treatment is a relative one, i.e. it does not constitute an absolute treatment standard, but is conditional on the treatment accorded to other foreign investors.

In the issue under consideration here, the following aspects of the Third Energy Package could raise issues under the MFN treatment standard: (1) individual ownership unbundling exemption decisions; (2) the certification procedure in relation to

[70] *LG&E Energy Corp. LG&E Capital Corp. and LG&E International, Inc. v. Argentine Republic*, Decision on Liability (3 October 2006) ICSID Case No. ARB/02/1 [147]. The treaty provision prohibited arbitrary and discriminatory measures, which goes beyond nationality-based discrimination. See also *Methanex Corporation v. United States of America* (n 55), part IV(B), [12].

[71] For an analogous argument in the context of (domestic) public vs. (foreign) private companies, see Anatole Boute, *Russian Electricity and Energy Investment Law* (Law in Eastern Europe, Brill 2015) 620.

[72] Gudkov (n 15) 65; Anufrieva (n 15) 86.

[73] See Sect. 4.9.2.

[74] See also Boute (n 16) [3.47] (who writes that 'Member States that, for energy security reasons, refuse to certify existing foreign operators that comply with the unbundling requirements will have to provide strong arguments to substantiate this decision').

[75] United Nations Conference on Trade and Development, *Most-Favoured-Nation Treatment* (UNCTAD Series on Issues in International Investment Agreements II, United Nations 2010) 12.

third countries; and (3) the unbundling requirements as such. Although these points have already been addressed in the context of Article II:1 GATS, a fresh analysis is needed here, since the MFN standard in international investment law differs slightly from that under the GATS.

In investment arbitration practice, MFN clauses have commonly been invoked in order to 'import' more favorable substantive treatment obligations or more favorable procedural provisions from other IIAs.[76] The present issue under examination does not, however, concern the 'importation' of more favorable substantive or procedural provisions from third-party treaties. Rather, the issue is whether foreign investors can claim a treatment no less favorable than that *actually* accorded to other third-party investors *under domestic measures*. Although there are only a few cases of this kind in practice,[77] it is clear that MFN clauses also apply to the actual treatment of foreign investors from different countries.[78] In other words, like under the NT obligation, the host State is prohibited from discriminating *de jure* or *de facto*, through domestic measures, between investors benefiting from a treaty and other foreign investors.[79]

The operation of MFN clauses is similar to the application of NT provisions. First, it must be ascertained whether the foreign investors at issue are in 'like circumstances'. Second, the question arises whether there has been less favorable treatment.[80] Third, there is no MFN violation if a legitimate justification can be provided, i.e. 'if a State's legitimate objective justifies such different treatment in relation to the specificity of the investment.'[81]

As regards individual ownership unbundling exemption decisions, it is clear that the objective and non-discriminatory criteria contained in Article 36 of Directive 2009/73/EC and Article 17 of Regulation 714/2009 justifiably differentiate between different infrastructure projects. Consequently, any most-favored-nation treatment

---

[76]In *Bayindir v. Pakistan*, for example, an arbitration under the Turkey-Pakistan-BIT, which lacked a fair and equitable treatment provision, the ICSID tribunal accepted that Bayindir was entitled to rely on the FET obligation contained in the Pakistan-Switzerland BIT, see *Bayindir Insaat Turizm Ticaret Ve Sanayi A.S. v. Islamic Republic of Pakistan,* Decision on Jurisdiction (14 November 2005) ICSID Case No. ARB/03/29 [230ff]; *Bayindir Insaat Turizm Ticaret Ve Sanayi A.S. v. Islamic Republic of Pakistan* (n 68) [153ff]. In *Maffezini v. Spain*, a case under the Argentine-Spain BIT, the tribunal held that the MFN clause would allow the investor to take advantage of the fact that the Chile-Spain BIT did not require a waiting period of 18 months before arbitration proceedings could be instituted, see *Emilio Agustín Maffezini v. The Kingdom of Spain,* Award (13 November 2000) ICSID Case No. ARB/97/7 [38ff].

[77]For a rare example, see *Parkerings-Compagniet AS v. Republic of Lithuania* (n 53) [369ff].

[78]August Reinisch, 'Most Favoured Nation Treatment' in Marc Bungenberg and others (eds), *International Investment Law* (C.H. Beck; Hart; Nomos 2015) [23, 61]; Newcombe and Paradell (n 49) 226–227, 230; International Law Commission, Draft Articles on Most-Favoured-Nation Clauses with Commentaries (1978) YBILC 1978/II(2), 23 (Commentary (6) to Article 5).

[79]United Nations Conference on Trade and Development (n 75) 26, 28.

[80]Newcombe and Paradell (n 49) 226–227, 230.

[81]*Parkerings-Compagniet AS v. Republic of Lithuania* (n 53) [371]. See also Dolzer and Schreuer (n 50) 207; Newcombe and Paradell (n 49) 227.

claim will fail unless it can be shown that the individual exemption decision is not plausibly or reasonably connected to the exemption criteria. It should however be stressed that international investment tribunals will carry out an in-depth factual investigation in order to ascertain whether there is, in fact, such a plausible or reasonable connection.

With respect to the third country certification procedure in Article 11 of the Directives, it must be recalled that passing the security of supply test does not generally depend on (criteria related to) the country of origin of the foreign investor.[82] In principle, therefore, there is no MFN violation where two TSOs from third countries apply for certification under Article 11, but only one of them passes the security of supply test. What's more, even if origin-based criteria, such as general security of supply related agreements or the existence of energy trade relations, were taken into account by the national regulatory authorities and/or the European Commission, the objective of ensuring security of energy supply would provide an appropriate justification—assuming, of course, that the origin-based criteria were applied in a proportional and non-discriminatory manner.

Lastly, a foreign investor may also argue that the unbundling requirements as such are *de facto* discriminatory. This possible challenge relates to the fact that while in some EU Member States vertically integrated undertakings can choose the ITO model, other Member States have prescribed mandatory ownership unbundling. The chances of success of an MFN claim in these circumstances also depend on how the MFN obligation applies in relation to sub-(supra)national entities (*in casu*, EU Member States).[83] In other words, the question arises whether a foreign investor in EU Member State A, where the relevant measure is enacted, is in 'like circumstances' with another foreign investor in Member State B, or whether compliance with the MFN obligation requires treating the former no less favorably than the latter.

The difficulty in applying the MFN principle in relation to sub-(supra)national subdivisions has played a certain role in the investment law literature and in the investment treaty practice of some States. Canada, for example, included in its 2004 Model BIT a provision that '[f]or greater certainty, the treatment accorded by a Party

[82]See Sect. 4.7.2.3.

[83]The application of non-discrimination provisions to sub-(supra)national subdivisions is often difficult. For example, with respect to the national treatment obligation the question arose whether foreign investors should be granted 'best-in-sub-state treatment' or 'best out-of-sub-state treatment', see United Nations Conference on Trade and Development, *National Treatment* (UNCTAD Series on Issues in International Investment Agreements, United Nations 1999) 25–28; United Nations Conference on Trade and Development, *Lessons from the MAI* (UNCTAD Series on Issues in International Investment Agreements, United Nations 1999) 14; J. A VanDuzer, Penelope Simons and Graham Mayeda, *Integrating Sustainable Development into International Investment Agreements: A Guide for Developing Country Negotiators* (Commonwealth Secretariat 2013) 118; Newcombe and Paradell (n 49) 188–189.

under [the provision on MFN treatment] means, with respect to a sub-national government, treatment accorded, in like circumstances, by that sub-national government to investors, and to investments of investors, of a non-Party.'[84] This clarification defines in more detail the basis of comparison for the 'treatment no less favorable' standard. It specifies that where the treatment accorded by one sub-national government is at issue, investors cannot claim the treatment accorded by another sub-national government.[85] The investment chapters of recent PTAs—like the CETA between the EU and Canada—feature similar clarification provisions.[86] With respect to the clause in the CETA, one commentator stated that it 'effectively "homes in" the non-discrimination obligations on the basis of nationality to the regional or Member State level, thus allowing the relevant sub-national governments or Member States to remain in control of the treatment they accord to all investors within their jurisdiction.'[87]

Where a clarification is absent, it is unclear how the respective MFN provision will be interpreted. It cannot be completely ruled out that investment tribunals could find that a foreign investor in one sub-(supra)national entity must be treated no less favorably than another foreign investor in any other sub-(supra)national entity, regardless of the fact that the relevant measure was enacted not at the supranational or national but at the *sub*-(supra)national level. However, it is submitted here that compliance with the MFN obligation under IIAs does not require the EU to accord to a foreign investor in EU Member State A treatment no less favorable than that 'autonomously' granted by Member State B in its territory to another foreign investor. Such a requirement would imply a requirement of regulatory homogeneity not intended by the MFN principle. Apart from that, it seems that the less favorable treatment flowing from the adoption of different unbundling models among EU Member States could in any event be justified. In particular, the justification could be that an EU Member State should be able to exercise its legislative competences within its territorial jurisdiction in a manner independent of the other Member States.

---

[84]Government of Canada, '2004 Canada Model Foreign Investment Promotion and Protection Agreement' (2004) <http://www.italaw.com/documents/Canadian2004-FIPA-model-en.pdf> accessed 13 April 2015. See also Céline Lévesque and Andrew Newcombe, 'Canada' in Chester Brown (ed), *Commentaries on Selected Model Investment Treaties* (Oxford Commentaries on International Law. Oxford University Press 2013) 76–77.

[85]For a similar argument of the Mexican government with respect to Article 1102(3) NAFTA, see Bjorklund (n 51) 55–56 (referring to *Pope & Talbot Inc. v. The Government of Canada,* Submissions of the United Mexican States (3 April 2000) [63–65]).

[86]Comprehensive Economic and Trade Agreement between the European Union and Canada – Consolidated text (2016) <http://trade.ec.europa.eu/doclib/docs/2014/september/tradoc_152806.pdf> accessed 20 January 2018, 46.

[87]Antonios Tzanakopoulos, 'National Treatment and MFN in the (Invisible) EU Model BIT' (2014) 15 Journal of World Investment & Trade 484, 500.

5.6 Protection from Direct or Indirect Expropriation

5.6.1 Introduction

This section analyzes whether the ownership unbundling measures, as set out in Directives 2009/72/EC and 2009/73/EC, amount to expropriation. International investment agreements consistently contain a standard of protection against expropriation without compensation.[88] It is widely believed to be the 'core' of international investment law. Although the wording of the relevant provisions may differ in some details, investment agreements generally cover both direct and indirect (i.e. *de facto*) expropriations. An act of direct expropriation occurs where the legal title to the ownership is formally transferred by a State measure. In contrast, an indirect expropriation 'leaves the investor's title untouched but deprives him of the possibility of utilizing the investment in a meaningful way.'[89] In the case of ownership unbundling requirements, there is no formal transfer of property rights. Until OU is implemented by the investor himself, his legal title over the relevant assets in the energy sector remains unaffected.[90] The central question is therefore whether OU measures are tantamount to an indirect or *de facto* expropriation. Providing an answer to this question involves the difficulty of drawing a dividing line between non-compensable regulatory measures and measures that amount to indirect expropriation, and thus are compensable.

In some instances the foreign investor may be able to invoke more favorable provisions on expropriation. There are over a dozen BITs in force which contain expropriation provisions that specifically address the type of divestment occurring in the case of OU measures.[91] Many of these BITs have been concluded with EU

---

[88]Markus Perkams, 'The Concept of Indirect Expropriation in Comparative Public Law – Searching for Light in the Dark' in Stephan W Schill (ed), *International Investment Law and Comparative Public Law* (Oxford University Press 2010) 109; United Nations Conference on Trade and Development, *Expropriation* (UNCTAD Series on Issues in International Investment Agreements II, United Nations 2012) 5.

[89]Dolzer and Schreuer (n 50) 101.

[90]Non-compliance with the OU requirements will usually be dealt with through the imposition of fines; see Article 37(4)(d) of Directive 2009/72/EC of the European Parliament and of the Council concerning common rules for the internal market in electricity and repealing Directive 2003/54/EC (13 July 2009) OJ 2009/L 211/55; Article 41(4)(d) of Directive 2009/73/EC of the European Parliament and of the Council concerning common rules for the internal market in natural gas and repealing Directive 2003/55/EC (13 July 2009) OJ 2009/L 211/94.

[91]See Article 5(6) of the Agreement between the Government of the Republic of Slovenia and the Government of the State of Kuwait on the Promotion and Reciprocal Protection of Investments (26 April 2002) <https://www.uradni-list.si/glasilo-uradni-list-rs/vsebina/2002-02-0075> accessed 20 January 2018; Paragraph 4(a) of the Protocol to the Agreement between the Swiss Confederation and the State of Kuwait for the Encouragement and Reciprocal Protection of Investments (31 October 1998) <http://investmentpolicyhub.unctad.org/download/treatyfile/4819> accessed 20 January 2018; Article 7(4) of the Agreement between the State of Kuwait and the Republic of India for the Encouragement and Reciprocal Protection of Investment

Member States. To give an example, Article 6(4) on expropriation of the BIT between Latvia and Kuwait provides as follows:

> For the purposes of this Agreement, the term 'expropriation' shall also include interventions or regulatory measures by a Contracting Party that have a de facto expropriatory effect, in that their effect results in depriving the investor in fact from his ownership, control or substantial benefits over his investment or which may result in loss or damage to the economic value of the investment, *such as* the freezing or blocking of the investment, levying of arbitrary or excessive taxes on the investment, *compulsory sale of all or part of the investment*, or other comparable measures.[92]

It is obvious that according to this provision the 'compulsory sale of all or part of the investment' is *ipso facto* an expropriation. Therefore, under the Latvia-Kuwait BIT, the OU requirements foreseen in Directives 2009/72/EC and 2009/73/EC would clearly constitute an expropriation. Similarly strong provisions can also be found in the BITs concluded between Kuwait or the United Arab Emirates, on the

---

(27 November 2001) <http://investmentpolicyhub.unctad.org/download/treatyfile/1569> accessed 20 January 2018; Article 6(4) of the Agreement between the Government of the Republic of Latvia and the Government of the State of Kuwait for the Encouragement and Reciprocal Protection of Investments (05 October 2001) <investmentpolicyhub.unctad.org/download/treatyfile/5014> accessed 20 January 2018; Article 6(2) of the Agreement between the Government of the Kingdom of the Netherlands and the Government of the State of Kuwait for the Encouragement and Reciprocal Protection of Investments (29 May 2001) <investmentpolicyhub.unctad.org/download/treatyfile/1851> accessed 20 January 2018; Article 6(4) of the Agreement between Bosnia and Herzegovina and the State of Kuwait for the Encouragement and Reciprocal Protection of Investments (13 June 2001) <investmentpolicyhub.unctad.org/download/treatyfile/478> accessed 20 January 2018; Article 6(5) of the Agreement between the Republic of Lithuania and the State of Kuwait for the Encouragement and Reciprocal Protection of Investments (05 June 2001) <investmentpolicyhub.unctad.org/download/treatyfile/1849> accessed 20 January 2018; Article 6(4) of the Agreement between the Republic of Croatia and the State of Kuwait for the Promotion and Reciprocal Protection of Investments (08 March 1997) <investmentpolicyhub.unctad.org/download/treatyfile/869> accessed 20 January 2018; Article 6(4) of the Agreement between the Republic of Austria and the State of Kuwait for the Encouragement and reciprocal Protection of Investments (16 November 1996) <http://investmentpolicyhub.unctad.org/download/treatyfile/3315> accessed 20 January 2018; Article 6(4) of the Agreement between the Federal Democratic Republic of Ethiopia and the State of Kuwait for the Encouragement and Reciprocal Protection of Investments (14 September 1996) <investmentpolicyhub.unctad.org/download/treatyfile/1169> accessed 20 January 2018; Paragraph 3 of the Protocol to the Agreement between the Republic of Hungary and the State of Kuwait for the Encouragement and Reciprocal Protection of Investments (08 November 1989) <investmentpolicyhub.unctad.org/download/treatyfile/1529> accessed 20 January 2018; Article 5(2) of the Agreement between the Government of the United Arab Emirates and the Government of the Kingdom of Sweden on the Promotion and Reciprocal Protection of Investments (10 November 1999) <investmentpolicyhub.unctad.org/download/treatyfile/2306> accessed 20 January 2018; Article 6(1)(i) of the Agreement between the Government of the United Arab Emirates and the Government of Romania on the Promotion and Protection of Investments (11 April 1993) <http://investmentpolicyhub.unctad.org/download/treatyfile/2217> accessed 20 January 2018; Article 6(2) of the Agreement between the Government of the Czech Republic and the Government of the United Arab Emirates for the Promotion and Protection of Investments (23 November 1994) <investmentpolicyhub.unctad.org/download/treatyfile/992> accessed 20 January 2018.

[92]Emphasis added.

one part, and Austria, Croatia, the Czech Republic, Hungary, Lithuania, the Netherlands, Romania, Slovenia and Sweden, respectively, on the other part. These more favorable provisions on expropriation not only benefit investors from Kuwait or the United Arab Emirates, but also, and particularly, investors from other third countries that have invested in the EU internal energy market. Unless explicitly stated otherwise,[93] a commonly worded MFN clause in a BIT between one of the EU Member States concerned and another third country would generally allow investors to 'import' the more favorable substantive obligations into the BIT.[94]

However, where such provisions explicitly addressing the situation of a compulsory sale of investment assets cannot be relied upon, it is necessary to carefully analyze the scope of indirect or *de facto* expropriations.

5.6.2 Compulsory Sale of an Investment: Taking Stock

Given that compulsory disinvestments have given rise to expropriation claims under international law in the past, it is useful to examine how this issue has been addressed in the existing case-law, State practice, and the academic literature. This will provide the background for the subsequent discussion of ownership unbundling measures.

First of all, compulsory sales of investment assets have taken place in the form of the so-called 'indigenization' measures which were taken by many African and Asian countries, mainly after the end of colonialism. Indigenization measures effected the transfer of economic ownership from foreign to domestic shareholders by way of divestment.[95] In Nigeria, the 'Nigerian Enterprises Promotion Decrees' of 1972 and 1977 required between 40 and 100% indigenous ownership, depending on the industry concerned.[96] In Zimbabwe, the 'Indigenisation and Economic Empowerment Act' was adopted in 2008 in order to ensure that, in the long run, at least 51% of the shares of every company will be owned by indigenous Zimbabweans.[97] Sornarajah stated, with respect to indigenization, that 'the transfer of the ownership

[93]See Article 8.7(4) CETA – Consolidated text (n 86) 46. The provision states that '[s]ubstantive obligations in other international investment treaties and other trade agreements do not in themselves constitute "treatment", and thus cannot give rise to a breach of this Article, absent measures adopted or maintained by a Party pursuant to those obligations'.

[94]Dolzer and Schreuer (n 50) 209–211; *Vladimir Berschader and Moïse Berschader v. The Russian Federation,* Award (21 April 2006) SCC Case No. 080/2004 [179] (stating that 'it is universally agreed that the very essence of an MFN provision in a BIT is to afford to investors all material protection provided by subsequent treaties'). It is unclear whether a foreign investor could also rely upon already existing third-party treaties, see Reinisch (n 78) [16–17].

[95]Muthucumaraswamy Sornarajah, *The International Law on Foreign Investment* (3rd edn, Cambridge University Press 2010) 380–382.

[96]Fiona C Beveridge, 'Taking Control of Foreign Investment: A Case Study of Indigenisation in Nigeria' (1991) 40 International and Comparative Law Quarterly 302, 307–321.

[97]Reuters, 'Zimbabwe PM Says Indigenisation Not Expropriation' (16 September 2010) <http://af.reuters.com/article/topNews/idAFJOE68F0EQ20100916> accessed 30 May 2015.

is involuntary and the timing of the transfer of the shares in the venture owned by the foreigner is not left to him. As a result, he may not be able to secure the optimum price for his shares.'[98] However, without delving into a detailed legal analysis, Sornarajah also opined that the indigenization policy 'falls within the regulatory controls a state establishes in pursuance of its sovereign rights over economic matters rather than into the category of takings for which the state [has] to pay compensation.'[99] In support of his conclusion, he noted that, first, depending on the degree of indigenous ownership required, the foreign investor may remain in control of his enterprise and that, second, indigenization measures serve an important political and economic objective in that they seek to remedy economic inequality.[100]

Another author, Beveridge, specifically dealt with the relationship between indigenization policies in Nigeria and international law rules on the protection of foreign investment.[101] Beveridge wrote in 1991 that although the compulsory divestment of business interests or shareholdings would constitute a *prima facie* case of expropriation, there was a 'general acceptance' on the part of the affected investors of the indigenization measures. In view of this acceptance (or acquiescence) and given the fact that there was no 'duress', which she defined narrowly as the 'threat or use of physical force or compulsion', Beveridge concluded that the sale agreements reached in order to comply with the provisions of the Nigerian Enterprises Promotion Decrees 'must be assumed to have been voluntary'.[102] She thus rejected a case of expropriation. Beveridge further stated that, even assuming *arguendo* that an expropriatory act occurred, the revenue generated through the sale transactions would almost always fulfill the standard of compensation required under international law.[103]

Apart from the academic treatment of indigenization measures, there is also some State practice concerning this matter. For example, Zaire (today known as the Democratic Republic of the Congo) faced compensation claims by Belgium and Switzerland on behalf of affected nationals. As regards Belgium, the Zairian government recognized its obligation to pay compensation and in 1976 the two countries signed a treaty which contained provisions to that effect.[104] The claims of the Swiss government were based on the Switzerland-Zaire BIT of 1972, and in particular

[98]Sornarajah (n 95) 381.

[99]Ibid.

[100]Ibid 381–382.

[101]Beveridge (n 96) 321–328.

[102]Ibid 322–324. Regarding the concept of 'duress' in relation to the question of expropriation under international law, Beveridge referred to Detlev F Vagts, 'Coercion and Foreign Investment Rearrangements' (1978) 72 American Journal of International Law 17.

[103]Beveridge (n 96) 324–325.

[104]Ahowanou A Agbessi, *Les mesures d'indigénisation des investissements privés étrangers au Nigeria et au Zaïre* (Doctoral Thesis No. 511, University of Geneva, 1993) 159ff, 205–207.

Article 4 thereof, relating to expropriation.[105] In accordance with the provisions of that BIT, which did not provide for the possibility of investor-State dispute settlement, a mixed Swiss-Zairian commission was established in 1976. Finally, in 1980, a compensation agreement was signed.[106] The indigenization measures taken by the government of Nigeria, in contrast, have not triggered any compensation claims. Even though British investors were affected, the government of the United Kingdom did not intervene.[107]

Another case of compulsory divestment measures concerns the South African mining sector. In 2006, a group of European investors requested the institution of arbitration proceedings against South Africa (*Piero Foresti v. South Africa*).[108] They claimed that the entry into force in 2004 of the Mineral and Petroleum Resources Development Act (MPRDA)[109] amounted to, *inter alia*, a violation of the prohibition of expropriation. The investment arbitration action was brought under the South Africa-Italy[110] and the South Africa-Belgium/Luxembourg[111] BITs. As part of the Broad Based Black Economic Empowerment legislation, the MPRDA had restructured the ownership of mining industry assets with a view to alleviating the effects of past discrimination against historically disadvantaged persons resulting from the Apartheid regime. In particular the MPRDA, in conjunction with the Broad-Based Socio-Economic Empowerment Charter for the South African Mining Industry,[112] required mining companies to sell 26% of their shares to historically disadvantaged South Africans (HDSAs).[113] The claimants alleged that this 'equity

---

[105]Accord entre la Confédération suisse et la République du Zaïre relatif à la protection et à l'encouragement des investissements (10 March 1972) <investmentpolicyhub.unctad.org/download/treatyfile/827> accessed 20 January 2018.

[106]Agbessi (n 104) 175ff.

[107]Ibid 100, 204.

[108]*Piero Foresti, Laura de Carli & Others v. The Republic of South Africa,* Award (4 August 2010) ICSID Case No. ARB(AF)/07/01.

[109]Republic of South Africa, Mineral and Petroleum Resources Development Act (2002) No. 28.

[110]Agreement between the Government of the Italian Republic and the Government of the Republic of South Africa on the Promotion and Protection of Investments (09 June 1997) <investmentpolicyhub.unctad.org/download/treatyfile/3216> accessed 20 January 2018.

[111]Agreement between the Belgo-Luxembourg Economic Union and the Republic of South Africa on the Reciprocal Promotion and Protection of Investments (14 August 1998) <investmentpolicyhub.unctad.org/download/treatyfile/414> accessed 20 January 2018.

[112]Republic of South Africa, Broad-Based Socio-Economic Empowerment Charter for the South African Mining Industry (11 October 2002).

[113]Section 23(l)(h) in conjunction with section 100 of the South African Mineral and Petroleum Resources Development Act (n 109). The Mining Charter provides: 'In order to increase participation and ownership by HDSA's in the mining industry, mining companies agree ... [t]o achieve 26% HDSA ownership of the mining industry assets in 10 years by each mining company', see section 4.7 of the Broad-Based Socio-Economic Empowerment Charter for the South African Mining Industry (n 112). See also Peter Leon, 'A Fork in the Investor-State Road: South Africa's New Mineral Regulatory Regime Four Years On' (2008) 42 Journal of World Trade 671, 681f, 685f.

divestiture scheme' constituted a direct or indirect expropriation of the claimants' shares in certain mining enterprises.[114] Moreover, they argued that the expropriation was unlawful due to, *inter alia*, the lack of compensation.[115] The South African government rejected these contentions and argued that there was neither a direct nor an indirect expropriation.[116] More specifically, the government stated that 'there could be no indirect expropriation ... because, even if there was a 26% divestment ..., the Claimants would still retain control over their investments.'[117] In 2008, the claimants and the South African government concluded an agreement according to which the requirement to sell 26% of the shares to HDSAs would not be fully applied.[118] In 2010, following a request of the claimants, the arbitral proceedings were discontinued with *res judicata* effect.[119] In consequence, the tribunal had no opportunity to address the claims on the merits.

In discussing the *Piero Foresti v. South Africa* case, one author observed that the requirement to sell a 26% equity stake 'may constitute a forced divestiture' due to the fact that 'government actions may constitute an expropriation even if they do not completely deprive the owner of his property rights, including so-called "forced" or "involuntary sales"'.[120] In this connection he made reference to a number of cases of forced sales during the Nazi regime in Germany.[121] After the Nazi government had been overthrown, these cases were handled by special tribunals, such as the Court of Restitution Appeals under Allied Military Government Law No. 59. It is evident that the respective sales of property all took place in an atmosphere of anti-Semitism and persecution. Due to these extraordinary circumstances, the corresponding case-law is not relevant to the issue under consideration here.[122] It does not lend support to the proposition that the measures giving rise to the *Piero Foresti v. South Africa* case, or, for that matter, the ownership unbundling requirements in the EU energy sector, amount to an expropriatory act.

[114] *Piero Foresti, Laura de Carli & Others v. The Republic of South Africa* (n 108) [64–65].

[115] Ibid [66].

[116] Ibid [67–77].

[117] Ibid [77].

[118] Ibid [79]. The award notes that '[i]nstead, pursuant to the Offset Agreement, the Operating Companies would be deemed to have complied with the Mining Charter by (i) making a 21% beneficiation offset (i.e., beneficiating – processing and adding value to the quarried stone – in South Africa 21% of the stone that it mined in South Africa); and (ii) providing a 5% employee ownership program for employees of the Operating Companies'. The possibility to reduce the percentage of the equity ownership requirement through beneficiation activities was provided for in section 4.8 of the Mining Charter, see Broad-Based Socio-Economic Empowerment Charter for the South African Mining Industry (n 112).

[119] See Republic of South Africa, Department of Mineral Resources, *Successful Conclusion to SA – Foresti Arbitration Proceedings* (2010).

[120] Leon (n 113) 685–686.

[121] Reference is made to George C Christie, 'What Constitutes a Taking of Property under International Law?' (1994) 88 American Journal of International Law 307, 324–329.

[122] See also Vagts (n 102) 24–25, who likewise questions the transferability of these cases.

The issue of compulsory sale of investments has received some additional, albeit limited, treatment in the academic literature. One author stated that the 'compulsory sale of the investment or parts thereof' would be a 'typical' example of indirect expropriation.[123] In support of this contention, she cites the Fedorchak Claim of 1962, which was decided by the United States Foreign Claims Settlement Commission (FCSC).[124] The FCSC is a quasi-judicial agency within the US Department of Justice which hears and adjudicates claims of US citizens against foreign governments. The claim of Irene Toman Fedorchak against the government of Czechoslovakia related to the acquisition by the government of a piece of land which she owned in Czechoslovakia at the beginning of the 1950s. The FCSC's decision states that the Czechoslovakian government 'purported to purchase' the land by a contract and that the land was subsequently recorded in the State's name.[125] Furthermore, the decision notes that '[i]t appears that no payments were ever made on account of said "contract"'.[126] Ultimately, the Commission held 'that the transaction by which the Government of Czechoslovakia acquired title to the land was not a voluntary sale of property, as that term is customarily understood, but rather that the action of the Government of Czechoslovakia constituted a taking of property without compensation.'[127] It seems clear that FCSC's decision does not lend support to the broad assertion that the compulsory sale of an investment constitutes an indirect expropriation. The involuntary nature of the transaction did not relate to the fact that Irene Fedorchak was under a legal obligation to sell the land, but to the fact that she had never signed a contract[128] and/or that no payments were ever made under said 'contract'.

Other authors have likewise dealt with the category of 'forced' or 'involuntary' sales. Drawing upon cases from the late nineteenth and early twentieth century, such as *Gowen and Copeland* and *Ellerman c. Etat Polonais*, they developed the general principle that '[a]ssuming they are price-deficient, "involuntary sales" of foreign wealth should be considered the functional equivalents of deprivations giving rise to

[123]Claudia Wendrich, 'Ten Years After: The World Bank Guidelines on Foreign Direct Investment: In Need of Revision?' (2002) 3 Journal of World Investment & Trade 831, 848. See also United Nations Conference on Trade and Development, *The Protection of National Security in IIAs* (UNCTAD Series on International Investment Policies for Development, United Nations 2009) 115–116 (stating that '[a] forced disinvestment for national security reasons . . . would amount to an expropriation of the investor, with the result that the host country would have to pay compensation').

[124]Foreign Claims Settlement Commission of the United States, *Fedorchak Claim,* Amended Final Decision (11 April 1962) Claim No. CZ-4634 40 ILR 96. See also Newcombe and Paradell (n 49) 327 (who also mention the Fedorchak case as an example of a 'forced sale').

[125]*Fedorchak Claim* (n 124) 96.

[126]Ibid 97.

[127]Ibid.

[128]But see Oliver R Jones and Chido Dunn, 'Consent, Forced Renegotiation and Expropriation in International Law' (2010) 26 Arbitration International 391, 401 (who write that 'it is . . . evident that at the time Fedorchak transferred her title to the property she was voluntarily agreeing to that transfer').

compensatory responsibility.'[129] This general assertion also seems to be confirmed by an award of the Iran-US Claims Tribunal. In the case *Emanuel Too v. Greater Modesto Insurance Associates and the United States of America*,[130] the tribunal was faced with the claim of an Iranian national who demanded compensation for, *inter alia*, the forced sale of a liquor license at an auction by the United States Internal Revenue Service in order to satisfy overdue taxes. Although the facts of the case are rather specific, the tribunal's reasoning is worthwhile noting here. It held that a State does not bear responsibility for loss of property or for other economic disadvantage resulting from bona fide general taxation or any other action that is commonly accepted as within the police power of States, unless it is 'designed to cause the alien ... to sell [the property] at a distress price.'[131]

Finally, the case-law of the European Court of Human Rights may also provide a further source of guidance, provided that the structural differences between human rights law and international investment law are taken into account. In fact, international investment tribunals have in a number of cases made references to the jurisprudence of the ECtHR, *inter alia* in order to define the notion of expropriation under international law.[132] Among the many judgments dealing with Article 1 of the First Protocol to the ECHR, the ECtHR's decision in *James and Others v. United Kingdom*[133] is of particular relevance. Several scholars have taken the view that this case is relevant to the determination of whether ownership unbundling measures constitute an expropriation under EU law.[134]

---

[129]Burns H Weston, '"Constructive Takings" under International Law: A Modest Foray into the Problem of "Creeping Expropriation"' (1975) 16 Virginia Journal of International Law 103, 148. See also the 'general conclusion' of Christie (n 121) 338 and Rosalyn Higgins, 'The Taking of Property by the State' (1982) 176 Recueil des Cours 259, 326.

[130]*Emanuel Too v. Greater Modesto Insurance Associates and the United States of America*, Award (29 December 1989) Case No. 880 23 Iran-US C.T.R. 378.

[131]Ibid [26]. See also OECD, Draft Convention on the Protection of Foreign Property (1967) 7 I.L.M. 117 (1968). The notes and comments to Article 3 (Taking of Property) of the Draft Convention state that 'prohibiting the national to sell his property or forcing him to do so at a fraction of the fair market price' is considered as a taking.

[132]See *Técnicas Medioambientales Tecmed, S.A. v. The United Mexican States*, Award (29 May 2003) ICSID Case No. ARB (AF)/00/2 [116], footnote 134; *Ronald S. Lauder v. The Czech Republic*, Final Award (3 September 2001) [200]; *Azurix Corp. v. The Argentine Republic*, Award (14 July 2006) ICSID Case No. ARB/01/12 [311–312]; *Saipem S.p.A. v. The People's Republic of Bangladesh*, Decision on Jurisdiction and Recommendation on Provisional Measures (21 March 2007) ICSID Case No. ARB/05/07 [130].

[133]European Court of Human Rights, *James and Others v. The United Kingdom*, Judgment (21 February 1986) Application No. 8793/79.

[134]See Jürgen F Baur and others, *Eigentumsentflechtung der Energiewirtschaft durch Europarecht: Mittel, Schranken und Rechtsfolgen* (Veröffentlichungen des Instituts für Energierecht an der Universität zu Köln vol 138, Nomos 2008) 36; Kim Talus, *EU Energy Law and Policy: A Critical Account* (Oxford University Press 2013) 87; Kim Talus and Michaël Hunt, 'Ownership Unbundling: What End to the Saga?' in Dirk Buschle, Simon Hirsbrunner and Christine Kaddous (eds), *European Energy Law: Droit européen de l'énergie* (Dossier de droit européen vol 22. Helbing Lichtenhahn 2011) 38; Sabrina Praduroux and Kim Talus, 'The Third Legislative Package

In *James v. UK* the applicants had been deprived of their ownership of a number of properties by virtue of a piece of legislation (the Leasehold Reform Act 1967, as amended) that gave tenants living in houses on the basis of long-term leases the right, under certain circumstances, to purchase, under force of compulsion, the freehold interest in the property.[135] As it is important to understand the rationale and functioning of the law, it merits quoting at some length a government paper outlining the central problem addressed by the case:

> In the case of [residential] long leases, experience has shown that the system has worked very unfairly against the occupying leaseholder. The freeholder has provided the land; but in the great majority of cases it is the leaseholder or his predecessor in title who at their own expense have built the house on the land. Whether this is so or not in all cases, it is almost universally true that over the years it is the lessee and his predecessors who have borne the cost of improvements and maintenance, and these will probably have cost far more than the original building itself. ... It is in such cases quite indefensible, if justice is to be done as between freeholder and occupying leaseholder, that at the end of the term, the law should allow the ownership of the house to revert to the freeholder without his paying anything for it so that he gets not only the land but also the house, the improvements and everything the leaseholder and his predecessors have added to it. ... The Bill will be based on the principle that the land belongs in equity to the landowner and the house belongs in equity to the occupying leaseholder.[136]

The applicants argued before the ECtHR that the Leasehold Reform Act 1967, as amended, 'compelled [them] to sell the properties, against their will, to private individuals for the benefit of those individuals.'[137] Without much ado, the Court concluded 'that the applicants were "deprived of [their] possessions", within the meaning of the second sentence of Article 1 (P1-1), by virtue of the contested legislation' and added that '[t]his point was not disputed before the Court.'[138] The subsequent analysis of the Court focused on the question of whether the violation could be justified, which it ultimately answered in the positive.

As already indicated, many authors have explicitly or implicitly asserted that the measures at issue in *James and Others v. United Kingdom* and ownership unbundling measures are comparable.[139] However, it should be noted that there are significant factual differences between the two cases. In the *James* case, the legislation provided that the purchase price of the freehold was to be determined in accordance with one or the other of two bases of valuation (the '1967 basis of valuation' and the '1974 basis of valuation'). In other words, the price of the property was not the outcome of a bargaining process between a buyer and a seller on the open market, as in the case of ownership unbundling measures, but rather the

---

and Ownership Unbundling in Light of the European Fundamental Rights Discourse' (2008) 9 Competition and Regulation in Network Industries 3, 20–21.

[135] *James and Others v. The United Kingdom* (n 133) [10–11].

[136] Ibid [18].

[137] Ibid [34].

[138] Ibid [38].

[139] See sources cited in footnote 134 (this chapter).

result of government interference. Furthermore, the 1967 basis of valuation reflected the equity considerations outlined above. According to this approach, the amount of money to be paid by the tenant approximately equaled the site value, but excluded the value of the buildings on the site.[140] In the view of the ECtHR, this 'clearly and deliberately favour[ed] the tenant.'[141] Therefore, the transactions did not even come close to a compulsory sale at market value. Considering the foregoing, it is apparent that the *James v. UK* case has only limited relevance for the determination of whether the OU requirements in the EU energy sector entail the expropriation of foreign investors.

The preceding review of theoretically applicable case-law leads to some general conclusions. There is a whole universe of governmental measures that can give rise to 'compulsory', 'involuntary' or 'forced' sales. In some cases that fall within this overly broad category, the sales occurred in a climate of racial discrimination (World War II cases). In other cases, the divestments took place in accordance with the rule of law, but went far beyond a mere legal obligation to sell, because the governmental regulations even determined the buyer and the sales price, thus excluding a bargaining process on the open market (*James v. UK* case). In yet other cases, such as with the indigenization measures or the South African divestiture obligations for the benefit of HDSAs, the relevant State conduct was aimed at remedying past economic, social and political inequities and not 'simply' to foster competition.

This 'diversity' in terms of the presence of special circumstances, and the specific nature of the respective governmental measures, has also colored the legal assessment of whether there was an expropriation. All of this makes it very difficult to formulate generally applicable principles.[142] What is clear is that there is no clear precedent in international law that would make it possible to draw any firm conclusions as to the expropriatory nature of the ownership unbundling measures in the EU energy sector. Nevertheless, a few points will be made here. First of all, the argument has been raised more than once that the fact that the foreign investor can remain in control of his investment would militate against finding an expropriation.[143] Second, and with respect to the revenue generated through the sale of the investment assets, there is some authority for the proposition that 'compulsory', 'involuntary' or 'forced' sales at a price substantially below the market value would constitute an expropriation.[144] Third, and on a related point, it has been highlighted that even if an expropriation occurred, the price obtained through the sale of the investment could be considered as an offset toward the fulfilment of an international law requirement

[140] *James and Others v. The United Kingdom* (n 133) [23, 56].

[141] Ibid [56].

[142] See also Higgins (n 129) 326 (noting that the 'case law in this area turns very much on the particular facts and it is not easy to extrapolate general principles').

[143] Sornarajah (n 95) 382; *Piero Foresti, Laura de Carli & Others v. The Republic of South Africa* (n 108) [77].

[144] See footnotes 129–131 (this chapter) and accompanying text.

of payment of compensation.[145] Fourthly and finally, it can be concluded, in particular based on the *James v. UK* case, that the more the governmental measure at issue prescribes the manner in which the compulsory sale has to be carried out (e.g. time frame, determination of buyer, determination of the sales price) and thus limits the room for maneuver of the affected investors, the more likely it is that the measure amounts to an expropriation under international law.

5.6.3 Ownership Unbundling Measures as a Compulsory Sale of Investments

Next it is necessary to analyze whether ownership unbundling measures do in fact amount to an indirect expropriation. An assessment of the severity of the impact of OU requirements on foreign investors' property rights is the logical starting point of this analysis. Arbitral tribunals use different terminology to describe the threshold of interference required to establish an indirect expropriation.[146] In *Generation Ukraine v. Ukraine*, the applicable standard was said to be a 'persistent or irreparable obstacle to the Claimant's use, enjoyment or disposal of its investment.'[147] In *Tecmed v. Mexico*, the tribunal held that there is an indirect *de facto* expropriation if the governmental measure results in the disappearance of 'any form of exploitation' of the property rights and thus destroys or neutralizes 'the economic value of the use, enjoyment or disposition of the assets or rights affected.'[148] Finally, in *Metalclad v. Mexico*, the notion of indirect expropriation was defined so as to include 'covert or incidental interference with the use of property which has the effect of depriving the owner, in whole or in significant part, of the use or reasonably-to-be-expected economic benefit of property.'[149] Thus it can be seen that although different tribunals use different wording, they all consistently require a significant interference with property rights.[150] A concise criterion, which is consistently used in many awards, is the 'substantial deprivation' of the investment.[151]

---

[145]Beveridge (n 96) 324–326.

[146]For an overview, see L. Y Fortier and Stephen L Drymer, 'Indirect Expropriation in the Law of International Investment: I Know It When I See It, or Caveat Investor' (2004) 19 ICSID Review – Foreign Investment Law Journal 293, 305.

[147]*Generation Ukraine, Inc. v. Ukraine,* Award (16 September 2003) ICSID Case No. ARB/00/9 [20.32].

[148]*Técnicas Medioambientales Tecmed, S.A. v. The United Mexican States* (n 132) [116].

[149]*Metalclad Corporation v. The United Mexican States,* Award (30 August 2000) ICSID Case No. ARB(AF)/97/1 [103].

[150]Ursula Kriebaum, 'Expropriation' in Marc Bungenberg and others (eds), *International Investment Law* (C.H. Beck; Hart; Nomos 2015) [87].

[151]*Pope & Talbot Inc. v. The Government of Canada,* Interim Award (26 June 2000) [102]; *Occidental Exploration and Production Company v. The Republic of Ecuador* (n 68) [89]; *CMS Gas Transmission Company v. The Republic of Argentina* (n 12) [263]; *Merrill & Ring Forestry*

Ownership unbundling measures legally compel the foreign investor to divest its shareholding in the transmission system operator (or, alternatively, in the production/generation or supply undertaking). This 'compulsory', 'involuntary' or 'forced' sale affects the use, enjoyment, and disposal of the investment. From one perspective, it could be argued that the rights of disposal are to some extent retained, at least initially, since the investor is able to decide on the selling arrangements, including the business partner,[152] the exact date of the sale, and the selling price.[153] It could be further reasoned that the foreign investor could also seek to renounce all rights to take part in the decision-making process in the TSO so that it holds only entirely passive financial rights.[154] However, the *right* to dispose of one's property is subject to limitation if the owner *must* dispose of the property.[155] Furthermore, OU measures do not give much leeway to the affected investor. First of all, he is not free to decide 'whether' to divest the assets.[156] Second, he cannot monitor the market for such a time that he considers reasonable and only sell if the price is adequate in his view.[157] Instead, he has to sell within the time frame mandated by the law, which for example was two-and-a-half years in the case of Estonia.[158] Thirdly, and most importantly, subsequent to the compulsory sale of the assets the owner is deprived of all rights and possibilities of disposal over them.[159] In the same vein, he is also completely prevented from using and exploiting the property, in particular from reaping the benefits from it. The permanence or irreversibility of OU is a factor that intensifies its detrimental impact on property rights.[160]

L.P. v. The Government of Canada, Award (31 March 2010) [145, 152]; *Deutsche Bank AG v. Democratic Socialist Republic of Sri Lanka,* Award (31 October 2012) ICSID Case No. ARB/09/2 [503]; Dolzer and Schreuer (n 50) 104.

[152]See Winfried Rasbach, *Unbundling-Regulierung in der Energiewirtschaft: Gemeinschaftsrechtliche Vorgaben und deren Umsetzung in die deutsche Energierechtsordnung* (C.H. Beck 2009) 348.

[153]See Ralf Müller-Terpitz and Michaela Weigl, 'Ownership Unbundling – ein gemeinschaftsrechtlicher Irrweg?' [2009] Europarecht 348, 363.

[154]This option was temporarily chosen by Gazprom in the case of the gas interconnector between the United Kingdom and Belgium, see Sect. 2.3.1.5.

[155]See Stefan Storr, 'Die Vorschläge der EU-Kommission zur Verschärfung der Unbundling-Vorschriften im Energiesektor' [2007] Europäische Zeitschrift für Wirtschaftsrecht 232, 236.

[156]See Rasbach (n 152) 348.

[157]See Baur and others (n 134) 36.

[158]See Sect. 2.3.1.5.

[159]Rasbach (n 152) 348.

[160]Despite the fact that a 'temporary' measure may suffice under certain circumstances (see *Consortium RFCC v. Royaume du Maroc* (n 53) [68]) and that arbitral tribunals have generally taken a flexible approach regarding the required duration (see Anne K Hoffmann, 'Indirect Expropriation' in August Reinisch (ed), *Standards of Investment Protection* (Oxford University Press 2008) 159–160), it can be clearly deduced from the case-law that a lasting deprivation would more readily be considered to amount to an expropriation, see *S.D. Myers, Inc. v. Government of Canada,* Partial Award (13 November 2000) [283]; *Generation Ukraine, Inc. v. Ukraine* (n 147)

The argument, advanced by the South African government in the *Piero Foresti* case[161]—as well as in the academic literature[162]—that a divestment obligation does not amount to an expropriation if the investor retains control over the investment is not applicable in the case of OU requirements. Here there is a 100% divestment obligation, which results in a total loss of control. Furthermore, it cannot be argued that ownership unbundling measures are not expropriatory because the direct beneficiary is a private person and not the State. Already in the *Tippets* case of 1984, the Iran-US Claims Tribunal emphasized that for an expropriation to occur, it is not required that the government 'has acquired something of value'.[163] Indeed, it is the prevailing view in arbitral jurisprudence that a transfer of rights or an economic benefit to the host State is not a prerequisite for finding an expropriation.[164] It is also unconvincing to assert that the sales agreements reached in order to comply with the OU obligations were 'voluntary', i.e. that no physical force or compulsion was used, and that this precludes any finding that an expropriation occurred. While this legal position was taken in the academic literature in the context of the African indigenization measures,[165] it is clearly based on an overly broad understanding of 'consent', which runs the risk of rendering the underlying property rights 'unreal'.[166] Finally, it cannot be argued that OU measures affect only part of the vertically integrated undertaking (the transmission branch or, alternatively, the production/generation or supply branch) and that these measures should thus not be seen as being capable of leading to a substantial deprivation of the investment in the VIU.[167] It is true that some arbitral tribunals reject the notion of 'partial expropriation' and therefore refuse to view particular elements of a larger investment operation in isolation, even though

---

[20.32]; *Técnicas Medioambientales Tecmed, S.A. v. The United Mexican States* (n 132) [116]; *BG Group Plc. v. The Republic of Argentina,* Final Award (24 December 2007) [268].

[161] *Piero Foresti, Laura de Carli & Others v. The Republic of South Africa* (n 108) [77].

[162] Sornarajah (n 95) 382.

[163] *Tippetts, Abbett, McCarthy, Stratton v. TAMS-AFFA Consulting Engineers of Iran,* Award (22 June 1984) Case No. 7 6 Iran-US C.T.R. 219 225.

[164] Kriebaum (n 150) [201]. See also *Amco Asia Corporation and others v. Republic of Indonesia,* Award (20 November 1984) ICSID Case No. ARB/81/1 1 ICSID Rep. 413 (1993) [158].

[165] Beveridge (n 96) 321–324.

[166] For an analysis of the notion of 'consent' in relation to expropriation claims, see Jones and Dunn (n 128) 396–401.

[167] See Boute (n 16) [3.45] (who mentions that 'tribunals are reluctant to consider specific assets in isolation from the overall investment transaction' and then writes: 'To be successful under the expropriation standard, companies affected by ownership unbundling will therefore have to prove that this forced restructuring destroyed their entire investment. This could be challenging to demonstrate. Only some arbitral tribunals have accepted that, when the main investment remains unaffected, a specific right associated with this investment could be individually protected under the expropriation standard. In line with this "partial expropriation" doctrine, companies affected by ownership unbundling could argue that the asset that they are forced to sell – or the vertical integration of their energy supply business – was a "key element" of their investments without which they would not have entered the market.'; footnotes omitted).

these individual elements would benefit from protection under the applicable IIA.[168] However, it seems to be undisputed that a partial expropriation will be accepted if the specific assets concerned have a 'stand-alone' character, in the sense that they are capable of an 'independent economic exploitation'.[169] This fully applies to the vertically integrated transmission system operator and the vertically integrated production/generation or supply assets, respectively. It should also be noted that any other interpretation of the investment protection standard of 'no expropriation without compensation' would lead to the patently unreasonable result that, in the case of a general disinvestment obligation in a specific sector, a foreign investor in a vertically integrated undertaking would receive less protection than a foreign investor who has invested directly in one of the affected companies.[170]

In conclusion, it is submitted that the ownership unbundling requirements as set out in Directives 2009/72/EC and 2009/73/EC involve a substantial deprivation of property rights. This is not to say, however, that there is *ipso facto* an expropriation. It is precisely at this point that the variations in the arbitral case-law become relevant. There are three main approaches in investment jurisprudence with respect to the concept of indirect or *de facto* expropriation.[171] The first approach focuses only on the effect of the governmental measure on the investment (the 'sole effects' doctrine). The second approach posits that non-discriminatory regulations for a public purpose do not constitute an expropriation (the 'police powers' doctrine). The third approach seeks to find a middle ground between the first two positions by taking into consideration both the purpose and effect of the host State measures.

Whether OU measures amount to an expropriation therefore depends to a large extent on which approach an arbitral tribunal will employ in a particular case.[172] Nevertheless, despite the fact that a measure of uncertainty remains, there is much to suggest that preference will be given to the third strand of the jurisprudence. In order

---

[168] Case-law cited by ibid [3.27] includes *Enron Corporation and Ponderosa Assets, L.P. v. Argentine Republic,* Decision on Jurisdiction (14 January 2004) ICSID Case No. ARB/01/3 [70]; *Ceskoslovenska Obchodni Banka, A.S. v. The Slovak Republic,* Decision of the Tribunal on Objections to Jurisdiction (24 May 1999) ICSID Case No. ARB/97/4 [72]; *Electrabel S.A. v. Republic of Hungary* (n 10) [5.52–3, 5.58, 6.53, 6.57–8]. See also cases cited in Kriebaum (n 150) [121].

[169] Ursula Kriebaum, 'Partial Expropriation' (2007) 8 Journal of World Investment & Trade 69, 83–84.

[170] For a similar argument, see ibid 83.

[171] Burkhard Schöbener, Jochen Herbst and Markus Perkams, *Internationales Wirtschaftsrecht* (C.F. Müller 2010) [279–289]; Thilo Rensmann, 'Völkerrechtlicher Enteignungsschutz' in Dirk Ehlers, Hans-Michael Wolffgang and Ulrich J Schröder (eds), *Rechtsfragen internationaler Investitionen: Tagungsband zum 13. Münsteraner Außenwirtschaftsrechtstag 2008* (Verlag Recht und Wirtschaft 2009) 45–46; Perkams (n 88) 110; Caroline Henckels, 'Indirect Expropriation and the Right to Regulate: Revisiting Proportionality Analysis and the Standard of Review in Investor-State Arbitration' (2012) 15 Journal of International Economic Law 223, 225.

[172] The resulting uncertainty for both the investor and the host State has rightly been criticized in academic literature, see Perkams (n 88) 110.

to understand why this is so, below it will be explained how OU measures would be assessed under each of the three approaches to indirect expropriation.

Under the 'sole-effects' doctrine, the detrimental impact of the governmental measure on the investment is the only and exclusive factor in the determination of whether an indirect expropriation occurred.[173] Accordingly, given that it has been established above that OU brings about a substantial deprivation of property rights, there clearly would be an expropriation. However, the main disadvantage of the sole effects doctrine is that it does not permit taking into consideration the public interests underlying the host State measure.[174] The fact that OU requirements are generally applicable regulatory measures that pursue an important public policy objective, namely ensuring non-discriminatory network access, would not play any part in the expropriation analysis under the sole effects doctrine. It is therefore submitted that the sole effects doctrine should not be applied to adjudicate an expropriation claim with respect to OU measures.[175] This is in line with the recent 'strong tendency' among arbitral tribunals not to focus exclusively on the interference with property rights, but to also take into account the regulatory purpose, at least to some extent.[176]

In stark contrast to the 'sole effects' approach, the 'police powers' doctrine views a measure's public purpose as the 'decisive criterion'.[177] In accordance with this doctrine, arbitral tribunals have held that States are not liable to pay compensation for certain non-discriminatory regulations, enacted in accordance with due process, which serve a legitimate public purpose.[178] In other words, they denied the existence of an expropriation in these circumstances, irrespective of the gravity of the interference on property rights. One of the most prominent cases in this regard is *Methanex v. US*.[179] In that case, which revolved around the challenge by a Canadian producer of methanol to California's ban on methyl tertiary-butyl ether (MTBE), in which methanol is a primary ingredient, the tribunal sweepingly declared that:

> [A]s a matter of general international law, a non-discriminatory regulation for a public purpose, which is enacted in accordance with due process and, which affects, inter alios, a

---

[173]See e.g. *Metalclad Corporation v. The United Mexican States* (n 149) [103–111]; *Compañiá de Aguas del Aconquija S.A. and Vivendi Universal S.A. v. Argentine Republic,* Award (20 August 2007) Award [7.5.21]; Rudolf Dolzer, 'Indirect Expropriation: New Developments?' (2002) 11 - New York University Environmental Law Journal 64, 79ff; Fortier and Drymer (n 146) 308–309.

[174]Ursula Kriebaum, 'Regulatory Takings: Balancing the Interests of the Investor and the State' (2007) 8 Journal of World Investment & Trade 717, 725.

[175]See also Hoffmann (n 160) 168 (who writes that the sole effects doctrine 'results in a rather one-sided focus upon the interests of and the harm done to the investor').

[176]Matthias Herdegen, *Principles of International Economic Law* (Oxford University Press 2013) 408.

[177]Kriebaum (n 174) 726.

[178]Schöbener, Herbst and Perkams (n 171) [285, 287]; Rensmann (n 171) 45–46; Fortier and Drymer (n 146) 298.

[179]*Methanex Corporation v. United States of America* (n 55).

foreign investor or investment is not deemed expropriatory and compensable unless specific commitments had been given ....[180]

Similar pronouncements were later made in *Saluka v. Czech Republic*[181] (relating to the decision of the Czech banking regulator to impose forced administration on a bank whose payment ability was rapidly and significantly deteriorating) and in *Chemtura v. Canada*[182] (relating to the cancellation of a registration, on health and environmental grounds, to produce and sell the pesticide 'lindane'). The police power doctrine, as developed by these arbitral tribunals, has been criticized in the academic literature on the grounds that it would render the concept of indirect expropriation largely meaningless. In fact, given the extreme reluctance of investment tribunals to find that a domestic measure has not been enacted in the public interest, regulatory measures would almost never entail a duty to compensate.[183]

Applied to the present context, the application of the police powers doctrine would mean that the ownership unbundling measures in the EU energy sector do not qualify as an indirect expropriation.[184] There are, however, three main reasons why the police powers doctrine cannot serve as an 'easily available escape'.[185] First, it seems that the scope of the police powers doctrine is not unlimited.[186] This can already be deduced from the *Saluka v. Czech Republic* award, which is considered as one of the principal exponents of the police powers doctrine. Drawing upon the formulation of the United States Third Restatement of the Law of Foreign Relations, the *Saluka* tribunal stated that a State is not liable to pay compensation when it adopts 'general regulations that are "*commonly accepted* as within the police power of States"'.[187] It added that what could be considered 'permissible' and 'commonly accepted' as falling within the State's police power has not yet been clarified under international law, and later explicitly stated that there are 'exceptions to the permissibility of regulatory action.'[188] Therefore, while property forfeiture for crime, seizure of illegal goods (such as drugs, weapons or pornography), seizure for

180Ibid, Part IV, Chapter D, [7].

181*Saluka Investments B.V. v. The Czech Republic,* Partial Award (17 March 2006) [254–265; 275–276].

182*Chemtura Corporation v. Government of Canada,* Award (2 August 2010) [266].

183Kriebaum (n 174) 725–727.

184In the *Piero Foresti* case, the South African government also attempted to invoke the police powers exception in order to argue that the 26% divestment requirement in the mining sector does not constitute an indirect expropriation. It claimed that a 'generally applicable and non-discriminatory regulation cannot be expropriatory absent a specific, prior promise that the regulation would not be adopted'; see *Piero Foresti, Laura de Carli & Others v. The Republic of South Africa* (n 108) [75].

185August Reinisch, 'Expropriation' in Peter Muchlinski, Federico Ortino and Christoph Schreuer (eds), *The Oxford Handbook of International Investment Law* (Oxford University Press 2008) 437.

186See Newcombe and Paradell (n 49) 360 (stating that 'the extent to which regulatory powers may be used to deprive investors of their investments is unclear').

187*Saluka Investments B.V. v. The Czech Republic* (n 181) [260, 262] (emphasis added).

188Ibid [263, 275].

non-payment of taxes, duties or fines, certain measures to protect human health or the environment, and general taxation could be regarded as examples where the deprivation of an investment does not trigger a duty to compensate,[189] it is unclear whether competition-related measures in the energy sector would be considered as within the boundaries of permissible regulatory action and thus 'eligible' to benefit from the police powers exception. It seems important to note in this context that while general competition laws that seek to ensure fair market practices are becoming ever more prevalent and reflecting a 'consistent and general comparative practice in a variety of states',[190] ownership unbundling measures have so far only been adopted by a relatively small number of States[191] and thus cannot be considered as universally accepted. Therefore, even though property deprivations flowing from the application of general competition laws could be said to fall within the ambit of the police powers doctrine, the opposite seems to apply to OU measures. Second, and more importantly, the police powers doctrine should be rejected from a doctrinal point of view. Under the police powers approach, the criteria of public purpose, due process, and non-discrimination are used to determine whether an expropriation has taken place *at all*. Traditionally, however, and under most current IIAs, these criteria are used to examine whether an expropriation could be considered as *lawful*.[192] The police powers doctrine is unable to resolve this doctrinal contradiction.[193]

Third, a considerable number of arbitral awards, rendered both before[194] and after[195] the *Methanex* decision, have emphatically rejected the proposition that regulatory measures, taken in the public interest, cannot amount to an expropriation. The *Pope & Talbot* tribunal, for example, reasoned that a 'blanket exception for regulatory measures would create a gaping loophole in international protections against expropriation.'[196] In the same vein, the *Vivendi II* tribunal warned that '[i]f public purpose automatically immunises the measure from being found to be expropriatory, then there would never be a compensable taking for a public purpose.'[197] In conclusion, the correct view should be that measures taken in the public

[189] Newcombe and Paradell (n 49) 358.

[190] Ibid 360–361.

[191] See Sect. 1.4.

[192] Kriebaum (n 174) 726.

[193] Rensmann (n 171) 46; Hoffmann (n 160) 166.

[194] See, for example, *Compañiá del Desarrollo de Santa Elena, S.A. v. The Republic of Costa Rica*, Final Award (17 February 2000) ICSID Case No. ARB/96/1 [72]; *Técnicas Medioambientales Tecmed, S.A. v. The United Mexican States* (n 132) [121–122]; *Pope & Talbot Inc. v. The Government of Canada* (n 151) [99].

[195] See, for example, *Compañiá de Aguas del Aconquija S.A. and Vivendi Universal S.A. v. Argentine Republic* (n 173) [7.5.21]; *El Paso Energy International Company v. The Argentine Republic*, Award (31 October 2011) ICSID Case No. ARB/03/15 [234]; *Azurix Corp. v. The Argentine Republic* (n 132) [310].

[196] *Pope & Talbot Inc. v. The Government of Canada* (n 151) [99].

[197] *Compañiá de Aguas del Aconquija S.A. and Vivendi Universal S.A. v. Argentine Republic* (n 173) [7.5.21].

interest are not *a priori* excluded from being regarded as a compensable taking of property. There is thus no blanket exception for ownership unbundling measures.

At the same time, the central concern of the police powers approach, namely to give greater weight to the public purpose of a measure in the consideration of an expropriation claim, has nonetheless found its way into a growing number of arbitral awards. This 'third approach' to the concept of indirect expropriation takes into account *both* the measure's effect on a foreign investment and its purpose, and thus reconciles to a certain extent the 'sole effects' and 'police powers' doctrines.[198]

In order to achieve a balance between the level of interference with investors' property rights on the one hand, and a measure's public purpose on the other, some form of proportionality test is gaining traction, both in international investment arbitration[199] and among legal commentators.[200] In the *Tecmed v. Mexico* case, for example, the tribunal explained that:

> [T]he Arbitral Tribunal will consider, in order to determine if [regulatory actions and measures] are to be characterized as expropriatory, whether such actions or measures are proportional to the public interest presumably protected thereby and to the protection legally granted to investments, taking into account that the significance of such impact has a key role upon deciding the proportionality.[201]

Therefore, it seems that the question of whether ownership unbundling measures constitute an expropriation under international law could, and should, ultimately hinge on the application of a proportionality test. The issue of proportionality has also played a pivotal role in the academic discussion on the compatibility of ownership unbundling measures with the right to property under EU law, as well as in the *Essent* case. The arbitral case-law indicates that the proportionality analysis must employ a standard of review that is sufficiently deferential toward national regulatory autonomy. In this regard the *Tecmed* award referred to a '*reasonable* relationship of proportionality'[202] and the *LG&E v. Argentina* tribunal held that the measure must not be '*obviously* disproportionate'[203] to the objective being pursued.

---

[198]See Herdegen (n 176) 408 (identifying a 'strong tendency to focus on the balance between the interference with the investment and the public interest in terms of proportionality'); Henckels (n 171) 225 (stating that 'more recent case law indicates that both purpose and effect of host state measures will be taken into account when determining whether an indirect expropriation has occurred').

[199]See, for example, *LG&E Energy Corp. LG&E Capital Corp. and LG&E International, Inc. v. Argentine Republic* (n 70) [195]; *Azurix Corp. v. The Argentine Republic* (n 132) [311–312]; *El Paso Energy International Company v. The Argentine Republic* (n 195) [241, 243]; *Deutsche Bank AG v. Democratic Socialist Republic of Sri Lanka* (n 151) [522].

[200]See Henckels (n 171) 228 (with further references).

[201]*Técnicas Medioambientales Tecmed, S.A. v. The United Mexican States* (n 132) [122]. In a footnote, the tribunal referred to European Court of Human Rights, *Matos e Silva, Lda. and Others v. Portugal,* Judgment (16 September 1996) Application No. 15777/89.

[202]*Técnicas Medioambientales Tecmed, S.A. v. The United Mexican States* (n 132) [122] (emphasis added).

[203]*LG&E Energy Corp. LG&E Capital Corp. and LG&E International, Inc. v. Argentine Republic* (n 70) [195] (emphasis added).

While a detailed proportionality analysis is provided below in the context of the fair and equitable treatment standard,[204] the main findings can be summarized as follows. Ownership unbundling measures clearly contribute to enhancing non-discriminatory network access and thereby to the smooth functioning of the EU's internal energy market. Behavioral policies, i.e. network access regulation, have inherent limitations and thus cannot completely eliminate the ability of integrated TSOs to deny or hinder network access. Behavioral measures do not, therefore, represent a less-restrictive alternative option. Furthermore, in addition to being more effective than functional or legal unbundling, OU is the only regulatory solution that completely and structurally removes the inherent incentive of integrated transmission system operators to discriminate against non-affiliated competitors. Other unbundling models, such as ITO, retain the possibility of vertical integration and are not therefore equally effective in ensuring non-discriminatory network access. This assessment is not changed by the fact that the Preambles to Directives 2009/72/EC and 2009/73/EC[205] and European Commission documents[206] contain the legal presumption that all unbundling models contained in the TEP (OU, ISO and ITO) are equally effective in terms of separating the network activities from other activities not related to transmission. The EU Member States that have adopted ownership unbundling through national implementing measures are not bound to this assumption of equal effectiveness, and have generally provided reasons for their decision to mandate the OU instead of the ISO or ITO models. Apart from necessity, OU is also proportionate *stricto sensu*, provided that the seller of the transmission assets receives an adequate price. In conclusion, and also taking into consideration that the applicable standard of review should not be too 'interventionist', OU requirements are proportionate, which means that they do not constitute an expropriation.

---

[204]See Sect. 5.7.3.2.

[205]9th, 11th-12th, 16th and 19th recital of the preamble to Directive 2009/72/EC (n 90); 6th, 8th-9th, 13th and 16th recital of the preamble to Directive 2009/73/EC (n 90). See also Cabau (n 38) [4.24]; Dirk Buschle, 'Unbundling of State-owned Transmission System Operators – Effective Remedy or Eyewash?' [2013] European Networks Law and Regulation Quarterly 49, 54, 62.

[206]European Commission, 'Commission Staff Working Paper – Interpretative Note on Directive 2009/72/EC concerning common Rules for the Internal Market in Electricity and Directive 2009/73/EC concerning common Rules for the Internal Market in Natural Gas – The Unbundling Regime' (22 January 2010) 4 <https://ec.europa.eu/energy/sites/ener/files/documents/2010_01_21_the_unbundling_regime.pdf> accessed 24 September 2016; European Commission, Commission Decision pursuant to Article 3(1) of Regulation (EC) No 714/2009 and Article 10(6) of Directive 2009/72/EC Ireland Eirgrid/ESB (12 April 2013) C(2013) 2169 final, [17]; European Commission, Commission Decision on the application of Article 9(9) of Directive 2009/72/EC to Transmission System Operation in Scotland (14 May 2012) C(2012) 3284 final, [8]; European Commission, Commission Decision pursuant to Article 3(1) of Regulation (EC) No 714/2009 and Article 10(6) of Directive 2009/72/EC – United Kingdom (Northern Ireland) – SONI/NIE (12 April 2013) C(2013) 2170 final, [11].

5.6.4 Legality of Expropriations

In the previous section it was concluded that ownership unbundling measures do not constitute an indirect expropriation under most IIAs, provided that (1) the arbitral tribunal does not follow the 'sole effects' doctrine and (2) the foreign investor is unable to invoke more favorable provisions on expropriation that specifically provide that compulsory sales are expropriatory in nature.

However, even if *arguendo* OU amounts to an indirect expropriation, such a finding would not conclusively answer the question of whether the EU or EU Member States incur responsibility under their respective instruments. IIAs generally recognize the host State's prerogative to expropriate foreign-owned assets if certain requirements are fulfilled. In such cases the expropriation will be deemed lawful and no damages for an internationally wrongful act can be claimed.[207] IIAs commonly stipulate four requirements for the legality of an expropriation. The expropriation must be:

- for a public purpose;
- carried out under due process of law;
- non-discriminatory; and
- accompanied by the payment of prompt, adequate and effective compensation.[208]

In the academic literature it has been stated that an indirect expropriation would 'almost by definition' fall within the category of *unlawful* expropriations.[209] The reason given for this position is that the host State generally does not recognize that the measure at issue amounts to an expropriation and consequently fails to provide for the payment of compensation.[210] At first glance the same would seem to apply to ownership unbundling measures (again on the assumption that there is an expropriation), given that the EU does not acknowledge their expropriatory nature.[211]

[207]Although the decision-making practice of arbitral tribunals is somewhat inconsistent, it seems that the award of compensation for unlawful expropriations is governed not by the provisions on expropriation contained in IIAs but by customary international law on State responsibility for internationally wrongful acts, see Sergey Ripinsky, *Damages in International Investment Law* (Kevin Williams tr, British Institute of International and Comparative Law 2008) 65–66; 83ff; Dolzer and Schreuer (n 50) 100. This has important consequences for the amount of compensation. As explained by an arbitral tribunal, the '[damages standard under customary international law] permits, if the facts so require, a higher rate of recovery than that prescribed in Article 5(2) [of the Argentina-France BIT] for *lawful* expropriations' (emphasis in the original), see *Compañiá de Aguas del Aconquija S.A. and Vivendi Universal S.A. v. Argentine Republic* (n 173) [8.2.5]. For a similar statement, see also *Siemens A.G. v. The Argentine Republic* (n 68) [352].

[208]August Reinisch, 'Legality of Expropriations' in August Reinisch (ed), *Standards of Investment Protection* (Oxford University Press 2008) 176–178; United Nations Conference on Trade and Development (n 88) 27.

[209]Ripinsky (n 207) 69. See also Dolzer and Schreuer (n 50) 100.

[210]Ripinsky (n 207) 69.

[211]See European Commission, 'Reply to Questions from Mr Shmatko on the Third Package' (29 June 2010) 10 <http://www.asktheeu.org/de/request/168/response/558/attach/3/Annex%

However, OU measures can arguably constitute a *lawful* indirect expropriation because, in the case of such 'compulsory', 'involuntary' or 'forced' sales, the revenue generated through the sale of the property could, under certain circumstances, be regarded as meeting the compensation requirement. Against this background, the remainder of this sub-section will deal successively with the four criteria for a lawful expropriation, i.e. public purpose, due process, non-discrimination, and compensation.

The first criterion for a lawful expropriation is that the respective measure must serve a public purpose. In arbitral practice, the existence of a public purpose was generally not disputed.[212] As the Iran-US Claims Tribunal pointed out in the case *Amoco International Finance Corporation v. Iran*, States enjoy 'extensive discretion' as to whether an expropriation was motivated by the pursuit of public policy objectives.[213] Only in a relatively small number of cases have tribunals found an expropriation to be unlawful based on the absence of a valid public purpose. One rare example is the expropriation of a foreign oil company as an act of retaliation for British foreign policy behavior.[214] Against this background, there is no doubt that the ownership unbundling measures in the EU energy sector fulfil the public purpose requirement as they are designed to enhance competition in the gas and electricity sectors and thus to benefit European energy consumers.[215]

The second criterion for an expropriation to be considered legal is that it meets the requirements of due process. These requirements can be said to encompass at least the following elements: (1) compliance with domestic law[216] and (2) the obligation to ensure that affected investors have an opportunity to have the measure at issue reviewed before an independent body.[217] In the present case, the due process requirements are clearly satisfied. First of all, OU measures have a solid legal basis in EU and national law. Furthermore, as evidenced by the proceedings in the *Essent* case, legal remedies are available to challenge the implementation of OU requirements.

According to the third criterion an expropriation must be non-discriminatory. Investment tribunals have found instances of discrimination between domestic and

20reply%20GHP%20Shmatko%203rd%20package%202.pdf> accessed 24 September 2016 (stating that '[r]equirements for unbundling do not have the same effect as expropriation').

212 Kriebaum (n 150) [219]; Newcombe and Paradell (n 49) 371; Reinisch (n 208) 179.

213 *Amoco International Finance Corporation v. The Government of the Islamic Republic of Iran,* Award (14 July 1987) Case No. 56 15 Iran-US C.T.R. 189 [145].

214 See *British Petroleum Exploration Co. (BP) v. Libyan Arab Republic,* Award (10 October 1973) 53 I.L.R. 297 (1979).

215 See also Boute (n 16) [3.46].

216 Newcombe and Paradell (n 49) 375–376.

217 *ADC Affiliate Limited and ADC & ADMC Management Limited v. The Republic of Hungary,* Award of the Tribunal (2 October 2006) ICSID Case No. ARB/03/16 [435]; *Ioannis Kardassopoulos v. The Republic of Georgia,* Award (3 March 2010) ICSID Case No. ARB/05/18 [394–396]; United Nations Conference on Trade and Development (n 88) 36ff.

foreign investors[218] and between different (groups of) foreign nationals.[219] In general, discrimination is present where distinctions are made exclusively on the basis of, for instance, race, religion, ethnicity or nationality.[220] The (ownership) unbundling requirements in the TEP apply equally to both EU and non-EU undertakings.[221] The fact that compliance with them is ensured through a certification procedure that distinguishes between EU and third-country-controlled companies is not relevant here, given that the expropriation does not result from the provisions setting forth the compliance procedure, but from the provisions laying down the substantive unbundling obligations. The OU measures therefore comply with the non-discrimination requirement.

The fourth requirement for the legality of an expropriation, the payment of compensation, is more complicated. For a long period of time there has been significant controversy as to the correct standard of compensation for expropriations under customary international law.[222] Whereas capital-exporting States have generally advocated the so-called 'Hull formula', which requires prompt, adequate and effective compensation, capital-importing States have espoused other standards, for example that of 'appropriate'[223] compensation. For the purposes of this book, however, it is not necessary to determine the state of customary international law on this issue, as most IIAs prescribe the above-mentioned Hull formula.[224] As already mentioned, the Hull formula mandates 'adequate' compensation, which translates into the fair market value of the investment.[225]

The question that invariably arises is thus whether the price obtained through the compulsory sale of the transmission system assets must be taken into account in this context. It seems unreasonable to contend that because the revenues generated through the sale are not part of an official compensation scheme of the State, they must be deemed irrelevant. The selling price must certainly be factored in when determining whether the expropriated foreign investor received compensation. In

---

[218] *Eureko B.V. v. Republic of Poland,* Partial Award (19 August 2005) [242].

[219] *Liberian Eastern Timber Corporation (LETCO) v. Republic of Liberia,* Award (31 March 1986) ICSID Case No. ARB/83/2.

[220] Newcombe and Paradell (n 49) 373; Kriebaum (n 150) [245].

[221] 24th recital of the preamble to Directive 2009/72/EC (n 90); 21st recital of the preamble to Directive 2009/73/EC (n 90).

[222] See Ripinsky (n 207) 71–77.

[223] United Nations General Assembly, Resolution 1803 – Permanent Sovereignty over Natural Resources (14 December 1962) A/RES/1803(XVII); United Nations General Assembly, Resolution 3281 – Charter of Economic Rights and Duties of States (12 December 1974) A/RES/3281(XXIX).

[224] United Nations Conference on Trade and Development (n 88) 40.

[225] Irmgard Marboe, 'Valuation in Cases of Expropriation' in Marc Bungenberg and others (eds), *International Investment Law* (C.H. Beck; Hart; Nomos 2015) [21]; Ripinsky (n 207) 72, footnote 39.

other words, the compensation requirement would be met if the selling price is equivalent to the fair market value of the investment.[226]

Accordingly, it becomes necessary to examine in some detail the notion of 'fair market value' as applied in international investment arbitration. Tribunals have regularly relied on the following definition of the term[227]:

> The price, expressed in terms of cash equivalents, at which property would change hands between a hypothetical willing and able buyer and a hypothetical willing and able seller, acting at arm's length in an open and unrestricted market, when neither is under compulsion to buy or sell and when both have reasonable knowledge of the relevant facts.

It is immediately noticeable that this definition envisages an ideal market situation, where neither the hypothetical willing and able buyer nor the hypothetical willing and able seller 'is under compulsion to buy or sell'. Therefore, on the abstract level of strict definition, the price realized through the sale of transmission system assets following the adoption of ownership unbundling requirements cannot reflect the 'fair market value' of the respective assets, since the seller is clearly under compulsion to sell.

On a factual level, however, the situation is more complex. On one hand, the market environment in which the divestiture of transmission system assets takes place may indeed be distorted to some extent by the ownership unbundling measures. Taking into account that there is a limited number of potential buyers which could speculate about declining prices due to the fact that there is a predetermined date by which the divestiture must have taken place, it is in principle conceivable that the bargaining process is constrained and that the affected foreign investors may sell at less than fair market value.[228] On the other hand, it is also plausible that profitable

---

[226]See Beveridge (n 96) 325 (with respect to the indigenization measures in Nigeria). See also Boute (n 16) [3.46] (who cautiously states, with respect to OU, that the market price of the infrastructure 'could be considered to fulfil the international law requirement of payment of prompt, adequate, and effective compensation – as required for the lawfulness of expropriation under international law').

[227]Ripinsky (n 207) 184. Tribunals that have relied on this definition include *CMS Gas Transmission Company v. The Republic of Argentina* (n 12) [402]; *Azurix Corp. v. The Argentine Republic* (n 132) [424]; *Sempra Energy International v. The Argentine Republic,* Award (28 September 2007) ICSID Case No. ARB/02/16 [405].

[228]Baur and others (n 134) 68; Jürgen F Baur and Matthias Schmidt-Preuß, 'Europarechtliche Grundlagen des Unbundling' in Jürgen F Baur, Kai U Pritzsche and Stefan Simon (eds), *Unbundling in der Energiewirtschaft: Ein Praxishandbuch* (Carl Heymanns Verlag 2006) [80]; Matthias Schmidt-Preuß, 'Die Zukunft der Netze – Szenarien, Modelle, rechtliche Implikationen' in Ulrich Ehricke (ed), *Die neuen Herausforderungen im Lichte des Energierechts* (Nomos 2009) 93. Similar circumstances were observed in the case of indigenization measures in African countries, see Leslie L Rood, 'Compensation for Takeovers in Africa' (1977) 11 Journal of International Law and Economics 521, 527.

transmission system assets are in great demand and that investors are competing for them.[229] Against this background, it cannot be assumed *in general* that foreign investors are not able to secure the full market value for their transmission system assets.[230] Factual evidence would need to be submitted to the tribunal in order to show that, in the individual case at issue, the selling price was actually below the fair market value.

Furthermore, even assuming that it is established, based on the facts on record, that there is a certain discrepancy between the price actually obtained and the full fair market value of the respective assets, it is questionable whether this would automatically lead to the conclusion that the respective EU Member State or the EU failed to meet the compensation requirement. It has been convincingly argued in the academic literature that the compensation requirement is complied with even if the compensation paid to the investor does not exactly match the required standard. The argument is as follows:

> It would hardly be reasonable to suggest that for an expropriation to be considered lawful, compensation actually paid must meet the required standard *precisely*. There is an inherent uncertainty underlying the matter of compensation: international law does not provide a formula to calculate an exact amount to be paid in a specific case that would reduce the calculation to a simple mathematical exercise. At most, international law can be said to establish basic guidelines for the determination of compensation, and even a good faith application of these guidelines can *objectively* lead to diverging results.[231]

Thus, except for cases in which the price obtained through the compulsory sale of transmission system assets is manifestly below their actual market value, it would be difficult to substantiate a claim that adequate compensation has not been paid. Hence the fourth prerequisite for a lawful expropriation will be fulfilled in the vast majority of cases.

By way of summary, even assuming *arguendo* that OU measures constitute an indirect expropriation, such an expropriation would be lawful under IIAs. Accordingly, there is no internationally wrongful act for which additional compensation might be due.

---

[229] Alan Riley, 'Ownership Unbundling – A Logic Outage for the Anti-Energy Liberalisers?' (2008) 2 <http://www.ceps.eu/system/files/book/1641.pdf> accessed 18 July 2016.

[230] See also the statement by the Lithuanian Prime Minister Algirdas Butkevičius made in connection with the plans of the Lithuanian government to buy Gazprom's shares in the transmission system operator Amber Grid: 'I think that, first of all, the value shall be the market value and next there are talks... I think we should pay as much as the shares are worth', see 'Lithuania Ready to Buy Amber Grid's Shares from E.ON and Gazprom' *Lithuania Tribune* (6 September 2013) <http://www.lithuaniatribune.com/49776/lithuania-ready-to-buy-amber-grids-shares-from-e-on-and-gazprom-201349776/> accessed 3 June 2015.

[231] Ripinsky (n 207) 68 (emphasis in the original).

5.7 The Fair and Equitable Treatment Standard

5.7.1 Introduction

The ownership unbundling measures set out in Directives 2009/72/EC and 2009/73/EC may also be incompatible with the investment protection standard of fair and equitable treatment (FET). The FET principle, which is contained in almost all modern BITs,[232] has become one of the most frequently invoked treatment standards in international investment arbitration. Furthermore, the majority of damages awarded in investment arbitrations are based on a finding of violation of the FET standard.[233] This can be explained by the fact that the concept of fair and equitable treatment has been given a fairly broad interpretation in arbitral jurisprudence. Like the standard of 'no expropriation without compensation', fair and equitable treatment embodies an absolute treatment standard that applies irrespective of the treatment given to other investments or investors.

It is important to note at the outset that although the notion of fair and equitable treatment appears in almost all contemporary IIAs, there are variations regarding the exact formulation of the provision. Two main categories can be identified. IIAs in the first category simply refer to 'fair and equitable treatment', without qualifying these words in any way.[234] These agreements thus contain a self-standing treaty obligation. IIAs in the second category, rather than containing an unqualified reference to FET, speak of 'treatment in accordance with customary international law, including fair and equitable treatment'[235] or 'treatment in accordance with international law, including fair and equitable treatment.'[236] Under these investment agreements, the principle of FET is limited to the customary international law minimum standard of treatment of aliens.

However, as there is some authority for the proposition that the international minimum standard is constantly evolving over time,[237] one can assume that there is a tendency toward convergence between the treaty-based FET principle and the

---

[232]United Nations Conference on Trade and Development, *Fair and Equitable Treatment* (UNCTAD Series on Issues in International Investment Agreements II, 2012) 17.

[233]Dolzer and Schreuer (n 50) 130.

[234]See Article 2(2) of the '2009 German Model Bilateral Investment Treaty' (n 44). Article 2 (2) provides: 'Each Contracting State shall in its territory in every case accord investments by investors of the other Contracting State fair and equitable treatment as well as full protection under this Treaty.'

[235]See Article 5(1) of the '2012 U.S. Model Bilateral Investment Treaty' (n 42).

[236]See Article 1105(1) NAFTA (n 3).

[237]*Pope & Talbot Inc. v. The Government of Canada,* Award in Respect of Damages (31 May 2002) [58–59]; *ADF Group Inc. v. United States of America,* Award (9 January 2003) ICSID Case No. ARB (AF)/00/1 [179]; *Waste Management, Inc. II v. United Mexican States,* Award (30 April 2004) ICSID Case No. ARB(AF)/00/3 [92]; *Gami Investments, Inc. v. The Government of the United Mexican States* (n 61) [95].

customary law standard.[238] For example, the tribunal in *Deutsche Bank v. Sri Lanka* held that 'the actual content of the Treaty standard of fair and equitable treatment is *not materially different* from the content of the minimum standard of treatment in customary international law.'[239] Having said that, in almost all EU Member State BITs 'fair and equitable treatment' is in any event incorporated as a self-standing treaty clause.[240] The same applies to the Energy Charter Treaty.[241]

The FET principle has been interpreted to include a number of substantive and procedural protections. These include protection against denial of justice, due process, protection against arbitrary and discriminatory measures, prohibition of abusive treatment such as coercion and harassment, protection of legitimate expectations, and an obligation of reasonableness and proportionality.[242] For the purposes of the present analysis of OU measures, the last two elements of FET take center stage.

5.7.2 Legitimate Expectations and the Stability of the Legal Framework

The concept of 'legitimate expectations' has become one of the most relevant and indeed most controversial features of FET. The tribunal in *Electrabel v. Hungary* stated that it is 'widely accepted that the *most important function* of the fair and equitable treatment standard is the protection of the investor's reasonable and legitimate expectations.'[243] The tribunal in *Saluka v. Czech Republic* called it the 'dominant element' of the FET standard.[244] The protection of legitimate expectations is not extraneous to general public international law. The principle of *estoppel*

---

[238]Stephan W Schill, 'Fair and Equitable Treatment, the Rule of Law, and Comparative Public Law' in Stephan W Schill (ed), *International Investment Law and Comparative Public Law* (Oxford University Press 2010) 152–154; *CMS Gas Transmission Company v. The Republic of Argentina* (n 12) [284]; *Saluka Investments B.V. v. The Czech Republic* (n 181) [291]; *Occidental Exploration and Production Company v. The Republic of Ecuador* (n 68) [189–190]; United Nations Conference on Trade and Development (n 232) 59–60.

[239]*Deutsche Bank AG v. Democratic Socialist Republic of Sri Lanka* (n 151) [419] (emphasis added).

[240]Ursula Kriebaum, 'FET and Expropriation in the (Invisible) EU Model BIT' (2014) 15 Journal of World Investment & Trade 454, 468–469.

[241]See Article 10(1) Energy Charter Treaty (n 4).

[242]See Dolzer and Schreuer (n 50) 145; Schill (n 238) 159–160; Roland Kläger, *'Fair and Equitable Treatment' in International Investment Law* (Cambridge University Press 2011) 116–119; Newcombe and Paradell (n 49) 279.

[243]*Electrabel S.A. v. Republic of Hungary* (n 10) [7.75] (emphasis added).

[244]*Saluka Investments B.V. v. The Czech Republic* (n 181) [302].

and the concept that unilateral declarations can create binding international obligations embody this idea to some extent at the inter-State level.[245]

It is recognized in arbitral jurisprudence that the legitimate expectations of an investor can be based on: (1) contractual obligations between the foreign investor and the host State; (2) any explicit or implicit representations by the host State; and (3) the legal framework as such.[246] In the case of ownership unbundling requirements, it is first and foremost the general legislative and regulatory framework which might provide the basis for a FET claim. The main question is thus to what extent foreign investors could have had a legitimate expectation that the regulatory framework in the EU energy sector, as it stood before the adoption and implementation of Directives 2009/72/EC and 2009/73/EC, would remain stable, and whether the introduction of ownership unbundling requirements frustrated such legitimate expectations, thereby possibly resulting in a breach of the FET standard.

5.7.2.1 An Obligation Not to Modify the Regulatory Framework?

A significant number of arbitral awards have accepted that the stability and predictability of the host State's legal order forms part and parcel of FET and the protection of legitimate expectations. The tribunal in *CMS v. Argentina* held, for example, that '[t]here can be no doubt ... that a stable legal and business environment is an essential element of fair and equitable treatment.'[247] In *Occidental Exploration and Production Company v. Ecuador*, the tribunal emphasized that 'there is certainly an obligation not to alter the legal and business environment in which the investment has been made.'[248] Similar statements to this effect abound.[249] In fact the provision on fair and equitable treatment in the Energy Charter Treaty even expressly links the FET standard to the obligation of each contracting party to 'encourage and create stable ... conditions' for investors of other contracting parties.[250] In light of the above, one might gain the impression that investors are completely shielded from changes to the legislation as it stands at the time when the investment is made. Indeed, *CMS v. Argentina* and *Occidental v. Ecuador* have been interpreted to the effect that 'any' regulatory change, in and of itself, may frustrate investors'

[245]See Newcombe and Paradell (n 49) 279; Schill (n 238) 164. See also International Court of Justice, *Nuclear Tests (Australia v. France)*, Judgment (20 December 1974) I.C.J. Reports 1974, 253 [46].

[246]Kläger (n 242) 164–165.

[247]*CMS Gas Transmission Company v. The Republic of Argentina* (n 12) [274].

[248]*Occidental Exploration and Production Company v. The Republic of Ecuador* (n 68) [191, 183].

[249]See, for instance, *LG&E Energy Corp. LG&E Capital Corp. and LG&E International, Inc. v. Argentine Republic* (n 70) [124–125, 131]; *Enron Corporation and Ponderosa Assets, L.P. v. Argentine Republic*, Award (22 May 2007) ICSID Case No. ARB/01/3 [260]; *BG Group Plc. v. The Republic of Argentina* (n 160) [307].

[250]Article 10(1) Energy Charter Treaty (n 4).

legitimate expectations of predictability and stability and thereby constitute a violation of the FET standard.[251]

Although it will be shown below that international investment law is much more nuanced in this regard, it must be pointed out at the outset that the FET principle limits not only the discretion of the executive branch. As a matter of principle, a host State's legislative bodies are not exempted from scrutiny under IIAs. As the tribunal in *Paushok v. Mongolia* succinctly put it: 'Actions by legislative assemblies are not beyond the reach of bilateral investment treaties. A State is not immune from claims by foreign investors in connection with legislation passed by its legislative body, unless a specific exemption is included in the relevant treaty.'[252]

In order to determine whether the adoption of ownership unbundling legislation implementing Directives 2009/72/EC and 2009/73/EC violate the FET obligation by undermining foreign investors' legitimate expectations of a predictable and stable legal framework,[253] it is necessary to conduct a more detailed analysis of the relevant arbitral jurisprudence. A good starting point in this regard is the *CMS v. Argentina* case.[254] This case revolved around the adoption of emergency measures by the Argentine government in the period 2000–2002 in response to a severe economic crisis. In particular, the government terminated the US dollar-based calculation of tariffs in the gas and electricity sectors and froze the adjustment of such tariffs in accordance with the United States Producer Price Index (US PPI). In upholding the claimant's fair and equitable treatment claim, the tribunal stated:

> There can be no doubt, therefore, that a stable legal and business environment is an essential element of fair and equitable treatment. ... The *measures that are complained of did in fact entirely transform and alter the legal and business environment under which the investment was decided and made*. ... It has also been established that the guarantees given in this connection under the legal framework and its various components were crucial for the investment decision. ... In addition to the specific terms of the Treaty, the significant number of treaties, both bilateral and multilateral, that have dealt with this standard also

---

[251] See United Nations Conference on Trade and Development (n 232) 64–67. The awards mentioned in the text above do not *expressis verbis* link the stability and predictability of the host State's legal order to the obligation to protect investors' legitimate expectations. For this reason, these awards could be interpreted to establish an 'independent element' of FET, which is 'absolute'; see Newcombe and Paradell (n 49) 287; Caroline Henckels, 'Proportionality and the Standard of Review in Fair and Equitable Treatment Claims: Balancing Stability and Consistency with the Public Interest' (SIEL Working Paper No 2012/27 2012) 4–5 <http://papers.ssrn.com/sol3/papers.cfm?abstract_id=2091474> accessed 12 April 2016. Nevertheless, the factual contexts in which the stability and predictability of the host State's legal order came to play a role and the tribunals' reasoning show that the tribunals essentially analyzed whether the change of the legal framework frustrated any legitimate expectations on the part of the affected investors; see Newcombe and Paradell (n 49) 287–288; United Nations Conference on Trade and Development (n 232) 67.

[252] *Sergei Paushok, CJSC Golden East Company and CJSC Vostokneftegaz Company v. The Government of Mongolia*, Award on Jurisdiction and Liability (28 April 2011) [298].

[253] This possibility is mentioned by Gudkov (n 15) 65; Anufrieva (n 15) 85.

[254] *CMS Gas Transmission Company v. The Republic of Argentina* (n 12).

unequivocally shows that fair and equitable treatment is inseparable from stability and predictability. Many arbitral decisions and scholarly writings point in the same direction.[255]

Several other tribunals which dealt with similar cases in connection with the Argentine crisis also found a violation of FET, on the basis that the government 'completely',[256] 'substantially',[257] 'entirely'[258] or 'fundamentally'[259] altered the legal framework which had formed the basis for claimants' investments. The tribunals consistently highlighted that Argentina had given 'specific commitments'[260] and 'specific guarantees'[261] that the tariffs would be calculated in US dollars and adjusted in accordance with the US PPI. In the tribunals' view, the existence of specific commitments and guarantees could be derived from the fact that the favorable regulatory conditions had been specifically devised by the Argentine government to 'attract',[262] 'induce',[263] 'solicit'[264] or 'seduce'[265] foreign investments and investors. In other words, the tribunals opined that the purposeful construction of an attractive regulatory framework, which contained certain key features designed to address and allay the specific concerns of foreign investors, amounted to a specific commitment on behalf of the State. It is this element of the awards which is particularly controversial, given that it contains the notion that specific commitments can be derived from general legislation. Although there is wide agreement that legitimate expectations may arise on the basis of State conduct in form of, *inter alia*, representations, commitments or specific conditions which are *specifically* directed at the investor and in reliance upon which the investor makes the investment,[266] this can nevertheless be seen as a sweeping extension of the

[255] Ibid [274–276] (emphasis added).

[256] *LG&E Energy Corp. LG&E Capital Corp. and LG&E International, Inc. v. Argentine Republic* (n 70) [139].

[257] *Enron Corporation and Ponderosa Assets, L.P. v. Argentine Republic* (n 249) [264]; *Sempra Energy International v. The Argentine Republic* (n 227) [303].

[258] *BG Group Plc. v. The Republic of Argentina* (n 160) [307].

[259] *National Grid plc v. The Argentine Republic,* Award (3 November 2008) [179].

[260] *CMS Gas Transmission Company v. The Republic of Argentina* (n 12) [277]; *BG Group Plc. v. The Republic of Argentina* (n 160) [310].

[261] *LG&E Energy Corp. LG&E Capital Corp. and LG&E International, Inc. v. Argentine Republic* (n 70) [133]; *Enron Corporation and Ponderosa Assets, L.P. v. Argentine Republic* (n 249) [264].

[262] *LG&E Energy Corp. LG&E Capital Corp. and LG&E International, Inc. v. Argentine Republic* (n 70) [139]; *Enron Corporation and Ponderosa Assets, L.P. v. Argentine Republic* (n 249) [264]; *BG Group Plc. v. The Republic of Argentina* (n 160) [304]; *National Grid plc v. The Argentine Republic* (n 259) [176].

[263] *Enron Corporation and Ponderosa Assets, L.P. v. Argentine Republic* (n 249) [267].

[264] *National Grid plc v. The Argentine Republic* (n 259) [179].

[265] *Enron Corporation and Ponderosa Assets, L.P. v. Argentine Republic* (n 249) [266].

[266] *National Grid plc v. The Argentine Republic* (n 259) [173]; *International Thunderbird Gaming Corporation v. The United Mexican States* (n 68) [147]; *Waste Management, Inc. II v. United Mexican States* (n 237) [98]; *CME Czech Republic B.V. v. The Czech Republic,* Partial Award (13 September 2001) [611]; *Parkerings-Compagniet AS v. Republic of Lithuania* (n 53) [331];

legitimate expectation doctrine. At the same time however, it is important to draw attention to the fact that the tariff regime was not only enshrined in general legislation but also formed an integral part of the licenses granted to the individual companies.[267] Moreover, the licenses explicitly provided that their basic rules could not be changed without the licensee's consent. Given their specificity, the licenses and their provisions were much more likely to give rise to legitimate expectations on the part of the foreign investor. However, as one commentator has rightly pointed out, it is 'difficult to evaluate exactly what role the presence of such licences ... played for the tribunals' finding of [a] breach of the fair and equitable treatment.'[268] Viewed from this perspective, the *CMS v. Argentina* and related awards may not be as far-reaching as one might initially think.

Another important case is *Occidental Exploration and Production Company (OEPC) v. Ecuador.*[269] Beginning in 1985, the US company OEPC provided oil services to Petroecuador, an Ecuadorian State-owned enterprise. Under their contractual arrangements, Petroecuador reimbursed OEPC for the Value-Added Tax (VAT) that OEPC paid on local acquisitions. In 1999, the two companies signed a new contract. Under the new contract, OEPC's VAT payments were no longer reimbursed through Petroecuador, but OEPC had to deal directly with the *Servicio de Rentas Internas* (SRI), Ecuador's tax authority. This constituted an important change, because OEPC would now incur liability for any taxes collected and not refunded. Therefore, before signing the contract, OEPC sought clarification from the SRI on the applicability of VAT on goods necessary to fulfil the contract by means of a '*consulta*'. Presuming that it would be eligible for reimbursement of VAT payments under the tax laws, OEPC did not raise the issue of refundability in the *consulta.*[270] In addition, the *consulta* did not touch upon the question of VAT levied on services. Thus the SRI's answer did not address this point either, despite the fact that a tax law reform was underway (which took effect in 1999) that made services

Enron Corporation and Ponderosa Assets, L.P. v. Argentine Republic (n 249) [262]; *LG&E Energy Corp. LG&E Capital Corp. and LG&E International, Inc. v. Argentine Republic* (n 70) [127].

[267]Newcombe and Paradell (n 49) 281–282 (writing that in *CMS*, *LG&E*, *Enron*, *BG* and *Sempra* 'there were specific representations that were crystallized into the terms of licenses or concession contracts under which the foreign investment operated').

[268]Michele Potestà, 'Legitimate Expectations in Investment Treaty Law: Understanding the Roots and the Limits of a Controversial Concept' (2013) 28 ICSID Review – Foreign Investment Law Journal 88, 112. See also Henckels, 'Proportionality and the Standard of Review in Fair and Equitable Treatment Claims: Balancing Stability and Consistency with the Public Interest' (n 251) 5, footnote 21. For an explicit reference to the importance of the licenses in connection with the legitimacy of the investor's expectations, see *BG Group Plc. v. The Republic of Argentina* (n 160) [306–307] (stating that '[c]onsidering also the incorporation of provisions relating to the stability of the Regulatory Framework in the MetroGAS License, BG could reasonably rely on the Regulatory Framework').

[269]*Occidental Exploration and Production Company v. The Republic of Ecuador* (n 68). For a discussion of that case, see Susan D Franck, 'Occidental Exploration & Production Co. v. Republic of Ecuador' (2005) 99 American Journal of International Law 675.

[270]*Occidental Exploration and Production Company v. The Republic of Ecuador* (n 68) [102].

subject to VAT. Another feature of the 1999 contract was that OEPC was granted a share in Ecuadorian oil production in accordance with a participation formula described as 'Factor X'. As OEPC exported the oil it received under the new contract, it applied to SRI for refunds of VAT payments. These claims were initially granted. Later however, in mid-2001, SRI denied further reimbursements and ordered OEPC to return previous VAT refunds.[271] The SRI believed that the contract's participation formula, i.e. Factor X, already included a reimbursement of VAT paid by OEPC. Furthermore, it took the view that OEPC had no right to VAT refunds under its interpretation of Ecuador's revised tax laws.

On both of these issues the tribunal decided against the respondent. Regarding the latter issue, the tribunal took into consideration judgments by the Ecuadorian Supreme Court and concluded that even after the above-mentioned tax reform, which had introduced some modifications with respect to tax refunds, oil exploration and exploitation companies were entitled to a VAT refund for their exports.[272] However, it emanates from the arbitral award that the revised tax law was quite contradictory in this regard,[273] which may explain the divergent interpretation by the SRI.

Regarding the applicant's FET claim, the tribunal relied on the *Metalclad*[274] and *Tecmed*[275] awards in holding that 'there is certainly an obligation not to alter the legal and business environment in which the investment has been made'.[276] Subsequently, it stated the following:

> The Tribunal must note in this context that the framework under which the investment was made and operates has been changed in an important manner by the actions adopted by the SRI. It was explained above that the Contract has been interpreted by the SRI in a manner that ended up being manifestly wrong as there is no evidence that VAT reimbursement was ever built into Factor X. The clarifications that OEPC sought on the applicability of VAT by means of a 'consulta' made to the SRI received a wholly unsatisfactory and thoroughly vague answer. The tax law was changed without providing any clarity about its meaning and extent and the practice and regulations were also inconsistent with such changes.[277]

Some commentators have given a broad interpretation to this finding. According to Hirsch, for example, '[t]he *Occidental* tribunal ... found that legislative changes undertaken by Ecuador (regarding tax refund) led to a breach of the FET clause.'[278]

[271] Ibid [32, 134–135].

[272] Ibid [143].

[273] Ibid [119ff].

[274] *Metalclad Corporation v. The United Mexican States* (n 149) [99].

[275] *Técnicas Medioambientales Tecmed, S.A. v. The United Mexican States* (n 132) [154].

[276] *Occidental Exploration and Production Company v. The Republic of Ecuador* (n 68) [191, 183].

[277] Ibid [184].

[278] Moshe Hirsch, 'Between Fair and Equitable Treatment and Stabilization Clause: Stable Legal Environment and Regulatory Change in International Investment Law' (2011) 12 Journal of World Investment & Trade 783, 799. Hirsch, however, admits that there was additional negative behaviour by the host State, which was 'highly significant' to the tribunal's finding of a FET breach (ibid 800).

A similar reading of the award can be found in an UNCTAD publication.[279] The facts of the case, however, do not seem to support such a broad reading. Indeed, nothing in the award suggests that the tax law reform as such amounted to a violation of FET. Rather, it was the conduct of the Ecuadorian tax authority SRI that was found to be incompatible with the obligation to ensure a stable legal and business environment.[280]

To summarize, the cases reviewed above (*CMS v. Argentina* & other early Argentine cases, and *Occidental v. Ecuador*) do not indicate that changes in the regulatory system of the host State automatically frustrate legitimate expectations protected by the FET standard. Furthermore, there is a powerful stream of arbitral jurisprudence which rejects the notion that investors can legitimately rely on the stability of laws and regulations that are not specifically addressed to them, and which emphasizes the host State's right to regulate in the public interest.[281] In *El Paso v. Argentina*, the tribunal made the following vigorous statement:

> [I]t is inconceivable that any State would accept that, because it has entered into BITs, it can no longer modify pieces of legislation which might have a negative impact on foreign investors, in order to deal with modified economic conditions and must guarantee absolute *legal stability*. ... FET cannot be designed to ensure the immutability of the legal order, the economic world and the social universe and play the role assumed by stabilisation clauses specifically granted to foreign investors with whom the State has signed investment agreements.[282]

Likewise, in *Parkerings-Compagniet v. Lithuania*, the tribunal observed that:

> It is each State's undeniable right and privilege to exercise its sovereign legislative power. A State has the right to enact, modify or cancel a law at its own discretion. Save for the existence of an agreement, in the form of a stabilisation clause or otherwise, there is nothing objectionable about the amendment brought to the regulatory framework existing at the time an investor made its investment. As a matter of fact, any businessman or investor knows that laws will evolve over time.[283]

---

[279]United Nations Conference on Trade and Development (n 232) 67.

[280]Similarly also Kläger (n 242) 170 (who states cautiously: 'Whether the regulatory changes alone, without the ambiguous conduct of the tax authority, would have sufficed for a breach of fair and equitable treatment remained unanswered by the tribunal'). *Cf.* also Franck (n 269) 680 (who writes that '[u]nless *Occidental* is limited to its peculiar facts, the tribunal's analysis ... may *inadvertently* establish liability whenever governments either fail to provide clear legal and business frameworks, or change those frameworks during the life of an investment'; emphasis added).

[281]Dolzer and Schreuer (n 50) 148–149.

[282]*El Paso Energy International Company v. The Argentine Republic* (n 195) [367–368]. See also ibid [350, 352].

[283]*Parkerings-Compagniet AS v. Republic of Lithuania* (n 53) [332].

Similar statements have been made in *Saluka v. Czech Republic*,[284] *AES v. Hungary*,[285] *EDF v. Romania*,[286] *Plama v. Bulgaria*,[287] *Total v. Argentina*[288] and *Continental v. Argentina*.[289] On the basis of these, it can be safely concluded that foreign investors cannot legitimately rely, under the FET standard, on the stability of the general regulatory framework without any specific commitments (such as in the form of a stabilization clause) or any particular behavior on behalf of the host State. The recent 2016 award in the case *Charanne and Construction Investments v. Spain* reinforces this proposition. In that case, European investors in a Spanish company, which was engaged in the generation and sale of electricity produced by photovoltaic solar plants, claimed that Spain breached the standard of FET under Article 10(1) of the ECT by modifying its regulatory and economic framework pertaining to the promotion of renewable energy generation through feed-in tariffs and thereby undermined their legitimate expectations.[290] In 2010, the Spanish government, confronted with rapidly increasing costs for its photovoltaic support scheme, decided to change the regulatory regime introduced in 2007/2008. In particular, regulated tariffs for solar photovoltaic facilities were eliminated after 30 years of operation and the yearly hours eligible for the tariff were limited.

In line with the well-established case-law, the arbitral tribunal acknowledged that a State cannot make commitments in order to induce foreign investment, thereby generating legitimate expectations, and later frustrate such expectations. However, it rejected claimants' contention that the 2007/2008 legal instruments could be interpreted as specific commitments on behalf of Spain given that they were directed at a particular, limited group of eligible photovoltaic investors. In the tribunal's view, a regulatory standard of *general* application could not be transformed into a *specific* commitment.[291] Subsequently, the tribunal analyzed advertising material issued by the Spanish government, but concluded that it did not include any indication that the regulated tariffs would remain unchanged for the rest of the lifespan of the plants.[292] In a final step, the tribunal ruled that 'in the absence of a specific commitment, the Claimants could not have a reasonable expectation that the

---

[284] *Saluka Investments B.V. v. The Czech Republic* (n 181) [305].

[285] *AES Summit Generation Limited and AES-Tisza Erömü Kft v. The Republic of Hungary* (n 11) [9.3.29].

[286] *EDF (Services) Limited v. Romania*, Award (8 October 2009) ICSID Case No. ARB/05/13 [217].

[287] *Plama Consortium Limited v. Republic of Bulgaria*, Award (27 August 2008) ICSID Case No. ARB/03/24 [219].

[288] *Total S.A. v. The Argentine Republic* (n 53) [115, 117, 309].

[289] *Continental Casualty Company v. The Argentine Republic*, Award (5 September 2008) ICSID Case No. ARB/03/9 [258].

[290] *Charanne and Construction Investments v. Spain* (n 9) [475ff].

[291] Ibid [491–493].

[292] Ibid [494–497].

regulatory framework established by RD 661/2007 and RD 1578/2008 remain frozen.'[293]

On the basis of the jurisprudence outlined above, the adoption of ownership unbundling legislation under the Third Energy Package cannot, and does not, amount to a violation of the standard of fair and equitable treatment. First of all, the legal and functional unbundling requirements as set out in the Second Energy Package were contained in generally applicable legislation, the immutability of which foreign investors cannot legitimately rely on. Secondly, there were no specific commitments, nor any other guarantees, that this unbundling regime would be subject to a 'freeze' or that OU would not be introduced.[294] Thirdly, even under the more far-reaching legitimate expectations doctrine embodied in the *CMS v. Argentina* award, there is no FET violation because the 2003 unbundling regime in the EU energy sector was not put in place with a view to attracting foreign investment.[295]

Furthermore, foreign investors should have been aware of the possibility of further changes even after the implementation of legal and functional unbundling. Indeed, already before the adoption of the Second Energy Package in June 2003, the concept of ownership unbundling was discussed in the EU.[296] In particular, during the legislative process leading to the adoption of the SEP, the European Parliament in 2002 called for full ownership unbundling in electricity in principle.[297] These circumstances certainly have an influence on the legitimacy of investors'

[293]Ibid [504] (citing *Electrabel S.A. v. Republic of Hungary* (n 10) [7.77]; *CMS Gas Transmission Company v. The Republic of Argentina* (n 12) [277]; *El Paso Energy International Company v. The Argentine Republic* (n 195) [350, 352]).

[294]It is true that Article 10(1) of Directive 2003/54/EC of the European Parliament and of the Council concerning common rules for the internal market in electricity and repealing Directive 96/92/EC (26 June 2003) OJ 2003/L 176/37 and Article 9(1) of Directive 2003/55/EC of the European Parliament and of the Council concerning common rules for the internal market in natural gas and repealing Directive 98/30/EC (26 June 2003) OJ 2003/L 176/57 explicitly stated that the rules on legal and functional unbundling 'shall not create an obligation to separate the ownership of assets of the transmission system from the vertically integrated undertaking'. However, it would be a far-fetched argument to say that this statement amounts to a 'specific commitment' that OU would not be introduced. The provisions were inserted exclusively for the purpose of clarifying the unbundling obligations applicable to vertically integrated undertakings, with a view to ensuring legal certainty.

[295]See also footnote 294 (this chapter).

[296]European Commission, Proposal for a Directive of the European Parliament and of the Council amending Directives 96/92/EC and 98/30/EC concerning common rules for the internal market in electricity and natural gas (13 March 2001) COM(2001) 125 final, 36–37; European Commission, Amended proposal for a Directive of the European Parliament and of the Council amending Directives 96/92/EC and 98/30/EC concerning rules for the internal markets in electricity and natural gas (07 June 2002) COM(2002) 304 final, 11.

[297]European Parliament, Position of the European Parliament adopted at first reading on 13 March 2002 with a view to the adoption of European Parliament and Council Directive 2002/.../EC amending Directive 96/92/EC concerning common rules for the internal market in electricity (13 March 2002) OJ 2003/C 47 E/351, 359.

expectations. In *Methanex v. United States*, a case which concerned a ban on the use or sale in California of the gasoline additive methyl tertiary-butyl ether (MTBE) on environmental grounds, the tribunal discussed whether the claimant could invoke any specific commitments relating to the (future) regulation of MTBE. In what can be understood as a general requirement that foreign investors must be aware of the regulatory and political environment in which they operate,[298] the tribunal stated that the applicant had entered into a political economy 'in which it was widely known, if not notorious, that governmental environmental and health protection institutions at the federal and state level . . . continuously monitored the use and impact of chemical compounds and commonly prohibited or restricted the use of some of those compounds for environmental and/or health reasons.'[299] Similarly, in *Glamis Gold v. United States*, the arbitrators rejected the claim that legitimate expectations had been frustrated because the claimant was operating in a climate that was becoming increasingly sensitive to the potential environmental dangers associated with open-pit mining.[300] Finally, in *Charanne and Construction Investments v. Spain*, an arbitral tribunal held that changes in the regulatory framework can only violate the legitimate expectations of the investor if these changes were not 'reasonably foreseeable' at the time of the investment.[301] In the increasingly regulated EU energy market, it should have been clear to every reasonable investor that the EU would take additional steps to address the problems posed by the vertical integration of energy companies if the existing legislation proved to be insufficient.

To sum up, the (preliminary) conclusion must be that the implementation of ownership unbundling measures in the EU energy sector cannot be said to have frustrated any legitimate expectations on the part of foreign investors. The same would apply to a potential 'Fourth Energy Package' introducing mandatory OU on an EU-wide basis.

5.7.2.2 Possible Exceptions to the General Rule

A very intricate question is whether 'special circumstances' can cause changes to the regulatory framework to be in violation of legitimate expectations, even in the absence of a stabilization clause or other specific commitments. While the case-law described above makes it clear that, as a rule, such specific commitments are indispensable, there may be two narrow exceptions: (1) a complete alteration of the existing framework; and (2) rapid and constant legislative changes.

Even in the absence of a stabilization clause or the like, there is some limited authority for the proposition that a complete and absolute alteration of the legal framework may infringe legitimate expectations, and thus possibly result in a

[298] United Nations Conference on Trade and Development (n 232) 71.

[299] *Methanex Corporation v. United States of America* (n 55) Part IV, Chapter D, [9].

[300] *Glamis Gold, Ltd. v. The United States of America,* Award (8 June 2009) [767].

[301] *Charanne and Construction Investments v. Spain* (n 9) [505].

violation of the FET standard. In the case of *El Paso v. Argentina*, the tribunal made the following pronouncement:

> There can be no legitimate expectation for anyone that the legal framework will remain unchanged in the face of an extremely severe economic crisis. No reasonable investor can have such an expectation unless very specific commitments have been made towards it *or unless the alteration of the legal framework is total.*[302]

Applying this standard to the facts of the case, the tribunal concluded that the cumulative impact of all measures taken by Argentina in the energy sector 'completely altered the overall framework'[303] and brought about a 'total alteration of the entire legal setup for foreign investments',[304] amounting to a breach of the FET standard. These statements particularly stand out given that the arbitrators' overall approach to construing the FET principle was rather cautious.[305] However, it seems that in the end the *El Paso* tribunal relied not only on the totality of the change, but also on the existence of a specific commitment by Argentina. After having found that the measures had brought about a total alteration of the legal framework, the tribunal hastened to add that 'all the different elements and guarantees just mentioned can be analysed as a *special commitment of Argentina that such a total alteration would not take place*'.[306] Thus it is open to doubt whether, in that case, the 'total alteration' of the legal framework alone would have sufficed for a finding of a breach of FET.

Toto v. Lebanon is another relevant case. In its 2012 award, the tribunal held that, in the absence of a stabilization clause or similar commitment, 'changes in the regulatory framework would be considered as breaches of the duty to grant ... fair and equitable treatment only in case of a *drastic ... change in the essential features of the transaction*'.[307] In applying this standard to the facts of the case, the arbitrators concluded that the increased taxes and customs duties were small in comparison to the overall cost of the project and that, consequently, the changes in the corresponding legislation did not reach the threshold of a 'drastic' modification of the legal framework.[308]

It must be stressed that until now no arbitral tribunal has found a violation of the FET standard on the basis of a 'total' or 'drastic' alteration of the host State's legal order: In *El Paso v. Argentina* a specific commitment by the State was identified, and

[302]*El Paso Energy International Company v. The Argentine Republic* (n 195) [374] (emphasis added).

[303]Ibid [515].

[304]Ibid [517].

[305]Potestà (n 268) 115.

[306]*El Paso Energy International Company v. The Argentine Republic* (n 195) [517] (emphasis added). The tribunal used the terms 'specific commitment' and 'special commitment' interchangeably.

[307]*Toto Costruzioni Generali S.p.A. v. Republic of Lebanon,* Award (7 June 2012) ICSID Case No. ARB/07/12 [244] (emphasis added).

[308]Ibid.

in *Toto v. Lebanon* no violation was found. Thus there is only a flimsy basis for the proposition that there exists an exception to the general rule that changes to the legal and business framework do not in and of themselves frustrate any legitimately held expectations. Furthermore, the notions of 'total' and 'drastic' are very elusive. Their practical application to the implementation of ownership unbundling requirements set out in Directives 2009/72/EC and 2009/73/EC remains ambiguous. On the one hand, one could certainly argue that accounting, legal and functional unbundling largely preserve ownership rights, whereas ownership unbundling entails a paradigm shift in that it obliges investors to completely divest their ownership. In this sense, the OU model in the TEP could be portrayed as a radical departure from, rather than a continuation of, the approach under the First and Second Energy Packages. On the other hand, the counterargument could be made that the introduction of unbundling requirements was gradual: First accounting unbundling (1996/1998), then legal and functional unbundling (2003), and only as a third step, ownership unbundling (2009). According to this view the change would be incremental rather than total or drastic.

The second possible exception to the rule that changes to the regulatory framework do not automatically undermine legitimate expectations relates to situations of rapid and constant legislative changes. In *PSEG v. Turkey*, the tribunal recognized that endless normative changes to the detriment of the foreign investor can amount to a violation of FET. In particular, it held that '[s]tability cannot exist in a situation where the law kept changing continuously and endlessly, as did its interpretation and implementation',[309] and found that 'the fair and equitable treatment obligation was seriously breached by ... the *"roller-coaster" effect of the continuing legislative changes*.'[310] However, in finding a violation of the FET standard, the tribunal also relied on (1) serious administrative negligence; (2) abuse of authority; and (3) failure to respect rights granted by law as a matter of policy or practice.[311] Thus it remains an open question whether the rapid and constant legislative changes alone, without the presence of special circumstances, would have sufficed for a breach of FET.

The *PSEG v. Turkey* award undoubtedly shows that investors have a strong interest in ensuring that legislative reforms which have only just taken effect are not immediately superseded by new regulatory frameworks without adequate transition periods. In fact, from the perspective of vertically integrated energy undertakings, the decision in 2003 not to introduce ownership unbundling, but only legal and functional unbundling,[312] could be interpreted as having two effects: First, it

---

[309] *PSEG Global, Inc. The North American Coal Corporation, and Konya Ingin Electrik Üretim ve Ticaret Limited Sirketi v. Republic of Turkey,* Award (19 January 2007) ICSID Case No. ARB/02/5 [254].

[310] Ibid [250] (emphasis added).

[311] Ibid [246–252].

[312] This political decision is reflected in Article 10(1) of Directive 2003/54/EC (n 294); Article 9 (1) of Directive 2003/55/EC (n 294). These provisions stated: 'These rules [on legal and functional unbundling] shall not create an obligation to separate the ownership of assets of the transmission

provided increased certainty for, and thereby incentivized, further investment in the maintenance and development of their transmission system assets. Second, all necessary expenditures in connection with the implementation of functional and legal unbundling requirements were made in reliance on the expectation that such regulations would stay in place at least for a certain period of time.[313] However, even if *PSEG v. Turkey* were interpreted to the effect that investors may actually have a legitimate expectation that they are not subject to 'roller-coaster' changes in the law, the successive adoption of the Second and Third Energy Packages cannot be deemed to have frustrated such expectations. Directives 2009/72/EC and 2009/73/EC were adopted on 13 July 2009, i.e. more than 5 years after the deadline for the transposition of the Second Energy Package rules on unbundling of TSOs had elapsed.[314] In addition, the new rules on unbundling were to be applied only from 3 March 2011.[315] There was, therefore, an adequate transition period of almost 7 years from the old to the current unbundling regime.

As a final observation, it must be emphasized that legislative or regulatory changes contravening the legitimately held expectations of an investor will not necessarily lead to liability under an FET provision. A number of awards have stressed that investors' expectations, once found to be legitimate, need to be balanced against the host State's right to regulate.[316] Therefore, to the extent that *El Paso v. Argentina*, *Toto v. Lebanon*, and *PSEG v. Turkey* stand for the proposition that a foreign investor can legitimately expect that the existing legal framework will be neither totally altered nor subject to rapid and constant legislative changes, it may be required to balance these expectations with the State's sovereign right to enact legislation in the public interest.

---

system from the vertically integrated undertaking.' See also 8th recital of the preamble to Directive 2003/54/EC (n 294); 10th recital of the preamble to Directive 2003/55/EC (n 294).

[313]See Matthias Wohlfahrt, *Ownership Unbundling: Die Vereinbarkeit verschärfter Entflechtungsvorgaben für die leitungsgebundenen Sektoren Elektrizität und Gas mit dem Gemeinschaftsrecht* (Berliner Wissenschafts-Verlag 2009) 212 (from the perspective of EU law). See also Rasbach (n 152) 334–335; Ulrich Büdenbender and Peter Rosin, *Einführung eines Ownership Unbundling bzw. Independent System Operator in der Energiewirtschaft: Rechtliche und rechtspolitische Würdigung der wesentlichen Argumente der Europäischen Kommission* (Verlag Energiewirtschaft und Technik 2007) 67ff.

[314]See Article 30(1) of Directive 2003/54/EC (n 294); Article 33(1) of Directive 2003/55/EC (n 294).

[315]Article 49(1) of Directive 2009/72/EC (n 90); Article 54(1) of Directive 2009/73/EC (n 90).

[316]*Saluka Investments B.V. v. The Czech Republic* (n 181) [305–306]; *Suez, Sociedad General de Aguas de Barcelona S.A.and InterAgua Servicios Integrales del Agua S.A. v. The Argentine Republic,* Decision on Liability (30 July 2010) ICSID Case No. ARB/03/17 [216]; *AWG Group Ltd. v. The Argentine Republic,* Decision on Liability (30 July 2010) [236].

5.7.3 Unreasonable and Disproportionate Changes to the Legal Framework

In the previous sub-section it was demonstrated that foreign investors could not have had a legitimate expectation that the unbundling requirements set out in Directives 2003/54/EC and 2003/55/EC would not be changed in the normal course of legislative activity. It could, however, be argued that the ownership unbundling rules in the TEP violate the legitimate expectation that, when modifying existing legislative or regulatory frameworks, the State will not act 'unreasonably' or 'disproportionately'.

5.7.3.1 Proportionality as an Element of FET

A number of arbitral awards have linked the FET obligation with the notions of reasonableness and proportionality.[317] In *Total v. Argentina*, for example, the tribunal stated that the circumstances and reasons for carrying out changes to the legal framework in the energy sector on one hand, and the seriousness of the negative impact on the foreign investor's operations on the other, must be 'compared in the light of a standard of reasonableness and proportionality'.[318] In *EDF v. Romania*, which concerned legislation that resulted in the revocation of licenses to operate duty-free businesses within airports, the tribunal called for a legitimate aim in the public interest and subsequently examined whether there was a 'reasonable relationship of proportionality between the means employed and the aim sought to be realized.'[319] Finally, the 2016 award in *Charanne v. Spain* can be cited as one of the most recent examples of a fair and equitable treatment analysis that focused on whether the State had acted unreasonably, disproportionately or against the public interest in modifying the legislative framework applicable to photovoltaic operators.[320]

The notion of reasonableness, like the concept of proportionality, seems to require a balancing exercise between the interests of foreign investors and those of the host State, and an objective nexus between the measure in question and the goal

---

[317] Apart from the cases cited in the main text, see also *MTD Equity Sdn. Bhd. and MTD Chile S.A. v. Republic of Chile,* Award (25 May 2004) ICSID Case No. ARB/01/7 [109]; *El Paso Energy International Company v. The Argentine Republic* (n 195) [373]; *Occidental Petroleum Corporation and Occidental Exploration and Production Company v. The Republic of Ecuador,* Award (5 October 2012) ICSID Case No. ARB/06/11 [404ff, 450, 452]; *Impregilo S.p.A. v. Argentine Republic,* Award (21 June 2011) ICSID Case No. ARB/07/17 [291].

[318] *Total S.A. v. The Argentine Republic* (n 53) [123]. See also ibid [333].

[319] *EDF (Services) Limited v. Romania* (n 286) [293] (quoting the ECtHR's judgment in the case of *James and Others v. The United Kingdom* (n 133) [50, 63]).

[320] *Charanne and Construction Investments v. Spain* (n 9) [513–539].

it pursues.[321] However, whereas the notion of reasonableness has been criticized for failing to provide a clear analytical structure which would enable the arbitrator to assess a measure's legality in a transparent and methodologically coherent manner,[322] a full-blown proportionality analysis typically entails an assessment of the legitimacy of a measure's objective, followed by an elaborate three-tiered test relating to the suitability of the particular measure at issue, its necessity and, ultimately, its proportionality *stricto sensu*.

In the present context of ownership unbundling measures, the central question is *how* the proportionality test will be applied. Two points can be raised here. First, if the arbitral tribunal conducts a comprehensive proportionality test, the State bears a higher burden of justification. If, in contrast, the proportionality test is applied only in a rudimentary fashion (leaving out one or more of the steps of suitability, necessity and balancing), it will be easier for the State to justify the implementation of ownership unbundling legislation. Second, the standard of review applied by arbitral tribunals will have a great influence on whether ownership unbundling requirements can be effectively challenged. If the arbitrators accord a high degree of deference to the host State's institutions in evaluating factual and legal issues, it is more likely that the relevant legislation will pass muster. If, on the other hand, strict scrutiny is applied at every stage of the proportionality test, foreign investors will have a greater chance of proving a breach of the FET standard.

Against this background, it is important to point out that (1) arbitral tribunals do not consistently address all consecutive analytical steps embedded in the principle of proportionality[323]; and (2) a coherent standard of review has not yet emerged.[324] While some arbitral awards focus exclusively on whether the measure at issue pursues a legitimate regulatory objective, others proceed to the stages of necessity[325] (is there a less restrictive alternative?) and proportionality *stricto sensu*.[326] Furthermore, while some tribunals adopt a deferential standard of review, others take a rather strict approach, in particular with respect to the availability of less restrictive alternative measures. The case of *S.D. Myers v. Canada*, which revolved around

[321]Henckels, 'Proportionality and the Standard of Review in Fair and Equitable Treatment Claims: Balancing Stability and Consistency with the Public Interest' (n 251) 13; Kläger (n 242) 239.

[322]Marc Jacob and Stephan W Schill, 'Fair and Equitable Treatment: Content, Practice, Method' in Marc Bungenberg and others (eds), *International Investment Law* (C.H. Beck; Hart; Nomos 2015) [93]; Henckels, 'Proportionality and the Standard of Review in Fair and Equitable Treatment Claims: Balancing Stability and Consistency with the Public Interest' (n 251) 13.

[323]Kläger (n 242) 245.

[324]Henckels, 'Proportionality and the Standard of Review in Fair and Equitable Treatment Claims: Balancing Stability and Consistency with the Public Interest' (n 251) 11–19, passim.

[325]*S.D. Myers, Inc. v. Government of Canada* (n 160) [255] (The proportionality analysis was conducted under Article 1102 (national treatment) of the NAFTA. However, the tribunal relied on its findings under Article 1102 NAFTA in concluding that Canada had breached the FET standard, see ibid [266]); *Pope & Talbot Inc. v. The Government of Canada* (n 55) [123, 125, 128, 155].

[326]*Occidental Petroleum Corporation and Occidental Exploration and Production Company v. The Republic of Ecuador* (n 317) [450, 452]; *EDF (Services) Limited v. Romania* (n 286) [293]; *Total S.A. v. The Argentine Republic* (n 53) [122–123, 159–165, 309, 317–318, 325–335].

Canada's ban on the export of toxic polychlorinated biphenyl (PCB) waste to the US between 1995 and 1997, exemplifies the more intrusive approach. While the tribunal accepted that the goal of maintaining the ability to dispose of PCB within Canadian borders was legitimate, it thereafter considered whether there were less restrictive alternatives than the export ban on PCB waste and ruled that Canada's 'right to source all government requirements and to grant subsidies to the Canadian industry are but two examples of legitimate alternative measures'.[327] On that basis, the Canadian measure was judged to fail the necessity test.[328] An example of a more deferential approach can be found in *Pope & Talbot v. Canada*, which concerned certain regulatory measures taken by the Canadian government with a view to executing the US-Canada Softwood Lumber Agreement. There, the tribunal emphasized that Canada 'might have chosen another approach' to implementing a particular aspect of the agreement, i.e. 'one that shared the burden more equitably' across the range of softwood lumber producers in British Colombia, but nevertheless accepted the necessity of the measure, holding that 'it is not the place of this Tribunal to substitute its judgment on the choice of solutions for Canada's.'[329]

Some arbitral tribunals have devised tailor-made proportionality tests in the form of a context-specific balancing exercise. In *Total v. Argentina*, for example, it was held that any change to the regulatory regime in the energy sector needed to respect certain fundamental features, in particular 'basic principles of economic equilibrium and business viability.'[330] In the view of the arbitrators, this would require States to refrain from taking measures that effectively prevent investors from covering their costs and making a reasonable return over time. The tribunal considered this to be particularly important in the case of 'utility or general interest sectors' subject to government regulation, which are characterized by capital intensive and long-term investments.[331]

An assessment of ownership unbundling measures in light of the proportionality obligation enshrined in the FET standard reveals the following picture: Much will depend on (1) whether the tribunal engages in a complete (suitability, necessity, and balancing) or only partial analysis; and (2) the kind of standard of review which is adopted. There are good reasons for arbitrators to adopt a high measure of deference vis-à-vis the decision-making institutions of the host State, in particular where such institutions can show that they have carefully considered possible alternatives as well as the appropriate balance between host State's regulatory objective and the

---

[327] *S.D. Myers, Inc. v. Government of Canada* (n 160) [255, 266].

[328] See also *Suez, Sociedad General de Aguas de Barcelona S.A.and InterAgua Servicios Integrales del Agua S.A. v. The Argentine Republic* (n 316) [215]; *AWG Group Ltd. v. The Argentine Republic* (n 316) [235].

[329] *Pope & Talbot Inc. v. The Government of Canada* (n 55) [155]. See also ibid [123, 125, 128] (where the tribunal applied a 'reasonable necessity' test).

[330] *Total S.A. v. The Argentine Republic* (n 53) [168].

[331] Ibid [122, 167–168, 312–313, 333].

measure's effect on (foreign) investors.[332] However, even if a strict test is applied, ownership unbundling measures will not be found to be disproportionate (as shown in the next sub-section). If OU policies are evaluated against an energy-sector-specific proportionality test, inspired by the 'economic equilibrium and business viability' doctrine in *Total v. Argentina*, one of the main questions will presumably be whether the investor is able to show that he was forced to sell the transmission system assets at a price substantially below the market value as a direct result of the OU legislation.

5.7.3.2 Proportionality and Ownership Unbundling Measures

In this sub-section a full proportionality analysis of ownership unbundling measures will be provided. As has become evident throughout this book the proportionality of OU policies plays a very important role not only in the context of FET, but also in connection with the principle of 'no expropriation without compensation' and Article VI:4/5 of the GATS (disciplines for domestic regulation). While OU measures are designed to contribute to the realization of a number of different public policy objectives, including non-discriminatory investment decisions, security of supply, prevention of cross-subsidization and prevention of the misuse of commercially sensitive information, the main aim of OU is to ensure non-discriminatory network access. Therefore it will be analyzed here whether OU requirements are proportionate to this objective.

As part of the first prong of the proportionality test, it must be asked whether OU measures are *suitable* to enhance non-discriminatory network access. A number of points have been raised concerning this matter. First of all, it has been argued that OU does not, and cannot, remove the potential for discrimination in the transmission sector, because transmission is and will remain a natural monopoly. From that perspective, it is the natural monopoly character of transmission networks that is the cause of discrimination, not vertical integration *per se*.[333]

It is certainly true that the possibility of abusive pricing is inherent to the natural monopoly position of the TSO and in that sense independent of ownership

[332]See Henckels, 'Proportionality and the Standard of Review in Fair and Equitable Treatment Claims: Balancing Stability and Consistency with the Public Interest' (n 251) passim.

[333]Baur and others (n 134) 48–49; Thomas Mayen and Ulrich Karpenstein, 'Eigentumsrechtliche Entflechtung der Energieversorgungsnetze: Verfassungs- und gemeinschaftsrechtliche Aspekte des Eigentumsschutzes' [2008] Recht der Energiewirtschaft 33, 39; Müller-Terpitz and Weigl (n 153) 365; Christian Koenig, Kristina Schreiber and Kristin Spiekermann, 'Defizitäres Entflechtungsregime? Eine kritische Analyse der Entflechtungsvorschriften in dem Entwurf des dritten Liberalisierungspakets der Kommission der Europäischen Gemeinschaften' [2008] Netzwirtschaften & Recht 7, 11; Bernd Holznagel and Pascal Schumacher, 'Großer Eingriff, k(l)eine Wirkung – Die Pläne der Kommission zur eigentumsrechtlichen Entflechtung der Energienetzbetreiber' [2007] Netzwirtschaften & Recht 96, 101; Jürgen Kühling and Guido Hermeier, 'Eigentumsrechtliche Leitplanken eines Ownership Unbundlings in der Energiewirtschaft' (2008) 58 Energiewirtschaftliche Tagesfragen 134, 137.

structures.[334] Therefore, extensive regulation would be needed even after the introduction of OU, and transmission system operators would not be 'neutralized'.[335] Nevertheless, this argument against the suitability of ownership unbundling is unconvincing. OU is not designed to eliminate the *ability* of TSOs to engage in anti-competitive behavior. It rather addresses the *incentives* of TSOs to discriminate.

However, there is another fundamental argument against the suitability (and necessity) of unbundling solutions in general, and ownership unbundling measures in particular, which takes its cue from the above-mentioned considerations. Ultimately, what matters is that the possibility of discrimination in network access, which results from the natural monopoly character of the transmission system, is effectively eliminated. If behavioral measures, i.e. network access regulation, can make such discrimination impossible, then the existence of an incentive to discriminate would be irrelevant.[336] Accordingly, unbundling measures would not be suitable (nor necessary) to increase competition in the electricity and gas sectors.

The ability of TSOs to discriminate in network access has been significantly reduced through network access regulation. Throughout the EU all transmission system operators are subject to regulated TPA, which means that all customers can seek network access on the basis of published and non-discriminatory tariffs. The national regulatory authorities have to approve at least the methodologies used to calculate the tariffs.[337] A TSO can only refuse access if it lacks the necessary capacity or (in the case of gas) where granting access would (1) prevent it from carrying out public service obligations, or (2) lead to 'serious economic and financial difficulties' with take-or-pay contracts.[338] When a refusal of access takes place, duly substantiated reasons must be provided. In addition, the annexes to the Electricity and Gas Regulations already contain the first specific provisions on non-discriminatory capacity allocation and congestion management.[339] Moreover, highly elaborate network codes are currently being developed and will become binding in the form of directly applicable regulations. These network codes will cover the following twelve areas, in both the electricity and gas markets: (1) network security and reliability rules; (2) network connection rules; (3) third-party access rules; (4) data exchange and settlement rules; (5) interoperability rules; (6) operational procedures in an emergency; (7) capacity allocation and congestion management rules; (8) rules for trading related to the technical and operational provision of network access services and system balancing; (9) transparency rules; (10) balancing

---

[334] Kühling and Hermeier (n 333) 137; Koenig, Schreiber and Spiekermann (n 333) 11.

[335] Baur and others (n 134) 49.

[336] See Koenig, Schreiber and Spiekermann (n 333) 11.

[337] Article 32 and Article 37(1)(a), (6) and (10) of Directive 2009/72/EC (n 90); Article 32 and Article 41(1)(a), (6) and (10) of Directive 2009/73/EC (n 90).

[338] Article 32(2) of Directive 2009/72/EC (n 90); Article 35(1) of Directive 2009/73/EC (n 90).

[339] The annex to the Gas Regulation has already been modified, see in particular European Union, Commission Decision 2012/490/EU on amending Annex I to Regulation (EC) No 715/2009 of the European Parliament and of the Council on conditions for access to the natural gas transmission networks (24 August 2012) OJ 2012/L 231/16.

rules; (11) rules regarding harmonized transmission tariff structures; and (12) energy efficiency regarding electricity/gas networks.[340] In the gas sector, the Network Code on Capacity Allocation Mechanisms in Gas Transmission Systems already entered into force in November 2015.[341] The regulatory policies in the areas of action listed above all focus on the creation of non-discriminatory access arrangements. Thus it can be expected that with more detailed regulation, there will be less room for anti-competitive practices in the future.

However, although third party access rights constitute the cornerstone of the toolbox of modern network industry regulation,[342] it is generally assumed that behavioral rules in the form of access regulation are 'almost always imperfect'.[343] If the incentive to engage in discriminatory behavior is not suppressed or removed through unbundling measures, even a well-resourced regulatory authority with strong enforcement powers will face an uphill struggle against the actions of an integrated operator. Given that gas and electricity transmission are highly complex businesses from both an economic and technical perspective, and that the integrated operator will always have an information advantage over the regulator, it will be challenging for the latter to try and detect subtle and constantly-changing forms of discrimination.[344] The regulation of third party access in the energy sector can therefore be 'only partially effective'.[345] Against this background, it becomes evident that unbundling measures have an important role to play in the creation of fully competitive energy markets.

The suitability of structural separation measures is confirmed by the fact that this instrument has been and continues to be used to create competitive industry structures. It was already provided for in the Treaty Establishing the European Coal and Steel Community[346]; it is contained in Regulation 1/2003 on the implementation of

---

[340]Article 8(6) of Regulation (EC) No 714/2009 of the European Parliament and of the Council on conditions for access to the network for cross-border exchanges in electricity and repealing Regulation (EC) No 1228/2003 (13 July 2009) OJ 2009/L 211/15; Article 8(6) of Regulation (EC) No 715/2009 of the European Parliament and of the Council on conditions for access to the natural gas transmission networks and repealing Regulation (EC) No 1775/2005 (13 July 2009) OJ 2009/L 211/36.

[341]Commission Regulation (EU) No 984/2013 establishing a Network Code on Capacity Allocation Mechanisms in Gas Transmission Systems and supplementing Regulation (EC) No 715/2009 of the European Parliament and of the Council (14 October 2013) OJ 2013/L 273/5.

[342]Jürgen Kühling, *Sektorspezifische Regulierung in den Netzwirtschaften* (Energie- und Infrastrukturrecht vol 4, C.H. Beck 2004) 359 ('Herzstück der Netzwirtschaftsregulierung').

[343]Thomas W Wälde and Andreas Gunst, 'International Energy Trade and Access to Networks: The Case of Electricity' in Janusz Bielecki and Melaku G Desta (eds), *Electricity Trade in Europe – Review of the Economic and Regulatory Changes* (Kluwer Law International 2004) 185. See also Cabau (n 38) [4.4] ('inadequate').

[344]OECD, 'Restructuring Public Utilities for Competition' (2001) 20ff, 53 <http://www.oecd.org/competition/sectors/19635977.pdf> accessed 20 January 2016.

[345]Ibid 21.

[346]Article 66(5) of the Treaty Establishing the European Coal and Steel Community (18 April 1951) 261 U.N.T.S. 140.

the rules on competition in Articles 101 and 102 TFEU[347]; and it also features in national competition legislation, such as the German Restriction of Competition Act.[348,349] It is irrelevant in this connection that the regulatory measures foreseen in Directives 2009/72/EC and 2009/73/EC are different in scope because they bring about across-the-board ownership unbundling applicable to all actors in the electricity and gas sectors.[350] Last but not least, it should be recalled that several countries around the world have adopted OU in order to create competitive energy markets.[351]

The second prong of the proportionality test requires a necessity analysis. This involves an assessment regarding the availability of less restrictive alternative measures. In the academic literature much of the criticism has focused on the fact that the Commission's proposal for a Third Energy Package in 2007 was premature, in the sense that it had not yet been conclusively determined whether the unbundling and third party access regulation of the Second Energy Package would adequately address the competition concerns related to vertically integrated undertakings. According to this view, the existing regulatory framework under the SEP (including regulated TPA; *ex ante* control of transmission tariffs; and legal and functional unbundling) needed sufficient time to 'take shape' and show its effects, considering that the deadline for transposition of the SEP had elapsed only on the 1st of July 2004[352] and that most Member States transposed the 2003 Directives only with (significant) delay.[353,354] However, as some measure of deference must be accorded

[347]Article 7 of Council Regulation (EC) No 1/2003 on the implementation of the rules on competition laid down in Articles 81 and 82 of the Treaty (16 December 2002) OJ 2003/L 1/1. See also Sect. 2.4.

[348]Article 41 of the Federal Republic of Germany, Restriction of Competition Act (Gesetz gegen Wettbewerbsbeschränkungen) (26 June 2013) BGBl. I S. 1750, 3245.

[349]Frank Schorkopf, 'Eigentumsrechtliche Entflechtung aus verfassungs- und europarechtlicher Sicht' in Wolfgang Löwer (ed), *Neue rechtliche Herausforderungen für den Strommarkt: Bonner Gespräch zum Energierecht – Band 3* (Bonner Gespräch zum Energierecht vol 3. V & R unipress 2008) 127.

[350]But see Matthias Schmidt-Preuß, 'Der Wandel der Energiewirtschaft vor dem Hintergrund der europäischen Eigentumsordnung' (2006) 41 Europarecht 463, 485; Baur and Schmidt-Preuß (n 228) [79] (who sweepingly state that ownership unbundling has a non-market character ('marktfremdes Mittel') and is thus not suitable to enhance competition).

[351]See Sect. 1.4.

[352]Article 30(1) of Directive 2003/54/EC (n 294); Article 33(1) of Directive 2003/55/EC (n 294).

[353]At the end of 2005 the Commission noted that 'most Member States have transposed the new Directives only with delay and some not yet at all', see European Commission, Report on progress in creating the internal gas and electricity market (15 November 2005) COM(2005) 568 final, 2–3.

[354]Mayen and Karpenstein (n 333) 39–40, 45; Baur and others (n 134) 56ff; Rasbach (n 152) 333ff, 350; Müller-Terpitz and Weigl (n 153) 366; Holznagel and Schumacher (n 333) 102–103; Johann-Christian Pielow and Eckart Ehlers, 'Rechtsfragen zum "Ownership Unbundling"' [2007] InfrastrukturRecht 259, 261–262; Kühling and Hermeier (n 333) 137; Büdenbender and Rosin (n 313) 109–110, 115. See also Schorkopf (n 349) 127–128; Iñigo del Guayo, Gunther Kühne and Martha M Roggenkamp, 'Ownership Unbundling and Property Rights in the EU Energy Sector' in Aileen McHarg and others (eds), *Property and the Law in Energy and Natural Resources* (Oxford University Press 2010) 343.

in the necessity analysis, it can be concluded here that the 2009 assessment of the Union legislator that the unbundling requirements in the Second Energy Package 'have not ... led to effective unbundling of the transmission system operators'[355] should not be called into question. The assessment was based on substantial factual evidence adduced by the European Commission,[356] and an international investment tribunal should not supplant its own judgment of this factual material for that of the EU institutions.

Apart from that, the assertion that in other network industries, such as telecommunications and railways, competition was successfully increased without the need to introduce (ownership) unbundling[357] is not persuasive. Despite their network-bound character, the telecommunications, railways, electricity and gas sectors have important differences. It is therefore only natural that regulatory tools are of greater importance in one sector and less significant in another.[358] Moreover, as regards the railway sector, the European Commission recently proposed the implementation of an 'institutional separation' between railway undertakings and infrastructure managers as part of the Fourth Railway Package, a concept almost identical to the OU model in the TEP.[359]

Next, the argument has been raised that ownership unbundling measures are not necessary, because the effectiveness of the existing regulatory framework can be improved.[360] To the extent that this argument related to improved network access regulation, reference can be made to the general comments above on the inherent limited effectiveness of behavioral measures. To the extent that the argument was aimed at enhancing the effectiveness of the unbundling rules in Directives 2003/54/EC and 2003/55/EC, this ties in with the overarching objection that the necessity of OU is questionable given that Directives 2009/72/EC and 2009/73/EC explicitly provide for two other models of unbundling, ISO and ITO.

Indeed, the inclusion of the ISO and ITO models could suggest that these are less restrictive but equally effective alternatives to ownership unbundling.[361] On the

---

355 10th recital of the preamble to Directive 2009/72/EC (n 90); 7th recital of the preamble to Directive 2009/73/EC (n 90).

356 European Commission, Inquiry pursuant to Article 17 of Regulation (EC) No 1/2003 into the European gas and electricity sectors (Final Report) (10 January 2007) COM(2006) 851 final; European Commission, DG Competition Report on Energy Sector Inquiry (10 January 2007) SEC(2006) 1724.

357 For this position, see Jürgen F Baur, Kai U Pritzsche and Stefan Klauer, *Ownership Unbundling: Wesen und Vereinbarkeit mit Europarecht und Verfassungsrecht* (Veröffentlichungen des Instituts für Energierecht an der Universität zu Köln vol 121, Nomos 2006) 83; Müller-Terpitz and Weigl (n 153) 366.

358 See in particular Peter Abegg and others, 'Entflechtung in Netzsektoren – ein Vergleich' [2014] Bremen Energy Working Papers No. 19, 30, 35 (who show that unbundling measures are less relevant in the telecoms sector, as compared to electricity and gas, *inter alia* due to the higher degree of infrastructure competition in that sector).

359 See Sect. 1.4.

360 Baur and others (n 134) 58ff.

361 See, in the EU law context, Müller-Terpitz and Weigl (n 153) 366.

other hand, what could speak against the equal effectiveness of all three unbundling models in the TEP is that the preambles to the Electricity and Gas Directives reproduce a statement from a 2007 resolution of the European Parliament[362] stating that ownership unbundling is '*the most effective tool* by which to promote investments in infrastructure in a nondiscriminatory way, fair access to the network for new entrants and transparency in the market.'[363] However, this statement only reveals the position of the European Parliament, which is only one of the institutions involved in the ordinary legislative procedure. It does not mean that the Union legislator endorsed the Parliament's position. In the same vein, the statements of the European Commission, in both its report on the energy sector inquiry and in its legislative proposals for a Third Energy Package, asserting that full ownership unbundling is '*the most effective means* to ensure choice for energy users and encourage investment'[364] are similarly inconclusive. They all pre-date the TEP and thus cannot represent the consensus reached to achieve the final version.

There are in fact also a number of indications that the Union legislator proceeded from the assumption that all three unbundling models in the TEP are equally effective. In an interpretative note by the European Commission on the unbundling rules in the Third Energy Package, as adopted, the Commission expressed the view that '[a]lthough [all three unbundling models] provide for different degrees of structural separation of network operation from production and supply activities, *each of them is expected to be effective in removing any conflict of interests* between producers, suppliers and transmission system operators.'[365] The Commission has reiterated this point on several occasions.[366] The Commission's interpretation is in line with the preambles to Directives 2009/72/EC and 2009/73/EC, which recognize that all three unbundling models are capable of delivering 'effective unbundling' and thus clearly reflect an assumption of equal effectiveness.[367] A comparison with the draft preambles impressively highlights the significant change from the notion of 'OU is the most effective tool' (2007 Commission proposals) to 'OU, ISO and ITO are equally effective' (TEP as adopted). Whereas the initial Commission proposals

[362] European Parliament, Resolution on Prospects for the Internal Gas and Electricity Market (10 July 2007) P6_TA(2007)0326, [2].

[363] 11th recital of the preamble to Directive 2009/72/EC (n 90); 8th recital of the preamble to Directive 2009/73/EC (n 90) (emphasis added).

[364] Inquiry into the European gas and electricity sectors (n 356) [55]; European Commission, Prospects for the internal gas and electricity market (10 January 2007) COM(2006) 841 final, 12; European Commission, An Energy Policy for Europe (10 January 2007) COM(2007) 1 final, 7.

[365] European Commission, 'Commission Staff Working Paper – Interpretative Note on Directive 2009/72/EC concerning common Rules for the Internal Market in Electricity and Directive 2009/73/EC concerning common Rules for the Internal Market in Natural Gas – The Unbundling Regime' (n 206) 4 (emphasis added).

[366] Commission Decision – Eirgrid/ESB (n 206) [17]; Commission Decision on the application of Article 9(9) of Directive 2009/72/EC to TSOs in Scotland (n 206) [8]; Commission Decision – SONI/NIE (n 206) [11].

[367] 9th, 11th-12th, 16th and 19th recital of the preamble to Directive 2009/72/EC (n 90); 6th, 8th-9th, 13th and 16th recital of the preamble to Directive 2009/73/EC (n 90).

posited that OU is 'clearly *the most* effective and stable way'[368] to solve the inherent conflict of interest of vertically integrated undertakings, the corresponding preambular paragraphs in the Third Energy Package simply state that OU is 'clearly *an* effective and stable way'[369] to achieve this goal. Against this background, it has been correctly pointed out that 'for the [Union] legislator, the three options are meant to achieve effective unbundling.'[370]

On the basis of this assumption of equal effectiveness, it would clearly be difficult to accept that ownership unbundling is 'necessary', even if a measure of deference is exercised. However, it is important to recall that the TEP leaves the choice of the unbundling model to the Member States. It is the Member States that may decide to prescribe mandatory OU. Therefore, it would need to be assessed whether the respective Member State put forward sufficient reasons to justify the adoption of OU legislation. Importantly, the Member States are not bound by the EU legislator's expectation of equal effectiveness expressed in the Gas and Electricity Directives. Rather, they can make their own assessment of the effectiveness of the three models provided for in the TEP. Thus the Lithuanian parliament, for example, opted for the implementation of ownership unbundling in the gas sector. In the explanatory memorandum accompanying its implementing law, it declares that OU will be most beneficial for the Lithuanian gas sector in the long term.[371] The memorandum explicitly refers to the 2007 Commission report on the competition sectoral inquiry[372] and the European Parliament resolution of 2007,[373] both of which, as mentioned above, characterized ownership unbundling as 'the most effective' tool to achieve the desired objectives. While these documents have no relevance for determining how the Union legislator ranked the unbundling models in terms of effectiveness, they can be used by national parliaments of the EU Member States to substantiate their view that OU will make the largest contribution to the creation of competitive energy markets. The Lithuanian explanatory memorandum also highlights that the ISO and ITO models were evaluated by the Lithuanian legislator, and that it was concluded that both models would not be able to achieve the same or even

[368]European Commission, Proposal for a Directive of the European Parliament and of the Council amending Directive 2003/54/EC concerning common rules for the internal market in electricity (19 September 2007) COM(2007) 528 final, 22; European Commission, Proposal for a Directive of the European Parliament and of the Council amending Directive 2003/55/EC concerning common rules for the internal market in natural gas (19 September 2007) COM(2007) 529 final, 22 (emphasis added).

[369]11th recital of the preamble to Directive 2009/72/EC (n 90); 8th recital of the preamble to Directive 2009/73/EC (n 90) (emphasis added).

[370]Cabau (n 38) [4.24]. See also Buschle (n 205) 54, 62.

[371]Republic of Lithuania, 'Law on the Amendment of the Law on Natural Gas and Law on the Implementation of the Law on the Amendment of the Law on Natural Gas – Explanatory Notes' (2011) <http://www3.lrs.lt/pls/inter2/dokpaieska.showdoc_l?p_id=391924&p_tr2=2> accessed 17 September 2015.

[372]See Inquiry into the European gas and electricity sectors (n 356) [53–56].

[373]Resolution on Prospects for the Internal Gas and Electricity Market (n 362) [2].

comparable benefits, in terms of opening of the market to competition, as ownership unbundling.[374]

Estonia is another example in point. In 2012, the Parliament of Estonia adopted a law that required companies in the gas sector to comply with ownership unbundling. In the context of an assessment of the constitutionality of OU, the memorandum accompanying the law specifically touches upon the question whether it is possible to achieve the goal of promoting competition by virtue of other less burdensome measures, i.e. through the adoption of the ISO or ITO model. As in the case of Lithuania, the memorandum posits that, based on the European Commission's findings in the sector inquiry, models other than ownership unbundling would not guarantee effective competition and that OU would therefore be a necessary measure for the introduction of competition into the Estonian gas market.[375]

To sum up, it may be said that the evaluations carried out by national parliaments within the framework of their respective legislative procedures, effectively replace or supersede the assumption of equal effectiveness that is embodied in the TEP. While there is a certain tension between the conflicting assessments of national legislators on the one hand, and the Union legislator on the other, national legislators must be able to deviate from the position taken at the EU level; otherwise all EU Member States would be prevented from adopting ownership unbundling because of the principle of proportionality. Therefore, if an international tribunal conducting the necessity test with respect to OU applies a deferential standard of review, and thus respects the ranking of policy options made by the respective legislator, in terms of their effect on the objectives pursued, OU could be considered to be 'necessary' to achieve non-discriminatory network access.

However, the international tribunal could also conduct a more thorough analysis of the necessity of OU policies. How, then, would OU measures be assessed under a more stringent standard of review? In this connection the judgment of the Dutch Supreme Court (*Hoge Raad*) in the *Essent* case comes to the forefront. In particular, the Supreme Court accepted the argument of the government that the risk of cross-subsidization is (theoretically) always present in vertically integrated energy companies and that the 'group prohibition' (i.e. the OU measures in the Dutch energy sector) sought to ensure that the possibility of cross-subsidization between a

[374] Republic of Lithuania, 'Law on the Amendment of the Law on Natural Gas and Law on the Implementation of the Law on the Amendment of the Law on Natural Gas – Explanatory Notes' (n 371).

[375] Republic of Estonia, 'Law on the Amendment of the Natural Gas Act – Explanatory Memorandum – Original Proposal' (2012) <http://www.riigikogu.ee/tegevus/eelnoud/eelnou/5dea306a-39a3-43c7-9d74-e20d79ad6527/Maagaasiseaduse%20muutmise%20seadus/> accessed 18 September 2015.

On second reading, a proposed amendment aiming to introduce the ITO model was rejected, see Republic of Estonia, 'Law on the Amendment of the Natural Gas Act – Explanatory Memorandum – Second Reading' (2012) <http://www.riigikogu.ee/tegevus/eelnoud/eelnou/5dea306a-39a3-43c7-9d74-e20d79ad6527/Maagaasiseaduse%20muutmise%20seadus/> accessed 18 September 2015.

distribution system operator and a commercial gas or electricity company is structurally excluded.[376] In rejecting the ruling of the Court of Appeal, it held that more regulation and greater oversight do not constitute an equally effective alternative, given that this solution would not structurally rule out the risk of cross-subsidization.[377] The same reasoning was also applied with respect to the issue of security of energy supply. Here the *Hoge Raad* ruled that only OU could ensure that the grid is completely structurally independent of commercial energy activities so that investment in commercial activity cannot be made at the expense of network management and development.[378] On that basis, the Supreme Court accepted that the group prohibition did not go beyond what was necessary to achieve the stated objectives.[379]

The judgment of the *Hoge Raad* is of great importance because it shows that the EU and its Member States will be able to argue that no unbundling model (other than OU) has the same effectiveness as ownership unbundling. Only OU can ensure that the incentive for vertically integrated undertakings to discriminate against competitors as regards network access is structurally excluded. The prohibition of holding a majority shareholding[380] or more than a 10% share[381] and other unbundling models[382] (such as the ISO and ITO models in the TEP) are therefore, while less-restrictive, not equally effective. This assessment, which could also become relevant for a potential Fourth Energy Package implementing mandatory ownership unbundling on an EU-wide level, is not altered by the fact that the European Commission came to the (preliminary) conclusion in 2014 that 'most requirements related to the ITO model seem to work in practice and are usually sufficient and adequate to ensure effective separation of the transmission business from generation and supply activities in the day-to-day business.'[383]

Under the third prong of the proportionality test, ownership unbundling policies must be proportionate *stricto sensu*. In other words, there must be a proper balance between the objective(s) pursued by ownership unbundling and its adverse effects on

[376] Hoge Raad der Nederlanden, *Staat der Nederlanden v. Essent N.V.* Judgment (26 June 2015) 10/03851 [3.17.2].

[377] Ibid.

[378] Ibid [3.22.2].

[379] Ibid [4.9.1].

[380] See Martin Wachovius, *Ownership Unbundling in der Energiewirtschaft: Vereinbarkeit einer eigentumsrechtlichen Entflechtung in der Energiewirtschaft mit den Grundrechten des Grundgesetzes und des Gemeinschaftsrechts deutscher vertikal integrierter Energieversorgungsunternehmen* (VWEW Energieverlag 2008) 83, 167.

[381] See Christian Kahle, 'Die Eigentumsrechtliche Entflechtung (Ownership Unbundling) der Energieversorgungsnetze aus europarechtlicher und verfassungsrechtlicher Sicht' [2007] Recht der Energiewirtschaft 293, 296.

[382] See Schmidt-Preuß (n 350) 485; Baur and Schmidt-Preuß (n 228) [79] (who refer, *inter alia*, to the solution of trusteeship, which is akin to the ISO model in the TEP).

[383] European Commission, Commission Staff Working Document – Report on the ITO Model (13 October 2014) SWD(2014) 312 final, 6.

individual interests. Some authors have argued that the expected benefits of OU are out of proportion to the serious infringement of the right to property it entails.[384] This conclusion is based on an assessment of the expected competition-related effects on the one hand, and the impact on the investor on the other.

As regards the former, it is undoubtedly the case that the most egregious forms of discrimination are already ruled out through third party access regulation in conjunction with less far-reaching forms of unbundling. However, the importance attached to reducing persistent subtle forms of discrimination with respect to network access reflects a value judgment that should not be second-guessed by international adjudicators. Moreover, the existence of competition-related benefits of OU cannot be discounted on the basis that a further decrease in network access charges will have only an insignificant effect on consumer prices.[385] The primary intended effect of ownership unbundling policies is not to reduce network access charges, but to eliminate incentives for discrimination in order to spur competition on the generation/production side, which ideally leads, *ceteris paribus*, to benefits for consumers.

Furthermore, as regards the impact of OU legislation on the investor, it seems that its proportionality *stricto sensu* depends to a large extent on the revenue generated from the sale of the transmission assets.[386] Where the owner is able to sell the transmission assets at (almost) full market value, it will be extremely difficult to argue that the benefits of ownership unbundling are manifestly disproportionate to the impact on investors' property rights.

Finally, the argument has been put forward that if ownership unbundling is only rarely considered as a (proportionate) remedy under Article 7 of Regulation 1/2003, where it can be used with respect to individual companies for a proven infringement of Article 101 or 102 TFEU, it cannot *a fortiori* be applied across-the-board to the whole energy sector.[387] This line of reasoning, however, is unconvincing. The fact that the European Commission has not yet imposed structural remedies under Article 7 of Regulation 1/2003[388] does not mean that this option is unavailable or disproportionate. Thus a comparison with disinvestment obligations as a structural remedy under general EU competition law cannot be used to show that OU is disproportionate in the strict sense.

---

[384]Baur and Schmidt-Preuß (n 228) [79]; Baur, Pritzsche and Klauer (n 357) 84; Baur and others (n 134) 69; Mayen and Karpenstein (n 333) 40; Müller-Terpitz and Weigl (n 153) 367.

[385]But see Müller-Terpitz and Weigl (n 153) 367.

[386]*Cf.* Baur and Schmidt-Preuß (n 228) [80]; Müller-Terpitz and Weigl (n 153) 367–368 (who stress the importance of the sales price for the proportionality *stricto sensu* in the context of the discussion on OU and the fundamental right to property under EU law).

[387]This is argued by Baur and others (n 134) 68 (who initially reject an analogy between structural measures as a remedy under general EU competition law and the broader discussion on OU as a regulatory instrument).

[388]See Sect. 2.4.

To sum up, it may be said that a good case can be made that ownership unbundling measures are proportionate to achieve the objective of ensuring non-discriminatory network access.

5.8 Conclusions

The unbundling and unbundling-related measures set out in the Third Energy Package have to comply with the general treatment standards applicable to foreign investors under BITs and other IIAs (such as the ECT) to which the EU and/or its Member States are a party. The relevant post-entry investment protection standards include national treatment, most-favored-nation treatment, no expropriation without compensation and fair and equitable treatment. Given that the applicable IIAs generally follow a 'controlled entry' approach, the adoption or maintenance of unbundling and unbundling-related legislation is not in any way limited as regards the pre-entry stage.

The substantive unbundling requirements in Directives 2009/72/EC and 2009/73/EC constitute the first dimension of the TEP's unbundling regime. First of all, and most importantly, the OU requirements could come into conflict with the standard of 'no expropriation without compensation'. Apart from cases where the foreign investor is able to invoke favorable provisions on expropriation, contained in a limited number of EU Member State BITs, according to which the compulsory sale of an investment or part thereof *ipso facto* constitutes an expropriation, the difficult question is whether OU requirements should be considered as an indirect or *de facto* expropriation, or as a non-compensable regulatory measure. Existing case-law, State practice, and the academic literature do not give a clear answer to the question whether 'compulsory', 'involuntary' or 'forced' sales of investments amount to an indirect expropriation under international law. Having said that, the significant detrimental impact on an investor's right to use, enjoy and dispose of his property shows that the OU measures in the EU energy sector lead to a substantial deprivation of property rights and that the required threshold of interference is thus met. However, given that there are different approaches in international investment jurisprudence with respect to the concept of indirect expropriation, this finding is not conclusive on its own. Following the 'sole effects' doctrine, there would be an expropriation as the effect of OU on the investor is the only relevant criterion. Under the 'police powers' doctrine, in contrast, OU requirements would not constitute an expropriation because they are non-discriminatory, respect due process requirements and serve a legitimate public purpose. In turn, according to the third approach used in arbitral awards, the qualification of ownership unbundling policies as expropriatory ultimately depends on the application of a proportionality test, considering both the purpose of OU and its impact on foreign investors. This is arguably the most convincing approach. It is submitted here that ownership unbundling requirements are proportionate to the objective of ensuring non-discriminatory network access, considering in particular that international investment tribunals usually apply a deferential standard of review. In particular, OU is 'necessary' because other unbundling options, such as the ISO and ITO models, are less effective. Thus in conclusion OU does not rise to the level of an expropriation. Furthermore, even if *arguendo* an expropriation occurs, it would generally be lawful, essentially because the price obtained through the compulsory sale of the transmission system assets will only in very rare cases be manifestly below the actual market value. Therefore there is no internationally wrongful act for which additional compensation might be due.

As regards the fair and equitable treatment standard, foreign investors affected by OU legislation could argue that they had a legitimate expectation in the stability of the legal and regulatory framework as it existed before the adoption of the TEP. Some arbitral awards, such as *CMS v. Argentina* and *Occidental v. Ecuador*, have in fact been interpreted to the effect that regulatory changes in and of themselves can frustrate investors' legitimate expectations. However, the legal reasoning in both awards reveals that they are not as far-reaching as sometimes assumed. Moreover, there is a powerful stream of arbitral jurisprudence which supports the idea that the legal and business environment cannot give rise to legitimate expectations in the absence of accompanying *specific* commitments, representations or assurances. While it may turn out that two narrow exceptions to this prevailing view gradually emerge, covering (1) 'total' or 'drastic' alterations of the existing framework and (2) rapid and constant legislative changes, the case-law to this effect is very limited and its application to the implementation of ownership unbundling would not necessarily lead to an FET violation. Apart from that, affected investors could seek to rely on the emerging obligation of proportionality as a basis for their claim. Several arbitral tribunals have linked the doctrine of legitimate expectations with the notions of reasonableness and proportionality. However, although a coherent standard of review has not yet been developed in the existing case-law, ownership unbundling requirements are in any case proportionate to the objective of ensuring non-discriminatory access to gas and electricity transmission networks. In conclusion, the adoption of OU requirements as set out in Directives 2009/72/EC and 2009/73/EC does not violate any legitimate expectations protected by the FET standard.

The special ownership unbundling requirements for public undertakings in Article 9(6) of the Directives do not violate the national treatment standard in IIAs, because domestic public investors have no advantage over foreign private ones as a result of Article 9(6). Finally, the unbundling requirements as set out in the Directives may come into conflict with the EU's MFN obligation due to the variety of unbundling models among the EU Member States (OU, ISO & ITO). However, even assuming that the 'treatment no less favorable' standard applies to the relationship between a foreign investor in EU Member State A, where the relevant measure is enacted, and another foreign investor in EU Member State B (which is questionable), any less favorable treatment could most likely be justified on the basis that any EU Member State should be able to exercise its legislative powers within its territory in a manner independent of the other Member States.

The second dimension of the unbundling regime in the TEP relates to the procedure for exemption of energy infrastructure from the OU requirements. Here, the MFN and national treatment obligations could play a role with respect to individual exemption decisions, for example where the exemption request of a foreign investor is rejected. However, the objective and non-discriminatory exemption criteria contained in Article 36 Gas Directive and Article 17 Electricity Regulation justifiably differentiate between different exemption requests. Therefore, the MFN and NT standards are not violated, unless the individual exemption decision is not plausibly or reasonably connected to the exemption criteria.

The third and final dimension of the unbundling regime in the TEP concerns the certification procedure in relation to third countries in Article 11 of the Directives. Given that the additional 'security of supply' test applies exclusively to foreign-controlled transmission system owners or operators, the third-country certification procedure clearly involves less favorable treatment for foreign investors. However, given that the additional test is designed to ensure the security of energy supply of the EU and its Member States, this less favorable treatment can arguably be justified. Furthermore, the third-country certification procedure is also in line with the MFN treatment standard. Passing the security of supply test does not generally depend on the country of origin of the foreign investor. However, even if origin-based criteria, such as general security of supply related agreements or the existence of energy trade relations, are taken into account, the objective of ensuring security of energy supply would provide an appropriate justification.

Chapter 6
International Economic Law as a Possible Vehicle for the Implementation of Unbundling Measures

6.1 Introduction

So far the focus has been on the question of whether and to what extent WTO law and international investment law prohibit or limit the implementation of unbundling and unbundling-related measures in the EU energy sector. It was this perspective that guided the analysis in Chaps. 4 and 5. In contrast, this chapter will sketch the 'positive' role that WTO law *could* play in the formulation of unbundling policies at both the national and supra-national levels. In other words, this chapter considers how the existing general WTO framework deals with the anti-competitive practices flowing from vertical integration and to what extent it imposes a positive obligation upon Members to bring about some degree of vertical separation in the energy sector. In addition, it will be shown how the existing WTO disciplines could be complemented by additional pro-competitive regulatory commitments, including in particular common rules on unbundling of energy companies.

At the outset it is important to once again highlight the aim of unbundling rules as well as the circumstances under which they can serve a useful purpose. Unbundling policies address *private* conduct that impedes cross-border trade in energy goods and services, with discriminatory network access being the main issue in this context. It is, however, essential to recall that it is *governmental* restraints which have traditionally formed the most significant limitations on world trade.[1] Even in the case of the European Union it was not too long ago that the energy markets of EU Member States were controlled by public monopolies.[2] Only in 1991 did the European Commission open infringement procedures against nine Member States in order to challenge the existence of exclusive rights for the import and export of gas and

[1]This is the reason why existing multilateral trade regulation focuses first and foremost on governmental restrictions on trade.

[2]Kim Talus, *EU Energy Law and Policy: A Critical Account* (Oxford University Press 2013) 15ff.

T. M. Dralle, *Ownership Unbundling and Related Measures in the EU Energy Sector*, European Yearbook of International Economic Law 5,
https://doi.org/10.1007/978-3-319-77797-9_6

electricity.[3] It is evident that where governmental trade barriers exist, i.e. where competition from foreign suppliers and products is categorically ruled out, the issue of network access does not even arise in the first place. Therefore, in order for unbundling measures to actually become relevant and take effect, it is necessary to ensure that there are no governmentally-imposed barriers to energy trade. Only then can unbundling measures play a meaningful role, i.e. prevent private market actors from impeding market access.

As regards trade in goods, the GATT has removed the most significant State-imposed restraints. WTO Members are prohibited from maintaining quantitative restrictions on the importation of energy goods (Article XI GATT). Likewise, they cannot treat foreign energy goods less favorably than like domestic products (Article III:4 GATT), particularly in terms of network access and network access tariffs. Finally, WTO Members must ensure the transit of energy products through their respective territories (Article V GATT).[4] Therefore, if a cross-border pipeline or electricity transmission line with sufficient capacity exists,[5] which is of course a *conditio sine qua non* for the importation of goods in the case of network-bound industries, private anti-competitive practices resulting from vertical integration become relevant.

As regards trade in services, the situation is slightly different. The adoption of the GATS has not automatically led to a legal, formal across-the-board liberalization. This is mainly due to the peculiar structure of the GATS, under which key obligations such as market access and national treatment only apply if and to the extent that the respective WTO Member has undertaken specific commitments in its country-specific schedule of commitments. With respect to the energy sector, WTO Members have generally been rather reluctant to make such commitments.[6] Furthermore, a significant part of the segment of the energy sector that is, in principle, open to competition is arguably not even subject to the GATS. As discussed, it seems that the production/generation of electricity and gas does not constitute a service within the

[3]European Commission, Second Progress Report on the Internal Energy Market (02 July 1993) COM(93) 261 final, 12; Peter Cameron, *Competition in Energy Markets – Law and Regulation in the European Union* (1st edn, Oxford University Press 2002) [3.81–3.87].

[4]Christopher Frey, 'Die Bedeutung des Welthandelsrechts für die Einfuhr von Strom aus Drittländern in den Energiebinnenmarkt' in Thilo Rensmann and Stefan Storr (eds), *Die Energiewende im rechtlichen Mehrebenensystem: Regionale, nationale und internationale Herausforderungen* (Verlag Österreich 2015) 119–125. Specifically on transit see also Danae Azaria, 'Energy Transit under the Energy Charter Treaty and the General Agreement on Tariffs and Trade' (2009) 27 Journal of Energy & Natural Resources Law 559; Vitaliy Pogoretskyy, 'Freedom of Transit and the Principles of Effective Right and Economic Cooperation: Can Systemic Interpretation of GATT Article V Promote Energy Security and the Development of an International Gas Market?' (2013) 16 Journal of International Economic Law 313.

[5]There is no positive obligation under WTO law to develop cross-border energy transmission capacity, see Karolis Gudas, *Intersection of WTO and EU law in International Electricity Trade: Analysis of the Regulatory Environment for Electricity Systems Development* (PhD Dissertation, forthcoming).

[6]See Sect. 4.4.

meaning of the GATS.[7] This means that measures relating to production/generation are not covered by the GATS and that WTO Members cannot undertake specific market access and national treatment commitments in this part of the energy sector.[8] Therefore, in the absence of relevant specific commitments and autonomous liberalization, all segments of the electricity/gas sector of a WTO Member may be dominated by a State monopoly. In such a situation, there would be no scope for international competition. Accordingly, in the case of trade in services unbundling measures can only become relevant and actually improve market access if the WTO Member concerned has opened up its energy market to competition from foreign suppliers (through mode 1 or mode 3) in the first place, either as a consequence of corresponding specific commitments under the GATS or autonomous liberalization measures.[9]

Having described the framework conditions for the successful operation of unbundling policies, it is appropriate to briefly consider the relationship between WTO law on the one hand, and competition policy and regulation on the other. From the observations above it can be seen that the existing multilateral trade rules primarily deal with hindrances to the flows of goods and services trade erected by countries. From its inception this has been the primary focus of international trade regulation.[10] However, the gradual removal of governmental tariff and non-tariff barriers has revealed that private market actors have a similarly significant potential to restrict or distort trade through anti-competitive practices.[11] In the absence of effective competition laws or pro-competitive regulations, there is thus a real risk that the market access achieved through trade liberalization will remain undermined.[12] In this sense an inadequate competition policy and competition regulation can constitute an important 'non-tariff barrier' to trade.[13] Against this

[7]See Sect. 4.2.

[8]Simonetta Zarrilli, 'Multilateral Rules and Trade in Energy Goods and Services: The Case of Electricity' in Janusz Bielecki and Melaku G Desta (eds), *Electricity Trade in Europe – Review of the Economic and Regulatory Changes* (Kluwer Law International 2004) 249–250; WTO, Council for Trade in Services, Energy Services – Background Note by the Secretariat (09 September 1998) S/C/W/52, [40–41].

[9]See also Energy Services – Background Note by the Secretariat (n 8) [6] (stating that '*[o]nce [WTO] Members have chosen to liberalize [the energy] sector*, major regulatory aspects need to be addressed in order to ensure that such liberalizing effort is not nullified by the market power of existing suppliers, especially those who control the transmission and distribution networks'; emphasis added).

[10]WTO, *Special Topic: Trade and Competition Policy* (Annual Report 1997 vol 1, 1997) 30.

[11]Maher M Dabbah, *International and Comparative Competition Law* (Cambridge University Press 2010) 581–582.

[12]Jürgen Basedow, *Weltkartellrecht: Ausgangslage und Ziele, Methoden und Grenzen der internationalen Vereinheitlichung des Rechts der Wettbewerbsbeschränkungen* (Beiträge zum ausländischen und internationalen Privatrecht vol 63, Mohr Siebeck 1998) 2; Energy Services – Background Note by the Secretariat (n 8) [6].

[13]Michael Trebilcock, 'Competition Policy and Trade Policy' (1996) 30 Journal of World Trade 71, 74.

background it should come as no surprise that competition policy issues have always been 'on the radar' of international trade negotiators. In fact, as will become apparent in the next section below, substantive obligations on competition issues are frequently found in bilateral or multilateral trade agreements.

The ways in which private anti-competitive practices manifest themselves are manifold. First, a company may abuse its dominant position to deter foreign competitors from entering the market. Similar impediments to trade can result from the concerted action of a number of companies at the same level of the market ('horizontal restraints'), e.g. collectively undercutting prices or boycotting other firms that do business with a foreign rival trying to establish itself on the domestic market. Furthermore, vertical restraints can prevent a level playing field between foreign and domestic competitors. This includes, for example, exclusive dealing arrangements between incumbent manufacturers and distributors or retailers.[14]

As regards specifically the anti-competitive practices resulting from the vertical integration of energy companies, it is clear that these practices pose considerable barriers to international trade by limiting the 'ability of foreign goods, services or service suppliers to supply downstream markets, access to which depends on the use of facilities controlled by [enterprises that enjoy monopolies or positions of market power].'[15] In essence, it seems that what is true for the 'micro cosmos' of the EU is also true at the global level. The WTO Secretariat, for example, has noted that the fact that most industries in the energy sector have traditionally been dominated by vertically integrated companies has left 'little margin for trade and competition'[16] and often 'prevented trade in energy services.'[17] In the same vein it has been highlighted that the cross-border trade of energy goods is constrained by restrictive business practices in the form of 'vertical foreclosure of transmission and distribution networks in the destination country.'[18] The unbundling of vertically integrated undertakings was therefore considered to be the 'first market access issue on the road of multilateral liberalization' in the energy sector.[19] Moreover, the importance of unbundling policies for enabling international trade has also become visible in WTO accession negotiations, where some acceding countries have faced demands from other WTO Members for the unbundling of their vertically integrated energy companies.[20]

Although it was noted at the beginning of this book that a number of WTO Members have already implemented some form of unbundling, particularly in the

---

[14]See Michael Trebilcock, Robert Howse and Antonia Eliason, *The Regulation of International Trade* (Routledge 2013) 759–760; Trebilcock (n 13) 87.

[15]WTO (n 10) 60–61.

[16]Energy Services – Background Note by the Secretariat (n 8) [3].

[17]Ibid [31]. See also ibid [44].

[18]Ibid [37].

[19]Ibid [6].

[20]Yulia Selivanova, *The WTO and Energy: WTO Rules and Agreements of Relevance to the Energy Sector* (Issue paper vol 1, International Centre for Trade and Sustainable Development 2007) 32.

electricity sector,[21] unbundling requirements are still far from becoming a global standard in the energy industry. Therefore, given the trade-restrictiveness of vertical integration, WTO Members wanting to export energy goods and services will have an interest in the adoption and enforcement, by other WTO Members, of effective competition policies or regulations aimed at gradually unbundling vertically integrated energy companies. Thus the question that naturally arises is whether WTO law requires, or at least promotes, the implementation of such policies.

6.2 The Development of International Competition Law

Before delving into an analysis of competition-related provisions in WTO law, a brief overview of the development and state of international competition law is necessary.

The first serious attempts to develop a set of multilateral competition rules were made after the Second World War. The Havana Charter for an International Trade Organization ('Havana Charter') of 1948 contained provisions on restrictive business practices.[22] In accordance with Article 46(1), each Member had to take appropriate measures and co-operate with the proposed International Trade Organization in order to 'prevent, on the part of private or public commercial enterprises, business practices affecting international trade which restrain competition, limit access to markets, or foster monopolistic control, whenever such practices have harmful effects on the expansion of production or trade and interfere with the achievement of any of the other objectives [of the International Trade Organization].' Business conduct considered as restrictive business practices under the Havana Charter included, *inter alia*, fixing prices, excluding enterprises from territorial markets or fields of business activity, discriminating against certain enterprises, limiting production or establishing production quotas, preventing the development or application of technology or invention, and extending the use of rights under patents, trademarks or copyrights beyond their scope.[23]

Under the Havana Charter, Member States were to be entitled to file a complaint with the International Trade Organization regarding restrictive business practices. In response to such a complaint, the International Trade Organization was to be empowered to open a formal investigation procedure, request information and, if necessary, recommend remedial action to the members concerned. However, the Havana Charter never entered into force, essentially due to opposition in the US Congress.[24] The GATT, which salvaged parts of the multilateral trading regime

[21]See Sect. 1.4.

[22]Havana Charter for an International Trade Organization (24 March 1948) UN Doc. E/CONF.2/78.

[23]Ibid, Article 46(3).

[24]Trebilcock (n 13) 88.

agreed upon in the Havana Charter, does not contain any competition law provisions comparable to those envisaged in the Charter.[25]

In the 1950s, there were further attempts to reach international agreement on competition law principles. But the works undertaken within the Economic and Social Council (ECOSOC) of the United Nations and committees of the GATT did not lead to any tangible results.[26] The first multilateral instrument to contain competition-related provisions was the UNCTAD-sponsored 'Set of Multilaterally Agreed Principles and Rules for the Control of Restrictive Business Practices',[27] which was adopted by the United Nations General Assembly in 1980.[28] The UNCTAD Code calls upon governments to adopt and effectively enforce appropriate legislation and implement judicial and administrative procedures in order to combat restrictive business practices, which are defined as 'acts or behaviour of enterprises which, through an abuse or acquisition and abuse of a dominant position of market power, limit access to markets or otherwise unduly restrain competition, having or being likely to have adverse effects on international trade, ... or which through formal, informal, written or unwritten agreements or arrangements among enterprises, have the same impact.'[29] In addition, the instrument also contains provisions on inter-State cooperation. However, the UNCTAD Code merely has the status of soft law; it lacks binding legal force.[30]

The establishment of the WTO in 1995 did not go hand in hand with the creation of strong competition law disciplines. However, this does not mean that the WTO agreements do not have any bearing on competition matters.[31] The GATT and GATS include rules on state trading enterprises (STEs) as well as monopoly and exclusive service suppliers.[32] The Agreement on Trade-Related Investment Measures mandates the WTO Council for Trade in Goods to consider whether the Agreement should be complemented with provisions on competition policy.[33] The

[25]The GATT only features provisions on state trading enterprises, which are of some relevance in the present context and will be discussed below.

[26]Basedow (n 12) 63–64.

[27]United Nations Conference on Trade and Development, The Set of Multilaterally Agreed Equitable Principles and Rules for the Control of Restrictive Business Practices (1980) A/C.2/35/6, annex.

[28]United Nations General Assembly, Restrictive business practices (05 December 1980) A/RES/35/63.

[29]Set of Multilaterally Agreed Equitable Principles and Rules for the Control of Restrictive Business Practices (n 27).

[30]Friedl Weiss, 'From World Trade Law to World Competition Law' (2000) 23 Fordham International Law Journal 250, 255.

[31]For a brief overview of the interlinkages between the WTO agreements and competition policy, see Trebilcock, Howse and Eliason (n 14) 761–762.

[32]Article XVII WTO, General Agreement on Tariffs and Trade (15 April 1994) 55 U.N.T.S. 194; Articles VIII WTO, General Agreement on Trade in Services (15 April 1994) 1869 U.N.T.S. 183.

[33]Article 9 WTO, Agreement on Trade-Related Investment Measures (15 April 1994) 1868 U.N.T.S. 186.

Agreement on Trade-Related Aspects of Intellectual Property Rights requires WTO Members to enter into negotiations, if requested, with a view to eliminating anti-competitive licensing practices or conditions pertaining to intellectual property rights.[34] Similarly, the GATS provides for a consultation mechanism with respect to anti-competitive business practices in the area of trade in services.[35] All in all however, the 'competition dimension' of the WTO provisions is quite limited. The only narrow exception is the sector-specific 'Reference Paper on Basic Telecommunications Services', which has been adopted by many WTO Members as an additional commitment under Article XVIII GATS.[36] It contains a number of pro-competitive regulatory principles for the telecom sector, some of which have already been applied by the WTO dispute settlement bodies in the *Mexico – Telecoms*[37] dispute.

After the creation of the WTO in 1995, the decision was taken at the Ministerial Conference in Singapore to establish a Working Group on the Interaction Between Trade and Competition Policy.[38] In 2001, the Doha Ministerial Conference recognized the case for a multilateral framework to enhance the contribution of competition policy to international trade and development and directed the Working Group to focus on three areas: (1) core principles (including transparency, non-discrimination and procedural fairness, as well as provisions on hardcore cartels); (2) a framework for voluntary cooperation; and (3) capacity building for competition institutions in developing countries.[39] However, as a result of the failure of the 2003 Cancún Ministerial meetings, the WTO's General Council decided a year later that the intersection between trade and competition policy would not form part of the work program of the Doha Round and that, therefore, no negotiations would take place on these issues.[40]

Despite the lack of progress at the multilateral level, there are a number of bilateral agreements which establish cooperation principles in competition matters. Such bilateral agreements have been concluded by, *inter alia*, the US, Canada, Australia, Germany and the EU. In addition to notification and consultation duties,

---

[34]Article 40 WTO, Agreement on Trade-Related Aspects of Intellectual Property Rights (15 April 1994) 1869 U.N.T.S. 299.

[35]Article IX GATS (n 32).

[36]Ibid, Article XVIII reads: 'Members may negotiate commitments with respect to measures affecting trade in services not subject to scheduling under Articles XVI or XVII, including those regarding qualifications, standards or licensing matters. Such commitments shall be inscribed in a Member's Schedule.'

[37]WTO, *Mexico – Measures Affecting Telecommunications Services*, Report of the Panel (2 April 2004) WT/DS204/R.

[38]World Trade Organization, Singapore Ministerial Declaration: Adopted on 13 December 1996 (18 December 1996) WT/MIN(96)/DEC, 20.

[39]World Trade Organization, Ministerial Declaration: Adopted on 14 November 2001 (20 November 2001) WT/MIN(01)/DEC/1, 23.

[40]World Trade Organization, Doha Work Programme: Decision Adopted by the General Council on 1 August 2004 (02 August 2004) WT/L/579, 3.

they usually contain negative, but increasingly also positive, comity obligations regarding the enforcement of domestic competition laws.[41] Bilateral antitrust cooperation also occurs through so-called 'Mutual Legal Assistance Treaties' (which are non-competition specific cooperation instruments) and 'Antitrust Mutual Assistance Agreements'. Both of these types of agreements have the advantage that the requested State can provide assistance in the enforcement of competition laws regardless of whether the particular anti-competitive behavior is likewise prohibited under its domestic law.[42]

In addition, certain competition disciplines are also contained in the great majority of bilateral and regional trade agreements.[43] In substantive terms, many of these FTAs impose obligations upon the respective parties to prohibit anti-competitive agreements and concerted practices and/or abuses of market power. At the same time, however, FTAs frequently exclude disputes relating to the competition-specific provisions from their general dispute settlement mechanism.[44] In this context attention must also be drawn to the Energy Charter Treaty. Article 6 ECT provides a 'best efforts' obligation, according to which each contracting party shall 'work to alleviate market distortions and barriers to competition.' Furthermore, each party is obliged to 'ensure that within its jurisdiction it has and enforces such laws as are necessary and appropriate to address unilateral and concerted anti-competitive conduct.' However, the Treaty later clarifies that the unilateral and concerted anti-competitive conduct referred to is to be defined by each contracting party 'in accordance with its laws'.[45] Against this background, and also taking into consideration that Article 6(5) ECT only features a non-binding information and consultation mechanism,[46] it has been stated that the ECT merely 'confirms the applicability' of existing domestic competition rules and thus fails to 'establish a common competition regime between [the] Contracting Parties.'[47]

---

[41]Basedow (n 12) 34ff; Florian Wagner-von Papp, '§ 11 Internationales Wettbewerbsrecht' in Christian Tietje (ed), *Internationales Wirtschaftsrecht* (De Gruyter 2015) [90ff]. The *negative* comity principle means that a State refrains from enforcing its competition laws in a cross-border context in order to respect the legitimate sovereign interests of the other State party. The *positive* comity principle means that a State can request the other State party to initiate competition proceedings against certain anti-competitive practices that occur outside the jurisdiction of the requesting State.

[42]Wagner-von Papp (n 41) [95ff].

[43]François-Charles Laprévote, Sven Frisch and Burcu Can, 'Competition Policy within the Context of Free Trade Agreements' (2015) 1 <http://e15initiative.org/publications/competition-policy-within-the-context-of-free-trade-agreements/> accessed 23 August 2016.

[44]Ibid 5, 12.

[45]Understanding 7(a) Energy Charter Treaty (17 December 1994) 2080 U.N.T.S. 95.

[46]See on this Katherine Holmes, 'Legal Implications of the Energy Charter Treaty, Competition – Rules and Liberalisation' in Thomas W Wälde (ed), *The Energy Charter Treaty: An East-West Gateway for Investment and Trade* (International Energy and Resources Law and Policy Series. Kluwer Law International 1996) 550–551.

[47]Yulia Selivanova, 'The Energy Charter and the International Energy Governance' in Yulia Selivanova (ed), *Regulation of Energy in International Trade Law: WTO, NAFTA and Energy Charter* (Kluwer Law International 2012) 390.

6.3 Existing Competition Law Provisions in the WTO Agreements

6.3.1 Article VIII GATS

The GATS contains some provisions dealing with anti-competitive practices of companies. The most significant provision in this respect is Article VIII GATS, which deals with the supply of services by monopoly and exclusive service suppliers. Article VIII:1 GATS provides that each WTO Member must ensure that monopoly service suppliers in its territory do not, 'in the supply of the monopoly service in the relevant market, act in a manner inconsistent with that Member's obligations under Article II and specific commitments.' Furthermore, according to Article VIII:2 GATS, where a monopoly service supplier competes in the supply of a service which is 'outside the scope of its monopoly rights' and subject to a WTO Member's specific commitments, that WTO Member is under an obligation to ensure that 'such a supplier does not abuse its monopoly position to act in its territory in a manner inconsistent with such commitments.' Paragraphs 1 and 2 of Article VIII GATS also apply to exclusive service suppliers.[48] Article VIII:3 GATS relates to information requests by the Council for Trade in Services.

It is primarily Article VIII:2 GATS that is relevant to the issue herein discussed. In contrast to the first paragraph, which focuses exclusively on the behavior of monopoly service suppliers in the respective monopoly market, the second paragraph of Article VIII GATS regulates the behavior of service suppliers that have monopoly rights in a non-competitive service sector and, at the same time, compete with service suppliers in another, competitive market segment. Thus the scope of Article VIII:2 GATS also includes vertically integrated undertakings in the energy sector. Nevertheless, it would be an overstatement to say that Article VIII:2 GATS was specifically designed to apply to cases of vertical integration in network-bound industries. The application of Article VIII:2 GATS does not presuppose the existence of a vertically integrated undertaking (defined as a company that controls several or all of the production and/or distribution steps required for the creation of a specific product or service). A monopoly service supplier competing in a market segment that has no connection whatsoever with the monopoly right also falls within the scope of the Article's provisions. For example, a company that has a monopoly in postal services and, at the same time, owns a bank would likewise come within the scope of Article VIII:2 GATS.[49] It also follows from this that Article VIII:2 GATS does not necessarily envisage a network-bound industry, such as gas or electricity. However, it seems that network-bound industries are indeed a prominent example of

[48] Article VIII:5 GATS (n 32).

[49] The example is taken from Martin Michaelis, '§ 20 Dienstleistungshandel (GATS)' in Meinhard Hilf and Stefan Oeter (eds), *WTO-Recht: Rechtsordnung des Welthandels* (2nd edn. Nomos 2010) [84, 86].

the type of situation covered by that provision,[50] because they (1) often feature a combination of monopolistic/oligopolistic and competitive market structures, and (2) thus provide strong incentives to companies that are active in both sectors to abuse their monopoly position on the transport market in order to increase their profits on the downstream market. In conclusion, while Article VIII:2 GATS was not specifically drafted to deal with the anti-competitive effects resulting from vertical integration, the problem that the provision tries to address certainly encompasses the challenges associated with vertically integrated undertakings in the energy sector.

The principal aim of Article VIII:2 GATS is to ensure that the market power of monopoly or exclusive service suppliers in the non-competitive market segment does not negatively affect services trade in a competitive services market.[51] Similar to the function of the unbundling requirements in Directives 2009/72/EC and 2009/73/EC, Article VIII:2 GATS could therefore have the potential to prevent vertically integrated undertakings from taking advantage of their monopoly position by discriminating against competing foreign energy suppliers via their monopoly network service.[52] In particular, it has been submitted in the academic literature that Article VIII:2 GATS prohibits cross-subsidization, in the sense that vertically integrated undertakings may not use monopoly rents to cross-subsidize services which are provided on a competitive basis.[53] Furthermore, it has been discussed whether, in order to comply with Article VIII:2 GATS, WTO Members need to ensure 'access to essential facilities [e.g. transmission and distribution networks], controlled by a monopolist, which are necessary to provide services in adjacent markets which are liberalized and indicated in the Members' Schedules.'[54] One could argue that the attainment of both of these objectives—preventing cross-subsidization and ensuring access to essential facilities—is greatly facilitated through the introduction of some type of unbundling measures.

[50]See Aaditya Mattoo, 'Dealing with Monopolies and State Enterprises: WTO Rules for Goods and Services' in Thomas Cottier and Petros C Mavroidis (eds), *State Trading in the Twenty-First Century* (University of Michigan Press 1998) 44; Mireille Cossy, 'Water Services at the WTO' in Edith B Weiss, Laurence Boisson de Chazournes and Nathalie Bernasconi-Osterwalder (eds), *Fresh Water and International Economic Law* (Oxford University Press 2005) 128 (referring to transport, telecommunications and energy).

[51]Werner Zdouc, *Legal Problems Arising under the General Agreement on Trade in Services – Comparative Analysis of GATS and GATT* (Dissertation Nr. 2608, Difo-Druck 2002) 269; Sadeq Z Bigdeli and Stefan Rechsteiner, 'Article VIII GATS' in Rüdiger Wolfrum, Peter-Tobias Stoll and Clemens Feinäugle (eds), *WTO – Trade in Services* (Max Planck Commentaries on World Trade Law vol 6. Martinus Nijhoff Publishers 2008) [16]; Nellie Munin, *Legal Guide to GATS* (Global Trade Law Series vol 31, Kluwer Law International 2010) 258.

[52]OECD, *Assessment of WTO and Competition Rules for Enterprises with Exclusive or Special Rights* (COM/TD/DAFFE/CLP(2000)45/FINAL, 2000) [70].

[53]Michaelis (n 49) [86]; Pierre Sauvé, 'Assessing the General Agreement on Trade in Services: Half-Full or Half-Empty?' (1995) 29 Journal of World Trade 125, 131; Bigdeli and Rechsteiner (n 51) [32].

[54]Bigdeli and Rechsteiner (n 51) [28].

However, there are three factors that need to be taken into account when judging the potential of the disciplines contained in Article VIII:2 GATS vis-à-vis the implementation of unbundling measures and, more generally, vis-à-vis the implementation of the objectives pursued by such measures. First, the application of Article VIII:2 GATS is limited by the definitions of the terms 'monopoly supplier' and 'exclusive service supplier'. According to Article XXVIII(h) GATS, a 'monopoly supplier of a service' is defined as 'any person, public or private, which in the relevant market of the territory of a Member is authorized or established formally or in effect by that Member as the sole supplier of that service.' Similarly, 'exclusive service suppliers' exist where a WTO Member, 'formally or in effect, (a) authorizes or establishes a small number of service suppliers and (b) substantially prevents competition among those suppliers in its territory.'[55] Both definitions require that the monopoly or exclusive service supplier be 'authorized or established' formally or in effect by a WTO Member. This requirement of authorization or establishment means that there must be some degree of government involvement, and that natural monopolies which have been created by market failure and which exist without any such government involvement fall outside the scope of Article VIII:2 GATS. This is widely recognized, both in the academic literature[56] and by the WTO Secretariat.[57] The exclusion of purely private activities is also in line with the general caveat that, according to Article I:1 GATS, the agreement only applies to *governmental* measures.[58]

In order to boost the effectiveness of Article VIII GATS, one could argue that the words 'in effect' justify a broad interpretation, according to which *the failure of a government to take measures* to prevent the emergence of or to remedy an existing natural monopoly situation is sufficient to conclude that the incumbent natural monopolist has been authorized or established 'in effect' by a WTO Member.[59] It may be recalled at this point that in *US – Gambling*, the Appellate Body emphasized the inclusion of the words 'formally *or in effect*' in the definitions of monopoly and

[55]Article VIII:5 GATS (n 32).

[56]Bigdeli and Rechsteiner (n 51) [4]; Rudolf Adlung, 'Public Services and the GATS' (2006) 9 Journal of International Economic Law 455, 473; Mattoo (n 50) 38–39; Christoph Herrmann, Wolfgang Weiß and Christoph Ohler, *Welthandelsrecht* (C.H. Beck 2007) [877]; Clemens Feinäugle, 'Article XXVIII GATS' in Rüdiger Wolfrum, Peter-Tobias Stoll and Clemens Feinäugle (eds), *WTO – Trade in Services* (Max Planck Commentaries on World Trade Law vol 6. Martinus Nijhoff Publishers 2008) [32]; Cossy (n 50) 128. But see Yulia Selivanova, 'The WTO Agreements and Energy' in Kim Talus (ed), *Research Handbook on International Energy Law* (Research Handbooks in International Law. Edward Elgar 2014) 297, who seems to assume that Article VIII GATS would apply to the 'incumbent natural monopolist' in the gas transportation and distribution market.

[57]Energy Services – Background Note by the Secretariat (n 8) [39], in particular footnote 17.

[58]This is highlighted by Markus Krajewski, *National Regulation and Trade Liberalization in Services: The Legal Impact of the General Agreement on Trade in Services (GATS) on National Regulatory Autonomy* (Kluwer Law International 2003) 87.

[59]See Mattoo (n 50) 66, note 2; Zdouc (n 51) 267.

exclusive service suppliers.[60] However, such an interpretation seems too expansive, because then the words ‘authorized or established’ would have no independent meaning,[61] contrary to the general rule of treaty interpretation as set out in Article 31(1) VCLT. As a consequence, a Member’s ‘mere tolerance or inaction’ is insufficient to trigger the application of Article VIII GATS.[62] This finding is also supported by the fact that a broad interpretation of the terms ‘monopoly supplier’ and ‘exclusive service supplier’ would have negative ‘spill-over’ effects. The twin notions of ‘monopoly supplier’ and ‘exclusive service supplier’ appear not only in Article VIII GATS, but also in Article XVI GATS (market access obligation). According to Article XVI:2(a) GATS, limitations on the number of service suppliers in the form of, *inter alia*, monopolies and exclusive service suppliers are *per se* prohibited, if and to the extent that specific market access commitments have been undertaken. In the *US – Gambling* case, the Appellate Body suggested that the terms ‘monopoly’ and ‘exclusive service supplier’ as used in Article XVI:2(a) GATS have the same meaning as used in Article VIII GATS.[63] This means that while a broad interpretation of the two notions would expand the scope of application of the competition law disciplines in Article VIII GATS (which would have the positive effect of contributing to the prevention of the abuse of monopoly or exclusive rights beyond their scope), it would also broaden the scope of the *per se* prohibition contained in Article XVI:2(a) GATS (which would have a clear negative impact on national regulatory autonomy).

In conclusion, in the absence of active government involvement, incumbent natural monopolists are not subject to Article VIII GATS. Precisely what kind or degree of State action is necessary for a natural monopolist to be considered as ‘authorized or established formally or in effect’ by a WTO Member cannot be determined on a purely abstract level. The mere fact that the operation of energy transmission systems is subject to licensing is certainly insufficient to bring a service supplier within the scope of Article VIII GATS. A licensing requirement does not in any way prevent competition from other service suppliers. What would trigger the application of Article VIII GATS is if the State explicitly grants a licensee or a concessionaire exclusive rights related to the operation of electricity/gas transmission networks, either nationwide or within a specific geographic area.[64] It is difficult

[60]WTO, *United States – Measures Affecting the Cross-Border Supply of Gambling and Betting Services,* Report of the Appellate Body (7 April 2005) WT/DS285/AB/R [228–230].

[61]Mattoo (n 50) 66, note 2.

[62]Feinäugle (n 56) [32]; Bigdeli and Rechsteiner (n 51) [5].

[63]*United States – Measures Affecting the Cross-Border Supply of Gambling and Betting Services* (n 60) [228–230]. See also Panagiotis Delimatsis and Martín Molinuevo, ‘Article XVI GATS’ in Rüdiger Wolfrum, Peter-Tobias Stoll and Clemens Feinäugle (eds), *WTO – Trade in Services* (Max Planck Commentaries on World Trade Law vol 6. Martinus Nijhoff Publishers 2008) [48].

[64]In Lithuania, for example, a license to transport gas is limited to a certain territory where the respective operator enjoys exclusive rights. The current licensee, Amber Grid, is granted the exclusive right to supply gas transmission services throughout the entire territory of the Republic of Lithuania; see Amber Grid, ‘AB Amber Grid Corporate Strategy 2015–2020’ (2015) 11 <https://

to determine to what degree such legal monopolies are still prevalent. A certain degree of transparency results from the fact that measures which are inconsistent with Article XVI GATS have to be inscribed in the market access column of the relevant country-specific schedule of specific commitments.[65] Therefore, if a WTO Member has undertaken specific market access commitments on energy transmission services, but wishes to maintain a monopoly or establish exclusive service suppliers (Article XVI:2(a) GATS), this must be specified in its schedule. Out of the 14 WTO Members that have made market access commitments on pipeline transmission services,[66] only two have scheduled limitations that can be considered to provide cover for government-mandated monopolies. On the face of it, this would seem to suggest that 'legal' monopolies are rather scarce. On the other hand, the overall small number of MA commitments by WTO Members in the energy transmission sector could also be interpreted to the effect that the respective governments 'may have a role in the persistence of monopolies beyond areas where it is a technological necessity.'[67] The general trend towards liberalization in the energy industry could be taken to imply a concomitant reduction of legal monopoly rights in the transmission sector as well.[68]

In sum, the narrow definition of 'monopoly supplier' and 'exclusive service supplier' considerably limits the reach of the obligation provided for in Article VIII:2 GATS.[69] The provision fails to discipline vertically integrated energy undertakings in general, but applies only to those vertically integrated companies that have legal monopoly or exclusive rights, as defined by the GATS, in the energy transmission sector. Vertically integrated undertakings that are in a position, *as a natural monopoly*, to discriminate against non-affiliated competitors as regards network

www.ambergrid.lt/uploads/structure/docs/318_fb0afbcac104e270ce2e52d63b42ba33.pdf> accessed 24 August 2016. In Portugal, REN Rede Elétrica Nacional and REN Gasodutos have exclusive rights to the transmission of electricity/gas in continental Portugal under corresponding public service concessions; see European Commission, Commission Opinion pursuant to Article 3 (1) of Regulation (EC) No 714/2009 and Article 10(6) of Directive 2009/72/EC and to Article 3 (1) of Regulation (EC) No 715/2009 and Article 10(6) of Directive 2009/73/EC – Portugal – Certification of REN Rede Elétrica Nacional S.A. and REN Gasodutos S.A. (12 May 2014) C (2014) 3255 final, 1.

[65]See Mattoo (n 50) 41, 45, 48.

[66]Australia, Cambodia, Croatia, Hungary, Kyrgyz Republic, Lithuania, Moldova, Montenegro, Nepal, New Zealand, Saudi Arabia, Tajikistan, Macedonia and Ukraine have made market access commitments (mode 3) on CPC 7131.

[67]Mattoo (n 50) 48. It could, however, also be argued that the lack of GATS commitments in this area is due to the fact that, generally speaking, energy transmission is a sensitive activity for many WTO Members.

[68]See Sadeq Z Bigdeli and Mira Burri Nenova, 'Article IX GATS' in Rüdiger Wolfrum, Peter-Tobias Stoll and Clemens Feinäugle (eds), *WTO – Trade in Services* (Max Planck Commentaries on World Trade Law vol 6. Martinus Nijhoff Publishers 2008) [5] (stating that 'government-mandated monopolies or exclusive service suppliers in the sense of Art. VIII:5 are gradually disappearing'). Similarly also Mattoo (n 50) 44, 48, 64.

[69]Bernard Hoekman and Petros C Mavroidis, 'Economic Development, Competition Policy and the World Trade Organization' (2003) 37 Journal of World Trade 1, 12.

access as a result of their control over the transmission network fall outside the scope of Article VIII:2 GATS.

Second, the potential of the disciplines in Article VIII:2 GATS is also limited by the fact that they only apply if and to the extent that specific commitments have been undertaken, by the WTO Member concerned, with respect to the service that is supplied in competition with other service suppliers.[70] The services that vertically integrated incumbents would typically supply in competition with other service providers are mainly wholesale and retail services, given that the generation/production of energy is considered not to be a service within the meaning of the GATS.[71] However, it must be noted that the Services Sectoral Classification List (W/120), which was used by WTO Members to formulate their specific commitments, does not contain an entry for wholesale and retail services of electricity.[72] Although these services fall within the scope of application of the GATS, their absence from the W/120 has led to a situation where no WTO Member has undertaken corresponding specific commitments. As the application of Article VIII:2 GATS necessarily requires the existence of such commitments, vertically integrated *electricity* companies are essentially free to exploit their monopoly position in the network sector to the detriment of foreign providers of wholesale or retail services of electricity. In the gas sector, around 55 WTO Members have undertaken commitments on wholesale and retail services of natural gas (CPC 62271 and CPC 63297),[73] so here the application of Article VIII:2 GATS is not barred.

Third, Article VIII:2 GATS is only violated if the WTO Member fails to prevent the monopoly service supplier (or the exclusive service supplier) from abusing its monopoly position in order 'to act in its territory *in a manner inconsistent with [that Member's specific commitments]*'. This shows that the drafters of the GATS were not primarily concerned about the effects of private anti-competitive behavior as such, but wanted to make sure that monopoly service suppliers do not undermine the specific market access and national treatment commitments.[74] As a consequence, 'the gravity of abusive conduct or the degree of anti-competitive effects caused by it do not matter in and of themselves, but rather whether, as a result of the abuse of the monopoly right, foreign services or service suppliers are facing less favourable treatment or forego market access opportunities in scheduled sectors and/or modes of supply.'[75] Therefore, the issue of whether a vertically integrated undertaking

---

[70]Mattoo (n 50) 40.

[71]See Sect. 4.2.

[72]Mireille Cossy, 'Energy Services under the General Agreement on Trade in Services' in Yulia Selivanova (ed), *Regulation of Energy in International Trade Law: WTO, NAFTA and Energy Charter* (Kluwer Law International 2012) 153; WTO, Council for Trade in Services, Energy Services – Background Note by the Secretariat (12 January 2010) S/C/W/311, [47].

[73]Energy Services – Background Note by the Secretariat (n 72) [71].

[74]Lee Tuthill, 'The GATS and New Rules for Regulators' (1997) 21 Telecommunications Policy 783, 792; Mattoo (n 50) 37.

[75]Zdouc (n 51) 271. But see Bigdeli and Rechsteiner (n 51) [23–32], who focus exclusively on the notion of abuse of a monopoly position.

abused its monopoly position contrary to Article VIII:2 GATS is determined exclusively by reference to Articles XVI and XVII GATS.

It will in many cases be difficult to show that anti-competitive practices result in a violation of market access or national treatment commitments. As has been shown above,[76] an *individual* denial of market access or an individual instance of less favorable treatment is not, as such, inconsistent with the requirements of Article XVI or Article XVII GATS. With regard to Article XVI GATS, it could be argued that market access commitments are violated if a vertically integrated undertaking controlling the entire gas network of a WTO Member refuses all network access requests by foreign independent suppliers of gas over a significant period of time, thereby completely preventing them from making use of the market access concessions made with respect to wholesale and retail services of natural gas. Some authors have stated in this connection that '[w]ithout access to the essential facilities, such as . . . pipelines . . ., the concessions on market access could not be realized particularly in services markets adjacent to monopolized markets.'[77] It is clear that the refusal of network access by a vertically integrated undertaking does not take the form of one of the prohibited market access restrictions contained in Article XVI:2 GATS. It would thus be necessary to focus on the *effect* of the network access refusal. Along the lines of the *US – Gambling* jurisprudence it could be argued that, for example, the behavior of the vertically integrated incumbent amounts to a 'zero quota' on foreign providers of energy supply services. However, it seems quite unlikely that the WTO dispute settlement bodies will find a violation of market access commitments in such circumstances.[78]

With regard to Article XVII GATS, it would need to be demonstrated that *overall*, foreign services or service suppliers are accorded less favorable treatment than like domestic services or like service suppliers. If the incumbent monopoly supplier abuses its position vis-à-vis both foreign and domestic service suppliers, this would arguably not amount to a case of *de jure* or *de facto* discrimination. Therefore, anti-competitive conduct such as denial of network access or cross-subsidization is only captured by Article VIII GATS if it disproportionately affects foreign service suppliers.

Based on the foregoing considerations, it becomes evident that the scope of the competition provisions in Article VIII GATS is very limited in practice,[79] and that

---

[76]See Sects. 4.5.1, 4.5.3, and 4.6.2.2.

[77]Bigdeli and Rechsteiner (n 51) [28].

[78]But see Zdouc (n 51) 269–270 (who writes that if the monopoly supplier 'boycotts suppliers with which it competes outside the scope of its monopoly rights from the supply of the monopolised services', it is 'likely' that this *de facto* undermines market access commitments within the meaning of Article XVI GATS).

[79]See also WTO (n 10) 63 ('very basic rules on competition').

they do not place an obligation on WTO Members to implement unbundling measures.[80]

6.3.2 Article IX GATS

Apart from Article VIII, Article IX GATS ('Business Practices') also relates to anti-competitive business conduct. Article IX has a broad scope of application, covering all business practices of service suppliers which may restrain competition and thereby restrict trade in services and which do not fall under Article VIII GATS. However, the provision contains only soft information-sharing and consultation duties.[81] Therefore, while Article IX GATS fully covers discriminatory network access practices which result from vertical integration, it does not provide a satisfactory solution.

6.3.3 Article XVII GATT

In the area of trade in goods, Article XVII GATT ('State Trading Enterprises') has a (limited) competition dimension and could thus be relevant in the present context. In particular, Article XVII:1 GATT imposes substantive obligations on WTO Members with respect to State enterprises and enterprises with exclusive or special privileges. WTO Members must ensure that such State trading enterprises (STEs) act, in their purchases or sales involving either imports or exports, 'in a manner consistent with the general principles of non-discriminatory treatment prescribed [in the GATT] for governmental measures affecting imports or exports by private traders' (Article XVII:1(a) GATT).[82] The provision further clarifies that this non-discrimination obligation shall be interpreted to require that STEs 'shall, having due regard to the other provisions of [the GATT], make any such purchases or sales solely in accordance with commercial considerations, including price, quality, availability, marketability, transportation and other conditions of purchase or sale, and shall afford the enterprises of the other contracting parties adequate opportunity, in accordance with customary business practice, to compete for participation in such

[80]See also David Luff, 'Current International Trade Rules Relevant to Telecommunications Services' in Damien Geradin and David Luff (eds), *The WTO and Global Convergence in Telecommunications and Audio-Visual Services* (Cambridge University Press 2004) 42 (who, in a discussion on telecommunications services, states that Article VIII GATS 'would not by itself mandate positive regulation by governments such as ... accounts separation or vertical divestiture').

[81]For a general overview, see Bigdeli and Burri Nenova (n 68).

[82]Article XVII:1(a) GATT (n 32).

purchases or sales' (Article XVII:1(b) GATT).[83] In *Canada – Wheat Exports and Grain Imports*, the Appellate Body explained that the thrust of Article XVII:1 GATT as an '"anti-circumvention" provision' is to ensure that WTO Members cannot, through State trading enterprises, undertake or facilitate conduct that would be considered discriminatory under the GATT if such conduct were carried out directly by the Member itself.[84]

Based on the considerations discussed below, it will become clear that Article XVII GATT has only a limited ability to ensure that vertically integrated energy undertakings provide non-discriminatory network access for energy products from third countries or, more specifically, that they implement unbundling measures to achieve this end.

First of all, not all vertically integrated undertakings will qualify as State enterprises or enterprises with exclusive or special privileges within the meaning of Article XVII GATT. While wholly or predominantly State-owned or State-controlled companies are automatically covered by the provision,[85] the same does not apply to private entities. Here it is necessary to show that 'exclusive or special privileges' have been granted. Selivanova argues that 'rights or privileges can be considered exclusive or special if they enable the enterprise to *influence trade flows*.'[86] On that basis, she concludes that the mere fact of having 'control over a transportation network' is sufficient to meet the definition of 'exclusive or special privileges'.[87] However, it seems that this interpretation is incorrect. The ability to 'influence ... the level or direction of imports or exports', to which Selivanova refers, is mentioned in the 'working definition' of STEs provided in the Understanding on the Interpretation of Article XVII of the General Agreement on Tariffs and Trade 1994. However, the working definition in the 1994 Understanding was included for notification purposes only and is thus 'without prejudice' to the substantive obligations in Article XVII GATT.[88] Furthermore, even under the 1994 Understanding, the ability to 'influence ... the level or direction of imports or exports' is only a necessary, but not a sufficient, condition to qualify as a STE.

---

[83] Ibid, Article XVII:1(b).

[84] WTO, *Canada – Measures Relating to Exports of Wheat and Treatment of Imported Grain*, Report of the Appellate Body (30 August 2004) WT/DS276/AB/R [85].

[85] See Tania Voon, 'Article XVII GATT' in Rüdiger Wolfrum, Peter-Tobias Stoll and Holger Hestermeyer (eds), *WTO – Trade in Goods* (Max Planck Commentaries on World Trade Law vol 5. Martinus Nijhoff Publishers 2011) [4].

[86] Yulia Selivanova, *Energy Dual Pricing in the WTO: Analysis and Prospects in the Context of Russia's Accession to the World Trade Organization* (Cameron May 2008) 100 (emphasis added). See also Selivanova (n 56) 291.

[87] Selivanova (n 56) 291–292; Selivanova (n 20) 19.

[88] See also Ernst-Ulrich Petersmann, 'GATT Law on State Trading Enterprises: Critical Evaluation of Article XVII and Proposals for Reform' in Thomas Cottier and Petros C Mavroidis (eds), *State Trading in the Twenty-First Century* (University of Michigan Press 1998) 80, 92–93 (who explicitly notes that the requirement that STEs influence the level or direction of trade through purchases or sales is not contained in Article XVII:1(a) GATT).

The granting of exclusive or special privileges is still required.[89] Therefore, a vertically integrated energy undertaking that has control over a country's transmission network cannot be considered a State trading enterprise just because its network-related activities affect imports and exports of electricity or gas. In my view, some level of facilitating State action is needed in order for a natural monopoly situation to fall under Article XVII GATT. Any other interpretation would render superfluous the requirement of a WTO Member having '*grant[ed]* to any enterprise, formally or in effect, exclusive or special privileges.'[90] The requirement of government involvement is thus a shared feature of both Article VIII GATS and Article XVII GATT.[91] This interpretation of Article XVII GATT is also supported by the writings of other authors, who have argued that situations of control over bottleneck or essential facilities should not be dealt with under Article XVII GATT but under 'generally applicable national competition policy rules.'[92]

Thus only a subset of all private vertically integrated energy undertakings fall within the scope of application of Article XVII GATT. For example, this would include VIUs that have (1) a legal monopoly or exclusive rights to buy energy from generators and to distribute and sell this energy to end users; and/or (2) a legal monopoly or exclusive rights to import/export energy.[93] Examples of the second category would include the French companies Gaz de France and Électricité de France, which for a long time had a monopoly on the import and export of natural gas and electricity.[94] Exclusive or special privileges would also exist where the vertically integrated undertaking is given an exclusive license to operate a country's national transmission system.[95]

[89]The working definition reads in full: 'Governmental and non-governmental enterprises, including marketing boards, which have been granted exclusive or special rights or privileges, including statutory or constitutional powers, in the exercise of which they influence through their purchases or sales the level or direction of imports or exports.'

[90]Emphasis added.

[91]See above Sect. 6.3.1.

[92]Bernard Hoekman and Patrick Low, 'State Trading: Rule Making Alternatives for Entities with Exclusive Rights' in Thomas Cottier and Petros C Mavroidis (eds), *State Trading in the Twenty-First Century* (University of Michigan Press 1998) 328–329, 341.

[93]Andras Lakatos, 'Overview of the Regulatory Environment for Trade in Electricity' in Janusz Bielecki and Melaku G Desta (eds), *Electricity Trade in Europe – Review of the Economic and Regulatory Changes* (Kluwer Law International 2004) 131. See also Energy Charter Secretariat, 'Trade in Energy – WTO Rules Applying under the Energy Charter Treaty' (2001) [148] <http://www.energycharter.org/fileadmin/DocumentsMedia/Thematic/WTO_Rules_applying_to_the_ECT_2002_en.pdf> accessed 13 May 2016.

[94]Both companies were notified as State trading enterprises within the meaning of Article XVII GATT, see WTO, Working Party on State Trading Enterprises, New and Full Notification Pursuant to Article XVII:4(a) of the GATT 1994 and Paragraph 1 of the Understanding on the Interpretation of Article XVII – European Communities (26 February 1999) G/STR/N/4/EEC, 2–3.

[95]Lakatos (n 93) 132 ('territorial franchise rights'); Energy Charter Secretariat, 'Trade in Energy – WTO Rules Applying under the Energy Charter Treaty' (n 93) [148].

The second factor limiting the effectiveness of Article XVII GATT in the present context relates to the substantive obligations contained in that provision. The language in Article XVII:1(b) GATT which provides that State trading enterprises shall make purchases or sales involving either imports or exports solely in accordance with 'commercial considerations' and that they shall afford 'adequate opportunity' to compete for participation in such purchases or sales does not constitute an independent, self-standing obligation. This was clarified by the Appellate Body in *Canada – Wheat Exports and Grain Imports*.[96] According to the AB, the main obligation of the provision on State trading enterprises is contained in Article XVII:1 (a) GATT, namely to act in a manner consistent with the 'general principles of non-discriminatory treatment' prescribed in the GATT. Subparagraph (b) merely serves to clarify the scope of subparagraph (a). Thus if a State trading enterprise offers to buy electricity or gas from foreign companies at an unreasonable price, thereby essentially foreclosing access to its transmission networks, it cannot be argued that, in doing so, the State trading enterprise failed to afford 'adequate opportunity' to compete for participation in that purchase or failed to act 'commercially' in a broad sense and that this gives rise to a violation of Article XVII:1 (b) GATT.[97] In fact, the Appellate Body emphasized in *Canada – Wheat Exports and Grain Imports* that the language in Article XVII:1(b) GATT cannot be read 'as imposing comprehensive competition-law-type obligations on STEs', as had been advocated by the United States in that dispute.[98]

Third, and most importantly, it is unclear whether the reference to the 'general principles of non-discriminatory treatment' in Article XVII:1(a) GATT relates only to MFN or also to national treatment. The GATT/WTO dispute settlement practice is divided on this point[99] and some eminent authors defend the view that, based on the negotiating history of Article XVII GATT,[100] the provision only implies a prohibition against discrimination between products of other countries on the basis of their origin, but not a national treatment obligation.[101] It is quite evident that if the vertically integrated undertaking controlling the transmission networks is only

[96] *Canada – Measures Relating to Exports of Wheat and Treatment of Imported Grain* (n 84) [100, 106].

[97] See on this also Selivanova (n 56) 292.

[98] *Canada – Measures Relating to Exports of Wheat and Treatment of Imported Grain* (n 84) [145].

[99] In favor of interpreting Article XVII GATT as covering also the national treatment obligation: WTO, *Korea – Measures Affecting Imports of Fresh, Chilled and Frozen Beef,* Report of the Panel (31 July 2000) WT/DS161/R, WT/DS169/R [753]. Contra: GATT, *Canada – Administration of the Foreign Investment Review Act,* Panel Report (7 February 1984) [5.16].

[100] See e.g. GATT, Article XVII (State Trading Enterprises) – Note by the Secretariat (11 August 1987) MTN.GNG/NG7/W/15, [20].

[101] John H Jackson, *The World Trading System: Law and Policy of International Economic Relations* (MIT Press 1991) 284 (cited by Mattoo (n 50) 39–40); Selivanova (n 56) 292–293; Vitaliy Pogoretskyy, 'Energy Dual Pricing in International Trade: Subsidies and Anti-dumping Perspectives' in Yulia Selivanova (ed), *Regulation of Energy in International Trade Law: WTO, NAFTA and Energy Charter* (Kluwer Law International 2012) 197–198.

required to provide MFN treatment, this would hardly be of any value, given that the TSO could deny network access to all foreign energy products.[102]

In my view, the general obligation on STEs to undertake their activities in accordance with the 'general principles of non-discriminatory treatment' prescribed in the GATT does not include the provisions of Article III GATT. The reason for this is quite straightforward. According to the text of Article XVII GATT, a State trading enterprise must act in a manner consistent with the general principles of non-discrimination only 'in its purchases or sales involving either imports or exports.' Considering the ordinary meaning of this phrase, it is clear that there is no obligation to actually import or export energy products. Consequently, only if the STE decides to trade in foreign goods must it respect the general principles referred to in Article XVII GATT. In contrast, there is no such obligation with respect to purchases or sales involving neither imports nor exports, i.e. domestic purchases/ sales. This strongly supports the view that Article XVII GATT only requires MFN and not national treatment.[103] Therefore, even if a vertically integrated energy company qualifies as a State trading enterprise within the meaning of Article XVII GATT, it is not required to grant any particular form of access to the gas or electricity transmission networks that it controls.

All in all, the potential of Article XVII GATT to ensure that vertically integrated energy undertakings provide non-discriminatory network access to foreign energy goods is very limited.[104] It does not require any unbundling of VIUs.

6.4 A Reference Paper for Energy Services Within the WTO Framework

It has been shown in the previous section that the reach of existing competition-related provisions in the GATS and the GATT is extremely limited. As it stands, general WTO law does not effectively address the anti-competitive potential stemming from vertical integration. Therefore, this section will discuss the possibility and desirability of additional pro-competitive disciplines on energy services at the multilateral level. To this end, it will be useful to first describe existing regulatory approaches and initiatives in the telecommunications and tourism sectors. In both of these sectors WTO Members have felt the need to push for additional rules within the framework of the WTO in order to deal with network access issues and/or anti-competitive practices directly linked to natural monopolies or *de facto* monopoly

[102]See Selivanova (n 56) 293.

[103]The same argument is also mentioned by Pogoretskyy (n 101) 197.

[104]See also Energy Services – Background Note by the Secretariat (n 8) [37] (stating that the 'cross-border trade of energy goods encounters obstacles ... such as vertical foreclosure of transmission and distribution networks in the destination country' and that this type of obstacles 'falls out of the scope of WTO agreements').

situations and, specifically, vertical integration. In a second step, bilateral and regional agreements that contain provisions in this regard will be examined. On that basis, it will be shown that there are several options to impose constraints upon the operations of vertically integrated undertakings in a future 'Energy Reference Paper'.

6.4.1 *Experience in the Telecommunications Sector*

In the years preceding the adoption of the GATS, the national telecommunications markets were liberalized and privatized on a worldwide level.[105] In many cases former monopoly suppliers retained their dominant position in the sector. Therefore, apart from 'locking-in' existing autonomous liberalization measures and achieving additional liberalization commitments, the multilateral trade negotiations on telecommunications services faced the challenge of developing safeguards against anti-competitive practices by incumbent network operators. Both the Annex on Telecommunications[106] and the Reference Paper on Basic Telecommunications Services,[107] which will be described below, reflect the concern that abuses of market power by dominant market players could undermine the value of market access and national treatment commitments in both the telecommunications and other services sectors.[108] The creation of provisions which would supplement and strengthen the rather weak disciplines found in Articles VIII and IX GATS was considered to be a particularly vital task due to the 'dual role' of the telecommunications sector: First, it is an important economic sector of its own. Second, telecommunications services provide the underlying means of transport for many other economic activities, such as banking and insurance.[109]

6.4.1.1 The Annex on Telecommunications

The Annex on Telecommunications, which was agreed upon during the Uruguay Round and which forms an integral part of the GATS in accordance with Article XXIX thereof, is the first instrument which includes additional regulatory provisions tailored to the specificities of the telecommunications sector. It is not concerned with

---

[105] Juliane Hernekamp, '§ 21 Ausgewählte Dienstleistungssektoren' in Meinhard Hilf and Stefan Oeter (eds), *WTO-Recht: Rechtsordnung des Welthandels* (2nd edn. Nomos 2010) [18].

[106] Annex on Telecommunications (15 April 1994) 33 I.L.M. 1192 (1994).

[107] Reference Paper on Basic Telecommunications Services (24 April 1996) 36 I.L.M. 367 (1997).

[108] For the Annex on Telecommunications, see Lee Tuthill, 'Users' Rights? The Multilateral Rules on Access to Telecommunications' (1996) 20 Telecommunications Policy 89, 90–91.

[109] Annex on Telecommunications (n 106), Section 1.

the liberalization of telecommunications services,[110] which is the subject of the services schedules, but aims to ensure fair access for suppliers of the liberalized services to public telecommunications transport networks and services. The Annex has a broad scope of application, covering 'all measures of a Member that affect access to and use of public telecommunications transport networks and services.'[111] Given that this phrase is not in any way limited to certain categories of services or service suppliers, *all* services and service suppliers, including value-added and basic telecommunications services as well as any other services, can in principle benefit from the provisions of the Annex.[112] Moreover, the definitions provided for 'public telecommunications transport service' and 'public telecommunications transport network' clarify that the term 'public' does not imply public ownership, but rather refers to the existence of some kind of universal service obligation.[113]

In substantive terms, the core obligation of the Annex on Telecommunications is found in Section 5(a). This provision stipulates that each WTO Member 'shall ensure that any service supplier of any other Member is accorded access to and use of public telecommunications transport networks and services on reasonable and non-discriminatory terms and conditions, for the supply of a service included in its Schedule.' The term 'non-discriminatory' is further defined in a footnote to the Annex. The footnote specifies that, apart from referring to the MFN and NT principles as set out in Articles XVI and XVII GATS, the term also has a sector-specific meaning in that it requires terms and conditions to be 'no less favourable than those accorded to any other user of like public telecommunications transport networks or services under like circumstances.' The general obligation in Section 5 (a) is complemented by a number of more specific provisions (lit (b)–(g)), which spell out in more detail what the 'reasonable and non-discriminatory access and use' principle entails in practice.

Before comparing to what extent the obligations contained in the Annex on Telecommunications go beyond the rules on competition in Article VIII:2 GATS, their somewhat different regulatory perspectives should first be examined. Article VIII:2 GATS envisages a situation where a service supplier which has monopoly or exclusive rights in one market also becomes active in another market, outside the

---

[110]See ibid, Sections 2(c)(i) and 5(e)(iii).

[111]Ibid, Section 2(a).

[112]In the *Mexico – Telecoms* case, Mexico had argued that 'the Annex applies only to access to and use of public telecommunications transport networks and services as a *transport* means for other economic activities, and not to the supply of basic telecommunications services *per se*'. However, this contention was rejected by the Panel, see *Mexico – Measures Affecting Telecommunications Services* (n 37) [7.274ff].

[113]Annex on Telecommunications (n 106), Section 3(b) and (c); Tuthill (n 108) 95; Bobjoseph Mathew, *The WTO Agreements on Telecommunications* (Studies in Global Economic Law vol 6, Peter Lang 2003) 89. The term 'public telecommunications transport service' (lit (b)) is defined as 'any telecommunications transport service required, explicitly or in effect, by a Member *to be offered to the public generally*' (emphasis added). A 'public telecommunications transport network' (lit (a)) is defined as 'the public telecommunications infrastructure which permits telecommunications between and among defined network termination points'.

scope of its monopoly rights, where it competes with other service suppliers. In contrast, the Annex on Telecommunications addresses the reverse situation, where the provider of a service, which is supplied on a competitive basis, seeks access to certain transport networks or services which are indispensable for the supply of that service (an 'essential facility').[114] Furthermore, while Article VIII:2 GATS invariably requires the existence of competition between the monopoly service supplier and other service providers in the liberalized sector, the Annex contemplates economic relations which do not necessarily involve a competitive relationship. Its focus is on the *users* of telecommunications services.[115] Many of these users (such as banking or insurance companies) will not in any way be competing with the operators of public telecommunications transport networks and services. However, the group of users may also include competing suppliers of telecommunications services. For this sub-set of companies, which likewise benefit from the guarantees of reasonable and non-discriminatory access and use, the Annex constitutes a pro-competitive instrument.[116]

With regard to its substantive obligations, the Annex on Telecommunications clearly goes beyond what Article VIII:2 GATS requires. A number of points can be mentioned here. First of all, from the perspective of ensuring non-discriminatory network access, the Annex directly tackles the issue by dealing with 'access to and use of public telecommunications transport networks and services.' Under Article VIII:2 GATS, in contrast, the positive effects with respect to network access (if any) are only an indirect result of the fact that monopoly and exclusive service suppliers must not act inconsistently with national treatment and market access commitments in the liberalized sectors. Second, whereas Article VIII:2 GATS only covers monopoly and exclusive service suppliers as defined in the agreement, and thereby presupposes both a specific market structure (a monopoly or non-competing oligopoly) and a certain degree of facilitating government action, the Annex applies irrespective of whether the relevant telecommunications market of a WTO Member is monopolistic, oligopolistic or fully competitive.[117] Third, whereas the application of Article VIII:2 GATS completely depends on the existence and scope of specific commitments in the liberalized sector, the Annex guarantees access to, and use of, public telecommunications transport networks or services on reasonable and non-discriminatory terms and conditions, even if the WTO Member concerned has not undertaken a national treatment commitment with respect to the particular service at issue.[118] The only two requirements are that the service be 'included' in

[114] Zdouc (n 51) 284–285.

[115] Tuthill (n 108) 89.

[116] See Patrick Low and Aaditya Mattoo, 'Reform in Basic Telecommunications and the WTO Negotiations: The Asian Experience' (Staff Working Paper 1997) 7 <https://www.wto.org/english/res_e/reser_e/pera9801.pdf> accessed 18 July 2016.

It is this 'pro-competitive' dimension of the Annex on Telecommunications which is particularly relevant for the problem of vertical integration in the energy sector.

[117] Mattoo (n 50) 55; Zdouc (n 51) 282–283.

[118] Tuthill (n 108) 92; Mattoo (n 50) 55–56; Zdouc (n 51) 284–285.

the country-specific schedule (i.e. the WTO Member must have made commitments in the service *sector* concerned)[119] and that foreign service suppliers are permitted to supply the service pursuant to (market access) commitments in the Member's schedule.[120] If these two conditions are met, the obligations of the Annex apply in full. Fourth, unlike Article VIII:2 GATS, the Annex on Telecommunications contains its own, sector-specific non-discrimination disciplines, which do not require services and service suppliers to be 'like' (as is the case with Article XVII GATS),[121] and establishes the principle of 'reasonable' terms and conditions, which creates obligations going beyond the requirement of non-discrimination.[122]

To the extent that the Annex on Telecommunications benefits users of telecom services which are, at the same time, also competitors of the incumbent supplier of public telecommunications transport networks and services, the Annex (indirectly) establishes a 'third party access' regime like in the energy sector. However, inasmuch as the Annex belongs to the category of 'behavioral' policies, the obligations in the Annex fail to require any vertical separation and thus do not tackle the discriminatory incentives resulting from vertical integration.

6.4.1.2 The Reference Paper on Basic Telecommunications Services

The second instrument which establishes additional regulatory rules for the telecommunications sector is the 'Reference Paper on Basic Telecommunications Services.'[123] The Reference Paper is the result of prolonged post-Uruguay Round negotiations on basic telecommunications,[124] which were finally concluded on 15 February 1997, i.e. almost 3 years after the signing of the Marrakesh agreement establishing the WTO, and which culminated in the adoption of the 'Fourth Protocol to the GATS'. In addition to (improved) national treatment and market access commitments on basic telecommunications services, which were annexed to the Fourth Protocol and subsequently integrated into the country-specific schedules of specific commitments, fifty-seven out of the sixty-nine countries taking part in the negotiations agreed to adopt the Reference Paper, either in its entirety or with only minor modifications, as an additional commitment according to Article XVIII

[119]Henry Gao, 'Annex on Telecommunications' in Rüdiger Wolfrum, Peter-Tobias Stoll and Clemens Feinäugle (eds), *WTO – Trade in Services* (Max Planck Commentaries on World Trade Law vol 6. Martinus Nijhoff Publishers 2008) [30, 32].

[120]*Cf.* Annex on Telecommunications (n 106), Section 5(e)(iii).

[121]This is highlighted by Gao (n 119) [37]. It must, however, be kept in mind that there are two novel likeness requirements: 'like public telecommunications transport networks or services' and 'like circumstances'. Depending on how these likeness criteria are interpreted, the sector-specific non-discrimination disciplines could lose much of their practical value.

[122]*Mexico – Measures Affecting Telecommunications Services* (n 37) [7.330].

[123]Reference Paper on Basic Telecommunications Services (n 107).

[124]See WTO, Decision on Negotiations on Basic Telecommunications (15 April 1994) LT/UR/D-5/4.

GATS. Following an 'à la carte' approach, six participating governments decided to 'pick and choose' certain parts of the Reference Paper or to incorporate their own language. Another six declined to accept the additional commitments on regulation.[125] As of today, at least 82 WTO Members have committed to abide by the regulatory principles contained in the Reference Paper.[126]

The rationale behind the negotiation of the Reference Paper can be explained as follows. For a long time, the basic telecommunications sector was in many countries subject to a public monopoly.[127] Thus, only one or a small number of operators had the exclusive right to supply basic telecommunications services. In the mid-1990s, as alluded to above, many WTO Members entered into national treatment and market access commitments under the Fourth Protocol to the GATS. However, there was a general concern that the national treatment and market access commitments would themselves be insufficient to ensure genuine liberalization of telecom services. The reason for this concern was that even after the legal, formal liberalization of the basic telecommunications sector, former monopoly operators would, by and large, continue to have a dominant position in the market. In particular, they would still be in a position to control the essential telecommunications network facilities.[128] At the same time, new market entrants crucially depended on access to these essential facilities, which for economic and/or technical reasons cannot be easily duplicated.[129] It was against this background that many WTO Members decided to draft the Reference Paper in order to establish a pro-competitive regulatory framework designed to prevent private anti-competitive practices by dominant market players.[130] The considerations leading to the negotiation of the Reference Paper thus fully correspond to the rationale behind the adoption of third party access and unbundling legislation in formally liberalized energy markets.

The Reference Paper on Basic Telecommunications Services is made up of six sections. They relate to (1) competitive safeguards; (2) interconnection; (3) universal service obligations; (4) public availability of licensing criteria; (5) independent regulators; and (6) allocation and use of scarce resources. While the last four sections address issues of a general regulatory nature, the first two directly govern the behavior of 'major suppliers'. Given the focus of this book, the following analysis will concentrate on the rules regarding competitive safeguards and interconnection. First of all, however, some necessary definitions must be provided. For the purposes

[125]Tuthill (n 74) 786.

[126]WTO, 'Telecommunications Services' (no date) <https://www.wto.org/english/tratop_e/serv_e/telecom_e/telecom_e.htm> accessed 11 December 2015.

[127]Marco C Bronckers and Pierre Larouche, 'Telecommunications Services and the World Trade Organization' (1997) 31 Journal of World Trade 5, 23.

[128]Mattoo (n 50) 56.

[129]Henry Gao, 'Telecommunications Services: Reference Paper' in Rüdiger Wolfrum, Peter-Tobias Stoll and Clemens Feinäugle (eds), *WTO – Trade in Services* (Max Planck Commentaries on World Trade Law vol 6. Martinus Nijhoff Publishers 2008) [1].

[130]For an examination of the 'object and purpose' of the Reference Paper, see *Mexico – Measures Affecting Telecommunications Services* (n 37) [7.237].

of the Reference Paper, a 'major supplier' is defined as a supplier 'which has the ability to materially affect the terms of participation (having regard to price and supply) in the relevant market for basic telecommunications services as a result of: (a) control over essential facilities; or (b) use of its position in the market.' The term 'essential facilities', in turn, denotes 'facilities of a public telecommunications transport network or service that (a) are exclusively or predominantly provided by a single or limited number of suppliers; and (b) cannot feasibly be economically or technically substituted in order to provide a service.' It is important to note that according to the definitions provided above, and in contrast to Article VIII:2 GATS, facilitating action on the part of a government is not required for a supplier to qualify as a 'major supplier'.

Section 1 of the Reference Paper deals with competitive safeguards. It enunciates the general rule that '[a]ppropriate measures shall be maintained for the purpose of preventing suppliers who, alone or together, are a major supplier from engaging in or continuing anti-competitive practices' (paragraph 1 of Section 1). Although the phrase 'anti-competitive practices' is not defined in the text, paragraph 2 of Section 1 lists three examples of such practices: (1) anti-competitive cross-subsidization (lit (a)); (2) use of information obtained from competitors with anti-competitive results (lit (b)); and (3) failure to make available to other service suppliers technical information about essential facilities and commercially relevant information which are necessary for them to provide services (lit (c)). As the list is preceded by the words 'shall include in particular', it is not exhaustive and thus does not cover all 'anti-competitive practices' that come within the ambit of the general obligation in Section 1(1).[131]

It is worthwhile examining the first two examples of 'anti-competitive practices' listed in Section 1(2). The first example is anti-competitive cross-subsidization. 'Cross-subsidization' refers to the practice of subsidizing a loss-making area of operations with profits made in another, profit-making area.[132] It is important to note that the language of Section 1(2) does not speak of cross-subsidization *per se*, but rather of *anti-competitive* cross-subsidization. While there are therefore certain forms of permissible cross-subsidization, a good case could be made that such practices become anti-competitive if the major supplier at issue has a dominant position in the profit-making industry.[133] However, the fact that the Reference Paper does not provide any guidance on how to identify cross-subsidization that is detrimental to competition is likely to have a negative impact on the effectiveness of this provision.[134]

---

[131]Ibid [7.232].

[132]Gao (n 129) [34].

[133]Bronckers and Larouche (n 127) 27.

[134]Georg Koopmann, 'Competition Policies and Telecommunication Regimes' in Paolo Guerrieri and Hans-Eckart Scharrer (eds), *Trade, Investment and Competition Policies in the Global Economy: The Case of International Telecommunications Regime* (Veröffentlichungen des Hamburgischen Welt-Wirtschafts-Archivs vol 69. Nomos 2002) 383.

Furthermore, the Reference Paper does not spell out the specific measures that must be taken in order to comply with the obligation to combat cross-subsidization (Section 1(1) in conjunction with Section 1(2)(a)). Rather, it leaves the choice of the measures to be adopted to the individual WTO Member. This reflects the general approach of the Reference Paper, which requires a specific result but does not specify the means by which this particular goal must or ought to be achieved.[135] What's more, given that Section 1(1) broadly refers to 'appropriate' measures that shall be maintained for the prevention of anti-competitive practices, a WTO Member is in principle free to adopt either general competition law provisions or sector-specific regulations.[136] Although a good case can be made that the prevention of anti-competitive cross-subsidization requires effective *ex ante* regulation,[137] a WTO Member may therefore also implement *ex post* competition law.[138]

Despite the general lack of specificity of the Reference Paper it is clear that, as regards anti-competitive cross-subsidization, compliance with Section 1 invariably requires the adoption of some kind of regulatory unbundling measures. Indeed, several authors have pointed out that the elimination of anti-competitive cross-subsidization under Section 1 of the Reference Paper necessitates accounting unbundling, or even 'structural separation',[139] which seems to be equivalent at least to legal or functional unbundling in the EU energy context. It is also interesting to note in this connection that the United States' draft proposal for a Reference Paper, which was circulated to the members of the Negotiating Group on Basic Telecommunications in 1995, explicitly referred to accounting and 'structural

[135] Gao (n 129) [2]; Laura B Sherman, '"Wildly Enthusiastic" About the First Multilateral Agreement on Trade in Telecommunications Services' (1998) 51 Federal Communications Law Journal 61, 73.

[136] Mira Burri Nenova, 'The Law of the World Trade Organization and the Communications Law of the European Community: On a Path of Harmony or Discord?' (2007) 41 Journal of World Trade 833, 851; Bronckers and Larouche (n 127) 26–27; Gao (n 129) [27].

[137] Bronckers and Larouche (n 127) 27.

[138] But see Eunike Prokop-Elkettani, 'Internationales und Europäisches Telekommunikationsrecht' in Franz J Säcker (ed), *Berliner Kommentar zum Telekommunikationsgesetz* (2nd edn. Verlag Recht und Wirtschaft 2009) [42] (who argues that Section 1(1) in conjunction with Section 1(2)(a)–(c) establishes *ex ante* regulatory obligations).

[139] Shin-yi Peng, 'Trade in Telecommunications Services: Doha and Beyond' (2007) 41 Journal of World Trade 293, 300; Mathew (n 113) 154; Sherman (n 135) 77; Bronckers and Larouche (n 127) 27–28; Rachel Frid, 'The Telecommunications Pact under the GATS: Another Step Towards the Rule of Law' (1997) 24 Legal Issues of Economic Integration 67, 84–85; Irene Öhlinger, *Internationaler Dienstleistungshandel und Wettbewerbsaspekte: Lösungsansätze im Telekommunikationsbereich* (Verlag Österreich 2001) 254–255; Markus Fredebeul-Krein and Andreas Freytag, 'The Case for a More Binding WTO Agreement on Regulatory Principles in Telecommunication Markets' (1999) 23 Telecommunications Policy 625, 628–629; Damien Geradin and Michel Kerf, 'Levelling the Playing Field: Is the WTO Adequately Equipped to Prevent Anti-Competitive Practices in Telecommunications?' in Damien Geradin and David Luff (eds), *The WTO and Global Convergence in Telecommunications and Audio-Visual Services* (Cambridge University Press 2004) 149.

separation' policies.[140] That the final text of the Reference Paper does not include such a reference to unbundling measures seems to be mainly due to the fact that it would have been contrary to the 'idea of establishing broad principles'.[141]

The importance of unbundling measures for the effective prevention of anti-competitive cross-subsidization is also highlighted by developments in the area of preferential trade agreements. The Canada-US FTA (1988, which was superseded by NAFTA),[142] NAFTA (1992),[143] the Canada-Chile FTA (1996),[144] the Panama-Taiwan FTA (2003)[145] and the Korea-Chile FTA (2003)[146] all mention accounting requirements and requirements for 'structural separation' as appropriate means to combat anti-competitive conduct in the telecommunications sector. However, as already alluded to above, the Reference Paper fails to prescribe even a minimal level of unbundling, such as accounting unbundling. This can be seen as one of its main weaknesses.[147]

The second example in Section 1(2) of anti-competitive practices is the 'use of information from competitors with anti-competitive results.' Where a major supplier controls bottleneck facilities such as telecom networks, service suppliers seeking access to such infrastructure will have to provide certain commercially sensitive information to the major supplier in order to be able to supply their services.[148] This information can then be used by the major supplier to gain a competitive advantage over those service suppliers. By way of example, if a national telecom operator supplies leased lines to data communications providers and, at the same time,

---

[140]WTO, Negotiating Group on Basic Telecommunications, Communication from the United States: Draft Offer on Basic Telecommunications (31 July 1995) S/NGBT/W/12/Add.3, 5. The draft proposal stated that '[a] dominant local exchange carrier with annual revenues in excess of a minimum level defined by the regulatory authority will adopt structural separation or cost accounting safeguards to prevent the allocation of costs of non-regulated services to regulated services'. See also WTO, Negotiating Group on Basic Telecommunications, Communication from the United States: Draft Offer on Basic Telecommunications – Revision (26 February 1996) S/NGBT/W/12/Add.3/Rev.1, 6; WTO, Negotiating Group on Basic Telecommunications, Communication from the United States: Pro-competitive Regulatory and other Measures for Effective Market Access in Basic Telecommunications Services (09 February 1995) S/NGBT/W/5, 2–3.

[141]Sherman (n 135) 76–77.

[142]Canada – United States Free Trade Agreement (02 January 1988) 27 I.L.M. 281 (1989), Annex 1404 to Chapter 14, Sectoral Annex on Computer Services and Telecommunications-Network-Based Enhanced Services, Article 5(2).

[143]North American Free Trade Agreement (17 December 1992) 32 I.L.M. 289 (1993), Article 1305 (2).

[144]Canada – Chile Free Trade Agreement (05 December 1996) <http://www.sice.oas.org/trade/chican_e/chcatoc.asp> accessed 20 January 2018, Chapter I (Telecommunications), Article I-05 (2).

[145]Panama – Taiwan Free Trade Agreement (21 August 2003) <http://www.sice.oas.org/trade/panrc/panrc_e.asp> accessed 20 January 2018, Article 13.06(2).

[146]Chile – Korea Free Trade Agreement (15 February 2003) <http://www.sice.oas.org/trade/chiskorea_e/chikoreaind_e.asp> accessed 20 January 2018, Article 12.6(2).

[147]Fredebeul-Krein and Freytag (n 139) 628–629, 641.

[148]Gao (n 129) [35].

provides data communications services in competition with those providers, the 'network division' of the operator will have a strong incentive to pass on valuable competitor information to the 'data communications division' of the operator.[149]

There are compelling arguments that preventing the misuse of competitor information, as required by Section 1(1) in conjunction with Section 1(2)(b) of the Reference Paper, also entails the implementation of some form of regulatory unbundling. Although the mere unbundling of accounts would not help protect proprietary information, various academic commentators have called for the introduction of a 'legal separation of business divisions operating in different markets.'[150] However, as with cross-subsidization, the Reference Paper fails to mention unbundling measures as a possible means to achieve the objective of combating the misuse of competitor information. It also does not specify which kinds of rules are to be adopted in this regard (*ex ante* regulation or *ex post* competition law).[151]

Section 2 of the Reference Paper deals with interconnection. Supplementing Section 5 of the Annex on Telecommunications,[152] it obliges major suppliers of public telecommunications transport networks or services to interconnect providers of basic telecom services with their networks and services (Section 2(2)), to the extent that corresponding commitments have been undertaken by the respective WTO Member.[153] The term 'interconnection' is broadly defined in Section 2(1) as the 'linking with suppliers providing public telecommunications transport networks or services in order to allow the users of one supplier to communicate with users of another supplier and to access services provided by another supplier.'[154] The use of the words 'linking *with* suppliers' instead of 'linking *of* suppliers' emphasizes that the interconnection obligation guarantees access to the networks or services necessary to provide services.[155]

Section 2(2) further specifies that interconnection must be provided at any technically feasible point in the network and in a timely fashion. The terms, conditions, and rates of such interconnection must be non-discriminatory, transparent, and reasonable. The major supplier is also under an obligation to ensure that the quality of interconnection is no less favorable than that provided to its own like services or to like services of non-affiliated service suppliers or to its subsidiaries or other affiliates. Furthermore, the interconnection must be 'sufficiently unbundled so

[149]Bronckers and Larouche (n 127) 27–28.

[150]Bronckers and Larouche (n 127) 27–28; Mathew (n 113) 156. See also Prokop-Elkettani (n 138) [122].

[151]But see Prokop-Elkettani (n 138) [122] (stating that the nature of the obligation is such that the establishment of a 'firewall' between the respective divisions of the company is the 'only measure' which can ensure compliance with it).

[152]On the 'residual importance' of the Annex on Telecommunications in comparison with the Reference Paper, see Bronckers and Larouche (n 127) 32f.

[153]Gao (n 129) [42].

[154]See *Mexico – Measures Affecting Telecommunications Services* (n 37) [7.102].

[155]Sherman (n 135) 78; Mathew (n 113) 159.

that the supplier need not pay for network components or facilities that it does not require for the service to be provided.'[156] Finally, there is a requirement that interconnection rates must be 'cost-oriented'.[157]

With a view to enhancing the transparency of interconnection arrangements, Section 2(4) further stipulates that major suppliers have to publicize a reference interconnection offer. Moreover, Section 2(5) provides that interconnection-seeking service providers may initiate dispute settlement proceedings before an independent domestic body.

The provisions contained in Sections 1 and 2 of the Reference Paper have already been applied by the WTO dispute settlement bodies. In the *Mexico – Telecoms* case, the Panel found that Mexico maintained measures which legally required Telmex, the dominant telecommunications company in Mexico, to engage in practices which amounted, in effect, to a price-fixing cartel and a market sharing arrangement, and thus violated its obligation to prevent such anti-competitive practices under Section 1(1) of the Reference Paper.[158] Furthermore, the Panel held that Mexico was in breach of its commitments under Section 2(2) of the Reference Paper, because the interconnection rates charged by Telmex to US service suppliers were not cost-oriented within the meaning of the provision, as they were 'substantially higher' than the costs actually incurred in providing the interconnection.[159]

The *Mexico – Telecoms* ruling was hailed as the WTO's 'first antitrust case'[160] which would 'give[] life'[161] to the disciplines in the Reference Paper and which would demonstrate that the WTO is 'able to adopt competition-relevant measures and to engage in competition-related work with material results.'[162,163]

In conclusion, the interconnection obligation in Section 2 of the Reference Paper establishes a 'third party access' regime for suppliers of basic telecom services. While clearly contributing to enhanced non-discriminatory network access, it constitutes a classic example of behavioral policies[164] and thus falls short of removing the *incentive* of major suppliers to discriminate against competitors. The obligation to prevent anti-competitive practices in Section 1 of the Reference Paper directly

[156]In this context, the term 'unbundling' does not refer to the vertical separation of different activities within vertically integrated undertakings.

[157]In *Mexico – Telecoms*, the Panel held that the term 'cost-oriented' would refer to the 'costs incurred in supplying the service' (*Mexico – Measures Affecting Telecommunications Services* (n 37) [7.177]).

[158]Ibid [7.262, 7.264, 7.269].

[159]Ibid [7.216].

[160]Eleanor M Fox, 'The WTO's First Antitrust Case – Mexican Telecom: A Sleeping Victory for Trade and Competition' (2006) 9 Journal of International Economic Law 271, 271.

[161]Ibid 292.

[162]Dabbah (n 11) 616.

[163]For a more critical account of the *Mexico – Telecoms* case, see Damien J Neven and Petros C Mavroidis, 'El mess in TELMEX: A Comment on Mexico – Measures Affecting Telecommunications Services' (2006) 5 World Trade Review 271.

[164]Koopmann (n 134) 382.

deals with certain forms of anti-competitive behavior typically resulting from vertical integration (anti-competitive cross-subsidization; misuse of competitor information), but fails to mention, let alone require, unbundling measures in this connection.

6.4.2 Experience in the Tourism Sector

There has also been some discussion about the introduction of sector-specific international regulatory disciplines at the WTO level in the tourism sector. This discussion was closely connected with the adoption of the Reference Paper on Basic Telecommunications Services, which was referred to as a 'precedent'.[165]

The push towards the development of regulatory principles for the tourism sector came from developing countries. Especially after the liberalization of the services trade brought about by the entry into force of the GATS in 1995, the domestic tourism industries of developing countries suffered from anti-competitive practices by foreign, often European, tourism service providers. One of the main problems was that the originating tourism markets were dominated by only a small number of large suppliers and that there was a high level of vertical (and horizontal) integration. Frequently, tour operators in developed countries engaged in vertical integration both up and down the supply chain, i.e. they merged with or acquired airlines and travel agencies.[166] At the time, travel agencies played a vital role in the tourism market, because they acted as the intermediaries between the consumers of tourism services on one hand, and the tourism destinations in developing countries on the other. Only later did this dominant role of the travel agent became less important due to the emergence of the internet as a primary source of information. But prior to the internet, travel agencies were able to exert a great deal of influence on the flow of tourists, which they could direct to specific destinations. For example, a travel agency had the discretion to decide on the selection of brochures it put on display, the so-called 'racking policy'. In order to fully appreciate the importance of the travel agent's display rack at that time, it is interesting to note that it was even described as an 'essential facility', drawing on the terminology used for a bottleneck infrastructure in the energy sector.[167]

Under these circumstances, the effect of vertical integration was at least twofold: First, vertically integrated tourism service providers were in a position to demand larger commissions from destination providers (e.g. local hotels, resorts or tourist

[165] WTO, Council for Trade in Services, Communication from the Dominican Republic, El Salvador and Honduras: Replies to the Comments on the Proposed Annex on Tourism (27 October 2000) S/CSS/W/9, 1–2.

[166] See Michael B Renshaw, 'Consequences of Integration in UK Tour Operating' (1995) 15 Tourism Management 243.

[167] Phillip Evans, *Recent Developments in Trade and Competition Issues in the Services Sector: A Review of Practices in Travel and Tourism* (UNCTAD/ITCD/CLP/Misc.13, UNCTAD Series on Issues in Competition Law and Policy, 1999) [24].

guides), thereby driving down the latter's profit margin. Second, vertically integrated tourism providers were also at a clear advantage in relation to independent travel operators from developing countries, which did not have control over the racking policy of travel agencies in developed countries. It is relatively clear that a vertically integrated travel agency was likely to channel tourists to an affiliated tour operator.[168]

Against this background, a 1998 UNCTAD expert meeting on 'Strengthening the Capacity for Expanding the Tourism Sector in Developing Countries' raised the possibility of negotiating an annex on tourism services under the GATS, which would, *inter alia*, contain competitive safeguards, and concluded that '[e]ffective mechanisms ... to deal with anti-competitive practices in the tourism sector and related sectors should be identified, in order to deal with the effects on trade of contractual practices relating to exclusive dealing, vertical integration and the abuse of dominance, particularly as regards new entrants to the industry.'[169] This UNCTAD report was taken up by the Dominican Republic, El Salvador and Honduras, which tabled a Draft Annex on Tourism in 1999.[170] Later, in 2001, an updated version of the Draft Annex was communicated to the Members of the Council for Trade in Services, which also enjoyed the support of Bolivia, Ecuador, Nicaragua, Panama, Peru and Venezuela.[171]

The Draft Annex on Tourism addresses several issues, including, *inter alia*, competitive safeguards, protection of consumer rights, access to and use of information, and access to air transport infrastructure and ancillary services. As regards competitive safeguards, Section 3(1) of the Draft Annex stipulates the general obligation that adequate measures shall be adopted to prevent anti-competitive practices in the tourism industries. Section 3(2) then goes on to state that the prevention of anti-competitive practices in the tourism industries shall require measures to address several forms of conduct, including, *inter alia*, discriminatory use of information networks, ancillary services to air transport, predatory pricing, or the allocation of scarce resources (lit (a)); abuse of dominance through exclusivity

[168]Evans (n 167) [23ff]; David Diaz, 'The Viability and Sustainability of International Tourism in Developing Countries' (2001) <https://www.wto.org/english/tratop_e/serv_e/diaz.doc> accessed 20 December 2015; Massimo G Grosso, Molly Lesher and Enrico Pinali, *Services Trade Liberalisation and Tourism Development: OECD Trade Policy Working Paper No. 57* (TD/TC/WP(2006)37/FINAL, 2007) 25ff.

[169]United Nations Conference on Trade and Development, Expert Meeting on Strengthening the Capacity for Expanding the Tourism Sector in Developing Countries, with Particular Focus on Tour Operators, Travel Agencies and Other Suppliers (07 July 1998) TD/B/COM.1/17, TD/B/COM.1/EM.6/3, 2.

[170]WTO, Council for Trade in Services, Preparations for the 1999 Ministerial Conference: Proposal Regarding the GATS – Communication from the Dominican Republic, El Salvador and Honduras (14 October 1999) WT/GC/W/372, S/C/W/127.

[171]WTO, Council for Trade in Services, Communication by Bolivia, Dominican Republic, Ecuador, El Salvador, Honduras, Nicaragua, Panama, Peru and Venezuela – Draft Annex on Tourism (26 September 2001) S/CSS/W/107.

clauses, refusal to deal, tied sales, quantity restrictions, or *vertical integration* (lit (b)); and misleading or discriminatory use of information by companies (lit (c)).[172]

It thus follows that the abuse of dominance through vertical integration is an anti-competitive practice under Section 3(2)(b) of the Draft Annex on Tourism. It must, however, be noted that the focus of the provision is on general competition law rather than sector-specific regulation. The central concept is the 'abuse of dominance' (through exclusivity clauses, refusal to deal, tied sales, quantity restrictions or vertical integration). Such language is generally found in antitrust legislation, such as Article 102 TFEU. The obligation to take measures to deal with situations of abuse of dominance is thus of an antitrust nature. Given that general competition law is always case-specific, the Draft Annex on Tourism falls short of requiring sector-wide regulation that would lead to some degree of unbundling of all tourism service suppliers across-the-board. Rather, it seems to envisage a situation where unbundling measures could be imposed in individual cases by the national competition authority in order to settle an ongoing antitrust investigation against a VIU.[173]

After having been introduced, the proposed annex on tourism services received some comments from other WTO Members, but was not further pursued in the services negotiations. One of the reasons for this might be that, in contrast to the Reference Paper on basic telecom services, the annex would have formed an integral part of the GATS in accordance with Article XXIX GATS and thus been binding on all WTO Members, irrespective of specific commitments undertaken.[174] Nevertheless, the Draft Annex on Tourism is a good reflection of the conviction held by a number of WTO Members that vertical integration can, under certain circumstances, produce behavior that distorts domestic and international competition.

Finally, it is also important to take into account related developments in the area of preferential trade agreements. In 2008, the EU concluded an Economic Partnership Agreement (EPA) with members of the Caribbean Forum (CARIFORUM),

[172]Ibid 2–3. The phrasing of Section 3 of the Draft Annex on Tourism is somewhat unfortunate. Section 3(2) provides that the prevention of anti-competitive practices in the tourism industries, as mandated by Section 3(1), shall require measures to 'address' certain specific forms of corporate behavior subsequently enumerated in the provision. Based on this wording, it is not entirely clear whether the types of conduct listed under Section 3(2) automatically qualify as 'anti-competitive practices' within the meaning of Section 3(1) and, therefore, whether the WTO Member concerned would have to adopt adequate measures to actually 'prevent' such conduct. In the original draft of the proposed annex on tourism, Section 3(2) unambiguously provided that '*[a]nti-competitive practices such as the ones referred to above [in Section 3(1)] will include*, inter alia, *the following*: ... b) Abuse of dominance through exclusivity clauses, refusal to deal, tied sales, quantity restrictions, or vertical integration', see Preparations for the 1999 Ministerial Conference: Proposal Regarding the GATS – Communication from the Dominican Republic, El Salvador and Honduras (n 170) 6.

[173]For an account of ownership unbundling obligations as a remedy in abuse of dominance cases under general EU competition law, see Sect. 2.4.

[174]See for example the statement of the representative of Mexico, WTO, Council for Trade in Services, Report of the Meeting held on 5 and 6 October 2000: Note by the Secretariat (01 December 2000) S/CSS/M/5, [103].

including Antigua and Barbuda, the Bahamas, Barbados, Belize, Dominica, Grenada, Guyana, Jamaica, Saint Lucia, Saint Vincent and the Grenadines, Saint Kitts and Nevis, Surinam, Trinidad, Tobago and the Dominican Republic. Article 111 of the EU-CARIFORUM EPA,[175] which is part of the section on tourism services, provides that 'appropriate measures shall be maintained or introduced ... for the purpose of preventing suppliers ... to affect materially the terms of participation in the relevant market for tourism services by engaging in or continuing anti-competitive practices, including, *inter alia*, abuse of dominant position through imposition of unfair prices, exclusivity clauses, refusal to deal, tied sales, quantity restrictions or *vertical integration*.'[176] This innovative provision, which has attracted significant research interest, seems to have been included particularly at the request of the CARIFORUM States, where oftentimes vertically integrated European providers with great market power exerted considerable anti-competitive pressures.[177] Like the Draft Annex on Tourism, Article 111 of the EU-CARIFORUM EPA envisages a case-specific application of general competition law principles. Therefore, as mentioned above, the national competition authority may, but is not required to, impose a requirement to unbundle in individual cases. Hence no obligation to introduce some kind of regulatory unbundling for all actors in the tourism sector can be read into Article 111 of the EU-CARIFORUM EPA.

6.4.3 *Experience from Bilateral and Regional Agreements with Energy-Specific Provisions*

The discussion on a reference paper for energy services within the WTO framework can also be guided by bilateral and regional preferential trade agreements that feature energy-specific provisions. However, there are only a small number of PTAs that specifically deal with issues relating to non-discriminatory access to gas and electricity transmission systems,[178] despite the fact that recent PTAs often include

[175]Economic Partnership Agreement between the CARIFORUM States, of the one part, and the European Community and its Member States, of the other part (2008) OJ 2008/L 289/3.

[176]Emphasis added.

[177]Hannes Schloemann and Christian Pitschas, 'Cutting the Regulatory Edge? Services Regulation Disciplines in the CARIFORUM-EU Economic Partnership Agreement' in Regine Qualmann (ed), *How to Ensure Development Friendly Economic Partnership Agreements – Lessons Across Regions* (Deutsche Gesellschaft für Technische Zusammenarbeit 2009) 131–132.

[178]See Mireille Cossy, 'The Liberalization of Energy Services: Are PTAs More Energetic than the GATS?' in Juan A Marchetti and Martin Roy (eds), *Opening Markets for International Trade in Services: Countries and Sectors in Bilateral and WTO Negotiations* (Cambridge University Press 2009) 415 (who writes, in 2009, that disciplines on non-discriminatory third party access and the prevention of anti-competitive practices are 'not found in any PTA so far'); Ilaria Espa and Kateryna Holzer, 'Negotiating an Energy Deal under TTIP: Drivers and Impediments to U.S. Shale Exports to Europe' 43 Denver Journal of International Law and Policy 357, 360. See also Thomas W Wälde and Andreas Gunst, 'International Energy Trade and Access to Networks:

so-called 'WTO-plus' or 'WTO-extra' provisions, i.e. provisions that build on, or go beyond, what is currently covered by the WTO agreements (including for example competition, labor, environment, investment and government procurement).

The EU-Georgia Association Agreement of 2014 is one of the rare examples of a PTA that separately addresses energy issues. It entered into force on 1 July 2016. Apart from trade-related energy provisions covering, *inter alia*, general transit matters, unauthorized taking of goods in transit, interruptions of transit, transit obligations for private operators, regulatory authorities and organization of energy markets, Article 217 ('Access to Energy Transport Facilities') of the agreement provides that each party 'shall ensure on its territory the implementation of a system of third party access to energy transport facilities ... applicable to all users and applied in a transparent, objective and non-discriminatory manner.'[179] The inclusion of this TPA obligation is mainly important for the time period until Georgia becomes a full member of the Energy Community (negotiations with respect thereto were launched in February 2014). As a member of the Energy Community, Georgia will have to implement the entire EU energy *acquis*, including the detailed third party access rules.

Similarly to the EU-Georgia Association Agreement, Article 145 ('Access to High-Voltage Electric Energy Transmission Grids and Lines') of the EU-Kazakhstan Enhanced Partnership and Cooperation Agreement (EPCA) of 2015 obliges each party to 'provide the enterprises of the other Party, established as juridical persons in the territory of the Party granting the access, with non-discriminatory access to high-voltage electric energy transmission grids and lines, which are partly or fully owned and regulated by the Party granting the access within the available capacities of such grids and lines.'[180] Moreover, the access shall be allocated in a 'fair and equitable manner'.[181] It is also worth noting that the EU-Kazakhstan EPCA contains another separate provision on connection and access to electric energy transmission grids for energy from renewable sources.[182]

Lastly, the EU has also been pushing for the inclusion of a TPA obligation in the EU-US Transatlantic Trade and Investment Partnership (TTIP), with a view to

The Case of Electricity' in Janusz Bielecki and Melaku G Desta (eds), *Electricity Trade in Europe – Review of the Economic and Regulatory Changes* (Kluwer Law International 2004) 199 (who state that '[i]t is hard to identify a norm in international law ... which imposes third-party access').

[179]Article 217(1) Association Agreement between the European Union and the European Atomic Energy Community and their Member States, of the one part, and Georgia, of the other part (27 June 2014) OJ 2014/L 261/4, 86.

[180]Enhanced Partnership and Cooperation Agreement between the European Union and its Member States, of the one part, and the Republic of Kazakhstan, of the other part (21 December 2015) OJ 2016/L 29/3, Article 145(1).

[181]Ibid.

[182]Ibid, Article 147(2)(f).

ensuring access to US crude oil and natural gas resources.[183] In July of 2016, the Commission made a textual proposal, and the wording of the proposed provision was as follows:

> Each Party shall ensure that operators of transmission systems in its territory grant access to their systems to entities of the other Party for the transport of gas and electricity. Such access shall be granted on commercial terms that are reasonable, transparent and non-discriminatory, and at cost-reflective tariffs. Each party shall publish the terms, conditions and tariffs for the access to and use of energy transport infrastructure.[184]

However, even assuming that the TTIP negotiations will be successfully concluded at some point in the future, it remains unclear whether the agreement will in fact contain a stand-alone chapter dedicated to energy issues. It seems that the US side questions the necessity of such a chapter.[185]

Apart from the examples mentioned above there are no other PTAs or sectorial agreements that specifically deal with access to energy infrastructure. Even the 1994 Energy Charter Treaty, which is the most important regional agreement relating directly to energy investment, trade and transit, does not contain pro-competitive disciplines on network access. An 'Understanding' appended to the text of the agreement, apparently as a result of pressure by major energy companies at that time,[186] explicitly clarifies that the provisions of the ECT 'do not … oblige any Contracting Party to introduce mandatory third party access.'[187] Furthermore, the Energy Charter Secretariat has clarified that while the ECT seeks to promote transparency and efficiency in energy markets, 'it is for governments to define the structure of their national energy sector' and that there is 'no obligation … to break up vertically integrated energy companies.'[188] This clarification can be seen as a response to former opponents of Russia ratifying the ECT, who had claimed for some time that the ECT required the unbundling of vertically integrated energy undertakings.[189] The NAFTA, which has a separate energy-related chapter

[183]European Commission, 'EU-US TTIP: Raw Materials and Energy: Initial EU Position Paper' (2013) <http://trade.ec.europa.eu/doclib/docs/2013/july/tradoc_151624.pdf> accessed 5 April 2016.

[184]European Commission, 'Transatlantic Trade and Investment Partnership – EU Textual Proposal: Energy and Raw Materials' (2016) 4 <http://trade.ec.europa.eu/doclib/docs/2016/july/tradoc_154801.pdf> accessed 30 August 2016. The provision further states that under certain conditions, limited derogations from the right to TPA may be introduced.

[185]For a general account of the energy-related negotiations with respect to TTIP, see Espa and Holzer (n 178).

[186]Wälde and Gunst (n 178) 200.

[187]Understanding 1(b)(i) of the Energy Charter Treaty (n 45).

[188]Energy Charter Secretariat, 'Frequently Asked Question about the Energy Charter Process' (no date) <http://www.energycharter.org/process/frequently-asked-questions/> accessed 6 August 2016.

[189]Andrey Konoplyanik, 'A Common Russia–EU Energy Space: The New EU–Russia Partnership Agreement, Acquis Communautaire and the Energy Charter' (2009) 27 Journal of Energy & Natural Resources Law 258, 278; Andrey Konoplyanik, 'Борьба с мифами – О мнимых выгодах и угрозах Договора к Энергетической Хартии' (2006) 21 Политический журнал 32, passim.

(Chapter 6 on 'Energy and Basic Petrochemicals'), also fails to address issues of access to infrastructure, in particular third party access obligations.[190]

In conclusion, it has been shown that there are only a small number of bilateral preferential trade agreements that deal with non-discriminatory network access to energy transmission networks. However, the fact that these are a recent phenomenon, starting only in 2014, could nevertheless suggest that the topic will play an increasingly important role in the future. So far, the respective PTAs only contain rules that impose obligations in the form of a third party access regime. Sector-specific safeguards against anti-competitive behaviors (particularly those resulting from vertical integration) or provisions dealing more directly with the unbundling of vertically integrated energy undertakings have not yet been included. The developments at the bilateral level will certainly have consequences for the creation of international rules on energy trade within the WTO. The inclusion of disciplines on third party access in the TTIP, for example, would show that network access issues can be subject to global governance and would serve as a stepping stone for future negotiations at the multilateral level.[191]

It is interesting to take a look at the draft Transit Protocol to the ECT, which is the preliminary outcome of negotiations between the contracting parties of the ECT and whose main purpose is to supplement the ECT's existing transit provisions (Article 7). The relevant provisions of the draft Transit Protocol are contained in Article 10(2), which provides that each contracting party shall 'ensure that Transit Tariffs and other conditions are not affected by market distortions, in particular those resulting from abuse of a dominant position by any owner or operator of Energy Transport Facilities used for Transit' (see Energy Charter Secretariat, 'Last Formal Version of the Draft Transit Protocol as Discussed by the Charter Conference in 2003' (2003) <http://www.energycharter.org/fileadmin/DocumentsMedia/CC_251_ENG.pdf> accessed 10 March 2016). The rationale of this obligation is clear: The incumbent natural monopolist in country A can abuse its control over the transit transmission line in order to charge excessively high prices from country C energy companies that rely on country A as a transit country. Unbundling policies would be suitable to reduce the incentive of TSOs to distort transit tariffs and, thus, an important step towards ensuring compliance with the corresponding obligation of the protocol. However, it is clear that the objective may also be achieved through alternative means, in particular behavioral measures.

[190]Roberto Rios Herrán and Pietro Poretti, 'Energy Trade and Investment under the North American Free Trade Agreement' in Yulia Selivanova (ed), *Regulation of Energy in International Trade Law: WTO, NAFTA and Energy Charter* (Kluwer Law International 2012) 336.

[191]See Espa and Holzer (n 178) 358–360, 376; European Commission, 'EU-US TTIP: Raw Materials and Energy: Initial EU Position Paper' (n 183) 2.

6.4.4 *The Way Forward: Developing a Reference Paper for Energy Services*

6.4.4.1 General Observations

The discussion on the need for a reference paper on energy services is not new. Already in 1998 the WTO Secretariat raised the question whether it would be desirable to negotiate a set of additional regulatory principles for the energy sector, following the example of the Reference Paper on telecom services.[192]

The rationale for an 'Energy Reference Paper' is clear. Gas and electricity transmission networks are considered to be a natural monopoly and thus not open to competition. The resulting regulatory challenges are compounded by the fact that energy transmission systems are often controlled by vertically integrated energy companies, which have a strong incentive to discriminate against non-affiliated competitors, in particular as regards network access. The removal of State-imposed market access barriers and national treatment barriers is therefore insufficient to ensure effective liberalization of cross-border energy trade. Additional rules are needed in order to guarantee access on reasonable and non-discriminatory terms to transmission (and distribution) networks.[193]

In 2000 and 2001 the United States[194] and Norway[195] proposed the development of a reference paper on energy services and identified substantive issues that should be covered by such an instrument. Based on these submissions, an 'Energy Reference Paper' could include the following elements: (1) transparency in the adoption and implementation of rules, regulations and technical standards; (2) -non-discriminatory third-party access to, and interconnection with, networks, grids and other essential facilities; (3) establishment of a regulator that is independent of, and not accountable to, any supplier; (4) provision of non-discriminatory and timely information on data relevant for transmission of energy (such as, *inter alia*, prices and transmission capacity); and (5) prevention of anti-competitive practices in general.[196] The idea of drafting a reference paper on energy services has also found support among many academics.[197] The proposals of the United States and

[192]Energy Services – Background Note by the Secretariat (n 8) [39, 71].

[193]See Sects. 1.1 and 6.1.

[194]WTO, Council for Trade in Services, Communication from the United States: Energy Services (18 December 2000) S/CSS/W/24, [14–16]. See also WTO, Committee on Specific Commitments, Communication from the United States – Classification of Energy Services (18 May 2000) S/CSC/W/27, [15, 22].

[195]WTO, Council for Trade in Services, Communication from Norway: The Negotiations on Trade in Services (21 March 2001) S/CSS/W/59, 10.

[196]Energy Services – Background Note by the Secretariat (n 72) [82].

[197]See for example Peter C Evans, *Liberalizing Global Trade in Energy Services* (The AEI Press 2002) 43ff; Pietro Poretti and Roberto Rios Herrán, 'A Reference Paper On Energy Services: The Best Way Forward?' (2006) 3 Manchester Journal of International Economic Law 2; Selivanova (n 56) 297.

Norway have not, however, been taken up yet by other WTO Members and thus have not led to serious negotiations. It should not be expected that this situation will change in the near future, given the current state of the Doha Round. Nevertheless, the issue is still on the agenda of the WTO.[198] In the course of discussions within the Council for Trade in Services in February 2010, for example, one delegation explicitly supported the idea of developing a reference paper on energy services 'as an area for further work'.[199]

One important issue that has received repeated attention is whether the Reference Paper in the telecoms sector could and should be used as a model for future disciplines with respect to energy services. In the Council for Trade in Services, some WTO Members cautioned that the disciplines in the telecom Reference Paper should not be automatically transposed to the energy sector, arguing that there are significant differences between telecom and energy networks and also among the different energy industries themselves.[200] However, in the academic literature it has been correctly pointed out that there also are many similarities between the telecommunications and energy sectors (network-bound industries with dominant incumbent suppliers), resulting in similar regulatory challenges (most notably access to the existing network; anti-competitive behavior).[201] Moreover, the differences between the gas and electricity industries themselves are not such that different requirements regarding transparency, independence of regulators or third party access would be needed.[202] Nevertheless, rules specifically tailored to the needs of the energy sector would be needed in order to address certain issues relating to the environment, energy efficiency, and security of supply.[203] Therefore, while most of the provisions in the Reference Paper on Basic Telecommunications Services can be considered as important points for developing similar disciplines in the sphere of energy services, supplementary provisions would be needed to deal with issues specific to the energy sector.

6.4.4.2 A Reference Paper on Energy Services and Unbundling Requirements

The first essential element of an 'Energy Reference Paper' would be network access regulation, i.e. behavioral rules.[204] In other words, transmission system operators should be obliged to grant access to their systems for the transport of gas or

[198]Energy Services – Background Note by the Secretariat (n 72) [79–83].

[199]WTO, Council for Trade in Services, Report of the Meeting Held on 11 February 2010 (05 March 2010) S/C/M/97, [83].

[200]Ibid [74, 83].

[201]Poretti and Rios Herrán (n 197) 33ff; Selivanova (n 56) 297.

[202]Cossy (n 72) 168.

[203]Selivanova (n 20) 22; Selivanova (n 56) 297.

[204]For the distinction between behavioral and structural regulation, see Sect. 1.3.

electricity on the basis of reasonable and non-discriminatory terms. The importance of such network access regulation is demonstrated by Section 2 on interconnection in the Reference Paper on Basic Telecommunications Services, the energy chapters of recent preferential trade agreements, the proposals of Norway and the United States, as well as the experience from the EU context. Furthermore, non-discriminatory third party access obligations have already been undertaken by some WTO Members as additional commitments under Article XVIII GATS[205] and as commitments forming part of their respective accession protocols to the WTO.[206]

However, even though international disciplines on TPA would go a long way in promoting cross-border energy trade, it is argued here that any future reference paper on energy services should also address the obstacles to non-discriminatory network access resulting from vertical integration. The need for corresponding disciplines is evidenced by, *inter alia*, Section 1 of the telecom Reference Paper and Section 3 of the Draft Annex on Tourism, which represent initial (limited) attempts to deal with the anti-competitive behavior of VIUs.

There are three main approaches to tackle the problems deriving from vertical integration in the energy sector: (1) through a provision on cross-subsidization and misuse of competitor information; and/or (2) through a provision on abuse of dominant position; and/or (3) through a provision explicitly mandating some level of unbundling. The first two options draw on the experiences with the Reference Paper on Basic Telecommunications Services and the Draft Annex on Tourism. The third option would be a significant innovation. All three approaches will be briefly discussed in turn.

The first option would be to include a provision on anti-competitive cross-subsidization and misuse of competitor information, such as that found in Section 1 of the telecom Reference Paper. As analyzed above,[207] the main weakness of such a provision is that it fails to illustrate, much less prescribe, the concrete measures that a WTO Member has to take in order to prevent such conduct. Against this background, the proposed reference paper on energy services could explicitly refer to accounting, functional and/or legal unbundling as a suitable regulatory measure.[208] The advantage of this first approach is that a great number of WTO

---

[205] In its GATS schedule of specific commitments and with respect to the transportation via pipeline of petroleum and natural gas, Ukraine undertook to 'ensure adherence to the principles of non-discriminatory treatment in access to and use of pipeline networks under its jurisdiction, within the technical capacities of these networks, with regard to the origin, destination or ownership of product transported, without imposing any unjustified delays, restrictions or charges, as well as without discriminatory pricing based on the differences in origin, destination or ownership'; see WTO, Ukraine – Schedule of Specific Commitments (10 March 2008) GATS/SC/144, 34. An identically worded commitment was also made by Montenegro; see WTO, Montenegro – Schedule of Specific Commitments (05 June 2012) GATS/SC/146, 28–29.

[206] See WTO, Report of the Working Party on the Accession of the Republic of Kazakhstan to the World Trade Organization (23 June 2015) WT/ACC/KAZ/93, [87].

[207] See Sect. 6.4.1.2.

[208] See also Poretti and Rios Herrán (n 197) 38.

Members have already accepted an almost identical proviso in the telecom Reference Paper. In contrast, the drawback of this approach is that WTO Members would not be obliged to actually implement unbundling measures, even if they are mentioned as a possible means to secure compliance with the obligation. Considering furthermore the ambiguity surrounding the concept of '*anti-competitive* cross-subsidization', there are significant doubts as to the effectiveness of this solution.

The second approach would be the inclusion of a provision on abuse of dominant position similar to the one in the Draft Annex on Tourism (and the EU-CARIFORUM EPA). The provision could read as follows: 'Appropriate measures shall be maintained or introduced for the purpose of preventing abuse of dominant position through [. . .] vertical integration.' Such a provision would highlight the fact that the abuse of dominance may in some cases result from vertical integration. It could thus provide the basis for the national competition authorities to impose a requirement to unbundle in individual cases, following general competition law procedures. However, the downside of this approach is that the creation of a competitive, non-discriminatory environment in the energy sector would very much depend on the action or inaction of the national competition authorities. Given that investigations into allegations of abuse of dominance are very fact-intensive and case-specific, and that competition authorities must enjoy a certain margin of appreciation, it is questionable whether compliance with this obligation could be adequately reviewed by the WTO dispute settlement bodies. Furthermore, it is often extremely difficult to garner sufficient evidence in order to actually prove abuses of dominance in the energy sector. The transmission of electricity and gas involves highly complex economic and technical transactions, which are a challenge in themselves, but which in addition enable vertically integrated undertakings to easily hide anti-competitive conduct.[209] Hence, there are doubts as to the actual effectiveness of such an obligation.[210]

The third option would be to include a provision that explicitly requires some degree of unbundling, on a regulatory level, of the transmission sector from other energy-related business activities.[211] Such an additional commitment under Article XVIII GATS would have no precedent, neither in the telecom Reference Paper, in the Draft Annex on Tourism, nor in bilateral or regional preferential trade

[209]Hubertus von Rosenberg, 'Unbundling Through the Back Door. . .the Case of Network Divestiture as a Remedy in the Energy Sector' (2009) 30 European Competition Law Review 237, 240.

[210]Even in the EU, where the European Commission actively enforces EU competition law, there are only a handful of Article 102 TFEU cases which led to the imposition of ownership unbundling measures on private companies. In fact, until today, ownership unbundling remedies have only been imposed under Article 9 of Regulation 1/2003, i.e. after the undertakings concerned had made voluntary commitments to this effect. See Sect. 2.4.

[211]See Thomas Cottier, Sofya Matteotti-Berkutova and Olga Nartova, 'Third Country Relations in EU Unbundling of Natural Gas Markets: The "Gazprom Clause" of Directive 2009/73 EC and WTO Law' in Dirk Buschle, Simon Hirsbrunner and Christine Kaddous (eds), *European Energy Law: Droit européen de l'énergie* (Dossier de droit européen vol 22. Helbing Lichtenhahn 2011) 284 (stating that '[i]n the field of energy, access to energy grids calls for *shared disciplines on unbundling*, comparable to the reference paper in telecommunication'; emphasis added).

agreements, but would be the most straightforward way to deal with the difficulties resulting from vertical integration.[212] A provision on common basic unbundling principles, inspired by the relevant EU legislation, could read as follows[213]:

> Unbundling
>
> In order to ensure non-discriminatory network access and to avoid cross-subsidization and distortion of competition, it is necessary to separate the transmission activities from other energy-related activities such as production/generation and supply.
>
> Appropriate measures shall be maintained in order to ensure that energy companies comply with accounting and functional unbundling. In particular, it will be ensured that (i) energy companies, in their internal accounting, keep separate accounts for their transmission activities; (ii) transmission system operators are independent at least in terms of their organization and decision making from other activities not relating to transmission.

Only this third option would ensure that the incentive of vertically integrated energy undertakings to discriminate against non-affiliated competitors as regards network access is to some extent suppressed. Although the experience in the EU context has shown that functional unbundling can only be partially successful in bringing about a structural separation between energy transmission activities on the one hand and energy production/generation and supply activities on the other, it is certainly a first step in the right direction. Moreover, the unbundling of accounts would lay the basis for the detection of cross-subsidization and would thereby also contribute to increased competition in the competitive segments of the energy industry. Finally, it should also be noted that it is perfectly justifiable to go beyond the limited disciplines in the Reference Paper on basic telecom services, given that unbundling requirements play a much more important role in the regulation of energy industries as compared to the telecom sector.[214]

---

[212]As regards the telecom sector, several authors have in fact proposed an explicit accounting unbundling requirement; see Fredebeul-Krein and Freytag (n 139) 641; Geradin and Kerf (n 139) 149–150.

[213]See also Olga Nartova, *Energy Services and Competition Policies under WTO Law* (Научная Мысль, INFRA-M 2010) 251; Jayant Parimal, 'Energy Services in WTO – A Recommended Course' (Master's Thesis 2004) 94 <http://www.peacepalacelibrary.nl/ebooks/files/WTI_PARIMAL_Energy-Services.pdf> accessed 15 January 2016. Nartova proposes the following formulation: 'Members recognise the importance of unbundling in furtherance of competition, efficiency and transparency. In view of this, all members shall endeavour to ensure full legal and functional separation of energy transport activity from other activities such as the sale of energy goods or services, in which energy service is consumed. At a minimum, the members shall ensure functional unbundling of the integrated companies, which will include, inter alia, separate budgeting, accounting and decision-making facilities.'

[214]Peter Abegg and others, 'Entflechtung in Netzsektoren – ein Vergleich' [2014] Bremen Energy Working Papers No. 19, 30, 35; see also Sect. 1.4.

6.5 Conclusions

This chapter has analyzed the extent to which WTO law could play a 'positive role' in promoting the formulation of unbundling policies at the level of WTO Members. The early Havana Charter for an International Trade Organization as well as the work subsequently undertaken within the UN's ECOSOC, GATT 1947 committees, UNCTAD and the WTO show that there is a widespread awareness and consensus that trade and competition policies are intimately interrelated. Where effective competition laws or pro-competitive regulations are not put into place, there is a real risk that the benefits of trade liberalization are eroded by private anti-competitive practices. As regards the energy sector, it is equally clear that the removal of State-imposed market access and national treatment barriers may be insufficient to ensure genuine liberalization. In particular, private barriers to international energy trade may result from the anti-competitive practices of vertically integrated energy undertakings.

The horizontal competition-related provisions in the GATS and GATT are relatively weak. In particular, both Article VIII GATS and Article XVII GATT do not regulate pure natural monopolies. Their application is conditioned on some degree of active State involvement in the creation of or persistence of the monopoly situation. Moreover, the disciplines contained in these two Articles were not designed to, and cannot, ensure that vertically integrated undertakings provide non-discriminatory network access or implement even a basic level of unbundling.

Sector-specific developments within the WTO show that there is a need for, and the possibility of, pro-competitive regulation which goes beyond the rudimentary competition obligations in the GATS/GATT. In the telecommunications sector, the Annex on Telecommunications and the Reference Paper on Basic Telecommunications Services establish rules on third party access and on anti-competitive practices, including those closely linked to vertical integration (such as cross-subsidization and misuse of competitor information). In the tourism sector, WTO Members have likewise tabled proposals to address, *inter alia*, abuse of dominance through vertical integration. Furthermore, there are also a small number of preferential trade agreements outside of the WTO that specifically address network access issues in the energy sector.

The idea of developing an 'Energy Reference Paper' within the WTO framework has received support from WTO Members as well as from academics. In addition to issues such as transparency, non-discriminatory TPA, and independence of regulators, it is argued that a future Energy Reference Paper should contain provisions that deal with the negative effects on international energy trade resulting from vertical integration. While several drafting options are available, some of which are based on existing experiences in the telecommunications and tourism sectors, the most straightforward way would be to explicitly require some basic level of structural separation, i.e. unbundling, in the energy transmission sector.

Chapter 7
Final Conclusions: Unbundling as a Competition Instrument in the Light of International Trade and Investment Law

The objective of this book has been to examine how WTO law and international investment law interact with the unbundling and unbundling-related measures in the EU energy sector introduced through the Third Energy Package in 2009. Following the provision of the necessary background information (Chaps. 2 and 3), the analysis was divided into two main parts. First, it was analyzed whether, and if so to what extent, WTO law and international investment law *set limits* on the adoption and maintenance of unbundling and unbundling-related measures (Chaps. 4 and 5). Second, in an effort to change the perspective, it was asked whether WTO law could *serve as a vehicle* for the implementation of unbundling measures. In other words, it was considered whether general WTO law could be utilized so as to impose certain (rudimentary) unbundling requirements upon the operations of vertically integrated energy undertakings, and whether additional pro-competitive regulatory principles might be needed at the multilateral level (Chap. 6). The relevance of the findings summarized below is not limited to the EU nor to the energy sector, but extend to many other countries around the world that have implemented, or plan to implement, unbundling regimes either in the energy industry or in other network-bound industries, such as railways and telecommunications.

7.1 The First Direct Legal Challenge to Unbundling Is Based on International Economic Law

The unbundling requirements themselves, the corresponding certification procedure, and the exemption regime provided for in the Third Energy Package, directly affect third-country companies operating in the EU energy sector. The most visible consequences of the TEP have been that foreign commercial energy companies were forced to sell their shares in energy transmission networks, and that major new infrastructure projects, such as South Stream, which were sponsored by foreign

T. M. Dralle, *Ownership Unbundling and Related Measures in the EU Energy Sector*, European Yearbook of International Economic Law 5,
https://doi.org/10.1007/978-3-319-77797-9_7

energy producers/suppliers, could not be built as planned. The third country that has been most affected by the implementation of the TEP's unbundling regime is the Russian Federation. Over the last few years the Russian government and the State-owned gas company Gazprom have sought to invoke international economic law in order to test the legality of the EU energy legislation. While Gazprom's investment arbitration against Lithuania was discontinued, the *EU – Energy Package* case before the WTO dispute settlement bodies is moving forward and the report of the Panel is expected to be released in 2018. Therefore, the first direct (and relatively comprehensive) legal challenge to the EU's unbundling and unbundling-related measures is unfolding not at the level of EU and national constitutional law, but before an international judicial institution on the basis of international economic law.

7.2 The EU and Its Member States Are Free to Impose OU, Subject to Conditions

The inclusion of an 'Ownership Unbundling Clarification' into the market access obligation of the EU-Canada CETA and the pending *EU – Energy Package* case before the WTO dispute settlement bodies show that there is considerable uncertainty with respect to the reach of GATS-type market access obligations in general, and Article XVI GATS in particular. The ownership unbundling requirements set out in Article 9 of Directives 2009/72/EC and 2009/73/EC clearly have a significant restrictive impact on market access opportunities. Under OU, companies engaged in the production/generation or supply of gas or electricity are prohibited from supplying energy transmission services. Conversely, companies that control a transmission system cannot provide wholesale or retail services of gas or electricity.

However, despite the fact that market access for foreign services and service suppliers is limited as a result of OU, this book has shown that such measures are not covered by any of the prohibited MA restrictions in Article XVI GATS. The same applies *a maiore ad minus* to the ISO and ITO models. The *EU – Energy Package* case will be an important opportunity for the WTO dispute settlement bodies to clarify the scope of Article XVI GATS in this connection, especially after the far-reaching ruling in *US – Gambling*. A determination that the ownership unbundling requirements in the EU energy sector are in conformity with the GATS market access provision will also be of significant importance for the regulation of public services in general and will, at least to a certain extent, allay the concerns of critics that Article XVI GATS excessively encroaches upon the regulatory autonomy of WTO Members.

Ownership unbundling policies as set out in the Third Energy Package are also in conformity with the substantive domestic regulation disciplines under Article VI:4/5 GATS, which are provisionally applicable pending the outcome of negotiations under Article VI:4. Neither do OU requirements 'nullify or impair' market access commitments on energy services (in fact, it could be argued that they preserve the value of such commitments), nor are they more 'burdensome', i.e. trade-restrictive, than necessary to ensure non-discriminatory network access. In particular, in terms of proportionality it has been shown that behavioral measures in the form of network access regulation cannot entirely rule out the possibility that integrated transmission system operators discriminate against competitors as regards network access. It is thus necessary to introduce some degree of structural separation between the network activities on the one hand, and the production/generation or supply activities on the other, in order to ensure that the *natural* incentive of the network operator, namely to stimulate demand for its services by promoting competition in the competitive market segment, is not supplanted by conflicting interests of the other branches of the vertically integrated undertaking. This can only be achieved by unbundling policies. Moreover, unbundling solutions other than ownership unbundling do not constitute a less trade-restrictive alternative that is reasonably available, because such unbundling models do not have the same effectiveness as OU. Only OU can guarantee that TSOs are completely structurally independent from production/generation or supply interests. Arguably, the outcome under a horizontal necessity test, which is the most controversial but also most important aspect of the prospective, yet-to-be-negotiated horizontal disciplines under Article VI:4 GATS, would not be any different.

Similarly as with Articles XVI and VI:4/5 of the GATS, the investment protection standards of 'no expropriation without compensation' and 'fair and equitable treatment' likewise do not constitute (insurmountable) barriers to the introduction of ownership unbundling legislation in the EU. In general, even though the investor's right to use, enjoy and dispose of his property is severely curtailed, reaching the level of a 'substantial deprivation', at the same time OU serves an important public purpose, namely non-discriminatory network access. Although there are different approaches among arbitral tribunals with respect to the determination of an indirect expropriation, the most convincing approach is to find a middle ground between the 'sole effects' and 'police powers' doctrines by taking into account both the effects and purposes of host State measures. According to this view, OU measures would not constitute an indirect expropriation under the vast majority of IIAs, because they are proportionate to the aim sought to be achieved. In any event the expropriation will almost always be lawful, because the price obtained through the compulsory sale of the transmission system assets will almost always be sufficient to constitute adequate compensation.

Moreover, foreign investors could not have had a legitimate expectation, protected by the FET standard, that the legal and regulatory framework as it existed before the adoption of the Third Energy Package would remain unchanged. Although certain awards suggest that a total or drastic alteration of the existing framework and/or rapid and constant legislative changes could constitute exceptions to this 'general rule', the case law to this effect is very limited and its application to the implementation of ownership unbundling would not necessarily lead to an FET violation. To the extent that the doctrine of legitimate expectations can be interpreted as embodying an obligation of proportionality, the OU requirements in the EU energy sector meet the proportionality test—even under a relatively strict standard of review.

At the same time, however, it is clear that, in particular, international investment law sets important limits on the design of OU policies. Notably, States will incur international liability if foreign investors are forced to sell their transmission system assets at a price significantly below the market value. This means that an investor will always need to be given sufficient time to comply with the compulsory sale obligation. Moreover, States cannot give specific assurances to foreign investors that ownership unbundling legislation will not be introduced, e.g. with a view to encouraging investment into the transmission networks, and then later ignore such commitments. Finally, international investment law requires that host State institutions evaluate the necessity of ownership unbundling and thus the availability of potential alternatives.

7.3 EU Member States Cannot Be Forced to Privatize Their TSOs/Commercial Energy Companies

Article 9(6) of Directives 2009/72/EC and 2009/73/EC provides that in the case of State-owned entities, the ownership unbundling rules are met if 'two separate public bodies' exercise control over network operations on the one hand, and generation/production or supply activities on the other. As a result, no EU Member State is forced to privatize either their transmission or production/generation and supply assets. WTO law and international investment law authorize such a regulatory solution. In particular, the special OU regime for public undertakings does not amount to a national treatment violation under Article XVII GATS and IIAs, because neither the public TSOs nor the public commercial energy companies have any competitive advantage vis-à-vis their (foreign) privately owned counterparts. States can therefore implement OU policies and, at the same time, retain key industries within public ownership. Having said that, it is also clear that WTO law and international investment law may prevent States from enacting legislation under which (foreign) private vertically integrated undertakings have to implement ownership unbundling, while (domestic) public companies can remain fully integrated.

7.4 The Plurality of Unbundling Models Among EU Member States Can Be Preserved

The Third Energy Package does not prescribe a specific unbundling solution, but allows the EU Member States to choose from three different unbundling models (OU, ISO and ITO), subject to certain conditions. Thus, as regards the gas sector for example, companies in Germany can choose the ITO model, whereas Lithuania has introduced mandatory OU in the sector. This variety of unbundling models among EU Member States does not violate the EU's MFN obligation under the GATS and IIAs. The MFN principle cannot be used as a mechanism to impose a requirement of regulatory uniformity on countries or regional integration organizations with a federalist or supranational structure (such as Canada, Switzerland, the United States, or the EU). This interpretation applies irrespective of the governmental measure and industry involved.

7.5 The Application of Unbundling Requirements to Offshore Gas Pipelines Should Be Clarified

Directive 2009/73/EC fails to specify whether the unbundling requirements (and the third party access rules) also apply to the offshore sections of international gas import pipelines running through the territorial waters of EU Member States. Recent developments surrounding the South Stream and Nord Stream 2 projects show that the absence of a corresponding clarification has created a substantial degree of legal uncertainty. Nevertheless, the EU's current administration of the unbundling requirements in the Gas Directive does not reach the threshold of being unreasonable, non-objective, or partial. Therefore, there is no inconsistency with the domestic regulation disciplines in Article VI:1 GATS. However, if the external dimension of the EU's energy policy is to follow a rule-based approach, it is necessary to establish a legal framework that governs the applicability of core provisions of the TEP to offshore gas import pipelines.

At the end of 2017, the European Commission actually proposed amendments to Directive 2009/73/EC in order to clarify the scope of application of the Gas Directive to pipelines to and from third countries (COM(2017) 660 final). The legal background for the Commission's initiative is that the legal services of both the European Commission and the Council of the EU have come to the shared conclusion that the provisions of the Gas Directive—as they currently stand—do not apply to offshore pipelines. With the amendments tabled by the Commission, Directive 2009/73/EC and the related legal instruments would unambiguously apply in their entirety to such pipelines up to the border of EU jurisdiction, including—in particular—the provisions on unbundling, third party access, and tariff regulation. The amendments would also introduce explicit language to the effect that new pipelines linking EU Member States with third countries can be granted an exemption from said provisions under the well-established procedure provided for in Article 36 of the Gas Directive. In addition, acknowledging the lack of specific rules governing the applicability of Directive 2009/73/EC to gas pipelines to and from third countries and the corresponding 'legitimate expectations of existing operators', the Commission proposal provides for the possibility for Member States to grant derogations with respect to existing infrastructure already in operation, i.e. infrastructure completed before the entry into force of the amendments. Such derogations can, however, only be granted if they are not 'detrimental to competition on or the effective functioning of the internal market in natural gas in the Union, or the security of supply in the Union'. Moreover, and importantly, they must be limited in time.

It is certainly a welcome development that the situation of legal uncertainty will end, and that the rules of the Gas Directive will be made explicitly applicable to all gas pipelines to and from third countries, including offshore pipelines coming from outside the EU. However, the timing, time frame and overall context of the Commission's proposal may create the impression that the new rules were designed with a 'special focus' on the controversial Nord Stream 2 project. To be more specific, if the proposed amendments to Directive 2009/73/EC enter into force before the completion of the Nord Stream 2 project, which seems to be the desired outcome, Germany would be unable to independently grant a derogation from ownership unbundling, third party access etc. Therefore, the only viable route would be to apply for an exemption under Article 36 of the Gas Directive, which would be subject to a series of strict conditions and, ultimately, to the approval of the Commission. The Commission's proposal could thus be seen as reflecting a rule-based approach in the EU's external energy policy, or simply as a tool to achieve political objectives.

Finally, and apart from the particular Nord Stream 2 issue, it should be recognized that the legislative changes, if adopted, will have significant competitive effects for the European gas market as a whole, taking into account that the gas pipelines impacted by the modifications to the Gas Directive include existing pipelines entering the EU from Norway, Algeria, Libya, Tunisia, Morocco and Russia. Given that the corresponding EU Member States would only be able to grant time-limited (and market-compatible) derogations, all pipelines as well as their respective TSOs would—after a certain period of time—become subject to the full weight of the Gas Directive.

7.6 The EU's Ownership Unbundling Exemption Regime Can Be Maintained As It Is

The Third Energy Package provides for the possibility to obtain an exemption from the requirements of ownership unbundling and third party access. This OU exemption regime in Article 36 of Directive 2009/73/EC and Article 17 of Regulation 714/2009 is of great significance for energy producers/generators and suppliers seeking to build and operate new transmission lines in accordance with their specific commercial needs, because in principle all new infrastructure projects built after 3 September 2009 must comply with the stringent OU rules. This book finds that individual exemption decisions, as a result of which a particular foreign energy company receives less advantageous treatment (e.g. denial of the request to be exempted), do not violate the MFN or NT principles under the GATS. The group-based approach of the GATS, which focuses on the underlying conditions of competition, disregards individual instances of less favorable treatment. The only situation whereby individual exemption decisions can be found to infringe Articles II or XVII GATS is when there is tangible evidence as to the existence of discriminatory intent. Except for clear-cut cases, the WTO dispute settlement bodies are unlikely to make such a determination.

Moreover, the interpretation and application of the central concept of 'interconnector' in all existing gas exemption decisions complies with the domestic regulation disciplines provided for in Article VI:1 GATS. None of the decisions reflect an unreasonable, non-objective or partial administration of the exemption regime in this regard. Besides, even if a complainant were able to show that the administration of the exemption regime in a particular case was unreasonable, non-objective or partial, this would generally be insufficient to find a violation of Article VI:1 GATS, as that provision only applies to measures of general application. Apart from the specific interconnector requirement, the more general conclusion is that it is almost impossible to (indirectly) challenge an individual OU exemption decision by arguing that the interpretation and application of one of the exemption requirements in that particular case constitutes a departure from the law or settled practice and that, consequently, the exemption regime is administered in a manner inconsistent with Article VI:1 GATS.

Thus, considering the limited usefulness of Articles II, VI:1 and XVII GATS with respect to individual measures, it seems that the judicial review of individual OU exemption decisions by international investment tribunals is more effective than that provided by the WTO dispute settlement bodies. The structural reason for this is that international investment law is specifically focused on protecting individual investors. The MFN or NT standard in IIAs would already be violated if a difference in treatment cannot be plausibly or reasonably connected to a legitimate public policy goal (*in casu*, the exemption criteria listed in the Gas Directive and Electricity Regulation).

Finally, the TEP's exemption regime as a whole is not discriminatory within the meaning of Article XVII GATS. It does not contain any criteria that relate to origin and the existing exemption practice does not allow for the conclusion that there is an asymmetric impact to the detriment of foreign services or service suppliers.

7.7 The Third-Country Certification Procedure Is Discriminatory but Can Nevertheless Be Justified

Due to the sensitive nature of the energy sector in general, and of energy transmission networks in particular, Directives 2009/72/EC and 2009/73/EC contain a separate certification procedure that is applicable in the case of third-country-controlled transmission system owners or operators. Apart from compliance with the unbundling requirements, the procedure in Article 11 of the Directives obliges third-country-controlled TSOs to demonstrate to the national regulatory authority that granting certification will not put at risk the security of energy supply of the granting Member State and the EU. This additional requirement clearly violates the national treatment obligation in Article XVII GATS and IIAs. Nevertheless, as regards the GATS, the discrimination is justifiable on security of supply grounds as a measure that is necessary to maintain public order (Article XIV(a) GATS). The underlying reason is that it is more difficult enforce EU energy law against a company that is located in a third country. The security of supply rationale also provides an appropriate justification under international investment law.

Apart from the national treatment obligation, the third-country certification procedure is fully consistent with the GATS and the treatment standards in international investment law. In particular, there is no violation of the MFN principle, as the additional security of supply test does not generally depend on criteria which are related to the home State of the respective service supplier or investor.

7.8 Vertical Integration Is a Barrier to Energy Trade, and WTO Law As It Stands Is Unable to Provide a Solution

In the absence of effective competition laws or pro-competitive regulations, private anti-competitive practices have the potential to erode the benefits of trade liberalization. As a consequence, the elimination of State-imposed market access and national treatment barriers may fall short of ensuring genuine liberalization. The energy industry is a sector wherein this becomes particularly obvious. Due to their control over gas/electricity transmission systems, which constitute a natural monopoly, vertically integrated energy companies have both the incentive and the ability to discriminate against non-affiliated competitors as regards, *inter alia*, network access. Vertical integration in the energy sector therefore constitutes a significant private barrier to international energy trade. WTO law as it stands, however, does not contain strong competition disciplines. The horizontal competition-related disciplines contained in Articles VIII GATS and XVII GATT are unable to effectively guarantee that vertically integrated energy undertakings provide non-discriminatory network access. Furthermore, they do not require any unbundling of vertically integrated energy undertakings. The inadequacy of the existing competition disciplines in the GATS/GATT demonstrates the need to develop a sector-specific reference paper on energy services, on the basis of Article XVIII GATS.

7.9 A Future Energy Reference Paper Should Contain Common Disciplines on Unbundling

Sector-specific developments within the WTO prove that it is feasible to devise additional pro-competitive regulatory principles for energy services. The Annex on Telecommunications and the Reference Paper on Basic Telecommunications Services regulate the access to, use of, and interconnection with public telecommunications transport networks and services on fair and non-discriminatory terms, and establish rules on anti-competitive practices which are closely linked to vertical integration, including cross-subsidization and misuse of competitor information. Moreover, proposals with respect to the tourism sector have included an obligation for WTO Members to address abuse of dominance through vertical integration. Apart from that, recently concluded preferential trade agreements outside of the WTO contain provisions that specifically address network access issues.

Multilateral regulatory solutions for the energy sector can build on these experiences. In addition to transparency, non-discriminatory TPA, and independence of regulators, an 'Energy Reference Paper' should deal with the negative effects on competition that follow from vertical integration. While there are several regulatory options available, the most direct and effective way would be to include a provision explicitly mandating some basic level of separation between energy transmission activities on the one hand and energy production/generation and supply activities on the other.

Table of Cases

WTO Panel and Appellate Body Reports

WTO, Argentina – Measures Affecting the Export of Bovine Hides and the Import of Finished Leather, Report of the Panel (19 December 2000) WT/DS155/R
WTO, Argentina – Measures Relating to Trade in Goods and Services, Report of the Panel (30 September 2015) WT/DS453/R
WTO, Argentina – Measures Relating to Trade in Goods and Services, Report of the Appellate Body (14 April 2016) WT/DS453/AB/R
WTO, Brazil – Measures Affecting Imports of Retreaded Tyres, Report of the Appellate Body (3 December 2007) WT/DS332/AB/R
WTO, Canada – Certain Measures Affecting the Automotive Industry, Report of the Panel (11 February 2000) WT/DS139/R, WT/DS142/R
WTO, Canada – Certain Measures Affecting the Automotive Industry, Report of the Appellate Body (31 May 2000) WT/DS139/AB/R, WT/DS142/AB/R
WTO, Canada – Certain Measures concerning Periodicals, Report of the Panel (14 March 1997) WT/DS31/R
WTO, Canada – Certain Measures concerning Periodicals, Report of the Appellate Body (30 June 1997) WT/DS31/AB/R
WTO, Canada – Measures Relating to Exports of Wheat and Treatment of Imported Grain, Report of the Panel (6 April 2004) WT/DS276/R
WTO, Canada – Measures Relating to Exports of Wheat and Treatment of Imported Grain, Report of the Appellate Body (30 August 2004) WT/DS276/AB/R
WTO, China – Certain Measures Affecting Electronic Payment Services, Report of the Panel (16 July 2012) WT/DS413/R
WTO, China – Measures Affecting Trading Rights and Distribution Services for Certain Publications and Audiovisual Entertainment Products, Report of the Panel (12 August 2009) WT/DS363/R
WTO, China – Measures Related to the Exportation of Various Raw Materials, Reports of the Panel (5 July 2011) WT/DS394/R, WT/DS395/R, WT/DS398/R
WTO, Dominican Republic – Measures Affecting the Importation and Internal Sale of Cigarettes, Report of the Panel (26 November 2004) WT/DS302/R

(continued)

T. M. Dralle, *Ownership Unbundling and Related Measures in the EU Energy Sector*, European Yearbook of International Economic Law 5,
https://doi.org/10.1007/978-3-319-77797-9

WTO, European Communities – Measures Affecting Asbestos and Asbestos-Containing Products, Report of the Panel (18 September 2000) WT/DS135/R
WTO, European Communities – Measures Affecting Asbestos and Asbestos-Containing Products, Report of the Appellate Body (12 March 2001) WT/DS135/AB/R
WTO, European Communities – Measures Affecting the Approval and Marketing of Biotech Products, Reports of the Panel (29 September 2006) WT/DS291/R, WT/DS292/R, WT/DS293/R
WTO, European Communities – Measures Affecting the Importation of Certain Poultry Products, Report of the Panel (12 March 1998) WT/DS69/R
WTO, European Communities – Measures Affecting the Importation of Certain Poultry Products, Report of the Appellate Body (13 July 1998) WT/DS69/AB/R
WTO, European Communities – Measures Prohibiting the Importation and Marketing of Seal Products, Reports of the Appellate Body (22 May 2014) WT/DS400/AB/R, WT/DS401/AB/R
WTO, European Communities – Regime for the Importation, Sale and Distribution of Bananas, Report of the Panel (22 May 1997) WT/DS27/R/ECU, WT/DS27/R/USA, WT/DS27/R/MEX
WTO, European Communities – Regime for the Importation, Sale and Distribution of Bananas, Report of the Appellate Body (9 September 1997) WT/DS27/AB/R
WTO, European Communities – Regime for the Importation, Sale and Distribution of Bananas – Recourse to Article 21.5 by Ecuador, Report of the Panel (12 April 1999) WT/DS27/RW/ECU
WTO, European Communities – Selected Customs Matters, Report of the Panel (16 June 2006) WT/DS315/R
WTO, European Communities – Selected Customs Matters, Report of the Appellate Body (13 November 2006) WT/DS315/AB/R
WTO, European Communities and its Member States – Tariff Treatment of Certain Information Technology Products, Reports of the Panel (16 August 2010) WT/DS375/R, WT/DS376/R, WT/DS377/R
WTO, Japan – Measures Affecting Consumer Photographic Film and Paper, Report of the Panel (31 March 1998) WT/DS44/R
WTO, Japan – Taxes on Alcoholic Beverages, Report of the Appellate Body (4 October 1996) WT/DS8/AB/R, WT/DS10/AB/R, WT/DS11/AB/R
WTO, Korea – Measures Affecting Imports of Fresh, Chilled and Frozen Beef, Report of the Panel (31 July 2000) WT/DS161/R, WT/DS169/R
WTO, Korea – Measures Affecting Imports of Fresh, Chilled and Frozen Beef, Report of the Appellate Body (11 December 2000) WT/DS161/AB/R, WT/DS169/AB/R
WTO, Mexico – Measures Affecting Telecommunications Services, Report of the Panel (2 April 2004) WT/DS204/R
WTO, Peru – Additional Duty on Imports of Certain Agricultural Products, Report of the Panel (27 November 2014) WT/DS457/R
WTO, Thailand – Customs and Fiscal Measures on Cigarettes from the Philippines, Report of the Appellate Body (17 June 2011) WT/DS371/AB/R
WTO, United States – Anti-Dumping Measures on Certain Hot-Rolled Steel Products from Japan, Report of the Panel (28 February 2001) WT/DS184/R
WTO, United States – Anti-Dumping measures on Stainless Steel Plate in Coils and Stainless Steel Sheet and Strip from Korea, Report of the Panel (22 December 2000) WT/DS179/R
WTO, United States – Certain Country of Origin Labelling (COOL) Requirements, Reports of the Panel (18 November 2011) WT/DS384/R, WT/DS386/R
WTO, United States – Certain Country of Origin Labelling (COOL) Requirements, Reports of the Appellate Body (29 June 2012) WT/DS384/AB/R, WT/DS386/AB/R

(continued)

WTO, United States – Countervailing Duty Investigation on Dynamic Random Access Memory Semiconductors (DRAMS) from Korea, Report of the Appellate Body (27 June 2005) WT/DS296/AB/R
WTO, United States – Measures Affecting the Cross-Border Supply of Gambling and Betting Services, Report of the Panel (10 November 2004) WT/DS285/R
WTO, United States – Measures Affecting the Cross-Border Supply of Gambling and Betting Services, Report of the Appellate Body (7 April 2005) WT/DS285/AB/R

GATT Case Law

GATT, Canada – Administration of the Foreign Investment Review Act, Panel Report (7 February 1984)
GATT, EEC – Regulation on Imports of Parts and Components, Report of the Panel (16 May 1990) L/6657 - 37S/132
GATT, European Economic Community – Payments and Subsidies Paid to Processors and Producers of Oilseeds and Related Animal-Feed Proteins, Report of the Panel (25 January 1990) L/6627 - 37S/86
GATT, Follow-Up on the Panel Report "European Economic Community – Payments and Subsidies Paid to Processors and Producers of Oilseeds and Related Animal-Feed Proteins", Report of the Members of the Original Oilseeds Panel (31 March 1992) DS28/R - 39S/91
GATT, United States – Measures Affecting Alcoholic and Malt Beverages, Report of the Panel (19 June 1992) DS23/R - 39S/206
GATT, United States – Taxes on Automobiles, Report of the Panel (11 October 1994) DS31/R (unadopted)
GATT, United States – Taxes on Petroleum and Certain Imported Substances (Superfund), Report of the Panel (17 June 1987) L/6175 - 34S/136
GATT, United States – Trade Measures Affecting Nicaragua, Report by the Panel (13 October 1986) L/6053

Arbitral Awards of International Investment Tribunals

ADC Affiliate Limited and ADC & ADMC Management Limited v. The Republic of Hungary, Award of the Tribunal (2 October 2006) ICSID Case No. ARB/03/16
ADF Group Inc. v. United States of America, Award (9 January 2003) ICSID Case No. ARB (AF)/00/1
AES Summit Generation Limited and AES-Tisza Erömü Kft v. The Republic of Hungary, Final Award (23 September 2010) ICSID Case No. ARB/07/22
Alex Genin, Eastern Credit Limited, Inc. and A.S. Baltoil v. The Republic of Estonia, Award (25 June 2001) ICSID Case No. ARB/99/2
Amco Asia Corporation and others v. Republic of Indonesia, Award (20 November 1984) ICSID Case No. ARB/81/1 1 ICSID Rep. 413 (1993)
Archer Daniels Midland Company v. Mexico, Award (21 November 2007) ICSID Case No. ARB (AF)/04/05
AWG Group Ltd. v. The Argentine Republic, Decision on Liability (30 July 2010)
Azurix Corp. v. The Argentine Republic, Award (14 July 2006) ICSID Case No. ARB/01/12
Bayindir Insaat Turizm Ticaret Ve Sanayi A.S. v. Islamic Republic of Pakistan, Award (27 August 2009) ICSID Case No. ARB/03/29

(continued)

Bayindir Insaat Turizm Ticaret Ve Sanayi A.S. v. Islamic Republic of Pakistan, Decision on Jurisdiction (14 November 2005) ICSID Case No. ARB/03/29
BG Group Plc. v. The Republic of Argentina, Final Award (24 December 2007)
Cementownia "Nowa Huta" S.A. v. Republic of Turkey, Award (17 September 2009) ICSID Case No. ARB(AF)/06/2
Ceskoslovenska Obchodni Banka, A.S. v. The Slovak Republic, Decision of the Tribunal on Objections to Jurisdiction (24 May 1999) ICSID Case No. ARB/97/4
Charanne and Construction Investments v. Spain, Final Award (translation) (21 January 2016) SCC Case No. 062/2012
Chemtura Corporation v. Government of Canada, Award (2 August 2010)
CME Czech Republic B.V. v. The Czech Republic, Partial Award (13 September 2001)
CMS Gas Transmission Company v. The Republic of Argentina, Award (12 May 2005) ICSID Case No. ARB/01/8
Compañiá de Aguas del Aconquija S.A. and Vivendi Universal S.A. v. Argentine Republic, Award (20 August 2007) Award
Compañiá del Desarrollo de Santa Elena, S.A. v. The Republic of Costa Rica, Final Award (17 February 2000) ICSID Case No. ARB/96/1
Consortium RFCC v. Royaume du Maroc, Arbitration Award (22 December 2003) ICSID Case No. ARB/00/6
Continental Casualty Company v. The Argentine Republic, Award (5 September 2008) ICSID Case No. ARB/03/9
Deutsche Bank AG v. Democratic Socialist Republic of Sri Lanka, Award (31 October 2012) ICSID Case No. ARB/09/2
EDF (Services) Limited v. Romania, Award (8 October 2009) ICSID Case No. ARB/05/13
El Paso Energy International Company v. The Argentine Republic, Award (31 October 2011) ICSID Case No. ARB/03/15
Electrabel S.A. v. Republic of Hungary, Decision on Jurisdiction, Applicable Law and Liability (30 November 2012) ICSID Case No. ARB/07/19
Emilio Agustín Maffezini v. The Kingdom of Spain, Award (13 November 2000) ICSID Case No. ARB/97/7
Enron Corporation and Ponderosa Assets, L.P. v. Argentine Republic, Decision on Jurisdiction (14 January 2004) ICSID Case No. ARB/01/3
Enron Corporation and Ponderosa Assets, L.P. v. Argentine Republic, Award (22 May 2007) ICSID Case No. ARB/01/3
Eureko B.V. v. Republic of Poland, Partial Award (19 August 2005)
Gami Investments, Inc. v. The Government of the United Mexican States, Final Award (15 November 2004)
Generation Ukraine, Inc. v. Ukraine, Award (16 September 2003) ICSID Case No. ARB/00/9
Glamis Gold, Ltd. v. The United States of America, Award (8 June 2009)
Impregilo S.p.A. v. Argentine Republic, Award (21 June 2011) ICSID Case No. ARB/07/17
International Thunderbird Gaming Corporation v. The United Mexican States, Arbitral Award (26 January 2006)
Ioannis Kardassopoulos v. The Republic of Georgia, Award (3 March 2010) ICSID Case No. ARB/05/18
LG&E Energy Corp. LG&E Capital Corp. and LG&E International, Inc. v. Argentine Republic, Decision on Liability (3 October 2006) ICSID Case No. ARB/02/1
Liberian Eastern Timber Corporation (LETCO) v. Republic of Liberia, Award (31 March 1986) ICSID Case No. ARB/83/2

(continued)

Loewen Group, Inc. v. United States, Award (26 June 2003) ICSID Case No. ARB(AF)/98/3
Marvin Feldman v. Mexico, Award (16 December 2002) ICSID Case No. ARB(AF)/99/1
Merrill & Ring Forestry L.P. v. The Government of Canada, Award (31 March 2010)
Metalclad Corporation v. The United Mexican States, Award (30 August 2000) ICSID Case No. ARB(AF)/97/1
Methanex Corporation v. United States of America, Final Award of the Tribunal on Jurisdiction and Merits (3 August 2005)
MTD Equity Sdn. Bhd. and MTD Chile S.A. v. Republic of Chile, Award (25 May 2004) ICSID Case No. ARB/01/7
National Grid plc v. The Argentine Republic, Award (3 November 2008)
Nykomb Synergetics Technology Holding AB v. The Republic of Latvia, Arbitral Award (16 December 2003)
Occidental Exploration and Production Company v. The Republic of Ecuador, Final Award (1 July 2004) LCIA Case No. UN 3467
Occidental Petroleum Corporation and Occidental Exploration and Production Company v. The Republic of Ecuador, Award (5 October 2012) ICSID Case No. ARB/06/11
Parkerings-Compagniet AS v. Republic of Lithuania, Award (11 September 2007) ICSID Case No. ARB/05/8
Piero Foresti, Laura de Carli & Others v. The Republic of South Africa, Award (4 August 2010) ICSID Case No. ARB(AF)/07/01
Plama Consortium Limited v. Republic of Bulgaria, Award (27 August 2008) ICSID Case No. ARB/03/24
Pope & Talbot Inc. v. The Government of Canada, Submissions of the United Mexican States (3 April 2000)
Pope & Talbot Inc. v. The Government of Canada, Interim Award (26 June 2000)
Pope & Talbot Inc. v. The Government of Canada, Award on the Merits of Phase 2 (10 April 2001)
Pope & Talbot Inc. v. The Government of Canada, Award in Respect of Damages (31 May 2002)
PSEG Global, Inc. The North American Coal Corporation, and Konya Ingin Electrik Üretim ve Ticaret Limited Sirketi v. Republic of Turkey, Award (19 January 2007) ICSID Case No. ARB/02/5
Ronald S. Lauder v. The Czech Republic, Final Award (3 September 2001)
S.D. Myers, Inc. v. Government of Canada, Partial Award (13 November 2000)
Saipem S.p.A. v. The People's Republic of Bangladesh, Decision on Jurisdiction and Recommendation on Provisional Measures (21 March 2007) ICSID Case No. ARB/05/07
Saluka Investments B.V. v. The Czech Republic, Partial Award (17 March 2006)
Sempra Energy International v. The Argentine Republic, Award (28 September 2007) ICSID Case No. ARB/02/16
Sergei Paushok, CJSC Golden East Company and CJSC Vostokneftegaz Company v. The Government of Mongolia, Award on Jurisdiction and Liability (28 April 2011)
Siemens A.G. v. The Argentine Republic, Award (17 January 2007) ICSID Case No. ARB/02/8
Slovak Gas Holding BV, GDF International SAS and E.ON Ruhrgas International GmbH v. Slovak Republic, Settlement Deed (14 December 2012) ICSID Case No. ARB/12/7
Suez, Sociedad General de Aguas de Barcelona S.A. and InterAgua Servicios Integrales del Agua S.A. v. The Argentine Republic, Decision on Liability (30 July 2010) ICSID Case No. ARB/03/17
Técnicas Medioambientales Tecmed, S.A. v. The United Mexican States, Award (29 May 2003) ICSID Case No. ARB (AF)/00/2

(continued)

Total S.A. v. The Argentine Republic, Decision on Liability (27 December 2010) ICSID Case No. ARB/04/01
Toto Costruzioni Generali S.p.A. v. Republic of Lebanon, Award (7 June 2012) ICSID Case No. ARB/07/12
Vattenfall AB and others v. Federal Republic of Germany ICSID Case No. ARB/12/12
Vladimir Berschader and Moïse Berschader v. The Russian Federation, Award (21 April 2006) SCC Case No. 080/2004
Waste Management, Inc. II v. United Mexican States, Award (30 April 2004) ICSID Case No. ARB(AF)/00/3
William Ralph Clayton, William Richard Clayton, Douglas Clayton, Daniel Clayton and Bilcon of Delaware Inc. v. Government of Canada, Award on Jurisdiction and Liability (17 March 2015) PCA Case No. 2009-04

Other Arbitral Awards

Amoco International Finance Corporation v. The Government of the Islamic Republic of Iran, Award (14 July 1987) Case No. 56 15 Iran-US C.T.R. 189
British Petroleum Exploration Co. (BP) v. Libyan Arab Republic, Award (10 October 1973) 53 I.L.R. 297 (1979)
Emanuel Too v. Greater Modesto Insurance Associates and the United States of America, Award (29 December 1989) Case No. 880 23 Iran-US C.T.R. 378
Foreign Claims Settlement Commission of the United States, Fedorchak Claim, Amended Final Decision (11 April 1962) Claim No. CZ-4634 40 ILR 96
Tippetts, Abbett, McCarthy, Stratton v. TAMS-AFFA Consulting Engineers of Iran, Award (22 June 1984) Case No. 7 6 Iran-US C.T.R. 219

International Court of Justice

International Court of Justice, Nuclear Tests (Australia v. France), Judgment (20 December 1974) I.C.J. Reports 1974, 253

Court of Justice of the European Union

European Court of Justice, Alessandrini, Judgment (30 June 2005) C-295/03 P
European Court of Justice, Campus Oil, Judgment (10 July 1984) C-72/83
European Court of Justice, Commission v. Belgium, Judgment (4 June 2002) C-503/99
European Court of Justice, Commission v. Germany, Judgment (18 July 2007) C-503/04
European Court of Justice, Commission v. Greece, Judgment (8 November 2012) C-244/11
European Court of Justice, Commission v. Italy, Judgment (2 June 2005) C-174/04
European Court of Justice, Commission v. Poland, Judgment (21 December 2011) C-271/09
European Court of Justice, Commission v. Portugal, Judgment (4 June 2002) C-367/98
European Court of Justice, Commission v. Portugal, Judgment (8 July 2010) C-171/08
European Court of Justice, Commission v. Spain, Judgment (13 May 2003) C-463/00

(continued)

European Court of Justice, European Commission v. Alrosa Company Ltd, Judgment (29 June 2010) C-441/07 P
European Court of Justice, Fearon v. Irish Land Commission, Judgment (6 November 1984) 182/83
European Court of Justice, Flughafen Hannover-Langenhagen, Judgment (16 October 2003) C-363/01
European Court of Justice, French Republic v. Commission, Judgment (16 May 2002) C-482/99
European Court of Justice, 'Gazprom' OAO, Opinion of Advocate General Wathelet (4 December 2014) C-536/13
European Court of Justice, Germany v. Parliament and Council (Tobacco Advertising), Judgment (5 October 2000) C-376/98
European Court of Justice, Hauer, Judgment (13 December 1979) C-44/79
European Court of Justice, Italy v. Commission, Judgment (21 March 1991) C-305/89
European Court of Justice, Konle v. Austria, Judgment (1 June 1999) C-302/97
European Court of Justice, Kraus v Land Baden-Württemberg, Judgment (31 March 1993) C-19/92
European Court of Justice, Ospelt and Schlössle Weissenberg, Judgment (23 September 2003) C-452/01
European Court of Justice, Regione autonoma Friuli-Venezia Giulia and ERSA, Judgment (12 May 2005) C-347/03
European Court of Justice, Reinhard Gebhard v Consiglio dell'Ordine degli Avvocati e Procuratori di Milano, Judgment (30 November 1995) C-55/94
European Court of Justice, Rewe v Bundesmonopolverwaltung für Branntwein, Judgment (20 February 1979) C-120/78
European Court of Justice, Ruckdeschel and Others v Hauptzollamt Hamburg-St. Annen, Judgment (19 October 1977) C-117/76 and 16/77
European Court of Justice, Schräder, Judgment (11 July 1989) C-265/87
European Court of Justice, Staat der Nederlanden v Essent NV and Others, Judgment (22 October 2013) C-105/12 to C-107/12
European Court of Justice, Staat der Nederlanden v Essent NV and Others, Opinion of Advocate General Jääskinen (16 April 2013) C-105/12 to C-107/12
European Court of Justice, Wachauf, Judgment (13 July 1989) C-5/88
General Court of the European Union, Alrosa Company Ltd v. European Commission, Judgment (11 July 2007) T-170/06

European Court of Human Rights

European Court of Human Rights, James and Others v. The United Kingdom, Judgment (21 February 1986) Application No. 8793/79
European Court of Human Rights, Matos e Silva, Lda. and Others v. Portugal, Judgment (16 September 1996) Application No. 15777/89

National Courts

German Federal Constitutional Court, Bananenmarkt (7 June 2000) BVerfGE 102, 147
German Federal Constitutional Court, Baulandumlegung (22 May 2001) BVerfGE 104, 1
German Federal Constitutional Court, Denkmalschutz (2 March 1999) BVerfGE 100, 226
German Federal Constitutional Court, Pflichtexemplar (14 July 1981) BVerfGE 58, 137

(continued)

German Federal Constitutional Court, Treibhausgas-Emissionsberechtigung (13 March 2007) BVerfGE 118, 79
German Federal Constitutional Court (21 July 2010) BVerfGE 126, 331
Gerechtshof Amsterdam, Delta N.V. v. Staat der Nederlanden, Judgment (1 November 2016) 200 176 186/01
Gerechtshof Amsterdam, Eneco Holding N.V. v. Staat der Nederlanden, Judgment (1 November 2016) 200 175 864/01
Gerecchtshof Amsterdam, Delta N.V. v. Staat der Nederlanden, Judgment (25 July 2017) 200 176 186/01
Gerechtshof Den Haag, Essent N.V. v. Staat der Nederlanden, Judgment (22 June 2010) 200 035 392/01
Hoge Raad der Nederlanden, Staat der Nederlanden v. Delta N.V. Judgment (26 June 2015) 10/03853
Hoge Raad der Nederlanden, Staat der Nederlanden v. Eneco Holding N.V. Judgment (26 June 2015) 10/03852
Hoge Raad der Nederlanden, Staat der Nederlanden v. Essent N.V. Judgment (26 June 2015) 10/03851
Hoge Raad der Nederlanden, Staat der Nederlanden v. Essent N.V. Judgment (24 February 2012) 10/03851
Rechtbank Den Haag, Essent N.V. v. Staat der Nederlanden, Judgment (11 March 2009) 306 147/ HA ZA 08-756

Legislation

WTO Agreements

Agreement Establishing the World Trade Organization (15 April 1994) 1867 U.N.T.S. 154
Agreement on Trade-Related Aspects of Intellectual Property Rights (15 April 1994) 1869 U.N.T.S. 299
Agreement on Trade-Related Investment Measures (15 April 1994) 1868 U.N.T.S. 186
Annex on Telecommunications (15 April 1994) 33 I.L.M. 1192 (1994)
General Agreement on Tariffs and Trade (15 April 1994) 55 U.N.T.S. 194
General Agreement on Trade in Services (15 April 1994) 1869 U.N.T.S. 183
Reference Paper on Basic Telecommunications Services (24 April 1996) 36 I.L.M. 367 (1997)

International Investment Agreements

Accord entre la Confédération suisse et la République du Zaïre relatif à la protection et à l'encouragement des investissements (10 March 1972) <investmentpolicyhub.unctad.org/download/treatyfile/827> accessed 20 January 2018
Agreement between Bosnia and Herzegovina and the State of Kuwait for the Encouragement and Reciprocal Protection of Investments (13 June 2001) <investmentpolicyhub.unctad.org/download/treatyfile/478> accessed 20 January 2018
Agreement between the Belgo-Luxembourg Economic Union and the Republic of South Africa on the Reciprocal Promotion and Protection of Investments (14 August 1998) <investmentpolicyhub.unctad.org/download/treatyfile/414> accessed 20 January 2018
Agreement between the Federal Democratic Republic of Ethiopia and the State of Kuwait for the Encouragement and Reciprocal Protection of Investments (14 September 1996) <investmentpolicyhub.unctad.org/download/treatyfile/1169> accessed 20 January 2018
Agreement between the Government of the Czech Republic and the Government of the United Arab Emirates for the Promotion and Protection of Investments (23 November 1994) <investmentpolicyhub.unctad.org/download/treatyfile/992> accessed 20 January 2018

(continued)

T. M. Dralle, *Ownership Unbundling and Related Measures in the EU Energy Sector*, European Yearbook of International Economic Law 5,
https://doi.org/10.1007/978-3-319-77797-9

Agreement between the Government of the Italian Republic and the Government of the Republic of South Africa on the Promotion and Protection of Investments (09 June 1997) <investmentpolicyhub.unctad.org/download/treatyfile/3216> accessed 20 January 2018
Agreement between the Government of the Kingdom of the Netherlands and the Government of the State of Kuwait for the Encouragement and Reciprocal Protection of Investments (29 May 2001) <investmentpolicyhub.unctad.org/download/treatyfile/1851> accessed 20 January 2018
Agreement between the Government of the Republic of Latvia and the Government of the State of Kuwait for the Encouragement and Reciprocal Protection of Investments (05 October 2001) <investmentpolicyhub.unctad.org/download/treatyfile/5014> accessed 20 January 2018
Agreement between the Government of the Republic of Nicaragua and the Government of the Italian Republic on the Promotion and Protection of Investments (20 April 2004) <investmentpolicyhub.unctad.org/download/treatyfile/3591> accessed 20 January 2018
Agreement between the Government of the Republic of Slovenia and the Government of the State of Kuwait on the Promotion and Reciprocal Protection of Investments (26 April 2002) <https://www.uradni-list.si/glasilo-uradni-list-rs/vsebina/2002-02-0075> accessed 20 January 2018
Agreement between the Government of the Russian Federation and the Government of the Republic of Lithuania on the Promotion and Reciprocal Protection of Investments (29 June 1999) <investmentpolicyhub.unctad.org/download/treatyfile/1921> accessed 20 January 2018
Agreement between the Government of the United Arab Emirates and the Government of Romania on the Promotion and Protection of Investments (11 April 1993) <http://investmentpolicyhub.unctad.org/download/treatyfile/2217> accessed 20 January 2018
Agreement between the Government of the United Arab Emirates and the Government of the Kingdom of Sweden on the Promotion and Reciprocal Protection of Investments (10 November 1999) <investmentpolicyhub.unctad.org/download/treatyfile/2306> accessed 20 January 2018
Agreement between the Republic of Austria and the State of Kuwait for the Encouragement and reciprocal Protection of Investments (16 November 1996) <http://investmentpolicyhub.unctad.org/download/treatyfile/3315> accessed 20 January 2018
Agreement between the Republic of Croatia and the State of Kuwait for the Promotion and Reciprocal Protection of Investments (08 March 1997) <investmentpolicyhub.unctad.org/download/treatyfile/869> accessed 20 January 2018
Agreement between the Republic of Hungary and the State of Kuwait for the Encouragement and Reciprocal Protection of Investments (08 November 1989) <investmentpolicyhub.unctad.org/download/treatyfile/1529> accessed 20 January 2018
Agreement between the Republic of Lithuania and the State of Kuwait for the Encouragement and Reciprocal Protection of Investments (05 June 2001) <investmentpolicyhub.unctad.org/download/treatyfile/1849> accessed 20 January 2018
Agreement between the State of Kuwait and the Republic of India for the Encouragement and Reciprocal Protection of Investment (27 November 2001) <http://investmentpolicyhub.unctad.org/download/treatyfile/1569> accessed 20 January 2018
Agreement between the Swiss Confederation and the State of Kuwait for the Encouragement and Reciprocal Protection of Investments (31 October 1998) <http://investmentpolicyhub.unctad.org/download/treatyfile/4819> accessed 20 January 2018

Trade-Related Agreements

Association Agreement between the European Union and the European Atomic Energy Community and their Member States, of the one part, and Georgia, of the other part (27 June 2014) OJ 2014/L 261/4

(continued)

Association Agreement between the European Union and the European Atomic Energy Community and their Member States, of the one part, and the Republic of Moldova, of the other part (27 June 2014) OJ 2014/L 260/4

Australia – Chile Free Trade Agreement (30 July 2008) <http://dfat.gov.au/trade/agreements/aclfta/pages/australia-chile-fta.aspx> accessed 20 January 2018

Canada – Chile Free Trade Agreement (05 December 1996) <http://www.sice.oas.org/trade/chican_e/chcatoc.asp> accessed 20 January 2018

Canada – United States Free Trade Agreement (02 January 1988) 27 I.L.M. 281 (1989)

Chile – Korea Free Trade Agreement (15 February 2003) <http://www.sice.oas.org/trade/chiskorea_e/chikoreaind_e.asp> accessed 20 January 2018

Comprehensive Economic and Trade Agreement between the European Union and Canada – Consolidated text (2016) <http://trade.ec.europa.eu/doclib/docs/2014/september/tradoc_152806.pdf> accessed 20 January 2018

Economic Partnership Agreement between the CARIFORUM States, of the one part, and the European Community and its Member States, of the other part (2008) OJ 2008/L 289/3

Energy Charter Treaty (17 December 1994) 2080 U.N.T.S. 95

Enhanced Partnership and Cooperation Agreement between the European Union and its Member States, of the one part, and the Republic of Kazakhstan, of the other part (21 December 2015) OJ 2016/L 29/3

North American Free Trade Agreement (17 December 1992) 32 I.L.M. 289 (1993)

Panama – Taiwan Free Trade Agreement (21 August 2003) <http://www.sice.oas.org/trade/panrc/panrc_e.asp> accessed 20 January 2018

US – Chile Free Trade Agreement (06 June 2003) 42 I.L.M. 1026 (2003)

US – Singapore Free Trade Agreement (06 May 2003) 42 I.L.M. 1026 (2003)

Other Public International Law Agreements

Vienna Convention on the Law of Treaties (23 May 1969) 1155 U.N.T.S. 331

Primary EU Legislation

Charter of Fundamental Rights of the European Union OJ 2012/C 326/391

Treaty Establishing the European Coal and Steel Community (18 April 1951) 261 U.N.T.S. 140

Treaty on European Union (consolidated version) OJ 2012/C 326/13

Treaty on the Functioning of the European Union (consolidated version) OJ 2012/C 326/47

Secondary EU Legislation

Directive 2002/19/EC of the European Parliament and of the Council on access to, and interconnection of, electronic communications networks and associated facilities (07 March 2002) OJ 2002/L 108/7

Directive 2003/54/EC of the European Parliament and of the Council concerning common rules for the internal market in electricity and repealing Directive 96/92/EC (26 June 2003) OJ 2003/L 176/37

(continued)

Directive 2003/55/EC of the European Parliament and of the Council concerning common rules for the internal market in natural gas and repealing Directive 98/30/EC (26 June 2003) OJ 2003/L 176/57
Directive 2009/140/EC of the European Parliament and of the Council amending Directives 2002/21/EC on a common regulatory framework for electronic communications networks and services, 2002/19/EC on access to, and interconnection of, electronic communications networks and associated facilities, and 2002/20/EC on the authorisation of electronic communications networks and services (25 November 2009) OJ 2009/L 337/37
Directive 2009/72/EC of the European Parliament and of the Council concerning common rules for the internal market in electricity and repealing Directive 2003/54/EC (13 July 2009) OJ 2009/L 211/55
Directive 2009/73/EC of the European Parliament and of the Council concerning common rules for the internal market in natural gas and repealing Directive 2003/55/EC (13 July 2009) OJ 2009/L 211/94
Directive 2012/34/EU of the European Parliament and of the Council establishing a single European railway area (21 November 2012) OJ 2012/L 343/32
Directive 2016/2370/EU of the European Parliament and of the Council amending Directive 2012/34/EU as regards the opening of the market for domestic passenger transport services by rail and the governance of the railway infrastructure (14 December 2016) OJ 2016/L 352/1
Directive 96/92/EC of the European Parliament and of the Council concerning common rules for the internal market in electricity (19 December 1996) OJ 1997/L 27/20
Directive 98/30/EC of the European Parliament and of the Council concerning common rules for the internal market in natural gas (22 June 1998) OJ 1998/L 204/1
Commission Regulation (EU) No 984/2013 establishing a Network Code on Capacity Allocation Mechanisms in Gas Transmission Systems and supplementing Regulation (EC) No 715/2009 of the European Parliament and of the Council (14 October 2013) OJ 2013/L 273/5
Council Regulation (EC) No 1/2003 on the implementation of the rules on competition laid down in Articles 81 and 82 of the Treaty (16 December 2002) OJ 2003/L 1/1
Council Regulation (EC) No 139/2004 on the control of concentrations between undertakings (20 January 2004) OJ 2004/L 24/1
Regulation (EC) No 1228/2003 of the European Parliament and of the Council on conditions for access to the network for cross-border exchanges in electricity (26 June 2003) OJ 2003/L 176/1
Regulation (EC) No 713/2009 of the European Parliament and of the Council establishing an Agency for the Cooperation of Energy Regulators (13 July 2009) OJ 2009/L 211/1
Regulation (EC) No 714/2009 of the European Parliament and of the Council on conditions for access to the network for cross-border exchanges in electricity and repealing Regulation (EC) No 1228/2003 (13 July 2009) OJ 2009/L 211/15
Regulation (EC) No 715/2009 of the European Parliament and of the Council on conditions for access to the natural gas transmission networks and repealing Regulation (EC) No 1775/2005 (13 July 2009) OJ 2009/L 211/36
Regulation (EU) No 1219/2012 of the European Parliament and of the Council establishing transitional arrangements for bilateral investment agreements between Member States and third countries (12 December 2012) OJ 2012/L 351/40

National Legislation

Republic of Peru, Electric Concessions Law (Ley de Concesiones Eléctricas) (19 November 1992) Decree Law No. 25844

Republic of Lithuania, Law on the Amendment of the Law on Natural Gas (Gamtinių dujų įstatymo pakeitimo įstatymas) (01 August 2011) Official Gazette, 14.07.2011, No. 87-4186

Republic of Lithuania, Law on Natural Gas (Gamtinių dujų įstatymas) (01 July 2001) Official Gazette, 25.10.2000, No. 89-2743

The Netherlands, Intervention and Implementation Act (Interventie- en Implementatiewet) (01 July 2004) Stb. 328

The Netherlands, Independent Network Operation Act (Wet onafhankelijk netbeheer) (23 November 2006) Stb. 614

Hellenic Republic, Law 4001/2011 on the Operation of Electricity and Gas Energy Markets, for Exploration, Production and Transmission Networks of Hydrocarbons and other provisions (όμος 4001/2011 για τη λειτουργία Ενεργειακών Αγορών λεκτρισμού και Φυσικού Αερίου, για Έρευνα, Παραγωγή και δίκτυα μεταφοράς δρογονανθράκων και άλλες ρυθμίσεις) (2011) Government Gazette, 22.8.2011, No. 179 A

Hellenic Republic, Law 4286/2014 (όμος 4286/2014) (2014) Government Gazette, 19.9.2014, No. 194 A

Republic of Estonia, Natural Gas Act (Maagaasiseadus) (07 May 2014) Riigi Teataja I, 06.05.2014, 11

Republic of Estonia, Amendment to the Natural Gas Act (Maagaasiseaduse muutmise seadus) (08 July 2012) Riigi Teataja I, 28.06.2012, 2

Republic of South Africa, Mineral and Petroleum Resources Development Act (2002) No. 28

Republic of Bulgaria, Draft Law on the Amendment and Supplement of the Energy Act (Законопроект за изменение и допълнение на Закона за енергетиката) (2014) 454-01-23

Federal Republic of Germany, Energy Industry Act (Gesetz über die Elektrizitäts- und Gasversorgung) (07 July 2005) BGBl. I S. 1970, 3621

Federal Republic of Germany, Restriction of Competition Act (Gesetz gegen Wettbewerbsbeschränkungen) (26 June 2013) BGBl. I S. 1750, 3245

Federal Republic of Germany, Act concerning the Agreement of 15 April 1994 Establishing the World Trade Organization and concerning the Amendment of other Laws (Gesetz zu dem Übereinkommen vom 15. April 1994 zur Errichtung der Welthandelsorganisation und zur Änderung anderer Gesetze) (09 September 1994) BGBl. II S. 1438

Documents

GATT/WTO Documents

Armenia – Schedule of Specific Commitments (29 April 2004) GATS/SC/137
Article VI:4 of the GATS: Disciplines on Domestic Regulation Applicable to All Services – Note by the Secretariat (01 March 1999) S/C/W/96
Article XVII (State Trading Enterprises) – Note by the Secretariat (11 August 1987) MTN.GNG/NG7/W/15
'Australian Responses to Panel Questions to Third Parties: China – Publications and Audiovisual Products: WT/DS363/R' (11 August 2008) <http://dfat.gov.au/international-relations/international-organisations/wto/wto-dispute-settlement/pages/china-measures-affecting-trading-rights-and-distribution-services-for-certain-publications-and-audiovisual-entertainment-pr.aspx> accessed 28 January 2016
Austria – Schedule of Specific Commitments (15 April 1994) GATS/SC/7
Chile – Schedule of Specific Commitments (15 April 1994) GATS/SC/18
Communication by Bolivia, Dominican Republic, Ecuador, El Salvador, Honduras, Nicaragua, Panama, Peru and Venezuela – Draft Annex on Tourism (26 September 2001) S/CSS/W/107
Communication from Australia (19 July 1999) S/WPDR/W/1
Communication from Norway: The Negotiations on Trade in Services (21 March 2001) S/CSS/W/59
Communication from the Dominican Republic, El Salvador and Honduras: Replies to the Comments on the Proposed Annex on Tourism (27 October 2000) S/CSS/W/9
Communication from the European Communities and its Member States – Certification: Draft consolidated GATS Schedule (09 October 2006) S/C/W/273
Communication from the European Communities and their Member States – GATS 2000: Energy Services (23 March 2001) S/CSS/W/60
Communication from the United States – Classification of Energy Services (18 May 2000) S/CSC/W/27
Communication from the United States: Draft Offer on Basic Telecommunications (31 July 1995) S/NGBT/W/12/Add.3

(continued)

T. M. Dralle, *Ownership Unbundling and Related Measures in the EU Energy Sector*, European Yearbook of International Economic Law 5,
https://doi.org/10.1007/978-3-319-77797-9

Communication from the United States: Draft Offer on Basic Telecommunications – Revision (26 February 1996) S/NGBT/W/12/Add.3/Rev.1
Communication from the United States: Energy Services (18 December 2000) S/CSS/W/24
Communication from the United States: Pro-competitive Regulatory and other Measures for Effective Market Access in Basic Telecommunications Services (09 February 1995) S/NGBT/W/5
Croatia – Schedule of Specific Commitments (22 December 2000) GATS/SC/130
Czech Republic – Schedule of Specific Commitments (15 April 1994) GATS/SC/26
Decision on Disciplines Relating to the Accountancy Sector – Adopted by the Council for Trade in Services on 14 December 1998 (15 December 1998) S/L/63
Decision on Domestic Regulation – Adopted by the Council for Trade in Services on 26 April 1999 (28 April 1999) S/L/70
Decision on Negotiations on Basic Telecommunications (15 April 1994) LT/UR/D-5/4
Decision on Professional Services – Adopted by the Council for Trade in Services on 1 March 1995 (04 April 1995) S/L/3
Disciplines on Domestic Regulation in the Accountancy Sector – Adopted by the Council for Trade in Services on 14 December 1998 (17 December 1998) S/L/64
Disciplines on Domestic Regulation Pursuant to GATS Article VI:4 – Chairman's Progress Report (14 April 2011) S/WPDR/W/45
Doha Work Programme: Decision Adopted by the General Council on 1 August 2004 (02 August 2004) WT/L/579
Energy Services – Background Note by the Secretariat (09 September 1998) S/C/W/52
Energy Services – Background Note by the Secretariat (12 January 2010) S/C/W/311
Energy Services – Information Note by the Secretariat (22 September 2005) JOB(05)/204
Environmental Services – Background Note by the Secretariat (06 July 1998) S/C/W/46
Estonia – Schedule of Specific Commitments (05 October 1999) GATS/SC/127
European Communities and their Member States – Schedule of Specific Commitments (15 April 1994) GATS/SC/31
'European Union and its Member States – Certain Measures Relating to the Energy Sector' (3 December 2015) <https://www.wto.org/english/tratop_e/dispu_e/cases_e/ds476_e.htm> accessed 13 April 2016
European Union and its Member States – Certain Measures Relating to the Energy Sector, Request for Consultations by the Russian Federation (8 May 2014) WT/DS476/1, S/L/409, G/L/1067, G/SCM/D102/1, G/TRIMS/D/40
European Union and its Member States – Certain Measures Relating to the Energy Sector, Request for the Establishment of a Panel by the Russian Federation (28 May 2015) WT/DS476/2
Finland – Schedule of Specific Commitments (15 April 1994) GATS/SC/33
GATT Analytical Index: Guide to GATT Law and Practice (Articles I - XXI vol 1, 6th updated edition, 1995)
Guidelines for the Scheduling of Specific Commitments under the General Agreement on Trade in Services (GATS), S/L/92 (28 March 2001)
Hungary – Schedule of Specific Commitments (15 April 1994) GATS/SC/40
Lao PDR – Schedule of Specific Commitments (22 April 2013) GATS/SC/150
Latvia – Schedule of Specific Commitments (22 April 1999) GATS/SC/126
Lithuania – Schedule of Specific Commitments (21 December 2001) GATS/SC/133
Ministerial Declaration: Adopted on 14 November 2001 (20 November 2001) WT/MIN(01)/DEC/1
Montenegro – Schedule of Specific Commitments (05 June 2012) GATS/SC/146

(continued)

Negotiations on Trade in Services – Report by the Chairman, Ambassador Fernando de Mateo, to the Trade Negotiations Committee (21 April 2011) TN/S/36
New and Full Notification Pursuant to Article XVII:4(a) of the GATT 1994 and Paragraph 1 of the Understanding on the Interpretation of Article XVII – European Communities (26 February 1999) G/STR/N/4/EEC
Poland – Schedule of Specific Commitments (15 April 1994) GATS/SC/71
Preparations for the 1999 Ministerial Conference: Proposal Regarding the GATS – Communication from the Dominican Republic, El Salvador and Honduras (14 October 1999) WT/GC/W/372, S/C/W/127
'Reply of the European Communities to Third Party Questions: China – Publications and Audiovisual Products: WT/DS363/R' (4 August 2008) <http://trade.ec.europa.eu/doclib/docs/2008/august/tradoc_140294.pdf> accessed 28 January 2016
Report of the Meeting Held on 11 February 2010 (05 March 2010) S/C/M/97
Report of the Meeting Held on 11 July 2000 – Note by the Secretariat (11 September 2000) S/CSC/M/16
Report of the Meeting Held on 22 March 2001 – Note by the Secretariat (27 April 2001) S/CSC/M/19
Report of the Meeting Held on 28 November 2000 – Note by the Secretariat (24 April 2001) S/CSC/M/18/Rev.1
Report of the Meeting Held on 4 October 2000 – Note by the Secretariat (24 November 2000) S/CSC/M/17
Report of the Meeting held on 5 and 6 October 2000: Note by the Secretariat (01 December 2000) S/CSS/M/5
Report of the Working Party on the Accession of the Republic of Kazakhstan to the World Trade Organization (23 June 2015) WT/ACC/KAZ/93
Report on the Meeting Held on 11 May 2001 – Note by the Secretariat (07 June 2001) S/WPDR/M/11
Report on the Meeting Held on 29 November 2000 – Note by the Secretariat (12 March 2001) S/WPDR/M/9
Romania – Schedule of Specific Commitments (15 April 1994) GATS/SC/72
Scheduling of Initial Commitments in Trade in Services: Explanatory Note, MTN.GNS/W/164 (03 September 1993)
Singapore Ministerial Declaration: Adopted on 13 December 1996 (18 December 1996) WT/MIN(96)/DEC
Slovak Republic – Schedule of Specific Commitments (15 April 1994) GATS/SC/77
Slovenia – Schedule of Specific Commitments (30 August 1995) GATS/SC/99
Slovenia – Schedule of Specific Commitments - Supplement 1 (26 February 1998) GATS/SC/99/Suppl.1
Special Topic: Trade and Competition Policy (Annual Report 1997 vol 1, 1997)
Sweden – Schedule of Specific Commitments (15 April 1994) GATS/SC/82
'Telecommunications Services' (no date) <https://www.wto.org/english/tratop_e/serv_e/telecom_e/telecom_e.htm> accessed 11 December 2015
'Third Party Written Submission by the European Communities: China – Publications and Audiovisual Products: WT/DS363/R' (4 July 2008) <http://trade.ec.europa.eu/doclib/docs/2008/august/tradoc_140292.pdf> accessed 28 January 2016
Trade Policy Review – European Union – Minutes of the Meeting (28 November 2013) WT/TPR/M/284/Add.1/Rev.1

(continued)

Trade Policy Review – Report by the Secretariat – China – Revision (12 August 2008) WT/TPR/S/199/Rev.1
Trade Policy Review – Report by the Secretariat – Japan – Revision (06 May 2015) WT/TPR/S/310/Rev.1
Trade Policy Review – Report by the Secretariat – Switzerland and Liechtenstein – Revision (16 August 2013) WT/TPR/S/280/Rev.1
Trade Policy Review – Report by Zimbabwe (14 September 2011) WT/TPR/G/252
Trade Policy Review – Turkey – Report by the Secretariat (19 November 2003) WT/TPR/S/125
Ukraine – Schedule of Specific Commitments (10 March 2008) GATS/SC/144

EU Documents

Amended proposal for a Directive of the European Parliament and of the Council amending Directives 96/92/EC and 98/30/EC concerning rules for the internal markets in electricity and natural gas (07 June 2002) COM(2002) 304 final
An Energy Policy for Europe (10 January 2007) COM(2007) 1 final
Antitrust: Commission welcomes ENI's structural remedies proposal to increase competition in the Italian gas market (MEMO/10/29, 2010)
Antitrust: Commission welcomes E.ON proposals for structural remedies to increase competition in German electricity market (MEMO/08/132, 2008)
Antitrust: Commission welcomes RWE proposals for structural remedies to increase competition in German gas market (MEMO/08/355, 2008)
Ausnahmegenehmigung der Bundesnetzagentur für die OPAL-Gasleitung gemäß Art. 22 der Richtlinie 2003/55 (12 June 2009) C(2009) 4694
Commission Consolidated Jurisdictional Notice under Council Regulation (EC) No 139/2004 on the control of concentrations between undertakings (no date) OJ 2008/C 95/1
Commission Decision 2012/490/EU on amending Annex I to Regulation (EC) No 715/2009 of the European Parliament and of the Council on conditions for access to the natural gas transmission networks (24 August 2012) OJ 2012/L 231/16
Commission Decision on the application of Article 9(9) of Directive 2009/72/EC to Transmission System Operation in Scotland (14 May 2012) C(2012) 3284 final
Commission Decision on the exemption of Adria Link s.r.l. (Italy) , Holding Slovenske Elektrarne d.o.o. (Slovenia) and E3 d.o.o. (Slovenia) under Article 17 of Regulation (EC) No. 714/2009 for two electricity interconnectors between Italy and Slovenia (17 December 2014) C(2014) 9904 final
Commission Decision on the exemption of ElecLink Limited under Article 17 of Regulation (EC) No. 714/2009 for an electricity interconnector between France and Great Britain (28 July 2014) C(2014) 5475 final
Commission Decision on the exemption of the "Gazelle" interconnector from ownership unbundling within the meaning of Article 9 of Directive 2009/73/EC (01 December 2011) C(2011) 8777 final
Commission Decision on the exemption of the Slovakian-Hungarian natural gas interconnector from ownership unbundling rules in Article 9 of Directive 2009/73/EC (17 September 2013) C(2013) 6159 final
Commission Decision on the exemption of the Trans Adriatic Pipeline from the requirements on third party access, tariff regulation and ownership unbundling laid down in Articles 9, 32, 41(6), 41(8) and 41(10) of Directive 2009/73/EC (16 May 2013) C(2013) 2949 final

(continued)

Commission Decision pursuant to Article 3(1) of Regulation (EC) No 714/2009 and Article 10(6) of Directive 2009/72/EC – Ireland – Eirgrid/ ESB (12 April 2013) C(2013) 2169 final	
Commission Decision pursuant to Article 3(1) of Regulation (EC) No 714/2009 and Article 10(6) of Directive 2009/72/EC – United Kingdom (Northern Ireland) – SONI/ NIE (12 April 2013) C(2013) 2170 final	
Commission Decision relating to a proceeding under Article 102 TFEU and Article 54 of the EEA Agreement (29 September 2010) Case COMP/39.315 – ENI	
Commission Decision relating to a proceeding under Article 82 of the EC Treaty and Article 54 of the EEA Agreement (26 November 2008) Cases COMP/39.388 – German Electricity Wholesale Market, COMP/39.389 – German Electricity Balancing Market	
Commission Decision relating to a proceeding under Article 82 of the EC Treaty and Article 54 of the EEA Agreement (18 March 2009) Case COMP/39.402 – RWE Gas Foreclosure	
Commission Opinion correcting Opinion C(2014) 5483 final of 28 July 2014 pursuant to Article 3 (1) of Regulation (EC) No 715/2009 and Article 10(6) and 11(6) of Directive 2009/73/EC – Greece – Certification of DESFA (17 October 2014) C(2014) 7734 final	
Commission Opinion pursuant to Article 3(1) of Regulation (EC) No 714/2009 and Article 10 of Directive 2009/72/EC - Latvia - Certification of Augstsprieguma tikls (03 December 2012) C(2012) 9108 final	
Commission Opinion pursuant to Article 3(1) of Regulation (EC) No 714/2009 and Article 10(6) of Directive 2009/72/EC - Austria - Certification of Eneco Valcanale S.r.l. (05 March 2015) C(2015) 1547 final	
Commission Opinion pursuant to Article 3(1) of Regulation (EC) No 714/2009 and Article 10(6) of Directive 2009/72/EC - Austria - Certification of Vorarlberger Übertragungsnetze GmbH (29 March 2012) C(2012) 2244 final	
Commission Opinion pursuant to Article 3(1) of Regulation (EC) No 714/2009 and Article 10(6) of Directive 2009/72/EC - Czech Republic - Certification of ČEPS (electricity) (04 October 2012) C(2012) 7059 final	
Commission Opinion pursuant to Article 3(1) of Regulation (EC) No 714/2009 and Article 10(6) of Directive 2009/72/EC - Denmark - Certification of Energinet.dk (electricity) (09 January 2012) C(2012) 87 final	
Commission Opinion pursuant to Article 3(1) of Regulation (EC) No 714/2009 and Article 10(6) of Directive 2009/72/EC - Germany - Certification of 50 Hertz Transmission GmbH (06 September 2012) C(2012) 6260 final	
Commission Opinion pursuant to Article 3(1) of Regulation (EC) No 714/2009 and Article 10(6) of Directive 2009/72/EC - Slovak Republic - Certification of Slovenská elektrizačná prenosová sústava a.s (09 August 2013) C(2013) 5376 final	
Commission Opinion pursuant to Article 3(1) of Regulation (EC) No 714/2009 and Article 10 (6) of Directive 2009/72/EC – the Netherlands - Certification of TenneT TSO B.V. (01 July 2013) C(2013) 4206 final	
Commission Opinion pursuant to Article 3(1) of Regulation (EC) No 714/2009 and Article 10(6) of Directive 2009/72/EC and to Article 3(1) of Regulation (EC) No 715/2009 and Article 10(6) of Directive 2009/73/EC - Portugal - Certification of REN Rede Elétrica Nacional S.A. and REN Gasodutos S.A. (12 May 2014) C(2014) 3255 final	
Commission Opinion pursuant to Article 3(1) of Regulation (EC) No 714/2009 and Article 10(6) of Directive 2009/72/EC and to Article 3(1) of Regulation (EC) No 715/2009 and Article 10(6) of Directive 2009/73/EC - United Kingdom - Certification of National Grid Electricity Transmission plc, National Grid Gas plc and National Grid Interconnectors Limited (19 April 2012) C(2012) 2735 final	

(continued)

Commission Opinion pursuant to Article 3(1) of Regulation (EC) No 714/2009 and Articles 10 (6) and 11(6) of Directive 2009/72/EC - United Kingdom - Certification of TC Westermost Rough OFTO Limited (15 February 2016) C(2016) 975 final
Commission Opinion pursuant to Article 3(1) of Regulation (EC) No 715/2009 and Article 10 of Directive 2009/73/EC - Germany - Certification of the Operators of the Nordeuropäische Erdgas Leitung (NEL) (18 October 2013) C(2013) 7019 final
Commission Opinion pursuant to Article 3(1) of Regulation (EC) No 715/2009 and Article 10(6) and 11(6) of Directive 2009/73/EC - Poland - Certification of Gaz-System as the operator of the Polish section of Yamal-Europe Pipeline (09 September 2014) C(2014) 6463 final
Commission Opinion pursuant to Article 3(1) of Regulation (EC) No 715/2009 and Article 10(6) and 11(6) of Directive 2009/73/EC - Poland - Certification of Gaz-System as the operator of the Polish section of Yamal-Europe Pipeline (19 March 2015) C(2015) 2008 final
Commission Opinion pursuant to Article 3(1) of Regulation (EC) No 715/2009 and Article 10(6) of Directive 2009/73/EC – Austria – NABUCCO Gas Pipeline International GmbH (11 December 2012) C(2012) 9575 final
Commission Opinion pursuant to Article 3(1) of Regulation (EC) No 715/2009 and Article 10 (6) of Directive 2009/73/EC - Denmark - Certification of Energinet.dk (gas) (09 January 2012) C(2012) 88 final
Commission Opinion pursuant to Article 3(1) of Regulation (EC) No 715/2009 and Article 10(6) of Directive 2009/73/EC – France – Certification of TIGF (04 June 2014) C(2014) 3837 final
Commission Opinion pursuant to Article 3(1) of Regulation (EC) No 715/2009 and Article 10(6) of Directive 2009/73/EC - Germany - Certification of Thyssengas GmbH (30 January 2013) C(2013) 570 final
Commission Opinion pursuant to Article 3(1) of Regulation (EC) No 715/2009 and Article 10(6) of Directive 2009/73/EC – Italy - Greece - Certification of TAP AG (28 January 2016) C(2016) 538 final
Commission Opinion pursuant to Article 3(1) of Regulation (EC) No 715/2009 and Article 10(6) of Directive 2009/73/EC - Lithuania - Amber Grid (23 March 2015) C(2015) 2135 final
Commission Opinion pursuant to Article 3(1) of Regulation (EC) No 715/2009 and Article 10(6) of Directive 2009/73/EC - Spain - Certification of ENAGAS, S.A. (gas) (15 June 2012) C(2012) 4171 final
Commission Opinion pursuant to Article 3(1) of Regulation (EC) No 715/2009 and Article 10(6) of Directive 2009/73/EC - Sweden - Certification of Swedegas AB (30 April 2012) C(2012) 3009 final
Commission Opinion pursuant to Article 3(1) of Regulation (EC) No 715/2009 and Article 10(6) of Directive 2009/73/EC – the Netherlands - Certification of Gas Transport Services B.V. (01 July 2013) C(2013) 4205 final
Commission Opinion pursuant to Article 3(1) of Regulation (EC) No 715/2009 and Article 10(6) of Directive 2009/73/EC – United Kingdom – Interconnector UK Limited (26 March 2013) C(2013) 1872 final
Commission Proposal for the Modernisation of the Treatment of Public Services in EU Trade Agreements (26 October 2011) TRADE.B.1/SC/am D(2011)
Commission Staff Working Document accompanying the legislative package on the internal market for electricity and gas – Impact Assessment (19 September 2007) SEC(2007) 1179
Commission Staff Working Document on Article 22 of Directive 2003/55/EC concerning common rules for the internal market in natural gas and Article 7 of Regulation (EC) No 1228/2003 on conditions for access to the network for cross-border exchanges in electricity – New Infrastructure Exemptions (06 May 2009) SEC(2009)642 final

(continued)

Commission Staff Working Document – Ownership Unbundling – The Commission's Practice in Assessing the Presence of a Conflict of Interest including in Case of Financial Investors (8 May 2013) SWD(2013) 177 final

Commission Staff Working Document: Ten Years of Antitrust Enforcement under Regulation 1/2003 (09 July 2014) SWD(2014) 230 final

Commission Staff Working Document – Report on the ITO Model (13 October 2014) SWD (2014) 312 final

'Commission Staff Working Paper – Interpretative Note on Directive 2009/72/EC concerning common Rules for the Internal Market in Electricity and Directive 2009/73/EC concerning common Rules for the Internal Market in Natural Gas – The Unbundling Regime' (22 January 2010) <http://ec.europa.eu/energy/gas_electricity/interpretative_notes/doc/implementation_notes/2010_01_21_the_unbundling_regime.pdf> accessed 24 September 2016

Commission Staff Working Paper: Report on the functioning of Regulation 1/2003 (29 April 2009) SEC(2009) 574 final

Council and Commission Decision on the conclusion, by the European Communities, of the Energy Charter Treaty and the Energy Charter Protocol on energy efficiency and related environmental aspects (23 September 1997) OJ 1998/L 69/1

Decision No 1364/2006/EC of the European Parliament and of the Council laying down guidelines for trans-European energy networks and repealing Decision 96/391/EC and Decision No 1229/2003/EC (06 September 2006) OJ 2006/L 262/1

DG Competition Report on Energy Sector Inquiry (10 January 2007) SEC(2006) 1724

Energising Europe: A real market with secure supply (MEMO/07/361, 2007)

Energy Markets in the European Union in 2011 (Publications Office of the European Union 2012)

'EU-US TTIP: Raw Materials and Energy: Initial EU Position Paper' (2013) <http://trade.ec.europa.eu/doclib/docs/2013/july/tradoc_151624.pdf> accessed 5 April 2016

Exemption decision on the Austrian section of the Nabucco pipeline (08 February 2008) CAB D (2008)142

Exemption decision on the Austrian section of the Nabucco pipeline (22 October 2008) CAB D (2008) 1094, C(2008) 6254

'Exemption Decisions and Pending Notifications of National Exemption Decisions for Gas and Electricity' (no date) <https://ec.europa.eu/energy/sites/ener/files/documents/exemption_decisions_15.pdf> accessed 24 September 2015

Final Decision on the Certification of the Transmission System Operator Gaz-System (19 May 2015) DRG-4720-2(28)/2014/2015/6154/KF

Inquiry pursuant to Article 17 of Regulation (EC) No 1/2003 into the European gas and electricity sectors (Final Report) (10 January 2007) COM(2006) 851 final

Mergers: Commission Opens in-depth Investigation into Proposed Acquisition of Greek Gas Transmission System Operator DESFA by SOCAR (IP/14/1442, 2014)

'Opinions and Decisions on Operator Certifications' (no date) <https://ec.europa.eu/energy/sites/ener/files/documents/certifications_decisions.pdf> accessed 24 September 2015

Position of the European Parliament adopted at first reading on 13 March 2002 with a view to the adoption of European Parliament and Council Directive 2002/. . ./EC amending Directive 96/92/EC concerning common rules for the internal market in electricity (13 March 2002) OJ 2003/C 47 E/351

Proposal for a Council Directive concerning common rules for the internal market in electricity (24 February 1992) OJ 1992/C 65/4

Proposal for a Council Directive concerning common rules for the internal market in electricity and for a Council Directive concerning common rules for the internal market in natural gas (21 February 1992) COM(91) 548 final

(continued)

Proposal for a Council Directive concerning common rules for the internal market in natural gas (24 February 1992) OJ 1992/C 65/14

Proposal for a Directive of the European Parliament and of the Council amending Directive 2003/54/EC concerning common rules for the internal market in electricity (19 September 2007) COM (2007) 528 final

Proposal for a Directive of the European Parliament and of the Council amending Directive 2003/55/EC concerning common rules for the internal market in natural gas (19 September 2007) COM (2007) 529 final

Proposal for a Directive of the European Parliament and of the Council amending Directive 2012/34/EU of the European Parliament and of the Council of 21 November 2012 establishing a single European railway area, as regards the opening of the market for domestic passenger transport services by rail and the governance of the railway infrastructure (30 January 2013) COM(2013) 29 final

Proposal for a Directive of the European Parliament and of the Council amending Directives 96/92/EC and 98/30/EC concerning common rules for the internal market in electricity and natural gas (13 March 2001) COM(2001) 125 final

Prospects for the internal gas and electricity market (10 January 2007) COM(2006) 841 final

Question for Written Answer E-001009/14 to the Commission – Radvilė Morkūnaitė-Mikulėnienė (PPE) – European Law Exemptions for Energy Infrastructure Projects with Russia (31 March 2014) OJ 2014/C 300/290

Recommendation for a Council Decision authorising the opening of negotiations on an Agreement between the European Union and the Republic of Azerbaijan on a legal framework governing the control of DESFA by SOCAR (12 February 2014) COM(2014) 68 final

'Reply to Questions from Mr Shmatko on the Third Package' (29 June 2010) <http://www.asktheeu.org/de/request/168/response/558/attach/3/Annex%20reply%20GHP%20Shmatko%203rd%20package%202.pdf> accessed 24 September 2016

Report on progress in creating the internal gas and electricity market (15 November 2005) COM (2005) 568 final

Resolution on Prospects for the Internal Gas and Electricity Market (10 July 2007) P6_TA(2007)0326

Second Progress Report on the Internal Energy Market (02 July 1993) COM(93) 261 final

Summary of Commission Decision (26 November 2008) C(2008) 7367 final; OJ 2009/C 36/8

Summary of Commission Decision (18 March 2009) C(2009) 1885; OJ 2009/C 133/10

Summary of Commission Decision (29 September 2010) C(2010) 6701; OJ 2010/C 352/8

The Economic Impact of Enforcement of Competition Policies on the Functioning of EU Energy Markets (Publications Office of the European Union 2016)

The Fourth Railway Package – Completing the Single European Railway Area to Foster European Competitiveness and Growth (30 January 2013) COM(2013) 25 final

Towards a Comprehensive European International Investment Policy (7 July 2010) COM(2010) 343 final

'Transatlantic Trade and Investment Partnership – EU Textual Proposal: Energy and Raw Materials' (2016) <http://trade.ec.europa.eu/doclib/docs/2016/july/tradoc_154801.pdf> accessed 30 August 2016

Other Documents

Amber Grid, 'AB Amber Grid Corporate Strategy 2015-2020' (2015) <https://www.ambergrid.lt/uploads/structure/docs/318_fb0afbcac104e270ce2e52d63b42ba33.pdf> accessed 24 August 2016

Bundesnetzagentur, Antrag auf Freistellung von der Regulierung – OPAL NEL Transport GmbH (25 February 2009) Az. BK7-08-009

—— Beschluss: Zertifizierung eines Fernleitungsnetzbetreibers – GASCADE Gastransport GmbH (05 February 2013) Az.: BK7-12-031

—— Beschluss: Zertifizierung eines Fernleitungsnetzbetreibers – NEL Gastransport GmbH (20 December 2013) Az.: BK7-12-188

—— Beschluss: Zertifizierung eines Fernleitungsnetzbetreibers – Thyssengas GmbH (12 March 2013) Az.: BK7-12-036

—— Beschluss: Zertifizierung eines Übertragungsnetzbetreibers – 50 Hertz Transmission GmbH (09 November 2012) Az.: BK6-12-040

—— 'Zertifizierungsverfahren – Hinweispapier zur Antragstellung' (BK6-11-157, BK7-11-157 12 December 2011) <http://www.bundesnetzagentur.de/DE/Service-Funktionen/Beschlusskammern/1BK-Geschaeftszeichen-Datenbank/BK7-GZ/2011/2011_0001bis0999/2011_100bis199/BK7-11-157_BKV/BK7-11-157_download.pdf?__blob=publicationFile&v=1> accessed 21 July 2015

Council of the European Economic Area, Conclusions of the 42nd meeting of the EEA Council (19 November 2014)

Council of European Energy Regulators, 'Status Review on the Implementation of Transmission System Operators' Unbundling Provisions of the 3rd Energy Package' (C15-LTF-43-04 2016) <http://www.ceer.eu/portal/page/portal/EER_HOME/EER_PUBLICATIONS/CEER_PAPERS/Cross-Sectoral/2016/C15-LTF-43-04_TSO-Unbundling_Status_Review-28-Apr-2016.pdf> accessed 27 September 2016

Council of the European Union, 'TTE (Energy) Council on 6 June 2008' (9512/1/08 - REV 1, Brussels 27 May 2008)

Deutscher Bundestag, 'Ausarbeitung: Nord Stream 2 – Vorgaben des europäischen Energierechts' (2016) <https://www.bundestag.de/blob/420194/7f62ba1e54f37cacaab01d4db4d1f65a/pe-6-027-16-pdf-data.pdf> accessed 1 August 2016

—— 'Entwurf eines Gesetzes zur Neuregelung energiewirtschaftsrechtlicher Vorschriften' (Drucksache 343/11 6 June 2011) <http://dipbt.bundestag.de/dip21/brd/2011/0343-11.pdf> accessed 26 August 2015

Eesti Gaas, 'History' (no date) <http://www.gaas.ee/en/group/history/> accessed 8 May 2015

Elering, Elering Acquires Gazprom's 37 per cent Stake in Estonian Gas Transmission Network (2015)

Energy Charter Secretariat, 'Frequently Asked Question about the Energy Charter Process' (no date) <http://www.energycharter.org/process/frequently-asked-questions/> accessed 6 August 2016

—— 'Last Formal Version of the Draft Transit Protocol as Discussed by the Charter Conference in 2003' (2003) <http://www.energycharter.org/fileadmin/DocumentsMedia/CC_251_ENG.pdf> accessed 10 March 2016

—— 'List of all Investment Dispute Settlement Cases' (no date) <http://www.energycharter.org/what-we-do/dispute-settlement/all-investment-dispute-settlement-cases/> accessed 6 August 2016

—— 'The Energy Charter Treaty' (no date) <http://www.energycharter.org/process/energy-charter-treaty-1994/energy-charter-treaty/> accessed 6 August 2016

(continued)

—— 'Trade in Energy – WTO Rules Applying under the Energy Charter Treaty' (2001) <http://www.energycharter.org/fileadmin/DocumentsMedia/Thematic/WTO_Rules_applying_to_the_ECT_2002_en.pdf> accessed 13 May 2016

Energie-Control Kommission, Bescheid – Nabucco Gas Pipeline International GmbH (09 April 2008) GZ K NIS G 01/07

—— Bescheid – Nabucco Gas Pipeline International GmbH (26 November 2008) GZ K NIS G 01/08

Eni, 'Interim Consolidated Report' (30 June 2016) <https://www.eni.com/docs/en_IT/enicom/publications-archive/publications/reports/reports-2016/interim-consolidated-report-as-of-june-30-2016.pdf> accessed 31 July 2016

Estonian Competition Authority, 'Annual Report to the European Commission – Estonian Electricity and Gas Market 2012' (Tallinn 2013)

Fluxys, 'Fluxys Acquires Gazprom Stake in Interconnector (UK)' (17 December 2015) <http://www.fluxys.com/group/en/NewsAndPress/2015/151217_Interconnector> accessed 23 June 2016

French Regulatory Authority for Energy CRE, Délibération de la Commission de régulation de l'énergie portant décision de certification de la société TIGF (03 July 2014)

Gazprom, Gazprom seeks international arbitration against Lithuanian Government (2012)

Government of Canada, 'Electricity Infrastructure: About Electricity' (2014) <http://www.nrcan.gc.ca/energy/electricity-infrastructure/about-electricity/7359> accessed 13 September 2016

—— '2004 Canada Model Foreign Investment Promotion and Protection Agreement' (2004) <http://www.italaw.com/documents/Canadian2004-FIPA-model-en.pdf> accessed 13 April 2015

Greek Regulatory Authority for Energy RAE, 'Final Decision on the Certification of the Hellenic Gas Transmission System Operator (DESFA) SA as an Independent Natural Gas Transmission Operator' (Decision No 523/2014 25 September 2014) <http://www.desfa.gr/wp-content/uploads/2015/10/%CF%84%CE%B5%CE%BB%CE%B9%CE%BA%CE%AE-%CE%91%CF%80%CF%8C%CF%86%CE%B1%CF%83%CE%AE-%CF%84%CE%B7%CF%82-%CE%A1%CE%91%CE%95.pdf> accessed 29 June 2015

ILC, Draft Articles on Most-Favoured-Nation Clauses with Commentaries (1978) YBILC 1978/II (2)

ILC, Draft Articles on Responsibility of States for Internationally Wrongful Acts, with commentaries (2001) YBILC 2001/II(2)

ICSID, 'The ICSID Caseload - Statistics (Issue 2016-1)' (2016) <https://icsid.worldbank.org/apps/ICSIDWEB/resources/Documents/ICSID%20Web%20Stats%202016-1%20(English)%20final.pdf> accessed 25 April 2016

Italian Regulatory Authority for Energy AEEG, Albanian Regulatory Authority for Energy ERE and Greek Regulatory Authority for Energy RAE, 'Final Joint Opinion of the Energy Regulators on TAP AG's Exemption Application' (2013) <http://www.autorita.energia.it/allegati/docs/13/249-13all.pdf> accessed 21 September 2016

Latvijas Gāze, 'Shares and Trading' (no date) <http://www.lg.lv/index.php?id=189&lang=eng> accessed 23 June 2016

—— 'Reorganisation Prospectus' (1 July 2016) <http://www.lg.lv/uploads/filedir/File/Jaunumi/2016/Reorganizacija/2016_Latvijas_Gaze_Reorganisation_Prospectus.pdf> accessed 9 September 2016

Lithuanian National Control Commission for Prices and Energy, 'Annual Report on Electricity and Natural Gas Markets of the Republic of Lithuania to the European Commission' (Vilnius 2013) <http://www.regula.lt/en/SiteAssets/ncc-reports/NCC-report-2012.pdf>

(continued)

MENA Chambers, 'South Stream Intergovernmental Agreements: A Compendium' (2014) <http://www.menachambers.com/expertise/energy/South-Stream-IGAs.pdf> accessed 1 May 2015

Ministerial Council of the Energy Community, 'Decision 2011/02/MC-EnC on the Implementation of Directive 2009/72/EC, Directive 2009/73/EC, Regulation (EC) 714/2009 and Regulation (EC) 715/2009 and amending Articles 11 and 59 of the Energy Community Treaty' (6 October 2011) <https://www.energy-community.org/portal/page/portal/ENC_HOME/DOCS/1146182/0633975AB3B67B9CE053C92FA8C06338.PDF> accessed 8 March 2016

Ministry of Economy, Trade and Industry of Japan, 'Electricity Market Reform in Japan' (2013) <http://www.meti.go.jp/english/policy/energy_environment/electricity_system_reform/pdf/201311EMR_in_Japan.pdf> accessed 7 September 2016

Ministry of Energy of the Republic of Lithuania, 'Comment of the Minister of Energy on Gazprom's Decision to Sell its Stake in Lithuanian Utilities' (12 June 2014) <https://enmin.lrv.lt/en/news/comment-of-the-minister-of-energy-on-gazprom-s-decision-to-sell-its-stake-in-lithuanian-utilities> accessed 25 June 2015

Ministry of Foreign Affairs of the Russian Federation, 'Speech by the Minister of Foreign Affairs of Russia Sergey Lavrov During a Meeting with Representatives of the Association of European Businesses in the Russian Federation' (8 October 2012) <http://archive.mid.ru//bdomp/brp_4.nsf/0/52A9A0EC716E909344257A94002EBF18> accessed 5 August 2016

—— 'Interview by the Russian Foreign Minister Sergey Lavrov to the Serbian Newspaper "Politics"' (3 February 2014) <http://www.mid.ru/brp_4.nsf/0/5B3D4C4DD2B0BE5744257C75005E82AC>

—— 'Speech by the Russian Foreign Minister, Sergey Lavrov, and his Answers to Questions from the Mass Media during the Press Conference Summarising the Results of the Negotiations with the Bulgarian Foreign Minister, Kristian Vigenin' (7 July 2014) <http://www.mid.ru/brp_4.nsf/0/E1E909450FC0862F44257D10005BA3C4>

—— 'Foreign Minister Sergey Lavrov's Address and Annual News Conference on Russia's Diplomatic Performance in 2014' (2015) <http://www.mid.ru/brp_4.nsf/0/D1AFD0A22ABD9AB443257DD4004F33B5>

Monopolkommission, 'Strom und Gas 2007: Wettbewerbsdefizite und zögerliche Regulierung' (2007), Sondergutachten 49

Nord Stream, 'The Pipeline' (no date) <https://www.nord-stream.com/the-project/pipeline/> accessed 21 April 2015

—— Nord Stream: "The First Three Kilometres Are Laid" (2010)

Nord Stream 2, Gazprom and ENGIE Modify Nord Stream 2 Shareholdings, Equalizing EU-Russian Ownership (2015)

OECD, Assessment of WTO and Competition Rules for Enterprises with Exclusive or Special Rights (COM/TD/DAFFE/CLP(2000)45/FINAL, 2000)

—— Draft Convention on the Protection of Foreign Property (1967) 7 I.L.M. 117 (1968)

—— OECD Benchmark Definition of Foreign Direct Investment (4th edn, OECD 2008)

—— 'Recommendation of the Council Concerning Structural Separation in Regulated Industries' (C(2011)135 and CORR1 13 December 2011) <http://www.oecd.org/daf/competition/50119298.pdf> accessed 24 June 2015

—— 'Report on Experiences with Structural Separation' (2012) <http://www.oecd.org/daf/competition/50056685.pdf> accessed 24 June 2015

—— 'Restructuring Public Utilities for Competition' (2001) <http://www.oecd.org/competition/sectors/19635977.pdf> accessed 20 January 2016

Permanent Court of Arbitration, 'OAO Gazprom v. The Republic of Lithuania' (no date) <https://pcacases.com/web/view/47> accessed 14 September 2016

(continued)

Republic of Estonia, 'Law on the Amendment of the Natural Gas Act – Explanatory Memorandum – Original Proposal' (2012) <http://www.riigikogu.ee/tegevus/eelnoud/eelnou/5dea306a-39a3-43c7-9d74-e20d79ad6527/Maagaasiseaduse%20muutmise%20seadus/> accessed 18 September 2015
—— 'Law on the Amendment of the Natural Gas Act – Explanatory Memorandum – Second Reading' (2012) <http://www.riigikogu.ee/tegevus/eelnoud/eelnou/5dea306a-39a3-43c7-9d74-e20d79ad6527/Maagaasiseaduse%20muutmise%20seadus/> accessed 18 September 2015
Republic of Lithuania, 'Law on the Amendment of the Law on Natural Gas and Law on the Implementation of the Law on the Amendment of the Law on Natural Gas – Explanatory Notes' (2011) <http://www3.lrs.lt/pls/inter2/dokpaieska.showdoc_l?p_id=391924&p_tr2=2> accessed 17 September 2015
Republic of South Africa, Broad-Based Socio-Economic Empowerment Charter for the South African Mining Industry (11 October 2002)
—— Department of Mineral Resources, Successful Conclusion to SA – Foresti Arbitration Proceedings (2010)
UN, Central Product Classification, Ver. 2.1 (2015)
—— Havana Charter for an International Trade Organization (24 March 1948) UN Doc. E/CONF.2/78
—— Provisional Central Product Classification (1991) ST/ESA/STAT/SER.M/77
UNCTAD, Energy Services in International Trade: Development Implications – Note by the UNCTAD Secretariat (18 June 2001) TD/B/COM.1/EM.16/2
—— Expert Meeting on Strengthening the Capacity for Expanding the Tourism Sector in Developing Countries, with Particular Focus on Tour Operators, Travel Agencies and Other Suppliers (07 July 1998) TD/B/COM.1/17, TD/B/COM.1/EM.6/3
—— Expropriation (UNCTAD Series on Issues in International Investment Agreements II, United Nations 2012)
—— Fair and Equitable Treatment (UNCTAD Series on Issues in International Investment Agreements II, 2012)
—— Lessons from the MAI (UNCTAD Series on Issues in International Investment Agreements, United Nations 1999)
—— National Treatment (UNCTAD Series on Issues in International Investment Agreements, United Nations 1999)
—— Most-Favoured-Nation Treatment (UNCTAD Series on Issues in International Investment Agreements II, United Nations 2010)
—— The Protection of National Security in IIAs (UNCTAD Series on International Investment Policies for Development, United Nations 2009)
—— The Set of Multilaterally Agreed Equitable Principles and Rules for the Control of Restrictive Business Practices (1980) A/C.2/35/6, annex
—— World Investment Report 2016: Investor Nationality: Policy Challenges (United Nations 2016)
UN General Assembly, Resolution 1803 – Permanent Sovereignty over Natural Resources (14 December 1962) A/RES/1803(XVII)
—— Resolution 3281 – Charter of Economic Rights and Duties of States (12 December 1974) A/RES/3281(XXIX)
—— Restrictive business practices (05 December 1980) A/RES/35/63
U.S. International Trade Commission, Electric Power Services – Recent Reforms in Selected Foreign Markets (USITC Publication 3370, 2000)

(continued)

'2004 Canadian Model Foreign Investment Protection Agreement' <http://www.italaw.com/documents/Canadian2004-FIPA-model-en.pdf> accessed 9 June 2015

'2009 German Model Bilateral Investment Treaty' (no date) <http://www.iilcc.uni-koeln.de/fileadmin/institute/iilcc/Dokumente/matrechtinvest/VIS_Mustervertrag.pdf> accessed 9 June 2015

'2012 U.S. Model Bilateral Investment Treaty' (no date) <http://www.state.gov/documents/organization/188371.pdf> accessed 24 September 2016

Bibliography

Peter Abegg and others, 'Entflechtung in Netzsektoren – ein Vergleich' [2014] Bremen Energy Working Papers No. 19

Aly K Abu-Akeel, 'The MFN as it Applies to Service Trade: New Problems for an Old Concept' (1999) 33 Journal of World Trade 103

Rudolf Adlung and others, 'Fog in GATS Commitments – Boon or Bane?' (Staff Working Paper ERSD-2011-04 2011) <https://www.wto.org/english/res_e/reser_e/ersd201104_e.pdf> accessed 29 January 2016

———, 'Public Services and the GATS' (2006) 9 Journal of International Economic Law 455

Rudolf Adlung and Martin Roy, 'Turning Hills into Mountains? Current Commitments Under the General Agreement onTrade in Services and Prospects for Change' (2005) 39 Journal of World Trade 1161

Rudolf Adlung and Weiwei Zhang, 'Trade Disciplines with a Trapdoor: Contract Manufacturing' (2013) 16 Journal of International Economic Law 383

Ahowanou A Agbessi, Les mesures d'indigénisation des investissements privés étrangers au Nigeria et au Zaïre (Doctoral Thesis No. 511, University of Geneva, 1993)

Dapo Akande and Sope Williams, 'International Adjudication on National Security Issues: What Role for the WTO?' (2003) 43 Virginia Journal of International Law 365

Lars Albath, Handel und Investitionen in Strom und Gas: Die internationalen Regeln (Schriftenreihe Energie- und Infrastrukturrecht vol 7, Beck 2005)

Alexandra Anufrieva, Регулирование иностранных инвестиций в ЕС: Общие вопросы и инвестирование в энергетический сектор (Зерцало-М 2014)

Danae Azaria, 'Energy Transit under the Energy Charter Treaty and the General Agreement on Tariffs and Trade' (2009) 27 Journal of Energy & Natural Resources Law 559

Martin Banks, 'Battle Rages between Bulgaria and Brussels over Future of Energy Supplies' EU Reporter (7 May 2014) <http://www.eureporter.co/world/2014/05/07/battle-rages-between-bulgaria-and-brussels-over-future-of-energy-supplies/>

Lorand Bartels, 'The Separation of Powers in the WTO: How to Avoid Judicial Activism' (2004) 53 International and Comparative Law Quarterly 861

——— 'The WTO Legality of the Application of the EU's Emission Trading System to Aviation' (2012) 23 European Journal of International Law 429

Dietrich Barth, 'Das Allgemeine Übereinkommen über den internationalen Dienstleistungshandel (GATS)' [1994] Europäische Zeitschrift für Wirtschaftsrecht 455

T. M. Dralle, *Ownership Unbundling and Related Measures in the EU Energy Sector*, European Yearbook of International Economic Law 5,
https://doi.org/10.1007/978-3-319-77797-9

Jürgen Basedow, Weltkartellrecht: Ausgangslage und Ziele, Methoden und Grenzen der internationalen Vereinheitlichung des Rechts der Wettbewerbsbeschränkungen (Beiträge zum ausländischen und internationalen Privatrecht vol 63, Mohr Siebeck 1998)

Jürgen F Baur and others, Eigentumsentflechtung der Energiewirtschaft durch Europarecht: Mittel, Schranken und Rechtsfolgen (Veröffentlichungen des Instituts für Energierecht an der Universität zu Köln vol 138, Nomos 2008)

——— Baur and Andreas Lückenbach, Fortschreitende Regulierung der Energiewirtschaft: Eine kritische Stellungnahme zu den Kommissionsvorschlägen zur Änderung der Binnenmarktrichtlinie Erdgas (98/30/EG) (Nomos 2002)

——— Baur, Kai U Pritzsche and Stefan Klauer, Ownership Unbundling: Wesen und Vereinbarkeit mit Europarecht und Verfassungsrecht (Veröffentlichungen des Instituts für Energierecht an der Universität zu Köln vol 121, Nomos 2006a)

——— Baur and Matthias Schmidt-Preuß, 'Europarechtliche Grundlagen des Unbundling' in Jürgen F Baur, Kai U Pritzsche and Stefan Simon (eds), Unbundling in der Energiewirtschaft: Ein Praxishandbuch (Carl Heymanns Verlag 2006b)

Jürgen F Baur, Kai U Pritzsche and Sebastian Pooschke, 'Ownership Unbundling von Energienetzen und der europäische Schutz des Eigentums' [2008] Deutsches Verwaltungsblatt 483

Jürgen F Baur, 'Ausschließliche Nutzungsrechte an bestimmten Großinvestitionen im Gas- und im Elektrizitätsbereich' in Jürgen F Baur and others (eds), Festschrift für Gunther Kühne zum 70. Geburtstag (Verlag Recht und Wirtschaft 2009)

Karel Beckman, 'Can Nord Stream 2 Be Stopped?' (14 April 2016) <http://www.energypost.eu/can-nord-stream-2-stopped/> accessed 23 June 2016

Norbert Bernsdorff, 'Artikel 17 – Eigentumsrecht' in Jürgen Meyer (ed), Charta der Grundrechte der Europäischen Union (4th edn. Nomos 2014)

Fiona C Beveridge, 'Taking Control of Foreign Investment: A Case Study of Indigenisation in Nigeria' (1991) 40 International and Comparative Law Quarterly 302

Jagdish Bhagwati, 'International Trade in Services and Its Relevance for Economic Development' in Douglas A Irwin (ed), Political Economy and International Economics (The MIT Press 1991)

Sadeq Z Bigdeli and Mira Burri Nenova, 'Article IX GATS' in Rüdiger Wolfrum, Peter-Tobias Stoll and Clemens Feinäugle (eds), WTO – Trade in Services (Max Planck Commentaries on World Trade Law vol 6. Martinus Nijhoff Publishers 2008a)

——— Bigdeli and Stefan Rechsteiner, 'Article VIII GATS' in Rüdiger Wolfrum, Peter-Tobias Stoll and Clemens Feinäugle (eds), WTO – Trade in Services (Max Planck Commentaries on World Trade Law vol 6. Martinus Nijhoff Publishers 2008b)

Jan A Bischoff, 'Just a Little BIT of "Mixity"? The EU's Role in the Field of International Investment Protection Law' (2011) 48 Common Market Law Review 1527

Andrea K Bjorklund, 'National Treatment' in August Reinisch (ed), Standards of Investment Protection (Oxford University Press 2008)

Armin von Bogdandy and Joseph Windsor, 'Understanding on Commitments in Financial Services' in Rüdiger Wolfrum, Peter-Tobias Stoll and Clemens Feinäugle (eds), WTO – Trade in Services (Max Planck Commentaries on World Trade Law vol 6. Martinus Nijhoff Publishers 2008)

Achim-R Börner, 'Investment Law and Energy' in Marc Bungenberg and others (eds), International Investment Law (C.H. Beck; Hart; Nomos 2015)

Anatole Boute, Russian Electricity and Energy Investment Law (Law in Eastern Europe, Brill 2015)

——— 'Energy Trade and Investment Law: International Limits to EU Energy Law and Policy' in Martha M Roggenkamp and others (eds), Energy Law in Europe - National, EU and International Regulation (3rd edn. Oxford University Press 2016)

——— 'Wederkerigheid in Europese en Russische energie-investeringen: Een juridische analyse van de "Gazprom-clausule"' [2007] Tijdschrift voor Energierecht 247

Marco C Bronckers and Pierre Larouche, 'Telecommunications Services and the World Trade Organization' (1997) 31 Journal of World Trade 5

Ulrich Büdenbender and Peter Rosin, Einführung eines Ownership Unbundling bzw. Independent System Operator in der Energiewirtschaft: Rechtliche und rechtspolitische Würdigung der wesentlichen Argumente der Europäischen Kommission (Verlag Energiewirtschaft und Technik 2007)

Oliver Budzinski, The Governance of Global Competition: Competence Allocation in International Competition Policy (Edward Elgar 2008)

'Bulgaria, Commission, Lost in Translation over South Stream' EurActiv (25 April 2014) <http://www.euractiv.com/sections/energy/bulgaria-commission-lost-translation-over-south-stream-301751>

Marc Bungenberg, 'Going Global? The EU Common Commercial Policy After Lisbon' in Christoph Herrmann and Jörg P Terhechte (eds), European Yearbook of International Economic Law 2010 (Springer 2010)

Mira Burri Nenova, 'The Law of the World Trade Organization and the Communications Law of the European Community: On a Path of Harmony or Discord?' (2007) 41 Journal of World Trade 833

Dirk Buschle, 'Unbundling of State-owned Transmission System Operators – Effective Remedy or Eyewash?' [2013] European Networks Law and Regulation Quarterly 49

Emmanuel Cabau, 'Unbundling of Transmission System Operators' in Christopher Jones (ed), The Internal Energy Market – The Third Liberalisation Package (EU Energy Law Series vol 1, 3rd edn. Claeys & Casteels Publishing 2010)

Christian Calliess, Entflechtung im europäischen Energiebinnenmarkt: Zur Vereinbarkeit der europäischen Pläne für ein Ownership Unbundling mit der Kompetenzordnung des EG-Vertrages, insbesondere Art. 295 EGV, und dem allgemeinen Gleichheitssatz (Bochumer Beiträge zum Berg- und Energierecht vol 50, Boorberg 2008)

——— 'Ownership Unbundling für alle?: Kritische Überlegungen zu den aktuellen Entflechtungsvorhaben der Europäischen Kommission' (2007) 57 Energiewirtschaftliche Tagesfragen 92

Peter Cameron, Competition in Energy Markets – Law and Regulation in the European Union (1st edn, Oxford University Press 2002)

Nichola Cho and Fausta Geelhoed, 'The Nord Stream Pipeline Project – A Brief Overview of its Legal and European Relevance for Supply Security' in Ulf Hammer and Martha M Roggenkamp (eds), European Energy Law Report VI (Energy & Law vol 8. Intersentia 2009)

George C Christie, 'What Constitutes a Taking of Property under International Law?' (1994) 88 American Journal of International Law 307

Katherine Connolly, 'Finding Space for Regulatory Autonomy in GATS Article XVII after EC – Seals: Public Services and the 'Likeness' of Public and Private Service Providers' (2015) 42 Legal Issues of Economic Integration 57

Mireille Cossy, 'Water Services at the WTO' in Edith B Weiss, Laurence Boisson de Chazournes and Nathalie Bernasconi-Osterwalder (eds), Fresh Water and International Economic Law (Oxford University Press 2005)

——— 'Some Thoughts on the Concept of "Likeness" in the GATS' in Marion Panizzon, Nicole Pohl and Pierre Sauvé (eds), GATS and the Regulation of International Trade in Services (Cambridge University Press 2008)

——— 'The Liberalization of Energy Services: Are PTAs More Energetic than the GATS?' in Juan A Marchetti and Martin Roy (eds), Opening Markets for International Trade in Services: Countries and Sectors in Bilateral and WTO Negotiations (Cambridge University Press 2009)

——— 'Energy Transport and Transit in the WTO' in Joost Pauwelyn (ed), Global Challenges at the Intersection of Trade, Energy and the Environment (Center for Economic and Policy Research 2010)

——— 'Energy Services under the General Agreement on Trade in Services' in Yulia Selivanova (ed), Regulation of Energy in International Trade Law: WTO, NAFTA and Energy Charter (Kluwer Law International 2012a)

——— 'Energy Trade and WTO Rules: Reflexions on Sovereignty over Natural Resources, Export Restrictions and Freedom of Transit' in Christoph Herrmann and Jörg P Terhechte (eds), European Yearbook of International Economic Law 2012 (European Yearbook of International Economic Law vol 3. Springer 2012b)

Thomas Cottier and others, 'Energy in WTO Law and Policy' in Thomas Cottier and Panagiotis Delimatsis (eds), The Prospects of International Trade Regulation: From Fragmentation to Coherence (Cambridge University Press 2011a)

Thomas Cottier and Panagiotis Delimatsis, 'Article XIVbis GATS' in Rüdiger Wolfrum, Peter-Tobias Stoll and Clemens Feinäugle (eds), WTO – Trade in Services (Max Planck Commentaries on World Trade Law vol 6. Martinus Nijhoff Publishers 2008)

Thomas Cottier, Panagiotis Delimatsis and Nicolas F Diebold, 'Article XIV GATS' in Rüdiger Wolfrum, Peter-Tobias Stoll and Clemens Feinäugle (eds), WTO – Trade in Services (Max Planck Commentaries on World Trade Law vol 6. Martinus Nijhoff Publishers 2008)

———, Sofya Matteotti-Berkutova and Olga Nartova, 'Third Country Relations in EU Unbundling of Natural Gas Markets: The "Gazprom Clause" of Directive 2009/73 EC and WTO Law' in Dirk Buschle, Simon Hirsbrunner and Christine Kaddous (eds), European Energy Law: Droit européen de l'énergie (Dossier de droit européen vol 22. Helbing Lichtenhahn 2011b)

Paul Craig and Gráinne de Búrca, EU Law: Text, Cases, and Materials (5th edn, Oxford University Press 2011)

Robert W Crandal, Jeffrey A Eisenach and Robert E Litan, 'Vertical Separation of Telecommunications Networks: Evidence from Five Countries' (2010) 62 Federal Communications Law Journal 493

James Crawford, Brownlie's Principles of Public International Law (8th edn, Oxford University Press 2012)

Eugene Cross and others, 'EU Energy Law' in Martha M Roggenkamp and others (eds), Energy Law in Europe – National, EU and International Regulation (2nd edn. Oxford University Press 2007)

Maher M Dabbah, International and Comparative Competition Law (Cambridge University Press 2010)

Bart De Meester, Liberalization of Trade in Banking Services: An International and European Perspective (Cambridge University Press 2014)

———, 'The Global Financial Crisis and Government Support for Banks: What Role for the GATS?' (2010) 13 Journal of International Economic Law 27

Bart De Meester and Dominic Coppens, 'Mode 3 of the GATS: A Model for Disciplining Measures Affecting Investment Flows?' in Zdenek Drabek and Petros C Mavroidis (eds), Regulation of Foreign Investment: Challenges to International Harmonization (World Scientific Studies in International Economics vol 21. World Scientific 2013)

Christopher Decker, Modern Economic Regulation: An Introduction to Theory and Practice (Cambridge University Press 2015)

Iñigo del Guayo, Gunther Kühne and Martha M Roggenkamp, 'Ownership Unbundling and Property Rights in the EU Energy Sector' in Aileen McHarg and others (eds), Property and the Law in Energy and Natural Resources (Oxford University Press 2010)

Panagiotis Delimatsis, International Trade in Services and Domestic Regulations: Necessity, Transparency, and Regulatory Diversity (International Economic Law Series, Oxford University Press 2007a)

——— 'Towards a Horizontal Necessity Test for Services: Completing the GATS Article VI:4 Mandate' in Marion Panizzon, Nicole Pohl and Pierre Sauvé (eds), GATS and the Regulation of International Trade in Services (Cambridge University Press 2008)

Panagiotis Delimatsis and Martín Molinuevo, 'Article XVI GATS' in Rüdiger Wolfrum, Peter-Tobias Stoll and Clemens Feinäugle (eds), WTO – Trade in Services (Max Planck Commentaries on World Trade Law vol 6. Martinus Nijhoff Publishers 2008)

Panagiotis Delimatsis, 'Due Process and "Good" Regulation Embedded in the GATS – Disciplining Regulatory Behaviour in Services Through Article VI of the GATS' (2007b) 10 Journal of International Economic Law 13

David Diaz, 'The Viability and Sustainability of International Tourism in Developing Countries' (2001) <https://www.wto.org/english/tratop_e/serv_e/diaz.doc> accessed 20 December 2015

Nicolas F Diebold, Non-Discrimination in International Trade in Services: 'Likeness' in WTO/GATS (Cambridge International Trade and Economic Law, Cambridge University Press 2010)

——— 'Standards of Non-Discrimination in International Economic Law' (2011) 60 International and Comparative Law Quarterly 831

Nicholas DiMascio and Joost Pauwelyn, 'Nondiscrimination in Trade and Investment Treaties: Worlds Apart or Two Sides of the Same Coin?' (2008) 102 American Journal of International Law 48

Rudolf Dolzer and Christoph Schreuer, Principles of International Investment Law (2nd edn, Oxford University Press 2012)

Rudolf Dolzer, 'Indirect Expropriation: New Developments?' (2002) 11 New York University Environmental Law Journal 64

'EC: Russia Should Apply for South Stream Exemption' Natural Gas Europe (7 December 2013) <http://www.naturalgaseurope.com/south-stream-pipeline-exemption-eu-rules> accessed 17 July 2016

Piet Eeckhout, 'Constitutional Concepts for Free Trade in Services' in Gráinne de Búrca and Joanne Scott (eds), The EU and the WTO: Legal and Constitutional Issues (Hart Publishing 2001)

Claus-Dieter Ehlermann and Lothar Ehring, 'WTO Dispute Settlement and Competition Law: Views from the Perspective of the Appellate Body's Experience' (2002) 26 Fordham International Law Journal 1505

Lothar Ehring, 'De Facto Discrimination in World Trade Law: National and Most-Favoured-Nation Treatment – or Equal Treatment?' (2002) 36 Journal of World Trade 921

Andrew Emmerson, 'Conceptualizing Security Exceptions: Legal Doctrine or Political Excuse?' (2008) 11 Journal of International Economic Law 135

Ilaria Espa and Kateryna Holzer, 'Negotiating an Energy Deal under TTIP: Drivers and Impediments to U.S. Shale Exports to Europe' 43 Denver Journal of International Law and Policy 357

Phillip Evans, Recent Developments in Trade and Competition Issues in the Services Sector: A Review of Practices in Travel and Tourism (UNCTAD/ITCD/CLP/Misc.13, UNCTAD Series on Issues in Competition Law and Policy, 1999)

Peter C Evans, Liberalizing Global Trade in Energy Services (The AEI Press 2002)

Paolo D Farah and Elena Cima, 'Energy Trade and the WTO: Implications for Renewable Energy and the OPEC Cartel' (2013) 16 Journal of International Economic Law 707

Ole K Fauchald, Environmental Taxes and Trade Discrimination (International Environmental Law & Policy Series vol 50, Kluwer Law International 1998)

Clemens Feinäugle, 'Article XXVIII GATS' in Rüdiger Wolfrum, Peter-Tobias Stoll and Clemens Feinäugle (eds), WTO – Trade in Services (Max Planck Commentaries on World Trade Law vol 6, Martinus Nijhoff Publishers 2008)

Ulrich Forsthoff, 'AEUV Art. 49 Niederlassungsfreiheit' in Eberhard Grabitz, Meinhard Hilf and Martin Nettesheim (eds), Das Recht der Europäischen Union: EUV/AEUV (54th edn. C.H. Beck 2014)

L. Y Fortier and Stephen L Drymer, 'Indirect Expropriation in the Law of International Investment: I Know It When I See It, or Caveat Investor' (2004) 19 ICSID Review – Foreign Investment Law Journal 293

Eleanor M Fox, 'The WTO's First Antitrust Case – Mexican Telecom: A Sleeping Victory for Trade and Competition' (2006) 9 Journal of International Economic Law 271

Susan D Franck, 'Occidental Exploration & Production Co. v. Republic of Ecuador' (2005) 99 American Journal of International Law 675

Markus Fredebeul-Krein and Andreas Freytag, 'The Case for a More Binding WTO Agreement on Regulatory Principles in Telecommunication Markets' (1999) 23 Telecommunications Policy 625

Christopher Frey, 'Die Bedeutung des Welthandelsrechts für die Einfuhr von Strom aus Drittländern in den Energiebinnenmarkt' in Thilo Rensmann and Stefan Storr (eds), Die Energiewende im rechtlichen Mehrebenensystem: Regionale, nationale und internationale Herausforderungen (Verlag Österreich 2015)

Rachel Frid, 'The Telecommunications Pact under the GATS: Another Step Towards the Rule of Law' (1997) 24 Legal Issues of Economic Integration 67

Sanford E Gaines and Birgitte E Olsen, 'Trade and Social Objectives' in Sanford E Gaines, Birgitte E Olsen and Karsten E Sørensen (eds), Liberalising Trade in the EU and the WTO: A Legal Comparison (Cambridge University Press 2012)

Carlo Gamberale, 'Energy Services', Guide to the GATS: An Overview of Issues for Further Liberalization of Trade in Services (Kluwer Law International 2001)

Henry Gao, 'Annex on Telecommunications' in Rüdiger Wolfrum, Peter-Tobias Stoll and Clemens Feinäugle (eds), WTO – Trade in Services (Max Planck Commentaries on World Trade Law vol 6. Martinus Nijhoff Publishers 2008a)

——— 'Telecommunications Services: Reference Paper' in Rüdiger Wolfrum, Peter-Tobias Stoll and Clemens Feinäugle (eds), WTO – Trade in Services (Max Planck Commentaries on World Trade Law vol 6. Martinus Nijhoff Publishers 2008b)

Bryan A. Garner (ed), Black's Law Dictionary (9th edn)

'Gazprom Drops One Arbitration Case Against Lithuania' Natural Gas Europe (5 April 2015) <http://www.naturalgaseurope.com/gazprom-lithuania-arbitration-case-23046>

Felix Geiger, Beschränkungen von Direktinvestitionen aus Drittstaaten (Schriften zum Öffentlichen Wirtschaftsrecht vol 4, Nomos 2013)

Damien Geradin, 'Introduction' in Damien Geradin (ed), The Liberalization of Electricity and Natural Gas in the European Union (Kluwer Law International 2001)

Damien Geradin and Michel Kerf, 'Levelling the Playing Field: Is the WTO Adequately Equipped to Prevent Anti-Competitive Practices in Telecommunications?' in Damien Geradin and David Luff (eds), The WTO and Global Convergence in Telecommunications and Audio-Visual Services (Cambridge University Press 2004)

Claas F Germelmann, 'Der gemeinschaftsrechtliche Rahmen für Schutzmaßnahmen gegenüber Investitionen aus Drittstaaten im Energiesektor' (2009) 124 Deutsches Verwaltungsblatt 78

Silke Goldberg and Henrik Bjørnebye, 'Introduction and Comment' in Bram Delvaux, Michaël Hunt and Kim Talus (eds), EU Energy Law and Policy Issues (vol 3. Intersentia 2012)

Ignacio Gómez-Palacio and Peter Muchlinski, 'Admission and Establishment' in Peter Muchlinski, Federico Ortino and Christoph Schreuer (eds), The Oxford Handbook of International Investment Law (Oxford University Press 2008)

D. V Gordon, K. Gunsch and C. V Pawluk, 'A Natural Monopoly in Natural Gas Transmission' (2003) 25 Energy Economics 473

Floris Gräper and Christof Schoser, 'Third Party Access' in Christopher Jones (ed), The Internal Energy Market – The Third Liberalisation Package (EU Energy Law Series vol 1, 3rd edn. Claeys & Casteels Publishing 2010)

Massimo G Grosso, Molly Lesher and Enrico Pinali, Services Trade Liberalisation and Tourism Development: OECD Trade Policy Working Paper No. 57 (TD/TC/WP(2006)37/FINAL, 2007)

Rainer Grote, 'Article XXIII GATS' in Rüdiger Wolfrum, Peter-Tobias Stoll and Clemens Feinäugle (eds), WTO – Trade in Services (Max Planck Commentaries on World Trade Law vol 6. Martinus Nijhoff Publishers 2008)

Karolis Gudas, Intersection of WTO and EU law in International Electricity Trade: Analysis of the Regulatory Environment for Electricity Systems Development (PhD Dissertation, forthcoming)

Ivan Gudkov, 'Третий энергетический пакет ЕС: разъединение вертикально интегрированных компаний и ограничение прав инвесторов из третьих стран' [2007] НефтьГазПраво 53

——— 'Третий энергетический пакет Европейского союза' [2010] НефтьГазПраво 58

——— 'Газовый диалог России и ЕС: взаимодействие и конфликт международного и европейского права' [2014] Научный журнал Российского газового общества 49

——— 'Проблемы международноправовового регулирования энергетических отношений на примере взаимодействия России и Европейского союза' [2015] Закон 84

Klaus Gugler, Margarethe Rammerstorfer and Stephan Schmitt, 'Ownership Unbundling and Investment in Electricity Markets – A Cross Country Study' (2013) 40 Energy Economics 702

Jörg Gundel and Claas F Germelmann, 'Kein Schlussstein für die Liberalisierung der Energiemärkte' [2009] Europäische Zeitschrift für Wirtschaftsrecht 763

Anca Gurzu, 'Nord Stream 2's Opponents Look for Legal Ammunition' (30 December 2015) <http://www.politico.eu/article/nord-stream-2s-opponents-look-for-legal-ammunition/> accessed 23 June 2016

Sanam S Haghighi, Energy Security: The External Legal Relations of the European Union with Major Oil and Gas Supplying Countries (Modern Studies in European Law vol 16, Hart 2007)

——— 'Establishing an External Policy to Guarantee Energy Security in Europe?: A Legal Analysis' in Ulf Hammer and Martha M Roggenkamp (eds), European Energy Law Report VI (Energy & Law vol 8. Intersentia 2009)

Michael J Hahn, 'Vital Interests and the Law of GATT: An Analysis of GATT's Security Exception' (1991) 12 Michigan Journal of International Law 558

——— Die einseitige Aussetzung von GATT-Verpflichtungen als Repressalie (Beiträge zum ausländischen öffentlichen Recht und Völkerrecht vol 122, Springer 1996)

Leigh Hancher and Francesco M Salerno, 'Energy Policy after Lisbon' in Andrea Biondi, Piet Eeckhout and Stefanie Ripley (eds), EU Law After Lisbon (Oxford University Press 2012)

Richard Happ, 'The Legal Status of the Investor vis-a-vis the European Communities: Some Salient Thoughts' (2007) 10 International Arbitration Law Review 74

Katrin Harjes, '§ 4b Zertifizierung in Bezug auf Drittstaaten' in Franz J Säcker (ed), Berliner Kommentar zum Energierecht (vol 1, 3rd edn. Dt. Fachverl. Fachmedien Recht und Wirtschaft 2014)

Tim Heitling and Ann-Christin Wiegemann, 'Fallstrick für Finanzinvestoren? – Die eigentumsrechtliche Entflechtung von Transportnetzbetreibern nach dem neuen EnWG' [2011] Netzwirtschaften & Recht 233

Hans Heller, Neue Erdgasinfrastrukturen und Freistellung von der Regulierung: Ein legitimes Instrument der Investitionsförderung? (Nomos 2013)

——— 'Neue Erdgasinfrastrukturen und Freistellung von der Regulierung: Art. 36 der Erdgasrichtlinie 2009/73/EG (§ 28a EnWG) als legitimes Instrument der Investitionsförderung?' (2015) 12 Netzwirtschaften & Recht 66

Caroline Henckels, 'Proportionality and the Standard of Review in Fair and Equitable Treatment Claims: Balancing Stability and Consistency with the Public Interest' (SIEL Working Paper No 2012/27 2012a) <http://papers.ssrn.com/sol3/papers.cfm?abstract_id=2091474> accessed 12 April 2016

——— 'Indirect Expropriation and the Right to Regulate: Revisiting Proportionality Analysis and the Standard of Review in Investor-State Arbitration' (2012b) 15 Journal of International Economic Law 223

Matthias Herdegen, Principles of International Economic Law (Oxford University Press 2013)

Juliane Hernekamp, '§ 21 Ausgewählte Dienstleistungssektoren' in Meinhard Hilf and Stefan Oeter (eds), WTO-Recht: Rechtsordnung des Welthandels (2nd edn. Nomos 2010)

Christoph Herrmann, Wolfgang Weiß and Christoph Ohler, Welthandelsrecht (C.H. Beck 2007)

Sebastian M Heselhaus, '§32 Eigentumsgrundrecht' in Sebastian M Heselhaus and Carsten Nowak (eds), Handbuch der Europäischen Grundrechte (C.H. Beck 2006)

Holger Hestermeyer, 'Article XXI GATT' in Rüdiger Wolfrum, Peter-Tobias Stoll and Holger Hestermeyer (eds), WTO – Trade in Goods (Max Planck Commentaries on World Trade Law vol 5. Martinus Nijhoff Publishers 2011)

Rosalyn Higgins, 'The Taking of Property by the State' (1982) 176 Recueil des Cours 259

T. P Hill, 'On Goods and Services' (1977) 23 Review of Income and Wealth 315

Steffen Hindelang, The Free Movement of Capital and Foreign Direct Investment: The Scope of Protection in EU Law (Oxford University Press 2009)

Moshe Hirsch, 'Between Fair and Equitable Treatment and Stabilization Clause: Stable Legal Environment and Regulatory Change in International Investment Law' (2011) 12 Journal of World Investment & Trade 783

Bernard Hoekman and Patrick LOW, 'State Trading: Rule Making Alternatives for Entities with Exclusive Rights' in Thomas Cottier and Petros C Mavroidis (eds), State Trading in the Twenty-First Century (University of Michigan Press 1998)

Bernard Hoekman and Petros C MAVROIDIS, 'Economic Development, Competition Policy and the World Trade Organization' (2003) 37 Journal of World Trade 1

Anne K Hoffmann, 'Indirect Expropriation' in August Reinisch (ed), Standards of Investment Protection (Oxford University Press 2008)

Frank Hoffmeister, 'Litigating against the European Union and Its Member States – Who Responds under the ILC's Draft Articles on International Responsibility of International Organizations?' (2010) 21 European Journal of International Law 723

Katherine Holmes, 'Legal Implications of the Energy Charter Treaty, Competition - Rules and Liberalisation' in Thomas W Wälde (ed), The Energy Charter Treaty: An East-West Gateway for Investment and Trade (International Energy and Resources Law and Policy Series. Kluwer Law International 1996)

Bernd Holznagel and Pascal Schumacher, 'Großer Eingriff, k(l)eine Wirkung – Die Pläne der Kommission zur eigentumsrechtlichen Entflechtung der Energienetzbetreiber' [2007] Netzwirtschaften & Recht 96

Robert E Hudec, 'GATT/WTO Constraints on National Regulation: Requiem for an "Aim and Effects" Test' (1998) 32 The International Lawyer 619

Michaël Hunt, 'Ownership Unbundling: The Main Legal Issues in a Controversial Debate' in Bram Delvaux, Michaël Hunt and Kim Talus (eds), EU Energy Law and Policy Issues (1st edn. Euroconfidentiel 2008)

Douglas A Irwin and Joseph Weiler, 'Measures Affecting the Cross-Border Supply of Gambling and Betting Services (DS 285)' (2008) 7 World Trade Review 71

Alexey S Ispolinov and Tatiana Dvenadtcatova, 'Принудительное выделение сетевого бизнеса в рамках Третьего Энергопакета ЕС (unbundling): практика применения' [2014] Закон 111

John H Jackson, The World Trading System: Law and Policy of International Economic Relations (MIT Press 1991)

Marc Jacob and Stephan W Schill, 'Fair and Equitable Treatment: Content, Practice, Method' in Marc Bungenberg and others (eds), International Investment Law (C.H. Beck; Hart; Nomos 2015)

Hans D Jarass, Charta der Grundrechte der Europäischen Union: Kommentar (2nd edn, C.H. Beck 2013)

——— Jarass and Bodo Pieroth, Grundgesetz für die Bundesrepublik Deutschland – Kommentar (13th edn, C.H. Beck 2014)

Angus Johnston, 'Ownership Unbundling: Prolegomenon to a Legal Analysis' in Mielle Bulterman and others (eds), Views of European Law from the Mountain: Liber Amicorum Piet Jan Slot (Wolters Kluwer Law & Business 2009)

Angus Johnston and Guy Block, EU Energy Law (Oxford University Press 2012)

Christopher Jones and William Webster, 'Derogations and Exemptions' in Christopher Jones (ed), The Internal Energy Market – The Third Liberalisation Package (EU Energy Law Series vol 1, 3rd edn. Claeys & Casteels Publishing 2010)

Oliver R Jones and Chido Dunn, 'Consent, Forced Renegotiation and Expropriation in International Law' (2010) 26 Arbitration International 391

Christian Kahle, 'Die Eigentumsrechtliche Entflechtung (Ownership Unbundling) der Energieversorgungsnetze aus europarechtlicher und verfassungsrechtlicher Sicht' [2007] Recht der Energiewirtschaft 293

Roland Kläger, 'Fair and Equitable Treatment' in International Investment Law (Cambridge University Press 2011)
Marcus Klamert, Services Liberalization in the EU and the WTO: Concepts, Standards and Regulatory Approaches (Cambridge Studies in European Law and Policy, Cambridge University Press 2015)
Andreas Klees, 'Das Instrument der Zusagenentscheidung der Kommission und der Fall "E.ON" – Ein (weiterer) Sündenfall' [2009] Wirtschaft und Wettbewerb 374
Henrik Klement, 'Verstaatlichung statt Regulierung?' [2014] Europäische Zeitschrift für Wirtschaftsrecht 57
Günter Knieps, Wettbewerbsökonomie: Regulierungstheorie, Industrieökonomie, Wettbewerbspolitik (3rd edn, Springer 2008)
——— 'Wettbewerb auf den Ferntransportnetzen der deutschen Gaswirtschaft: Eine netzökonomische Analyse' (2003) 26 Zeitschrift für Energiewirtschaft 171
Matthias Koehler, Das Allgemeine Übereinkommen über den Handel mit Dienstleistungen (GATS): Rahmenregelung zur Liberalisierung des internationalen Dienstleistungsverkehrs unter besonderer Berücksichtigung des grenzüberschreitenden Personenverkehrs von Dienstleistungsanbietern (Schriften zum Internationalen Recht vol 106, Duncker & Humblot 1999)
Christian Koenig, Jürgen Kühling and Winfried Rasbach, Energierecht (3rd edn, Nomos 2013)
Christian Koenig, Kristina Schreiber and Kristin Spiekermann, 'Defizitäres Entflechtungsregime? Eine kritische Analyse der Entflechtungsvorschriften in dem Entwurf des dritten Liberalisierungspakets der Kommission der Europäischen Gemeinschaften' [2008] Netzwirtschaften & Recht 7
Andrey Konoplyanik, 'Борьба с мифами – О мнимых выгодах и угрозах Договора к Энергетической Хартии' (2006) 21 Политический журнал 32
——— 'A Common Russia–EU Energy Space: The New EU–Russia Partnership Agreement, Acquis Communautaire and the Energy Charter' (2009) 27 Journal of Energy & Natural Resources Law 258
——— 'Russia and the Third EU Energy Package: Regulatory Changes for Internal EU Energy Markets in Gas and Possible Consequences for Suppliers (Including Non-EU Suppliers) and Consumers' [2011] International Energy Law Review 24
Georg Koopmann, 'Competition Policies and Telecommunication Regimes' in Paolo Guerrieri and Hans-Eckart Scharrer (eds), Trade, Investment and Competition Policies in the Global Economy: The Case of International Telecommunications Regime (Veröffentlichungen des Hamburgischen Welt-Wirtschafts-Archivs vol 69. Nomos 2002)
Markus Krajewski, National Regulation and Trade Liberalization in Services: The Legal Impact of the General Agreement on Trade in Services (GATS) on National Regulatory Autonomy (Kluwer Law International 2003a)
——— 'Disziplinen für innerstaatliche Regulierung nach Artikel VI GATS' in Dirk Ehlers, Hans-Michael Wolffgang and Marc Lechleitner (eds), Rechtsfragen des internationalen Dienstleistungsverkehrs: Tagungsband zum 10. Münsteraner Außenwirtschaftsrechtstag 2005 (Verlag Recht und Wirtschaft 2006)
——— 'Article VI GATS' in Rüdiger Wolfrum, Peter-Tobias Stoll and Clemens Feinäugle (eds), WTO – Trade in Services (Max Planck Commentaries on World Trade Law vol 6. Martinus Nijhoff Publishers 2008)
——— 'Public Services in Bilateral Free Trade Agreements of the EU' (2011) <http://papers.ssrn.com/sol3/papers.cfm?abstract_id=1964288>
——— 'The Impact of International Investment Agreements on Energy Regulation' in Christoph Herrmann and Jörg P Terhechte (eds), European Yearbook of International Economic Law 2012 (European Yearbook of International Economic Law vol 3. Springer 2012)
——— 'Public Services and Trade Liberalization: Mapping the Legal Framework' (2003b) 6 Journal of International Economic Law 341

——— 'Playing by the Rules of the Game?: Specific Commitments after US – Gambling and Betting and the Current GATS Negotiations' (2005) 32 Legal Issues of Economic Integration 417

Markus Krajewski and Maika Engelke, 'Article XVII GATS' in Rüdiger Wolfrum, Peter-Tobias Stoll and Clemens Feinäugle (eds), WTO – Trade in Services (Max Planck Commentaries on World Trade Law vol 6. Martinus Nijhoff Publishers 2008)

Markus Krajewski and Britta Kynast, 'Impact of the Transatlantic Trade and Investment Partnership (TTIP) on the Legal Framework for Public Services in Europe' (2014) <http://papers.ssrn.com/sol3/papers.cfm?abstract_id=2576079> accessed 8 May 2016

Brigitta Kratz and Frederik Kreuzer, 'Ownership Unbundling – A Swiss Perspective' in Dirk Buschle, Simon Hirsbrunner and Christine Kaddous (eds), European Energy Law: Droit européen de l'énergie (Dossier de droit européen vol 22. Helbing Lichtenhahn 2011)

Ursula Kriebaum, 'Expropriation' in Marc Bungenberg and others (eds), International Investment Law (C.H. Beck; Hart; Nomos 2015)

——— 'Partial Expropriation' (2007a) 8 Journal of World Investment & Trade 69

——— 'Regulatory Takings: Balancing the Interests of the Investor and the State' (2007b) 8 Journal of World Investment & Trade 717

——— 'FET and Expropriation in the (Invisible) EU Model BIT' (2014) 15 Journal of World Investment & Trade 454

Neelie Kroes, 'Improving Competition in European Energy Markets Through Effective Unbundling' (2007) 31 Fordham International Law Journal 1387

Jürgen Kühling, Sektorspezifische Regulierung in den Netzwirtschaften (Energie- und Infrastrukturrecht vol 4, C.H. Beck 2004)

Jürgen Kühling and Guido Hermeier, 'Eigentumsrechtliche Leitplanken eines Ownership Unbundlings in der Energiewirtschaft' (2008) 58 Energiewirtschaftliche Tagesfragen 134

Jürgen Kurtz, 'The Merits and Limits of Comparativism: National Treatment in International Investment Law and the WTO' in Stephan W Schill (ed), International Investment Law and Comparative Public Law (Oxford University Press 2010)

George Lagaris and Alexia Trokoudi, 'Application of Article 11 of the Gas Directive – TSOs Controlled by Companies from Non-Member States' (2014) <https://www.energy-community.org/portal/page/portal/ENC_HOME/DOCS/2950031/0633975AD7C27B9CE053C92FA8C06338.PDF> accessed 18 April 2016

Andras Lakatos, 'Overview of the Regulatory Environment for Trade in Electricity' in Janusz Bielecki and Melaku G Desta (eds), Electricity Trade in Europe – Review of the Economic and Regulatory Changes (Kluwer Law International 2004)

François-Charles Laprévote, Sven Frisch and Burcu Can, 'Competition Policy within the Context of Free Trade Agreements' (2015) <http://e15initiative.org/publications/competition-policy-within-the-context-of-free-trade-agreements/> accessed 23 August 2016

Sergey Lavrov, 'State of the Union Russia–EU: Prospects for Partnership in the Changing World' (2013) 51 Journal of Common Market Studies 6

Helmut Lecheler and Claas F Germelmann, Zugangsbeschränkungen für Investitionen aus Drittstaaten im deutschen und europäischen Energierecht (Energierecht vol 1, Mohr Siebeck 2010)

Peter Leon, 'A Fork in the Investor-State Road: South Africa's New Mineral Regulatory Regime Four Years On' (2008) 42 Journal of World Trade 671

Eric H Leroux, 'From Periodicals to Gambling: A Review of Systemic Issues Addressed by WTO Adjudicatory Bodies under the GATS' in Marion Panizzon, Nicole Pohl and Pierre Sauvé (eds), GATS and the Regulation of International Trade in Services (Cambridge University Press 2008)

——— 'What is a "Service Supplied in the Exercise of Governmental Authority" Under Article I:3 (b) and (c) of the General Agreement on Trade in Services?' (2006) 40 Journal of World Trade 345

LETA, 'Latvijas Gaze shareholders back creation of new company in charge of gas transmission, storage' (2 September 2016) <http://www.leta.lv/eng/home/important/133A1865-48EF-844B-16AB-349B536F4803/> accessed 9 September 2016

Céline Lévesque and Andrew Newcombe, 'Canada' in Chester Brown (ed), Commentaries on Selected Model Investment Treaties (Oxford Commentaries on International Law. Oxford University Press 2013)

'Lithuania Ready to Buy Amber Grid's Shares from E.ON and Gazprom' Lithuania Tribune (6 September 2013) <http://www.lithuaniatribune.com/49776/lithuania-ready-to-buy-amber-grids-shares-from-e-on-and-gazprom-201349776/> accessed 3 June 2015

Anne Looijestijn-Clearie, 'Breaking up Is Hard to Do: Dutch Unbundling Legislation and the Free Movement of Capital' (2014) 15 European Business Organization Law Review 337

Patrick Low and Aaditya Mattoo, 'Reform in Basic Telecommunications and the WTO Negotiations: The Asian Experience' (Staff Working Paper 1997) <https://www.wto.org/english/res_e/reser_e/pera9801.pdf> accessed 18 July 2016

David Luff, 'Regulation of Health Services and International Trade Law' in Aaditya Mattoo and Pierre Sauvé (eds), Domestic Regulation and Service Trade Liberalization (Oxford University Press 2003)

——— 'Current International Trade Rules Relevant to Telecommunications Services' in Damien Geradin and David Luff (eds), The WTO and Global Convergence in Telecommunications and Audio-Visual Services (Cambridge University Press 2004)

Thorsten Mäger, 'Einführung und Grundlagen' in Thorsten Mäger (ed), Europäisches Kartellrecht (2nd edn. Nomos 2011)

Irmgard Marboe, 'Valuation in Cases of Expropriation' in Marc Bungenberg and others (eds), International Investment Law (C.H. Beck; Hart; Nomos 2015)

Gabrielle Marceau, 'The WTO in the Emerging Energy Governance Debate' in Joost Pauwelyn (ed), Global Challenges at the Intersection of Trade, Energy and the Environment (Center for Economic and Policy Research 2010)

Mario Martini, 'Zu Gast bei Freunden?: Staatsfonds als Herausforderung an das europäische und internationale Recht' (2008) 61 Die Öffentliche Verwaltung 314

Bobjoseph Mathew, The WTO Agreements on Telecommunications (Studies in Global Economic Law vol 6, Peter Lang 2003)

Aaditya Mattoo, 'Dealing with Monopolies and State Enterprises: WTO Rules for Goods and Services' in Thomas Cottier and Petros C Mavroidis (eds), State Trading in the Twenty-First Century (University of Michigan Press 1998)

——— 'National Treatment in the GATS – Corner-Stone or Pandora's Box?' (1997) 31 Journal of World Trade 107

Thomas Mayen and Ulrich Karpenstein, 'Eigentumsrechtliche Entflechtung der Energieversorgungsnetze: Verfassungs- und gemeinschaftsrechtliche Aspekte des Eigentumsschutzes' [2008] Recht der Energiewirtschaft 33

Joshua Meltzer, 'Climate Change and Trade – The EU Aviation Directive and the WTO' (2012) 15 Journal of International Economic Law 111

Armand de Mestral, 'Pre-Entry Obligations under International Law' in Marc Bungenberg and others (eds), International Investment Law (C.H. Beck; Hart; Nomos 2015)

Martin Michaelis, '§ 20 Dienstleistungshandel (GATS)' in Meinhard Hilf and Stefan Oeter (eds), WTO-Recht: Rechtsordnung des Welthandels (2nd edn. Nomos 2010)

Andrew Mitchell and Tania Voon, 'Reasonableness, Impartiality and Objectivity' in Aik H Lim and Bart De Meester (eds), WTO Domestic Regulation and Services Trade: Putting Principles into Practice (Cambridge University Press 2014)

Nikolay Mizulin, 'EC Experience in Creating an Internal Energy Market: Lessons for the WTO' in Joost Pauwelyn (ed), Global Challenges at the Intersection of Trade, Energy and the Environment (Center for Economic and Policy Research 2010)

Martín Molinuevo, Protecting Investment in Services: Investor-State Arbitration versus WTO Dispute Settlement (Global Trade Law Series vol 38, Kluwer Law International 2012)

Teresa M Moschetta, Il mercato comunitario del gas naturale: Investimenti esteri diretti e diritto internazionale (Giuffrè 2009)
Ralf Müller-Terpitz and Michaela Weigl, 'Ownership Unbundling – ein gemeinschaftsrechtlicher Irrweg?' [2009] Europarecht 348
Nellie Munin, Legal Guide to GATS (Global Trade Law Series vol 31, Kluwer Law International 2010)
Irene Musselli and Simonetta Zarrilli, 'Oil and Gas Services: Market Liberalization and the Ongoing GATS Negotiations' (2005) 8 Journal of International Economic Law 551
Olga Nartova, Energy Services and Competition Policies under WTO Law (Научная Мысль, INFRA-M 2010)
Martin Nettesheim, 'Unternehmensübernahmen durch Staatsfonds: Europarechtliche Vorgaben und Schranken' (2008) 172 Zeitschrift für das gesamte Handels- und Wirtschaftsrecht 729
Damien J Neven and Petros C Mavroidis, 'El mess in TELMEX: A Comment on Mexico - Measures Affecting Telecommunications Services' (2006) 5 World Trade Review 271
Andrew Newcombe and Lluís Paradell, Law and Practice of Investment Treaties: Standards of Treatment (Wolters Kluwer Law & Business 2009)
Kalypso Nicolaïdis and Joel P Trachtman, 'From Policed Regulation to Managed Recognition in GATS' in Pierre Sauvé and Robert M Stern (eds), GATS 2000: New Directions in Services Trade Liberalization (Brookings Institution Press 2000)
'Nord Stream: A View from Poland' Natural Gas Europe (9 November 2011) <http://www.naturalgaseurope.com/nord-stream-a-view-from-poland-3421>
Philipp Offenberg, 'The European Neighbourhood and the EU's Security of Supply with Natural Gas' (2016) <http://www.institutdelors.eu/media/euneighbourhoodandgas-offenberg-jdib-jan16.pdf?pdf=ok> accessed 31 January 2016
Irene Öhlinger, Internationaler Dienstleistungshandel und Wettbewerbsaspekte: Lösungsansätze im Telekommunikationsbereich (Verlag Österreich 2001)
Christian Oliver and Jack Farchy, 'Gazprom Criticises EU over South Stream Gas Pipeline' Financial Times (30 May 2014) <http://www.ft.com/intl/cms/s/0/949eb796-e7f2-11e3-9af8-00144feabdc0.html>
Federico Ortino, 'The Principle of Non-Discrimination and its Exceptions in GATS: Selected Legal Issues' in Kern Alexander and Mads Andenas (eds), The World Trade Organization and Trade in Services (Martinus Nijhoff Publishers 2008)
——— 'Treaty Interpretation and the WTO Appellate Body Report in US–Gambling: A Critique' (2006) 9 Journal of International Economic Law 117
Jayant Parimal, 'Energy Services in WTO – A Recommended Course' (Master's Thesis 2004) <http://www.peacepalacelibrary.nl/ebooks/files/WTI_PARIMAL_Energy-Services.pdf> accessed 15 January 2016
Joost Pauwelyn, 'Comment: The Unbearable Lightness of Likeness' in Marion Panizzon, Nicole Pohl and Pierre Sauvé (eds), GATS and the Regulation of International Trade in Services (Cambridge University Press 2008)
——— 'Rien Ne Va Plus? Distinguishing Domestic Regulation from Market Access in GATT and GATS' (2005) 4 World Trade Review 131
Shin-yi Peng, 'Trade in Telecommunications Services: Doha and Beyond' (2007) 41 Journal of World Trade 293
Markus Perkams, 'The Concept of Indirect Expropriation in Comparative Public Law – Searching for Light in the Dark' in Stephan W Schill (ed), International Investment Law and Comparative Public Law (Oxford University Press 2010)
Ernst-Ulrich Petersmann, The GATT/WTO Dispute Settlement System: International Law, International Organizations and Dispute Settlement (Kluwer Law International 1997)
——— 'GATT Law on State Trading Enterprises: Critical Evaluation of Article XVII and Proposals for Reform' in Thomas Cottier and Petros C Mavroidis (eds), State Trading in the Twenty-First Century (University of Michigan Press 1998)

Johann-Christian Pielow, Gert Brunekreeft and Eckart Ehlers, 'Legal and Economic Aspects of Ownership Unbundling in the EU' (2009) 2 Journal of World Energy Law & Business 96
Johann-Christian Pielow and Eckart Ehlers, 'Rechtsfragen zum "Ownership Unbundling"' [2007] InfrastrukturRecht 259
Michael Pießkalla, 'Die Kommissionsvorschläge zum "full ownership unbundling" des Strom- und Gasversorgungssektors im Lichte der Eigentumsneutralität des EG-Vertrags (Art. 295 EG)' [2008] Europäische Zeitschrift für Wirtschaftsrecht 199
Denis Pinchuk and Nerijus Adomaitis, Gazprom takes on Lithuania in EU policy test case (Reuters 2012)
Simon Pirani and Katja Yafimava, Russian Gas Transit Across Ukraine Post-2019: Pipeline Scenarios, Gas Flow Consequences, and Regulatory Constraints (Oxford Institute for Energy Studies 2016)
Christian Pitschas, 'Allgemeines Übereinkommen über den Handel mit Dienstleistungen (GATS)' in Prieß, Hans-Joachim and Georg M Berrisch (eds), WTO-Handbuch (C.H. Beck 2003)
André Plourde, 'Canada's International Obligations in Energy and the Free-Trade Agreement with the United States' (1990) 24 Journal of World Trade 35
Vitaliy Pogoretskyy, 'Energy Dual Pricing in International Trade: Subsidies and Anti-dumping Perspectives' in Yulia Selivanova (ed), Regulation of Energy in International Trade Law: WTO, NAFTA and Energy Charter (Kluwer Law International 2012)
——— 'Freedom of Transit and the Principles of Effective Right and Economic Cooperation: Can Systemic Interpretation of GATT Article V Promote Energy Security and the Development of an International Gas Market?' (2013) 16 Journal of International Economic Law 313
Michael Pollitt, 'The Arguments For and Against Ownership Unbundling of Energy Transmission Networks' (2008) 36 Energy Policy 704
Pietro Poretti and Roberto Rios Herrán, 'A Reference Paper On Energy Services: The Best Way Forward?' (2006) 3 Manchester Journal of International Economic Law 2
Michele Potestà, 'Legitimate Expectations in Investment Treaty Law: Understanding the Roots and the Limits of a Controversial Concept' (2013) 28 ICSID Review – Foreign Investment Law Journal 88
Sabrina Praduroux and Kim Talus, 'The Third Legislative Package and Ownership Unbundling in Light of the European Fundamental Rights Discourse' (2008) 9 Competition and Regulation in Network Industries 3
Eunike Prokop-Elkettani, 'Internationales und Europäisches Telekommunikationsrecht' in Franz J Säcker (ed), Berliner Kommentar zum Telekommunikationsgesetz (2nd edn. Verlag Recht und Wirtschaft 2009)
Winfried Rasbach, Unbundling-Regulierung in der Energiewirtschaft: Gemeinschaftsrechtliche Vorgaben und deren Umsetzung in die deutsche Energierechtsordnung (C.H. Beck 2009)
Tobias Reimold, Der Handel mit Bildungsdienstleistungen nach dem GATS (Mohr Siebeck 2010)
August Reinisch, 'Expropriation' in Peter Muchlinski, Federico Ortino and Christoph Schreuer (eds), The Oxford Handbook of International Investment Law (Oxford University Press 2008a)
——— 'Legality of Expropriations' in August Reinisch (ed), Standards of Investment Protection (Oxford University Press 2008b)
——— 'Protection of or Protection Against Foreign Investment? The Proposed Unbundling Rules of the EC Draft Energy Directives' in Christoph Herrmann and Jörg P Terhechte (eds), European Yearbook of International Economic Law 2010 (Springer 2010)
——— 'Most Favoured Nation Treatment' in Marc Bungenberg and others (eds), International Investment Law (C.H. Beck; Hart; Nomos 2015a)
——— 'National Treatment' in Marc Bungenberg and others (eds), International Investment Law (C.H. Beck; Hart; Nomos 2015b)
——— 'How Narrow are Narrow Dispute Settlement Clauses in Investment Treaties?' (2011) 2 Journal of International Dispute Settlement 115
Michael B Renshaw, 'Consequences of Integration in UK Tour Operating' (1995) 15 Tourism Management 243

Thilo Rensmann, 'Völkerrechtlicher Enteignungsschutz' in Dirk Ehlers, Hans-Michael Wolffgang and Ulrich J Schröder (eds), Rechtsfragen internationaler Investitionen: Tagungsband zum 13. Münsteraner Außenwirtschaftsrechtstag 2008 (Verlag Recht und Wirtschaft 2009)

——— 'Völkerrechtliche Grenzen extraterritorialer Wirtschaftssanktionen' in Dirk Ehlers and Hans-Michael Wolffgang (eds), Recht der Exportkontrolle: Bestandsaufnahme und Perspektiven (R & W Verlag 2015)

Georg Ress and Jörg Ukrow, 'AEUV Art. 63 Freier Kapital- und Zahlungsverkehr' in Eberhard Grabitz, Meinhard Hilf and Martin Nettesheim (eds), Das Recht der Europäischen Union: EUV/AEUV (54th edn. C.H. Beck 2014)

Reuters, 'Zimbabwe PM Says Indigenisation Not Expropriation' (16 September 2010) <http://af.reuters.com/article/topNews/idAFJOE68F0EQ20100916> accessed 30 May 2015

Alan Riley, 'Ownership Unbundling – A Logic Outage for the Anti-Energy Liberalisers?' (2008) <http://www.ceps.eu/system/files/book/1641.pdf> accessed 18 July 2016

——— 'Nordstream 2: Too Many Obstacles, Legal, Economic, and Political to be Delivered?' (2015) <http://www.atlanticcouncil.org/images/publications/Nordstream_2_web_1125.pdf> accessed 31 July 2016

Roberto Rios Herrán and Pietro Poretti, 'Energy Trade and Investment under the North American Free Trade Agreement' in Yulia Selivanova (ed), Regulation of Energy in International Trade Law: WTO, NAFTA and Energy Charter (Kluwer Law International 2012)

Sergey Ripinsky, Damages in International Investment Law (Kevin Williams tr, British Institute of International and Comparative Law 2008)

Michel Rivier, Ignacio J Pérez-Arriaga and Luis Olmos, 'Electricity Transmission' in Ignacio J Pérez-Arriaga (ed), Regulation of the Power Sector (Springer 2013)

Frieder Roessler, 'The Concept of Nullification and Impairment in the Legal System of the World Trade Organization' in Ernst-Ulrich Petersmann (ed), International Trade Law and the GATT/WTO Dispute Settlement System (Kluwer Law International 1997)

Martha M Roggenkamp, 'Energy Law in the Netherlands' in Martha M Roggenkamp and others (eds), Energy Law in Europe – National, EU and International Regulation (2nd edn. Oxford University Press 2007)

——— 'Ownership Unbundling in the Netherlands: More Haste and Less Speed?' in Jürgen F Baur and others (eds), Festschrift für Gunther Kühne zum 70. Geburtstag (Verlag Recht und Wirtschaft 2009)

Leslie L Rood, 'Compensation for Takeovers in Africa' (1977) 11 Journal of International Law and Economics 521

Hubertus von Rosenberg, 'Unbundling Through the Back Door. . .the Case of Network Divestiture as a Remedy in the Energy Sector' (2009) 30 European Competition Law Review 237

Wulf-Henning Roth, Investitionsbeschränkungen im deutschen Außenwirtschaftsrecht – Europa- und völkerrechtliche Probleme (Rechtspolitisches Forum – Legal Policy Forum vol 47, Institut für Rechtspolitik an der Universität Trier 2009)

'Russia Confirms Decision to Abandon South Stream' EurActiv (10 December 2014) <http://www.euractiv.com/sections/energy/russia-confirms-decision-abandon-south-stream-final-310712> accessed 26 June 2015

'Russia Says South Stream project is Over' EurActiv (2 December 2014) <http://www.euractiv.com/sections/global-europe/russia-says-south-stream-project-over-310491> accessed 26 June 2015

Giorgio Sacerdoti, 'The Admission and Treatment of Foreign Investment under Recent Bilateral and Regional Treaties' (2000) 1 Journal of World Investment 105

Franz J Säcker and Jochen Mohr, '§ 8 Eigentumsrechtliche Entflechtung' in Franz J Säcker (ed), Berliner Kommentar zum Energierecht (vol 1, 3rd edn. Dt. Fachverl. Fachmedien Recht und Wirtschaft 2014)

Otto Sandrock, 'The Right of Foreign Investors to Access German Markets: The Meaning of Article 2(1) of the German Model Treaty for the Promotion and Protection of Foreign Investments' (2010) 25 ICSID Review – Foreign Investment Law Journal 268

Pierre Sauvé, 'Assessing the General Agreement on Trade in Services: Half-Full or Half-Empty?' (1995) 29 Journal of World Trade 125

Michael Schäfer and Thomas Voland, 'Staatsfonds: Die Kontrolle ausländischer Investitionen auf dem Prüfstand des Verfassungs-, Europa- und Welthandelsrechts' [2008] Europäisches Wirtschafts- und Steuerrecht 166

Stephan W Schill, The Multilateralization of International Investment Law (Cambridge University Press 2009)

——— 'Fair and Equitable Treatment, the Rule of Law, and Comparative Public Law' in Stephan W Schill (ed), International Investment Law and Comparative Public Law (Oxford University Press 2010)

Hannes Schloemann and Christian Pitschas, 'Cutting the Regulatory Edge? Services Regulation Disciplines in the CARIFORUM-EU Economic Partnership Agreement' in Regine Qualmann (ed), How to Ensure Development Friendly Economic Partnership Agreements – Lessons Across Regions (Deutsche Gesellschaft für Technische Zusammenarbeit 2009)

Hannes L Schloemann and Stefan Ohlhoff, '"Constitutionalization" and Dispute Settlement in the WTO: National Security as an Issue of Competence' (1999) 93 American Journal of International Law 424

Matthias Schmidt-Preuß, 'Verfassungsrechtliche Rahmenbedingungen des Unbundling' in Jürgen F Baur, Kai U Pritzsche and Stefan Simon (eds), Unbundling in der Energiewirtschaft: Ein Praxishandbuch (Carl Heymanns Verlag 2006a)

——— 'Die Zukunft der Netze – Szenarien, Modelle, rechtliche Implikationen' in Ulrich Ehricke (ed), Die neuen Herausforderungen im Lichte des Energierechts (Nomos 2009)

——— 'Die Kontrolle des Verkaufs bzw. des Erwerbs von Netzen (Erwerb durch Nicht-EU-Ausländer gem. §4b EnWG; Außenwirtschaftsrecht; Fusionskontrolle)' in Jürgen F Baur, Peter Salje and Matthias Schmidt-Preuß (eds), Regulierung in der Energiewirtschaft: Ein Praxishandbuch (2nd edn. Carl Heymanns Verlag 2016)

——— 'Der Wandel der Energiewirtschaft vor dem Hintergrund der europäischen Eigentumsordnung' (2006b) 41 Europarecht 463

——— 'Energieversorgung als Aufgabe der Außenpolitik?: Rechtliche Aspekte' [2007] Recht der Energiewirtschaft 281

Burkhard Schöbener, Jochen Herbst and Markus Perkams, Internationales Wirtschaftsrecht (C.F. Müller 2010)

Rupert Scholz, 'Freiheitlicher Binnenmarkt oder diktierte Marktstruktur?: Zur neuen Gasrichtlinie der EG' [2001] Energiewirtschaftliche Tagesfragen 678

——— 'Eigentumsschutz und Entflechtung – Zu den Unbundling-Plänen der Europäischen Kommission' (2007) 57 Energiewirtschaftliche Tagesfragen 76

Frank Schorkopf, 'Eigentumsrechtliche Entflechtung aus verfassungs- und europarechtlicher Sicht' in Wolfgang Löwer (ed), Neue rechtliche Herausforderungen für den Strommarkt: Bonner Gespräch zum Energierecht - Band 3 (Bonner Gespräch zum Energierecht vol 3. V & R unipress 2008)

——— '"Energie" als Thema des Welthandelsrechts' in Christian Walter, Stefan Leible and Michael Lippert (eds), Die Sicherung der Energieversorgung auf globalisierten Märkten (Mohr Siebeck 2012)

Christoph Schreuer, 'The Protection of Investments in Armed Conflicts' in Freya Baetens (ed), Investment Law within International Law: Integrationist Perspectives (Cambridge University Press 2013)

Ignaz Seidl-Hohenveldern, International Economic Law (3rd edn, Kluwer Law International 1999)

Yulia Selivanova, The WTO and Energy: WTO Rules and Agreements of Relevance to the Energy Sector (Issue paper vol 1, International Centre for Trade and Sustainable Development 2007)

——— Energy Dual Pricing in the WTO: Analysis and Prospects in the Context of Russia's Accession to the World Trade Organization (Cameron May 2008)

——— 'The Energy Charter and the International Energy Governance' in Yulia Selivanova (ed), Regulation of Energy in International Trade Law: WTO, NAFTA and Energy Charter (Kluwer Law International 2012)

——— 'The WTO Agreements and Energy' in Kim Talus (ed), Research Handbook on International Energy Law (Research Handbooks in International Law. Edward Elgar 2014)

Sergey S Seliverstov and Ivan Gudkov, Энергетическое право Европейского союза (Аспект Пресс 2014)

Wenhua Shan and Sheng Zhang, 'The Treaty of Lisbon: Half Way toward a Common Investment Policy' (2010) 21 European Journal of International Law 1049

Malcolm N Shaw, International Law (7th edn, Cambridge University Press 2014)

Laura B Sherman, '"Wildly Enthusiastic" About the First Multilateral Agreement on Trade in Telecommunications Services' (1998) 51 Federal Communications Law Journal 61

Ibrahim F I Shihata, 'Recent Trends Relating to Entry of Foreign Direct Investment' (1994) 9 ICSID Review – Foreign Investment Law Journal 47

Karl Sidhu, Die Regelung von Direktinvestitionen in der WTO: Das TRIMs-Abkommen und das GATS (Schriften zum europäischen und internationalen Recht vol 12, V & R unipress 2004)

Piet J Slot, 'Energy and Competition' (1994) 31 Common Market Law Review 511

——— Slot and Andrew Skudder, 'Common Features of Community Law Regulation in the Network-Bound Sectors' (2001) 38 Common Market Law Review 87

Hanna Smith, 'Russian Foreign Policy and Energy: The Case of the Nord Stream Gas Pipeline' in Pami Aalto (ed), Russia's Energy Policies – National, Interregional and Global Levels (Edward Elgar 2012)

Jukka Snell, 'The Notion of Market Access: A Concept or a Slogan?' (2010) 47 Common Market Law Review 437

Muthucumaraswamy Sornarajah, The International Law on Foreign Investment (3rd edn, Cambridge University Press 2010)

'South Stream Bilateral Deals Breach EU Law, Commission Says' EurActiv (4 December 2013) <http://www.euractiv.com/energy/commission-south-stream-agreemen-news-532120>

Jonathan Stern, Simon Pirani and Katja Yafimava, 'Does the Cancellation of South Stream Signal a Fundamental Reorientation of Russian Gas Export Policy?' (2015) <http://www.oxfordenergy.org/wpcms/wp-content/uploads/2015/01/Does-cancellation-of-South-Stream-signal-a-fundamental-reorientation-of-Russian-gas-export-policy-GPC-5.pdf>

Peter-Tobias Stoll, 'Article 3 DSU' in Rüdiger Wolfrum, Peter-Tobias Stoll and Karen Kaiser (eds), WTO – Institutions and Dispute Settlement (Max Planck Commentaries on World Trade Law vol 2. Martinus Nijhoff Publishers 2006)

Stefan Storr, 'Ownership Unbundling und alternative Entflechtungsmodelle' in Jürgen F Baur, Peter Salje and Matthias Schmidt-Preuß (eds), Regulierung in der Energiewirtschaft: Ein Praxishandbuch (Kölner Handbücher zum Energiewirtschaftsrecht. Carl Heymanns Verlag 2011)

——— 'Die Vorschläge der EU-Kommission zur Verschärfung der Unbundling-Vorschriften im Energiesektor' [2007] Europäische Zeitschrift für Wirtschaftsrecht 232

Wolfgang Ströbele, Wolfgang Pfaffenberger and Michael Heuterkes, Energiewirtschaft: Einführung in Theorie und Politik (Oldenbourg Verlag 2012)

Torje Sunde, Möglichkeiten und Grenzen innerstaatlicher Regulierung nach Art. VI GATS (Beiträge zum Transnationalen Wirtschaftsrecht vol 59, 2006)

Andrius Sytas, Lithuania Completes Buy of Gas Utility Shares from Gazprom (Reuters 2014)

Marek Szydło, 'Regulatory Exemptions for New Gas Infrastructure. A Key Challenge for European Energy Policy' (2009) 18 European Energy and Environmental Law Review 254

Kim Talus, Vertical Natural Gas Transportation Capacity, Upstream Commodity Contracts and EU Competition Law (Kluwer Law International 2011)

——— EU Energy Law and Policy: A Critical Account (Oxford University Press 2013)

Kim Talus and Michaël Hunt, 'Ownership Unbundling: What End to the Saga?' in Dirk Buschle, Simon Hirsbrunner and Christine Kaddous (eds), European Energy Law: Droit européen de l'énergie (Dossier de droit européen vol 22. Helbing Lichtenhahn 2011)

Kim Talus and Angus Johnston, 'Comment on Pielow, Brunekreeft and Ehlers on "Ownership Onbundling"' (2009) 2 Journal of World Energy Law & Business 149

Simon Taylor, 'EU Struggles to Agree on Anti-Gazprom Clause' Politico (21 May 2008) <http://www.politico.eu/article/eu-struggles-to-agree-on-anti-gazprom-clause/> accessed 21 June 2016

Christian Tietje, Die Außenwirtschaftsverfassung der EU nach dem Vertrag von Lissabon (Beiträge zum Transnationalen Wirtschaftsrecht vol 83, 2009)

——— Bilaterale Investitionsschutzverträge zwischen EU-Mitgliedstaaten (Intra-EU-BITs) als Herausforderung im Mehrebenensystem des Rechts (Beiträge zum Transnationalen Wirtschaftsrecht vol 104, 2011)

——— 'Beschränkungen ausländischer Unternehmensbeteiligungen zum Schutz vor „Staatsfonds": Rechtliche Grenzen eines neuen Investitionsprotektionismus' [2007] Policy Paper on Transnational Economic Law

Elena Timofeeva, Unbundling in der russischen Elektrizitätswirtschaft im Vergleich zum deutschen und europäischen Energierecht (Veröffentlichungen des Instituts für deutsches und europäisches Wirtschafts-, Wettbewerbs- und Regulierungsrecht der Freien Universität Berlin vol 34, Peter Lang 2012)

Joel P Trachtman, 'United States – Measures Affecting the Cross-Border Supply of Gambling and Betting Services' (2005a) 99 American Journal of International Law 861

——— 'Lessons for the GATS from Existing WTO Rules on Domestic Regulation' in Aaditya Mattoo and Pierre Sauvé (eds), Domestic Regulation and Service Trade Liberalization (Oxford University Press 2003)

——— 'Negotiations on Domestic Regulation and Trade in Services (GATS Article VI): A Legal Analysis of Selected Current Issues' in Ernst-Ulrich Petersmann and James Harrison (eds), Reforming The World Trading System: Legitimacy, Efficiency, and Democratic Governance (Oxford University Press 2005b)

Michael Trebilcock, Robert Howse and Antonia Eliason, The Regulation of International Trade (Routledge 2013)

Michael Trebilcock, 'Competition Policy and Trade Policy' (1996) 30 Journal of World Trade 71

Todd Tucker, 'How to Reform WTO and FTA Rules to Confront Too-Big-To-Fail Banks' (2011) <https://www.citizen.org/documents/memo-gats-conflict-with-bank-size-limits-may-10-2011.pdf> accessed 24 September 2016

Lee Tuthill, 'Users' Rights? The Multilateral Rules on Access to Telecommunications' (1996) 20 Telecommunications Policy 89

——— 'The GATS and New Rules for Regulators' (1997) 21 Telecommunications Policy 783

Antonios Tzanakopoulos, 'National Treatment and MFN in the (Invisible) EU Model BIT' (2014) 15 Journal of World Investment & Trade 484

Ott Ummelas, 'Estonian Parliament Approves Natural-Gas Unbundling Bill' Bloomberg (6 June 2012) <http://www.bloomberg.com/news/2012-06-06/estonian-parliament-approves-natural-gas-unbundling-bill-1-.html> accessed 23 June 2016

Detlev F Vagts, 'Coercion and Foreign Investment Rearrangements' (1978) 72 American Journal of International Law 17

Caroline Van den bergh, 'Reciprocity Clause and International Trade Law' (2009) 27 Journal of Energy & Natural Resources Law 228

Peter van den Bossche and Werner Zdouc, Law and Policy of the World Trade Organization (3rd edn, Cambridge University Press 2013)

Guillaume Van Der Loo, 'EU-Russia Trade Relations: It Takes WTO to Tango?' (2013) 40 Legal Issues of Economic Integration 7

Victor van Hoorn, '"Unbundling", "Reciprocity" and the European Internal Energy Market: WTO Consistency and Broader Implications for Europe' (2009) 1 European Energy and Environmental Law Review 51

Cécile van Vyve, 'Financial Investors and the Unbundling Provisions for TSOs' (2014) 23 - European Energy and Environmental Law Review 63

Isabelle Van Damme, 'What Role is there for Regional International Law in the Interpretation of the WTO Agreements?' in Lorand Bartels and Federico Ortino (eds), Regional Trade Agreements and the WTO Legal System (Oxford University Press 2006)

J. A VanDuzer, Penelope Simons and Graham Mayeda, Integrating Sustainable Development into International Investment Agreements: A Guide for Developing Country Negotiators (Commonwealth Secretariat 2013)

Gaëtan Verhoosel, National Treatment and WTO Dispute Settlement: Adjudicating the Boundaries of Regulatory Autonomy (Hart Publishing 2002)

Tania Voon, 'Article XVII GATT' in Rüdiger Wolfrum, Peter-Tobias Stoll and Holger Hestermeyer (eds), WTO – Trade in Goods (Max Planck Commentaries on World Trade Law vol 5. Martinus Nijhoff Publishers 2011)

Tania Voon and Andrew Mitchell, 'Open for Business? China's Telecommunications Service Market and the WTO' (2010) 13 Journal of International Economic Law 321

Ulrich Vosgerau, 'Art. 17 – Eigentumsrecht' in Klaus Stern and Michael Sachs (eds), Europäische Grundrechte-Charta – Kommentar (C.H. Beck 2016)

Erich Vranes, 'The WTO and Regulatory Freedom: WTO Disciplines on Market Access, Non-Discrimination and Domestic Regulation Relating to Trade in Goods and Services' (2009) 12 Journal of International Economic Law 953

——— 'State Measures Protecting Against "Undesirable" Foreign Investment: Issues in EU and International Law' (2012) 67 Zeitschrift für Öffentliches Recht 639

Martin Wachovius, Ownership Unbundling in der Energiewirtschaft: Vereinbarkeit einer eigentumsrechtlichen Entflechtung in der Energiewirtschaft mit den Grundrechten des Grundgesetzes und des Gemeinschaftsrechts deutscher vertikal integrierter Energieversorgungsunternehmen (VWEW Energieverlag 2008)

Florian Wagner-von Papp, '§ 11 Internationales Wettbewerbsrecht' in Christian Tietje (ed), Internationales Wirtschaftsrecht (De Gruyter 2015)

Thomas W Wälde, 'International Investment under the 1994 Energy Charter Treaty' in Thomas W Wälde (ed), The Energy Charter Treaty: An East-West Gateway for Investment and Trade (International Energy and Resources Law and Policy Series. Kluwer Law International 1996)

——— Wälde and Andreas Gunst, 'International Energy Trade and Access to Networks: The Case of Electricity' in Janusz Bielecki and Melaku G Desta (eds), Electricity Trade in Europe – Review of the Economic and Regulatory Changes (Kluwer Law International 2004)

Monica Waloszyk, Law and Policy of the European Gas Market (Edward Elgar 2014)

Malcolm Webb, 'The Emergence of Functional Separation' in International Telecommunication Union (ed), Trends in Telecommunication Reform 2008: Six Degrees of Sharing (2008)

Hanno Wehland, 'Intra-EU Investment Agreements and Arbitration: Is European Community Law an Obstacle?' (2009) 58 International and Comparative Law Quarterly 297

Friedl Weiss, 'The General Agreement on Trade in Services 1994' (1995) 32 Common Market Law Review 1177

——— 'From World Trade Law to World Competition Law' (2000) 23 Fordham International Law Journal 250

Claudia Wendrich, 'Ten Years After: The World Bank Guidelines on Foreign Direct Investment: In Need of Revision?' (2002) 3 Journal of World Investment & Trade 831

Stephan Wernicke, 'AEUV Art. 345 Eigentumsordnung' in Eberhard Grabitz, Meinhard Hilf and Martin Nettesheim (eds), Das Recht der Europäischen Union: EUV/AEUV (54th edn. C.H. Beck 2014)

Jan G Westerhof, 'The Third Internal Energy Market Package' in Ulf Hammer and Martha M Roggenkamp (eds), European Energy Law Report VI (Energy & Law vol 8. Intersentia 2009)

Burns H Weston, '"Constructive Takings" under International Law: A Modest Foray into the Problem of "Creeping Expropriation"' (1975) 16 Virginia Journal of International Law 103

Jochem Wiers and James Mathis, 'The Report of the Appellate Body in the Asbestos Dispute: WTO Appellate Body Report 12 March 2001, WT/DS135/AB/R, European Communities – Measures Affecting Asbestos and Asbestos-containing Products' (2001) 28 Legal Issues of Economic Integration 211

Arnoud Willems, Jung-ui Sul and Yohan Benizri, 'Unbundling as a Defence Mechanism Against Russia: Is the EU Missing the Point?' in Kim Talus and Piero L Fratini (eds), EU – Russia Energy Relations (Euroconfidentiel 2010)

Matthias Wohlfahrt, Ownership Unbundling: Die Vereinbarkeit verschärfter Entflechtungsvorgaben für die leitungsgebundenen Sektoren Elektrizität und Gas mit dem Gemeinschaftsrecht (Berliner Wissenschafts-Verlag 2009)

Jan Wouters and Dominic Coppens, 'GATS and Domestic Regulation: Balancing the Right to Regulate and Trade Liberalization' in Kern Alexander and Mads Andenas (eds), The World Trade Organization and Trade in Services (Martinus Nijhoff Publishers 2008)

Moritz Wüstenberg, 'An Overview of the Dichotomy between EU Energy Market Liberalisation and the Multilateral Trading System: Case Review of WTO Case DS476 - Certain Measures Relating to the Energy Sector' (2016) 22 International Trade Law & Regulation 8

Christian de Wyl and Jasper Finke, 'Entflechtung von Energieversorgungsunternehmen' in Jens-Peter Schneider and Christian Theobald (eds), Recht der Energiewirtschaft (4th edn. C.H. Beck 2013)

Katja Yafimava, The Transit Dimension of EU Energy Security: Russian Gas Transit Across Ukraine, Belarus, and Moldova (Oxford University Press 2011)

——— The EU Third Package for Gas and the Gas Target Model: Major Contentious Issues Inside and Outside the EU (Oxford Institute for Energy Studies 2013)

——— 'Transit: The EU Energy Acquis and the Energy Charter Treaty' in Kim Talus (ed), Research Handbook on International Energy Law (Research Handbooks in International Law. Edward Elgar 2014)

Diana Zacharias, 'Article I GATS' in Rüdiger Wolfrum, Peter-Tobias Stoll and Clemens Feinäugle (eds), WTO – Trade in Services (Max Planck Commentaries on World Trade Law vol 6. Martinus Nijhoff Publishers 2008)

Simonetta Zarrilli, 'Multilateral Rules and Trade in Energy Goods and Services: The Case of Electricity' in Janusz Bielecki and Melaku G Desta (eds), Electricity Trade in Europe – Review of the Economic and Regulatory Changes (Kluwer Law International 2004)

Werner Zdouc, Legal Problems Arising under the General Agreement on Trade in Services – Comparative Analysis of GATS and GATT (Dissertation Nr. 2608, Difo-Druck 2002)

——— 'WTO Dispute Settlement Practice Relating to the General Agreement on Trade in Services' in Federico Ortino and Ernst-Ulrich Petersmann (eds), The WTO Dispute Settlement System 1995-2003 (Kluwer Law International 2004)

——— 'Streitigkeiten über den Dienstleistungsverkehr vor dem DSB' in Dirk Ehlers, Hans-Michael Wolffgang and Marc Lechleitner (eds), Rechtsfragen des internationalen Dienstleistungsverkehrs: Tagungsband zum 10. Münsteraner Außenwirtschaftsrechtstag 2005 (Verlag Recht und Wirtschaft 2006)

——— 'WTO Dispute Settlement Practice Relating to the GATS' (1999) 2 Journal of International Economic Law 295

Юрий Барсуков and Андрей Райский, '"Газпром" отказался судиться с Литвой' Kommersant (3 April 2015) <http://www.kommersant.ru/doc/2699980>

The manufacturer's authorised representative in the EU is Springer Nature Customer Service Centre GmbH, Europaplatz 3, 69115 Heidelberg, Germany. If you have any concerns regarding our products, please contact ProductSafety@springernature.com

Printed and bound by CPI Group (UK) Ltd, Croydon, CR0 4YY
05/10/2026
02228140-0016